Allusions–
Cultural, Literary, Biblical, and Historical: A Thematic Dictionary

Allusions—

Cultural, Literary, Biblical, and Historical: A Thematic Dictionary

Laurence Urdang
and Frederick G. Ruffner, Jr.

GALE RESEARCH COMPANY ● BOOK TOWER
DETROIT, MICHIGAN 48226

Editors: Jerome Ackerman, George C. Kohn, Janet Muller, Vincent Regan, John Vestali, Howard G. Zettler

with William Jarrett and Kern Longcope, whose help is gratefully acknowledged.

Library of Congress Cataloging in Publication Data

Main entry under title:

Allusions: cultural, literary, Biblical, and historical.

Includes index.
1. Allusions. I. Urdang, Laurence.
PN43.A4   081   82-1088
ISBN 0-8103-1124-0   AACR2

Editor's Foreword

If language can be considered a fabric, then the warp are its words, the weft its grammar. There are plain-weave fabrics with little color and elaborate tapestries that are works of art. Much of literary language falls into the latter category. Yet we cannot ignore the poetry and the rhetorical devices used by those of us who are not poets. Language is by nature metaphoric.

With a few exceptions, dictionaries persist in ignoring the most productive, evocative, emotive, descriptive aspects of language. They pay scant attention to the creative genius of its users, whether they be poets or peasants. Rather, they are concerned with a sterile distillate which robs the lexicon of its intimations of creativity. Lexicographers by tradition or discipline ignore the innate ability of speakers to perceive relationships between the realities of life and the symbolism of myth, literature, culture, and language. The rationale is that dictionaries record denotation, not connotation. Even cursory examination of any desk (or larger) dictionary will show that such a claim is errant, arrant nonsense: one need only read through a few longer entries like *take, run,* or *set* to see how false that position is, how many metaphoric senses are listed.

Lexicographers, it must be acknowledged, are (almost) human, too: no matter how disciplined the mind, it cannot avoid metaphor or allusion. Language is not a plain weave, an ecru fustian; it is a colorful tapestry. Depending on the weaver, it may not always turn out to be a panoramic work of art, but colorful it often is, frequently realistic in some areas and abstract in others. Even the "scientific" lexicographer succumbs to its magic, unable to separate his work from his nature: there can be no objectivity in the description of one's own language.

Nevertheless, that does not keep lexicographers from trying to be objective, chiefly by the arbitrary elimination of certain classes of words and meanings and the inclusion—just as arbitrary—of others. We may ask why, for example, the word *Superman* (in reference to the comic-strip character) is omitted: surely, it has not only denotative meaning but also a host of useful connotations and metaphoric senses that are far more familiar to (American) English speakers than are the kinds of obscure entries that one customarily finds in dictionaries.

There are thousands of such references that constantly occur in our language. Some may be drawn from the comic strips, as in the case of *Superman;* many are drawn from literature (*Babbitt, Scrooge*), from legend or mythology (*Midas, Hercules, Paul Bunyan*), from brand names (*Edsel, Coca-Cola [Coke]*), from symbols (*closed book, yin-yang*), from real people (*Shakespeare, Rockefeller*—on a formula like, "He's a regular Rockefeller"), from events (*Watergate, Boston Tea Party*), from the names of places, buildings, or the like (*Loch Ness, Empire State Building*), from music and the other arts (*Star-spangled Banner, Mona Lisa*), from animals (*dolphin, leopard, mule, rabbit*—all have their attributes), and from every other classification of information associated with culture. By what criteria may such references be omitted from a dictionary that purports to contain "all of the common words and meanings of English"? Even so-called "unabridged" dictionaries don't list them.

These lexical items cannot be omitted on the grounds of lack of frequency: they are often more frequent than words that are listed. They cannot be omitted because "everyone already knows them": a (general) dictionary is supposed to be "a description of the lexicon, or word stock of a language," and they clearly are a part of the lexicon. Many words, now spelled with small letters, were once allusive referents—*thersitical, pander.* Some are listed in dictionaries with capitals—*Midas, Jonah, Adam, Gargantuan.* Capitalization is an empty criterion if we consider language as primarily spoken, with any distinction between capital and small letters obviously inaudible. (It may be true that some proper names and adjectives are identifiable from their syntactic relationships, even in oral discourse, but that is not true of all: we speak of *Shakespeare,* "the" *George Washington Bridge,* and so on; but how can one analyze *a Shakespeare* 'a genius,' or *a Scrooge* 'a miser,' or *a Rockefeller* 'a wealthy man' as distinct from the senses for which they are equivalents? These are preceded by indefinite articles, hence are used metaphorically.)

Because we feel these words should be documented in their metaphoric senses, we have compiled this book. *Allusions—Cultural, Literary, Biblical, and Historical: A Thematic Dictionary,* contains more than 7000 such references: to the Bible, Shakespeare, Dickens; to Greek, Roman, Scandinavian, and other mythologies; to American, European, Eastern, and other legends; to music, the arts, industry, comics, motion pictures, television, radio—in fact, to all of the divers elements that make up what we classify under the general rubric of culture. These are our familiar, everyday references, the things we talk about and the things we use when we speak English, the veritable fabric of our lives, gathered in a single work for easy reference. Not everything is here, of course. There are probably hundreds of thousands of allusions (if they could all be counted), always arriving, always departing. Any reader of this book can find inclusions that may not be to his taste and omissions that he considers heinously unforgivable. We have attempted a broad coverage of a subject so vast and so mercurial that it is doubtful its documentation can ever be complete. We should be grateful for readers' comments, addenda, and corrigenda.

Laurence Urdang

Essex, Connecticut
August 1981

How To Use This Book

Allusions consists of three parts:

1. The main section, containing 628 thematic categories with more than 7000 references listed under them.

The thematic categories are listed in alphabetical order and are numbered consecutively. Under each category are listed, also in alphabetical order and also numbered consecutively, a number of allusions. If you are seeking a set of allusions dealing with, say, IRASCIBILITY, then you need only find that thematic category and the allusions will be listed below it:

346. IRASCIBILITY (See also ANGER, EXASPERATION, SHREW-ISHNESS.)

1. **Caius, Dr.** irritable physician. [Br. Lit.: *Merry Wives of Windsor*]

2. **Donald Duck** cantankerousness itself. [Comics: Horn, 216–217]

3. **Elisha** sics bears on boys for their jibing. [*O.T.: II Kings* 2:23–24]

4. **Findlay, Maude** out-spoken, oft-married, liberated woman. [TV: "Maude" in Terrace, II, 79–80]

Note that the bracketed text included with each entry contains several useful pieces of information:

(a) A broad category that gives the allusive reference some focus (e.g., "Br. Lit." for 1, "Comics" for 2, "O.T." for 3, and "TV" for 4).

Note: For the sake of brevity, broad categories are not repeated in the identification of the allusion itself. A list of abbreviations appears on the next page.

(b) The title of a primary source, shown in italic type (e.g., "*Merry Wives of Windsor*" for 1, "*II Kings*" for 3).

(c) The title of a secondary source, shown, in some cases, in a shortened form (e.g., "Horn" for 2, "Terrace, II" for 4).

(d) The page number or other localized reference where a particular citation can be found (e.g., "Horn, 216–217" for 2, "*II Kings* 2:23–24" for 3, "Terrace, II, 79–80" for 4).

Note: Except for references to the Bible, few localized references are provided in primary sources because the person or place used allusively often appears throughout the work.

(e) Most real people referred to are listed with their birth (and, where appropriate, death) dates (e.g., "Henry, Patrick (1736–1799)"). In some cases, where such a date is absent, look up the person in the Index to find another reference, where the date will appear. In rare cases, it has not been possible to determine an individual's dates.

2. The Bibliography contains the lists of sources consulted in the preparation of this book. These sources are listed in alphabetical order by the short reference or code that appears in square brackets following each listing in the main section. The editions referred to, for the sake of accuracy, are those used in the compilation of *Allusions*, but in a large number of cases, there may be many editions of the work cited, and it makes little difference which edition is consulted if you wish to refer to the actual source.

3. The third section consists of an Index in which can be found, in single alphabetical file, not only all of the allusions listed in the main body of the work but many cross references and variant forms. For example, the listing **flaming heart** will appear also (in its proper alphabetical place) as **heart, flaming**, with an appropriate numerical reference that will guide you to the thematic category and then to the numbered subentry following it. Thus, the reference **598.9** refers to thematic category **598** [**598. Villainy (See also Evil, Wickedness.)**] and to the fourth listing beneath it (**9. Iago**).

To aid in the search for these numbered items, each page in the main part of the book carries a heading, at the indicating the numerical interval appearing on that page.

If you wish to find an allusion to use in a speech or in writing, find the proper thematic category and choose from among the allusions listed there. Because the description provided for identification is, necessarily, brief, you may wish to have fuller information about the allusion, in order to make certain, for instance, that your selection has the correct nuances and connotations. You may then wish to turn to the Bibliography, find the source, and read more about the subject in the book itself.

On the other hand, in your reading you may encounter an allusion whose reference you are unsure of. In that case, you will be guided to the entry itself and to its reference in the Bibliography

Abbreviations Used in This Book

Am.	American	**Hagiog.**	Hagiography	**O.T.**	Old
Arab.	Arabic	**Hist.**	History		Testament
Arg.	Argentinian	**Hung.**	Hungarian	**Pers.**	Persian
Arth.	Arthurian	**Iconog.**	Iconography	**Phil.**	Philosophy
Aust.	Austrian	**Ind.**	Indian	**Pop.**	Popular
Babyl.	Babylonian	**Ital.**	Italian	**Port.**	Portuguese
Br.	British	**Jap.**	Japanese	**Rel.**	Religion
Can.	Canadian	**Jew.**	Jewish	**Ren.**	Renaissance
Class.	Classical	**Jour.**	Journalism	**Rom.**	Roman
Czech.	Czechoslovakian	**Lit.**	Literature	**Russ.**	Russian
Dan.	Danish	**Mex.**	Mexican	**Scot.**	Scottish
Egypt.	Egyptian	**Misc.**	Miscellaneous	**Span.**	Spanish
Eur.	European	**Myth.**	Mythology	**Swed.**	Swedish
Flem.	Flemish	**Nor.**	Norwegian	**Theol.**	Theology
Fr.	French	**N.T.**	New Testament	**Trad.**	Tradition
Ger.	German	**Nurs.**	Nursery	**TV**	Television
Gk.	Greek	**Rhyme**	Rhyme	**Yid.**	Yiddish

Table of Contents

Categories

A

1. Abandonment (See also Orphan.)
2. Abduction
3. Abundance (See also Fertility.)
4. Acting
   Adolescence (See Teenager, Youth.)
5. Adultery (See also Cuckoldry, Faithlessness.)
6. Adventurousness
   Adversity (See Failure.)
   Advice (See Counsel.)
   Affectation (See Pretension.)
   Affliction (See Suffering.)
7. Age, Old
8. Agelessness (See also Immortality.)
   Aggressiveness (See Conquest.)
9. Aid, Governmental (See also Generosity.)
10. Aid, Organizational (See also Generosity.)
    Aimlessness (See Wandering.)
11. Air
    Alarm (See Warning.)
12. Alcoholism (See also Drunkenness.)
    Allurement (See Temptation.)
13. Aloofness
14. Ambiguity
15. Ambition
16. America
17. Androgyny
18. Angel
19. Anger (See also Exasperation, Irascibility, Ranting.)
20. Annunciation
21. Anti-Heroism
22. Antimilitarism (See also Peace, Peacemaking.)
23. Antiquarian
24. Anti-Semitism (See also Bigotry.)
25. Antislavery
26. Aphrodisiac
27. Apocalypse
28. Apostasy (See also Sacrilege.)
29. Appearances, Deceiving (See also Illusion.)
30. Apple
31. Architecture
32. Argumentativeness
33. Aristocracy
34. Arrivism (See also Philistinism.)
35. Arrogance (See also Boastfulness, Conceit, Egotism.)
    Artfulness (See Cunning.)
    Artlessness (See Innocence, Naiveness.)
36. Ascension

H

287. Hair
Happiness (See Joy.)
288. Harmony
289. Hatred
Haughtiness (See Arrogance.)
290. Headlessness (See also
Decapitation.)
291. Healing (See also Medicine.)
292. Health
293. Heartlessness (See also Cruelty,
Ruthlessness.)
294. Heaven (See also Paradise.)
Height (See Giantism,
Tallness.)
295. Hell (See also Underworld.)
296. Helpfulness (See also
Kindness.)
297. Henpecked
Heresy (See Apostasy.)
298. Heroism (See also Bravery.)
299. Highspiritedness
300. Highwayman (See also
Outlawry, Thievery.)
301. Homecoming
302. Homosexuality
303. Honesty (See also
Righteousness, Virtuousness.)
304. Hope (See also Optimism.)
Hopelessness (See Despair.)
305. Horror
306. Horse
307. Hospitality
Hugeness (See Giantism.)
308. Humbuggery (See also
Trickery.)
309. Humility (See also Modesty.)
Humorousness (See Wittiness.)
310. Hunger
311. Hunting
312. Hypochondria
313. Hypocrisy (See also
Pretension.)

I

314. Identification
315. Idolatry
316. Ignorance (See also Stupidity.)
317. Illegitimacy
318. Illusion (See also Appearances,
Deceiving.)
319. Imbalance
320. Immortality (See also
Agelessness.)
321. Imperialism
322. Impertinence
Impetuousness (See Rashness.)
323. Impossibility (See also
Unattainability.)
Impotence (See Weakness.)
324. Imprisonment
325. Incest
Incorruptibility (See Honesty.)
326. Indecision
327. Independence
328. Indifference
329. Individualism (See also
Egotism.)
330. Inducement
331. Industriousness
332. Ineptitude (See also
Awkwardness.)
333. Inexpensiveness
334. Inexperience (See also
Innocence, Naiveness.)
Infertility (See Barrenness.)
Infidelity (See Adultery,
Cuckoldry, Faithlessness.)
335. Informer
336. Ingratitude
337. Inhospitality
338. Injustice
339. Innocence (See also
Inexperience, Naiveness.)
Inquisitiveness (See Curiosity.)
Insanity (See Madness.)
340. Insecurity
Inseparability (See Friendship.)
Insolence (See Arrogance.)

A

1. **ABANDONMENT** (See also ORPHAN.)

   1. **Auburn** agricultural village which loses inhabitants with onslaught of industry. [Br. Lit.: "The Deserted Village" in *Traveller*]

   2. **Cio-Cio-San** deserted by family for renouncing her religion. [Ital. Opera: Puccini, *Madama Butterfly*, Westerman, 357]

   3. **Helmer, Nora** deserts family to find "whole woman" identity. [Nor. Lit.: *A Doll's House*]

   4. **Henchard-Newson, Susan** Michael Henchard's deserted wife. [Br. Lit.: *The Mayor of Casterbridge*, Magill, I, 571–573]

   5. **Mary Celeste** brigantine found drifting with no hands aboard. [Br. Folklore: Leach, 683]

   6. **Santuzza** deserted by Turiddu after yielding to his advances. [Ital. Opera: Mascagni, *Cavalleria Rusticana*, Westerman, 338–339]

   7. **Smike** boy deserted and forgotten at Dotheboys Hall. [Br. Lit.: *Nicholas Nickleby*]

   8. **Snow White** deserted in forest; found by seven dwarfs. [Ger. Fairy Tale: Grimm, 184]

   9. **Thursday, Margaret** left on church doorstep as baby. [Children's Lit.: *Margaret Thursday*, Fisher, 199–200]

2. **ABDUCTION**

   1. **Balfour, David** expecting inheritance, kidnapped by uncle. [Br. Lit.: *Kidnapped*]

   2. **Bertram, Henry** kidnapped at age five; taken from Scotland. [Br. Lit.: *Guy Mannering*]

   3. **Cephalus** carried off in lusting Aurora's chariot. [Rom. Myth.: Hall, 36]

   4. **Conway, Hugh** kidnapped to the lamasery called Shangri-la. [Br. Lit.: *Lost Horizon*]

   5. **Gilda** abducted by Duke of Mantua's courtiers. [Ital. Opera: Verdi, *Rigoletto*, Westerman, 299–300]

   6. **Helen** carried off by Paris, thus precipitating Trojan war. [Gk. Lit.: *Iliad*, Hall, 147]

   7. **Prisoner of Zenda, The** King of Ruritania is held captive in castle of Zenda. [Br. Lit.: *The Prisoner of Zenda*]

8. **Proserpina** (Gk. **Persephone**) whisked away by lustful Pluto in chariot. [Rom. Lit.: *Metamorphoses; Fasti;* Art: Hall, 260]
9. **Raid of Ruthven** James VI kidnapped for ten months by Protestant nobles (1582–1583). [Scot. Hist.: Grun, 258]
10. **Resurrection Men** 1800s "body snatchers"; supplied cadavers for dissection. [Br. Hist.: Brewer *Note-Book,* 756]
11. **Sabine Women** menfolk absent, Romans carry off women for wives. [Rom. Hist.: Brewer *Dictionary,* 948; Flem. Art: Rubens, "Rape of the Sabine Women"]
12. **virgins of Jabesh-gilead** abducted by Israelites while dancing at Shiloh. [*O.T.: Judges* 21:12–24]

3. **ABUNDANCE (See also FERTILITY.)**
   1. **Amalthea's horn** horn of Zeus's nurse-goat which became a cornucopia. [Gk. Myth.: Walsh *Classical,* 19]
   2. **Copia** goddess of abundance. [Rom. Myth.: Kravitz, 65]
   3. **cornucopia** conical receptacle which symbolizes abundance. [Rom. Myth.: Kravitz, 65]
   4. **Cubbins, Bartholomew** head sports inexhaustible supply of hats. [Children's Lit.: *The Five Hundred Hats of Bartholomew Cubbins*]
   5. **Dagon** (**Dāgan**) fish-corn god symbolizing fertility and abundance. [Babyl. Myth.: Parrinder, 72; Jobes, 410]
   6. **Daikoku** god has inexhaustible sack of useful articles. [Jap. Myth.: *LLEI,* I: 325]
   7. **Dhisana** Vedic goddess of abundance. [Hinduism: Jobes, 439]
   8. **Doritis** epithet of Aphrodite, meaning "bountiful." [Gk. Myth.: Zimmerman, 25]
   9. **Goshen** Egyptian fertile land; salvation for Jacob's family. [*O.T.: Genesis* 46:28]
   10. **land of milk and honey** land of fertility and abundance. [*O.T.: Exodus* 3:8, 33:3; *Jeremiah* 11:5]
   11. **Thanksgiving Day** American holiday celebrating abundant harvest; originally observed by Pilgrims (1621). [Am. Culture: *NCE,* 2726]
   12. **wheat ears, garland of** symbol of agricultural abundance and peace. [Western Folklore: Jobes, 374]

4. **ACTING**
   1. **Thespis** first individual Greek performer; whence, *thespian.* [Gk. Drama: Espy, 46]
   2. **Vitus, St.** patron saint of actors. [Christian Hagiog.: Brewster, 291]

ADOLESCENCE (See TEENAGER, YOUTH.)

5. ADULTERY (See also CUCKOLDRY, FAITHLESSNESS.)

1. **Alcmena** unknowingly commits adultery when Jupiter impersonates husband. [Rom. Lit.: *Amphitryon*]

2. **Alison** betrays old husband amusingly with her lodger, Nicholas. [Br. Lit.: *Canterbury Tales*, "Miller's Tale"]

3. **Andermatt, Christiane** eventually has child by lover, not husband. [Fr. Lit.: *Mont-Oriol*, Magill, I, 618–620]

4. **Bathsheba** impregnated by David during husband's absence. [*O.T.: II Samuel* 11:4]

5. **Bovary, Emma** acquires lovers to find rapture marriage lacks. [Fr. Lit.: *Madame Bovary*, Magill, I, 539–541]

6. **Brant, Capt. Adam** fatefully falls for general's wife. [Am. Lit.: *Mourning Becomes Electra*]

7. **Buchanan, Tom** even with Daisy's knowledge, deliberately has affairs. [Am. Lit.: *The Great Gatsby*]

8. **Clytemnestra** takes Aegisthus as paramour. [Gk. Lit.: *Orestes*]

9. **Cunizza** amours with Sordello while married to first husband. [Br. Lit.: *Sordello*]

10. **currant** symbol of infidelity. [Flower Symbolism: Jobes, 398]

11. **Guinevere** King Arthur's unfaithful wife. [Br. Lit.: *Le Morte d'Arthur*]

12. **Herzog** insatiable husband plays the field. [Am. Lit.: *Herzog*]

13. **Julia, Donna** Alfonso's wife; gives herself to Don Juan. [Br. Lit.: "Don Juan" in Magill, I, 217–219]

14. **Karenina, Anna** commits adultery with Count Vronsky; scandalizes Russian society. [Russ. Lit.: *Anna Karenina*]

15. **Mannon, Christine** conspires with lover to poison husband; discovered, commits suicide. [Am. Lit.: *Mourning Becomes Electra*]

16. **Moechus** personification of adultery. [Br. Lit.: *The Purple Island*, Brewer *Handbook*, 715]

17. **Pozdnishef, Madame** bored with husband, acquires Trukhashevsky as lover. [Russ. Lit.: *The Kreutzer Sonata*, Magill, I, 481–483]

18. **Prynne, Hester** adulterous woman in Puritan New England; condemned to wear a scarlet letter. [Am. Lit.: *The Scarlet Letter*]

19. **scarlet letter** "A" for "adultery" sewn on Hester Prynne's dress. [Am. Lit.: *The Scarlet Letter*]

20. **Tonio** after Nedda's repulsion, tells husband of her infidelities. [Ital. Opera: Leoncavallo, *Pagliacci*, Westerman, 341–342]
21. **Wicked Bible** misprint gives Commandment: "Thou shalt commit adultery." [*sic*] [Br. Hist.: Brewer *Dictionary*, 108]

6. ADVENTUROUSNESS

1. **Baggins, Bilbo** hobbit-protagonist; has escapades with dwarfs. [Br. Lit.: *The Hobbit*]
2. **Bunny, Benjamin** Peter Rabbit's thrill-seeking cousin. [Children's Lit.: *The Tale of Benjamin Bunny*]
3. **Deadwood Dick** hero of Wild West dime novels. [Am. Folklore: Walsh *Modern*, 115]
4. **Fabio** 19th-century young runaway becomes gaucho; Argentinian Huckleberry Finn. [Arg. Lit.: *Don Segundo Sombra*]
5. **Finn, Huckleberry** 19th-century picaresque teenager travels down the Mississippi on a raft. [Am. Lit.: *Huckleberry Finn*]
6. **Fogg, Phileas** gentleman undertakes world trip on wager. [Fr. Lit.: *Around the World in Eighty Days*]
7. **Gulliver, Lemuel** 17th-century hero travels to fanciful lands on extraordinary voyages. [Br. Lit.: *Gulliver's Travels*]
8. **Hawkins, Jim** cabin boy on pirate ship. [Br. Lit.: *Treasure Island*]
9. **Kim** orphan wanders streets of India with lama. [Br. Lit.: *Kim*]
10. **Kon-Tiki** tale of raft trip taken to prove sea-borne migration of peoples and culture. [Nor. Hist.: *Kon-Tiki*]
11. **Lismahago, Lieutenant Obadiah** 19th-century sportsman with quixotic tales. [Br. Lit.: *Humphry Clinker*, Magill, I, 394–397]
12. **Münchhausen, Baron** picaresque traveler and teller of tall tales. [Ger. Lit.: *Baron Münchhausen*]
13. **Polo, Marco** 13th-century Venetian merchant; brought Oriental wonders to Europe. [Eur. Hist.: Bishop, 222–224]
14. **Pym, Arthur Gordon** journeys include mutiny, shipwreck, savages, and the supernatural. [Am. Lit.: "The Narrative of Arthur Gordon Pym" in Magill, I, 640–643]
15. **Sawyer, Tom** classic 19th-century adventuresome, all-American boy. [Am. Lit.: *Tom Sawyer*]
16. **Simplicissimus** from callowness to audacity on 18th-century battlefields. [Ger. Lit.: *Simplicissimus*]
17. **Tartarin** 19th-century French Quixote acts out his dreams of travel. [Fr. Lit.: *Tartarin de Tarascon*]
18. **Tarzan** jungle man leads adventurous life. [Am. Lit.: *Tarzan of the Apes*]

19. **Time Machine, The** inventor of time machine travels into future; sees degeneration of life. [Br. Lit.: *The Time Machine*]

ADVERSITY (See FAILURE.)

ADVICE (See COUNSEL.)

AFFECTATION (See PRETENSION.)

AFFLICTION (See SUFFERING.)

7. **AGE, OLD**
1. **Alberich** 500 years old, but still child-sized. [Ger. Legend: Walsh *Classical*, 13]
2. **Chuffey** old clerk. [Br. Lit.: *Martin Chuzzlewit*]
3. **Darby and Joan** happily settled elderly couple. [Br. Ballad: Brewer *Dictionary*, 300]
4. **Ezekiel** portrayed with flowing white beard. [Art: Hall, 118]
5. **Father Time** personification of the old year. [Folklore: Misc.]
6. **Geritol** leading brand of tonic for geriatric health. [Trademarks: Crowley *Trade*, 230]
7. **Methuselah** oldest man mentioned in Bible. [*O.T.: Genesis* 5:27]
8. **Parr, Thomas** husbandman; lived through reigns of ten sovereigns. [Br. Hist.: Brewer *Dictionary*, 805]
9. **Philemon and Baucis** fabled aged couple. [Rom. Lit.: *Metamorphoses*]
10. **Prufrock, J. Alfred** "I grow old, I grow old." [Br. Lit.: "The Love Song of J. Alfred Prufrock" in Hart, 497]

8. **AGELESSNESS (See also IMMORTALITY.)**
1. **Endymion** man kept immortally youthful through eternal sleep. [Gk. Myth.: Howe, 91; Br. Lit.: "Endymion" in Harvey, 271]
2. **Gray, Dorian** artist Basil Hallward's "ideal of youth." [Br. Lit.: *The Picture of Dorian Gray*, Magill, I, 746–748]
3. **Little Orphan Annie** teenage heroine who has not aged since strip started (1938). [Comics: "Little Orphan Annie" in Horn, 459]

AGGRESSIVENESS (See CONQUEST.)

9. **AID, GOVERNMENTAL (See also GENEROSITY.)**
1. **Berlin Airlift** free world's circumvention of Soviet blockade (1948–1949). [Eur. Hist.: Van Doren, 519]

2. **CARE** agency devoted to channeling relief to needy people abroad. [Am. Hist.: *NCE*, 456]

3. **G.I. Bill** WWII U.S. veterans' educational subsidy by government. [Am. Hist.: Van Doren, 499]

4. **Lend-Lease Act** provision of American materiel to beleaguered Allies in WWII. [Am. Hist.: Van Doren, 480]

5. **Marshall Plan** U.S.-led project to rebuild post-WWII Europe. [Eur. Hist.: Van Doren, 515]

6. **Medicare** U.S. program of health insurance for the aged. [Am. Hist.: *EB*, VI: 747]

7. **Peace Corps** U.S. agency devoted to assisting underdeveloped nations. [Am. Hist.: Van Doren, 575–576]

8. **Social Security Act** U.S. legislation providing for old-age benefits financed by payroll taxes; later expanded to include more extensive coverage. [Am. Hist.: *EB*, IX: 314]

9. **VISTA** (Volunteers in Service to America), government agency which fights poverty in the U.S. [Am. Hist.: *WB*, 1: 27]

10. **AID, ORGANIZATIONAL (See also GENEROSITY.)**

1. **Boy Scouts** organization of teenage boys dedicated to community service and character building. [Am. and Br. Hist.: *NCE*, 350]

2. **Girl Scouts** recreational and service organization for girls. [Am. and Br. Hist.: *NCE*, 1089]

3. **Red Cross** international philanthropic organization devoted to the alleviation of human suffering. [World Hist.: *NCE*, 2288]

4. **Salvation Army** nonsectarian Christian organization for philanthropic and evangelical work. [World Hist.: *NCE*, 2408–2409]

AIMLESSNESS (See WANDERING.)

11. **AIR**

1. **Aeolus** god of the winds. [Gk. Myth.: Zimmerman, 9]

2. **Aether** god of whole atmosphere. [Gk. Myth.: Jobes, 42]

3. **Aurae** winged nymphs of breezes. [Rom. Myth.: *LLEI*, I: 323]

4. **Juno** in allegories of elements, personification of air. [Art: Hall, 128]

5. **sylph** spirit inhabiting atmosphere in Rosicrucian philosophy. [Medieval Hist.: Brewer *Dictionary*, 1055]

ALARM (See WARNING.)

12. ALCOHOLISM (See also DRUNKENNESS.)

1. **Alcoholics Anonymous (AA)** society of ex-alcoholics who help alcoholics to stop drinking. [Am. Hist.: Flexner, 356]

2. **L'Assommoir** study of the demoralizing effects of alcohol. [Fr. Lit.: *L'Assommoir*]

3. **the Bowery** area in New York City known for its destitute and drunken population. [Am. Culture: Misc.]

4. **Brick** dipsomaniac; drinks until he feels a "click." [Am. Lit.: *Cat on a Hot Tin Roof*]

5. **Emery, Stan** drinking as only means to adjust to world. [Am. Lit.: *The Manhattan Transfer*]

6. **Iceman Cometh, The** portrayal of Harry Hope's rundown saloon which harbors alcoholics. [Am. Lit.: *The Iceman Cometh*]

7. **Lost Weekend, The** study of Don Birnam, an unsuccessful writer who drinks too much. [Am. Lit.: *The Lost Weekend*, Magill, I, 531–532]

8. **Prohibition** resurgence of American puritanism (1920–1933). [Am. Hist.: Allen, 14–15]

9. **skid row** a run-down area frequented by alcoholics. [Am. Culture: Misc.]

ALLUREMENT (See TEMPTATION.)

13. ALOOFNESS

1. **de Coverly, Major** so aloof that nobody dares to ask him his first name. [Am. Lit.: *Catch-22*]

2. **Gatsby, Jay** aloof from intimacy; addressed most often as "ol' sport." [Am. Lit.: *The Great Gatsby*]

3. **Hatteras, Captain** paranoid sea captain remains incognito for half a voyage. [Fr. Lit.: *Captain Hatteras*]

4. **Havisham, Miss** eccentric lady who resents men; maintains a detached attitude toward Pip. [Br. Lit.: *Great Expectations*]

5. **Miriam** mysteriously reluctant to reveal her past. [Am. Lit.: *The Marble Faun*]

6. **Morgan, Captain** officious officer; will not talk with enlisted men. [Am. Lit.: *Mister Roberts*, Magill, I, 605–607]

7. **Trot, Dame** "not troubled with other folks' strife." [Nurs. Rhyme: *Mother Goose*, 13]

8. **Winterbourne** distant from even his own feelings about Daisy. [Am. Lit.: *Daisy Miller*]

14. AMBIGUITY

1. **Catch-22** paradoxical statement; e.g., claiming insanity to escape military duty proves one's sanity. [Am. Lit.: *Catch-22*]

2. **Delphic oracle** ultimate authority in ancient Greece; often speaks in ambiguous terms. [Gk. Hist.: Leach, 305]

3. **Iseult's vow** pledge to husband has double meaning. [Arth. Legend: *Tristan*]

4. **Loxias** epithet of Apollo, meaning "ambiguous" in reference to his practically uninterpretable oracles. [Gk. Myth.: Zimmerman, 26]

5. **Pooh-Bah** different opinion for every one of his offices. [Br. Opera: *The Mikado*, Magill, I, 591–592]

15. AMBITION

1. **Alger, Horatio** author of a series of rags-to-riches stories. [Am. Lit.: *Ragged Dick*]

2. **Claudius** murders to gain throne; plots to keep it. [Br. Lit.: *Hamlet*]

3. **Constance** ambitious for her son Arthur. [Br. Lit.: *King John*]

4. **Faustus, Doctor** makes a pact with the devil to further his own ambitions. [Br. Lit.: *The Tragical History of Doctor Faustus*]

5. **hollyhock** traditional meaning. [Flower Symbolism: *Flora Symbolica*, 174]

6. **John, King** aspiring, self-assertive king of mediocre character. [Br. Lit.: *King John*]

7. **Macbeth** ruthlessly aspires to political power. [Br. Lit.: *Macbeth*]

8. **Macbeth, Lady** stops at nothing to gain political power for husband. [Br. Lit.: *Macbeth*]

9. **mountain laurel** traditional meaning. [Flower Symbolism: *Flora Symbolica*, 175]

10. **Ragged Dick** hero of a Horatio Alger rags-to-riches story. [Am. Lit.: *Ragged Dick*]

11. **Roxana** sleeps with the rich to get ahead in world. [Br. Lit.: *Roxana, The Fortunate Mistress*]

12. **What Makes Sammy Run** a dynamic but vicious opportunist attains success. [Am. Lit.: *What Makes Sammy Run*]

16. AMERICA

1. **apple pie** typical, wholesome American dessert. [Am. Culture: Flexner, 68]

2. **bald eagle** national bird of the U.S.; only eagle native to North America. [Am. Culture: *EB*, I: 753]

3. **baseball** traditional American sport and pastime. [Am. Sports: *EB*, I: 850]

4. **Brother Jonathan** the original Uncle Sam. [Am. Hist.: Hart, 110]

5. **Crossing of the Delaware** Washington's beleaguered army attacks Trenton; famous event in American history (1776). [Am. Hist.: Jameson, 138]

6. **e pluribus unum** motto of the U.S.: "one out of many." [Am. Culture: *RHD*, 481]

7. **Fourth of July** Independence Day; traditional U.S. holiday; anniversary of adoption of Declaration of Independence (July 4, 1776). [Am. Culture: *EB*, V: 326]

8. **Liberty Bell** symbol of American freedom; at Independence Hall, Philadelphia. [Am. Hist.: Jameson, 284]

9. **Mayflower** the ship of the founding Puritan fathers. [Am. Hist.: Jameson, 313]

10. **melting pot** America as the home of many races and cultures. [Am. Pop. Culture: Misc.]

11. **Peoria** byword for a typical American small town. [Am. Culture: Misc.]

12. **Plymouth Rock** site of pilgrim landing in Massachusetts (1620). [Am. Hist.: Jameson, 395–396]

13. **pumpkin pie** traditional dish, especially at Thanksgiving. [Am. Culture: Flexner, 68]

14. **Silent Majority** average Americans of middle class. [Am. Culture: Flexner, 375]

15. **Star-Spangled Banner, The** U.S. national anthem. [Am. Hist.: *EB*, IX: 532]

16. **Statue of Liberty** huge copper statue in New York harbor. [Am. Hist.: Jameson, 284]

17. **Thanksgiving** annual U.S. holiday celebrating harvest and yearly blessings; originated with Pilgrims (1621). [Am. Culture: *EB*, IX: 922]

18. **Uncle Sam** personifies people or government of the United States. [Am. Hist.: Hart, 870–871]

19. **Vespucci, Amerigo** (1454–1512) Italian navigator-explorer from whose name the name of the American continent is derived. [Am. Hist.: *EB*, X: 410]

20. **Washington, D.C.** focus of U.S. government, policies, etc. [Am. Hist.: Hart, 899]

21. **Washington, George** (1732–1799) "the Father of our country"; first U.S. President (1789–1797). [Am. Hist.: Jameson, 535–536]

22. **White House** official residence of the president of the U.S. in Washington, D.C. [Am. Culture: *EB*, X: 656]

23. **Yankee** to an American, a New Englander; to a Southern American, any Northerner; to a foreigner, any American. [Am. Hist.: Hart, 953]

17. ANDROGYNY

1. **Hermaphroditus** half-man, half-woman; offspring of Hermes and Aphrodite. [Gk. Myth.: Hall, 153]

2. **Iphis** Cretan maiden reared as boy because father ordered all daughters killed. [Gk. Myth.: Howe, 143]

3. **Tiresias** prophet who lived as man or woman. [Gk. Myth.: Zimmerman, 255–256]

18. ANGEL

1. **Abaddon** angel in charge of Sheol's bottomless pit. [*N. T.*: *Revelation* 9:11; 20:1–3]

2. **Abdiel** faithful seraph who withstood Satan when urged to revolt. [Br. Lit.: *Paradise Lost*]

3. **Gabriel** angel of the annunciation; tells Mary she will bear Christ child. [*N. T.*: *Luke* 1:26–38]

4. **guardian angel** believed to protect a particular person. [Folklore: Misc.]

5. **Michael** leader of angels against Satan. [*N.T.*: *Revelation* 12:7–9; Br. Lit.: *Paradise Lost*]

6. **Raphael** God's healer and helper in Book of Tobit. [*Apocrypha: Tobit*]

7. **Uriel** sent by God to instruct prophet Esdras. [*Apocrypha: II Esdras* 4]

8. **Zadkiel** angel of the planet Jupiter. [Jew. Myth.: Brewer *Handbook*, 1237]

19. **ANGER** (See also EXASPERATION, IRASCIBILITY, RANTING.)
1. **Alecto** one of the three Furies, vengeful deities who punish evil-doers. [Gk. Myth.: Zimmerman, 274]
2. **Almeira** scorned woman like whom "hell hath no fury." [Br. Drama: *The Mourning Bride*]
3. **Belinda** furious over loss of lock of hair. [Br. Lit.: *Rape of the Lock*]
4. **Brunhild** furiously vengeful concerning Kriemhild's accusations of promiscuity. [Ger. Lit.: *Nibelungenlied*]
5. **Erinyes (the Furies)** angry and avenging deities who pursue evil-doers. [Gk. Myth.: Leach, 347]
6. **Fudd, Elmer** hapless man seethes over Bugs Bunny's antics. [Comics: "Bugs Bunny" in Horn, 140]
7. **Hera (Rom. Juno)** known for her anger at Zeus's illicit sexual pleasure. [Rom. Myth.: Leach, 563]
8. **Herod** upon wise men's disobedience, orders slaughter of male infants. [*N.T.: Matthew* 2:16–17]
9. **the Hulk** character whose anger transforms him into monster. [Comics: Horn, 324–325]
10. **Megaera** one of the three Furies, vengeful deities who punish evil-doers. [Gk. Myth.: Zimmerman, 274]
11. **Nemesis** goddess of vengeance. [Gk. Myth.: Zimmerman, 173]
12. **Oronte** takes offense at Alceste's criticism of sonnet. [Fr. Lit.: *The Misanthrope*]
13. **Othello** smothers wife, Desdemona, in paroxysm of rage over her suspected adultery. [Br. Lit.: *Othello*]
14. **Rumpelstiltskin** stamps ground in rage over lass's discovery of his name. [Ger. Fairy Tale: *Rumpelstiltskin*]
15. **Tisiphone** one of the three Furies, vengeful deities who punish evil-doers. [Gk. Myth.: Zimmerman, 274]
16. **Volumnia** "in anger, Junolike." [Br. Lit.: *Coriolanus*]
17. **whin** indicates fury. [Flower Symbolism: *Flora Symbolica,* 178]

20. **ANNUNCIATION**
1. **dove and lily** pictured with Virgin and Gabriel. [Christian Iconography: Brewer *Dictionary,* 645]
2. **Elizabeth** Mary's old cousin; bears John the Baptist. [*N.T.: Luke* 1:36–80]
3. **Gabriel** messenger angel; tells Mary she will bear Christ child. [*N.T.: Luke* 1:26–38]
4. **Hail, Mary** prayer adapted from the words of Gabriel to Mary announcing the coming birth of Christ. [*N.T.: Luke* 1:26–36]

21. **ANTI-HEROISM**

1. **Brown, Charlie** bumbling boy with low self-esteem. [Comics: "Peanuts" in Horn, 542–543]
2. **Cooke, Ebenezer** his every move denies all things heroic. [Am. Lit.: *The Sot-Weed Factor*]
3. **Hoover, Dwayne** materially successful car dealer whose only friend is his dog. [Am. Lit.: *Breakfast of Champions*]
4. **Rosewater, Eliot** unemployed heir who spends day buying drinks for volunteer firemen. [Am. Lit.: *God Bless You, Mr. Rosewater*]
5. **Spade, Sam** semi-literate, tough-talking private eye; lacks culture. [Am. Lit.: *The Maltese Falcon*]

22. **ANTIMILITARISM (See also PEACE, PEACEMAKING.)**

1. **All Quiet on the Western Front** unromanticized novel of WWI and its unsung heroes. [Ger. Lit.: *All Quiet on the Western Front*]
2. **Arms and the Man** satirizes romantic view of war. [Br. Lit.: *Arms and the Man*]
3. **Farewell to Arms, A** novel of lovers who flee from war's horrors. [Am. Lit.: *A Farewell to Arms*]
4. **Quakers** known for service to peace. [Am. Hist.: *EB*, 7: 743–745]

23. **ANTIQUARIAN**

1. **Clutterbuck, Cuthbert** retired captain, devoted to study of antiquities. [Br. Lit.: *The Monastery*]
2. **Oldbuck, Jonathan** learned and garrulous antiquary. [Br. Lit.: *The Antiquary*]
3. **Teufelsdroeckh, Herr** eccentric German philosopher and professor. [Br. Lit.: *Sartor Resartus;* Brewer *Handbook*, 1088]

24. **ANTI-SEMITISM (See also BIGOTRY.)**

1. **Agobard** (799–840) Lyonnais archbishop, father of medieval anti-Jewish racism. [Fr. Hist.: Wigoder, 15]
2. **Anti-Defamation League** B'nai B'rith organization which fights anti-Semitism. [Am. Hist.: Wigoder, 33]
3. **Armleder** medieval bands; ravaged Alsatian Jewish communities. [Ger. Hist.: Wigoder, 41]
4. **Babi Yar** Russian site of WWII German massacre of the Jews. [Russ. Hist.: Wigoder, 56]
5. **Bernheim Petition** 1933 petition exposed Nazi treatment of Jews. [Jew. Hist.: Wigoder, 83]

6. **Black Death pogroms** plague blamed on Jews who were later murdered. [Jew. Hist.: Bishop, 382]

7. **Black Hundreds** early 20th-century armed squads ravaged Jews. [Russ. Hist.: Wigoder, 92]

8. **blood libel** trials of Jews who allegedly murdered non-Jews for Passover blood. [Jew. Hist.: Wigoder, 95]

9. **Bok, Yakov** victim of Russian anti-Semitism; falsely accused of murder. [Am. Lit.: *The Fixer*]

10. **Final Solution** Nazi plan to exterminate Jewish race. [Ger. Hist.: *Hitler*, 1037–1061]

11. **Frank, Anne** (1929–1945) young Dutch girl found and killed by Nazis after years in hiding. [Dutch Lit.: *Anne Frank*]

12. **Gentleman's Agreement** indictment of anti-Semiticism. [Am. Lit.: *Gentleman's Agreement*]

13. **Haman** convinces king to issue decree for Jewish extermination. [*O.T.*: *Esther* 3:1–11]

14. **Hep Hep riots** Jewish pogroms Germany (1819). [Ger. Hist.: Wigoder, 251]

15. **Hitler, Adolf** (1889–1945) Nazi dictator of Germany; eclipsed all predecessors' hatred for Jews. [World Hist.: *Hitler*]

16. **Jacobowsky and the Colonel** anti-Semitic Polish colonel refuses to recognize his rescuer because he is Jewish. [Ger. Lit.: *Jacobowsky and the Colonel*]

17. **Kishinev** Moldavian city; scene of pogroms and WWII genocide. [Jew. Hist.: Wigoder, 344]

18. **Kristallnacht** destruction of Jews' property anticipated later atrocities (November 9–10, 1938). [Ger. Hist.: *Hitler*, 689–694]

19. **Mein Kampf** Adolf Hitler's autobiography, including his theories on treatment of the Jews. [Ger. Hist.: *Mein Kampf*]

20. **Nuremberg Laws** stripped Jews of citizenship and civil rights (1935). [Ger. Hist.: Wigoder, 458]

21. **Protocols of the Elders of Zion** forged tract revealing Jewish conspiracy to control world. [Jew. Hist.: Wigoder, 170]

22. **Torquemada, Tomás de** (1420–1498) Inquisition head; expelled Jews from Spain (1492). [Span. Hist.: Wigoder, 600]

23. **Untermenschen** subhumans; Nazi conception of Jews and Slavs. [Ger. Hist.: Shirer, 1223]

24. **Volkischer Beobachter** Nazi party organ featuring Jew-baiting articles. [Ger. Hist.: Shirer, 75–78]

25. ANTISLAVERY

1. **Abolitionists** activist group working to free slaves. [Am. Hist.: Jameson, 1]
2. **Emancipation Proclamation** edict issued by Abraham Lincoln freeing the slaves (1863). [Am. Hist.: *EB*, III: 869]
3. **Free Soil Party** Abolitionist political party before Civil War. [Am. Hist.: Flexner, 3]
4. **Jayhawkers** antislavery guerrillas fighting on Union side in Civil War. [Am. Hist.: Jameson, 256]
5. **Laus Deo!** poem written to celebrate emancipation of slaves. [Am. Lit.: "Laus Deo!" in Hart, 460]
6. **Liberator** William Lloyd Garrison's virulently Abolitionist newspaper. [Am. Hist.: Van Doren, 142]
7. **Lincoln, Abraham** (1809–1865) sixteenth U.S. president; issued Emancipation Proclamation freeing the slaves. [Am. Hist.: Jameson, 286–287]
8. **North Star** newspaper supporting emancipation founded by Frederick Douglass. [Am. Hist.: Hart, 607]
9. **Shelby, George** vows to devote self to freeing slaves. [Am. Lit.: *Uncle Tom's Cabin*]
10. **Stowe, Harriet Beecher** (1811–1896) author of *Uncle Tom's Cabin*, influential Abolitionist novel. [Am. Hist.: Jameson, 481]
11. **Uncle Tom's Cabin** highly effective, sentimental Abolitionist novel. [Am. Lit.: Jameson, 513]
12. **Underground Railroad** system which helped slaves to escape to the North. [Am. Hist.: *EB*, X: 255]

26. APHRODISIAC

1. **cestus** Aphrodite's girdle made by Hephaestus; magically induces passion. [Gk. Myth.: Benét, 183]
2. **ginseng** induces passion. [Plant Symbolism: *EB*, IV: 549]
3. **lupin** leguminous plant; arouses passion. [Plant Folklore: Boland, 9]
4. **mandrake** a narcotic that arouses passion. [Western Folklore: Boland, 13]
5. **marjoram** used on bedsheets; Venus used it with Ascanius. [Rom. Myth.: Boland, 11–12]
6. **periwinkle, worms, and houseleek** combination induces passion. [Plant Folklore: Boland, 9]
7. **raw oysters** food consumed as a love potion. [Popular Folklore: Misc.]

8. **Spanish fly** preparation made of green blister beetles and used to incite cattle to mate. [Insect Symbolism: *EB*, IX: 399]

9. **willow seeds** taken in water, produce only sons. [Western Folklore: Boland, 11]

27. **APOCALYPSE**

1. **behemoth** king of animals whose flesh will provide feast for chosen when Messiah comes. [Jew. Tradition: Leach, 132]

2. **Four Horsemen of the Apocalypse** four riders symbolizing pestilence, war, famine, and death. [*N.T.: Revelation* 6:1–8]

3. **Gog and Magog** giant leaders in ultimate battle against God's people. [*N.T.: Revelation* 20:8]

4. **Götterdämmerung** day of great battle between Teutonic gods and forces of evil. [Ger. Folklore: Leach, 461]

5. **leviathan** sea monster; symbol of apocalypse. [Jew. Tradition: Leach, 67]

6. **Revelation** final book of the New Testament discussing the coming of the world's end. [*N.T.: Revelation*]

28. **APOSTASY** (See also SACRILEGE.)

1. **Aholah and Aholibah** symbolize Samaria's and Jerusalem's abandonment to idols. [*O.T.: Ezekiel* 23:4]

2. **Albigenses** heretical sect; advocated Manichaean dualism. [Fr. Hist.: *NCE*, 53]

3. **Arians** 4th-century heretical sect; denied Christ's divinity. [Christian Hist.: Brewer *Note-Book*, 43]

4. **Big-endians** heretical group; always break eggs unlawfully at large end. [Br. Lit.: *Gulliver's Travels*]

5. **Cathari** heretical Christian sect in 12th and 13th centuries; professed a neo-Manichaean dualism. [Christian Hist.: *EB*, II: 639]

6. **Donatists** Christian group in North Africa who broke with Catholicism (312). [Christian Hist.: *EB*, III: 618]

7. **Ebionites** 2nd- and 3rd-century Christian ascetic sect that retained a Jewish emphasis. [Christian Hist.: *EB*, III: 768]

8. **Erastianism** doctrine declaring state is superior to the church in ecclesiastical affairs (1524–1543). [Christian Hist.: *EB*, III: 937]

9. **Fires of Smithfield** Marian martyrs burnt at stake as heretics. [Br. Hist.: Brewer *Dictionary*, 1013]

10. **Gnosticism** heretical theological movement in Greco-Roman world of 2nd century. [Christian Hist.: *EB*, IV: 587]

11. **Inquisition** Roman Catholic tribunal engaged in combating and suppressing heresy. [Christian Hist.: *NCE*, 1352]

12. **Jansenism** unorthodox Roman Catholic movement of the 17th and 18th centuries led by Cornelius Jansen. [Christian Hist.: *EB*, V: 515]

13. **Lollards** in late medieval England, a name given to followers of unorthodox philosopher John Wycliffe. [Christian Hist.: *EB*, VI: 306]

14. **min** appellation of any heretic, Jew or non-Jew. [Judaism: Wigoder, 417]

15. **Monophysites** heretical Christian sect who questioned the divine and human nature of Jesus. [Christian Hist.: *EB*, VI: 1003]

16. **Montanism** 2nd-century heretical Christian movement led by prophet, Montanus. [Christian Hist.: *EB*, VI: 1012]

17. **Sabellianism** 3rd-century Christian heresy led by Sabellius. [Christian Hist.: *EB*, VIII: 747]

29. **APPEARANCES, DECEIVING (See also ILLUSION.)**

1. **Baldwin, George** "good" lawyer having affair with client's wife. [Am. Lit.: *The Manhattan Transfer*]

2. **Clinker, Humphry** admirable character concealed by shabby exterior. [Br. Lit.: *Humphry Clinker*]

3. **Cory, Richard** man "with everything" commits suicide. [Am. Lit.: "Richard Cory" in Hart, 711]

4. **daffodil** beautiful, but narcotic. [Plant Symbolism: *Flora Symbolica*, 168]

5. **Gray, Dorian** his portrait becomes the record of his life. [Br. Lit.: *The Picture of Dorian Gray*]

6. **Little Buttercup** apparently dumpy woman revealed as beautiful. [Br. Opera: *H.M.S. Pinafore*]

7. **Phaedra** pretends unkindness to Hippolytus to hide her passion for him. [Fr. Drama: *Phaedra*, Magill, I, 741–742]

8. **Sawyer, Tom** pretends punishment is reward to hoodwink friends. [Am. Lit.: *Tom Sawyer*]

9. **Tchitchikoff** swindler-adventurer, outwardly a philanthropist. [Russ. Lit.: *Dead Souls*]

10. **Valancourt** his gambling not a vice but attempt to secure money to aid friends. [Br. Lit.: *The Mysteries of Udolpho*, Magill, I, 635–638]

11. **Venus's-flytrap** lures insects with sweet odor. [Flower Symbolism: *Flora Symbolica*, 178]

30. **APPLE**

1. **Adam and Eve** original couple tempted to eat forbidden fruit. [*O.T.: Genesis* 2:17]

2. **Apple Annie** nickname for women who sold apples on street corners during the Depression. [Am. Culture: Flexner, 11]

3. **Appleseed, Johnny** (John Chapman, 1774–1845), missionary nurseryman who supplied apple seeds to pioneers. [Am. Folklore: *EB*, II: 746]

4. **Big Apple** nickname for New York City. [Am. Folklore: Misc.]

5. **forbidden fruit** fruit that God forbade Adam and Eve to eat; byword for tempting object. [*O.T.: Genesis* 3:1–6]

6. **Newton, Isaac** (1642–1727) English mathematician whose observation of apple's fall led to treatise on gravitation. [Br. Hist.: *EB*, 13: 16–21]

7. **Tell, William** Swiss folk hero condemned to shoot apple from atop son's head. [Swiss Folklore: *EB*, IX: 872]

31. **ARCHITECTURE**

1. **Daedalus** mythical Greek architect said to have built the labyrinth for King Minos of Crete. [Gk. Myth.: *EB*, III: 342]

2. **Roecus** architect of the early temple of Hera at Samos. [Architecture: *NCE*, 1799]

3. **Thomas, St.** patron saint of architects. [Christian Hagiog.: *Saints and Festivals*, 30]

32. **ARGUMENTATIVENESS**

1. **Absolute, Sir Anthony** warm-hearted but testy; always blames others. [Br. Drama.: *The Rivals*]

2. **Caterpillar** peevishly disputes with Alice. [Br. Lit.: *Alice's Adventures in Wonderland*]

3. **Lessways, Hilda** husband Edwin could never agree with her. [Br. Lit.: *The Clayhanger Trilogy*]

4. **Naggleton, Mr. and Mrs.** contentious and fault finding couple. [Br. Lit.: *Punch*, 1864–1865; Brewer *Handbook*, 742]

5. **Philadelphia lawyer** lawyer known for skill in arguing cases. [Am. Usage: Misc.]

33. **ARISTOCRACY**

1. **Almanach de Gotha** German social register. [Ger. Lit.: Benét, 26]

2. **Beaucaire, Monsieur** portrays English aristocracy as shallow, inept snobs. [Am. Lit.: *Monsieur Beaucaire*, Magill, I, 616–617]

3. **Brahmin** appellation accorded members of old, "aristocratic" New England families. [Am. Hist.: *EB*, II: 226]

4. **Cabala, The** portrays wealthy esoterics, mysteriously influential in governmental affairs. [Am. Lit.: *The Cabala*]

5. **First Families of Virginia** elite families of prestigious rank. [Am. Usage: Misc.]

6. **the Four Hundred** social elite; the number of people Mrs. Astor could accommodate in her ballroom. [Am. Usage: Misc.]

7. **gold on white** symbol of elite class. [Chinese Art: Jobes, 357]

8. **Junkers** Prussian elite. [Ger. Hist.: *Hitler*, 387]

9. **Social Register** book listing names and addresses of social elite. [Am. Usage: Misc.]

10. **St. Aubert, Emily** young French woman of wealth and position. [Br. Lit.: *The Mysteries of Udolpho*, Magill, I, 635–638]

11. **Winthrop** English upper-class family; America's parliamentary governors. [Am. Hist.: Hart, 937–938]

34. **ARRIVISM (See also PHILISTINISM.)**

1. **Beverly Hillbillies, The** hillbillies transplanted by wealth to Beverly Hills. [TV: Terrace, I, 93–94]

2. **Gatsby, Jay** nouveau riche entrepreneur displays wealth on Long Island. [Am. Lit.: *The Great Gatsby*]

3. **Jefferson, George** bumptious Black who thinks money is everything. [TV: "The Jeffersons" in Terrace, I, 409–410]

4. **Jiggs and Maggie** they flounder in seas of sudden wealth. [Comics: "Bringing up Father" in Horn, 132]

5. **Jourdain, Monsieur** elderly tradesman who spends wealth trying to raise his social status. [Fr. Lit.: *Le Bourgeois Gentilhomme*]

6. **Newman, Christopher** nouveau riche entrepreneur feels he deserves an aristocratic wife. [Am. Lit.: *The American*]

35. **ARROGANCE** (See also **BOASTFULNESS, CONCEIT, EGOTISM.**)

1. **amber** traditional meaning. [Gem Symbolism: Jobes, 81]

2. **Arachne** presumptuously challenges Athena to weaving contest; transformed into spider. [Gk. Myth.: Leach, 69]

3. **Citizen Kane** rich and powerful man drives away friends by use of power. [Am. Cinema: Halliwell, 149]

4. **Coriolanus** class-conscious and contemptuous leader. [Br. Lit.: *Coriolanus*]

5. **Darcy, Fitz William** proud of superior station. [Br. Lit.: *Pride and Prejudice*]

6. **Duck, Donald** overbearing comic strip character with a chip on his shoulder. [Comics: Horn, 216–217]

7. **Dundreary, Lord** his aristocratic haughtiness a trademark. [Br. Lit.: *Our American Cousin*]

8. **Fell, Dr.** object of unexplainable dislike ("I do not love thee, Dr. Fell.") [Br. Lit.: Tho. Brown, in *Golden Treasury*]

9. **Lucy** know-it-all cartoon character gives advice to other children. [Comics: "Peanuts" in Horn, 543]

10. **Niobe** for boasting of superiority, her children are killed. [Gk. Myth.: Hall, 224; Rom. Lit.: *Metamorphoses*]

11. **rue** traditional symbol. [Flower Symbolism: *Flora Symbolica*, 177]

12. **tall sunflower** indicates haughtiness. [Flower Symbolism: *Flora Symbolica*, 177]

13. **Uzziah** punished with leprosy for arrogantly burning incense. [*O.T.: II Chronicles* 16:20]

14. **veni, vidi, vici** Caesar's dispatch describing his subjugation of Pharnaces (47 B.C.). [Rom. Hist.: Brewer *Note-Book*, 923]

15. **Volumnia** magisterial mother of Coriolanus; molds his character. [Br. Lit.: *Coriolanus*]

16. **yellow carnation** traditional symbol. [Flower Symbolism: Jobes, 291]

17. **yellow sultan** indicates contempt. [Flower Symbolism: *Flora Symbolica*, 177]

ARTFULNESS (See CUNNING.)

ARTLESSNESS (See INNOCENCE, NAIVENESS.)

36. **ASCENSION**

1. **Assumption of Virgin Mary** belief that Mary was assumed bodily into heaven. [Christian Tradition: *NCE*, 1709]

2. **crescent moon** Mary often depicted standing on or above moon. [Christian Iconog.: Brewer *Dictionary*, 726]

3. **Elijah** transported to heaven in fiery chariot. [*O.T.: II Kings* 2:11]

4. **Jesus Christ** 40 days after Resurrection, ascended into heaven. [*N.T.: Acts* 1:1–11]

5. **Marguerite** borne to heaven by angels. [Fr. Opera: *Faust*, Westerman, 183–185]

6. **mi'raj** Mohammed's night journey to paradise. [Islam: Leach, 731]

7. **stars, garland of** emblem associated with the Assumption of the Virgin Mary. [Christian Iconog.: Jobes, 374]

37. **ASCETICISM (See also AUSTERITY, DISCIPLINE.)**

1. **Albigenses** heretical and ascetic Christian sect in France in 12th and 13th centuries. [Christian Hist.: *EB*, I: 201]

2. **Alexis, St.** patron saint of beggars and hermits. [Christian Hagiog.: Brewer *Dictionary*, 22]

3. **Anthony, St.** founder of monasticism. [Christian Hagiog.: Attwater, 49]

4. **Béguines** 12th-century French mendicant order. [Fr. Hist.: Espy, 98–99]

5. **Cathari** heretical and ascetic Christian sect in Europe in 12th and 13th centuries. [Christian Hist.: *EB*, II: 639]

6. **Cincinnatus** left farm to fight; returned to plow. [Rom. Hist.: Espy, 335]

7. **Cistercians** Roman Catholic monastic order observing strict asceticism, founded in 1098. [Christian Hist.: *EB*, II: 948]

8. **Clare, St.** founder of mendicant Order of Poor Clares. [Christian Hagiog.: Hall, 69]

9. **Crazy Ivar** lived in hole on side of river bed. [Am. Lit.: *O Pioneers!*, Magill, I, 663–665]

10. **Diogenes** (412–323 B.C.) despised worldly possessions; made his home in a tub. [Gk. Hist.: Hall, 104]

11. **Fakirs** fanatical mendicant sects found primarily in India. [Asian Hist.: Brewer *Note-Book*, 310]

12. **Franciscans** 13th-century religious order whose members lived in poverty. [Christian Hist.: *EB*, IV: 273]

13. **Gandhi, Mohandas K.** (1869–1948) Indian spiritual leader; embodied Hindu abstemiousness. [Indian Hist.: *NCE*, 1042]

14. **Jerome, St.** Christian monastic leader who searched for peace as hermit in desert. [Christian Hist.: *EB*, V: 545]

15. **Manichaean Sabbath** Manichaean observance of Sunday, demanding abstinence from food and sex. [Christian Hist.: *EB*, VIII: 746]

16. **Paul of Thebes, St.** first Christian hermit; cave-dweller most of life. [Christian Hagiog.: Attwater, 268]

17. **Priscillianism** rigorously ascetic Christian sect found in Europe until the 6th century. [Christian Hist.: *EB*, VIII: 219]

18. **Stoicism** philosophical school in Greco-Roman antiquity advocating rationality and austerity. [Gk. Hist.: *EB*, VIII: 746]

19. **Stylites, St. Simeon** Christian monk whose philosophy was so ascetic that he dwelt atop a column to meditate. [Christian Hist.: *EB*, IX: 216]

20. **Timon of Athens** lost wealth, lived frugally; became misanthropic when deserted by friends. [Br. Lit.: *Timon of Athens*]

21. **Waldenses** members of 12th-century French religious movement living in poverty. [Christian Hist.: *EB*, X: 519]

22. **Xenocrates** temperate philosopher, noted for contempt of wealth. [Gk. Hist.: Brewer *Dictionary*, 1169]

38. **ASS**

1. **Balaam's ass** ass which rebukes Balaam who then blesses the Israelites. [*O.T.: Numbers* 22:22–35]

2. **Bottom, Nick** oaf upon whom Puck fixes ass's head. [Br. Lit.: *Midsummer Night's Dream*]

3. **Dapple** Sancho's ass. [Span. Lit.: *Don Quixote*]

4. **Democratic Party** donkey; symbol of Democratic Party in U.S. politics. [Am. Culture: Misc.]

5. **Golden Ass, The** portrays wandering donkey observing foibles of mankind. [Rom. Lit.: Benét, 44]

6. **Midas** for judging Pan winner of flute contest, his ears are changed to ass's ears. [Gk. Myth.: Leach, 83]

7. **Pinocchio and Lampwick** naughtiness causes them to sprout donkey's ears and tails. [Am. Cinema: *Pinocchio* in *Disney Films*, 32–37]

39. **ASSASSIN**

1. **assassins** Fanatical Moslem sect that smoked hashish and murdered Crusaders (11th–12th centuries). [Islamic Hist.: Brewer *Note-Book*, 52]

2. **Brutus** conspirator and assassin of Julius Caesar. [Br. Lit.: *Julius Caesar*]

40. **ASSASSINATION (See also MURDER.)**

1. **Caesar, Julius** (102–44 B.C.) murdered by conspirators. [Br. Lit.: *Julius Caesar*]

2. **Ides of March** Caesar killed by opposing factions (44 B.C.). [Rom. Hist.: *EB*, 3: 575–580]

41. **ASTROLOGY**

1. **Chaldea** ancient Mesopotamian land where study of astrology developed. [Ancient Hist.: *NCE*, 499]

2. **Ecclitico** manipulator and false astrologer; dupes Buonafede. [Ger. Opera: Haydn, *The World of the Moon*, Westermark, 68–69]

3. **Mannering, Guy** cast fateful horoscope for young Bertram. [Br. Lit.: *Guy Mannering*]

4. **Nostradamus** (1503–1566) French astrologer/seer; wrote *Centuries* (1555), famous book of prognostications. [Fr. Hist.: *NCE*, 1969]

5. **Urania** muse of astrology. [Gk. Myth.: Brewer *Dictionary*, 1119]

42. ASTRONAUTICS

1. **Rogers, Buck** early spaceman in fantasy comics. [Comics: Horn, 137–138]

43. ASTRONOMY

1. **Aristarchus of Samos** (fl. c. 270 B.C.) Greek astronomer; first to maintain that Earth rotates and revolves around Sun. [Gk. Hist.: *EB*, I: 514]

2. **Copernicus, Nicholas** (1453–1543) Polish astronomer; author of the Copernican theory that planets orbit the sun. [Polish Hist.: *NCE*, 652]

3. **Galileo** (1564–1642) Italian mathematician, astronomer, and physicist. [Ital. Hist.: *EB*, IV: 388]

4. **Halley, Edmond** (1656–1742) British mathematician and astronomer; calculated orbit of comet named after him. [Br. Hist.: *EB*, IV: 860]

5. **Hipparchus** (fl. 146–127 B.C.) astronomer who calculated the year and discovered the precession of the equinoxes. [Turkish Hist.: *EB*, V: 55]

6. **Ptolemy** (85–165) eminent Greek astronomer. [Gk. Hist.: Hall, 255]

7. **Urania** muse of astronomy. [Gk. Myth.: Jobes, 374]

44. AUSTERITY (See also ASCETICISM, DISCIPLINE.)

1. **Amish** conservative Christian group in North America noted for its simple, orderly life and nonconformist dress. [Am. Hist.: *EB*, I: 316]

2. **Borromeo, Charles** archbishop; lived thriftily; gave money to poor. [Ital. Hist.: Hall, 65]

3. **Cato, Marcus Porcius** (234–149 B.C.) Roman statesman known for conservatism; taxed luxuries. [Rom. Hist.: *EB*, II: 645]

4. **Clennam, Mrs.** ascetic woman; wears only black. [Br. Lit.: *Little Dorrit*]

5. **common thistle** indicates starkness. [Flower Symbolism: *Flora Symbolica*, 178]

6. **Dotheboys Hall** Mr. Squeers's school: no extras, no vacations. [Br. Lit.: *Nicholas Nickleby*]

7. **Puritanism** 16th- and 17th-century religious reform movement noted for its moral earnestness and austerity. [Br. and Am. Hist.: *EB*, VIII: 309]

8. **Shakers** celibate religious sect flourishing in 19th-century U.S. [Am. Hist.: *EB*, IX: 105]

9. **Spartans** residents of Greek city known for its stern dedication to militarism. [Gk. Hist.: *EB*, IX: 403]

45. AUTHORITY

1. **cathedra** throne indicative of religious power. [Folklore: Jobes, 307]

2. **crook** staff carried as a symbol of office and authority. [Western Culture: Misc.]

3. **crosier** bishop's staff signifying his ruling power. [Christian Symbolism: Appleton, 21]

4. **cross and ball** signifies that spiritual power is above temporal. [Heraldry: Jobes, 387]

5. **crown** headpiece worn as symbol of royal authority. [Western Culture: Misc.]

6. **double bar cross** signifies archbishops, cardinals, and patriarchs. [Christian Iconog.: Jobes, 386]

7. **eagle** attribute of Zeus, thus of authority. [Art: Hall, 109]

8. **fasces** rods bundled about ax; emblem of magistrates, Fascists. [Rom. Hist.: Hall, 119; Ital. Hist.: Brewer *Dictionary*, 399]

9. **gavel** small mallet used by judge or presiding officer to signal order. [Western Culture: Misc.]

10. **globe** in Christ child's hands signifies power and dominion. [Christian Symbolism: de Bles, 25]

11. **keys** symbolic of St. Peter's spiritual authority. [Christian Symbolism: *N.T.: Matthew* 16:19]

12. **mace** ceremonial staff carried as a symbol of office and authority. [Western Culture: Misc.]

13. **nimbus** cloud of light signifying might, divinely imparted. [Gk. Lit.: *Iliad*]

14. **pectoral cross** worn by prelates on chain around neck. [Christian Iconog.: Child, 255; Jobes, 386]

15. **purple** color worn by persons of high rank. [Western Culture: Misc.]

16. **rod** wand or staff carried as a symbol of office and authority. [Western Culture: Misc.]

17. **scepter** symbol of regal or imperial power and authority. [Western Culture: Misc.]

18. **Stone of Scone** coronation stone where kings of Scotland were crowned. [Br. Hist.: Brewer *Dictionary*, 970]

19. **throne** seat of political or religious authority. [Western Folklore: Jobes, 1567]

20. **triple cross** three upper arms; symbolizes authority of the pope. [Christian Iconog.: Jobes, 386]

AUTOBIOGRAPHY (See BIOGRAPHY, AUTOBIOGRAPHY.)

46. **AUTUMN**

1. **Autumnus** personification; portrayed as mature and manly. [Rom. Myth.: *LLEI*, I: 322]

2. **Bacchus** god of this season. [Rom. Myth.: Hall, 130]

3. **Carpo** goddess of autumn and corn season. [Gk. Myth.: Kravitz, 53]

4. **cornucopia** conical receptacle full of the fruits of the harvest. [World Culture: Misc.]

5. **grapes and vine leaves** symbolize harvest of vineyards for wine. [Art: Hall, 130]

6. **Indian summer** a period of mild, dry weather occurring in U.S. and Canada in late autumn. [Am. Culture: Misc.]

47. **AVIATION**

1. **Kitty Hawk** site of first manned, powered flight (1903). [Am. Hist.: Jameson, 563]

2. **Lafayette Escadrille** American aviators assisting Allies in WWI. [Am. Hist.: Jameson, 273]

3. **Red Baron** nickname given to Baron Richthofen. [Aviation: *EB*, VIII: 574]

4. **Smilin' Jack** comic strip pilot who solves crimes. [Comics: "Smilin' Jack" in Horn, 624–625]

5. **Spirit of St. Louis** Charles Lindbergh's plane. [Am. Hist.: Jameson, 287]

6. **Wright brothers** creators-aviators of first manned aircraft (1903). [Am. Hist.: Jameson, 563]

48. **AWKWARDNESS (See also INEPTITUDE.)**

   1. **Clouseau, Inspector Jacques** bungling detective who inadvertently but always gets his man. [Am. Cinema: "The Pink Panther" in Halliwell, 565–566]
   2. **Crane, Ichabod** lanky Yankee schoolmaster who loves Katrina. [Am. Lit.: *The Legend of Sleepy Hollow*]
   3. **Dobbin, Captain William** tall, uncouth, awkward fellow with large feet. [Br. Lit.: *Vanity Fair*]
   4. **Goofy** bumbling, awkward dog; originally named Dippy Dawg. [Comics: "Mickey Mouse" in Horn, 492]
   5. **Gringoire** a penniless, stupid, and oafish poet. [Fr. Lit.: *The Hunchback of Notre Dame*]
   6. **Li'l Abner** ungainly comic strip oaf with height of six foot three. [Comics: Horn, 450]
   7. **Small, Lennie** simple-minded, clumsy giant; parasite of George. [Am. Lit.: *Of Mice and Men*]

B

49. **BACHELORDOM**

1. **bachelor's button** celibacy symbol. [Flower Symbolism: Jobes, 171]

2. **Dillon, Matt** bachelor U.S. Marshal fights for law and order in Old West. [TV: "Gunsmoke" in Terrace, I, 331–332]

3. **laurel** symbol of unmarried scholar; whence, *baccalaureate*. [Flower Symbolism: Emboden, 25]

4. **Mason, Perry** bachelor lawyer. [TV: Terrace, II, 199]

5. **Morgan, Rex** bachelor doctor stars in comic strip. [Comics: "Rex Morgan, M.D." in Horn, 580–581]

6. **Odd Couple, The** pair of bachelors living the good life in New York. [Am. Lit. and TV: Terrace, II, 160–161]

7. **Pumblechook** eminently "available" uncle of Joe Gargery. [Br. Lit.: *Great Expectations*]

BADNESS (See EVIL.)

50. **BALDNESS**

1. **bald eagle** U.S. national bird whose white head looks bald. [Am. Hist.: *EB*, I: 753]

2. **Mowgli** (the Frog) name given infant by wolves for hairlessness. [Children's Lit.: *The Jungle Book*]

51. **BALLOONING (See also AVIATION.)**

1. **Ferguson, Samuel** embarks with two others on air-borne journey over Africa. [Fr. Lit.: *Five Weeks in a Balloon*]

2. **Wizard of Oz** reaches and departs from Oz in circus balloon. [Children's Lit.: *The Wonderful Wizard of Oz*]

52. **BANISHMENT**

1. **Acadians** America's lost tribe; suffered expulsion under British. [Am. Hist.: Jameson, 2; Am. Lit.: "Evangeline" in Hart, 263]

2. **Adam and Eve** banished from the Garden of Eden for eating forbidden fruit. [*O.T.: Genesis* 3:23–24]

3. **anemone** ordered from Flora's court. [Gk. Myth.: *Flora Symbolica*, 172]

4. **Cain** cast out from homeland for murdering Abel. [*O.T.: Genesis* 4:12]

5. **Devil's Island** former French penal colony off French Guiana. [Fr. Hist.: *NCE*, 754]

6. **Elba** site of Napoleon's first exile (1814). [Fr. Hist.: *NCE*, 854]

7. **fire and water** Roman symbol of exile. [Rom. Hist.: Brewer *Note-Book*, 451]

8. **Hagar and Ishmael** Sarah orders Abraham to drive them out. [*O.T.: Genesis* 21:9–13]

9. **Ivanhoe** disinherited by father, Cedric the Saxon. [Br. Lit.: *Ivanhoe*]

10. **Jenik** banished by jealous stepmother. [Czech. Opera: Smetana, *Bartered Bride*, Westerman, 404]

11. **Nolan, Philip** treasonous man sentenced to live remainder of life at sea. [Am. Lit.: *Man Without a Country*]

12. **Oedipus** exiles himself for killing father and marrying mother. [Gk. Lit.: *Oedipus Rex*]

13. **Patmos** island of exile for St. John. [*N.T.: Revelation* 1:9]

14. **Posthumus** marries Cymbeline's daughter; Cymbeline banishes him. [Br. Lit.: *Cymbeline*]

15. **Pride's Purge** Cromwell's ejection of royalist MPs (1648). [Br. Hist.: Brewer *Note-Book*, 711]

16. **Rosalind** her sylvan exile sets scene for comedy. [Br. Lit.: *As You Like It*]

17. **Saint Helena** place of Napoleon's second exile (1815). [Fr. Hist.: *NCE*, 2397]

18. **Siberia** Soviet land of exile. [Geography. *NCE*, 2509–2510]

19. **Trail of Tears** forced march of 18,000 Cherokees westward to Indian Territory (Oklahoma); 4,000 die of disease and exposure (winter, 1838–1839). [Am. Hist.: *EB*, 2: 808]

20. **Tristram** expelled from Cornwall by King Mark for ten years. [Br. Lit.: *Le Morte d'Arthur*]

21. **Untouchables** lowest caste in India; social outcasts. [Ind. Culture: Brewer *Dictionary*, 1118]

53. **BANKRUPTCY (See also POVERTY.)**

1. **Birotteau, César** ruined by bad speculations and dissipated life. [Fr. Lit.: *Greatness and Decline of César Birotteau*, Walsh *Modern*, 58]

2. **Black Friday** day of financial panic (1869). [Am. Hist.: *RHDC*]

3. **Black Tuesday** day of stock market crash (1929). [Am. Hist.: Allen, 238]

4. **green cap** symbol. [Eur. Hist.: Brewer *Note-Book*, 390–391]

5. **Harland, Joe** drunk who loses fortune on Wall Street. [Am. Lit.: *The Manhattan Transfer*]

6. **Hassan, Abu** pretends to be dead to avoid debts. [Ger. Opera: von Weber, *Abu Hassan*, Westerman, 138–139]

7. **Henchard, Michael** loses business and social standing with bad financial planning. [Br. Lit.: *Mayor of Casterbridge*]

8. **Lydgate, Tertius** driven deeper into debt on daily basis. [Br. Lit.: *Middlemarch*]

9. **Panic of 1873** bank failures led to extended depression. [Am. Hist.: Van Doren, 267–268]

10. **Queer Street** condition of financial insolvency. [Am. Usage: Misc.]

54. BAPTISM

1. **Aenon** where St. John performed rites. [*N.T.: John* 3:23]

2. **Cornelius** Roman centurion baptized by Peter. [*N.T.: Acts* 10, 11]

3. **John the Baptist** prophet who baptized crowds and preached Christ's coming. [*N.T.: Matthew* 3:1–13]

4. **scallop shell** vessel used for conferral of sacrament. [Christian Symbolism: Appleton, 88]

55. BARRENNESS

1. **Andermatt, Christiane** takes series of baths hoping to cure childlessness. [Fr. Lit.: *Mont-Oriol*, Magill, I, 618–620]

2. **Barren Ground** novel portraying a woman's emotional sterility and her harsh labor on a farm. [Am. Lit.: *Barren Ground*]

3. **brown** symbol of unfruitfulness. [Color Symbolism: Jobes, 357]

4. **Death Valley** sterile, arid basin in Nevada and California. [Geography: *EB*, III: 417]

5. **Elizabeth** Virgin's kinswoman, blessed with pregnancy as old woman. [*N.T.: Luke* 1:5–25]

6. **Empty Quarter** vast desert in the Arabian peninsula. [Geography: *EB*, VIII: 703]

7. **Hannah** Elkanah's barren wife; prays to Lord who grants her a son, Samuel. [*O.T.: I Samuel* 1:6]

8. **Sahara** vast north African desert. [Geography: *EB*, VIII: 768]

9. **Sarah** Abraham's wife; unable to bear children. [*O.T.: Genesis* 11:30]

10. **Waste Land, The** portrays sterility and chaos of the contemporary world. [Br. Lit.: "The Waste Land" in Hart, 899–900]

BASHFULNESS (See TIMIDITY.)

56. **BATTLE (See also WAR.)**

1. **Actium** Octavian's naval defeat of Antony and Cleopatra (31 B.C.). [Rom. Hist.: *NCE*, 15]

2. **Agincourt** longbow helps British defeat French (1415). [Br. Lit.: *Henry V*; Br. Hist.: Harbottle *Battles*, 5]

3. **Alamo** fort at San Antonio that was site of Mexican massacre of Texans (1836). [Am. Hist.: Jameson, 8]

4. **Antietam** indecisive battle of the Civil War (1862). [Am. Hist.: Harbottle *Battles*, 15]

5. **Arbela** Alexander's rout of Darius (331 B.C.). [Classical Hist.: Harbottle *Battles*, 17]

6. **Armageddon** final battle between forces of good and evil. [*N.T.*: *Revelation* 16:16]

7. **Austerlitz** Napoleon's brilliant success over Austro-Russian coalition (1805). [Fr. Hist.: Harbottle *Battles*, 23–24]

8. **Balaclava** fought between Russians and British during Crimean War (1854). [Russ. Hist.: Harbottle *Battles*, 25–26]

9. **Battle of the Bulge** unsuccessful attempt by Germans to push Allies back from German territory (1944–1945). [Ger. Hist.: *EB*, II: 360–361]

10. **Belleau Wood** locale of significant American triumph in WWI (1918). [Am. Hist.: Jameson, 47]

11. **Bull Run** site of two important battles of the Civil War (1861) (1862). [Am. Hist.: Jameson, 68]

12. **Bunker Hill** "Don't shoot until you see the whites of their eyes"; American Revolutionary battle (1775). [Am. Hist.: Worth, 22]

13. **Cannae** perhaps Hannibal's greatest victory (216 B.C.). [Rom. Hist.: Harbottle *Battles*, 48]

14. **Coral Sea** first naval engagement exclusively involving planes versus ships (1942). [Am. Hist.: Van Doren, 488]

15. **Crécy** English over French; preeminence of longbow established (1346). [Fr. Hist.: Bishop, 382–385]

16. **Fort Sumter** site of opening blow of Civil War (1861). [Am. Hist.: Jameson, 486–487]

17. **Gettysburg** site of Pyrrhic victory for North in Civil War (1863). [Am. Hist.: Harbottle *Battles*, 97]

18. **Guadalcanal** Marines triumphed in first major U.S. offensive of WWII (1942–1943). [Am. Hist.: Van Doren, 490]

19. **Hastings** battle that determined the Norman Conquest of England (1066). [Br. Hist.: Harbottle *Battles*, 107]

20. **Iwo Jima** inspiring American triumph in the Pacific (1945). [Am. Hist.: Leonard, 472–480]

21. **Jutland** established British WWI naval supremacy (1916). [Br. Hist.: *EB*, 19: 954–955]

22. **Lexington** opening engagement of the American Revolution (1775). [Am. Hist.: Jameson, 283]

23. **Lindisfarne** object of first major Viking raid in Britain (792). [Br. Hist.: Grun, 86]

24. **Lucknow** Indian mutiny put down by British (1858). [Ind. Hist.: Harbottle *Battles*, 143]

25. **Marathon** Persian Goliath felled by Greek David (490 B.C.). [Classical Hist.: Harbottle *Battles*, 152]

26. **Midway** site of decisive battle between Japanese and Americans in WWII (1942). [Am. Hist.: *EB*, VI: 877–878]

27. **Mount Badon** here Arthur soundly defeated the Saxons (c. 520). [Arthurian Legend: Benét, 72]

28. **New Orleans** fought after treaty had been signed (1815). [Am. Hist.: Worth, 22]

29. **Normandy Invasion** Allied invasion of Europe during WWII; D-Day (June 6, 1944). [Eur. Hist.: *EB*, VII: 391]

30. **Okinawa** scene of American amphibian operations during WWII (1945). [Am. Hist.: *EB*, VII: 505]

31. **Orléans** Joan of Arc's inspired triumph over English (1429). [Fr. Hist.: Bishop, 392]

32. **Pearl Harbor** site of Japanese surprise attack (December 7, 1941). [Am. Hist.: *EB*, VII: 822]

33. **Plains of Abraham** English victory decided last of French and Indian wars (1759). [Br. Hist.: *NCE*, 7]

34. **Ravenna** site of battle between Greeks and Italians; Greeks were routed (729). [Gk. Hist.: Harbottle *Battles*, 207]

35. **Salamis** Xerxes' horde repulsed by numerically inferior Greek navy (480 B.C.). [Class. Hist.: Harbottle *Battles*, 219]

36. **Samarkand** Arabs defeated Chinese (751); precipitated westward spread of Chinese cultural/technological advances. [Chinese Hist.: Grun, 78]

37. **Saratoga (Stillwater)** fought between Americans and British during Revolution (1777). [Am. Hist.: Harbottle *Battles*, 237–238]

38. **Sedan** decisive battle of the Franco-German War (1870). [Fr. Hist.: Harbottle *Battles*, 225]

39. **Stalingrad** unsuccessful German assault on Stalingrad, Russia (1942–1943). [Ger. Hist.: *EB*, IX: 517]

40. **Thermopylae** 300 Spartans liquidated by Xerxes' horde (480 B.C.). [Classical Hist.: Harbottle *Battles*, 248]

41. **Trafalgar** defeat of French; zenith of British naval history (1805). [Br. Hist.: Harbottle *Battles*, 252–253]

42. **Trenton** Washington's brilliant surprise attack galvanized American morale (1776). [Am. Hist.: Jameson, 508]

43. **Valmy** battle fought between French and Prussians (1792). [Eur. Hist.: Harbottle *Battles*, 259]

44. **Verdun** site of numerous battles. [Fr. Hist.: *EB*, X: 395]

45. **Vicksburg** city held by Confederates; besieged several times (1862) (1863). [Am. Hist.: Harbottle *Battles*, 261–262]

46. **Waterloo** site of Napoleon's defeat (1815). [Fr. Hist.: Harbottle *Battles*, 266]

47. **Yorktown** site of Union victory in Civil War (1862). [Am. Hist.: Harbottle *Battles*, 271]

57. BEAUTY

1. **Aglaia** one of the Graces; embodiment of comeliness. [Gk. Myth.: Brewer *Dictionary*, 481]

2. **Amoret (Amoretta)** typical of female loveliness. [Br. Lit.: *Faerie Queene*, Brewer *Dictionary*, 30]

3. **Bathsheba** king David killed to gain her. [*O.T.: II Samuel* 11]

4. **Beauty** beautiful woman married to an enchanted beast who turns into a prince. [Fr. Fairy Tale: "Beauty and the Beast" in Walsh *Classical*, 49]

5. **Blodenwedd** created from oak flowers and meadowsweet. [Welsh Lit.: *Mabinogion*]

6. **cowslip** symbol. [Flower Symbolism: Jobes, 377]

7. **Deirdre** prophesied to become the most beautiful woman in Ireland. [Irish Legend: Benét, 259]

8. **Euphrosyne** one of the Graces; epitome of beauty in joy. [Gk. Myth.: Brewer *Dictionary*, 481]

9. **Graces** three daughters of Zeus and Eurynome; goddesses of charm and beauty. [Gk. Myth.: Howe, 61]

10. **hibiscus** symbol of beauty. [Flower Symbolism: *Flora Symbolica*, 174]

11. **Hora Quirini** goddess of loveliness. [Rom. Myth.: Kravitz, 44]

12. **Hypatia** (c. 370–415) Greek philosopher, renowned for beauty and wit. [Gk. Hist.: *NCE*, 1302]

13. **lilies of the field** more splendidly attired than Solomon. [*N.T.*: *Matthew* 6:28–29; *Luke* 12:27–31]

14. **Monday's child** fair of face. [Nurs. Rhyme: Opie, 309]

15. **peri** beautiful fairylike creatures, guided way to heaven. [Pers. Myth.: Brewer *Dictionary*, 822]

16. **Snow White** snow-toned flesh, ebony hair, blood-red lips. [Ger. Fairy Tale: Grimm, 184]

17. **Thalia** one of the Graces; bestowed charm on others. [Gk. Myth.: Brewer *Dictionary*, 481]

18. **Ugly Duckling** scorned as unsightly, grows to be graceful swan. [Dan. Fairy Tale: *Andersen's Fairy Tales*]

19. **white camellia** symbol of beauty. [Flower Symbolism: Jobes, 281]

58. BEAUTY, FEMININE

1. **Annabel Lee** poet's beautiful beloved. [Am. Lit.: "Annabel Lee" in *Portable Poe*]

2. **Aphrodite** (Rom. **Venus**) archetype of feminine beauty. [Gk. Myth.: Parrinder, 24]

3. **Astarte** beautiful goddess of fertility and sexual love. [Phoenician Myth.: Zimmerman, 33]

4. **Cleopatra** beautiful queen of Egypt; wins Marc Antony's heart. [Br. Lit.: *Antony and Cleopatra*]

5. **crabapple blossom** traditional symbol. [Chinese Flower Symbolism: Jobes, 377]

6. **Doone, Lorna** her good looks stir John Ridd and others. [Br. Lit.: *Lorna Doone*, Magill, I, 524–526]

7. **Duchess of Alba** Goya's lover and model, immortalized on canvas. [Span. Art: Wallechinsky, 192]

8. **Etain** most beautiful woman in Ireland. [Irish Folklore: Briggs, 123–125]

9. **Freya** goddess of love, beauty, and fecundity; beautiful, blue-eyed blonde. [Norse Myth.: Leach, 425]

10. **Galatea** statue so striking, Venus grants sculptor Pygmalion's wish that it live. [Gk. Myth.: *LLEI*, I: 286]

11. **Gibson girl** classic, comely woman of illustrations (1890s). [Am. Hist.: Flexner, 283]

12. **Golden Bells** epitome of the beautiful Chinese woman. [Irish Lit.: *Messer Marco Polo*, Magill, I, 584–585]

13. **Hebe** beautiful cupbearer to the gods. [Gk. Myth.: Zimmerman, 117]

14. **Helen of Troy** beautiful woman kidnapped by smitten Paris, precipitating Trojan war. [Gk. Lit.: *Iliad; Trojan Women;* Euripides, *Helene*]

15. **Kriemhild** Burgundian princess's beauty known throughout Europe. [Ger. Lit.: *Nibelungenlied*]

16. **Marcella** farmer's daughter; every bachelor fancies her. [Span. Lit.: *Don Quixote*]

17. **Marie Antoinette** (1755–1793) beautiful queen consort of King Louis XVI of France. [Fr. Hist.: *EB*, VI: 620]

18. **Miss America** annually selected most beautiful young woman in America. [Am. Hist.: Allen, 56–57]

19. **O'Hara, Scarlett** epitome of a beautiful Southern belle. [Am. Lit.: *Gone With the Wind*]

20. **Simonetta** Botticelli's hauntingly beautiful young model. [Ital. Art: Wallechinsky, 190]

21. **Teal Eye** "Her beauty remained forever in Boone's memory." [Am. Lit.: *The Big Sky*]

22. **Tehani** lovely Tahitian girl loved by Byam. [Br. Lit.: *Mutiny on the Bounty*]

23. **Van Tassel, Katrina** rich farmer's daughter, pursued by Ichabod Crane and Brom Bones. [Am. Lit.: *The Legend of Sleepy Hollow*]

24. **Venus de Milo** armless statue of pulchritudinous goddess. [Gk. Art: Brewer *Dictionary*, 1126]

59. BEAUTY, LASTING

1. **Célimène** beauty not diminished by character or age. [Fr. Drama: *The Misanthrope*]

2. **Mona Lisa** La Gioconda, da Vinci's enchanting portrait. [Ital. Art: Wallechinsky, 190]

3. **My Last Duchess** poem about a wife whose beauty is frozen in portrait. [Br. Lit.: "My Last Duchess" in Norton, 757–758]

4. **stock** symbolizes enduring loveliness. [Flower Symbolism: *Flora Symbolica*, 177]

60. BEAUTY, MASCULINE (See also VIRILITY.)

1. **Absalom** flawlessly handsome. [*O.T.: II Samuel* 14:25]

2. **Adonis** beautiful youth. [Gk. Myth.: Brewer *Dictionary*, 11]

3. **Andrews, Joseph** handsome, virtuous man admired by many ladies. [Br. Lit.: *Joseph Andrews*]

4. **Apollo** god of manly beauty. [Gk. Myth.: Leach, 67]

5. **Balder** god of light and joy; known for his beauty. [Norse Myth.: Leach, 106]

6. **Chateaupers, Phoebus de** gallant, handsome horseman eternally loved by Esmeralda. [Fr. Lit.: *The Hunchback of Notre Dame*]

7. **David** sculpture by Michelangelo depicting figure epitomizing male beauty. [Art: Osborne, 718]

8. **Glaucus** handsome, wealthy young Greek pursued by various ladies. [Br. Lit.: *The Last Days of Pompeii*, Magill, I, 490–492]

9. **Hylas** Hercules' servant; so captivates Naiads, they abduct him. [Gk. Myth.: Hall, 158]

10. **Hyperion** one of the Titans; known for his beauty. [Gk. Myth.: Zimmerman, 132]

11. **Narcissus** beautiful youth who falls in love with his own reflection. [Gk. Myth.: Zimmerman, 171–172]

61. BEAUTY, RUSTIC

1. **Amaryllis** a favorite subject of pastoral poets. [Rom. Lit.: *Eclogues*]

2. **Chloë** beautiful shepherdess beloved by Daphnis. [Rom. Lit.: "Daphne and Chloë" in Brewer *Handbook*, 204]

3. **Dulcinea** beautiful peasant woman idealized by Don Quixote. [Span. Lit.: *Don Quixote*]

4. **Pocahontas** natural beauty embodied in an Indian maiden. [Am. Hist.: *EB*, VIII: 57]

5. **Ragmaid** no one but the prince sees through her dishevelment. [Br. Fairy Tale: "The Little Ragmaid" in Macleod, 39–44]

6. **Tess of the D'Urbervilles** beautiful country girl. [Br. Lit.: *Tess of the D'Urbervilles*]

7. **Thestylis** embodiment of peasant prettiness. [Br. Lit.: *L'Allegro*, Brewer *Dictionary*, 1074]

62. BEAUTY, SENSUAL (See SEX SYMBOL.)

1. **Angelica** infidel princess of exquisite grace and charm. [Ital. Lit.: *Orlando Innamorato; Orlando Furioso*]

2. **Borgia, Lucrezia** (1480–1519) her beauty was as legendary as her rumored vices and heartlessness. [Ital. Hist.: Plumb, 59]

3. **Buchanan, Daisy** Jay Gatsby's femme fatale. [Am. Lit.: *The Great Gatsby*]

4. **Cleopatra** seductive queen of Egypt; beloved by Marc Antony. [Br. Lit.: *Antony and Cleopatra*]

5. **Helen of Troy** Faust's desire to possess her makes him faint. [Ger. Lit.: *Faust*]

6. **Jezebel** Phoenician princess; enemy of the prophets; name is a byword for wicked woman. [*O.T.: I Kings* 16:21, 31; *II Kings* 9:1–10, 30–37]

7. **Lolita** precociously seductive 12-year-old. [Am. Lit.: *Lolita*]

8. **Madeline** gazed at in awe by Porphyro. [Br. Lit.: "The Eve of St. Agnes" in Magill, I, 263–264]

9. **Montez, Lola** (c. 1818–1861) Irish singer and dancer; mistress to famous men. [Irish Hist.: *NCE*, 1821]

10. **Phryne** courtesan, acquitted of charge by baring bosom. [Gk. Hist.: Brewer *Dictionary*, 830]

11. **Playmate of the Month** nude girl provocatively gracing *Playboy's* centerfold. [Am. Culture: Flexner, 285]

12. **Queen of Sheba** sultry Biblical queen who visits Solomon. [*O.T.: I Kings* 10]

13. **Salome** seductive dancer who obtains head of John the Baptist as reward. [*N.T.: Matthew* 14:3, 11]

14. **Vye, Eustacia** capricious, seductive, trouble-making heroine. [Br. Lit.: *Return of the Native*, Harvey, 690]

63. BESTIALITY (See also PERVERSION.)

1. **Asterius** Minotaur born to Pasiphaë and Cretan Bull. [Gk. Myth.: Zimmerman, 34]

2. **Leda** raped by Zeus in form of swan. [Gk. Myth.: Zimmerman, 149]

3. **Lucius** transformed into ass, makes love with harlot. [Rom. Lit.: *The Golden Ass*]

4. **Pasiphaë** positioned inside hollow cow, consummates lust for bull. [Gk. Myth.: Hall, 234; Gk. Lit.: *Imagines* 1:16]

5. **Zeus** in form of a swan, seduces and impregnates Leda. [Gk. Myth.: Zimmerman, 149]

64. BIGOTRY (See also ANTI-SEMITISM.)

1. **Beaumanoir, Sir Lucas de** prejudiced ascetic; Grand Master of Templars. [Br. Lit.: *Ivanhoe*]

2. **Bunker, Archie** middle-aged bigot in television series. [TV: "All in the Family" in Terrace, I, 47–48]

3. **fiery cross** used as symbolic threat by Ku Klux Klan. [Am. Hist.: Jobes, 387]

4. **Grundy, Mrs.** unconventional actions evoked "What will Mrs. Grundy say?" [Br. Drama: Morton, *Speed the Plough*]

5. **Hitler, Adolf** (1889–1945) German dictator; his New Order excluded non-Aryans, e.g. Jews, Slavs. [Ger. Hist.: *Hitler*]

6. **Jim Crow** Negro stereotype popularized by 19th-century minstrel shows. [Am. Hist.: Van Doren, 138]

7. **John Birch Society** ultra-conservative, anti-Communist U.S. organization founded in 1958. [Am. Hist.: *NCE*, 1421]

8. **Ku Klux Klan** anti-Negro terrorist organization, started in southern U.S. [Am. Hist.: Allen, 46–49]

9. **Lebenshorn** Himmler's adoption/breeding scheme to produce master race. [Ger. Hist.: *Hitler*, 1046]

10. **Light in August** study of race problem in South. [Am. Lit.: *Light in August*]

11. **Little Rock, Arkansas** required military intervention to desegregate schools (1957–1958). [Am. Hist.: Van Doren, 556–557]

12. **Native Son** pictures underprivileged Negro as either churchgoer or criminal. [Am. Lit.: *Native Son*, Magill, I, 643–645]

13. **Nazi** *Nazionalsozialist;* rabid anti-Semite of Hitler's party. [Ger. Hist.: Shirer]

14. **New Order** partially fulfilled Nazification of Europe. [Eur. Hist.: *Hitler*, 935, 1055]

65. BIOGRAPHY, AUTOBIOGRAPHY

1. **Boswell, James** (1740–1793) Scottish author and devoted biographer of Samuel Johnson. [Br. Hist.: *NCE*, 341]

2. **Cellini, Benvenuto** (1500–1571) Italian sculptor and author of important autobiography. [Ital. Lit.: *NCE*, 488]

3. **Franklin, Benjamin** (1706–1790) American statesman; author of famous autobiography. [Am. Lit.: *NCE*, 1000]

4. **Pepys, Samuel** (1633–1703) English public official; author of diary. [Br. Lit.: *NCE*, 2103]

5. **Plutarch** (c. 46–c. 120) Greek biographer known for his *Lives*, a collection of biographies of Greek and Roman leaders. [Gk. Lit.: *NCE*, 2170]

6. **Venerable Bede** (c. 673–735) Benedictine monk; wrote memorable biographies of English saints. [Br. Hist.: *NCE*, 257]

66. BIRDS

1. **Birdman of Alcatraz** (Robert Stroud, 1890–1963) from jailbird to famous ornithologist. [Am. Hist.: Worth, 28]

2. **Halitherses** Ithacan seer; ornithologist. [Gk. Myth.: Kravitz, 46]

BIRTH (See CHILDBIRTH.)

67. BIRTHSTONE

1. **amethyst** February. [Am. Gem Symbolism: Kunz, 319–320]

2. **aquamarine** March alternate birthstone. [Am. Gem Symbolism: Kunz, 319]

3. **bloodstone** March. [Am. Gem Symbolism: Kunz, 319–320]
4. **diamond** April. [Am. Gem Symbolism: Kunz, 319–320]
5. **emerald** May. [Am. Gem Symbolism: Kunz, 319–320]
6. **garnet** January. [Am. Gem Symbolism: Kunz, 319–320]
7. **moonstone** June alternate birthstone. [Am. Gem Symbolism: Kunz, 319]
8. **opal** October. [Am. Gem Symbolism: Kunz, 319–320]
9. **pearl** June. [Am. Gem Symbolism: Kunz, 319–320]
10. **peridot** August alternate birthstone. [Am. Gem Symbolism: Kunz, 319]
11. **ruby** July. [Am. Gem Symbolism: Kunz, 319–320]
12. **sapphire** September. [Am. Gem Symbolism: Kunz, 319–320]
13. **sardonyx** August. [Am. Gem Symbolism: Kunz, 319–320]
14. **topaz** November. [Am. Gem Symbolism: Kunz, 319–320]
15. **tourmaline** October alternate birthstone. [Am. Gem Symbolism: Kunz, 320]
16. **turquoise** December. [Am. Gem Symbolism: Kunz, 319–320]

68. **BLACKMAIL (See also BRIBERY.)**
1. **elders of Babylon** try to bribe Susanna into making love with them. [*Apocrypha: Daniel and Susanna* 13]
2. **Iago** amasses circumstantial evidence to convince Othello of Desdemona's infidelity. [Br. Lit.: *Othello*]
3. **Rigaud** adventurer and extortionist. [Br. Lit.: *Little Dorrit*]
4. **Rudge, Barnaby** extorts to achieve personal ends. [Br. Lit.: *Barnaby Rudge*]
5. **Sextus** threatens murder and dishonor to bed Lucretia. [Rom. Lit.: *Fasti; Livy;* Br. Lit.: *The Rape of Lucrece*]
6. **Wegg, Silas** attempts to blackmail Boffin. [Br. Lit.: *Our Mutual Friend*]

BLACKNESS (See NIGHT.)

BLASPHEMY (See APOSTASY.)

69. **BLINDNESS**
1. **Agib** dervish who lost an eye. [Arab. Lit.: *Arabian Nights*]
2. **Anchises** blinded by lightning. [Gk. Myth.: Walsh *Classical,* 22]
3. **Blind Pew** David, the blind beggar. [Br. Lit.: *Treasure Island*]
4. **Braille, Louis** (1809–1852) teacher of blind; devised raised printing which is read by touch. [Fr. Hist.: *NCE,* 354]
5. **Cratus** Titan who blinded Prometheus. [Gk. Myth.: Kravitz, 67–68]

6. **Cupid** blindfolded god of love. [Rom. Myth.: Jobes, 397]

7. **Gloucester** cruelly blinded by those he served. [Br. Lit.: *King Lear*]

8. **the Graeae** share one eye among them. [Gk. Myth.: Gayley, 208–210]

9. **Homer** sightless writer of *Iliad* and *Odyssey*. [Gr. Hist.: Wallechinsky, 13]

10. **Keller, Helen** (1880–1968) Achieved greatness despite blindness and deafness. [Am. Hist.: Wallechinsky, 13]

11. **Lucy, St.** vision restored after gouging out of eyes. [Christian Hagiog.: Brewster, 20–21]

12. **mole** said to lack eyes. [Medieval Animal Symbolism: White, 95–96]

13. **Nydia** beautiful flower girl lacks vision but "sees" love. [Br. Lit.: *The Last Days of Pompeii*, Magill, I, 490–492]

14. **Odilia, St.** recovered vision; shrine, pilgrimage for visually afflicted. [Christian Hagiog.: Attwater, 257]

15. **Oedipus** blinded self on learning he had married his mother. [Gk. Lit.: *Oedipus Rex*]

16. **Paul, St.** blinded by God on road to Damascus. [*N.T.: Acts* 9:1–19]

17. **Plutus** healed by two serpents under purple mantle. [Gk. Lit.: *Plutus*]

18. **Polyphemus** Cyclops blinded by Odysseus. [Gk. Myth.: *Odyssey*]

19. **Samson** Israelite hero deceptively blinded by Philistines. [*O.T.: Judges* 16:4–21]

20. **Stagg** sightless roomkeeper. [Br. Lit.: *Barnaby Rudge*]

21. **three blind mice** sightless rodents; lost tails to farmer's wife. [Nurs. Rhyme: Opie, 306]

22. **Tiresias** made sightless by Athena for viewing her nakedness. [Gk. Myth.: Brewer *Dictionary*, 1086]

23. **Tobit** sparrow guano falls into his eyes while sleeping. [*Apocrypha: Tobit* 2:10]

24. **Zedekiah** eyes put out for revolting against Nebuchadnezzar. [*O.T.: II Kings* 25:7]

70. **BOASTFULNESS (See also ARROGANCE, CONCEIT, EGOTISM.)**

1. **Aglaonice** Thessalian who claimed power over moon. [Gk. Legend: Brewer *Dictionary*, 16]

2. **Ajax (the greater)** archetypal *Miles Gloriosus*. [Br. Lit.: *Troilus and Cressida*]

3. **Anchises** Trojan prince; crippled for boasting of intimacy with Aphrodite. [Gk. Myth.: Zimmerman, 22]

4. **Armado** verbose braggart and pedant. [Br. Lit.: *Love's Labour's Lost*]

5. **Basilisco** knight renowned for foolish bragging. [Br. Lit.: *Solomon and Persida*, Brewer *Dictionary*, 83]

6. **Bessus** braggart soldier in the *Miles Gloriosus* tradition. [Br. Lit.: Walsh *Modern*, 55]

7. **Bluffe, Captain** blustering braggart and spurious war veteran. [Br. Lit.: *The Old Batchelour*]

8. **Bobadill, Captain** blustering braggadocio of yellow stripe. [Br. Lit.: *Every Man in His Humour*]

9. **Braggadocchio** empty braggart. [Br. Lit.: *Faerie Queene*]

10. **Drawcansir** blustering bully, known for his extravagantly boastful speeches. [Br. Lit.: *The Rehearsal*]

11. **Falstaff** jovial knight and rascal of brazen braggadocio. [Br. Lit.: *Merry Wives of Windsor; I Henry IV; II Henry IV*]

12. **Gascon** inhabitant of Gascony, France; people noted for their bragging. [Fr. Hist.: *NCE*, 1049]

13. **Glendower, Owen** Welsh ally of the Percys; his boastfulness antagonizes Hotspur. [Br. Lit.: *I Henry IV*]

14. **Kay, Sir** rude and vainglorious knight of the Round Table. [Br. Lit.: *Le Morte d'Arthur; Idylls of the King*]

15. **Mahon, Christopher** runaway boy tells stories with self as epitome of bravery. [Irish Lit.: *The Playboy of the Western World*, Magill, I, 758–759]

16. **Miles Gloriosus** comedy about a military braggart. [Rom. Lit.: *Miles Gloriosus*, Benét, 668]

17. **Parolles** cowardly braggart and wastrel. [Br. Lit.: *All's Well That Ends Well*]

18. **Pistol** knight of the "killing tongue and quiet sword." [Br. Lit.: *II Henry IV*]

19. **Rodomont** gallant but blustering Saracen leader. [Ital. Lit.: *Orlando Furioso; Orlando Innamorato*]

20. **Roister Doister, Ralph** well-to-do dolt brags loud and long of bravery. [Br. Lit.: *Ralph Roister Doister*]

21. **Sacripant** noisy braggart. [Ital. Lit.: *Secchia Rapita*, Brewer *Handbook*, 945]

22. **Scaramouche** talks a good fight; never does. [Ital. Lit.: Espy, 125]

23. **Texan** resident of second largest U.S. state; known for his tall tales. [Am. Culture: Misc.]
24. **Thraso** swaggering but foolish soldier. [Rom. Lit.: *The Eunuch*]

71. BOHEMIANISM

1. **Greenwich Village** area of southern Manhattan long identified with artists and writers. [Am. Culture: Misc.]
2. **Haight-Ashbury** neighborhood in San Francisco associated with beatnicks and "flower people" in the 1960s. [Am. Culture: Misc.]
3. **Latin Quarter** section of Paris on left bank of the Seine; home of students, artists, and writers. [Fr. Culture: *EB*, VI: 71–72]
4. **Olenska, Countess Ellen** often considers divorce; likes "unacceptable" people. [Am. Lit.: *The Age of Innocence*]
5. **SoHo** bohemian neighborhood So(uth of) Ho(uston Street), New York City. [Am. Culture: Misc.]

72. BOREDOM (See also FUTILITY.)

1. **Aldegonde, Lord St.** bored nobleman, empty of pursuits. [Br. Lit.: *Lothair*]
2. **Baudelaire, Charles** (1821–1867) French poet whose dissipated lifestyle led to inner despair. [Fr. Lit.: *NCE*, 248]
3. **Bovary, Emma** housewife suffers from ennui. [Fr. Lit.: *Madame Bovary*]
4. **Des Esseintes, Jean** in dissipation and isolation, develops morbid ennui. [Fr. Lit.: *Against the Grain*]
5. **Harthouse, James** thorough gentleman, weary of everything. [Br. Lit.: *Hard Times*]
6. **Oblomov, Ilya** Russian landowner; embodiment of physical and mental sloth. [Russ. Lit.: *Oblomov*]
7. **Povey, Constance Baines** uneventful thoughts, marriage best described as routine. [Br. Lit.: *The Old Wives' Tale*, Magill, I, 684–686]

73. BORESOMENESS

1. **Bellenden, Lady Margaret** tiresomely repeats story of Charles II's visit. [Br. Lit.: *Old Mortality*]
2. **Bovary, Charles** "dull-witted husband reeked of medicine and drugs." [Fr. Lit.: *Madame Bovary*]
3. **Dryasdust, Rev.** imaginary preface writer with wooden style. [Br. Lit.: Wheeler, 108]
4. **Warburton, Lord** Isabel's kindly, thoughtful, but overly boring suitor. [Am. Lit.: *The Portrait of a Lady*, Magill, I, 766–768]

5. **Welland, May** "correct but unexciting personality." [Am. Lit.: *The Age of Innocence*]

74. BOYISHNESS (See also MANNISHNESS.)

1. **Drew, Nancy** tall, slender, boyish, girl detective. [Children's Lit.: *Bungalow Mystery*]
2. **Jo** tall, awkward tomboy in March family. [Am. Lit.: *Little Women*]
3. **Oakley, Annie** (1860–1926) American markswoman with boyish style. [Am. Hist.: *Century Cyclopedia*, 2993]

75. BRAVERY

1. **Achilles** foremost Greek hero of Trojan War; brave and formidable warrior. [Gk. Hist.: *NCE*, 12]
2. **Adrastus** courageous Indian prince; Rinaldo's enemy. [Ital. Lit.: *Jerusalem Delivered*]
3. **Agenor** Antenor's son; distinguished for his valor in battle. [Gk. Myth.: Zimmerman, 12]
4. **Bajazet** fierce, reckless, indomitable Sultan of Turkey; Tamerlane's captive. [Br. Lit.: *Tamerlane*, Walsh *Modern*, 39]
5. **Beowulf** singlehandedly fights firebreathing dragon. [Br. Lit.: *Beowulf*]
6. **Birch, Harvey** at great risk spies on British. [Am. Lit.: *The Spy*]
7. **black agate** makes athletes brave and invincible. [Gem Symbolism: Jobes, 45]
8. **black poplar** symbol of bravery. [Plant Symbolism: *Flora Symbolica*, 176]
9. **Boadicea (Boudicca)** British queen and female warrior; slew 80,000 Romans. [Br. Hist.: Walsh *Classical*, 58]
10. **Bold Beauchamp** 14th-century champion; British generic for *warrior*. [Br. Hist.: Walsh *Classical*, 49]
11. **Breck, Alan** while evading enemies, risks his life to save others. [Br. Lit.: *Kidnapped*]
12. **bull** heraldic symbol of courage. [Heraldry: Halberts, 21]
13. **carp** a pictorial symbol of bravery. [Chinese and Jap. Folklore: Jobes, 292]
14. **Clorinda** Amazonian, battles in armor. [Ital. Lit.: *Jerusalem Delivered*]
15. **David** audaciously stands before and slays Goliath. [*O.T.: I Samuel* 17:48–51]
16. **French willow** indicates courage. [Flower Symbolism: *Flora Symbolica*, 178]

17. **Fritchie, Barbara** her bravery impressed Stonewall Jackson. [Am. Lit.: "Barbara Fritchie" in Hart, 57]

18. **Gawain** bravery in the Castle of Wonders. [Arth. Legend: *Parsival*]

19. **Hale, Nathan** (1755–1776) Revolutionary war hero, calmly accepted fate. [Am. Hist.: Jameson, 215]

20. **Havelok** right makes might as gallant prince triumphs. [Dan. Lit.: *Havelok the Dane*]

21. **Hector** captain and chief hero of Trojan forces. [Rom. Lit.: *Aeneid; Metamorphoses*]

22. **Horatius** holds off Etruscan forces while Romans burn bridge. [Rom. Hist.: *Livy*]

23. **Iron Cross** German medal awarded for outstanding bravery in wartime. [Ger. Hist.: Misc.]

24. **Joan of Arc, St.** peasant leader of French rout of British. [Christian Hagiog.: Attwater, 187]

25. **larch** symbol of bravery. [Tree Symbolism: *Flora Symbolica*, 175]

26. **Medal of Honor** highest American military decoration for wartime gallantry. [Am. Hist.: Misc.]

27. **Nicephorus, St.** layman voluntarily executed to prevent priest's apostasy. [Christian Hagiog.: Attwater, 249]

28. **Pitcher, Molly** (1744–1832) took husband's place in battle during American Revolution. [Am. Hist.: Jameson, 393]

29. **Profiles in Courage** John F. Kennedy's anthology of biographies of brave statesmen. [Am. Lit.: *Profiles in Courage*]

30. **Purple Heart** U.S. medal awarded to those wounded in military action. [Am. Hist.: Misc.]

31. **red badge** symbol of the conquest of fear. [Am. Lit.: *Red Badge of Courage*]

32. **Richard the Lion-Hearted** (1159–1199) romantic warrior-king renowned for his bravery and prowess. [Br. Hist.: Bishop, 49]

33. **Roland** brave French hero of medieval chansons de geste. [Fr. Lit.: *NCE*, 2344]

34. **Samson** strong, brave judge of Israel; strength was in his hair. [O.T.: *Judges* 13–16]

35. **Theseus** displays bravery in facing Minotaur; against Procrustes. [Gk. Myth.: *Odyssey; Metamorphoses*]

36. **Victoria Cross** highest British military award for valor. [Br. Hist.: Brewer *Dictionary*, 1129]

37. **York, Sergeant Alvin** (1887–1964) hero of WWI; captured hundreds of Germans. [Am. Culture: Misc.]

76. **BRAWNINESS** (See also STRENGTH, VIRILITY.)

1. **Atlas, Charles** (1893–1972) American muscleman; successful selling body-building by mail order. [Am. Culture: Misc.]
2. **Big John** brawny, strapping miner who saves others in mine collapse. [Am. Music: Jimmy Dean, "Big Bad John"]
3. **Browdie, John** big Yorkshireman. [Br. Lit.: *Nicholas Nickleby*]
4. **Bunyan, Paul** lumberjack performs mighty deeds. [Am. Folklore: *The Wonderful Adventures of Paul Bunyan*]
5. **Goliath** gigantic, sinewy Philistine killed by David's slingshot. [O.T.: *I Samuel* 17; 21:9, 22:10; *II Samuel* 21:19]
6. **the Hulk** huge, raging, green-skinned strongman into which Dr. Banner is transformed. [Comics: Horn, 324–325]
7. **McTeague** brawn his chief asset; accompanied with little brains. [Am. Lit.: *McTeague*]
8. **Tarzan** muscle-bound English lord, reared by African apes, hero of novels and films. [Am. Lit.: *Tarzan of the Apes* (1914); Am. Cinema: Rovin, 105–106]

77. **BREVITY**

1. **Adonis' garden** of short life. [Br. Lit.: *I Henry IV*]
2. **bubbles** symbolic of transitoriness of life. [Art: Hall, 54]
3. **cherry fair** cherry orchards where fruit was briefly sold; symbolic of transience. [Folklore: Brewer *Dictionary*, 217]
4. **Gettysburg Address** speech given by President Lincoln at dedication of national cemetery (Gettysburg, Penn., 1863). [Am. Hist.: *EB*, IV: 515]
5. **Grey, Lady Jane** (1537–1554) queen of England for nine days. [Br. Hist.: *NCE*, 1146]
6. **night-blooming cereus** symbol of fading loveliness; blooms briefly. [Flower Symbolism: *Flora Symbolica*, 176]
7. **Six-Day War** Arab-Israeli war (1967). [Near East. Hist.: *EB*, I: 470]

78. **BRIBERY** (See also BLACKMAIL.)

1. **Black Sox** star White Sox players sold out to gamblers (1919). [Am. Sports: Turkin, 478]
2. **Frollo, Claude** offers to save Esmeralda if she will be his. [Fr. Lit.: *The Hunchback of Notre Dame*]
3. **Joel and Abiah** intent on gain, perverted justice as Israel judges. [O.T.: *I Samuel* 8:2–3]
4. **Judas Iscariot** betrays Jesus for a bribe of thirty pieces of silver. [N.T.: *Matthew* 26:15]

5. **Maltese Falcon, The** through large bribe, detective becomes involved in crime. [Am. Lit.: *The Maltese Falcon*, Magill, I, 551–553]

6. **Menahem** pays off Assyrian king to avoid Israel. [*O.T.: II Kings* 15:20]

7. **mess of pottage** hungry Esau sells birthright for broth. [*O.T.: Genesis* 25:29–34]

8. **Shemaiah** suborned to render false prophecy to Nehemiah. [*O.T.: Nehemiah* 6:10–14]

9. **Tweed Ring** bribery is their essential method for corrupting officials (1860–1871). [Am. Hist.: Jameson, 511]

79. BRIDGE

1. **Al Sirat** fine as razor's edge, over which all must pass to enter paradise. [Islam: *Koran*]

2. **Amaurote** Utopian crossing; means "faintly seen." [Br. Lit.: *Utopia*]

3. **Bifrost** rainbow of water and fire for gods' passage from Asgard to Midgard. [Norse Myth.: Leach, 139]

4. **Bridge of San Luis Rey** rope bridge in Andes which breaks, killing five people. [Am. Lit.: *Bridge of San Luis Rey*]

5. **Brooklyn Bridge** suspension bridge spanning the East River from Manhattan to Brooklyn. [Am. Hist.: *EB*, II: 301]

6. **Golden Gate Bridge** suspension bridge in San Francisco spanning the Golden Gate. [Am. Hist.: *EB*, IV: 607]

7. **London Bridge** any one of many successive bridges that spanned the Thames River in London. [Br. Hist.: *EB*, VI: 311]

8. **River Kwai Bridge** bridge built by British POWs under Japanese orders. [Jap. Hist.: *Bridge Over the River Kwai*]

9. **Xerxes** constructed famed pontoon crossing of Hellespont. [Gk. Hist.: Brewer *Dictionary*, 1169]

80. BRIGHTNESS

1. **Alpha Centauri** brightest star in Centaurus constellation; closest star to Earth. [Astronomy: *NCE*, 74]

2. **diamond** April birthstone, most reflective of gems. [Gem Symbolism: Jobes, 440–441]

3. **North Star** bright star visible to naked eye and nearest to the north celestial pole. [Astronomy: *EB*, VIII: 79]

4. **St. Elmo's fire** glow of electrical discharge appearing on towers and ships' masts. [Physics: *EB*, VIII: 780]

5. **Sirius** dog star; brightest star in the heavens. [Astronomy: *EB*, IX: 238]

6. **Venus** bright planet, second from the Sun. [Astronomy: *EB*, X: 392]

81. BRITAIN

1. **Albion** poetic name for England. [Br. Lit.: Benét, 19]

2. **beefeater** yeoman of the English royal guard, esp. at the Tower of London; slang for Englishman. [Br. Culture: Misc.]

3. **Bull, John** personification of Britain. [Br. Folklore: Benét, 45]

4. **Court of St. James's** British royal court. [Br. Hist.: Misc.]

5. **George, St.** patron saint of Britain. [Br. Hist.: *Golden Legend*]

6. **God Save the Queen** British national anthem. [Br. Culture: Scholes, 408]

7. **Nation of Shopkeepers** name disdainfully given by Napoleon Bonaparte. [Fr. Hist.: Wheeler, 256]

8. **Rule Britannia!** patriotic song of Britain. [Br. Culture: Scholes, 897–898]

9. **10 Downing Street** the British government; refers to location of Prime Minister's residence [Br. Culture: Benét, 286]

10. **Union Jack** British national flag. [Br. Culture: Misc.]

11. **Whitehall** many government offices on this street; synonymous with government. [Br. Hist.: *NCE*, 2970]

82. BRUTALITY (See also CRUELTY.)

1. **Black Prince** angered by Limoges' resistance, massacred three hundred inhabitants (1370). [Eur. Hist.: Bishop, 75]

2. **Cenci, Count** he delighted in making people suffer. [Br. Lit.: "The Cenci" in Magill, I, 131–133]

3. **Crown** a stevedore who deals with people by physical force. [Am. Lit.: *Porgy*, Magill, I, 764–766]

4. **Drancy** concentration camp; France's largest Jewish deportation center. [Jew. Hist.: Wigoder, 161]

5. **Eichmann, Adolph** (1906–1962) Nazi SS officer; directed "Final Solution" in Europe. [Jew. Hist.: Wigoder, 167]

6. **Enlil** ordered wholesale destruction of humanity by flood. [Babylonian Myth.: *Gilgamesh*]

7. **Gestapo** German secret police under Nazi regime. [Ger. History: *RHD*, 595]

8. **Herod Antipas** presents John the Baptist's head to Salome. [*N.T.: Mark* 6:17–28]

9. **Himmler, Heinrich** (1900–1945) architect-in-chief of the "Final Solution." [Ger. Hist.: Hitler, 1044–1052]

10. **Hitler, Adolf** (1889–1945) Nazi dictator; architect of "Final Solution" to exterminate Jews. [Ger. Hist.: *Hitler*]

11. **Jael** drove tent-peg through skull of Sisera. [*O.T.: Judges* 4:19–21]

12. **Koch, Ilse** "Bitch of Buchenwald"; had inmates skinned for lampshades (WWII). [Ger. Hist.: Shirer, 1280]

13. **Kramer, Josef** "Beast of Belsen"; camp exterminator (WWII). [Ger. Hist.: Shirer, 878]

14. **Mengele, Dr. Joseph** Auschwitz concentration camp doctor; experimented on inmates (WWII). [Ger. Hist.: Wallechinsky, 83]

15. **Nazi** Jew-baiting, murderous Aryan supremacist under Hitler. [Ger. Hist.: Shirer]

16. **Nero** coarse, conceited, brutal emperor of Rome (37–68). [Polish Lit.: *Quo Vadis*, Magill, I, 797–799]

17. **Procrustes** robber; stretches or amputates limbs of victims to fit his bed. [Class. Myth.: Zimmerman, 221]

18. **Reign of Terror** all roads led to the guillotine (1793–1794). [Fr. Hist.: *EB*, IX: 904]

19. **SAVAK** Iranian secret police [Iranian History: *Facts* (1979), 125]

83. BULL

1. **Apis** bull of Memphis, created in Osiris' image. [Egypt. Myth.: Benét, 41]

2. **Buchis** black bull worshiped as chief city god. [Egypt. Rel.: Parrinder, 52]

3. **Cretan bull** sacred to Poseidon; sent to Minos. [Gk. Myth.: Kravitz, 68]

4. **Ferdinand** daydreaming bull who refuses to fight in ring. [Children's Lit.: *The Story of Ferdinand*]

5. **Minotaur** fabulous monster of Crete, half-bull, half-man. [Gk. Myth.: *EB*, VI: 922]

6. **Taurus** constellation of the zodiac symbolized by the bull. [Astrology: *EB*, IX: 844]

84. BULLYING

1. **Chowne, Parson Stoyle** terrorizes parish; kidnaps children. [Br. Lit.: *The Maid of Sker*, Walsh *Modern*, 94–95]

2. **Claypole, Noah** bully; becomes thief in Fagin's gang. [Br. Lit.: *Oliver Twist*]

3. **Curley** he picks on feeble-minded Lennie. [Am. Lit.: *Of Mice and Men*]

4. **Flashman, Harry** unconscionably impudent and overbearing coward. [Br. Lit.: *Flashman; Tom Brown's Schooldays*]

5. **hector** member street gang (early 1600s). [Br. Hist.: Espy, 40]

6. **Kowalski, Stanley** crude humor, animal maleness; mating call: "Stella!" [Am. Lit.: *A Streetcar Named Desire*]

7. **McTeague** forbidden to practice dentistry, he becomes mean and surly. [Am. Lit.: *McTeague*]

85. BUREAUCRACY

1. **Brid'oison, Judge** jurist who loves red tape. [Fr. Lit.: *Marriage of Figaro*]

2. **Catch-22** concerned with the frustration of red-tape mechanisms. [Am. Lit.: *Catch-22*]

3. **the Circumlocution Office** department of efficient bureaucratic evasiveness. [Br. Lit.: *Little Dorrit*]

4. **Inspector General, The** drama highlighting foibles of petty officialdom. [Russ. Lit.: *The Inspector General*]

5. **M*A*S*H** bitter farce on bungling bureaucracy in a Korean Army hospital. [Am. Cinema and TV: Halliwell, 474–475]

6. **red tape** excessive formality; bureaucratic paperwork. [Am. and Br. Usage: Misc.]

7. **the Secretary** repeatedly refuses permission to see the Consul. [Am. Opera: Menotti, *The Consul*, Westerman, 552–553]

8. **Trial, The** novel of individual accused of crime by impersonal bureaucracy. [Ger. Lit.: *The Trial*]

86. BURIAL GROUND

1. **Aceldama** potter's field; burial place for strangers. [*N.T.*: Matthew 27:7–8, Acts 1:18–19]

2. **Arlington National Cemetery** final resting place for America's war heroes. [Am. Hist.: Flexner, 95]

3. **Boot Hill** Tombstone, Arizona's graveyard, where gunfighters are buried. [Am. Hist.: Flexner, 178]

4. **Escorial** former monastery in central Spain; mausoleum of Spanish sovereigns. [Span. Hist.: *NCE*, 890]

5. **Flanders Field** immortalized in poem; cemetery for WWI dead. [Eur. Hist.: Jameson, 176]

6. **Gettysburg** site of Civil War battle; cemetery for war dead. [Am. Culture: *EB*, IV: 515]

7. **Grant's Tomb** New York City burial place of General Ulysses S. Grant. [Am. Culture: *EB*, IV: 680]

8. **Great Pyramid of Cheops** enormous Egyptian royal tomb. [World Hist.: Wallechinsky, 255]

9. **Machpelah** cave where Abraham, Sarah, Isaac, Jacob are buried. [*O.T.: Genesis* 23:19, 25:9, 49:30, 50:13]

10. **potter's field** burial ground purchased with Judas's betrayal money. [*N.T.: Matthew* 27:6–8]

11. **Taj Mahal** fabulous tomb built by Shah Jahan for wife. [Ind. Hist.: Wallechinsky, 317]

12. **Tomb of Mausolus** Queen Artemisia's spectacular memorial to husband. [World Hist.: Wallechinsky, 256]

13. **Tomb of the Unknowns** in Arlington National Cemetery; commemorates nameless war dead. [Am. Hist.: Brewer *Dictionary*, 1118]

14. **Westminster Abbey** abbey filled with tombs and memorials of famous British subjects. [Br. Hist.: *EB*, X: 632–633]

87. BUTLER (See also SERVANT.)

1. **Balderstone, Caleb** archetypal faithful servant of the Ravenswoods. [Br. Lit.: *Bride of Lammermoor*]

2. **Bunter** Lord Peter Wimsey's foil and jack-of-all-trades. [Br. Lit.: *The Nine Tailors*]

3. **Crichton** resourceful and take-charge servant when household is marooned. [Br. Lit.: *The Admirable Crichton*]

4. **Davy** Justice Shallow's varlet; assumes identity of master. [Br. Lit.: *Henry IV*]

5. **Face** Lovewit's house servant; connives to make profit by alchemy. [Br. Lit.: *The Alchemist*]

6. **French, Mr.** gentleman's gentleman for architect and motherless children. [TV: "Family Affair" in Terrace, I, 254]

7. **Hudson, Mr.** nostalgic, punctilious master of "downstairs." [Br. TV: *Upstairs, Downstairs*]

8. **Jeeves** manservant who frequently rescues his master. [Am. Lit.: novels of P. G. Wodehouse; Espy, 337]

9. **Lurch** Addams's zombielike, extremely tall butler. [TV: "The Addams Family" in Terrace, I, 29]

10. **Passepartout** bungling foil to the punctilious Fogg. [Fr. Lit.: *Around the World in Eighty Days*]

88. BUXOMNESS

1. **Daisy Mae** Dogpatch beauty with enviable figure. [Comics: "Li'l Abner" in Horn, 450]

2. **Fotis** full-bosomed maid intrigues and attracts Lucius. [Rom. Lit.: *The Golden Ass*]

3. **Little Annie Fanny** buxom version of Little Orphan Annie. [Comics: *Playboy*, Horn, 442]

4. **Morpho** epithet of Aphrodite, meaning "shapely." [Gk. Myth.: Zimmerman, 25]

5. **West, Mae** (1892–1980) voluptuous American leading lady; archetypal sex symbol. [Am. Cinema: Halliwell, 759–760]

6. **Wife of Bath** well-endowed, lusty teller of tales. [Br. Lit.: *Canterbury Tales*]

C

89. **CANNIBALISM**

1. **Alive** account of cannibalism among air crash survivors. [Am. Lit.: *Alive*]

2. **Antiphates** chieftain of Laestrygones, man-eating giants of Italy. [Gk. Lit.: *Odyssey;* Rom. Lit.: *Metamorphoses*]

3. **Beane, Sawney** highwayman who fed his gang on victims' flesh. [Br. Culture: Misc.]

4. **Caliban** his name is anagram of *cannibal.* [Br. Lit.: *The Tempest*]

5. **Clymenus** eats child who is product of incestuous union with daughter Harpalyce. [Gk. Myth.: Howe, 114]

6. **Donner Party** of 89 emigrants to California, 47 survive by eating others (1846–1847). [Am. Hist.: *EB*, III: 623]

7. **Hansel and Gretel** fattened up for child-eating witch. [Ger. Fairy Tale: Grimm, 56]

8. **Laestrygones** man-eating giants encountered by Odysseus. [Gk. Lit.: *Odyssey*]

9. **Lamia** female spirit in serpent form; devours children. [Gk. Myth.: Zimmerman, 146; Br. Lit.: "Lamia" in Benét, 563]

10. **Lycaon** turned to wolf for cannibalistic activities; whence, *lycanthropy.* [Gk. Myth.: Espy, 37]

11. **Modest Proposal, A** Swift's satire suggesting that children of the poor be used as food for the rich (1729). [Br. Lit.: "A Modest Proposal" in Harvey, 793]

12. **Narrative of Arthur Gordon Pym, The** for four days, survivors feed on Parker's flesh. [Am. Lit.: "The Narrative of Arthur Gordon Pym" in Magill, I, 640–643]

13. **Pelops** quartered and served as meal to gods. [Gk. Myth.: Brewer *Dictionary,* 817]

14. **Tereus** wife Procne murders son Itys and serves him to Tereus. [Gk. Myth.: Howe, 144]

15. **Thyestean banquet** banquet where Atreus serves Thyestes' sons to him as food. [Gk. Myth.: Brewer *Dictionary,* 1081]

90. **CARELESSNESS (See also FORGETFULNESS, IRRESPONSIBIL-ITY, LAZINESS.)**

1. **Grasshopper** sings through summer, overlooking winter preparations. [Gk. Lit.: *Aesop's Fables,* "Ant and the Grasshopper"]

2. **Little Bo-peep** lost her sheep; found them tailless. [Nurs. Rhyme: Baring-Gould, 93]

3. **Little Boy Blue** sleeps while the sheep's in the corn. [Nurs. Rhyme: Baring-Gould, 46]

4. **Locket, Lucy** misplaced her pocket. [Nurs. Rhyme: *Mother Goose*, 23]

5. **Pickle, Peregrine** a reckless young man of London in the 1750s. [Br. Lit.: *Peregrine Pickle*, Magill, I, 731–734]

6. **Prism, Miss** nursemaid who misplaces manuscript and infant in railroad station. [Br. Lit.: *Importance of Being Earnest*]

7. **Wimpy** sloppily dressed comic strip character; always forgets to pay for hamburgers. [Comics: "Popeye" in Horn, 657–658]

91. CASTAWAY

1. **Arden, Enoch** shipwrecked sailor; lost for eleven years. [Br. Lit.: "Enoch Arden" in Benét, 316]

2. **Bligh, Captain** commander of H.M.S. *Bounty* who was cast adrift by mutinous crew. [Am. Lit.: *Mutiny on the Bounty*]

3. **Byam, Roger** crew member of the *Bounty* cast onto South Sea island. [Am. Lit.: *Mutiny on the Bounty*]

4. **Crichton** resourceful butler who leads master and his family through difficulties on deserted island. [Br. Lit.: *Admirable Crichton*]

5. **Crusoe, Robinson** shipwreck victim who lives on desert island with savage he names Friday. [Br. Lit.: *Robinson Crusoe*]

6. **Gilligan's Island** comedy about a party shipwrecked on a South Pacific island. [TV: Terrace, I, 312–313]

7. **Gunn, Ben** marooned pirate, helps secure treasure hidden on island. [Br. Lit.: *Treasure Island*]

8. **Lost in Space** family is shipwrecked in space. [TV: Terrace, II, 38–39]

9. **Selkirk, Alexander** real-life prototype of *Robinson Crusoe*. [Br. Hist.: *EB*, IX: 45]

10. **Smith, Cyrus** knowledgeable engineer makes life bearable for castaway party on deserted island. [Fr. Lit.: *Mysterious Island*]

11. **Swiss Family Robinson** family shipwrecked on a deserted island. [Br. Lit.: *Swiss Family Robinson*]

92. CASTRATION

1. **Abélard, Peter** castrated by irate father of lover, Héloise. [Fr. Lit.: *Héloise and Abélard*]

2. **Barnes, Jake** castrated journalist whom Brett Ashley loves. [Am. Lit.: *The Sun Also Rises*]

3. **Cybele** hermaphroditic goddess honored orgiastically, usually by emasculation. [Phrygian Myth.: Parrinder, 68]

93. CENSORSHIP

1. **blue laws** restrict personal action to improve community morality. [Am. Hist.: Hart, 87]

2. **Boston** arbiter of Puritanical taste as reflected in phrase "banned in Boston." [Am. Usage: Misc.]

3. **Bowdler, Thomas** (1754–1825) expurgated Shakespeare and Gibbon for family editions. [Br. Hist.: Wallechinsky, 164]

4. **Comstock, Anthony** (1844–1915) in *comstockery,* immortalized advocate of blue-nosed censorship. [Am. Hist.: Espy, 135]

5. **Hays, Will** (1879–1954) clean-minded arbiter of 1930s Hollywood tastes. [Am. Cinema: Griffith, 182]

6. **imprimatur** license given by Roman Catholic Church to publish a book. [Christian Hist.: Misc.]

7. **Index librorum prohibitorum** list of forbidden books compiled by Roman Catholic Church. [Christian Hist.: *NCE,* 1323]

8. **nihil obstat** Roman Catholic Church's inscription in books denoting no objection to literary content. [Christian Hist.: Misc.]

9. **Unigenitus** papal bull condemning Quesnel's Jansenist book (1713). [Christian Hist.: Brewer *Dictionary,* 1115]

94. CHANCE (See also FATE.)

1. **Bridoison, Taiel de** judge who casts dice to decide cases. [Fr. Lit.: *Pantagruel*]

2. **Fata Morgana** lake-dwelling sorceress and personification of chance. [Ital. Lit.: *Orlando Innamorato*]

3. **Fortuna** goddess of chance. [Rom. Myth.: Kravitz, 58]

4. **Jimmy the Greek** renowned American oddsmaker. [Am. Culture: Wallechinsky, 468]

5. **Russian roulette** suicidal gamble involving a six-shooter, loaded with one bullet. [Folklore: Payton, 590]

6. **Sors** god of chance. [Rom. Myth.: Espy, 42–43]

7. **Three Princes of Serendip** always make discoveries by accident. [Br. Lit.: *Three Princes of Serendip*]

8. **Urim and Thummin** oracular gems used for casting lots, set in Aaron's breastplate. [*O.T.: Exodus* 28:30; *Leviticus* 8:8]

CHARITY (See GENEROSITY.)

95. CHASTITY (See also MODESTY, PURITY, VIRGINITY.)

1. **Agnes, St.** virgin saint and martyr. [Christian Hagiog.: Brewster, 76]

2. **Artemis** (Rom. **Diana**) moon goddess; virgin huntress. [Gk. Myth.: Kravitz, 36]

3. **Bona Dea** goddess; so chaste no one but husband sees her after marriage. [Rom. Myth.: Zimmerman, 43]

4. **Britomart** embodiment of purity. [Br. Lit.: *Faerie Queene*]

5. **Claudia** proves innocence by rescuing goddess' ship. [Rom. Myth.: Hall, 70]

6. **Cunegunda** proves innocence by walking unharmed on hot ploughshares. [Christian Hagiog.: Hall, 86]

7. **lapis lazuli** emblem of sexual purity. [Gem Symbolism: Kunz, 370]

8. **mirror of Alasnam** by clearness or opacity shows woman's purity. [Arab. Lit.: *Arabian Nights,* "The Tale of Zayn Alasnam"]

9. **orange blossoms** symbolic of chastity when used in wedding ceremonies. [Flower Symbolism: *Flora Symbolica,* 176]

10. **phoenix** in Middle Ages, attribute of this virtue personified. [Art: Hall, 246]

11. **sapphire** emblem of sexual purity. [Gem Symbolism: Kunz, 370]

12. **tortoise** symbol of sexual purity. [Animal Symbolism: Mercatante, 21]

13. **unicorn** capturable only by virgins; thus, a test of chastity. [Christian Symbolism: Appleton, 105]

14. **Venus Verticordia** Venus invoked to make women pure once more. [Rom. Myth.: Brewer *Dictionary,* 1126]

96. CHAUVINISM (See also BIGOTRY, PATRIOTISM.)

1. **Chauvin, Nicolas** soldier who passionately admired Napoleon; whence, ultranationalism. [Fr. Hist.: *NCE,* 518]

2. **Helmer, Torvald** treats wife Nora as an inferior being. [Nor. Lit.: *A Doll's House*]

97. CHEERFULNESS (See also GAIETY, JOVIALITY, OPTIMISM.)

1. **L'Allegro** pastoral idyll; title means the cheerful or merry one. [Br. Lit.: "L'Allegro" in Benét, 24–25]

2. **blood** humor effecting temperament of sanguineness. [Medieval Physiology: Hall, 130]

3. **coreopsis** symbol; because of its bright yellow flowers. [Flower Symbolism: Jobes, 371]

4. **crocus** symbol of cheerfulness. [Flower Symbolism: Jobes, 383]

5. **Pollyanna** the "glad child," extraordinarily optimistic. [Children's Lit.: *Pollyanna*]

6. **Raggedy Ann** good-natured despite misadventures; doll with perpetual smile. [Children's Lit.: *Raggedy Ann Stories*]

7. **Sabbath's (Sunday's) child** bonny and blithe, good and gay. [Nurs. Rhyme: Opie, 309]

8. **Silver, Mattie** Zeena's cousin-companion; brightens Frome's gloomy house. [Am. Lit.: *Ethan Frome*]

9. **Singin' in the Rain** downpour doesn't dampen singer's spirits. [Pop. Music: Fordin, 355]

10. **Tapley, Mark** Martin's ever-jovial companion. [Br. Lit.: *Martin Chuzzlewit*]

11. **xeranthemum** symbolizes good-naturedness in adversity. [Flower Symbolism: *Flora Symbolica*, 178]

98. CHILDBIRTH

1. **Artemis** (Rom. **Diana**) goddess of childbirth. [Gk. Myth.: Kravitz, 59]

2. **Auge** Arcadian goddess of childbirth. [Arcadian Myth.: Kravitz, 59]

3. **Carmenta** one of Camenae; protectress of women in confinement. [Rom. Rel.: Zimmerman, 50]

4. **dittany** symbol of childbirth. [Herb Symbolism: *Flora Symbolica*, 173]

5. **Egeria** goddess of childbirth; protectress of the unborn. [Rom. Myth.: Avery, 425–426]

6. **Eileithyia** ancient Greek goddess of childbirth. [Gk. Myth.: Zimmerman, 92]

7. **Hera** (Rom. **Juno**) goddess of childbirth. [Gk. Myth.: Kravitz, 59]

8. **Lilith** demon; dangerous to women in childbirth. [Jew. Trad.: Benét, 586]

9. **Lucina** goddess of childbirth. [Rom. Myth.: Kravitz, 59]

10. **Mater Matuta** goddess of childbirth. [Rom. Myth.: Howe, 160]

11. **Parca** ancient Greek goddess of childbirth. [Gk. Myth.: Kravitz, 59]

12. **test-tube baby** Louise Brown; first successful fertilization outside the body (1978). [Br. Hist.: *Facts* (1978), 596–597]

13. **Themis** goddess of childbirth. [Gk. Myth.: Kravitz, 53]

99. CHILDREN (See also YOUTH.)

1. **olive branches** humorous appellation for children. [*O.T.: Psalms* 128:3]

2. **Pancras, St.** boy saint, patron of young boys. [Christian Hagiog.: Brewer *Dictionary,* 799]

3. **snaps, snails, and puppy-dogs' tails** "what little boys are made of." [Nurs. Rhyme: *Mother Goose,* 108]

4. **sugar and spice** "what little girls are made of." [Nurs. Rhyme: *Mother Goose,* 108]

100. CHIVALRY

1. **Amadis of Gaul** personification of chivalric ideals: valor, purity, fidelity. [Span. Lit.: Benét, 27]

2. **Arthur, King** king of England; head of the Round Table. [Br. Lit.: *Le Morte d'Arthur*]

3. **Bevis** chivalrous medieval knight, righting wrongs in Europe. [Br. Lit.: *Bevis of Hampton*]

4. **Book of the Courtier** Castiglione's discussion of the manners of the perfect courtier (1528). [Ital. Lit.: *EB,* II: 622]

5. **Calidore, Sir** personification of courtesy and chivalrous actions. [Br. Lit.: *Faerie Queene*]

6. **Cid, El** Spanish military leader who becomes a national hero through chivalrous exploits. [Span. Lit.: *Song of the Cid*]

7. **Courtenay, Miles** dashing and chivalrous Irishman. [Br. Lit.: *King Noanett,* Walsh *Modern,* 108]

8. **Coverley, Sir Roger de** ideal, early 18th-century squire. [Br. Lit.: "Spectator" in Wheeler, 85]

9. **Dantes, Edmond** chivalrous adventurer. [Fr. Lit.: *Count of Monte-Cristo*]

10. **D'Artagnan** Dumas's ever-popular chivalrous character. [Fr. Lit.: *The Three Musketeers*]

11. **Eglamour, Sir** "a knight well-spoken, neat, and fine." [Br. Lit.: *Two Gentlemen of Verona*]

12. **Gawain, Sir** King Arthur's nephew; model of knightly perfection and chivalry. [Br. Lit.: *Sir Gawain and the Green Knight*]

13. **Ivanhoe** the epitome of chivalric novels. [Br. Lit.: *Ivanhoe*]

14. **Knights of the Round Table** chivalrous knights in King Arthur's reign. [Br. Lit.: *Le Morte d'Arthur*]

15. **Lancelot, Sir** knight in King Arthur's realm; model of chivalry. [Br. Lit.: *Le Morte d'Arthur*]

16. **Morte d'Arthur, Le** monumental work of chivalric romance. [Br. Lit.: *Le Morte d'Arthur*]

17. **Orlando** gallant and steadfast hero of medieval romance. [Ital. Lit.: *Orlando Furioso; Orlando Inammorato; Morgante Maggiore*]

18. **Quixote, Don** knight-errant ready to rescue distressed damsels. [Span. Lit.: *Don Quixote*]

19. **Richard the Lion-Hearted** (1159–1199) king known for his gallantry and prowess. [Br. Hist.: *EB*, 15: 827]

20. **Roland** paragon of chivalry; unyielding warrior in Charlemagne legends. [Fr. Lit.: *Song of Roland*]

21. **sweet william** symbolizes chivalry. [Flower Symbolism: *Flora Symbolica*, 181]

22. **Valiant, Prince** comic strip character epitomizes chivalry. [Comics: Horn, 565]

101. CHRIST

1. **Agnus Dei** lamb of god. [Christian Tradition: Brewer *Dictionary*, 17]

2. **bread** symbol of Christ's body in Eucharist. [Christian Tradition: *Luke* 22:19]

3. **chi rho** monogram of first two letters of Christ's name in Greek. [Christian Symbolism: Appleton, 111]

4. **Emmanuel** Jesus, especially as the Messiah. [*N.T.: Matthew* 1:23]

5. **fish** Greek acronym for Jesus Christ, Son of God, Saviour. [Christian Symbolism: Child, 210]

6. **Galilee** Jesus's area of activity. [Christianity: Wigoder, 203]

7. **Good Shepherd** [*N.T.: John* 10:11–14]

8. **King of Kings** appellation for Jesus Christ. [*N.T.*: Revelation 17:14]

9. **lamb** the Lord as the sacrificial animal. [Christian Symbolism: *O.T.: Isaiah* 53:7; *N.T.: John* 1:29]

10. **lion** symbol expressing power and courage of Jesus. [Christian Symbolism: *N.T.: Revelation* 5:5]

11. **Lord of the Dance** "At Bethlehem I had my birth." [Br. Folk Music: Carter, "Lord of the Dance" in Taylor, 128]

12. **Man of Sorrows** epithet for the prophesied Messiah. [*O.T.: Isaiah* 53:3]

13. **Piers the Plowman** English plowman who becomes allegorical figure of Christ incarnate. [Br. Lit.: *The Vision of William, Concerning Piers the Plowman*, Magill, III, 1105–1107]

14. **star** token of the Lord and his coming. [Christian Symbolism: *O.T.: Numbers*, 24:17; *N.T.: Revelation* 22:16]

15. **vine** gives nourishment to branches or followers. [Christian Symbolism: Appleton, 107; *N.T.: John* 15:5]

16. **wine** symbol of Christ's blood in Eucharist. [Christian Tradition: "Eucharist" in Cross, 468–469]

102. CHRISTMAS

1. **Amahl and the Night Visitors** lame shepherd boy gives crutch as gift for Christ Child; first opera composed for television (1951). [Am. Opera: *EB*, VI: 792–793]

2. **Befana** fairy fills stockings with toys on Twelfth Night. [Ital. Legend: *LLEI*, I: 323]

3. **carols** custom originating in England of singing songs at Christmas. [Christian Tradition: *NCE*, 552]

4. **Child's Christmas in Wales, A** nostalgic remembrance of Welsh Christmases. [Brit. Lit.: *A Child's Christmas in Wales*]

5. **Christmas** feast of the nativity of Jesus Christ (December 25). [Christian Tradition: *NCE*, 552]

6. **Christmas, Father** legendary bringer of gifts; another name for Santa Claus. [Children's Lit.: *Father Christmas*]

7. **Christmas tree** custom originating in medieval Germany of decorating an evergreen tree at Christmas. [Christian Tradition: *NCE*, 552]

8. **Deck the Halls with Boughs of Holly** traditional Christmas carol. [Western Culture: "Deck the Halls with Boughs of Holly" in Rockwell, 146–147]

9. **First Noel, The** traditional Christmas carol. [Western Culture: "The First Noel" in Rockwell, 136–137]

10. **Gift of the Magi, The** O. Henry's Christmas story of love and self-sacrifice. [Am. Lit.: Rockwell, 77–80]

11. **gold, frankincense, and myrrh** given to the infant Jesus by the three Wise Men. [*N.T.: Matthew* 2:1–11]

12. **Hark! the Herald Angels Sing** traditional Christmas carol. [Western Culture: "Hark! the Herald Angels Sing" in Rockwell, 132–133]

13. **holly** symbol of Christmas. [Flower Symbolism: *Flora Symbolica*, 174; Kunz, 331]

14. **Jingle Bells** yuletide song composed by J. S. Pierpont. [Pop. Music: Van Doren, 200]

15. **Joy to the World!** traditional Christmas carol. [Western Culture: "Joy to the World!" in Rockwell, 138]

16. **Kringle, Kris** Santa Claus in Germany. [Ger. Folklore: *LLEI*, I: 277]

17. **Lord of Misrule** formerly, person chosen to lead Christmas revels and games. [Br. Folklore: Misc.]

18. **Miracle on 34th Street** film featuring benevolent old gentleman named Kris Kringle. [Am. Cinema: Halliwell, 493]

19. **mistletoe** traditional yuletide sprig under which kissing is obligatory. [Br. and Am. Folklore: Leach, 731]

20. **Night Before Christmas, The** poem celebrating activities of Christmas Eve. [Am. Lit.: "The Night Before Christmas"]

21. **O Come, All Ye Faithful** traditional Christmas carol. [Western Culture: "O Come, All Ye Faithful" in Rockwell, 142–143]

22. **O Little Town of Bethlehem** traditional Christmas carol. [Western Culture: "O Little Town of Bethlehem" in Rockwell, 120–121]

23. **red and green** traditional colors of Christmas. [Christian Tradition: Misc.]

24. **Rudolph, the Red-Nosed Reindeer** his nose lights Santa on his way. [Am. Music: "Rudolph, the Red-Nosed Reindeer"]

25. **Santa Claus** jolly, gift-giving figure who visits children on Christmas Eve. [Christian Tradition: *NCE*, 1937]

26. **Scrooge, Ebenezer** the great miser during season of giving. [Br. Lit.: *A Christmas Carol*]

27. **Silent Night** traditional Christmas carol. [Western Culture: "Silent Night" in Rockwell, 130–131]

28. **Star of Bethlehem** announces birth of the Christ child. [Christianity: *N.T.: Matthew* 2:2]

29. **We Three Kings of Orient Are** traditional Christmas carol. [Western Culture: "We Three Kings of Orient Are" in Rockwell, 122–123]

30. **yule log** log burned at Christmas. [Western Tradition: *NCE*, 552]

103. CIRCUMCISION

1. **Abraham** initiated rite in covenant with God. [*O.T.: Genesis* 17:11–14]

2. **Berith** Jewish rite of circumcising male child eight days after birth. [Judaism: Misc.]

3. **Elijah** traditionally represented at ceremony by empty chair. [Judaism: Wigoder, 172]

4. **Gibeath-haaraloth** Hill of Foreskins; where Joshua circumcised Israelites. [*O.T.: Joshua* 5:3]

104. CLEANLINESS (See also ORDERLINESS.)

1. **Berchta** unkempt herself, demands cleanliness from others, especially children. [Ger. Folklore: Leach, 137]

2. **cat** continually "washes" itself. [Animal Symbolism: Jobes, 296]

3. **Clean, Mr.** brand of household cleaner. [Trademarks: Crowley *Trade,* 379]

4. **hyssop** Biblical herb used for ceremonial sprinkling. [Flower Symbolism: *O.T. Psalms* 51:7]

5. **Mary Mouse** constantly sweeping and dusting. [Children's Lit.: *Mary Mouse and the Doll's House,* Fisher, 216]

6. **Spic and Span** brand of household cleaner. [Trademarks: Crowley *Trade,* 546]

7. **Wag-at-the-Wa'** brownie who is strict about neatness of houses. [Br. Folklore: Briggs, 425–426]

CLEVERNESS (See CUNNING.)

105. CLOCKS

1. **Big Ben** bell of Houses of Parliament clock in London keeps Britons punctual. [Br. Culture: Misc.]

2. **Nuremberg Egg** first watch; created by Peter Henlein (1502). [Ger. Hist.: Grun, 223]

3. **Strasbourg cathedral clock** famous clock in Strasbourg Cathedral. [Fr. Culture: *NCE,* 581]

106. CLOWN

1. **Bardolph** "coney-catching rascal"; follower of Falstaff. [Br. Lit.: *Merry Wives of Windsor*]

2. **Bertoldo** medieval jester, butt, and buffoon. [Ital. Folklore: Walsh *Classical,* 54–55]

3. **Feste** playful fool. [Br. Lit.: *Twelfth Night*]

4. **Geddes** jester in the court of Mary Queen of Scots. [Scot. Hist.: Brewer *Handbook,* 380]

5. **Gobbo, Launcelot** a "wit-snapper," a "merry devil." [Br. Lit.: *Merchant of Venice*]

6. **harlequin** comic character in commedia dell'arte; dressed in multicolored tights in a diamond-shaped pattern. [Ital. Drama: *NCE,* 1194]

7. **Hop-Frog** deformed dwarf; court fool. [Am. Lit.: "Hop-Frog" in *Portable Poe,* 317–329]

8. **Jocus** Cupid's companion and fool. [Rom. Lit.: *Psychomachia*]

9. **Joey** after Joseph Grimaldi, famous 19th-century clown. [Am. Hist.: Espy, 45]

10. **Jupe** a clown in Sleary's circus. [Br. Lit.: *Hard Times*]

11. **Kelly, Emmett** (1897–1979) foremost silent, sad-faced circus clown. [Am. Hist.: Flexner, 83]

12. **McDonald, Ronald** hamburger chain's Pied Piper. [Am. Culture: *Grinding*]

13. **Merry-Andrew** Andrew Borde, Henry VIII's physician. [Br. Hist.: Wheeler, 241]

14. **Patch** court fool of Elizabeth, wife of Henry VII. [Br. Hist.: Brewer *Handbook*, 380]

15. **Touchstone** a "motley-mined," "roynish" court jester. [Br. Lit.: *As You Like It*]

16. **Yorick** jester in the court of Denmark. [Br. Lit.: *Hamlet*]

CLUMSINESS (See AWKWARDNESS, INEPTITUDE.)

107. **COARSENESS**

1. **the Branghtons** Evelina's rude, coarse cousins. [Br. Lit.: *Evelina*]

2. **Catherine de Bourgh, Lady** coarse, vulgar lady. [Br. Lit.: *Pride and Prejudice*]

3. **Crawley, Sir Pitt** vulgar aristocrat. [Br. Lit.: *Vanity Fair*]

4. **Goops** naughty, balloon-headed children. [Am. Lit.: *Goops and How To Be Them*, Hart, 323]

5. **Neanderthal man** early form of man, Caucasoid and strongly built. [Anthropology: *NCE*, 1900]

6. **Ochs, Baron** vulgar, lecherous nobleman. [Aust. Opera: R. Strauss, *Rosenkavalier*, Westerman, 423–425]

7. **Pike** "he expectorates vehemently " [Am. Lit.: *At Home and Abroad*, Hart, 655]

8. **Tearsheet, Doll** prostitute with vitriolic vocabulary. [Br. Lit.: *II Henry IV*]

9. **Troglodytes** race of uncivilized cave dwellers. [Gk. Hist.: Brewer *Dictionary*, 1103]

10. **xanthium** symbolizes bad manners and rudeness. [Flower Symbolism: *Flora Symbolica*, 178]

11. **Yahoos** loutish, abusive brutes in shape of men. [Br. Lit.: *Gulliver's Travels*]

108. **COCKNEY**

1. **Bow Bells** famous bell in East End of London; "only one who is born within the bell's sound is a true Cockney." [Br. Hist.: *NCE*, 347]

2. **Capp, Andy** truculent little layabout who "touches a common cord to Cockneys." [Comics: Horn, 82]

3. **Doolittle, Eliza** Cockney girl taught by professor to imitate aristocracy. [Br. Lit.: *Pygmalion*]

109. **COLDNESS**

1. **Acis** blood turned into a "river of ice." [Gk. Myth.: *Metamorphoses*]

2. **Frost, Jack** personification of freezing cold. [Am. and Br. Folklore: Misc.]

3. **Hyperboreans** fabulous people living beyond North Wind, traditionally near North Pole. [Rom. Myth.: Zimmerman, 132]

4. **Lapland** northern region of Scandinavian peninsula, mostly within Arctic Circle. [Geography: Misc.]

5. **Lower Slobbovia** cartoon land of perpetual cold. [Comics: "Li'l Abner" in Horn, 450–451]

110. **COLONIZATION**

1. **Evander** Arcadian, founded settlement in Italy. [Gk. Myth.: Kravitz, 100]

2. **Jamestown, Virginia** first permanent English settlement in New World (1607). [Am. Hist.: Jameson, 255]

3. **Mayflower** ship which brought Pilgrims to New World (1620). [Am. Hist.: *NCE*, 1730]

4. **Plymouth Plantation** first English settlement in New England (1620). [Am. Hist.: *Major Bradford's Town*]

5. **Williamsburg** monument of American colonial period; settled in 1632. [Am. Hist.: Hart, 930]

COMEUPPANCE (See LAST LAUGH.)

COMFORT (See LUXURY.)

COMMERCE (See FINANCE.)

COMPANIONSHIP (See FRIENDSHIP.)

COMPASSION (See KINDNESS.)

COMPROMISE (See PEACEMAKING.)

111. **CONCEALMENT (See also REFUGE.)**

1. **Ali Baba** 40 thieves concealed in oil jars. [Arab. Lit.: *Arabian Nights*]

2. **ark of bulrushes** Moses hidden in basket to escape infanticide. [*O.T.: Exodus* 2:1–6]

3. **Inigo and Gonsalve** Concepción's would-be lovers; hides them in her husband's clocks. [Fr. Opera: Ravel, *The Spanish Hour,* Westerman, 198]

4. **Polonius** Hamlet stabs him through the arras. [Br. Lit.: *Hamlet*]

5. **sealed book** symbolic of impenetrable secrets. [Christian Symbolism: Appleton, 13]

6. **wilderness of Maon** where David sought refuge from Saul's pursuit. [*O.T.: I Samuel* 23:25–29]

7. **wilderness of Ziph** where David hid to escape Saul's search. [*O.T.: I Samuel* 23:14]

112. **CONCEIT** (See also **ARROGANCE, BOASTFULNESS, EGOTISM.**)

1. **Ajax (the lesser)** boastful and insolent; drowns due to vanity. [Gk. Myth.: Kravitz, 14]

2. **Bunthorne, Reginald** fleshly poet; "aesthetically" enchants the ladies. [Br. Lit.: *Patience*]

3. **Butler, Theodosius** thinks he is a wonderful person. [Br. Lit.: *Sketches by Boz*]

4. **Dalgetty, Rittmaster Dugald** self-aggrandizing, pedantic soldier-of-fortune. [Br. Lit.: *Legend of Montrose*]

5. **Dedlock, Sir Leicester** contemplates his own greatness. [Br. Lit.: *Bleak House*]

6. **Dogberry and Verges** ignorant and bloated constables. [Br. Lit.: *Much Ado About Nothing*]

7. **Grosvenor, Archibald** idyllic poet of no imperfections. [Br. Lit.: *Patience*]

8. **Henry VIII** inflated self-image parallels bloated body. [Br. Lit.: *Henry VIII*]

9. **Horner, Little Jack** pats his back with "What a good boy am I!" [Nurs. Rhyme: *Mother Goose,* 90]

10. **Lewis** self-important coxcomb full of hollow, ostentatious valor. [Br. Lit.: *Henry V*]

11. **Malvolio** Olivia's grave, self-important steward; "an affectioned ass." [Br. Lit.: *Twelfth Night*]

12. **Montespan, Marquis de** regards exile and wife's concubinage as honor. [Br. Lit.: *The Duchess of la Vallière,* Brewer *Handbook,* 721]

13. **narcissus** flower of conceit. [Plant Symbolism: *Flora Symbolica,* 170; Gk. Myth.: Zimmerman, 171–172]

14. **nettle** symbol of vanity and pride. [Flower Symbolism: *Flora Symbolica,* 176]

15. **Orion** scorpion stung him to death for his boasting. [Rom. Myth.: Brewer *Dictionary*, 971]

16. **Prigio, Prince** too clever prince; arrogance renders him unpopular. [Children's Lit.: *Prince Prigio*]

17. **Slurk, Mr.** had a "consciousness of immeasurable superiority" over others. [Br. Lit.: *Pickwick Papers*]

18. **Tappertit, Simon** boasted he could subdue women with eyes. [Br. Lit.: *Barnaby Rudge*]

113. CONDEMNATION

1. **bell, book, and candle** symbols of Catholic excommunication rite. [Christianity: Brewer *Note-Book*, 85]

2. **Bridge of Sighs** passage from Doge's court to execution chamber in Renaissance Venice. [Ital. Hist.: Brewer *Note-Book*, 121]

3. **Eurydice** doomed to eternal death when Orpheus disobeys Hades. [Gk. Myth.: Kravitz, 97]

4. **lions' mouths** Venetian receptacles for denunciations, character assassinations. [Ital. Hist.: Plumb, 259–260]

5. **Nathan** bitterly denounces David's killing of Bathsheba's husband. [*O.T.: II Samuel* 12:1–14]

6. **Prometheus** a Titan condemned by Zeus for giving fire to mortals. [Gk. Lit.: *Prometheus Bound*, Magill, I, 786–788]

7. **tell-tale heart** intolerable beatings behind wall drive narrator to confess murder. [Am. Lit.: "The Tell-tale Heart" in *Portable Poe*, 290–296]

114. CONFUSION

1. **Babel** where God confounded speech of mankind. [*O.T.: Genesis* 11:7–9]

2. **bedlam** from Hospital of St. Mary of Bethlehem, former English insane asylum. [Br. Folklore: Jobes, 193]

3. **Corybantes** half-divine priests of Cybele; celebrated noisy festivals in her honor. [Gk. Myth.: Howe, 67]

4. **Jude** "the other Judas, not Iscariot." [*N.T.: John* 14:22]

5. **Labyrinth** maze at Knossos where Minotaur lived. [Gk. Myth.: Hall, 185]

6. **Pandemonium** capital of the devils. [Br. Lit.: *Paradise Lost*]

7. **Pantagruelian Law Case** not understanding the defense, judgment given is incomprehensible.[Fr. Lit.: *Pantagruel*]

8. **Serbonian Bog** Egyptian morass, "where armies whole have sunk." [Br. Lit.: *Paradise Lost*]

9. **Star-Splitter, The** "We've looked and looked, but after all where are we?" [Am. Lit.: "The Star-Splitter" in Hart, 799]

115. CONQUEST

1. **Agricola** (40–93) enlightened governor and general; subdued all Britain. [Rom. Hist.: *NCE*, 35]

2. **Alaric** (c. 370–410) Visigoth chief; sacked Rome. [Eur. Hist.: Bishop, 14]

3. **Alexander the Great** (356–323 B.C.) Macedonian king and conqueror of much of Asia. [Gk. Hist.: *NCE*, 61]

4. **Attila** (d. 453) king of Huns. [Eur. Hist.: *NCE*, 182]

5. **Batu Khan** (d. 1255) Mongol conqueror of 13th century; grandson of Genghis Khan. [Asian Hist.: *NCE*, 248]

6. **Caesar, Julius** (102–44 B.C.) Roman statesman and general; reduced all of Gaul and Britain to Roman control. [Rom. Hist.: *NCE*, 416]

7. **Canute** (995–1035) Norseman; subjugator of England. [Br. Hist.: Bishop, 42]

8. **Charlemagne** (742–814) established the Carolingian empire. [Fr. Hist.: *NCE*, 507]

9. **Charles V** (1500–1558) Holy Roman Emperor; last to sack Rome (1527). [Ital. Hist.: Plumb, 43, 406–407]

10. **Cortés, Hernando** (1485–1547) annihilated Aztec culture, claiming Mexico for Spain. [Span. Hist.: *EB*, 5: 194–196]

11. **Cyrus II (the Great)** (d. 529 B.C.) creator of Persian empire (553–529). [Class. Hist.: Grun]

12. **Genghis Khan** (1167–1227) Mongol chieftain overran most of Asia and eastern Europe (1206–1227). [Asian Hist.: *EB*, 7: 1013–1016]

13. **Genseric** (c. 390–477) Vandal king; controlled large portion of Mediterranean. [Rom. Hist.: *NCE*, 1034]

14. **Golden Horde** 13th-century Mongol overlords of Russia. [Russ. Hist.: Grun, 170]

15. **Hitler, Adolf** (1889–1945) led Germany to conquer or destroy most of Europe. [Ger. Hist.: *Hitler*]

16. **Mohammed II** (1429–1481) Ottoman conqueror of Constantinople (1453). [Eur. Hist.: Plumb, 292–293]

17. **Napoleon** (1769–1821) vanquished most of Europe and North Africa. [Fr. Hist.: Harvey, 570]

18. **Nebuchadnezzar** (d. 562 B.C.) subjugated Jews, initiating Babylonian captivity (597–5 B.C.). [*O.T.: Daniel* 1:1–2]

19. **Pizarro, Francisco** (c. 1476–1541) with small force, destroyed Incan empire. [Span. Hist.: *EB*, 14: 487–488]

20. **Tamerlane** (1336–1405) Tartar; vanquished Persia and India. [Asian Hist.: Brewer *Dictionary*, 1061]

21. **William the Conqueror** (1027–1087) commanded Normans in conquest of Britain; victor at Hastings (1066). [Br. Hist.: Bishop, 42–46]

116. CONSCIENCE

1. **Aidos** ancient Greek personification of conscience. [Gk. Myth.: Zimmerman, 14]

2. **Cricket, Jiminy** dapper mite guides the callow Pinocchio. [Am. Cinema: *Pinocchio* in *Disney Films*, 32–37]

3. **Valdes and Cornelius** Good Angel and Evil Angel; symbolize Faustus's inner conflict. [Br. Lit.: *Doctor Faustus*]

4. **Wilson, William** his Doppelgänger irrupts at occasions of duplicity. [Am. Lit.: "William Wilson" in *Portable Poe*, 57–82]

117. CONSERVATISM

1. **Conservative party** British political party, once called the Tory party. [Br. Hist.: *NCE*, 632]

2. **Daughters of the American Revolution (D.A.R)** conservative society of female descendants of Revolutionary War soldiers. [Am. Hist.: Jameson, 132]

3. **elephant** symbol of the Republican party. [Am. Hist.: Misc.]

4. **John Birch Society** ultraconservative, anti-Communist organization. [Am. Hist.: *NCE*, 1421]

5. **laissez-faire** political doctrine that an economic system functions best without governmental interference. [Politics: Misc.]

6. **Luddites** arch-conservative workmen; smashed labor-saving machinery (1779). [Br. Hist.: Espy, 107]

7. **Republican Party** U.S. political party, generally espousing a conservative platform. [Am. Hist.: Jameson, 424]

118. CONSPIRACY (See also INTRIGUE.)

1. **Babington Plot** abortive plot to assassinate Elizabeth I; sealed Mary Stuart's fate (1586). [Br. Hist.: *NCE*, 202]

2. **Black Friday** (September 24, 1869) gold speculation led to financial panic. [Am. Hist.: Van Doren, 259]

3. **Brutus** plotted against Caesar with Cassius and Casea. [Br. Lit.: *Julius Caesar*]

4. **Cassius** intriguer and cohort in plot against Caesar. [Br. Lit.: *Julius Caesar*]

5. **Cinq-Mars** conspires against Cardinal Richelieu. [Fr. Lit.: *Cinq-Mars*]

6. **Doctors' Plot** physicians falsely tried for trying to poison Stalin. [Jew. Hist.: Wigoder, 160]

7. **Duke of Buckingham** Richard III's "counsel's consistory"; assisted him to throne. [Br. Lit.: *Richard III*]

8. **Fawkes, Guy** (1570–1606) leader of Gunpowder Plot to blow up Houses of Parliament (1605). [Br. Hist.: *EB, IV:* 70, 801]

9. **Gunpowder Plot** see Fawkes, Guy.

10. **Joseph's brothers** sold him into slavery out of hatred. [*O.T.: Genesis* 37:18–28]

11. **Pontiac** (1720–1769) brains behind widespread American Indian uprising (1762). [Am. Hist.: Jameson, 398]

12. **Shallum** plots and successfully executes overthrow of Zechariah. [*O.T.: II Kings* 15:10]

13. **Watergate** political intrigue leading to resignation of Pres. Nixon. [Am. Hist.: *EB*, X: 568–569]

CONSTANCY (See LOYALTY.)

119. CONTEMPLATION

1. **Compleat Angler, The** Izaak Walton's classic treatise on the *Contemplative Man's Recreation.* [Br. Lit.: *The Compleat Angler*]

2. **Thinker, The** sculpture by Rodin, depicting contemplative man. [Fr. Art: Osborne, 988]

120. CONTROVERSY (See also SCANDAL.)

1. **Avignon** location of alternate papacy (1309–1377). [Fr. Hist.: Bishop, 376]

2. **Birth of a Nation, The** film whose historical perspective elicits emotional response (1915). [Am. Cinema: Griffith, 36–39]

3. **Chicago 8 trial** alleged ringleaders of Chicago riots tried in circus atmosphere (1969). [Am. Hist.: Van Doren, 630]

4. **Dred Scott decision** Supreme Court decision concerning freedom of slaves (1857). [Am. Hist.: Jameson, 151–152]

5. **Origin of Species** once revolutionary theory of evolution and natural selection (1859). [Br. Science: *The Origin of Species*]

6. **Pentagon Papers** Defense Department's Vietnam policy papers leaked to press. [Am. Hist.: Flexner, 376]

7. **Rite of Spring** Stravinsky's score caused riot at premiere (1913). [Music Hist.: Thompson, 1900]

8. **Sacco and Vanzetti** (Nicola, 1891–1927) (Bartolomeo, 1888–1927) Italian immigrants tried and executed for murder in witch-hunt for anarchists. [Am. Hist.: *Sacco-Vanzetti Case: A Transcript*]

9. **Scopes trial** concerning the teaching of evolution in public schools (1925). [Am. Hist.: Allen, 142–146]

10. **Scottsboro Case** cause célèbre concerning nine Negro men, two white girls (1931). [Am. Hist.: Hart, 753]

11. **scrap of paper** pre-WWI Belgian neutrality; German disregard precipitated British involvement. [Am. Hist.: Jameson, 450]

12. **Stamp Act** legislative development contributing to American Revolution (1765). [Am. Hist.: Jameson, 475]

13. **Tonkin Gulf** disputed N. Vietnamese attacks escalated U.S. war effort (1964). [Am. Hist.: Van Doren, 595]

14. **Warren Report** government's much disputed conclusion that President Kennedy's assassin acted alone. [Am. Hist.: Van Doren, 594]

121. COOPERATION

1. **Common Market** association of western European countries designed to facilitate free trade among members. [Eur. Hist.: *EB*, III: 1001]

2. **Entente Cordiale** agreement between Great Britain and France to settle their disagreements over colonies as diplomatic partners. [Eur. Hist.: *WB*, 21: 367]

3. **Helsinki accord** agreement between Soviet bloc and the West for economic, commercial, and scientific cooperation and for respect of human rights and fundamental freedoms. [World Hist.: *News Directory* (1977), 177–179]

4. **League of Nations** world organization for international cooperation. [World Hist.: *EB*, 6: 102]

5. **NATO** free-world mutual security pact against Soviet bloc. [World Hist.: Van Doren, 520]

6. **Nazi-Soviet Pact** nonaggression treaty freed Hitler to invade Poland. [Ger. Hist.: Shirer, 685–705]

7. **OPEC** cartel of nations whose economic livelihood depends upon the export of petroleum. [World Hist.: *WB*, 14: 646]

8. **Pact of Steel** German-Italian treaty established common cause in future undertakings. [Eur. Hist.: Shirer, 646–648]

9. **Potsdam Conference** unconditional Japanese surrender demanded; war crimes trials planned (July, 1945). [World Hist.: Van Doren, 507]

10.   **SEATO** organization formed to assure protection against com-
      munist expansion in Southeast Asia (1955–1976). [World Hist.:
      EB, IX: 377]

11.   **Tinker to Evers to Chance** legendary baseball double-play
      combination (1902–1910). [Am. Sports: Turkin, 474]

12.   **Triple Entente** association among Great Britain, France, and
      Russia; nucleus of the Allied Coalition in WWI. [World Hist.:
      EB, 10: 128]

13.   **United Nations** world organization for international discussion
      and peacekeeping. [World Hist.: Brewer *Dictionary*, 1116]

14.   **Yalta Conference** Allies developed plan for reconstruction of
      Europe (February, 1945). [World Hist.: Van Doren, 504]

122. **COUNSEL (See also GUIDANCE.)**

1.   **Achitophel** sage adviser to David; subsequently to Absalom.
     [*O.T.: II Samuel* 16:23]

2.   **Antenor** counselor; advised Priam to return Helen to Menelaus.
     [Gk. Myth.: Zimmerman, 23]

3.   **Areopagus** hill near the Acropolis used for Athenian council
     deliberations. [Gk. Hist.: Benét, 46]

4.   **Consus** god of councils and advice; agricultural god. [Rom.
     Myth.: Kravitz, 65; Parrinder, 66]

5.   **Egeria** wife, instructress, and advisor of emperor Numa. [Rom.
     Myth.: Jobes, 491; Avery, 426]

6.   **Laurence, Friar** adviser to the lovers. [Br. Lit.: *Romeo and
     Juliet*]

7.   **Mentor** Odysseus's adviser; entrusted with care and education
     of Telemachus. [Gk. Lit.: *Odyssey*]

8.   **Nestor** a sage old counselor to the Greeks in the Trojan War.
     [Gk. Myth.: *Iliad*]

9.   **Poseidon Hippios** god of counsel and councils. [Gk. Myth.:
     Kravitz, 67]

COURAGE (See BRAVERY.)

123. **COURTESANSHIP (See also MISTRESS, PROSTITUTION.)**

1.   **Aspasia** mistress of Pericles; byword for cultured courtesan.
     [Gk. Hist.: Benét, 58]

2.   **Lais** celebrated Thessalonian courtesan, so beautiful the towns-
     women kill her out of jealousy. [Gk. Hist.: Benét, 561]

3.   **Lescaut, Manon** lives well by giving affections to noblemen.
     [Fr. Lit.: *Manon Lescaut*]

4. **Marneffe, Madame** as courtesan for barons, she obtains wealth. [Fr. Lit.: *Cousin Bette*, Magill, I, 166–168]

5. **Phryne** (4th century B.C.) wealthy Athenian hetaera of surpassing beauty. [Gk. Hist.: Benét, 784]

6. **Rosette** D'Albert's pliable, versatile, talented, acknowledged bedmate. [Fr. Lit.: *Mademoiselle de Maupin*. Magill, I, 542–543]

7. **Thaïs** Alexandrian courtesan, converts to Christianity. [Medieval Legend: Walsh *Classical*, 307]

124. COURTESY

1. **Boy Scouts** youth organization, ever ready to perform good deeds. [Am. Hist.: Jameson, 59]

2. **Castiglione, Baldassare** (1478–1529) author of *The Courtier*, Renaissance bible of etiquette. [Ital. Lit.: Plumb, 316–319]

3. **Dickon** one of "nature's gentlemen." [Children's Lit.: *The Secret Garden*]

4. **Post, Emily** (1873–1960) etiquette book author; preaches "consideration for others." [Am. Hist.: Flexner, 277]

5. **Shem and Japheth** cover father's nakedness without looking at him. [*O.T.*: *Genesis* 9:23–27]

125. COURTESY, EXCESSIVE

1. **Alphonse and Gaston** personifications of overdone politeness. [Comics: Horn, 77–78]

2. **Haskell, Eddie** hypocritical teenager, gracious toward adults, pugnacious toward children. [TV: "Leave it to Beaver" in Terrace, II, 18–19]

3. **Petruchio** his excessive kindness a stratagem to break Katharina. [Br. Lit.: *The Taming of the Shrew*]

COVETOUSNESS (See GREED.)

126. COWARDICE (See also BOASTFULNESS, TIMIDITY.)

1. **Acres, Bob** a swaggerer lacking in courage. [Br. Lit.: *The Rivals*]

2. **Bobadill, Captain** vainglorious braggart, vaunts achievements while rationalizing faintheartedness. [Br. Lit.: *Every Man in His Humour*]

3. **chicken** slang insult used toward the timid. [Western Folklore: Jobes, 322]

4. **Conachar** pathetically lacks courage. [Br. Lit.: *The Fair Maid of Perth*]

5. **Coup de Jarnac** to hit a man while he is down. [Fr. Folklore: Espy, 62]

6. **Cowardly Lion** king of the forest has yellow streak up back. [Am. Lit.: *The Wonderful Wizard of Oz*]

7. **Falstaff, Sir John** "the better part of valor is discretion." [Br. Lit.: *I Henry IV*]

8. **Indiana Volunteers** during Mexican war, ran when action began. [Am. Hist.: Espy, 183]

9. **Martano** poltroon claiming credit for another's feat. [Ital. Lit.: *Orlando Furioso*]

10. **Rogue's March** played in British Army to expel dishonored soldier. [Br. Music: Scholes, 885]

11. **Roister Doister, Ralph** foolish suitor repulsed by widow with household utensil. [Br. Lit.: *Ralph Roister Doister*]

12. **Scaramouche** stock character in commedia dell'arte; boastful poltroon. [Ital. Drama: Brewer *Dictionary*, 967]

13. **yellow** color symbolizing cowardice. [Western Culture: Misc.]

127. CRAFTSMANSHIP

1. **Alcimedon** a first-rate carver in wood. [Gk. Myth.: *Eclogues*, 00]

2. **Argus** skillful builder of Jason's Argo. [Gk. Myth.: Walsh *Classical*, 29]

3. **Athena** (Rom. **Minerva**) protector of craftsmen. [Gk. Myth.: Kravitz, 67]

4. **Bezalel and Oholiab** called to make tabernacle and accouterments for Moses. [O.T.: *Exodus* 31:1–11]

5. **Cyclopes** one-eyed, unruly giants; excellent metals craftsmen. [Gk. Lyth.: Parrinder, 68]

6. **Dactyls** fabulous smiths; discovered iron and how to work with it. [Gk. Myth.: Leach, 273]

7. **Daedalus** great craftsman; built Labyrinth and Pasiphaë's cow. [Gk. Myth.: Leach, 273]

8. **Epeius** designer and builder of the Trojan Horse. [Rom. Lit.: *Aeneid*]

9. **Hephaestus** (Rom. **Vulcan**) god of fire and metalworkers. [Gk. Myth.: Zimmerman, 121]

10. **Hiram** expert brazier commissioned by Solomon for temple work. [O.T.: *I Kings* 7:13–14]

11. **Joseph** storied carpenter and foster-father of Jesus. [*N.T.: Matthew* 1:18–25; Hall, 177]

12. **Pygmalion** sculpts beautiful image which comes to life. [Rom. Lit.: *Metamorphoses*]

13. **Sidonians** known for timber-felling skill. [*O.T.: I Kings* 5:6]

14. **Tubal-cain** master of copper and iron smiths. [*O.T.: Genesis* 4:22]

128. CREATION

1. **Adam and Eve** first man and woman. [*O.T.: Genesis* 1:26, 2:21–25]

2. **Allah** made man from flowing blood. [Islam: *Koran*, 96:2]

3. **Apsu** primeval waters, origin of all things. [Babyl. Myth.: Leach, 68]

4. **Aruru** goddess pinched man, Enkidu out of clay. [Assyrian Myth.: Gaster, 9, Babyl. Myth.: *Gilgamesh*]

5. **Askr** first man; created from ash tree. [Norse Myth.: Benét, 58]

6. **Ea** made man from primordial ocean clay. [Babyl. Myth.: Gaster, 9]

7. **Embla** first woman on earth. [Norse Myth.: Benét, 58]

8. **Genesis** Old Testament book dealing with world's creation. [*O.T.: Genesis*]

9. **God** created the world in six days. [*O.T.: Genesis* 1]

10. **the Hatchery** mass produces everything, including human beings. [Br. Lit.: *Brave New World*]

11. **Khnum** ram god, created man from clay on potter's wheel. [Egypt. Rel.: Parrinder, 155]

12. **Prometheus** molded man of clay, animated him with fire. [Gk. Myth.: Wheeler, 304]

13. **Shiva** Lord of creation; danced to begin life. [Hinduism: Binder, 23]

14. **Tocupacha** molded man from clay. [Aztec Myth.: Gaster, 18]

129. CRIME FIGHTING (See also SLEUTHING.)

1. **Canadian Mounties** (Royal Canadian Mounted Police) corps which gained a romantic reputation for daring exploits and persistence in trailing criminals. [Can. Hist.: *NCE*, 2367]

2. **Dragnet** radio show in which justice is always served. [Radio: Buxton, 73]

3. **Earp, Wyatt** (1848–1929) law officer and gunfighter of American West. [Am. Hist.: *NCE*, 819]

4. **Kojak** hard-boiled, Manhattan plainclothes detective. [TV: Terrace, I, 445]

5. **Lone Ranger** arch foe of criminals in early west. [Radio: "The Lone Ranger" in Buxton, 143–144; Comics: Horn, 460; TV: Terrace, II, 34–35]

6. **McGarrett, Steve** implacable nemesis of Hawaiian wrongdoers. [TV: "Hawaii Five-O" in Terrace, I, 342]

7. **Ness, Eliot** G-man successfully subdues Prohibition gangsters. [TV: "The Untouchables" in Terrace, II, 402–403]

8. **Peel, Sir Robert** (1788–1850) reorganized British police; established Irish constabulary. [Br. Hist.: Flexner, 276]

9. **Purvis, Melvin** gunned down Dillinger outside Chicago theater (1934). [Am. Hist.: Wallechinsky, 464]

10. **Scotland Yard** Criminal Investigation Department of Metropolitan Police. [Br. Hist.: Brewer *Dictionary*, 97]

11. **Starsky and Hutch** plainclothes L.A. detectives break cases and hearts. [TV: Terrace, II, 317]

12. **Superman** invincible scourge of crime. [Comics: Horn, 642–643]

13. **Texas Rangers** 19th-century constabulary thwarting villains. [Am. Hist.: Brewer *Dictionary*, 1071]

14. **Tracy, Dick** comicbook cop. [Comics: Horn, 206–207]

CRIMINALITY (See OUTLAWRY.)

130. **CRITICISM**

1. **Bludyer, Mr.** a "slashing" book reviewer with savage humor. [Br. Lit.: *Pendennis*]

2. **Bolo, Miss** "looked a small armoury of daggers" at those who made mistakes. [Br. Lit.: *Pickwick Papers*]

3. **Dutch uncle** strict elder who scolds and moralizes. [Br. Slang: Lurie, 122–123]

4. **Eliphaz, Bildad, and Zophar** rebuke Job for his complaints. [*O.T.: Job* 4–31]

5. **Joab** admonishes David for ingratitude to troops and servants. [*O.T.: II Samuel* 19:1–8]

6. **Michal** David's wife; castigates him for boyish exulting. [*O.T.: II Samuel* 6:20]

7. **Monday morning quarterback** football spectator who, in hindsight, points out where team went wrong. [Am. Sports and Folklore: Misc.]

8. **Sanballat and Tobiah** jeered Jews' attempt to rebuild Jerusalem's walls. [*O.T.: Nehemiah* 4:1–3]

9. **Theon** satirical poet of trenchant wit. [Rom. Lit.: Brewer *Dictionary*, 1073]

10. **Zoilus** malicious and contentious rhetorician; "Homer's scourge." [Gk. Hist.: Brewer *Dictionary*, 1175]

131. CRONYISM

1. **Tammany Hall** Manhattan Democratic political circle notorious for spoils system approach. [Am. Hist.: Jameson, 492]

132. CRUELTY (See also BRUTALITY.)

1. **Achren** mean, spiteful enchantress of Spiral Castle. [Children's Lit.: *The Castle of Llyr*]

2. **Blackbeard** nickname of pirate, Edward Teach (d. 1718). [Am. Hist.: Hart, 84]

3. **Bligh, Captain** tyrannical master of the ship *Bounty*. [Am. Lit.: *Mutiny on the Bounty*]

4. **bull** symbolizes cruelty in Picasso's *Guernica*. [Span. Art.: Mercatante, 99]

5. **Bumble, Mr.** abusive beadle, mistreats Oliver and other waifs. [Br. Lit.: *Oliver Twist*]

6. **Creakle, Mr.** headmaster at Salem House; enjoys whipping boys. [Br. Lit.: *David Copperfield*]

7. **cuscuta** symbol of cruelty. [Flower Symbolism; Jobes, 399]

8. **Diocletian** Roman emperor (284–305); instituted general persecutions of Christians. [Rom. Hist.: *EB*, 5: 805–807]

9. **Guilbert, Brian de Bois** dissolute and cruel commander of the Knights Templars. [Br. Lit.: *Ivanhoe*]

10. **Legree, Simon** harsh taskmaster; slavetrader. [Am. Lit.: *Uncle Tom's Cabin*]

11. **leopard** represents meanness, sin, and the devil. [Animal Symbolism: Mercatante, 56]

12. **Margaret of Anjou** hard, vicious, strong-minded, imperious woman. [Br. Lit.: *II Henry VI*]

13. **Mezentius** savagely cruel Etrurian king; killed by Aeneas. [Rom. Lit.: *Aeneid*]

14. **Murdstone, Edward** harsh and cruel husband of widow Copperfield. [Br. Lit.: *David Copperfield*]

15. **Slout, Mr.** punished Oliver for asking for more gruel. [Br. Lit.: *Oliver Twist*]

16. **Squeers, Wackford** brutal, abusive pedagogue; starves and maltreats urchins. [Br. Lit.: *Nicholas Nickleby*]

17. **Totenkopfverbande** tough Death's Head units maintaining concentration camps in Nazi Germany. [Ger. Hist.: Shirer, 375]

18. **Vlad the Impaler** (c. 980–1015) prince of Walachia; called Dracula; ruled barbarously. [Eur. Hist.: *NCE*, 2907]

133. CRYING

1. **Bokim** Hebrew toponym: 'Weepers'; Israelites bewail their wrong doings. [*O.T.: Judges* 2:1–5]
2. **Heraclitus** the weeping philosopher; melancholic personality. [Gk. Phil.: Hall, 98]
3. **Mary Magdalene** tearfully washes Christ's feet. [*N.T.: Luke* 7:37–38]
4. **Niobe** weeps when her children are slain, even after Zeus turns her to stone. [Gk. Myth.: *RHDC*]
5. **Rachel weeping for her children** Israel, for children slain by order of Herod. [*N.T.: Matthew* 2:16–18]
6. **tears of Eos** dewdrops; teardrops shed for slain son. [Gk. Myth.: Brewer *Dictionary*, 1065]

134. CUCKOLDRY (See also ADULTERY, FAITHLESSNESS.)

1. **Actaeon's horns** symbol of cuckoldry. [Medieval and Ren. Folklore: Walsh *Classical*, 5]
2. **antlers** metaphorical decoration for deceived husband. [Western Folklore: Jobes, 395]
3. **Arveragus** delivers wife to adulterer to keep promise. [Br. Lit.: *Canterbury Tales*, "The Franklin's Tale"]
4. **Camacho** cheated of bride after lavish wedding preparations. [Span. Lit.: *Don Quixote*]
5. **cuckoo** symbolizes adulterous betrayal by wife. [Western Folklore: Jobes, 395; Mercatante, 164]
6. **del Sarto, Andrea** cuckolded Florentine painter; protagonist of Browning's poem. [Art Hist.: Walsh *Modern*, 19–20; Br. Lit.: "Andrea del Sarto" in Norton, 778–783]
7. **Hildebrand, Old** sent away while wife and preacher play. [Ger. Fairy Tale: Grimm, 333]
8. **Mannon, Ezra** kindly general deceived by adulterous wife and murdered. [Am. Lit.: *Mourning Becomes Electra*]
9. **Mark, King** by Tristan after May-December marriage to Isolde. [Ger. Opera: Wagner, *Tristan and Isolde*, Westerman, 220]
10. **Menelaus** his wife, Helen, was also Paris's lover. [Gk. Lit.: *Iliad*]
11. **Rubin, Maximiliano** sickly pharmacist; wife's infidelities begin on wedding night. [Span. Lit.: *Fortunata and Jacinta*]
12. **Uriah the Hittite** while he is at war, wife sleeps with David. [*O.T.: II Samuel* 11:6]

135. CUNNING

1. **Artful Dodger** nickname for the sly pickpocket, John Dawkins. [Br. Lit.: *Oliver Twist*]

2. **Asmodeus** clever, hell-born hero. [Fr. Lit.: *Le Diable Boîteux*, Walsh *Modern*, 31]

3. **Autolycus** craftiest of thieves; stole neighbors' flocks by changing marks. [Gk. Myth.: *NCE*, 192]

4. **Bamber, Jack** law clerk with "strange wild slyness." [Br. Lit.: *Pickwick Papers*]

5. **Bolingbroke, Henry** cleverness and timing bring him England's crown. [Br. Lit.: *Richard II*]

6. **Borgia, Cesare** (1476–1507) unscrupulously plotted against friend and foe. [Ital. Hist.: Plumb, 59–61]

7. **Brer Fox** sly trickster; outwits everyone. [Children's Lit.: *Uncle Remus*]

8. **Bunny, Bugs** for whom no trap is too tricky. [Comics: Horn, 140]

9. **cheetah** pounces without warning on prey. [Western Folklore: Jobes, 320]

10. **Cleopatra** manipulates Antony through her "infinite variety." [Br. Lit.: *Antony and Cleopatra*]

11. **crow** symbolizes one who lives by his wits. [Western Folklore: Jobes, 388]

12. **Dido** in plotting the site of Carthage. [Rom. Lit.: *Aeneid;* Espy, 42]

13. **Dolius** epithet of Hermes, meaning 'crafty.' [Gk. Myth.: Zimmerman, 124]

14. **Fabius** delayed meeting Hannibal's troops; wore them down; hence, *fabian*. [Rom. Hist.: Espy, 177]

15. **Figaro** ingeniously contrives means to his own ends. [Fr. Lit.: *Barber of Seville; Marriage of Figaro*]

16. **fox** symbol of cleverness and deceit. [Animal Symbolism: Mercatante, 84–85]

17. **Helena** tricks husband into fulfilling marital duties. [Br. Lit.: *All's Well That Ends Well*]

18. **Isabella** frustrates captor while pretending compliance. [Ital. Opera: Rossini, *Italian Girl in Algeria*, Westerman, 118–119]

19. **jackal** outwits the tiger; imprisons him. [Hindu Folklore: Mercatante, 55]

20. **Malengin** carries net on back to "catch fools with." [Br. Lit.: *Faerie Queene*]

21. **Marion, Francis** (1732–1795) Revolutionary general, nicknamed the "Swamp Fox." [Am. Hist.: Jameson, 308]

22. **Morgiana** female slave cleverly dispatches 40 thieves. [Arab. Lit.: *Arabian Nights,* "Ali Baba and the Forty Thieves"]

23. **Odysseus** wily and noble hero of the *Odyssey.* [Gk. Lit.: *Odyssey*]

24. **Oriol, Father** shrewd landowner with admirable bargaining ability. [Fr. Lit.: *Mont-Oriol,* Magill, I, 618–620]

25. **Panurge** "received answers in twelve known and unknown tongues." [Fr. Lit.: *Gargantua and Pantagruel*]

26. **Road Runner** thrives on outwitting Wile E. Coyote. [Comics: "Beep Beep the Road Runner" in Horn, 105]

27. **Sawyer, Tom** hoodwinks friends into painting fence. [Am. Lit.: *Tom Sawyer*]

28. **Scheherazade** escapes being put to death by telling stories for 1001 nights. [Arab. Lit.: *Arabian Nights*]

29. **serpent** subtly deceives Eve in the Garden. [*O.T.: Genesis* 3:1]

30. **Sinon** induces Trojans to take in wooden horse. [Rom. Lit.: *Aeneid*]

31. **spider ophrys** indicates cleverness. [Flower Symbolism: *Flora Symbolica,* 177]

32. **third little pig** outwits Wolf; lures him into boiling water. [Children's Lit.: Bettelheim, 41–45]

33. **Whipple, Molly** outwits ferocious giant and gains his talismanic possessions. [Br. Fairy Tale: "Molly Whipple" in Macleod, 58–64]

34. **wolf** symbol on coats of arms. [Heraldry: Halberts, 16]

136. CURIOSITY

1. **Anselmo** so assured of wife's fidelity, asks friend to try to corrupt her; friend is successful. [Span. Lit.: *Don Quixote*]

2. **Cupid and Psyche** her inquisitiveness almost drives him away forever. [Gk. Myth.: Espy, 27]

3. **Curious George** inquisitive, mischievous monkey. [Children's Lit.: *Curious George*]

4. **Fatima** Bluebeard's 7th and last wife; her inquisitiveness uncovers his murders. [Fr. Fairy Tale: Harvey, 97–98]

5. **Faustus, Doctor** makes demonic compact to sate thirst for knowledge. [Br. Lit.: *Doctor Faustus*]

6. **Harker, Jonathan** uncovers vampiric and lycanthropic activities at Castle Dracula. [Br. Lit.: *Dracula*]

7. **Lot's wife** ignores God's command; turns to salt upon looking back. [*O.T.: Genesis* 19:26]

8. **Nosy Parker** after a meddlesome Elizabethan Archbishop of Canterbury. [Br. Hist.: Espy, 169]

9. **Pandora** inquisitively opens box of plagues given by Zeus. [Gk. Myth.: Zimmerman, 191]

10. **Pry, Paul** overly inquisitive journalist. [Br. Lit.: *Paul Pry;* Espy, 135]

11. **sycamore** symbolizes inquisitiveness. [Flower Symbolism: *Flora Symbolica,* 177]

12. **Vathek** journeys to Istakhar where world's secrets are revealed. [Br. Lit.: *Vathek*]

137. CURLYHEADEDNESS

1. **Little Orphan Annie** red, curly hair. [Comics: Horn, 459]

2. **Temple, Shirley** (1928–   ) blonde, curly-headed darling of America. [Am. Cinema: Browne, 100–111]

138. CUTENESS

1. **Bambi** adorable deer grows rhapsodically in beautiful forest. [Am. Cinema: *Bambi* in *Disney Films,* 53–56]

2. **teddy bear** cuddly commodity named after President Theodore Roosevelt. [Am. Hist.: Frank, 46]

3. **Thumper** Bambi's huggable rabbit sidekick. [Am. Cinema: *Bambi* in *Disney Films,* 53–56]

139. CYNICISM (See also PESSIMISM.)

1. **Antisthenes** (444–371 B.C.) Greek philosopher and founder of Cynic school. [Gk. Hist.: *NCE,* 121]

2. **Apemantus** churlish, sarcastic advisor of Timon. [Br. Lit.: *Timon of Athens*]

3. **Backbite, Sir Benjamin** sarcastic would-be poet and wit. [Br. Lit.: *School for Scandal*]

4. **Bierce, Ambrose** (1842–1914) acerbic journalist for *San Francisco Examiner;* nicknamed "Bitter Bierce." [Am. Lit.: Hart, 77]

5. **Diogenes** (412–323 B.C.) frustratedly looked everywhere for an honest man. [Gk. Hist.: Avery, 395]

6. **Lescaut** assured Geronte sister will succumb to his money. [Ital. Opera: Puccini, *Manon Lescaut,* Westerman, 346]

7. **Pandarus** jaded about good graces of women. [Br. Lit.: *Troilus and Cressida*]

D

140. **DANCE**

1. **Rockettes** precision dancers; a fixture at New York's Radio City; Music Hall. [Am. Dance: Payton, 576]

2. **Roseland Ballroom** New York dance hall. [Pop. Culture: Misc.]

3. **St. Denis, Ruth, and Ted Shawn** (1877–1968) (1891–1972) husband-and-wife team, founders of Denishawn dance schools. [Am. Dance: *NCE*, 2395]

4. **Salome** danced to obtain head of John the Baptist. [*N.T.: Matthew* 14:6–11]

5. **Terpsichore** muse of dancing. [Gk. Myth.: Brewer *Dictionary*, 849]

6. **Vitus, St.** patron saint of dancers. [Christian Hagiog: *Saints and Festivals*, 291]

7. **Ziegfeld Follies** beautiful dancing girls highlighted annual musical revue on Broadway (1907–1931). [Am. Theater: *NCE*, 3045]

141. **DANGER**

1. **Geiger counter** radiation detector named for inventor. [Am. Hist.: Flexner, 12]

2. **Mayday** international radiotelephone distress signal. [Maritime Hist.: Misc.]

3. **Perils of Pauline** cliff-hangers in which Pauline's life is recurrently in danger. [Am. Cinema: Halliwell, 559]

4. **red alert** final alert; attack believed imminent. [Military: Misc.]

5. **red flag** symbol of peril. [Folklore: Jobes, 413]

6. **rhododendron** symbol of approaching pitfalls. [Flower Symbolism: *Flora Symbolica*, 177]

7. **rhubarb** symbol of approaching pitfalls. [Flower Symbolism: *Flora Symbolica*, 177]

8. **Scylla and Charybdis** rocks and whirlpool, respectively, opposite each other in the Strait of Messina. [Classical Myth.: Zimmerman, 59, 235–236]

9. **skull and crossbones** alerts consumers to presence of poison; represents death. [Folklore: Misc.]

10. **SOS** Morse code distress signal. [World Culture: Flexner, 359]

11. **sword of Damocles** signifies impending peril; blade suspended over banqueter by a hair. [Gk. Myth.: Brewer *Dictionary*, 297]

12. **Symplegades** "Clashing Cliffs" at the entrance to the Black Sea, said to crush vessels. [Classical Myth.: *New Century*, 1043]

13. **Syrtes** quicksands off the coast of northern Africa; any part of the sea dangerous to ships because of natural phenomena. [Rom. Myth.: Zimmerman, 251]

14. **thin ice** universal symbol of possible danger. [Folklore: Misc.]

15. **Yuck, Mr.** pictorial symbol denoting poison; grimacing face with tongue sticking out. [Am. Culture: Misc.]

DARKNESS (See NIGHT.)

142. **DAWN**

1. **Aarvak** one of the horses of the sun. [Norse Myth.: Leach, 1]

2. **Aurora** goddess of dawn whose tears provide dew. [Rom. Myth.: Kravitz, 42]

3. **Daphne** Apollo's attempted rape represents dawn fleeing daylight. [Gk. Myth.: Parrinder, 72; Jobes, 414]

4. **Eos** goddess of dawn; announces Helios each morning. [Gk. Myth.: Kravitz, 89]

5. **Heimdall** god of dawn and protector of rainbow bridge, Bifrost. [Norse Myth.: Leach, 488]

6. **laughing jackass** bird whose cry brings in daylight. [Euahlayi Legend: *How the People Sang The Mountains Up*, 19]

7. **Octa** mountain from which sun rises. [Rom. Folklore: Wheeler, 7]

8. **rays, garland of** emblem of Aurora, dawn goddess. [Gk. Myth.: Jobes, 374]

9. **rooster** its crowing at dawn heralds each new day. [Western Folklore: Leach, 329]

143. **DEADLINESS**

1. **anaconda** South American boa constrictor; longest and deadliest of its kind. [Zoology: *NCE*, 317]

2. **basilisk** monstrous reptile; has fatal breath and glance. [Gk. Folklore: Jobes, 184]

3. **black widow spider** poisonous spider; consumes her mate after mating. [Zoology: *NCE*, 308]

4. **boa constrictor** largest of all snakes; squeezes its victims in a deadly grip. [Zoology: *NCE*, 317]

5. **cobra** bite believed to mean death. [Folklore: Jobes, 352]

6. **copperhead** deadly pit viper in eastern U.S. [Zoology: *NCE*, 652]

7. **coral snake** its bite is deadly. [Zoology: *NCE*, 654]

8. **Gila monster** small but venomous lizard found in U.S. desert. [Zoology: *NCE*, 1084]

9. **Hydra's gall** deadly; Hercules dipped his arrows in it. [Gk. and Rom. Myth.: Hall, 149]

10. **piranha** South American carnivorous fish. [Zoology: *EB*, VIII: 1]

11. **Portuguese man-of-war** a long-tentacled jellyfish whose sting can be deadly. [Zoology: *NCE*, 1408]

12. **python** nonvenomous jungle snake crushes its victims. [Zoology: *NCE*, 2252]

13. **rattlesnake** venomous snake, often deadly. [Zoology: *NCE*, 2281]

14. **shark** large and ferocious fish, sometimes man-eating. [Zoology: *NCE*, 2493]

15. **tarantula** spider with a deadly venom. [Zoology: *NCE*, 2695]

16. **viper (or adder)** poisonous snake family; puff adder is deadliest of all. [Zoology: *NCE*, 2898]

17. **water moccasin** (also **cottonmouth**) highly poisonous snake found in southern U.S. [Zoology: *NCE*, 2490]

144. DEAFNESS

1. **Aged P.** Wemmick's deaf father. [Br. Lit.: *Great Expectations*]

2. **Bell, Alexander Graham** (1847–1922) telephone inventor; renowned for studies of deafness. [Am. Hist.: *NCE*, 265]

3. **Keller, Helen** (1880–1968) overcame handicap of deafness as well as blindness. [Am. Hist.: *NCE*, 1462]

145. DEATH

1. **Ah Puch** deity of doom; represented as bloated corpse or skeleton. [Maya Myth.: Leach, 30]

2. **Ankou** gaunt driver of spectral cart; collects the dead. [Brittany Folklore: Leach, 62]

3. **Anubis** god and guardian of the dead. [Ancient Egyptian Rel.: Parrinder, 10]

4. **Arrow of Azrael** angel of death's way of summoning dead. [Islamic Myth.: Jobes, 129]

5. **asphodel flower** bloom growing in Hades. [Gk. Myth.: Kravitz, 37]

6. **Atropos** Fate who cuts thread of life. [Gk. and Rom. Myth.: Hall, 302]

7. **Azrael** angel of death; separates the soul from the body. [Islamic Myth.: Walsh *Classical*, 41]

8. **banshee** female specter, harbinger of death. [Irish and Welsh Myth.: Walsh *Classical*, 45]

9. **bell** passing bell; rung to indicate demise. [Christian Tradition: Jobes, 198]

10. **black** Western color for mourning. [Christian Color Symbolism: Leach, 242; Jobes, 357]

11. **Bodach Glas** gray specter; equivalent to Irish banshee. [Scot. Myth.: Walsh *Classical*, 45]

12. **Bran** god whose cauldron restored dead to life. [Welsh Myth.: Jobes, 241]

13. **Calvary (Golgotha)** where Christ was crucified. [*N.T.: Luke* 23:33]

14. **Cer** goddess of violent death. [Gk. Myth.: Kravitz, 75]

15. **Charun** god of death. [Etruscan Myth.: Jobes, 315]

16. **Conqueror Worm** the worm ultimately vanquishes man in grave. [Am. Lit.: "Ligeia" in *Tales of Terror*]

17. **danse macabre** Dance of Death; representation of procession in which living and dead participate. [Art: Osborne, 299–300, 677]

18. **dust and ashes** "I am become like dust and ashes." [*O.T.: Job* 30:19]

19. **Ereshkigal** goddess of death; consort of Nergal. [Sumerian and Akkadian Myth.: Parrinder, 93]

20. **extreme unction** Roman Catholic sacrament given to a person in danger of dying. [Christianity: *RHD*, 506]

21. **Grim Reaper** name given to personification of death. [Pop. Culture: Misc.]

22. **handful of earth** symbol of mortality. [Folklore: Jobes, 486]

23. **horse** symbol of agents of destruction. [Christian Tradition: *N.T.: Revelation* 6; Mercatante, 65]

24. **Kali** Hindu goddess to whom Thug sacrificed victims. [Hinduism: Brewer *Dictionary*, 600]

25. **Lenore** "saintly soul floats on the Stygian river." [Am. Lit.: "Lenore" in Hart, 468]

26. **Lord of the Flies** showing man's consciousness and fear of dying. [Br. Lit.: *Lord of the Flies*]

27. **manes** spirits of the dead. [Rom. Rel.: Leach, 672]

28. **Mania** ancient Roman goddess of the dead. [Rom. Myth.: Zimmerman, 159]

29. **nightingale** identified with mortality. [Animal Symbolism: Mercatante, 163]

30. **pale horse** ridden by death personified. [*N.T.: Revelation* 7:7–8]

31. **Requiem** religious mass (music or spoken) for the dead. [Christianity: Payton, 568]

32. **Sacco Benedetto** yellow robe worn going to the stake during Inquisition. [Span. Hist.: Brewer *Dictionary,* 948]

33. **scythe** carried by the personification of death, used to cut life short. [Art.: Hall, 276]

34. **skeleton** visual representation of death. [Western Folklore: Cirlot, 298]

35. **skull** representation of body's dissolution. [Christian Symbolism: Appleton, 92]

36. **skull and crossbones** symbolizing mortality; sign on poison bottles. [World Culture: Brewer *Dictionary,* 1009]

37. **Styx** chief river of Hades. [Gk. Myth.: Howe, 259]

38. **Thanatos (Mors)** god of death; brother of Somnos (sleep). [Gk. Myth.: Gayley, 54]

39. **Thoth** record-keeper of the dead. [Egyptian Myth.: Leach, 1109]

40. **Valdemar, M.** in hypnotic trance, recounts impressions from other side of death. [Am. Lit.: "The Facts in the Case of M. Valdemar" in *Portable Poe,* 268–280]

41. **viaticum** Eucharist given to one who is dying. [Christianity: Brewer *Dictionary,* 1128]

146. **DEATH, EARLY (See also LOVE, TRAGIC.)**

1. **Byron, Lord** (1788–1824) English poet died of fever at 36. [Br. Lit.: Harvey, 129]

2. **Dean, James** (1931–1955) leader of restless youth cult in early 50s. [Am. Cinema: *NCE,* 730]

3. **Frank, Anne** (1929–1945) young Dutch diarist, died in Bergen-Belsen camp during WWII. [Jew. Hist.: Wigoder, 196]

4. **Grey, Lady Jane** (1537–1554) English queen at 15; died at 17. [Br. Hist.: *NCE,* 1146]

5. **Keats, John** (1795–1821) English poet died of consumption at 25. [Br. Lit.: Harvey, 443]

6. **March, Beth** dies young; sensitive girl. [Children's Lit.: *Little Women*]

7. **Romeo and Juliet** star-crossed lovers die as teenagers. [Br. Lit.: *Romeo and Juliet*]

8. **Schubert, Franz** (1797–1828) brilliant composer, died at 31. [Music Hist.: Thompson, 1968]

9. **Shelley, Percy Bysshe** (1792–1822) English poet drowned at 30. [Br. Lit.: Harvey, 748]

10. **Valentino, Rudolph** (1895–1926) matinée idol; his death caused several suicides. [Am. Cinema: Halliwell, 734]

147. DEBAUCHERY (See also DISSIPATION, PROFLIGACY.)

1. **Alexander VI** Borgia pope infamous for licentiousness and debauchery. [Ital. Hist.: Plumb, 219–220]

2. **Bacchus** (Gk. **Dionysus**) god of wine; honored by Bacchanalias. [Gk. Myth.: Howe, 83]

3. **Behan, Brendan** (1923–1964) uninhibited Irish playwright who lived wildly. [Irish Lit.: *NCE*, 261]

4. **Bowery** Manhattan district, once notorious for brothels and gambling halls. [Am. Hist.: Hart, 97]

5. **Hell-fire Club** 18th-century British clique devoted to debauchery. [Br. Hist.: Brewer *Note-Book*, 411]

6. **Nero** (A.D. 37–68) hated as Roman emperor; led life of debauchery. [Rom. Hist.: *NCE*, 1909]

7. **Pandarus** a "honey-sweet lord"; go-between for lovers. [Br. Lit.: *Troilus and Cressida*]

8. **Pornocracy** period of unparalleled papal decadence (early 10th century). [Christian Hist.: Grun, 106]

9. **Rasputin** (1871–1916) debauchee who preached and practised doctrine mixing religious fervor with sexual indulgence. [Russ. Hist.: *NCE*, 1770]

10. **Saturnalia** licentious December 17th feast honoring Saturn. [Rom. Myth.: Espy, 19]

11. **Satyricon** tales of vice and luxury in imperial Rome. [Rom. Lit.: *Satyricon*]

12. **Sergius III** instituted the Pornocracy. [Christian Hist.: Grun, 106]

13. **Sodom and Gomorrah** ancient cities destroyed by God because of their wickedness. [*O.T.*: Genesis 19:1–29]

DEBT (See BANKRUPTCY, POVERTY.)

148. DECAPITATION (See also HEADLESSNESS.)

1. **Antoinette, Marie** (1755–1793) queen of France beheaded by revolutionists. [Fr. Hist.: *NCE*, 1697]

2. **Becket, Thomas à** (1118–1170) leader of Church of England; beheaded by King Henry II. [Br. Hist.: *NCE*, 2735]

3. **Boleyn, Anne** (1507–1536) beheaded by husband, Henry VIII, for adultery and incest. [Br. Hist.: *NCE*, 325]

4. **Grey, Lady Jane** (1537–1554) English queen beheaded at 17. [Br. Hist.: *NCE*, 1146]

5. **Guillotin, Joseph** (1738–1814) physician; advocated humane method of capital punishment. [Fr. Hist.: Wallechinsky, 164]

6. **Holofernes** Assyrian commander-in-chief beheaded by Judith. [*Apocrypha: Judith* 13:4–10]

7. **John the Baptist** head presented as gift to Salome. [*N.T.: Mark* 6:25–28]

8. **Medusa** beheaded by Perseus. [Gk. Myth.: Hall, 206; Rom. Lit.: *Metamorphoses*]

9. **More, Sir Thomas** (1478–1535) English statesman beheaded by King Henry VIII. [Br. Hist.: *NCE*, 1830]

149. DECAY

1. **Buddenbrooks** portrays the downfall of a materialistic society. [Ger. Lit.: *Buddenbrooks*]

2. **Diver, Dick** dissatisfied psychiatrist goes downhill on alcohol. [Am. Lit.: *Tender is the Night*]

3. **Great Gatsby, The** 1925 novel by F. Scott Fitzgerald symbolizes corruption and decadence. [Am. Lit.: *The Great Gatsby*]

4. **House of Usher** eerie old mansion collapses as master dies. [Am. Lit.: "Fall of the House of Usher" in *Tales of Terror*]

5. **Lonigan, Studs** Chicago Irishman whose life is one of physical and moral deterioration (1935). [Am. Lit.: *Studs Lonigan: A Trilogy*, Magill, III, 1028–1030]

6. **Manhattan Transfer** novel portraying the teeming greed of the city's inhabitants. [Am. Lit.: *Manhattan Transfer*]

7. **Nana** indictment of social decay during Napoleon III's reign (1860s). [Fr. Lit.: *Nana*, Magill, I, 638–640]

8. **Sun Also Rises, The** moral collapse of expatriots. [Am. Lit.: *The Sun Also Rises*]

9. **Warren, The** Haredale's house, "mouldering to ruin." [Br. Lit.: *Barnaby Rudge*]

10. **Yoknapatawpha County** northern Mississippi; decadent setting for Faulkner's novels. [Am. Lit.: Hart, 955]

150. DECEIT

1. **Aimwell** pretends to be titled to wed into wealth. [Br. Lit.: *The Beaux' Stratagem*]

2. **Ananias** lies about amount of money received for land. [*N.T.: Acts* 5:1–6]

3. **Ananias Club** all its members are liars. [Am. Lit.: Worth, 10]

4. **angel of light** false apostles are like Satan in masquerade. [*N.T.: II Corinthians* 11:14]

5. **Apaturia** epithet of Athena, meaning 'deceitful.' [Gk. Myth.: Zimmerman, 36]

6. **apples of Sodom** outwardly sound fruit; inwardly rotten. [Class. Myth.: Jobes, 114]

7. **Arbaces** priest who frames Glaucus. [Br. Lit.: *The Last Days of Pompeii*, Magill, I, 490–492]

8. **Archimago** uses sorcery to deceive people. [Br. Lit.: *Faerie Queene*]

9. **Arnolphe** plans marriage to ward; maintains guardianship under alias. [Fr. Lit.: *L'Ecole des Femmes*]

10. **bilberry** symbol for falsehood. [Flower Symbolism: *Flora Symbolica*, 172]

11. **Brunhild** outdone in athletic competition by Gunther with invisible assistance. [Ger. Myth.: *Nibelungenlied*]

12. **Buttermilk, Little Johnny** fools witch by substituting china for self in sack. [Br. Fairy Tale: Macleod, 21–24]

13. **Camilla, Mrs.** practises deception on Pip. [Br. Lit.: *Great Expectations*]

14. **clematis** symbol of deception. [Flower Symbolism: Jobes, 347; *Flora Symbolica*, 173]

15. **dogbane** symbol for deceit. [Flower Symbolism: Jobes, 458]

16. **Hlestakov, Ivan Alexandrovich** dissimulating gentleman hoodwinks town dignitaries as tsar's inspector. [Russ. Lit.: *The Inspector General*]

17. **hocus-pocus** magician's parody of *Hoc Est Corpus Domini*. [Western Folklore: Espy, 76]

18. **Judas goat** decoy for luring animals to slaughter. [Western Folklore: Espy, 80]

19. **Latch, William** Esther's betrayer; seduces her on marriage pretense. [Br. Lit.: *Esther Waters*, Magill, I, 254–256]

20. **Mak** Falstaffian figure; categorically maintains his innocence. [Br. Lit.: *The Second Shepherds' Play*]

21. **Malengin** personification of craftiness. [Br. Lit.: *Faerie Queene*]

22. **mask** a disguise; hence, symbol of deception. [Art: Hall, 204]

23. **Moncrieff, Algernon, and Jack Worthing** both assume fictitious name "Ernest" in wooing belles. [Br. Lit.: *The Importance of Being Earnest*]

24. **Montoni, Signor** marries Emily's aunt to secure her property. [Br. Lit.: *The Mysteries of Udolpho,* Magill, I, 635–638]

25. **nightshade** poisonous flower; symbol of falsehood. [Flower Symbolism: *Flora Symbolica,* 176]

26. **Nimue** cajoles Merlin to reveal secret of power. [Arth. Romance: *History of Prince Arthur,* Brewer *Handbook,* 756]

27. **Nixon, Richard** (1913–   ) 37th U.S. president (1969–1974); nicknamed "Tricky Dicky." [Am. Hist.: Kane, 523]

28. **Pharaoh** continually reneges on promise of Israelite freedom. [*O.T.: Exodus* 8:15-32; 9:34–35]

29. **Pinocchio** wooden nose lengthens when he lies. [Am. Cinema: *Pinocchio* in *Disney Films,* 32–37]

30. **Sinon** convinced Trojans to accept wooden horse. [Rom. Lit.: *Aeneid*]

31. **Trojan Horse** hollow horse concealed soldiers, enabling them to enter and capture Troy. [Gk. Myth.: *Iliad*]

32. **white flytrap** lures insects with sweet odor. [Flower Symbolism: *Flora Symbolica,* 178]

33. **winter cherry** inedible fruit symbolizes falsehood. [Plant Symbolism: Jobes, 319]

151. DEFEAT

1. **Appomattox Courthouse** scene of Lee's surrender to Grant (1865). [Am. Hist.: Jameson, 22]

2. **Armada, Spanish** defeat by English fleet marked Spain's decline and England's rise as a world power (1588). [Eur. Hist.: *EB*, 1: 521–522]

3. **Austerlitz** defeat of Austro-Russian coalition by Napoleon (1805). [Fr. Hist.: Harbottle *Battles,* 23–24]

4. **Bataan** Philippine peninsula where U.S. troops surrendered to Japanese (1942). [Am. Hist.: *NCE,* 245]

5. **Battle of the Boyne** sealed Ireland's fate as England's vassal state (1690). [Br. Hist.: Harbottle *Battles,* 39]

6. **Battle of the Bulge** final, futile German WWII offensive (1944–1945). [Eur. Hist.: *Hitler,* 1148–1153, 1154–1155]

7. **Culloden** consolidated English supremacy; broke clan system (1746). [Br. Hist.: Harbottle *Battles,* 70]

8. **Dien Bien Phu** Vietminh rout of French paved way for petition of Vietnam (1954). [Fr. Hist.: Van Doren, 541]

9. **Gallipoli** poorly conceived and conducted battle ending in British disaster (1915). [Br. Hist.: Fuller, III, 240–261]

10. **Little Bighorn** scene of General Custer's "last stand" (1876). [Am. Hist.: Van Doren, 274]

11. **Pearl Harbor** Japan's surprise attack destroys U.S. fleet (1941). [Am. Hist.: NCE, 2089]

12. **Salt River** up which losing political parties travel to oblivion. [Am. Slang: LLEI, I: 312]

13. **Sedan** decisive German defeat of French (1870). [Fr. Hist.: Harbottle Battles, 225]

14. **Stalingrad** German army succumbs to massive Soviet pincer movement (1942–1943). [Ger. Hist.: Fuller, III, 531–538]

15. **Pyrrhic victory** a too costly victory; "Another such victory and we are lost." [Rom. Hist.: "Asculum I" in Eggenburger, 30–31]

16. **Waterloo** British victory in Belgium signals end of Napoleon's domination (1815). [Fr. Hist.: Harbottle Battles, 266]

17. **white flag** a sign of surrender. [Western Folklore: Misc.]

152. DEFENDER

1. **Bryan, William Jennings** (1860–1925) battled Clarence Darrow in famous Scopes trial. [Am. Hist.: NCE, 383–384]

2. **Canisius, St. Peter** Jesuit theologian; buttressed Catholic faith against Protestantism. [Christian Hagiog.: Attwater, 276]

3. **Daniel** halts Susanna's execution; gets her acquitted. [Apocrypha: Daniel and Susanna]

4. **Darrow, Clarence** (1857–1938) lawyer; Bryan's nemesis in Scopes trial (1925). [Am. Hist.: Jameson, 131]

5. **Defender of the Faith** Henry VIII as defender of the papacy against Martin Luther (1521). [Br. Hist.: EB, 8: 769–772]

6. **Defenders, The** father-son lawyer team in early 1960s. [TV: Terrace, I, 197]

7. **Donatello** Miriam's ardent friend ever ready to defend her. [Am. Lit.: The Marble Faun]

8. **Mason, Perry** detective novels and TV series feature courtroom drama by lawyer. [Am. Lit.: Gardner, Erle Stanley, in EB, IV: 416; Radio: Buxton, 186–187; TV: Terrace, II, 199]

9. **Ridd, John** defender of the parish of Oare in Somerset. [Br. Lit.: Lorna Doone, Magill, I, 524–526]

10. **Zola, Emile** (1840–1902) attacked Army cover-up of Dreyfus affair in J'accuse (1898). [Fr. Hist.: Wallechinsky, 60]

DEFIANCE (See DISOBEDIENCE.)

153. DEFORMITY (See also LAMENESS.)

1. **Calmady, Sir Richard** born without lower legs. [Br. Lit.: *Sir Richard Calmady*, Walsh *Modern*, 84]

2. **Carey, Philip** embittered young man with club foot seeks fulfillment. [Br. Lit.: *Of Human Bondage*]

3. **Cyclopes** one-eyed monsters. [Gk. Lit.: *Odyssey*]

4. **Freaks** 1930s macabre movie about sideshow people. [Am. Cinema: Halliwell, 278]

5. **Mayeux** deformed man, both brave and witty. [Fr. Folklore: Wheeler *Dictionary*, 237]

6. **Priapus** son of Aphrodite and Dionysus; grotesque man with huge phallus. [Gk. Myth.: Howe, 233]

7. **Quasimodo** hunchbacked bell-ringer. [Fr. Lit.: *Hunchback of Notre Dame*]

8. **Sarn, Prudence** harelipped girl is servant on brother's farm. [Br. Lit.: *Precious Bane*, Magill, I, 778–780]

9. **thalidomide** supposedly harmless sedative resulted in disfigured babies. [Am. Hist.: Van Doren, 582–583]

10. **Toulouse-Lautrec, Henri de** (1864–1901) crippled and stunted; became great artist. [Fr. Hist.: Wallechinsky, 13]

154. DELIVERANCE (See also FREEDOM.)

1. **Aphesius** epithet of Zeus, meaning 'releaser.' [Gk. Myth.: Zimmerman, 292–293]

2. **Bolívar, Simón** (1783–1830) the great liberator of South America. [Am. Hist.: *NCE*, 325]

3. **Boru, Brian** freed Ireland from the Danes. [Irish Myth.: Walsh *Classical*, 61–62]

4. **Brown, John** (1800–1859) abolitionist; attempted to liberate slaves. [Am. Hist.: Jameson, 64]

5. **Ehud** freed Israelites from Moabites by murdering king. [O.T.: *Judges* 3:15]

6. **Emancipation Proclamation** Lincoln's declaration freeing the slaves (1863). [Am. Hist.: Jameson, 161]

7. **Gideon** with 300 men, saved Israel from Midianites. [O.T.: *Judges* 6:14, 7:19–21]

8. **Jephthah** routed the Ammonites to save Israelites. [O.T.: *Judges* 11:32]

9. **Lincoln, Abraham** (1809–1865) 16th U.S. president; the Great Emancipator. [Am. Hist.: Jameson, 286–287]
10. **Moses** led his people out of bondage. [*O.T.: Exodus*]
11. **Othniel** freed Israelites from bondage of Cushan-rishathaim. [*O.T.: Judges* 3:9]
12. **Parsifal** deliverer of Amfortas and the Grail knights. [Ger. Opera: Wagner, *Parsifal,* Westerman, 250]
13. **Passover** festival commemorating Exodus. [Judaism: Wigoder, 472; *O.T.: Exodus* 12]
14. **Purim** Jewish festival commemorating salvation from Haman's destruction. [*O.T.: Esther* 9:20–28]

155. DELUSION

1. **Borkman, John Gabriel** suffers from delusions of power. [Nor. Lit.: *John Gabriel Borkman*]
2. **Clamence, Jean-Baptiste** living with his own good and evil. [Fr. Lit.: *The Fall*]
3. **Jones, Brutus** self-styled island emperor experiences traumatic visions. [Am. Lit.: *Emperor Jones*]
4. **Lockit, Lucy** steals jailer-father's keys to free phony husband. [Br. Lit.: *The Beggar's Opera*]
5. **opium of the people** Marx's classic metaphor for religion. [Ger. Hist.: *Critique of Hegel's "Philosophy of Right"*]
6. **ostrich** hides head, thinking itself concealed. [Animal Symbolism: Brewer *Dictionary,* 788]
7. **Pan, Peter** little boy, refuses to grow up; resides in Never Never Land. [Children's Lit.: *Peter Pan*]

156. DEMAGOGUERY

1. **Hague, Frank** (1876–1956) corrupt mayor of Jersey City, N.J., for 30 years. [Am. Hist.: *NCE,* 1173]
2. **Long, Huey P.** (1893–1935) infamous "Kingfish" of Louisiana politics. [Am. Hist.: *NCE,* 1607]
3. **Pendergast, Thomas J.** (1872–1945) political boss in Kansas City, Mo.: convicted of income tax evasions. [Am. Hist.: *NCE,* 2096]
4. **Savonarola** (1452–1498) rabble-rousing bane of Renaissance Florence. [Ital. Hist.: Plumb, 141–142, 166–167]
5. **Stark, Willie** rises to top as graft-dealing political boss. [Am. Lit.: *All the King's Men*]
6. **Tweed, "Boss" William** (1823–1878) powerful Tammany Hall leader in New York City. [Am. Hist.: *NCE,* 2810]

157. **DEMON** (See also DEVIL.)

1. **Aello** Harpy; demon carrying people away, personifying a whirlwind. [Gk. Myth.: Jobes, 40]

2. **Apophis** the snake god; most important of demons. [Ancient Egypt. Rel.: Parrinder, 24]

3. **Ashmedai** king of friends. [Hebrew Myth.: Leach, 83]

4. **Asmodeus** king of the devils. [Talmudic Legend: Benét, 58]

5. **bat** bird that is the devil incarnate. [Western Folklore: Mercatante, 181]

6. **cat** evil being, demonic in nature. [Animal Symbolism: Mercatante, 46]

7. **crocodile** feared as spirit of evil. [African Folklore: Jobes, 382; Mercatante, 9]

8. **Demogorgon** mere mention of his name brings death and destruction. [Western Folklore: Benét, 263]

9. **Dives** ferocious spirits under sovereignty of Eblis. [Persian Myth.: *LLEI*, I: 326]

10. **Fideal** evil water spirit; dragged men under water. [Scot. Folklore: Briggs, 175]

11. **Great Giant of Henllys** ghost of dead man turned demon. [Br. Folklore: Briggs, 199–200]

12. **incubus** demon in the form of a man. [Western Folklore: Briggs, 232]

13. **jinn (genii)** class of demon assuming animal/human form. [Arab. Myth.: Benét, 13, 521]

14. **Old Bogy** nursery fiend invoked to frighten children. [Br. Folklore: Wheeler, 265]

15. **succubus** demon in the form of a woman. [Western Folklore: Briggs, 232]

16. **whale** symbol of demonic evil. [Animal Symbolism: Mercatante, 26]

158. **DESPAIR** (See also FUTILITY.)

1. **Achitophel** hanged self when his advice went unheeded. [*O.T.*: *II Samuel* 17:23]

2. **Aram, Eugene** scholar murders from pressure of poverty. [Br. Lit.: *Eugene Aram*]

3. **the Bowery** Manhattan skid row for alcoholics. [Am. Hist.: Hart, 97]

4. **Hrothgar** Danish king desperately distressed by warrior-killing monster. [Br. Lit.: *Beowulf*]

5. **Maurya** mother loses six sons in the sea. [Br. Lit.: *Riders to the Sea*]

6. **Melusina** fairy who despaired when husband discovered secret. [Fr. Folklore: Brewer *Handbook*, 695]

7. **Narcissus** wastes away yearning to kiss reflection of himself. [Gk. Myth.: Brewer *Handbook*, 745; Rom. Lit.: *Metamorphoses*]

8. **Slough of Despond** bog enmiring and discouraging Christian. [Br. Lit.: *Pilgrim's Progress*]

9. **Sullivan brothers** mother despairs over losing her five sons in WWII (1942). [Am. Hist.: *Facts* (1943), 106]

159. DESTRUCTION

1. **Abaddon** angel of the abyss; king of locusts. [*N.T.: Revelation* 9:11]

2. **abomination of desolation** epithet for the destructive or hateful. [Western Folklore: Benét, 3]

3. **Armageddon** final battle between forces of good and evil. [*N.T.: Revelation* 16:16]

4. **atomic bomb (A-bomb)** fission device of enormous destructive power. [Am. Sci.: *EB*, I: 628]

5. **Bikini and Eniwetok** Pacific atolls, sites of A-bomb testing. [Am. Hist.: Flexner, 12]

6. **Dresden, bombing of** allied incendiary bombs reduced city to inferno (February 13, 1945). [Ger. Hist.: *Hitler*, 1165; Am. Lit.: *Slaughterhouse-Five*]

7. **Enhil** storm god responsible for deluge. [Babyl. Myth.: Parrinder, 91]

8. **firebranded foxes** Samson unlooses them to scorch cornfields. [*O.T.: Judges* 15:3–6]

9. **Four Horsemen of the Apocalypse** allegorical figures representing pestilence, war, famine, death. [*N.T.: Revelation* 6:1–8]

10. **Götterdämmerung** great final battle between Teutonic pantheon and forces of evil. [Ger. Myth.: Leach, 461]

11. **Hiroshima** Japanese city destroyed by A-bomb (1945). [Am. Hist.: Fuller, III, 626]

12. **Hormah** Judah and his men level this Canaanite city. [*O.T.: Judges* 1:17]

13. **Hundred Years War** reduced much of France to wasteland (1337–1453). [Eur. Hist.: Bishop, 382–395]

14. **hydrogen bomb** or H-bomb thermonuclear device more destructive than A-bomb. [Am. Sci.: *EB*, IX: 949]

15. **Jericho, Walls of** razed on the seventh blowing of trumpets. [*O.T.: Joshua* 6]

16. **Juggernaut (Jagannath)** huge idol of Krishna drawn through streets annually, occasionally rolling over devotees. [Hindu Rel.: *EB*, V: 499]

17. **Kristallnacht** Nazi rampage against property of German Jews (November 9–10, 1938). [Ger. Hist.: *Hitler*, 689–694]

18. **Lidice** Czech town obliterated by Nazis (June 10, 1942). [Eur. Hist.: Van Doren, 489]

19. **Nagasaki** Japanese city destroyed by A-bomb (1945). [Am. Hist.: Fuller, III: 626]

20. **neutron bomb** causes limited havoc: kills people, preserves property. [World Hist.: *Facts* (1978), 103]

21. **Ragnarok** destruction of gods and all things in final battle with evil. [Norse Myth.: *NCE*, 1762]

22. **Rome, Sack of** destroyed by the German-Spanish army under Charles V (1527). [Ital. Hist.: Plumb, 43, 406–407]

23. **Sherman's "March to the Sea"** Confederate heartland ravaged by marauding Union army (1864). [Am. Hist.: Jameson, 307]

24. **Sodom and Gomorrah** Biblical cities destroyed by fire for wicked ways. [*O.T.: Genesis* 10:19; 13; 14; 18; 19]

25. **Thirty Years War** world war prototype reduced Germany to wasteland (1618–1648). [Eur. Hist.: *EB*, 18: 333–344]

26. **Vials of Wrath** seven plagues precipitating end of world. [*N.T.: Revelation* 16:1–17]

27. **Vulcan** god of destruction, placated by gifts of captured weapons. [Rom. Myth.: Howe, 294]

160. **DETERMINATION (See also PERSEVERANCE.)**

1. **Agathocles** (361–289 B.C.) Syracusan king; "burned his ships behind him" in attacking Carthage. [Gk. Hist.: Walsh *Classical*, 9]

2. **Balboa, Rocky** determined prize fighter takes on impossible dream. [Am. Cinema: "Rocky" in *EB* (1978), 552]

3. **bulldog** bred for doggedly refusing to let go. [Dog Breeding: Misc.]

4. **Dry Guillotine** book by French escapee from Devil's Island. [Fr. Lit.: *Dry Guillotine*]

5. **Ignatz** tenaciously refuses Krazy Kat's advances. [Comics: "Krazy Kat" in Horn, 436–437]

6. **Jones, John Paul** (1747–1792) Revolutionary War naval hero; remembered for saying; "I have not yet begun to fight!" [Am. Hist.: Jameson, 260–261]

7. **Keller, Helen** (1880–1968) though blind and deaf, becomes noted author and lecturer. [Am. Hist.: Hart, 439–440]

8. **Little Engine That Could** succeeds when others refuse to help. [Children's Lit.: *The Little Engine That Could*]

9. **Papillon** wily prisoner endeavors repeatedly to escape from Devil's Island. [Fr. Lit.: *Papillon*]

10. **Santiago** struggles long and hard for great fish. [Am. Lit.: *Old Man and the Sea*]

11. **tortoise** slow and steady, it wins the race against the hare. [Animal Symbolism: Mercatante, 22; Gk. Lit.: Aesop, "The Tortoise and the Hare"]

12. **Tovesky, Marie** outgoing and friendly, despite husband's insane jealousy. [Am. Lit.: *O Pioneers!*, Magill, I, 663–665]

161. **DEVIL (See also DEMON.)**

1. **Adramalech** leader of fallen angels. [Br. Lit.: *Paradise Lost*]

2. **adversary** traditional appellation of Satan. [*O.T.: Job* 1:6; *N.T.: I Peter* 5:8]

3. **Amaimon** king of eastern portion of hell. [Medieval Legend: Brewer *Dictionary*, 28]

4. **Apollyon** Biblical name for Satan. [*N.T.: Revelation* 9:11]

5. **Auld Ane** literally, 'old one'; nickname for demon. [Scot. Folklore: Walsh *Modern*, 35]

6. **Auld Hornie** Scottish appellation for the devil. [Scot. Folklore: Leach, 353]

7. **Azazel** Satan's standard bearer. [Br. Lit.: *Paradise Lost*]

8. **Beelzebub** prince of demons. [*N.T.: Matthew* 12:24]

9. **Belial** chief of fiends. [*O.T.: I Samuel* 2:12]

10. **Clootie** Scottish appellation for the devil. [Scot. Folklore: Leach, 353]

11. **Darkness, Prince of** "The Prince of Darkness," alias the Devil. [Br. Lit.: *All's Well That Ends Well*]

12. **the Deuce** New England appellation for the devil. [Am. Folklore: Leach, 353]

13. **Devils, Prince of the** biblical equivalent for Satan. [*N.T.: Matthew* 9:34]

14. **Iblis (Eblis)** Moslem prince of darkness; chief evil spirit. [Islam: Leach, 513]

15. **Lucifer** a Biblical name for Satan. [*O.T.: Isaiah* 14:12]

16. **Master Leonard** grand-master of sabbats and orgies. [Medieval Demonology: Brewer *Handbook,* 684]

17. **Mephistopheles** fiend to whom Faust sells his soul. [Ger. Lit.: *Faust*]

18. **Nickie-Ben** a Scottish name for Satan. [Scot. Folklore: Wheeler, 258]

19. **Old Nick** Satan himself. [Western Folklore: Brewer *Dictionary,* 755]

20. **Old Scratch** Satan. [Eng. Usage: Brewer *Dictionary,* 973; Am. Lit.: "The Devil and Daniel Webster"]

21. **Peter, Meister** German euphemism alluding to the devil. [Ger. Folklore: Leach, 353]

22. **Satan** the devil himself, source of all evil. [*O.T.: Job* 1–2]

DEVOTION (See FAITHFULNESS.)

162. **DICTION, FAULTY**

1. **Ace, Jane** (1905–1974) radio personality, remembered for sayings such as "up at the crank of dawn." [Radio: "Easy Aces" in Buxton, 74–75]

2. **Amos 'n' Andy** early radio buffoons who distorted language: "I'se regusted!" [Radio: Buxton, 13–14]

3. **Claudius** because he stammered, held in little esteem as emperor. [Br. Lit.: *I, Claudius*]

4. **Clouseau, Inspector Jacques** infamous, tongue-tripping French detective. [Am. Cinema: "The Pink Panther" in Halliwell, 565]

5. **Dean, Dizzy** (1911–1974) famous baseball pitcher turned sports announcer: "He slud inta t'ird." [Radio: Buxton, 223]

6. **Dean, James** (1931–1955) actor whose inarticulateness epitomized the anti-eloquence of American youth in the 1950s. [Am. Cinema: Griffith, 423]

7. **Doolittle, Eliza** Cockney flower girl transformed from guttersnipe to lady via better English. [Br. Lit.: *Pygmalion*]

8. **Ephraimites** identified as enemy by mispronunciation of "shibboleth." [*O.T.: Judges* 12:6]

9. **Fudd, Elmer** disgruntled little man, stammers out his frustration at impish rabbit. [TV: "The Bugs Bunny Show" in Terrace, I, 125]

10. **Malaprop, Mrs.** misuses words without mispronouncing them. [Br. Lit.: *The Rivals*]

11. **Pig, Porky** stuttering porcine character in film cartoons. [Comics: Horn, 562–563]

12. **Pip** how orphan Philip Pirrup says his name. [Br. Lit.: *Great Expectations*]

13. **Socrates** (469–399 B.C.) learned proper diction with mouth full of pebbles. [Gk. Hist.: *NCE*, 2553]

14. **Spooner, Rev. W. A.** (1844–1930) legendary for transposing initial sounds: "our queer dean Mary"; hence, *spoonerism*. [Br. Hist.: Brewer *Dictionary*, 1029]

15. **Sylvester** the lisping feline star of film cartoons. [TV: "The Bugs Bunny Show" in Terrace, I, 125]

163. **DIGNITY (See also NOBLEMINDEDNESS.)**

1. **cherub** celestial being symbolizing dignity, glory, and honor. [Heraldry: Halberts, 23]

2. **cloves** symbolic of stateliness. [Plant Symbolism and Folklore: Jobes, 350]

3. **dahlia** symbol of dignity. [Flower Symbolism: Jobes, 406]

4. **ermine** fur which represents nobility. [Heraldry: Halberts, 13]

5. **strawberry** symbolizes esteem. [Flower Symbolism: *Flora Symbolica*, 177]

164. **DIMWITTEDNESS (See also STUPIDITY.)**

1. **Allen, Gracie** (1906–1964) American comedienne who projected a scatterbrained image. [Radio, TV, Am. Cinema: Halliwell, 14]

2. **Bodine, Jethro** oafish mental midget of millionaire hillbilly family. [TV: "The Beverly Hillbillies" in Terrace, I, 93]

3. **Bullwinkle** dimwitted moose with penchant for pedantry. [TV: "Rocky and His Friends" in Terrace, II, 252–253]

4. **Bunker, Edith** Archie's lovable "dingbat." [TV: "All in the Family" in Terrace, I, 47–48]

5. **Costello, Lou** (1906–1959) dumpy American comedian; used dimwittedness to spark humor. [Am. Cinema: Halliwell, 171]

6. **Drummle, Bentley** "heavy in comprehension"; suspicious of new ideas. [Br. Lit.: *Great Expectations*]

7. **Elspeth** Flashman's air-headed but beguiling wife. [Br. Lit.: *Flashman*]

8. **Laurel, Stan** (1890–1965) deadpan foil for Oliver Hardy. [Am. Cinema: Halliwell, 425]

9. **Moose** the epitome of "the obtuse jock," or dimwitted athlete. [Comics: "Archie" in Horn, 87]

10. **Palooka, Joe** semi-literate boxer, wholesome and bungling. [Comics: Horn, 343–344]

11. **Rudge, Barnaby** grotesquely dressed, retarded son of a murderer. [Br. Lit.: *Barnaby Rudge*]

12. **Zero** army private whose name and IQ are almost equivalent. [Comics: "Beetle Bailey" in Horn, 105–106]

165. DIRTINESS (See also FILTH.)

1. **Daw, Margery** sold her bed and slept on dirt. [Nurs. Rhyme: Opie, 297]

2. **hoopoe** filthy bird; lines nest with dung. [Medieval Animal Symbolism: White, 150]

3. **Madison, Oscar** disheveled and sloppy sportswriter for *New York Herald*. [Am. Drama: *The Odd Couple*; TV: "The Odd Couple" in Terrace, II, 160]

4. **Pig Pen** "a walking dust storm." [Comics: "Peanuts" in Horn, 542–543]

166. DISAPPEARANCE (See also ABDUCTION.)

1. **Atlantis** submerged legendary island kingdom; never located. [Classical Folklore: Walsh *Classical*, 37]

2. **Bermuda Triangle** area of mysterious disappearance of ships and planes at sea. [Am. Hist.: *The Bermuda Triangle*]

3. **Bierce, Ambrose** (1842–1914?) journalist and short story writer; disappeared into Mexico in 1913. [Am. Hist.: *NCE*, 294]

4. **Crater, Judge** (Joseph Force Crater, 1889–1930?) Judge of N. Y. Supreme Court; vanished August 6, 1930. [Am. Hist.: *RHD*]

5. **Drood, Edwin** nephew of John Jasper; mysteriously vanishes. [Br. Lit.: *Edwin Drood*]

6. **Earhart, Amelia** (1897–1937?) aviatrix vanished in 1937 amid speculation and gossip. [Am. Hist.: *NCE*, 819]

7. **Hoffa, Jimmy** (1913–1975?) Teamsters' boss kidnapped and presumed dead. [Am. Hist.: *Facts* (1975), 573]

8. **Louis XVII** (1793–1795?) "lost dauphin"; heir to French kingship imprisoned and probably abducted. [Fr. Hist.: *NCE*, 1617]

9. **Mister Keen** tracer of lost persons. [Radio: "Keen" in Sharp, IV, 354]

10. **Roanoke** Carolina settlement that seemingly vanished into thin air (1587). [Am. Hist.: Jameson, 430]

167. DISASTER

1. **Amoco Cadiz** oil tanker broke up off Britanny coast; 1.6 million barrels spilled (1978). [Fr. Hist.: *Facts* (1978), 201, 202]

2. **Angur-boda** Utgard giantess, worker of disaster; literally, 'anguish-boding.' [Norse Myth.: Leach, 58]

3. **Chicago fire** conflagration destroyed most of city (1871). [Am. Hist.: Jameson, 94]

4. **Deluge** earth-covering flood that destroyed all but Noah's family and animals in the ark. [*O.T.: Genesis* 6–8]

5. **Deucalion's Flood** the Deluge of Greek legend. [Gk. Myth.: Benét, 266]

6. **Evangeline** concerns peaceful village vacated and destroyed during war. [Am. Lit.: "Evangeline" in Magill, I, 261–263]

7. **Fatal Vespers** 100 Jesuits killed in collapse of lecture hall. [Br. Hist.: Brewer *Dictionary*, 1127]

8. **Gilgamesh epic** Babylonian legend contains pre-Biblical account of Flood. [Near East. Myth.: *EB*, IV: 542]

9. **the Hindenburg** German airship blew up at mooring in New Jersey (1937). [Am. Hist.: *NCE*, 43]

10. **Johnstown Flood** Pennsylvania city destroyed by flood (May 31, 1889); 2,200 lives lost. [Am. Hist.: *NCE*, 1427]

11. **Pompeii** Roman city buried by eruption of Mt. Vesuvius (79). [Rom. Hist.: *NCE*, 2187]

12. **red cloud** indicates disaster is impending. [Eastern Folklore: Jobes, 350]

13. **San Francisco earthquake** disaster claiming many lives and most of city (1906). [Am. Hist.: Jameson, 443–444]

14. **Titanic** British passenger ship sinks on maiden voyage (1912). [Br. Hist.: *NCE*, 2753]

168. **DISBELIEF (See also SKEPTICISM.)**

1. **Capys** Trojan who mistrusted Trojan Horse; cautioned against bringing it into the city. [Gk. Myth.: Zimmerman, 50]

2. **Cassandra** no one gave credence to her prophecies of doom. [Gk. Myth.: Zimmerman, 51]

3. **Gerstein, Kurt** anti-Nazi German; nobody credited his story of atrocities. [Ger. Hist.: Wigoder, 210]

169. **DISCIPLINE**

1. **chicken** indicates martinetish authority. [Military Slang: Wentworth, 98]

2. **Patton, General George** (1885–1945) U.S. Army general known for imposing rigid discipline on his troops. [Am. Hist.: *NCE*, 2083]

3. **Puritans** strictly religious and morally disciplined colonists. [Am. Hist.: Payton, 551]

4. **spare the rod and spoil the child** axiomatic admonition. [*O.T.: Proverbs* 13:24]

5. **Spartans** Doric people noted for bravery, frugality, and stern self-discipline. [Gk. Hist.: Payton, 640]

6. **West Point** U.S. Military Academy focusing on discipline as part of training. [Am. Hist.: Payton, 729]

170. DISCORD (See also CONFUSION.)

1. **Andras** demon of discord. [Occultism: Jobes, 93]

2. **discord, apple of** caused conflict among goddesses; Trojan War ultimate result. [Gk. Myth.: Benét, 43]

3. **Discordia** goddess of strife and discord. [Gk. Myth.: Kravitz, 83]

4. **Eris** goddess of discord; threw apple of discord among Peleus's wedding guests. [Gk. Myth.: Howe, 95]

5. **54-40 or Fight!** slogan alluding to disputed borders of Oregon territory under joint British and U.S. occupation. [Am. Hist.: Payton, 241]

6. **Gaza Strip** small coastal desert on borders of Egypt and Israel, the control of which has been in continual dispute. [Middle East. Hist.: Payton, 264]

7. **the Great Schism** Catholic Church divided over papal succession (1378–1417). [Eur. Hist.: Bishop, 376–379]

8. **onyx** provokes disagreement and separates lovers. [Gem. Symbolism: Kunz, 98–99]

171. DISCOVERY

1. **Archimedes** (287–212 B.C.) uncovered fluid displacement principle while bathing. [Gk. Hist.: Wallechinsky, 272]

2. **Dead Sea scrolls** ancient manuscripts of Biblical commentaries found in cave. [Jew. Hist.: Wigoder, 152]

3. **Eureka!** exclaimed Archimedes, on discovering specific gravity principle. [Gk. Hist.: NCE, 137]

4. **Franklin, Benjamin** (1706–1790) used a simple kite to discover electricity. [Science: NCE, 1000]

5. **Kaldi** Arabian goatherd; alleged discoverer of coffee (850). [Arab. Hist.: Grun, 97]

6. **Newton, Sir Isaac** (1642–1727) a falling apple said to have inspired theory of gravitation. [Science: NCE, 1929]

7. **Rosetta Stone** inscribed in three languages; key to hieroglyphics. [Fr. Hist.: Brewer *Dictionary*, 935]

8. **Sutter's Mill** where James Marshall discovered California gold (1848). [Am. Hist.: NCE, 2662]

9. **Tutankhamun's tomb** incredible archaeological find unlocks the past. [Egypt. Hist.: *NCE*, 2809]

172. DISEASE

1. **Black Death** killed at least one third of Europe's population (1348–1349). [Eur. Hist.: Bishop, 379–382]

2. **Fiacre, St.** intercession sought by sick. [Christian Hagiog.: Attwater, 130]

3. **influenza epidemic** caused 500,000 deaths in U.S. alone (1918–1919). [Am. Hist.: Van Doren, 403]

4. **Joram** suffered for abandoning God's way. [*O.T.: II Chronicles* 21:15, 19]

5. **Lazarus** leper brought back to life by Christ. [*N.T.: John* 11:1–44]

6. **Legionnaires' disease** 28 American Legion conventioneers die of flu-like disease in Philadelphia (1976). [Am. Hist.: *Facts* (1976), 573, 656]

7. **Molokai** Hawaiian island; site of government leper colony. [Am. Hist.: *NCE*, 1807]

8. **Naaman** leprous Syrian commander healed by Elisha. [*O.T.: II Kings* 5]

9. **Rock, St.** legendary healer of plague victims. [Christian Hagiog.: Attwater, 299]

10. **St. Anthony's Fire** horrific 11th-century plague. [Eur. Hist.: Brewer *Note-Book*, 34]

11. **Syphilis** Fracastoro's epic concerning *Syphilis*, mythical first victim. [Ital. Lit.: *RHD*, 1443; Plumb, 342]

12. **Typhoid Mary** (Mary Mallon, 1870–1938) unwitting carrier of typhus; suffered 23-year quarantine. [Am. Hist.: Van Doren, 354]

173. DISGUISE

1. **Abigail** enters nunnery as convert to retrieve money. [Br. Lit.: *The Jew of Malta*]

2. **Batman** millionaire Bruce Wayne dresses in his batlike cape and cowl. [Comics: Horn, 101]

3. **Beaucaire, Monsieur** to escape marriage, nobleman pretends to be a barber. [Am. Lit.: *Monsieur Beaucaire*]

4. **Biron** masks self as Muscovite; woos wrong woman. [Br. Lit.: *Love's Labour's Lost*]

5. **Blakeney, Percy** outwits his opponents by his ingenious disguises. [Br. Lit.: *Scarlet Pimpernel*]

6. **Bones, Brom** impersonates Headless Horseman to scare off rival suitor. [Am. Lit.: *The Legend of Sleepy Hollow*]

7. **Brainworm** impersonates variety of characters in his trickery. [Br. Lit.: *Every Man in His Humour*]

8. **Burchell, Mr.** baronet passes himself off as beggar. [Br. Lit.: *The Vicar of Wakefield*]

9. **Burlingame, Henry** man with a thousand faces. [Am. Lit.: *The Sot-Weed Factor*]

10. **Cléonte** masquerades as Grand Turk to win pretentious man's daughter. [Fr. Lit.: *Le Bourgeois Gentilhomme*]

11. **Cupid** disguised as Ascanius, son of Aeneas. [Gk. Myth.: *Aeneid*]

12. **Demara, Ferdinand, Jr.,** "Great Impostor"; posed in professional roles. [Am. Hist.: Wallechinsky, 484]

13. **Despina** disguised doctor who supposedly restores lovers to life. [Ger. Opera: Mozart, *Cosi fan tutte*, Westerman, 98]

14. **Eugenia, St.** dressed as male, becomes abbot of Egyptian monastery. [Christian Hagiog.: Attwater, 120]

15. **Ford** assumes pseudonym to uncover adulterer. [Br. Lit.: *Merry Wives of Windsor*]

16. **Hautdesert, Sir Bercilak de** disguised as Green Knight, challenges Gawain's valor. [Br. Lit.: *Sir Gawain and the Green Knight*]

17. **Imogen** disguises self as a page. [Br. Lit.: *Cymbeline*]

18. **Jacob** dressed as Esau to obtain father's blessing. [*O.T.: Genesis* 27:15–16]

19. **the Joker** master of disguise confounds Batman. [Comics: "Batman" in Horn, 101]

20. **Julia** masks self as page. [Br. Lit.: *Two Gentlemen of Verona*]

21. **Kenneth, Sir** as Richard's slave, saves king from assassination. [Br. Lit.: *The Talisman*]

22. **Köpenick** tailor disguised as a captain, takes over city. [Ger. Lit.: *Captain from Köpenick*, Espy, 173]

23. **Leonora** masks as Fidelio to save imprisoned husband. [Ger. Opera: Beethoven, *Fidelio*, Scholes, 352–353]

24. **Leucippus** youth disguised as girl to be near Daphne; killed upon discovery. [Gk. Myth.: Zimmerman, 150]

25. **Lone Ranger** masked crime fighter hides true identity. [Radio: Buxton, 143–144; Comics: Horn, 460; TV: Terrace, II, 34–35]

26. **Nanki-Poo** emperor's son disguised as a minstrel. [Br. Opera: *The Mikado*, Magill, I, 591–592]

27. **Paolo, Don** political agitator dressed incognito as priest. [Ital. Lit.: *Bread and Wine*]

28. **Paris** disguised as priest of Venus to free Helen. [Fr. Operetta: Offenbach, *La Belle Hélène*, Westerman, 272–273]

29. **Pierre, Maître** a French merchant; in reality, King Louis XI. [Br. Lit.: *Quentin Durward*, Magill, I, 795–797]

30. **Rosalind** disguises herself as a male. [Br. Lit.: *As You Like It*]

31. **Saladin** Saracen leader, in doctor's garb, cures Richard's illness. [Br. Lit.: *The Talisman*]

32. **Serannes, Theodore de** "young man" in reality Mademoiselle de Maupin. [Fr. Lit.: *Mademoiselle de Maupin*, Magill, I, 542–543]

33. **Siegfried** disguised as Gunther, steals gold ring from Brunhild. [Ger. Opera: Wagner, *Götterdämmerung*, Westerman, 244]

34. **Superman** superhero under guise of Clark Kent, mild-mannered reporter. [Comics: Horn, 642]

35. **Thousandfurs** king's daughter works anonymously, cloaked in manypelted coat. [Ger. Fairy Tale: Grimm, 245]

36. **Toad of Toad Hall** passes as washerwoman to escape from jail. [Children's Lit.: *The Wind in the Willows*]

37. **Vicentio** masquerades as Friar Lodowick. [Br. Lit.: *Measure for Measure*]

38. **Viola** masquerades as Cesario. [Br. Lit.: *Twelfth Night*]

39. **Zeus** disguises himself as: satyr to lie with Antiope, Artemis with Callisto, shower of gold with Danaë, white bull with Europa, swan with Leda, flame of fire with Aegina, and cuckoo with Hera. [Gk. Myth.: Jobes, 1719; *New Century*, 1158; Zimmerman, 293]

40. **Zorro** masked swordsman, defender of weak and oppressed. [Am. Lit.: comic strip (1919); Am. Cinema: Halliwell, 794; TV: Terrace, II, 461–462]

DISHONESTY (See DECEIT.)

174. **DISILLUSIONMENT**

1. **Adams, Nick** loses innocence through WWI experience. [Am. Lit.: "The Killers"]

2. **Angry Young Men** disillusioned postwar writers of Britain, such as Osborne and Amis. [Br. Lit.: Benét, 37]

3. **Chuzzlewit, Martin** swindled, becomes disillusioned with Americans. [Br. Lit.: *Martin Chuzzlewit*]

4. **Dodsworth, Sam** disillusioned with wife, European tour, and American situation. [Am. Lit.: *Dodsworth*]

5. **Journey to the End of the Night** exposing the philosophy of post-war disillusionment. [Fr. Lit.: *Journey to the End of the Night,* Magill, I, 453–455]

6. **Krasov, Kuzma Ilich** frustrated writer considers life complete waste. [Russ. Lit.: *The Village*]

7. **Loman, Willy** salesman victimized by own and America's values. [Am. Lit.: *Death of a Salesman*]

8. **March, Augie** "everyone got bitterness in his chosen thing." [Am. Lit.: *The Adventures of Augie March*]

9. **O'Hanlon, Virginia** (1890–1971) *N.Y. Sun* editorial dispels her doubts about Santa Claus (1897). [Am. Hist.: Rockwell, 188]

10. **Smith, Winston** clerk loses out in totalitarian world. [Br. Lit.: *1984*]

11. **Voynitsky, Ivan and Sonya Alexandrovna** dedicate their lives to support worthless professor. [Russ. Lit.: *Uncle Vanya*]

175. DISOBEDIENCE

1. **Achan** defies God's ban on taking booty. [O.T.: *Joshua* 7:1]

2. **Adam and Eve** eat forbidden fruit of Tree of Knowledge. [O.T.: *Genesis* 3:1–7; Br. Lit.: *Paradise Lost*]

3. **Antigone** despite Creon's order, she buries Polynices. [Gk. Lit.: *Antigone*]

4. **Brunhild** disobeys father's order to let Siegmund die. [Ger. Opera: Wagner, *Valkyrie,* Westerman, 237]

5. **Saul** contravening God, takes spoils from conquered Amalekites. [O.T.: *I Samuel* 15:17–19]

6. **Vashti, Queen** loses queenship for not submitting to king's demands. [O.T.: *Esther* 1:10–22]

DISORDER (See CONFUSION.)

176. DISSIPATION (See also DEBAUCHERY.)

1. **Breitmann, Hans** lax indulger. [Am. Lit.: *Hans Breitmann's Ballads*]

2. **Burley, John** wasteful ne'er-do-well. [Br. Lit.: *My Novel,* Walsh *Modern,* 79]

3. **Camors** leads selfish, shameless life. [Fr. Lit.: *M. de Camors,* Walsh *Modern,* 84]

4. **Carton, Sidney** wasteful bohemian; does not use his talents. [Br. Lit.: *A Tale of Two Cities*]

5. **Castlewood, Francis Esmond** gambles away living. [Br. Lit.: *Henry Esmond*]

6. **Christian II** sybaritic king. [Fr. Lit.: *Kings in Exile*, Walsh *Modern*, 96]

7. **Chuzzlewit, Jonas** dissipated, wasteful person. [Br. Lit.: *Martin Chuzzlewit*]

8. **Clavering, Sir Francis** dissipated gambling baronet. [Br. Lit.: *Pendennis*]

9. **Dalgarno, Lord Malcolm of** wasteful and ruinous; destroys several people. [Br. Lit.: *Fortunes of Nigel*]

10. **Fitzgerald, F. Scott** (1896–1940) American novelist whose works reflect a life of dissipation. [Am. Lit.: *NCE*, 957]

11. **Jeshurun** citizens abandon God; give themselves up to luxury. [O.T.: *Deuteronomy* 32:15]

12. **Mite, Sir Matthew** dissolute merchant; displays wealth ostentatiously. [Br. Lit.: *The Nabob*, Brewer *Handbook*, 713]

13. **Pheidippides** his extravagant bets ruin father's wealth. [Gk. Lit.: *The Clouds*]

14. **prodigal son** squanders share of money in reckless living. [*N.T.*: *Luke* 15:13]

DIVINATION (See OMEN.)

177. **DOG**

1. **Boatswain** Byron's favorite dog. [Br. Hist.: Harvey, 239]

2. **Buck** wild canine hero. [Am. Lit.: *The Call of the Wild*]

3. **Bullet** Roy Rogers' dog. [TV: "The Roy Rogers Show" in Terrace, II, 260]

4. **Bull's-eye** Bill Sykes's dog. [Br. Lit.: *Oliver Twist*]

5. **Cerberus** three-headed beast guarding gates of hell. [Classical Myth.: Zimmerman, 55–56]

6. **Checkers** Richard Nixon's cocker spaniel; used in his defense of slush fund (1952). [Am. Hist.: Wallechinsky, 126]

7. **Diogenes** Dr. Blimber's clumsy dog. [Br. Lit.: *Dombey and Son*]

8. **Dominic** hound who travels widely. [Children's Lit.: *Dominic*]

9. **Fala** Franklin Roosevelt's dog. [Am. Hist.: Wallechinsky, 126]

10. **Hound of the Baskervilles** gigantic "fiend dog" of Sir Arthur Conan Doyle's tale. [Br. Lit.: *The Hound of the Baskervilles*]

11. **Jip** Dora's dog. [Br. Lit.: *David Copperfield*]

12. **Lassie** canine star of popular film and TV series. [TV: Terrace, II, 13–15; Radio: Buxton, 135]

13. **Peritas** Alexander the Great's dog. [Gk. Hist.: Harvey, 239]

14. **Rin-Tin-Tin** early film hero; German shepherd. [Radio: Buxton, 200]

15. **Sandy** Little Orphan Annie's dog. [Comics: "Little Orphan Annie" in Horn, 459]

16. **Snoopy** world's most famous beagle. [Comics: "Peanuts" in Horn, 542]

17. **Spot** dog accompanying Sally, Dick, and Jane in primers. [Am. Cult.: Misc.]

18. **Toto** pet terrier who accompanies Dorothy to Oz. [Am. Lit.: *The Wonderful Wizard of Oz*]

178. DOMESTICITY (See also WIFELINESS.)

1. **Crocker, Betty** leading brand of baking products; byword for one expert in homemaking skills. [Trademarks: Crowley *Trade*, 56]

2. **Dick Van Dyke Show, The** series on the vicissitudes of middle-class living. [TV: Terrace, I, 208–209]

3. **Donna Reed Show, The** joys and sorrows of a pediatrician and his family. [TV: Terrace, I, 220]

4. **Flintstones, The** family life in the Stone Age. [TV: Terrace, I, 271–273]

5. **hearth** symbol of home life. [Folklore: Jobes, 738]

6. **Honeymooners, The** nuts and bolts of American working-class life. [TV: Terrace, I, 365–366]

7. **Keep the Home Fires Burning** song of love of home popular during World War I. [Music: Scholes, 549]

8. **Leave It To Beaver** tranquil life in suburbia (1957–1963). [TV: Terrace II, 18]

9. **March, Meg** devoted wife and mother. [Children's Lit.: *Little Women*]

10. **Martha, St.** patroness of housewives and cooks. [Christian Hagiog.: Brewster, 345]

11. **My Three Sons** trials and tribulations of womanless household. [TV: Terrace, II, 131–132]

12. **Ozzie and Harriet** depicting home life, American style. [TV: "The Adventures of Ozzie and Harriet" in Terrace, I, 34–35]

13. **sage** symbolizes domestic virtue. [Flower Symbolism: *Flora Symbolica*, 177]

14. **silky** female spirit who does household chores. [Br. Folklore: Briggs, 364–365]

179. **DOUBLE** (See also TWINS.)

1. **Amphitryon and Jupiter** god assumes man's form to lie with his wife. [Rom. Lit.: *Amphitryon*]
2. **Darnay, Charles** physical duplicate of Carton. [Br. Lit.: *A Tale of Two Cities*]
3. **fetch** a Doppelgänger. [Irish Folklore: Leach, 376]
4. **Prince of Wales** switches places with his double, poor boy Tom Canty. [Am. Lit.: *The Prince and the Pauper*]
5. **Sam and Eric** their identities merge as "Samneric." [Br. Lit.: *Lord of the Flies*]
6. **Sosia and Mercury** god assumes slave's identity. [Rom. Lit.: *Amphitryon*]
7. **Wilson, William** his Doppelgänger ultimately kills him. [Am. Lit.: "William Wilson" in *Portable Poe*, 57–82]

180. **DRUG ADDICTION**

1. **Valley of the Dolls** portrays self-destruction of drug-addicted starlets. [Am. Lit.: *Valley of the Dolls*]

181. **DRUNKENNESS** (See also ALCOHOLISM.)

1. **Acrasia** self-indulgent in the pleasures of the senses. [Br. Lit.: *Faerie Queene*]
2. **Admiral of the red** a wine-bibber. [Br. Folklore: Brewer *Dictionary*, 11]
3. **Bacchus, priest of** a toper, perhaps originally because of ceremonial duties. [Western Folklore: Brewer *Dictionary*, 65]
4. **Barleycorn, John** humorous personification of intoxicating liquor. [Am. and Br. Folklore: Misc.]
5. **Booze** sold cheap whiskey in a log-cabin bottle. [Am. Hist.: Espy, 152–153]
6. **Capp, Andy** archetypal British working-class toper. [Comics: Horn, 82–83]
7. **Gambrinus** mythical Flemish king; reputed inventor of beer. [Flem. Myth.: *NCE*, 1041]
8. **Magnifico, Don** appointed Prince's butler, oversamples his wines. [Ital. Opera: Rossini, *Cinderella*, Westerman, 120–121]
9. **Noah** inebriated from wine, sprawls naked in tent. [*O.T.*: *Genesis* 9:20–23]
10. **Silenus** one of Bacchus's retinue; fat, always inebriated. [Gk. Myth.: Hall, 283]
11. **Sly, Christopher** identity changes during drunken stupor. [Br. Lit.: *Taming of the Shrew*]

12. **Vincent, St.** patron saint of drunks. [Christian Hagiog.: Brewer *Dictionary*, 1129]

182. DUPERY

1. **Bobchinsky and Dobchinsky** town squires bamboozled by inspector-impostor. [Russ. Lit.: *The Inspector General*]
2. **Buonafede** tricked into financing and approving daughters' marriages. [Ger. Opera: Haydn, *The World of the Moon*, Westerman, 68–69]
3. **Calandrino** duped by friends into believing heliotrope confers invisibility. [It. Lit.: *Decameron*, "Calandrino and the Heliotrope"]
4. **Cassio** fooled by Iago. [Br. Lit.: *Othello*]
5. **Dapper** lawyer's clerk; swindled into believing himself perfect gambler. [Br. Lit.: *The Alchemist*]
6. **Drugger, Abel** cozened by rogues in hopes of future riches. [Br. Lit.: *The Alchemist*]
7. **Fenella** mute beauty tricked, imprisoned, and abandoned by Alfonso. [Fr. Opera: Auber, *Dumb Girl of Portici*, Westerman, 163–164]
8. **Matthew, Master** "the town gull." [Br. Lit.: *Every Man in His Humour*]
9. **Pelleas** used by Ettarre; betrayed by Gawain. [Br. Lit.: *Idylls of the King*, "Pelleas and Ettarre"]
10. **Roderigo** foppish dupe and tool of Iago. [Br. Lit.: *Othello*]
11. **Skvoznik-Dmukhanovsky, Anton Antonovich** prefect kowtows to supposed inspector for good impression. [Russ. Lit.: *The Inspector General*]

183. DWARFISM (See also SMALLNESS.)

1. **Alberich** king of dwarfs; lives in subterranean palace. [Norse Myth.: Leach, 33; Ger. Lit.: *Nibelungenlied*]
2. **Andvari** sometimes considered king of dwarfs; kept Nibelung treasure. [Norse Myth.: Leach, 56]
3. **Dvalin** inventor of runes. [Norse Myth.: Leach, 330]
4. **Elbegast** king of dwarfs; dwelt in underground palace. [Norse Myth.: *LLEI*, I: 327]
5. **Hop-Frog** crippled, deformed court fool. [Am. Lit.: "Hop-Frog" in *Portable Poe*, 317–329]
6. **Nibelungs** race of dwarfs who possess a hoard of gold. [Norse Myth.: Payton, 477]
7. **Oakmen** squat, dwarfish people with red caps. [Br. Folklore: Briggs, 313–314]

8. **Rumpelstiltskin** homunculus spins gold for lass's first child. [Ger. Fairy Tale: Grimm, 196]

9. **Seven Dwarfs** Doc, Happy, Sleepy, Sneezy, Bashful, Grumpy, Dopey. [Am. Cinema: *Snow White and the Seven Dwarfs* in *Disney Films*, 25–32]

E

EAGERNESS (See ZEAL.)

184. EARTH

1. **Bona Dea** "goddess of earthly creatures." [Rom. Myth.: Parrinder, 48]

2. **Bona Mater** Fauna, goddess of wildlife. [Rom. Myth.: Kravitz, 24]

3. **Demogorgon** tyrant-genius of soil and life of plants. [Medieval Eur. Myth.: *LLEI*, I: 326]

4. **Dyava-Matar** Hindu earthmother, equivalent of Demeter. [Hindu Myth.: Jobes, 480]

5. **Frigga** Odin's wife; symbolizes the earth. [Norse Myth.: *LLEI*, I: 328]

6. **Gaea** goddess of the earth; mother of the mountains. [Gk. Myth.: Howe, 104]

7. **gnome** ground-dwelling spirit in Rosicrucian philosophy. [Medieval Hist.: Brewer *Dictionary*, 468]

8. **hobbits** benevolent, furry-footed people living in burrows. [Br. Lit.: *The Hobbit*]

9. **Midgard** region between heaven and hell where men live. [Norse Myth.: Wheeler, 242]

10. **Mother Nature** epitome of the earth, especially its more benevolent phenomena. [Pop. Cult.: Misc.]

11. **Tapio** Finnish woodland god; realm described in Sibelius' *Tapiola*. [Music Hist.: Thompson, 2239]

12. **Tellus Mater** in allegories of elements, personification of earth. [Art: Hall, 128]

13. **two circles linked** symbol of earth as bride of heaven. [Christian Tradition: Jobes, 343]

14. **Vertumnus** god of changing seasons. [Rom. Myth.: Kravitz, 58]

185. EASTER

1. **basket** filled with treats, representative of feast on Easter Sunday. [Folklore: Misc.]

2. **bonnet** usually worn along with new clothes on Easter Sunday ("Oh, I could write a sonnet about your Easter bonnet.") [Christian Tradition: Misc.; Am. Music: Irving Berlin, "Easter Parade"]

3. **daisy** a flower traditionally displayed in homes during Easter season. [Christian Tradition: Jobes, 487]

4. **egg** colored eggs as symbol of new life, adopted to reflect Resurrection. [Christian Tradition: Brewer *Dictionary*, 361]

5. **jelly beans** traditional treat for children on Easter Sunday; symbolize eggs. [Pop. Culture: Misc.]

6. **parade** of finery; most notable ones in New York and Atlantic City on Easter Sunday. [Pop. Culture: Misc.]

7. **purple and yellow** traditional colors seen in churches during Easter season. [Christian Color Symbolism: Jobes, 487]

8. **rabbit** bunny who delivers chocolates, etc., to children. [Western Folklore: Jobes, 487]

9. **spring flowers** a token of Christ's resurrection. [Christian Tradition: Jobes, 487]

10. **white and green** signifies color of Easter holidays. [Christian Color Symbolism: Jobes, 487]

11. **white lily** symbol of Resurrection. [Christian Tradition: Jobes, 487]

186. EAVESDROPPING (See also CURIOSITY, VOYEURISM.)

1. **Andret** eavesdrops through keyhole on Tristan and Isolde's conversation. [Arthurian Legend: Walsh *Classical,* 22]

2. **Peeping Tom** tailor who peeps through closed shutters at Lady Godiva as she rides naked through Coventry. [Medieval Legend: *Lady Godiva,* Payton, 516]

3. **Polonius** lurking behind arras, he is killed accidentally by Hamlet. [Br. Lit.: *Hamlet*]

4. **Pry, Paul** inquisitive, meddlesome character who "eavesdrops on everyone." [Br. Drama: *Paul Pry,* Payton, 514]

5. **Rumpelstiltskin** his name overheard by queen's messenger, allowing spell to be broken. [Ger. Fairy Tale: Grimm, 19]

187. ECCENTRICITY

1. **Addams Family** weird family, presented in grotesque domesticity. [TV: Terrace, I, 29]

2. **Boynton, Nanny** travels with set of *Encyclopaedia Britannica* to settle disputes. [Am. Lit.: "Percy" in *Stories,* 634–644]

3. **Dick, Mr.** odd but harmless old gentleman. [Br. Lit.: *David Copperfield*]

4. **Doolittle, Doctor** veterinarian who talks to animals. [Children's Lit.: *Dr. Doolittle*]

5. **Flite, Miss** "ancient" ward in Chancery. [Br. Lit.: *Bleak House*]

6. **Great-Aunt Dymphna** outlandish dresser who pointedly doesn't eat meat. [Children's Lit.: *The Growing Summer*, Fisher 124–127]

7. **Havisham, Miss** jilted bride turns into witchlike old woman. [Br. Lit.: *Great Expectations*]

8. **Longstocking, Pippi** outrageous, rebellious, imaginative child. [Children's Lit.: *Pippi Longstocking*]

9. **Madeline** individualist; only girl "out of line." [Children's Lit.: *Madeline*, Fisher, 196]

10. **Madwoman of Chaillot** delightfully pixilated old woman manages to exploit the Parisian exploiters. [Fr. Lit.: *The Madwoman of Chaillot*, Benét, 618]

11. **Pickwick, Mr. (Samuel)** jolly "conformist" who understands anything but the obvious. [Br. Lit.: *Pickwick Papers*]

12. **Poppins, Mary** English nanny who practises levitation, flies up chimneys, etc. [Children's Lit.: *Mary Poppins*, Fisher, 218]

13. **Salus, St. Simeon** behaved queerly to share outcasts' contempt. [Christian Hagiog.: Attwater, 311]

188. **EDUCATION (See also TEACHING.)**

1. **the Academy** Plato's school in Athens. [Gk. Hist.: Benét, 5]

2. **Cambridge** one of two leading British universities (since 1231); consists of 24 colleges. [Br. Education: Payton, 116]

3. **Catherine of Alexandria, St.** patroness of education. [Christian Hagiog.: Hall, 58]

4. **Émile** Rousseau's treatise on education of children (1762). [Fr. Lit.: *Émile*, Magill, III, 330–333]

5. **the Grand Tour** European tour as necessary part of education for British aristocrats. [Eur. Hist.: Plumb, 414]

6. **Instructions to a Son** papyrus document; one of earliest preserved writings (c. 2500 B.C.). [Classical Hist.: Grun, 2]

7. **Ivy League** select group of colleges: Brown, Columbia, Cornell, Dartmouth, Harvard, Pennsylvania, Princeton, Yale. [Am. Education: Payton, 343]

8. **Lyceum** a gymnasium where Aristotle taught in ancient Athens. [Gk. Hist.: Hart, 502]

9. **mortarboard** closefitting cap with flat square piece and tassel; part of academic costume. [Am. and Br. Culture: Misc.]

10. **Oxford** one of two leading British universities (c. 1167); consists of 34 colleges. [Br. Education: Payton, 502]

11. **Phi Beta Kappa** honorary scholarship society; eligibility restricted to best students. [Am. Hist.: Hart, 651]

12. **Seven Sisters** select group of colleges: Barnard, Bryn Mawr, Mount Holyoke, Radcliffe, Smith, Vassar, Wellesley. [Am. Education: Payton, 615]

13. **Sorbonne** University of Paris; long esteemed as educative center. [Fr. Hist.: Brewer *Dictionary*, 1019]

14. **Wanderjahr** a year's absence from one's schooling as period to reflect on learning. [Eur. Hist.: Plumb, 414]

189. EFFEMINACY

1. **Blue Boy** Gainsborough painting depicting princely lad with sissyish overtones. [Br. Art.: Misc.]

2. **Fauntleroy, Little Lord** title-inheriting, yellow-curled sissy in velvet. [Am. Lit.: *Little Lord Fauntleroy*]

3. **Percy** personification of "sissy." [Pop. Culture: Misc.]

190. EGOTISM (See also ARROGANCE, CONCEIT, INDIVID-UALISM.)

1. **Baxter, Ted** TV anchorman who sees himself as most important news topic. [TV: "The Mary Tyler Moore Show" in Terrace, II, 70]

2. **cat** symbol of egotism because of its aloofness and independence. [Animal Symbolism: Mercatante, 49]

3. **Milvain, Jasper** sees himself as extremely important in literary world. [Br. Lit.: *New Grub Street*, Magill, I, 647–649]

4. **narcissus** symbol of self-centeredness. [Flower Symbolism: *Flora Symbolica*, 176]

5. **Narcissus** falls in love with his reflection in pond. [Gk. Myth.: Brewer *Handbook*, 745; Rom. Lit.: *Metamorphoses*]

6. **Number One** portraying politician Crawford; self-gain as tour de force. [Am. Lit.: *Number One*]

7. **Skimpole, Horace** egocentric, wily fraud. [Br. Lit.: *Bleak House*]

8. **Templeton** self-centered rat. [Children's Lit.: *Charlotte's Web*]

191. ELEGANCE (See also GLAMOUR.)

1. **After Six, Inc.** makers of men's formal wear and accessories. [Trademarks: Crowley *Trade*, 9]

2. **Archer, Isabel** American heiress undergoes process of refinement amid European culture. [Am. Lit.: *The Portrait of a Lady*]

3. **Ashley, Lady Brett** heroine "as charming when drunk! as when sober." [Am. Lit.: *The Sun Also Rises*]

4. **dahlia** represents elegance. [Flower Symbolism: Jobes, 406]

5. **Darlington, Lord** epitome of London's man about town (1800s). [Br. Lit.: *Lady Windermere's Fan*, Magill, I, 488–490]

6. **locust** type of tree representing elegance. [Tree Symbolism: *Flora Symbolica*, 175]

192. ELOPEMENT

1. **Carker, James** with Dombey's wife. [Br. Lit.: *Dombey and Son*]

2. **Leonora** with Alvaro, rejected as suitor by her father. [Ital. Opera: Verdi, *La Forza del Destino*, Westerman, 315–317]

3. **Little Emily** with Steerforth, although engaged to Ham. [Br. Lit.: *David Copperfield*]

4. **Madeline** with Porphyro, who appears in dream. [Br. Lit.: "The Eve of St. Agnes" in Magill, I, 263–264]

193. ELOQUENCE

1. **Ambrose, St.** bees, prophetic of fluency, landed in his mouth. [Christian Hagiog: Brewster, 177]

2. **Antony, Mark** gives famous speech against Caesar's assassins. [Br. Lit.: *Julius Caesar*]

3. **bees on the mouth** pictorial and verbal symbol of eloquence. [Folklore and Christian Iconog.: Brewster, 177]

4. **Bragi** god of poetry and fluent oration. [Norse Myth.: *LLEI*, I: 324]

5. **Calliope** chief muse of poetic inspiration and oratory. [Gk. Myth.: Brewer *Dictionary*, 177]

6. **Churchill, Winston** (1874–1965) statesman whose rousing oratory led the British in WWII. [Br. Hist.: *NCE*, 556]

7. **Cicero** (106–43 B.C.) orator whose forcefulness of presentation and melodious language is still imitated. [Rom. Hist.: *NCE*, 558]

8. **Demosthenes** (382–322 B.C.) generally considered the greatest of the Greek orators. [Gk. Hist.: *NCE*, 559]

9. **Gettysburg Address** Lincoln's brief, moving eulogy for war dead (1863). [Am. Hist.: Jameson, 286–287]

10. **King, Martin Luther, Jr.** (1929–1968) civil rights leader and clergyman whose pleas for justice won support of millions. [Am. Hist.: *NCE*, 1134]

11. **lotus** symbol of eloquence. [Plant Symbolism: *Flora Symbolica*, 175]

12. **Paine, Thomas** (1737–1809) powerful voice of the colonies; wrote famous "Common Sense." [Am. Hist.: Jameson, 369–370]

13. **Webster, Daniel** (1782–1852) noted 19th-century American orator-politician. [Am. Hist.: Jameson, 539]

194. **ENCHANTMENT (See also FANTASY.)**

1. **Alidoro** fairy godfather to Italian Cinderella. [Ital. Opera: Rossini, *Cinderella*, Westerman, 120–121]

2. **Bottom** under spell, grows ass's head. [Br. Lit.: *A Midsummer Night's Dream*]

3. **Cinderella** enchantment lasts only till midnight. [Fr. Fairy Tale: *Cinderella*]

4. **Circe** enchantress who changes Odysseus's men into swine. [Gk. Lit.: *Odyssey;* Rom. Lit.: *Aeneid*]

5. **Land of Oz** bewitching realm of magic and mystery. [Am. Lit.: *The Wonderful Wizard of Oz*]

6. **Lorelei** water nymph of the Rhine; lured sailors to their doom with her singing. [Ger. Folklore: Leach, 645]

7. **Maugis** enchanter; one of Charlemagne's paladins. [Fr. Folklore: Harvey, 526]

8. **Miracle, Dr.** bewitches Antonia into singing despite doctor's orders. [Fr. Opera: Offenbach, *Tales of Hoffmann*, Westerman, 275–276]

9. **Oberon** fairy king orders love charm placed on wife. [Br. Lit.: *A Midsummer Night's Dream*]

10. **Orpheus** his singing opens the gates of the underworld. [Ger. Opera: Gluck, *Orpheus and Euridyce*, Westerman, 72]

11. **Pied Piper** charms children of Hamelin with music. [Children's Lit.: "The Pied Piper of Hamelin" in *Dramatic Lyrics*, Fisher, 279–281]

12. **pishogue** Irish fairy spell that distorts reality. [Irish Folklore: Briggs, 327–328]

13. **Scheherazade** spins yarns for Sultan for 1001 nights. [Arab. Lit.: *Arabian Nights*]

14. **Schwanda** Czech Orpheus; bagpipe music moves even Queen Iceheart. [Czech Opera: Weinberger, *Schwanda*, Westerman, 412]

15. **Sirens** with song, bird-women lure sailors to death. [Gk. Myth.: *Odyssey*]

16. **Sleeping Beauty** sleeps for 100 years. [Fr. Fairy Tale, *The Sleeping Beauty*]

17. **Titania** experiences spell-induced fascination over Bottom. [Br. Lit.: *A Midsummer Night's Dream*]

18. **Van Winkle, Rip** returns to village after sleep of 20 years. [Am. Lit.: *The Sketch Book of Geoffrey Crayon, Gent.*]

19. **vervain** indicates bewitching powers. [Flower Symbolism: *Flora Symbolica*, 178]

195. END

1. **Armageddon** battleground of good and evil before Judgment Day. [*N.T.: Revelation* 16:16]

2. **checkmate** end of game in chess: folk-etymology of *Shah-mat*, 'the Shah is dead.' [Br. Folklore: Espy, 217]

3. **fatal raven** indicates defeat or victory by arranging its wings. [Norse Legend: *Volsung Saga*]

4. **Judgment Day** final trial of all mankind. [*N.T.: Revelation*]

5. **Last Supper** Passover dinner the night before Christ died. [*N.T.: Matthew* 26:26–29; *Mark* 14:22–25; *Luke* 22:14–20]

196. ENDURANCE (See also LONGEVITY.)

1. **Atalanta** feminine name denotes power of endurance. [Gk. Myth.: Jobes, 148]

2. **Boston marathon** famous 26-mile race held annually for long-distance runners. [Am. Pop. Culture: Misc.]

3. **cedrala tree** symbol of longevity and endurance. [Eastern Folklore and Plant Symbolism: Jobes, 301]

4. **Denisovich, Ivan** prisoner persists through travails of Soviet camp. [Russ. Lit.: *One Day in the Life of Ivan Denisovich*]

· 5. **dromedary** able to cover a hundred miles in one day. [Medieval Animal Symbolism: White, 80–81]

6. **marathon dancing** dance contest with endurance as chief factor. [Am. Hist.: Sann, 57–69]

7. **Prometheus** epitome of stoic endurance. [Gk. Myth.: Gayley, 10–15]

8. **Steadfast Tin Soldier** one-legged toy survives multiple calamities; ultimately immolated. [Dan. Lit.: *Andersen's Fairy Tales*]

9. **Yossarian** always creating new ways to stay alive through long war. [Am. Lit.: *Catch-22*]

197. ENEMY

1. **Amalekites** Israel's hereditary foe and symbol of perpetual hatred. [Jew. Hist.: Wigoder, 24]

2. **Antichrist** principal antagonist of Christ. [Christianity: *NCE*, 117]

3. **Armilus** legendary name of anti-Messiah. [Judaism: Wigoder, 41]

4. **Satan** also called the Adversary or the Devil. [Christianity: Misc.]

198. ENLIGHTENMENT

1. **ball and cross** symbol of gradual universal evangelism. [Christian Tradition: Jobes, 176]
2. **Bodhisattva** "the enlightened one" deferring Nirvana to help others. [Buddhism: Parrinder, 48]
3. **Buddha** a mortal who's achieved Nirvana, particularly Gautama. [Buddhism: Parrinder, 53]
4. **Chloë** "fearful virgin" learns love's delights on wedding night. [Gk. Lit.: *Daphnis and Chloë*, Magill, I, 184]
5. **Gautama** sees "everything" and has "eyes on his feet." [Buddhism: Parrinder, 110]
6. **prajna** (Sanskrit) "wisdom," used in abstract sense or sometimes personified as a goddess. [Sanskrit: Parrinder, 222]
7. **Sanātana Dharma,** "eternal truth." [Hinduism: Parrinder, 122]
8. **scales falling from eyes** vision restored, Saul is converted. [*N.T.: Acts* 9:17–19]

199. ENTRAPMENT

1. **Fear of Flying** metaphor for housewife Isadora Wing's temporary inability to achieve self-awareness. [Am. Lit.: *Fear of Flying*]
2. **Frome, Ethan** chained to detestable wife and unsalable farm. [Am. Lit.: *Ethan Frome*]
3. **Loman, Willy** despite dreams of success, he is condemned to failure. [Am. Drama; *Death of a Salesman*, Payton, 397]
4. **Prufrock, J. Alfred** aware that his life is meaningless and empty, he struggles to rise above it, but cannot. [Br. Lit.: "The Love Song of J. Alfred Prufrock" in Payton, 548]
5. **Rochester, Edward** tied to insane wife; cannot marry Jane Eyre. [Br. Lit.: *Jane Eyre*]

200. ENVY (See also JEALOUSY.)

1. **Amneris** envious of Aïda. [Ital. Opera: Verdi, *Aïda*, Westerman, 325]
2. **Anastasia and Orizella** Cinderella's two step-sisters; jealous of her beauty, they treat her miserably. [Fr. Fairy Tale: *Cinderella*]
3. **coat of many colors** Jacob's gift to Joseph; object of jealousy. [*O.T.: Genesis* 37:3]

4. **green** symbol of envy; "the green-eyed monster." [Color Symbolism: Jobes, 357; Br. Lit.: *Othello*]

5. **Iago** Othello's ensign who, from malevolence and envy, persuades Othello that Desdemona has been unfaithful. [Br. Lit.: *Othello*]

6. **Joseph's brothers** resented him for Jacob's love and gift. [*O.T.*: *Genesis* 37:4]

7. **Lensky** envy of Onegin leads to his death in a duel. [Russ. Opera: Tchaikovsky, *Eugene Onegin*, Westerman, 395–397]

8. **Lisa** envious of Amina; tries unsuccessful stratagems. [Ital. Opera: Bellini, *The Sleepwalker*, Westerman, 128–130]

9. **Snow White's stepmother** envious of her beauty, queen orders Snow White's death. [Ger. Fairy Tale: Grimm, 184]

10. **Turnus** of Aeneas, whom Lavinia prefers. [Rom. Lit.: *Aeneid*]

201. **EPIC**

1. **Aeneid** Virgil's epic poem glorifying the origin of the Roman people. [Rom. Lit.: *Aeneid*]

2. **Beowulf** Old English epic poem of sixth-century Denmark. [Br. Lit.: *Beowulf*]

3. **Divine Comedy** Dante's epic poem in three sections: *Inferno*, *Purgatorio*, and *Paradiso*. [Ital. Lit.: *Divine Comedy*]

4. **Faerie Queene** allegorical epic poem by Edmund Spenser. [Br. Lit.: *Faerie Queene*]

5. **Gilgamesh** Babylonian epic of myth and folklore, centered on the king, Gilgamesh. [Babyl. Myth.: *Gilgamesh*]

6. **Iliad** Homer's epic detailing a few days near the end of the Trojan War. [Gk. Lit.: *Iliad*]

7. **Jerusalem Delivered** Tasso's celebrated romantic epic written during Renaissance. [Ital. Lit.: *Jerusalem Delivered*]

8. **Kalevala** alliterative epic poem of Finland. [Finn. Lit.: *Kalevala*]

9. **Lusiads** Cañoes' epic poem of the Portuguese and, principally, Vasco da Gama. [Port. Lit.: *Lusiads*]

10. **Mahabharata** Indian epic poem of the struggle between the Pandavas and the Kauravas. [Indian Lit.: *Mahabharata*]

11. **Nibelungenlied** medieval German epic poem of Siegfried and the Nibelung kings. [Ger. Lit.: *Nibelungenlied*]

12. **Odyssey** Homer's long, narrative poem centered on Odysseus. [Gk. Lit.: *Odyssey*]

13. **Orlando Furioso** Ariosto's romantic epic; actually a continuation of Boiardo's plot. [Ital. Lit.: *Orlando Furioso*]

14. **Orlando Innamorato** Boiardo's epic combining Carolingian chivalry and Arthurian motifs. [Ital. Lit.: *Orlando Innamorato*]

15. **Paradise Lost** Milton's epic poem of man's first disobedience. [Br. Lit.: *Paradise Lost*]

16. **Ramayana** epic poem of ancient India. [Indian Lit.: *Ramayana*]

17. **Song of Igor's Campaign** Old Russian epic poem of 12th-century Prince Igor. [Russ. Lit.: *Song of Igor's Campaign*]

18. **Song of Roland** chanson de geste of Roland and Charlemagne. [Fr. Lit.: *Song of Roland*]

19. **Song of the Cid** epic poem of Spain by an anonymous author. [Span. Lit.: *Song of the Cid*]

202. EPICUREANISM (See also FEAST.)

1. **Belshazzar** gave banquet unrivalled for sumptuousness. [*O.T.: Daniel* 5:1–4]

2. **Finches of the Grove** eating club established for expensive dining. [Br. Lit.: *Great Expectations*]

3. **Gatsby, Jay** modern Trimalchio, wines and dines the upper echelon. [Am. Lit.: *The Great Gatsby*]

4. **Lucullus, Lucius Licinius** (110–57 B.C.) hosted luxurious banquets. [Rom. Hist.: *New Century*, 650]

5. **Trimalchio** vulgar freedman gives lavish feast for noble guests. [Rom. Lit.: *Satyricon*]

203. EPILEPSY

1. **Vitus, St.** his chapel at Ulm famed for epileptic cures. [Christian Hagiog.: Brewster, 291]

204. EQUALITY (See also FEMINISM.)

1. **Augsburg, Peace of** German princes determined state religion; Lutherans granted equal rights (1555). [Ger. Hist.: *NCE*, 185]

2. **Bakke decision** "reverse discrimination" victim; entered medical school with Supreme Court's help. [Am. Hist.: *Facts* (1978), 483]

3. **Dred Scott decision** controversial ruling stating that Negroes were not entitled to "equal justice." [Am. Hist.: Payton, 203]

4. **Equal Employment Opportunity Commission** U.S. government agency appointed to promote the cause of equal opportunity for all U.S. citizens. [Am. Hist.: Payton, 224]

5. **Equality State** nickname of Wyoming, first state to give women the right to vote. [Am. Hist.: Payton, 224]

6. **Equal Rights Amendment (ERA)** the proposed 27th Amendment to the U.S. Constitution, stating that men and women must be treated equally by law. [Am. Hist.: Payton, 224]

7. **NAACP** (National Association for the Advancement of Colored People) vanguard of Negro fight for racial equality. [Am. Hist.: Van Doren, 548–549]

8. **Nantes, Edict of** granted Protestants same rights as Catholics in France (1598). [Fr. Hist.: *EB*, VII: 184]

9. **Nineteenth Amendment** granted women right to vote (1920). [Am. Hist.: Van Doren, 409]

205. **ESCAPE**

1. **Abiathar** only son of Ahimelech to avoid Saul's slaughter. [*O.T.: I Samuel* 22:20]

2. **Ariadne** Minos's daughter; gave Theseus thread by which to escape labyrinth. [Gk. Myth.: Zimmerman, 31]

3. **Cerambus** transformed into beetle in order to fly above Zeus's deluge. [Gk. Myth.: Zimmerman, 55]

4. **Christian** flees the City of Destruction. [Br. Lit.: *Pilgrim's Progress*]

5. **Deucalion** on Prometheus' advice, survived flood in ark. [Gk. Myth.: Gaster, 84–85]

6. **Dunkirk** 340,000 British troops evacuated against long odds (1941). [Eur. Hist.: Van Doren, 475]

7. **Fugitive, The** (Dr. Richard Kimble) tale of wrongfully-accused man fleeing imprisonment. [TV: Terrace, I, 290–291]

8. **Hansel and Gretel** woodcutter's children barely escape witch. [Ger. Fairy Tale: Grimm, 56]

9. **Hegira (Hijrah)** Muhammad's flight from Mecca to Medina (622). [Islamic Hist.: *EB*, V: 39–40]

10. **Houdini, Harry** (1874–1926) shackled magician could extricate himself from any entrapment. [Am. Hist.: Wallechinsky, 196]

11. **Jim** Miss Watson's runaway slave; Huck's traveling companion. [Am. Lit.: *Huckleberry Finn*]

12. **Jonah** delivered from fish's belly after three days. [*O.T.: Jonah* 1, 2]

13. **Noah** with family and animals, escapes the Deluge. [*O.T.: Genesis* 8:15–19]

14. **parting of the Red Sea** God divides the waters for Israelites' flight. [*O.T.: Exodus* 14:21–29]

15. **Phyxios** epithet of Zeus as god of escape. [Gk. Myth.: Kravitz, 94]

16. **Robin, John, and Harold Hensman** run away from "petticoat government" to live in forest. [Children's Lit.: *Brendon Chase,* Fisher, 306]

17. **Theseus** escapes labyrinth with aid from Ariadne. [Gk. Myth.: Zimmerman, 31]

18. **Tyler, Toby** runs away from cruel Uncle Daniel to join circus. [Children's Lit.: *Toby Tyler*]

19. **Ziusudra** Sumerian Noah. [Sumerian Legend: Benét, 1116]

206. EVANGELISM

1. **Gantry, Elmer** fire and brimstone, fraudulent revivalist. [Am. Lit.: *Elmer Gantry*]

2. **John** disciple closest to Jesus. [*N.T.: John*]

3. **Luke** early Christian; the "beloved physician." [*N.T.: Luke*]

4. **Mark** Christian apostle. [*N.T.: Mark*]

5. **Matthew** one of the twelve disciples. [*N.T.: Matthew*]

207. EVERYMAN

1. **A. N. Other** British *John Doe.* [Br. Usage: Misc.]

2. **Brother Jonathan** British slang for the typical American. [Br. Usage: Misc.]

3. **Ivan Ivanovich Ivanov** embodiment of ordinary Russian person. [Russ. Usage: *LLEI,* I: 292]

4. **Jane Doe** female counterpart of *John Doe.* [Am. Usage: Misc.]

5. **Jean Crapaud** personification of peculiarities of French people. [Fr. Usage: *LLEI,* I: 292]

6. **John a Noakes** fictitious, litigious character; used in legal proceedings. [Br. Legal Usage: Wheeler, 260]

7. **John a Styles** fictitious, litigious counterpart to John a Noakes. [Br. Legal Usage: Wheeler, 260]

8. **John Bull** any Englishman, or Englishmen collectively. [Br. Lit.: *History of John Bull,* Brewer *Dictionary,* 591]

9. **John Doe** formerly, any plaintiff; now just anybody. [Am. Pop. Usage: Brewer *Dictionary,* 329]

10. **John Q. Citizen** fictitious average man on the street. [Am. Jour.: Mathews, 910]

11. **John Q. Public** fictitious typical citizen. [Am. Jour.: Mathews, 910]

12. **John Q. Voter** fictitious typical citizen. [Am. Jour.: Mathews, 910]

13. **Richard Roe** formerly, any defendant; now just anybody. [Am. Pop. Usage: Brewer *Dictionary,* 329]

208.   **EVIL** (See also VILLAINY, WICKEDNESS.)

1. **Ahriman** represents principle of wickedness; will one day perish. [Persian Myth.: *LLEI*, I: 322; Zoroastrianism: Benét, 16]

2. **Alberich's curse** on the Rhinegold ring: possessor will die. [Ger. Opera: Wagner, *Rhinegold*, Westerman, 233]

3. **Apaches** name given to Parisian gangsters. [Fr. Hist.: Payton, 31]

4. **Apollyon** demon, personification of evil, vanquished by Christian's wholesomeness. [Br. Lit.: *Pilgrim's Progress*]

5. **Archimago** enchanter epitomizing wickedness. [Br. Lit.: *Faerie Queene*]

6. **Ate** goddess of wickedness, mischief, and infatuation. [Gk. Myth.: Parrinder, 32]

7. **Avidyā** cause of suffering through desire. [Hindu Phil.: Parrinder, 36]

8. **black** symbol of sin and badness. [Color Symbolism: Jobes, 357]

9. **black dog** symbol of the devil. [Rom. Folklore: Brewer *Dictionary*, 329]

10. **black heart** symbol of a scoundrel. [Folklore: Jobes, 223]

11. **black poodle** a transformation of Mephistopheles. [Ger. Lit.: *Faust*]

12. **crocodile** epitome of power of evil. [Medieval Animal Symbolism: White, 8–10]

13. **darkness** traditional association with evil in many dualistic religions. [Folklore: Cirlot, 76–77]

14. **dragon** archetypal symbol of Satan and wickedness. [Christian Symbolism: Appleton, 34]

15. **Drug** principle of evil. [Zoroastrianism: Leach, 325]

16. **Gestapo** Nazi secret police. [Ger. Hist.: *Hitler*, 453]

17. **Golden Calf** Mephisto's cynical and demoniacal tarantella. [Fr. Opera: Gounod, *Faust*, Westerman, 187]

18. **Iago** declaims "I believe in a cruel god." [Br. Lit.: *Othello;* Ital. Opera: Verdi, *Otello;* Westerman, 329]

19. **John, Don** plots against Claudio. [Br. Lit.: *Much Ado About Nothing*]

20. **Klingsor** enemy of Grail knights. [Ger. Opera: Wagner, *Parsifal*, Westerman, 248]

21. **lobelia** traditional symbol of evil. [Flower Symbolism: *Flora Symbolica*, 175]

22. **Mephistopheles** the cynical, malicious devil to whom Faust sells his soul. [Ger. Lit.: *Faust*, Payton, 436]

23. **Miles and Flora** apparently sweet children assume wicked miens mysteriously. [Am. Lit.: *The Turn of the Screw*]

24. **Monterone** after humiliation, curses both Duke and Rigoletto. [Ital. Opera: Verdi, *Rigoletto*, Westerman, 299]

25. **o'Nell, Peg** wicked spirit claiming victim every seven years. [Br. Folklore: Briggs, 323]

26. **Pandora's box** contained all evils; opened up, evils escape to afflict world. [Rom. Myth.: Brewer *Dictionary*, 799]

27. **Powler, Peg** wicked water-demon; lures children to death. [Br. Folklore: Briggs, 323–324]

28. **Quint, Peter** dead manservant who haunts James's story. [Am. Lit.: *Turn of the Screw*]

29. **Rasputin** immoral person of tremendous power and seeming invulnerability. [Russ. Hist.: Espy, 339–340]

30. **Satan** the chief evil spirit; the great adversary of man. [Christianity and Judaism: Misc.]

31. **Vandals** East German people known for their wanton destruction (533). [Ger. Hist.: Payton, 705]

32. **Wicked Witch of the West** the terror of Oz. [Am. Lit.: *The Wonderful Wizard of Oz*]

33. **Wolf's Glen** scene of macabre uproar. [Ger. Opera: von Weber, *Der Freischütz*, Westerman, 139–140]

209. EXAGGERATION

1. **Jenkins' ear** trivial cause of a great quarrel. [Br. Hist.: Espy, 336]

2. **Madison Avenue** New York street; home of advertising companies. [Am. Culture: Misc.]

3. **Mrs. O'Leary's cow** kicked over a lantern in Mrs. O'Leary's barn, supposedly starting fire that destroyed heart of Chicago (1871). [Am. Hist.: Payton, 141]

4. **Münchhausen, Baron von** (1720–1797) soldier, adventurer, and teller of tall tales. [Ger. Hist.: *EB*, VII: 99]

210. EXASPERATION (See also FRUSTRATION.)

1. **Carter, Sergeant** Marine corps sergeant exasperated by Gomer's ceaseless stupidity. [TV: "Gomer Pyle, U.S.M.C." in Terrace, I, 319]

2. **Dagwood** comic strip character exasperated over Blondie's sale purchases. [Comics: "Blondie" in Horn, 118–119]

3. **Dithers, Mr.** Dagwood's boss; ever exasperated over Dagwood's sloppy work habits. [Comics: "Blondie" in Horn, 118–119]

4. **Gildersleeve, Throckmorton P.** comic character exasperated by nephew Leroy's antics. [Radio: "The Great Gildersleeve" in Buxton, 101]

5. **Kowalski, Stanley** exasperated by Blanche DuBois' affected refinement. [Am. Lit.: *A Streetcar Named Desire*]

6. **Kramden, Ralph** frustrated busdriver projects exasperation toward his wife and Ed Norton. [TV: "The Honeymooners" in Terrace, I, 365–366]

7. **Lodge, Mr.** Veronica's wealthy father driven to distraction by Archie. [Comics: Horn, 87]

8. **Moe** continually exasperated at Larry and Curly for their mischievous pranks. [TV: "The Three Stooges" in Terrace, II, 366]

9. **Ricardo, Ricky** bandleader frustrated by Lucy's mischief. [TV: "I Love Lucy" in Terrace, I, 383–384]

10. **Smith, Ranger** park manager "driven bananas" by Yogi's incorrigibility. [TV: "Yogi Bear" in Terrace, II, 448–449]

211. EXECUTION

1. **Derrick** famous hangman; eponym of modern hoisting apparatus. [Br. Hist.: Espy, 170]

2. **Doeg the Edomite** dispatches priests of Nob under Saul's order. [*O.T.: I Samuel* 22:18–19]

3. **Ko-Ko** appointed by the Mikado as Lord High Executioner. [Br. Opera: *The Mikado*]

4. **Lord of the Manor of Tyburn** nickname for ordinary hangman at Tyburn gallows. [Br. Hist.: Brewer *Dictionary*, 1110]

212. EXPENSIVENESS

1. **Lais** charged Demosthenes 10,000 drachmas for night in bed. [Gk. Hist.: Wallechinsky, 328]

2. **100 Philistine foreskins** price David paid to marry Saul's daughter. [*O.T.: I Samuel* 18:25–27]

3. **Vincy, Rosamond** Lydgate's income did not meet her spendthrift habits. [Br. Lit.: *Middlemarch*, Magill, I, 588–591]

EXILE (See BANISHMENT.)

213. EXPLOITATION (See also OPPORTUNISM.)

1. **Barnum, P. T.** (1810–1891) circus impressario famous for his saying, "Never give a sucker an even break." [Am. Hist.: Van Doren, 825–826]

2. **Carpetbaggers** northern exploiters whose chicanery exacerbated Reconstruction problems. [Am. Hist.: Jameson, 84]

3. **Casby, Christopher** rack-renting proprietor of slum property. [Br. Lit.: *Little Dorrit*]

4. **Stromboli** wicked puppetmaster enslaves Pinocchio aboard troupe's caravan. [Am. Cinema: *Pinocchio* in *Disney Films*, 32–37]

214. EXPLORATION (See also FRONTIER.)

1. **Columbus, Christopher** (1446–1506) expeditions to West Indies, South and Central America; said to have "discovered" America in 1492. [Ital. Hist.: Jameson, 107–108]

2. **Polo, Marco** (1254–1324) Venetian traveler in China. [Ital. Hist.: *NCE*, 1695]

215. EXTINCTION

1. **bald eagle** once on verge of extinction, this bird is now protected; still an endangered species. [Ecology: Hammond, 290]

2. **dinosaur** dinosaurs died out, unable to adapt to environmental change. [Ecology: Hammond, 290]

3. **dodo** large, flightless bird exterminated on Mauritius. [Ecology: Wallechinsky, 131]

4. **great auk** hunters killed such large numbers, these birds became extinct in 1840s. [Ecology: Hammond, 290]

5. **heath hen** human settlement of U.S. Atlantic Coast contributed to the extinction of these birds. [Ecology: Hammond, 290]

6. **Last of the Barons, The** portrays England's brilliant aristocracy as dying breed (1470s). [Br. Lit.: *The Last of the Barons*, Magill, I, 492–494]

7. **Last of the Mohicans, The** novel foreseeing the extinction of various Indian tribes. [Am. Lit.: *The Last of the Mohicans*]

8. **mastodon** similar to the elephant, the mastodon is now extinct. [Ecology: Hammond, 290]

9. **moa** large ostrichlike bird, hunted chiefly for its food; it died out in 1914. [Ecology: Hammond, 290]

10. **passenger pigeon** hunted to extinction by 1914; vast numbers once darkened American skies during migratory flights. [Ecology: *EB*, VII: 786]

11. **saber-toothed tiger** wild cat that died out about 12,000 years ago. [Ecology: Hammond, 290]

12. **whale** many species in danger of extinction, owing to massive hunting. [Ecology: Hammond, 290]

216. EXTRAVAGANCE

1. **Bovary, Emma** spends money recklessly on jewelry and clothes. [Fr. Lit.: *Madame Bovary*, Magill, I, 539–541]

2. **Cleopatra's pearl** dissolved in acid to symbolize luxury. [Rom. Hist.: Jobes, 348]

217. EXTREMISM (See also FANATICISM.)

1. **drys** advocates of Prohibition in America. [Am. Hist.: Allen, 41]

2. **Jacobins** rabidly radical faction; principal perpetrators of Reign of Terror. [Fr. Hist.: *EB*, V: 494]

3. **John Birch Society** rabid right-wing group ideologically similar to the Ku Klux Klan. [Am. Hist.: Van Doren, 576]

4. **Ku Klux Klan (KKK)** group espousing white supremacy takes law into its own hands. [Am. Hist.: *EB*, V: 935]

5. **McCarthy, Senator Joseph** (1909–1957) anti-Communist zeal frequently resulted in injustice. [Am. Hist.: Van Doren, 522]

6. **the Mikado of Japan** demands Ko-Ko execute one person a month. [Br. Opera: *The Mikado*, Magill, I, 591–592]

F

218. FAD

1. **Barbie doll** most popular doll in 1950s; extremely conventional and feminine. [Am. Hist.: Sann, 179]

2. **Beatle cut** hairstyle with bangs, sides trimmed just below ears; banned by many school boards (1960s). [Am Hist.: Sann, 251–254]

3. **bee-stung lips** ruby red and puckered decor of female mouths (1920s). [Am. Hist.: Griffith, 198]

4. **bobbed hair** short, curly boyish hairstyle caused shock (1920s). [Am. Hist.: Griffith, 198]

5. **car-stuffing** one example: 23 bodies stuffed in a Volkswagen bug. (1950s–1960s). [Am. Hist.: Sann, 300]

6. **chain letters** at height in 1930s, craze crippled postal service. [Am. Hist.: Sann, 97–104]

7. **coonskin caps** raccoon cap with tail worn in recognition of Davy Crockett, Daniel Boone revival (1950s). [Am. Hist.: Sann, 30]

8. **flagpole sitting** sitting alone at the top of a flagpole; craze comes and goes. [Am. Hist.: Sann, 39–46]

9. **frisbees** tossing plastic disks was favorite pastime, especially among collegians (1970s). [Am. Hist.: Sann, 178]

10. **gold fish-swallowing** collegiate craze in 1930s. [Am. Hist.: Sann, 289–292]

11. **hip-flask** liquor bottle designed to fit into back pockets; indispensable commodity during Prohibition. [Am. Hist.: Allen, 70]

12. **hula hoops** large plastic hoops inside of which hips swiveled (1950s). [Am. Hist.: Sann, 145–149]

13. **Kewpie doll** designed by Rose O'Neill and modeled on her baby brother; millions were made (about 1910). [Am. Hist.: WB, 5: 240–241]

14. **marathon dancing** dance contests, the longest of which lasted 24 weeks and 5 days (1930s). [Am. Hist.: McWhirter, 461]

15. **marathon eating** contestants consume ridiculous quantities of food; craze comes and goes. [Am. Hist.: Sann, 77–78]

16. **miniskirt** skirts hemmed at mid-thigh or higher; heyday of the leg in fashion world (1960s). [Am. Hist.: Sann, 255–263]

17. **mud baths** warm mud applied on skin supposedly to retain "fresh, young" complexion (1940s). [Am. Hist.: Griffith, 198]

18. **panty raids** collegiate craze in the 1940s and 1950s. [Am. Hist.: Misc.]

19. **raccoon coats** popular attire for collegians (1920s). [Am. Hist.: Sann, 175]

20. **rolled stockings** worn by flappers to achieve risqué effect (1920s). [Am. Hist.: Griffith, 198]

21. **saddle shoes** an oxford, usually white, with a saddle of contrasting color, usually brown; a favorite fad of the 1940s and 1950s. [Am. Pop. Culture: Misc.]

22. **Silly Putty** synthetic clay; uses ranging from bouncing balls to false mustaches. [Am. Hist.: Sann, 165]

23. **skateboards** mini surfboard supported on roller skate wheels; 1960s craze enjoyed 1970s renaissance. [Am. Hist.: Sann, 151–152]

24. **telephone booth-stuffing** bodies piled on top of one another inside a telephone booth; 1950s and 1960s craze. [Am. Hist.: Sann, 297]

25. **tulipomania** tulip craze in Holland during which fortunes were lost. [Eur. Hist.: *WB*, 19: 394]

26. **yo-yo** child's toy that periodically overwhelms public's fancy. [Am. Hist.: Sann, 173]

27. **zoot suits** bizarre outfits with the "reet pleats" (1940s). [Am. Hist.: Sann, 275]

219. FAILURE

1. **Army Bomb Plot** attempted assassination of Hitler; his miraculous escape brought dreadful retaliation (1944). [Ger. Hist.: Van Doren, 500]

2. **Brown, Charlie** comic strip character for whom losing is a way of life. [Comics: "Peanuts" in Horn, 542–543]

3. **Bunion Derby** financially disastrous cross-country marathon. [Am. Hist.: Sann, 48–56]

4. **Carker, John** broken-spirited man occupying subordinate position. [Br. Lit.: *Dombey and Son*]

5. **Edsel** much bruited automobile fails on market (1950s). [Am. Hist.: Flexner, 78]

6. **English, Julian** contentious and unloved salesman; commits suicide in despair. [Am. Lit.: *Appointment in Samarra*]

7. **Gunpowder Plot** attempt to blow up the Parliament building; led to the execution of its leader, Guy Fawkes (1605). [Brit. Hist.: *EB*, IV: 70–71]

8. **Little Tramp** Chaplin's much-loved, much-imitated hapless, "I'm a failure" persona. [Am. Cinema: Griffith, 79]

9. **Loman, Willy** traveling salesman who gradually comes to realize that his life has been a complete failure; commits suicide. [Am. Lit.: *The Death of a Salesman*, Payton, 397]

10. **Mighty Casey** ignominiously strikes out in the clutch. [Am. Lit.: "Casey at the Bat" in Turkin, 642]

11. **Reardon, Edwin** very promising writer who, after unsuccessful publication, returns to clerical job. [Br. Lit.: *New Grub Street*, Magill, I, 647–649]

12. **Skid Row** district of down-and-outs and bums. [Am. Usage: Brewer *Dictionary*, 1008]

13. **WIN buttons** President Ford's scheme to reduce inflation: for the American public to wear shields stating "W.I.N." (Whip Inflation Now). [Am. Hist.: Misc.]

14. **World Football League** "ingenious" creation of a third professional football league that never materialized. [Am. Sports: Misc.]

220. FAITHFULNESS (See also LOYALTY.)

To Lovers

1. **Abigail** prostrates herself before David and vows devotion. [*O.T.: I Samuel* 25:40–41]

2. **Akawi-ko** waits eighty years for lover to return. [Jap. Legend: Jobes, 59]

3. **Amelia** despite financial woes, remains faithful to Booth. [Br. Lit.: *Amelia*]

4. **Andromache** devoted wife of Hector. [Gk. Lit.: *Iliad; Trojan Women; Andromache;* Fr. Lit.: *Andromaque*]

5. **Aramati** name of Vedic goddess means faithfulness. [Hindu Myth.: Jobes, 117]

6. **Arsinoë** Alcmaeon's wife; continues to love husband though he is unfaithful. [Gk. Myth.: Zimmerman, 32]

7. **Brandimante** loyal to lover and leader. [Ital. Lit.: *Orlando Innamorato*]

8. **Briseis** loved Achilles despite her capture by Ag. [Gk. Myth.: Walsh *Classical*, 62]

9. **Britomart** waits many years for true love, Artegall. [Br. Lit.: *Faerie Queene*]

10. **Candida** ever faithful to husband. [Br. Lit.: *Candida*]

11. **Charlotte** faithful to fiancé lost at sea. [Br. Lit.: *Fatal Curiosity*]

12. **China aster** symbol of fidelity. [Flower Symbolism: Jobes, 326]

13. **Clärchen** devoted to Egmont. [Ger. Lit.: *Egmont*]

14. **crow** faithful; does not mate again for nine generations. [Animal Symbolism: Mercatante, 161]

15. **doves** faithfulness reflected in their pairing for life. [Christian Symbolism: Child, 211]

16. **Dupre, Sally** Clay Wingate's fiancée quietly waits for his return. [Am. Lit.: "John Brown's Body" in Magill, I, 445–448]

17. **Enid** though falsely accused of infidelity, nurses husband through wounds. [Br. Lit.: *Idylls of the King*]

18. **Evangeline** lifelong search for lover, Gabriel. [Am. Lit.: *Evangeline*]

19. **heliotrope** also means "turn to the sun." [Flower Symbolism: *Flora Symbolica*, 174]

20. **Hypermnestra** only one of Danaides who did not murder husband on wedding night. [Gk. Myth.: Howe, 136]

21. **ivy** traditional symbol of faithfulness. [Plant Symbolism: *Flora Symbolica*, 175]

22. **key** attribute of the personified Fidelity. [Art: Hall, 184]

23. **Laodamia** commits suicide to join husband Protesilaus in underworld. [Gk. Lit.: *Iliad;* Rom. Lit.: *Aeneid*]

24. **Leonore** disguises as Fidelio to save imprisoned husband. [Ger. Opera: Beethoven, *Fidelio*, Westerman, 109–110]

25. **Micawber, Mrs. Emma** swears she will never desert husband. [Br. Lit.: *David Copperfield*]

26. **Nanna** immolated herself on pyre with husband, Baldur. [Norse Myth.: Wheeler, 256]

27. **Penelope** Odysseus' patient wife; faithful for 20 years while waiting for his return. [Gk. Lit.: *Iliad; Odyssey*]

28. **Perseus** ever devoted to wife, Andromeda. [Gk. Myth.: Zimmerman, 200]

29. **Pietas** goddess of faithfulness, respect, and affection. [Rom. Myth.: Kravitz, 192]

30. **plum** symbol of faithfulness. [Flower Symbolism: *Flora Symbolica*, 176]

31. **Portia** takes own life after husband, Brutus's, suicide. [Rom. Hist.: *Plutarch's Lives*]

32. **red on yellow** symbol of faithfulness. [Chinese Art: Jobes, 357]

33. **Rodelinda** faithful to her deposed husband, Bertarido. [Br. Opera: Handel, *Rodelinda*, Westerman, 50–52]

34. **Roxy** tries to "save" immoral husband. [Am. Lit.: *Roxy*]

35. **Sonia** young prostitute stays near prison to comfort Raskolnikov. [Russ. Lit.: *Crime and Punishment*]

36. **Valentine** a true friend and constant lover. [Br. Lit.: *Two Gentlemen of Verona*]

37. **veronica** symbol of faithfulness. [Flower Symbolism: *Flora Symbolica,* 178]

38. **violet** symbol of faithfulness. [Flower Symbolism: *Flora Symbolica,* 178; Kunz, 327]

39. **Zelda** shows devotion to Dobie, who manfully resists. [TV: "The Many Loves of Dobie Gillis" in Terrace, II, 64–66]

To God

40. **Abdiel** seraph who refused to join Satan's rebellion. [Br. Lit.: *Paradise Lost*]

41. **Abraham** in obedience to God, would sacrifice his only son. [*O.T.: Genesis* 22:1–18]

42. **Caleb** faithfully followed God in exploration of Canaan. [*O.T.: Numbers* 14:24–25]

43. **Canterbury bell** flower memorializing harness bells of Canterbury pilgrims. [Br. Hist.: Espy, 303]

44. **Hezekiah** brings people of Judah back to God. [*O.T.: II Chronicles* 29:3–11; 31:20–21]

45. **Jehoshaphat** destroyed idols; adjured men to follow God. [*O.T.: II Chronicles* 17:3–6; 19:9–11]

46. **Josiah** tenaciously follows Moses' law; orders keeping of Passover. [*O.T.: II Kings* 23:21–24]

221. **FAITHLESSNESS (See also ADULTERY, CUCKOLDRY.)**

1. **Angelica** betrays Orlando by eloping with young soldier. [Ital. Lit.: *Orlando Furioso*]

2. **Camilla** falls to temptations of husband's friend. [Span. Lit.: *Don Quixote*]

3. **Carmen** throws over lover for another. [Fr. Lit.: *Carmen;* Fr. Opera: Bizet, *Carmen,* Westerman, 189–190]

4. **Coronis** princess killed by Apollo for being unfaithful to him. [Gk. Myth.: Howe, 66]

5. **Cressida** unfaithful mistress of Troilus; byword for unfaithfulness. [Br. Lit.: *Troilus and Cressida*]

6. **Dear John** letter from woman informing boyfriend that relationship is over. [Am. Usage: Misc.]

7. **Frankie and Johnnie** Johnnie, unfaithful to Frankie, is shot by her; there are nearly 500 versions of the song. [Am. Music: Misc.]

8. **Goneril and Regan** Lear's disloyal offspring; "tigers, not daughters." [Br. Lit.: *King Lear*]

9. **Manon** indifferently allows lover to be abducted. [Fr. Opera: Massenet, *Manon*, Westerman, 194–195]

222. **FAME**

1. **cardinal flower** traditional symbol of eminence. [Flower Symbolism: Jobes, 290]

2. **daphne** traditional symbol of fame. [Plant Symbolism: Jobes, 414]

3. **Grauman's Chinese Theater** famous for the imprints of movie stars' footprints in its forecourt. [Am. Cinema: Payton, 284.]

4. **Halls of Fame** national shrines honoring outstanding individuals in a particular field (baseball, football, acting, Great Americans, etc.). [Am. Culture: *WB*, 9, 22–23]

5. **trumpet** attribute of fame personified. [Art: Hall, 119]

6. **trumpet flower** indicates notoriety. [Flower Symbolism: *Flora Symbolica*, 178]

7. **Who's Who** biographical dictionary of notable living people. [Am. Hist.: Hart, 922]

223. **FANATICISM (See also EXTREMISM.)**

1. **Adamites** various sects preaching a return to life before the fall. [Christian Hist.: Brewer *Note-Book*, 8]

2. **assassins** Moslem murder teams used hashish as stimulus (11th and 12th centuries). [Islamic Hist.: Brewer *Note-Book*, 52]

3. **Fakirs** mendicant Indian sects bent on self-punishment for salvation. [Asian Hist.: Brewer *Note-Book*, 310]

4. **flagellants** various Christian sects practising self-punishment. [Christian Hist.: Brewer *Note-Book*, 331–332]

5. **Harmony Society** Harmonists, also Rappites; subscribed to austere doctrines, such as celibacy, and therefore no longer exist (since 1960). [Am. Hist.: *NCE*, 910]

6. **Shakers** (or **Alethians**) received their name from the trembling produced by excesses of religious emotion; because of doctrine of celibacy, Shakers are all but extinct. [Am. Hist.: *NCE*, 1938]

224. **FANTASY (See also ENCHANTMENT.)**

1. **Aladdin's lamp** when rubbed, genie appears to do possessor's bidding. [Arab. Lit.: *Arabian Nights*, "Aladdin and the Wonderful Lamp"]

2. **Alice** undergoes incredible adventures, such as dealing with the "real" Queen of Hearts. [Br. Lit.: *Alice's Adventures in Wonderland; Through the Looking Glass*]

3. **Arabian Nights** compilation of Middle and Far Eastern tales. [Arab. Lit.: Parrinder, 26]

4. **Baggins, Bilbo** Hobbit who wanders afar and brings back the One Ring of Power to The Shire. [Br. Lit.: *The Hobbit*]

5. **Chitty Chitty Bang Bang** magical car helps track down criminals. [Children's Lit.: *Chitty Chitty Bang Bang*]

6. **Dorothy** flies via tornado to Oz. [Am. Lit.: *The Wonderful Wizard of Oz*]

7. **Fantasia** music comes to life in animated cartoon. [Am. Cinema: *Fantasia* in *Disney Films*, 38–45]

8. **Harvey** six-foot rabbit who appears only to a genial drunkard. [Am. Lit.: Benét, 444]

9. **Land of the Giants** a *Gulliver's Travels* in outer space. [TV: Terrace, II, 10–11]

10. **Little Prince, The** travels to Earth to learn what is important in life; fable by Antoine de Saint-Exupéry (1943). [Fr. Lit.: Benét, 889]

11. **Lord of the Rings, The** "feigned history" of the Hobbits; epic trilogy written by J. R. R. Tolkein. [Br. Lit.: Benét, 1013]

12. **Millionaire, The** mysterious Croesus bestows fortunes on unsuspecting individuals. [TV: Terrace, II, 97–98]

13. **Mitty, Walter** timid man who imagines himself a hero. [Am. Lit.: Benét, 1006; Am. Cinema and Drama: *The Secret Life of Walter Mitty*]

14. **Narnia** kingdom in which fantasy cycle of seven tales by C. S. Lewis takes place. [Children's Lit.: Fisher, 289–290]

15. **O'Gill, Darby** befriends dwarfdom. [Am. Cinema: *Darby O'Gill and the Little People* in *Disney Films*, 159–162]

16. **Pan, Peter** escapes to Never Never Land to avoid growing up. [Br. and Am. Drama: Benét, 778]

17. **Poppins, Mary** enchanted nanny guides her charges through fey adventures. [Children's Lit.: *Mary Poppins;* Am. Cinema: *Mary Poppins* in *Disney Films*, 226–232]

18. **Wonderful Wizard of Oz, The** adventures in land "somewhere over the rainbow." [Am. Lit.: *The Wonderful Wizard of Oz*]

225. **FAREWELL**

1. **Auld Lang Syne** closing song of New Year's Eve. [Music: Leach, 91]

2. **extreme unction (last rites)** anointing at the hour of death, sacrament of Orthodox Church and Roman Catholic Church. [Christianity: *NCE*, 689]

3. **golden handshake** token of gratitude bestowed on retiring employee after years of service. [Br. Pop. Culture: Misc.]

4. **gold watch** token of gratitude often bestowed on retiring employee after years of service. [Am. Pop. Culture: Misc.]

5. **Last Hurrah, The** portrays epitome of a politician's goodbye. [Am. Lit.: *The Last Hurrah*]

6. **Last Supper** Christ's final dinner with disciples before crucifixion. [*N.T.: Matthew* 26:26–29; *Mark* 14:22–25; *Luke* 22:14–20]

7. **MacArthur's goodbye** "Old soldiers never die; they just fade away." [Am. Hist.: Van Doren, 528]

8. **Mafia's kiss** gangsters' farewell ritual before murdering victim. [Am. Hist.: Misc.]

9. **Michaelmas daisy** traditional symbol of farewell. [Flower Symbolism: Jobes, 407]

226. **FARMING**

1. **Aristaeus** honored as inventor of beekeeping. [Gk. Myth.: *NCE*, 105]

2. **Ashnan** goddess of grain. [Sumerian Myth.: Benét, 57]

3. **Barren Ground** portrayal of inability to maintain standards on unproductive farm. [Am. Lit.: *Barren Ground*]

4. **Bergson, Alexandra** proves her ability above brothers' to run farm. [Am. Lit.: *O Pioneers!*, Magill, I, 663–665]

5. **bread basket** an agricultural area, such as the U.S. Midwest, that provides large amounts of food to other areas. [Am. Hist.: Misc.]

6. **Ceres** goddess of agriculture. [Rom. Myth.: Kravitz, 13]

7. **Chicomecoatl** goddess of maize. [Aztec Myth.: Jobes, 322]

8. **cow college** an agricultural college. [Pop. Culture: Misc.]

9. **Dea Dia** ancient Roman goddess of agriculture. [Rom. Myth.: Howe, 77]

10. **Demeter** goddess of corn and agriculture. [Gk. Myth.: Jobes, 429–430]

11. **Dionysus** god of fertility; sometimes associated with fertility of crops. [Gk. Myth.: *NCE*, 575]

12. **Fiacre, St.** extraordinary talent in raising vegetables; patron saint. [Christian Hagiog.: Attwater, 130]

13. **Freya** goddess of agriculture, peace, and plenty. [Norse Myth.: Payton, 257]

14. **Frome, Ethan** epitome of struggling New England farmer (1890s). [Am. Lit.: *Ethan Frome*]

15. **Gaea** goddess of the earth. [Gk. Myth.: *NCE*, 785]

16. **Giants in the Earth** portrayal of man's struggle with the stubborn earth. [Am. Lit.: *Giants in the Earth*, Magill, I, 303–304]

17. **Good Earth, The** portrayal of land as only sure means of survival. [Am. Lit.: *The Good Earth*]

18. **King Cotton** term personifying the chief staple of the South. [Am. Hist.: Hart, 445]

19. **Kore** name for Persephone as symbol of annual vegetation cycle. [Gk. and Rom. Myth.: *NCE*, 1637]

20. **Odin** god of farming. [Norse Myth.: Benét, 728]

21. **Persephone** goddess of fertility; often associated with crops. [Gk. and Rom. Myth.: *NCE*, 1637]

22. **Shimerda, Antonia** "like wavering grass, a child of the prairie and farm." [Am. Lit.: *My Ántonia*, Magill, I, 630–632]

23. **Silvanus** god of agriculture. [Rom. Myth.: Kravitz, 13]

24. **Triptolemus** an Eleusinian who learns from Demeter the art of growing corn. [Gk. Myth.: *NCE*, 557]

25. **Walstan, St.** English patron saint of husbandmen. [Christian Hagiog.: Brewer *Dictionary*, 1138]

26. **wheat ears, garland of** to Demeter, goddess of grain. [Gk. Myth.: Jobes, 374]

227. **FASHION**

1. **Brummel, George B. (Beau Brummel)** (1778–1840) set styles for men's clothes and manners for a quarter century. [Western Fashion: *NCE*, 926]

2. **Harper's Bazaar** leading fashion magazine. [Am. Culture: Misc.]

3. **Vogue** leading fashion magazine in France and America. [Fr. and Amer. Culture: Misc.]

228. **FASTIDIOUSNESS (See also PUNCTUALITY.)**

1. **Fogg, Phileas** entire life tuned to precise schedule. [Fr. Lit.: *Around the World in Eighty Days*]

2. **Linkinwater, Tim** handles minutest details with order and precision. [Br. Lit.: *Nicholas Nickleby*]

3. **Morris the cat** finicky eater; eats only "9-Lives." [TV: Wallechinsky, 129]

4. **Steva** Jenufa's new scar cools his adulterous ardor. [Czech Opera: Janáček, *Jenufa,* Westerman, 407]

5. **Unger, Felix** for him, godliness is next to cleanliness. [Am. Lit.: *The Odd Couple;* Am. Cinema: *The Odd Couple;* TV: "The Odd Couple" in Terrace, II, 160–161]

229. **FATE (See also CHANCE.)**

1. **Adrastea** goddess of inevitable fate. [Gk. Myth.: Jobes, 35]

2. **Atropos, Clotho, and Lachesis** the three Fates; worked the thread of life. [Gk. and Rom. Myth.: Bulfinch]

3. **Bridge of San Luis Rey, The** catastrophe as act of divine providence. [Am. Lit.: *The Bridge of San Luis Rey*]

4. **the dance of death** recurring motif in medieval art. [Eur. Culture: Bishop, 363–367]

5. **Destiny** goddess of destiny of mankind. [Gk. Myth.: Kravitz, 78]

6. **Jennie Gerhardt** novel of young girl trapped by life's circumstances (1911). [Am. Lit.: *Jennie Gerhardt,* Magill, III, 526–528]

7. **karma** one's every action brings inevitable results. [Buddhist and Hindu Trad.: *EB* (1963), 13: 283; Pop. Culture: Misc.]

8. **kismet** alludes to the part of life assigned one by his destiny. [Moslem Trad.: *EB* (1963), 13: 418; Pop. Culture: Misc.]

9. **Leonora** cursed by father; stabbed by brother. [Ital. Opera: Verdi, *La Forza del Destino,* Westerman, 316–317]

10. **Meleager** death would come when firebrand burned up. [Gk. Myth.: Walsh *Classical,* 186]

11. **Necessitas** goddess of the destiny of mankind. [Gk. Myth.: Kravitz, 78, 162]

12. **Nemesis** goddess of vengeance and retribution; *nemesis* has come to mean that which one cannot achieve. [Gr. Myth.: *WB,* 14: 116; Pop. Culture: Misc.]

13. **Norns** wove the fabric of human destiny. [Norse Myth.: Benét, 720]

14. **wool and narcissi, garland of** emblem of the three Fates. [Gk. Myth.: Jobes, 374]

230. **FATHERHOOD**

1. **Abraham** progenitor of a host of nations. [O.T.: *Genesis* 17:3–6]

2. **Adam** first man and progenitor of humanity. [*O.T.: Genesis* 5: 1–5]

3. **Dag(h)da** great god of Celts; father of Danu. [Celtic Myth.: Parrinder, 68; Jobes, 405]

4. **Vatea** the first man; the father of mankind. [Polynesian Legend: *How the People Sang the Mountains Up*, 85]

231. FATNESS

1. **Bagstock, Major** corpulent army officer. [Br. Lit.: *Dombey and Son*]

2. **Challenger, Professor** amusing and opinionated scientist of notable rotundity. [Br. Lit.: *The Lost World*]

3. **Domino, Antoine "Fats"** (1928–   ) popular singer of the 1950s, nicknamed for his size and shape. [Am. Music: Misc.]

4. **Double, Edmund** loves to eat; represents the Fattipuffs. [Children's Lit.: *Fattipuffs and Thinifers*, Fisher, 100–101]

5. **Eglon** obese Moabite king; sword engulfed by adiposity. [*O.T.: Judges* 3:17–22]

6. **Five by Five, Mr.** obese subject of song by Gene DePaul and Don Raye (1942). [Am. Pop. Music: Kinkle, 1, 379.]

7. **Gleason, Jackie** (1916–   ) heavyweight TV comedian. [TV: "The Jackie Gleason Show," "The Honeymooners" in Terrace, I, 402]

8. **Humpty Dumpty** "egg" in Mother Goose who, among other things, alludes to fatness. [Children's Lit.: *Mother Goose*]

9. **Joe ("Fat Boy")** sole employment consists in alternately eating and sleeping. [Br. Lit.: *Pickwick Papers*]

10. **king and his ministers** "large, corpulent, oily men." [Am. Lit.: "Hop-Frog" in *Portable Poe*, 317–329]

11. **Limkins, Mr.** large gentleman with "a very round red face." [Br. Lit.: *Oliver Twist*]

12. **Minnesota Fats** (Rudolph Walter Wanderone, Jr., 1903–   ) world champion billiard player easily recognized by his fleshy physique. [Am. Sports: Misc.]

13. **Robbin and Bobbin** "eat more victuals than threescore men." [Nurs. Rhyme: Baring-Gould, 33]

14. **Snuphanuph, Lady** obese visitor at Bath. [Br. Lit.: *Pickwick Papers*]

232. FEARSOMENESS

1. **Deimos** attendant of Ares; personification of fear. [Gk. Myth.: Howe, 77]

2. **Dracula** eerie tale of vampires and werewolves. [Br. Lit.: *Dracula*]

3. **Invasion from Mars** Orson Welles's broadcast; terrified a credulous America (1938). [Am. Hist.: Van Doren, 468]

4. **Iroquois** strongest, most feared of eastern confederacies. [Am. Hist.: Jameson, 250]

5. **Jaggers, Mr.** lawyer esteemed and feared by clients. [Br. Lit.: *Great Expectations*]

6. **Ko-Ko** holder of dread office of High Executioner. [Br. Opera: *The Mikado,* Magill, I, 591–592]

7. **Native Son** portrays oppressor and oppressed as both filled with fear. [Am. Lit.: *Native Son,* Magill, I, 643–645]

8. **Phobus** god of dread and alarm. [Gk. Myth.: Kravitz, 14, 84]

9. **Shere Khan** lame tiger who wants to devour Mowgli; causes fear throughout story. [Children's Lit.: *The Jungle Book*]

233. **FEAST (See also EPICUREANISM.)**

1. **Barmecide feast** a sham banquet, with empty plates, given to a beggar by wealthy Bagdad nobleman. [Arab. Lit.: *Arabian Nights,* "The Bamecide's Feast"]

2. **Belshazzar's Feast** lavish banquet, with vessels stolen from Jerusalem temple. [O.T.: *Daniel,* 5]

3. **Hanukkah** (Feast of Lights or Feast of Dedication) Jewish festival lasting eight days; abundance of food is characteristic. [Judaism: *NCE,* 1190]

4. **Lucullan feast** a lavish banquet; after Lucullus, roman general and gourmet. [Rom. Hist.: Espy, 236]

5. **Thanksgiving** national holiday with luxurious dinner as chief ritual. [Am. Pop. Culture: Misc.]

6. **Thyestean banquet** at which Atreus served his brother Thyestes' sons to him as main course. [Gk. Myth.: *Brewer Dictionary,* 1081]

7. **Trimalchio's Feast** lavishly huge banquet given by wealthy vulgarian. [Rom. Lit.: *Satyricon*]

234. **FEMININITY**

1. **Belphoebe** perfect maidenhood; epithet of Elizabeth I. [Br. Lit.: *Faerie Queene*]

2. **Darnel, Aurelia** personification of femininity. [Br. Lit.: *Sir Launcelot Greaves*]

3. **Miss America** winner of beauty contest; femininity high among virtues desired. [Am. Hist.: Payton, 445]

235. **FEMINISM** (See also EQUALITY.)

1. **Alving, Mrs.** feminist; unconventional widow. [Nor. Lit.: *Ghosts*]

2. **Bates, Belinda** intellectual and amiable advocate of women's rights. [Br. Lit.: "The Haunted House" in Fyfe, 16]

3. **Bloomer, Amelia** (1818–1894) dress reformer; designed bloomers. [Am. Hist.: Flexner, 391]

4. **blue-stocking** female intellectual; advocates nontraditional feminine talents. [Western Folklore: Brewer *Dictionary*, 127]

5. **Bostonians, The** suffragists for lost causes, vulnerable to romance. [Am. Lit.: *The Bostonians*]

6. **Doll's House, A** drama on the theme of women's rights. [Nor. Lit.: *A Doll's House*]

7. **Equal Rights Amendment** forbids discrimination against women. [Am. Hist.: Flexner, 397]

8. **Findlay, Maude** militant, outspoken women's libber. [TV: "Maude" in Terrace, II, 79–80]

9. **Lysistrata** Athenian exhorts fellow women to continence for peace. [Gk. Lit.: *Lysistrata*]

10. **Ms.** the magazine for the liberated woman. [Am. Culture: Misc.]

11. **Nora** rebellious heroine; leaves stultifying marriage. [Nor. Lit.: *A Doll's House*]

12. **Peel, Emma** early media manifestation of self-sufficient woman. [TV: "The Avengers" in Terrace, I, 71–73]

13. **Virginia Slims** cigarette trademark marketed to "independent women." "You've come a long way, baby," as slogan. [Trademarks: Crowley *Trade*, 630]

14. **Wisk, Miss** lady with a mission. [Br. Lit.: *Bleak House*]

15. **Women's Liberation Movement** appellation of modern day women's rights advocacy. [Am. Hist.: Flexner, 396]

16. **Wonder Woman** female comic strip heroine to offset Superman; she does everything a man can do and more. [Comics: Horn, 480]

236. **FERRYING**

1. **Charon** ferries dead across the river Styx. [Gk. and Rom. Myth.: Hall, 147; Ital. Lit.: *Inferno.*]

2. **Christopher, St.** took the Christ child and the weak across river. [Christian Hagiog.: Hall, 68]

3. **Julian the Hospitalor** carries leper across river. [Christian Hagiog.: Hall, 181]

4. **Phlegyas** conveyed Dante and Virgil through Stygian marsh. [Ital. Lit.: *Inferno*]

5. **Siddharta** "one who has attained goal," personified in ferryman role. [Ger. Lit.: *Siddharta*]

6. **Tuck, Friar** jolly member of Robin Hood's gang; carries Robin over stream but dumps him coming back. [Br. Lit.: *Robin Hood*]

237. **FERTILITY (See also ABUNDANCE.)**

1. **antler dance** archaic animal dance, preceding mating. [Br. Folklore: Brewer *Dictionary*, 1]

2. **Anu** Irish goddess of fecundity. [Irish Folklore: Briggs, 9]

3. **Aphrodite** goddess of fecundity. [Gk. Myth.: Parrinder, 24]

4. **Astarte** goddess of fecundity. [Phoenician Myth.: Jobes, 144]

5. **Astarte's dove** emblem of fecundity. [Phoenician Myth.: Jobes, 466]

6. **Atargatis' dove** emblem of fecundity. [Hittite Myth.: Jobes, 466]

7. **Athena** Athens' patroness; goddess of war and fecundity. [Gk. Myth.: Parrinder, 33; Kravitz, 40]

8. **Baal** chief male god of Phoenicians; the generative principle. [Phoenician Rel.: Parrinder, 38]

9. **Bacchus' cup** symbolizes fecundity. [Gk. Myth.: Jobes, 397]

10. **Bona Dea** goddess of fertility; counterpart of Faunus. [Rom. Myth.: Zimmerman, 43]

11. **breast** symbol of nourishment and fecundity. [Ren. Art: Hall, 52]

12. **Cernunnos** horned deity of fecundity, associated with snakes. [Celtic Myth.: Parrinder, 58]

13. **Cerridwen** nature goddess whose magical cauldron was misused. [Celtic Myth.: Parrinder, 58]

14. **Chloë** beloved maiden, goddess of new, green crops. [Gk. Myth.: Parrinder, 62]

15. **Clothru** Irish goddess of fertility. [Irish Myth.: Jobes, 349]

16. **clover** symbolizes fecundity. [Folklore: Jobes, 350]

17. **coconut** presented to women who want to be mothers. [Ind. Folklore: Binder, 85]

18. **Cybele** nature's fruitfulness assured by orgiastic rites honoring her. [Phrygian Myth.: Parrinder, 68; Jobes, 400]

19. **Dag(h)da** god of abundance, war, healing. [Celtic Myth.: Parrinder, 68; Jobes, 405]

20. **Dagon (Dāgan)** fish-corn god symbolizing fecundity and abundance. [Babyl. Myth.: Parrinder, 71; Jobes, 405]

21. **Demeter** goddess of fecundity. [Gk. Myth.: Jobes, 429–430]

22. **Dôn** goddess of fecundity; Welsh equivalent of Irish Danu. [Brythonic Myth.: Leach, 321; Jobes, 461]

23. **double ax** emblem of fecundity. [Folklore: Jobes, 163]

24. **figs, garland of** a traditional pictorial identification of Pan, pastoral god of fertility. [Gk. Myth.: Jobes, 373]

25. **fish** signifies fecundity. [Mexican Folklore: Binder, 17]

26. **flowers and fruit, garland of** traditional headdress of Pomona, goddess of fertility. [Rom. Myth.: Jobes, 373]

27. **flowers, garland of** traditional pictorial identification of Flora, goddess of flowers and fertility. [Rom. Myth.: Jobes, 373]

28. **Freya** goddess of agriculture, peace, and plenty. [Norse Myth.: Payton, 257]

29. **grape leaves, garland of** traditional headdress of Bona Dea, goddess of fertility. [Rom. Myth.: Jobes, 373]

30. **green** symbol of fruitfulness. [Color Symbolism: Jobes, 356]

31. **horn** believed to promote fertility. [Art: Hall, 157]

32. **horse** symbolizes fecundity. [Bengali Folklore: Binder, 67]

33. **Lavransdatter, Kristin** gives birth to eight sons in ten years. [Nor. Lit.: *Kristin Lavransdatter*, Magill, I, 483–486]

34. **Mylitta** goddess of fertility. [Babyl. Myth.: Leach, 776]

35. **old woman who lived in a shoe** what to do with so many children? [Nurs. Rhyme: Opie, 434]

36. **Ops** Sabine goddess of fecundity. [Rom. Myth.: Brewer *Dictionary*, 782]

37. **orange blossoms** symbolic of bride's hope for fruitfulness. [Br. and Fr. Tradition: Brewer *Dictionary*, 784]

38. **pomegranate** indicates abundance. [Heraldry: Halberts, 36]

39. **Pomona** goddess of gardens and fruit trees. [Rom. Myth.: Zimmerman, 218]

40. **rabbit** symbol of fecundity. [Animal Symbolism: Mercatante, 125–126]

41. **Rhea** worshiped orgy and fertility; mother of Zeus, Poseidon, Hera, Hades, Demeter, and Hestia. [Gk. Myth.: *NCE*, 1796]

42. **rhinoceros horn** in powdered form, considered powerful fertility agent. [Eastern Culture: Misc.]

43. **waxing moon** only effective time for sowing seeds. [Gardening Lore: Boland, 31]

44. **yellow** color of fecundity, relating to yellow sun and earth. [Eastern Color Symbolism: Binder, 78]

238. FESTIVAL, FILM

1. **Cannes** founded after WWII; the 1968 festival was the scene of demonstrations by political activists. [Cinema Hist.: *EB*, 12: 496]

239. FESTIVAL, MUSIC

1. **Bayreuth** since 1876, international center for Wagner's operas. [Opera Hist.: Thompson, 165]
2. **Berkshire Music Festival (Tanglewood)** summer home of Boston Symphony since 1934. [Music Hist.: Thompson, 202–203]
3. **Edinburgh Festival** internationally famous entertainment since 1947. [Music Hist.: Thompson, 617]
4. **Tanglewood** See Berkshire Music Festival.
5. **Woodstock** 300,000 rock music fans attended this festival held near Bethel, N.Y. (August 16, 1969). [Am. Music Hist.: *EB*, X: 741]

FIERCENESS (See SAVAGERY.)

240. FILTH (See also DIRTINESS.)

1. **Augean stables** held 3,000 oxen, uncleaned for 30 years; Hercules' fifth labor: washes out dung by diverting a river. [Gk. and Rom. Myth.: Hall, 149]
2. **Jungle, The** portrays the lack of hygiene among Chicago meatpacking plants (1906). [Am. Lit.: *The Jungle*, Payton, 356]
3. **Lake Erie** Great Lake; once so polluted, referred to as Lake Eerie. [Am. Hist.: *NCE*, 887]

241. FINANCE (See also MONEY.)

1. **Bourse** the Paris stock exchange. [Fr. Commerce: Misc.]
2. **Dow Jones** the best known of several U.S. indexes of movements in price on Wall Street. [Am. Hist.: Payton, 202]
3. **Lombard Street** London bankers' row; named for 13th-century Italian moneylenders. [Br. Hist.: Plumb, 15]
4. **Old Lady of Threadneedle Street** nickname for the Bank of England. [Br. Culture: Misc.]
5. **Praxidice** goddess of commerce. [Gk. Myth.: Kravitz, 88]
6. **Rockefeller, John D(avison)** (1839–1937) multimillionaire oil tycoon and financier, [Am. Hist.: *EB*, VIII: 623]
7. **Throgmorton Street** location of Stock Exchange; by extension, financial world. [Br. Hist.: Brewer *Dictionary*, 1079]

8. **Wall Street** N.Y.C. financial district. [Am. Hist.: Jameson, 530]

242. FIRE

1. **Agni** intermediary of the gods through sacrificial fire. [Hindu Myth.: Parrinder, 12]

2. **Caca** goddess of the hearth. [Rom. Myth.: Kravitz, 49]

3. **Dactyli** introduced fire to Crete. [Gk. Myth.: Kravitz, 74]

4. **Etticoat, Little Nancy** candle personified: longer she stands, shorter she grows. [Nurs. Rhyme: *Mother Goose*, 39]

5. **Florian** miraculously extinguished conflagration; popularly invoked against combustion. [Christian Hagiog.: Hall, 126]

6. **Great Chicago Fire** destroyed much of Chicago; it was supposedly started when Mrs. O'Leary's cow kicked over a lantern (1871). [Am. Hist.: Payton, 141]

7. **Hephaestus** Prometheus' kinsman and the god of fire. [Gk. Lit.: *Prometheus Bound*, Magill, I, 786–788]

8. **lucifer** kitchen match; from Lucifer, fallen archangel. [Br. Folklore: Espy, 66]

9. **Polycarp, St.** sentenced to immolation, flames unscathingly ensheathed him. [Christian Hagiog.: Attwater, 290]

10. **Prometheus** Titan who gave fire to man. [Gk. Myth.: Payton, 546]

11. **salamander** flamedwelling spirit in Rosicrucian philosophy. [Medieval Hist.: Brewer *Dictionary*, 956]

12. **Taberah** Israelite camp scorched by angry Jehovah. [*O.T.: Numbers* 11:1–3]

13. **Topheth** where parents immolated children to god, Moloch. [*O.T.: II Kings* 23:10; *Jeremiah* 7:31–32]

14. **Vesta** virgin goddess of hearth; custodian of sacred fire. [Rom. Myth.: Brewer *Dictionary*, 1127]

15. **Vulcan** blacksmith of gods; personification of fire. [Art: Hall, 128]

243. FIRST

1. **Adam** in the Bible, the first man. [*O.T.: Genesis* 1:26–5:5]

2. **Alalcomeneus** the first man. [Gk. Myth.: Zimmerman, 14]

3. **Aldine Classics** first standardized, comprehensive editions of the classics (16th century). [Ital. Hist.: Plumb, 267]

4. **Armstrong, Neil** (1930–   ) first person to set foot on the moon (July 20, 1969). [Am. Hist.: *NCE*, 172]

5. **Bannister, Roger** (1929–   ) first runner to break the four-minute mile. [Sports: *EB*, I: 795]

6. **Bay Psalm Book, The** first book published in U.S. (1640). [Am. Hist.: Van Doren, 784]

7. **Cabrini, St. Frances** (1850–1917) first U.S. saint; tirelessly helped new Italian Americans. [Christian Hagiog.: Attwater, 135–136]

8. **Caedmon** (b. 671) earliest English Christian poet. [Br. Hist.: Grun]

9. **Cincinnati Red Stockings** first all-professional baseball team (1869). [Am. Hist.: Van Doren, 260]

10. **Dafue** first true opera (Florence, 1597). [Ital. Opera: Westerman, 17]

11. **Dare, Virginia** (b. 1587) first English child born in New World. [Am. Hist.: Jameson, 131]

12. **Delaware** first colony to ratify the Constitution; thus, "the first state." [Am. Hist.: *NCE*, 738]

13. **Eve** in the Bible, the first woman. [*O.T.: Genesis* 1–5]

14. **Gagarin, Yury** (1934–1968) first man in space (1961). [Russ. Hist.: Wallechinsky, 116]

15. **Genesis** first book of the Old Testament. [*O.T.: Genesis*]

16. **Gertie the Dinosaur** first substantial animated cartoon (1909). [Am. Hist.: Van Doren, 362]

17. **the Great Exhibition** the first industrial exhibition, promoted by Prince Albert and held in Hyde Park in Crystal Palace. [Br. Hist.: Payton, 285]

18. **Great Train Robbery, The** considered the first "real" movie. [Am. Cinema: Griffith, 10]

19. **Gutenberg, Johannes** (1397–1468) German printer, supposedly the first European to print with movable type (c. 1436). [Ger. Hist.: *NCE*, 1166]

20. **Harvard** the first American college (1636). [Am. Hist.: *NCE*, 1200]

21. **Lindbergh, Charles** (1902–1974) U.S. aviator; made the first solo, nonstop transatlantic flight (1927). [Am. Hist.: *NCE*, 1586]

22. **Macy's** prototype of the department store. [Am. Hist.: Van Doren, 217–218]

23. **Montgolfier brothers** (Joseph, 1740–1810) (Jaques, 1745–1799) first to make practical, manned balloon flight (1783). [Fr. Hist.: *NCE*, 1821]

24. **La Navidad** first European settlement in New World (1492). [Am. Hist.: Van Doren, 2]

25. **Oberlin College** first college to admit Negroes and to give women degrees. [Am. Hist.: Hart, 612]

26. **Robinson, Jackie** (1919–1972) professional American baseball player; first Negro to play in the major leagues. [Am. Sports: *NCE*, 2335]

27. **Steamboat Willie** first animated cartoon with sound (Disney). [Am. Cinema: Van Doren, 431]

28. **Tom Thumb** first American steam locomotive. [Am. Hist.: Van Doren, 141]

29. **Virginia** first of the Thirteen Colonies. [Am. Hist.: *NCE*, 289]

30. **Washington, George** (1732–1799) first United States president. [Am. Hist.: Hart, 897]

31. **Wright Brothers** (Wilbur, 1867–1912) (Orville, 1871–1948) made the first controlled, sustained flight in a power-driven airplane (1903). [Am. Hist.: *NCE*, 3012]

FLAMBOYANCE (See ELEGANCE.)

244. **FLATTERY**

1. **Adams, Jack** toady to his employer. [Br. Lit.: *Dombey and Son*]

2. **Amaziah** fawningly complains of Amos to King Jeroboam. [*O.T.: Amos* 7:10]

3. **bolton** one who flatters by pretending humility. [Br. Hist.: Espy, 343]

4. **Chanticleer** cajoled by fox into singing; thus captured. [Br. Lit.: *Canterbury Tales*, "Nun's Priest's Tale"]

5. **Chilo** informs Nero of Christian activity. [Polish Lit.: *Quo Vadis*, Magill, I, 797–799]

6. **Clumsy, Sir Tunbelly** toadies towards aristocracy. [Br. Lit.: *The Relapse*, Walsh *Modern*, 102]

7. **Collins, Mr.** priggish, servile clergyman; toady to the great. [Br. Lit.: *Pride and Prejudice*]

8. **Damocles** for his sycophancy to Dionysus, seated under sword at banquet. [Gk. Myth.: *LLEI*, I: 278]

9. **Mutual Admiration Society** circle of mutual patters on the backs. [Br. Hist.: Wheeler, 254]

10. **oreo** cookie; pejoratively refers to obsequious Black with white aspirations. [Am. Culture: Flexner, 49]

11. **Ruach** island of people sustained by insincere praise. [Fr. Lit.: *Pantagruel*]

12. **Tom, Uncle** Stowe character came to signify subservient Black. [Am. Lit.: *Uncle Tom's Cabin*]

13. **Wren, Jenny** wooed by Robin Redbreast with enticing presents. [Nurs. Rhyme: *Mother Goose*, 23]

245.   **FLIRTATIOUSNESS** (See also SEDUCTION.)

1.   **Boop, Betty** comic strip character who flirts to win over boys. [Comics: Horn, 110]

2.   **can-can** boisterous and indecorous French dance designed to arouse audiences. [Fr. Hist.: Scholes, 151]

3.   **Célimène** unabashed coquette wooed by Alceste. [Fr. Lit.: *The Misanthrope*]

4.   **Columbine** light-hearted, flirtatious girl. [Ital. Lit.: Walsh *Classical*, 83]

5.   **dandelion** traditional symbol of flirtation. [Flower Symbolism: Jobes, 413]

6.   **daylily** traditional symbol of flirtation. [Flower Symbolism: *Flora Symbolica*, 175]

7.   **fan** symbol of coquetry. [Folklore: Jobes, 370]

8.   **Frasquita** woman character chiefly remembered for her flirtatiousness toward old Don Eugenio. [Ger. Opera: Wolf, *The Magistrate*, Westerman, 262]

9.   **Habanera** Carmen's "love is a wild bird" provokes hearers. [Fr. Opera: Bizet, *Carmen*, Westerman, 189–190]

10.   **Jiménez, Pepita** young widow coquettishly distracts seminarian; love unfolds. [Span. Lit.: *Pepita Jiménez*]

11.   **Julie, Miss** young gentlewoman high-handedly engages servant's love. [Swed. Lit.: *Miss Julie* in *Plays by August Strindberg*]

12.   **Musetta** leads on Alcindoro while pursuing Marcello. [Ital. Opera: Puccini, *La Bohème*, Westerman, 349]

13.   **O'Hara, Scarlett** hot-tempered heroine-coquette who wooed Southern Gentlemen. [Am. Lit.: *Gone With The Wind*]

14.   **Varden, Dolly** Watteau-style colorful costume: broad-brimmed hat and dress with deep cleavage; honors Dickens character. [Br. Costume: Misc.; Br. Lit.: *Barnaby Rudge*, Espy, 272]

15.   **West, Mae** (1892–1980) actress personified as a vamp; known for her famous line, "Come up and see me some time." [Am. Cinema: Halliwell, 759]

246.   **FLOWER or PLANT, NATIONAL**

1.   **almond blossom** of Israel. [Flower Symbolism: *WB*, 7: 264]

2.   **blue anemone** of Norway. [Flower Symbolism: *WB*, 7: 264]

3.   **blue cornflower** of West Germany. [Flower Symbolism: *WB*, 7: 264]

4.   **cantua** of Bolivia. [Flower Symbolism: *WB*, 7: 264]

5.   **carnation** of Egypt and Spain. [Flower Symbolism: *WB*, 7: 264]

6.   cattleya of Brazil. [Flower Symbolism: *WB*, 7: 264]

7.   ceibo of Argentina. [Flower Symbolism: *WB*, 7: 264]

8.   chrysanthemum of Japan. [Flower Symbolism: *WB*, 7: 264]

9.   cinchona of Ecuador. [Flower Symbolism: *WB*, 7: 264]

10.   dahlia of Mexico. [Flower Symbolism: *WB*, 7: 264]

11.   edelweiss of Switzerland. [Flower Symbolism: Jobes, 490]

12.   fern of New Zealand. [Flower Symbolism: *WB*, 7: 264]

13.   flame lily of Rhodesia. [Flower Symbolism: *WB*, 7: 264]

14.   fleur-de-lis of France. [Flower Symbolism: Halberts, 28]

15.   frangipani of Laos. [Flower Symbolism: *WB*, 7: 264]

16.   golden wattle of Australia. [Flower Symbolism: *WB*, 7: 264]

17.   hibiscus of Malaysia. [Flower Symbolism: *WB*, 7: 264]

18.   jasmine (also rose) of Indonesia. [Flower Symbolism: *WB*, 7: 264]

19.   leek of Wales. [Flower Symbolism: Brewer *Note-Book*, 334]

20.   lily of then city-state Florence. [Flower Symbolism: Brewer *Note-Book*, 334]

21.   lily of the valley of Finland. [Flower Symbolism: *WB*, 7: 264]

22.   linden of former Prussia. [Flower Symbolism: Brewer *Note-Book*, 334]

23.   lotus of India. [Flower Symbolism: *WB*, 7: 264]

24.   maple leaf of Canada. [Flower Symbolism: Jobes, 283]

25.   mignonette of the former Saxony. [Flower Symbolism: Brewer *Note-Book*, 334]

26.   orchid of Venezuela. [Flower Symbolism: *WB*, 7: 264]

27.   poppy of Greece. [Flower Symbolism: *WB*, 7: 264]

28.   protea of South Africa. [Flower Symbolism: *WB*, 7: 264]

29.   red rose of England. [Flower Symbolism: Brewer *Note-Book*, 334]

30.   rhododendron of Nepal. [Flower Symbolism: *WB*, 7: 264]

31.   rose of Honduras. [Flower Symbolism: *WB*, 7: 264]

32.   sampaguita of Philippines. [Flower Symbolism: *WB*, 7: 264]

33.   shamrock of Ireland. [Flower Symbolism: Brewer *Note-Book*, 334]

34.   thistle of Scotland. [Flower Symbolism: Halberts, 38]

35.   tulip of Netherlands. [Flower Symbolism: *WB*, 7: 264]

36.   violet of then city-state Athens. [Flower Symbolism: Brewer *Note-Book*, 334]

37.   white orchid of Guatemala. [Flower Symbolism: *WB*, 7: 264]

247. FLOWERS

1. **Anthea** epithet of Hera, meaning "flowery." [Gk. Myth.: Zimmerman, 121]
2. **Anthesteria** ancient Athenian festival, celebrating flowers and new wine. [Gk. Hist.: Misc.]
3. **Chloris** goddess of flowers. [Gk. Myth.: Kravitz, 59]
4. **Zephyr and Flora** wedded pair, scatter flowers from cornucopia. [Rom. Myth.: Hall, 125]

248. FLOWER, STATE

1. **American pasque flower** of South Dakota. [Flower Symbolism: Golenpaul, 642]
2. **apple blossom** of Arkansas and Michigan. [Flower Symbolism: Golenpaul, 626]
3. **bitterroot** of Montana. [Flower Symbolism: Golenpaul, 636]
4. **black-eyed susan** of Maryland. [Flower Symbolism: Golenpaul, 633]
5. **bluebonnet** of Texas. [Flower Symbolism: Golenpaul, 643]
6. **camellia** of Alabama. [Flower Symbolism: Golenpaul, 625]
7. **Carolina yellow jessamine** of South Carolina. [Flower Symbolism: Golenpaul, 642]
8. **Cherokee rose** of Georgia. [Flower Symbolism: Golenpaul, 629]
9. **dogwood** of North Carolina and Virginia. [Flower Symbolism: Golenpaul, 639]
10. **flower of saguaro cactus** of Arizona. [Flower Symbolism: Golenpaul, 626]
11. **forget-me-not** of Alaska. [Flower Symbolism: Golenpaul, 625]
12. **golden poppy** of California. [Flower Symbolism: Golenpaul, 627]
13. **goldenrod** of Kentucky and Nebraska. [Flower Symbolism: Golenpaul, 632]
14. **hawthorn** of Missouri. [Flower Symbolism: Golenpaul, 635]
15. **hibiscus** of Hawaii. [Flower Symbolism: Golenpaul, 629]
16. **Indian paintbrush** of Wyoming. [Flower Symbolism: Golenpaul, 646]
17. **iris** of Tennessee. [Flower Symbolism: Golenpaul, 642]
18. **magnolia** of Louisiana and Mississippi. [Flower Symbolism: Golenpaul, 632]
19. **mayflower** of Massachusetts. [Flower Symbolism: Golenpaul, 633]
20. **mistletoe** of Oklahoma. [Flower Symbolism: Golenpaul, 640]

21. **mountain laurel** of Connecticut and Pennsylvania. [Flower Symbolism: Golenpaul, 628]

22. **orange blossom** of Florida. [Flower Symbolism: Golenpaul, 628]

23. **Oregon grape** of Oregon. [Flower Symbolism: Golenpaul, 640]

24. **peach blossom** of Delaware. [Flower Symbolism: Golenpaul, 628]

25. **peony** of Indiana. [Flower Symbolism: Golenpaul, 631]

26. **purple lilac** of New Hampshire. [Flower Symbolism: Golenpaul, 637]

27. **red clover** of Vermont. [Flower Symbolism: Golenpaul, 644]

28. **rhododendron** of Washington and West Virginia. [Flower Symbolism: Golenpaul, 644]

29. **Rocky Mountain columbine** of Colorado. [Flower Symbolism: Golenpaul, 627]

30. **rose** of New York. [Flower Symbolism: Golenpaul, 638]

31. **sagebrush** of Nevada. [Flower Symbolism: Golenpaul, 636]

32. **scarlet carnation** of Ohio. [Flower Symbolism: Golenpaul, 639]

33. **sego lily** of Utah. [Flower Symbolism: Golenpaul, 643]

34. **showy lady slipper** of Minnesota. [Flower Symbolism: Golenpaul, 634]

35. **sunflower** of Kansas. [Flower Symbolism: Golenpaul, 631]

36. **syringa** of Idaho. [Flower Symbolism: Golenpaul, 630]

37. **violet** of Illinois, New Jersey, Rhode Island, and Wisconsin. [Flower Symbolism: Golenpaul, 630]

38. **white pine cone and tassel** of Maine. [Flower Symbolism: Golenpaul, 633]

39. **wild prairie rose** of North Dakota. [Flower Symbolism: Golenpaul, 639]

40. **wild rose** of Iowa. [Flower Symbolism: Golenpaul, 631]

41. **yucca** of New Mexico. [Flower Symbolism: Golenpaul, 638]

249. FLYING

1. **Daedalus** flew with wings of wax and feathers. [Gk. Myth.: Bulfinch]

2. **Dolor** possesses magic cloak which permits flight. [Children's Lit.: *The Little Lame Prince*]

3. **Dumbo** little elephant's huge ears take him up and away. [Am. Cinema: *Dumbo* in *Disney Films*, 49–53]

4. **Houssain** rode upon magic carpet that could fly. [Arab. Lit.: *Arabian Nights*, "Ahmed and Paribanou"]

5. **Icarus** Daedalus's son whose wings disintegrated inflight when approaching the sun. [Gk. Myth.: Kravitz, 126]

6. **Pegasus** winged horse. [Class. Myth.: Zimmerman, 195]

7. **Phaëthon** ill-fated driver of the chariot of sun. [Gk. Myth.: *Metamorphoses*]

250. FOLLY

1. **Abu Jahl** "father of folly"; opposes Mohammed. [Muslim Tradition: *Koran* 22:8]

2. **Alnaschar's daydream** spends profits before selling his goods. [Arab. Lit.: *Arabian Nights*, "The Barber's Fifth Night"]

3. **Le Bateau** Matisse's famous painting, displayed in the Museum of Modern Art for 47 days before someone discovered it was being shown upside down. [Am. Hist.: Wallechinsky, 472]

4. **the Bay of Pigs** disastrous U.S.-backed invasion of Cuba (1961). [Am. Hist.: Van Doren, 577]

5. **columbine** traditional symbol of folly. [Plant Symbolism: *Flora Symbolica*, 173]

6. **dog returning to his vomit** and so the fool to his foolishness. [*O.T.: Proverbs* 26:11]

7. **Fulton's Folly** the first profitable steamship, originally considered a failure. [Am. Hist.: *NCE*, 1025]

8. **Grand, Joseph** spends years writing novel; only finishes first sentence. [Fr. Lit.: *The Plague*]

9. **Hamburger Hill** bloody Viet Nam battle over strategically worthless objective (1969). [Am. Hist.: Van Doren, 631]

10. **Howard Hotel** after completing construction, the contractors installed boilers and started fires before discovering they had forgotten to build a chimney. [Am. Hist.: Wallechinsky, 470]

11. **Laputa and Lagada** lands where wise men conduct themselves inanely. [Br. Lit.: *Gulliver's Travels*]

12. **Seward's Folly** Alaska, once seemingly valueless territory which William Henry Seward bought for two cents an acre (1867), thirty years before the Klondike gold rush. [Am. Hist.: Payton, 610]

FOOLISHNESS (See DIMWITTEDNESS, STUPIDITY.)

251. FOPPISHNESS

1. **Acres, Bob** affected, vain, cowardly, blustery country gentleman. [Br. Lit.: *The Rivals*]

2. **Aguecheek, Sir Andrew** silly old fop, believes himself young. [Br. Lit.: *Twelfth Night*]

3. **Blakeney, Percy** rescuer of French revolution victims disguises himself as brainless fop. [Br. Lit.: *Scarlet Pimpernel*]

4. **Brummel, Beau** (George B. Brummel, 1778–1840) "prince of dandies." [Br. Hist.: *Century Cyclopedia*, 682]

5. **Flutter, Sir Fopling** witless dandy. [Br. Lit.: *The Man of Mode*]

6. **Foppington, Lord** a selfish coxcomb, most intent upon dress and fashion. [Br. Hist.: Brewer *Handbook*, 381]

7. **Kookie** teen idol of 1950s whose character was depicted by slick shirts, tight pants, and "wet look" hairstyle. [TV: "77 Sunset Strip" in Terrace, II, 282–283]

8. **Malyneaux** epitome of the British dandy. [Am. Lit.: *Monsieur Beaucaire*, Magill, I, 616–617]

9. **Yankee Doodle Dandy** feather-capped dandy; "handy" with the girls. [Nurs. Rhyme: Opie, 439]

252. FORGERY (See also FRAUDULENCE.)

1. **Acta Pilati** (Acts of Pilate) apocryphal account of Crucifixion. [Rom. Hist.: Brewer *Note-Book*, 7]

2. **Altamont, Col. Jack** convicted of forgery; sentenced to transportation; escapes. [Br. Lit.: *Pendennis*]

3. **Book of Mormon** golden plates revealed to Joseph Smith (1805–1844) by angel Mormon. [Am. Hist.: Brewer *Handbook*, 385]

4. **Chatterton** boy poet produced poems allegedly by 15th-century monk. [Br. Hist.: Brewer *Note-Book*, 164]

5. **Constitutum Constantini** so-called Donation of Constantine, a document in which Constantine gave Rome authority over his capital at least a decade before his capital was founded. [Rom. Hist.: Wallechinsky, 45]

6. **Mr. X** by definition, the identity of the greatest forger of all time. [Pop. Culture: Wallechinsky, 47]

7. **Piltdown man** missing link turned out to be orangutan. [Br. Hist.: Wallechinsky, 46; *Time*, October 13, 1978, 82]

253. FORGETFULNESS (See also CARELESSNESS.)

1. **Absent-Minded Beggars, The** ballad of forgetful soldiers who fought in the Boer War. [Br. Lit.: "The Absent-Minded Beggars" in Payton, 3]

2. **absent-minded professor** personification of one too contemplative to execute practical tasks. [Pop. Culture: Misc.]

3. **jujube** causes loss of memory and desire to return home. [Classical Myth.: Leach, 561–562]

4. **Lethe** river of Hades which induced forgetfulness. [Gk. Myth.: Brewer *Dictionary*, 687; Br. Lit.: *Paradise Lost*; Rom. Lit.: *Aeneid*]

5. **limbo** place or condition of neglect and inattention (from Dante). [Western Folklore: Espy, 124]

6. **Lotophagi** African people, eaters of an amnesia-inducing fruit. [Gk. Lit.: *Odyssey*; Br. Lit.: "The Lotus-Eaters" in Norton, 733 –736]

7. **Madison, Percival Wemys** character who no longer remembers his name. [Br. Lit.: *Lord of the Flies*]

8. **soma** drug that induces forgetfulness. [Br. Lit.: *Brave New World*]

9. **Winkle, Rip Van** character who continually forgets how things have changed. [Am. Lit.: *Sketch Book*, Payton, 574]

254. FORGIVENESS

1. **Angelica, Suor** is forgiven by the Virgin Mary for ill-considered suicide. [Ital. Opera: Puccini, *Suor Angelica*, Westerman, 364]

2. **Bishop of Digne** character who forgives Jean Valjean when latter steals the bishop's valuables. [Fr. Lit.: *Les Misérables*]

3. **Christ** forgives man for his sins. [Christianity: Misc.]

4. **fatted calf** killed to celebrate return of prodigal son. [*N.T.: Luke* 15:23]

5. **Matthias** of his brother, for twenty years' false imprisonment. [Ger. Opera: Kienzl, *The Evangelist*, Westerman, 264]

6. **Melibee** shepherd who pardons his enemies. [Br. Lit.: *Canterbury Tales*, "Tale of Melibee"]

7. **Porgy** of Bess's promiscuity with Crown. [Am. Opera: Gershwin, *Porgy and Bess*, Westerman, 555]

8. **prodigal son** received with open arms by forbearing father. [*N.T.: Luke* 15:20–21]

9. **Timberlane, Cass** receives Jinny after her extramarital venture. [Am. Lit.: *Cass Timberlane*]

10. **Titus** Roman emperor pardons those attempting his destruction. [Ger. Opera: Mozart, *La Clemenza di Tito*, Westerman, 100–101]

255. FORTITUDE (See also BRAVERY.)

1. **Asia** despite torture, refuses to deny Moses. [Islam: Walsh *Classical*, 35]

2. **Calantha** fulfills wifely and queenly duties despite losses. [Br. Lit.: *The Broken Heart*]

3. **Corey, Giles** martyred without flinching. [Am. Lit.: *New England Tragedies*, Walsh *Modern*, 106]

4. **helmeted warrior** representation in painting of cardinal virtue. [Art: Hall, 127]

5. **lion** personification of intrepidity. [Animal Symbolism: Hall, 193]

6. **Valley Forge** proving ground of American mettle. [Am. Hist.: Jameson, 519]

FRATRICIDE (See MURDER.)

256. **FRAUDULENCE (See also FORGERY.)**

1. **Cagliostro** lecherous peasant posing as count. [Ital. Hist.: Espy, 335]

2. **Gantry, Elmer** personifies hypocrisy and corruption in America's religious practices. [Am. Lit.: *Elmer Gantry*]

3. **the Mississippi Bubble** land speculation scam; ultimately backfired on creators. [Am. Hist.: Jameson, 326]

4. **Sabbatai Zevi** false messiah, head of Kabbalic movement in mid-1600s. [Jew. Hist.: Wigoder, 544]

5. **wooden nickel** cheap counterfeits circulating in 1850s America. [Am. Hist.: Brewer *Dictionary*, 1164]

6. **wooden nutmeg** sold by dishonest Connecticut peddlers as real thing. [Am. Hist.: Brewer *Dictionary*, 1164]

257. **FREEDOM (See also DELIVERANCE.)**

1. **Areopagitica** pamphlet supporting freedom of the press. [Br. Lit.: Benét, 46]

2. **Berihah** 1940s underground railroad for Jews out of East Europe. [Jew. Hist.: Wigoder, 80]

3. **Bill of Rights** (1791) term popularly applied to first 10 Amendments of U.S. Constitution. [Am. Hist.: Payton, 78]

4. **Declaration of Human Rights** (1948) declaration passed by the United Nations; the rights are the individual freedoms usually associated with Western democracy. [World Hist.: Payton, 186]

5. **Declaration of Independence** (1776) document declaring the independence of the North American colonies. [Am. Hist.: Payton, 186]

6. **Declaration of Indulgence** (1672) Charles II's attempt to suspend discrimination against Nonconformists and Catholics. [Br. Hist.: Payton, 186]

7. **Declaration of the Rights of Man** (1789) proclaimed legal equality of man. [Fr. Hist.: Payton, 186]

8. **eagle** widely used as national symbol. [Animal Folklore: Jobes, 213]

9. **Eleutherius** epithet of Zeus, meaning "god of freedom." [Gk. Myth.: Zimmerman, 292]

10. **Fourth of July** American independence day. [Am. Culture: Misc.]

11. **Go Tell It On The Mountain** message of love and release from bondage. [Am. Music: Misc.]

12. **Great Emancipator, The** sobriquet of Abraham Lincoln. [Am. Hist.: Hart, 329]

13. **Henry, Patrick** (1736–1799) famous American patriot known for his statement: "Give me liberty or give me death." [Am. Hist.: Hart, 367]

14. **Jubilee year** fiftieth year; liberty proclaimed for all inhabitants. [*O.T.: Leviticus* 25:8–13]

15. **Magna Charta** symbol of British liberty. [Br. Hist.: Bishop, 49–52, 213]

16. **Monroe Doctrine** consolidated South American independence; stonewalled European intervention. [Am. Hist.: Jameson, 329–330]

17. **Phrygian cap** presented to slaves upon manumission. [Rom. Hist.: Jobes, 287]

18. **Rienzi** liberator of Rome from warring Colonna and Orsini families. [Ger. Opera: Wagner, *Rienzi*, Westerman, 203]

19. **Runnymede** site of Magna Charta signing (1215). [Br. Hist.: Bishop, 49–52, 213]

20. **Rütli Oath** legendary pact establishing independence of Swiss cantons (1307). [Swiss Hist.: *NCE*, 2384]

21. **Statue of Liberty** perhaps the most famous monument to independence. [Am. Hist.: Jameson, 284]

22. **Underground Railroad** effective means of escape for southern slaves. [Am. Hist.: Jameson, 514]

23. **water willow** indicates independence. [Flower Symbolism: *Flora Symbolica*, 178]

258. **FRENZY**

1. **Beatlemania** term referring to the Beatles' (rock musicians) immense popularity; manifested by screaming fans in the 1960s. [Pop. Culture: Miller, 172–181]

2. **Big Bull Market** speculation craze precipitated stock market crash (1929). [Am. Hist.: Allen, 205–226]

3. **Gold Rush** lure of instant riches precipitated onslaught of prospectors (1848, 1886). [Am. Hist.: Jameson, 203]

4. **the Klondike** scene of wild rush for riches (1886). [Am. Hist.: Jameson, 269]

5. **Old Woman of Surrey** "morn, noon, and night in a hurry." [Nurs. Rhyme: *Mother Goose*, 117]

6. **Valentino's funeral** overwhelmed with grief, fans rioted. [Am. Hist.: Sann, 317–327]

7. **White Queen** in a perpetual dither. [Br. Lit.: *Through the Looking-glass*]

8. **White Rabbit** agitated rabbit in a perpetual hurry. [Br. Lit.: *Alice's Adventures in Wonderland*]

259. **FRIENDSHIP** (See also **LOYALTY.**)

1. **acacia** traditional symbol of friendship. [Flower Symbolism: *Flora Symbolica*, 172]

2. **Achilles and Patroclus** beloved friends and constant companions, especially during the Trojan War. [Gk. Myth.: Zimmerman, 194]

3. **Amos and Andy** dim-witted Andy Brown and level-headed partner Amos Jones, owners of the Fresh Air Taxi Cab Company. [Radio and TV: "The Amos and Andy Show" in Terrace, I, 54]

4. **Amys and Amylion** the Pylades and Orestes of the feudal ages. [Medieval Lit.: *LLEI*, I: 269]

5. **Biddy and Pip** "friends for life." [Br. Lit.: *Great Expectations*]

6. **Castor and Pollux** twin brothers who lived and died together. [Gk. Myth.: Zimmerman, 52]

7. **Chingachgook and Natty Bumppo** Chingachgook as Natty Bumppo's constant sidekick and advisor. [Am. Lit.: *The Pathfinder*, Magill, I, 715–717]

8. **Damon and Pythias** Damon agreed to die for his friend. [Gk. Hist.: Espy, 48]

9. **Diomedes and Sthenelus** Sthenelus was the companion and charioteer of Diomedes. [Gk. Myth.: Zimmerman, 248]

10. **Fannie and Edmund Bertram** while others ignored Fannie, he comforted her. [Br. Lit.: *Mansfield Park*, Magill, I, 562–564]

11. **Fred and Ethel** the Ricardos' true-blue pals. [TV: "I Love Lucy" in Terrace, I, 383–384]

12. **Friday and Robinson Crusoe** Friday was Robinson Crusoe's sole companion on desert island. [Br. Lit.: *Robinson Crusoe*]

13. **ivy leaves** symbolic of strong and lasting companionship. [Heraldry: Halberts, 31]

14. **Jane Frances de Chantal and Francis de Sales, Sts.** two of most celebrated in Christian annals. [Christian Hagiog.: Attwater, 183]

15. **Jonathan and David** swore compact of love and mutual protection. [*O.T.: I Samuel* 18:1–3; 20:17]

16. **Lightfoot, Martin and Hereward** Hereward's companion during various wanderings. [Br. Lit.: *Hereward the Wake*, Magill, I, 367–370]

17. **Marlow and Lord Jim** Marlow makes many efforts to help Jim. [Brit. Lit.: *Lord Jim*]

18. **Nisus and Euryalus** fought bravely together; Nisus dies rescuing Euryalus. [Rom. Hist.: Wheeler, 259; Rom. Lit.: *Aeneid*]

19. **Peggotty, Clara, and David Copperfield** lifelong friends. [Br. Lit.: *David Copperfield*]

20. **Petronius and Nero** Petronius as nobleman and intimate friend of Nero. [Polish Lit.: *Quo Vadis*, Magill, I, 797–799]

21. **Philadelphia** nicknamed "City of Brotherly Love." [Am. Hist.: *NCE*, 2127]

22. **Pylades and Orestes** Pylades willing to sacrifice life for Orestes. [Gk. Lit.: *Oresteia*, Kitto, 68–90]

23. **Rosencrantz and Guildenstern** two obsequious hypocritical courtiers in Denmark. [Br. Lit.: *Hamlet*]

24. **Standish, Miles and John Alden** best friends, despite their love for Priscilla. [Am. Lit.: "The Courtship of Miles Standish" in Magill, I, 165–166]

25. **Theseus and Pirithoüs** Pirithoüs, King of Lapithae, was intimate friend of Theseus, Athenian hero. [Gk. Myth.: Zimmerman, 195]

26. **Three Musketeers, The** three comrades known by motto, "All for one, and one for all." [Fr. Lit.: *The Three Musketeers*]

27. **Tiberge and the Chevalier** Tiberge as ever-assisting shadow of the chevalier. [Fr. Lit.: *Manon Lescaut*]

28. **Wilbur and Charlotte** spider and pig as loyal companions. [Children's Lit.: *Charlotte's Web*]

260.   FRIVOLITY

1. **Blondie** the gaffe-prone, frivolous wife of Dagwood Bumstead. [Comics: Horn, 118]

2. **grasshopper** sings instead of storing away food. [Animal Symbolism: Mercatante, 108]

3. **Lescaut, Manon** amorally chooses luxury above loyalty. [Ital. Opera: Puccini, *Manon Lescaut*, Westerman, 346]

4. **Merry Mount** colonists frolick around Maypole, causing Morton's arrest. [Am. Hist.: Hart, 543]

5. **Misanthrope** exposes frivolity and inconsistency of French society (1600s). [Fr. Lit.: *Le Misanthrope*]

6. **Nickleby, Mrs.** forever introducing inapposite topics into conversations. [Br. Lit.: *Nicholas Nickleby*]

261. FRONTIER

1. **Boone, Daniel** (1734–1820) American frontiersman in coonskin cap. [Am. Hist.: Hart, 90]

2. **Bowie, Jim** (1799–1836) frontiersman and U.S. soldier; developed large hunting knife named after him. [Am. Hist.: Payton, 95]

3. **Bumppo, Natty** also known as Leatherstocking, a tough backwoodsman. [Am. Lit.: *Deerslayer; Pathfinder*]

4. **California Joe** (Moses Embree Milner, 1829–1876) frontiersman and scout. [Am. Hist.: *NCE*, 424]

262. FRUSTRATION (See also EXASPERATION.)

1. **Angstrom, Harry "Rabbit"** former basketball star frustrated by demands of adult life. [Am. Lit.: *Rabbit, Run*, Magill, IV, 1042–1044]

2. **Barataria** dishes removed before Sancho tasted them. [Span. Lit.: *Don Quixote*]

3. **Bundren, Addie** family continually thwarted in 9-day attempt to bury her. [Am. Lit.: *As I Lay Dying*]

4. **coyote** foiled in attempts to enjoy prey. [Am. Ind. Folklore: Mercatante, 77–78]

5. **Henderson the Rain King** character's frustration shown by his continually saying, "I want, I want." [Am. Lit.: *Henderson the Rain King*]

6. **K.** continually hindered from gaining entrance to mysterious castle. [Ger. Lit.: *The Castle*]

7. **Old Mother Hubbard** foiled at all attempts to care for dog. [Nurs. Rhyme: Baring-Gould, 111–113]

8. **Raven, The** answer for quests of longing: "Nevermore." [Am. Lit.: "The Raven" in Hart, 656]

9. **Sharpless** frustrated in attempt to prepare Cio-Cio-San for disappointment. [Ital. Opera: Puccini, *Madame Butterfly*, Westerman, 358]

10. **Sisyphus** man condemned to roll up a hill a huge stone which always rolls back before he gets it to the top. [Gk. Myth.: Brewer *Dictionary*, 1006]

11. **Tantalus** condemned in Hades to thirst after receding water. [Gk. Myth.: Brewer *Dictionary*, 1062]

12. **Watty, Mr.** bankrupt; waits years for court action. [Br. Lit.: *Pickwick Papers*]

263. FUTILITY (See also DESPAIR.)

1. **American Scene, The** portrays Americans as having secured necessities; now looking for amenities. [Am. Lit.: *The American Scene*]

2. **Babio** performs the useless and supererogatory. [Fr. Folklore: Walsh *Classical*, 42]

3. **Bellamy, James** character who goes through phases "playboy, war hero" to suicide. [Br. TV: *Upstairs, Downstairs*]

4. **Danaides** fifty daughters, forty-nine of whom are condemned to Hades to collect water in sieves. [Rom. Myth.: *LLEI*, I: 326]

5. **Fall, The** tale of the monotonous life and indifference of modern man. [Fr. Lit.: *The Fall*]

6. **Grandet, Eugénie** lacking everything but wealth, she is indifferent to life. [Fr. Lit.: *Eugénie Grandet*, Magill, I, 258–260]

7. **Henry, Frederic** loses lover and child; nothing left. [Am. Lit.: *A Farewell to Arms*]

8. **Ocnus, the rope of** eaten by ass as quickly as it is made. [Gk. and Rom. Myth.: Wheeler, 767]

9. **Of Mice and Men** story of George Milton and Lennie Small's futile dream of having their own farm. [Am. Lit.: *Of Mice and Men*]

10. **Partington, Dame** tried to turn back tide with mop. [Br. Hist.: Brewer *Dictionary*, 807]

11. **pearls before swine** Jesus adjures one not to waste best efforts. [*N.T.*: *Matthew* 7:6]

12. **Pocket, Belinda** brought up chiefly to be highly ornamental. [Br. Lit.: *Great Expectations*]

13. **Sun Also Rises, The** story of American expatriots living a futile existence in Europe. [Am. Lit.: *The Sun Also Rises*]

14. **Tobacco Road** tale of Jeeter Lester and other oppressed, degraded lives. [Am. Lit.: *Tobacco Road*]

15. **Tregeagle** condemned to bail out Dozmary Pool with leaky shell. [Br. Legend: Brewer *Dictionary*, 1099]

G

264. **GAIETY** (See also **CHEERFULNESS, JOVIALITY.**)

1. **butterfly orchis** symbol of gaiety. [Plant Symbolism: *Flora Symbolica*, 172]

2. **Gay 90s** the 1890s, a decade of carefree and exciting days in America. [Am. Hist.: Flexner, 162]

3. **Mardi Gras** festive day celebrated at the close of the pre-Lenten season in France and in New Orleans. [Fr. and Am. Trad.: *EB*, VI, 608]

4. **the Roaring Twenties** the 1920s decade of the Jazz Age and the boom years before the depression. [Am. Hist.: Payton, 515]

5. **shamrock** indicates light-heartedness. [Flower Symbolism: *Flora Symbolica*, 177]

GALLANTRY (See **CHIVALRY.**)

265. **GAMBLING**

1. **Atlantic City** New Jersey city is quickly becoming the Las Vegas of the East. [Am. Hist.: Misc.]

2. **Balibari, Chevalier de** professional gambler and adventurer. [Br. Lit.: *Barry Lyndon*]

3. **Beaujeu, Monsieur de** known for his betting. [Br. Lit.: *Fortunes of Nigel*]

4. **Bet-a-million Gates** wealthy American industrialist John Warne Gates (1855–1911). [Am. Culture: Misc.]

5. **Brady, "Diamond Jim"** (1856–1917) diamond-attired rail magnate and financier who loved to gamble. [Am. Hist.: Payton, 192]

6. **Camptown Races** Foster's ode to betting. [Pop. Music: Van Doren, 192]

7. **the Cincinnati Kid** "one of the shrewdist gamblers east of the Mississippi." [Cinema: Halliwell, 462]

8. **Clonbrony, Lord** absentee landlord is compulsive gambler. [Br. Lit.: *The Absentee*]

9. **Consus** ancient Roman god of horse-racing and counsel. [Rom. Myth.: Zimmerman, 68]

10. **devil's bones** epithet for dice. [Folklore: Jobes, 436]

11. **Google, Barney** hopelessly in love with the ponies. [Comics: Horn, 99–100]

12. **Ivanovich, Alexei** irrevocably drawn to betting tables. [Russ. Lit.: *The Gambler*]

13. **Las Vegas** city in Nevada notorious for its gambling casinos since 1945. [Am. Hist.: Payton, 382]

14. **Lucky, Mr.** alias Joe Adams, gambler who owns the *Fortuna*, fancy supper club and gambling yacht. [TV: Terrace, II, 117]

15. **Maverick** family name of two brothers, Bret and Bart; self-centered and untrustworthy gentlemen gamblers. [TV: Terrace, II, 80]

16. **Minnie** plays poker to save Jack Johnson's life. [Ital. Opera: Puccini, *Girl of the Golden West*, Westerman, 361]

17. **Monte Carlo** town in Monaco principality, in southeast France; a famous gambling resort. [Fr. Hist.: *NCE*, 1819]

18. **Mutt and Jeff** hapless punters always looking for a quick buck. [Comics: Horn, 508–509]

19. **the Pit** Board of Trade's cellar, where all bidding occurs. [Am. Lit.: *The Pit*. Magill, I, 756–758]

20. **Queen of Spades, The** Aleksandr Pushkin's short story about the downfall of the gambler Germann. [Russ. Lit.: Benét, 833]

21. **Smiley, Jim** bets his frog can outjump any other; loses by sabotage. [Am. Lit.: *The Celebrated Jumping Frog of Calaveras County*]

266. **GANGSTERISM (See also OUTLAWRY.)**

    1. **the Black Hand** sobriquet for the Mafia. [Am. Hist.: *NCE*, 1657]

    2. **Capone, Al "Scarface"** (1899–1947) Chicago mobster, famous gangland bootleg king. [Am. Hist.: Flexner, 73]

    3. **Cosa Nostra** secret organization akin to the Mafia; operates in the U.S. [Am. Hist.: Misc.]

    4. **Detroit Purple Gang** gangster mob of the 1920s. [Am. Hist.: *NCE*, 2018]

    5. **Krik, Benya** tough Jewish gangster of Odessa. [Russ. Lit.: *Benya Krik, the Gangster*]

    6. **Godfather** "father figure" to the Mafia. [Am. Lit.: *The Godfather;* Am. Cinema: Halliwell, 297]

    7. **Little Caesar** archetypal gangster. [Am. Cinema: Griffith, 269]

    8. **Mafia** sinister crime syndicate promotes violence to achieve goals. [Am. Hist.: *NCE*, 1657]

    9. **Syndicate** organized crime unit throughout major cities of the United States. [Am. Hist.: *NCE*, 2018]

267. **GENEROSITY** (See also AID, ORGANIZATIONAL; KINDNESS.)

1. **Abbé Constantin** self-sacrificing priest; curé of Longueral. [Fr. Lit.: *The Abbé Constantin,* Walsh *Modern,* 105]

2. **Amelia** takes interest in Paul. [Br. Lit.: *Dombey and Son*]

3. **Antonio** lends money gratis. [Br. Lit.: *Merchant of Venice*]

4. **Appleseed, Johnny** (John Chapman, 1774–1845) gave settlers apple seeds and a helping hand. [Am. Hist.: Hart, 146]

5. **Baboushka** female Santa Claus on Feast of Epiphany. [Russ. Folklore: Walsh *Classical,* 50]

6. **Befana** female Santa Claus who comes at Epiphany. [Ital. Legend: Walsh *Classical,* 50]

7. **Bountiful, Lady** benevolent, beneficent, but a bit overbearing. [Br. Lit.: *Beaux' Stratagem,* Espy, 129]

8. **buffalo** heraldic symbol of unselfishness. [Heraldry: Halberts, 21]

9. **bull** heraldic symbol of magnanimity. [Heraldry: Halberts, 21]

10. **Burchell, Mr.** gave to the poor. [Br. Lit.: *Vicar of Wakefield*]

11. **Cinderella** feeds beggar whom sisters scorn. [Ital. Opera: Rossini, *Cinderella,* Westerman, 120–121]

12. **Dāna** almsgiving to poor, giftgiving to priests. [Hindu Rel.: Parrinder, 72]

13. **Ephron** tried unsuccessfully to give Abraham free burial-ground. [O.T.: *Genesis* 23:10–16]

14. **Hood, Robin** robbed rich to help poor. [Br. Lit.: *Robin Hood*]

15. **Maecenas** to poets, esp. Virgil, as a patron. [Rom. Hist.: Espy, 123]

16. **Nicholas, St.** bringer of presents to children on Christmas. [Folklore: Wheeler, 327]

17. **Rosie** could not deny love to anyone. [Am. Lit.: *Cakes and Ale*]

18. **Salvation Army** (officially called Volunteers of America) organization devoted to helping unfortunates. [Am. Hist.: Jameson, 443]

19. **Santa Claus** gives gifts to children on Christmas. [Folklore: Walsh *Classical,* 50]

20. **Trot, Tommy** sold bed to buy wife a mirror. [Nurs. Rhyme: Opie, 416]

21. **Twelve Days of Christmas** presents increase with each day of Yuletide. [Am. Music: "Twelve Days of Christmas" in Rockwell]

22. **Twm Shon Catti** Welsh Robin Hood. [Welsh Hist.: Brewer *Dictionary*, 1110]

23. **Unferth** offers Beowulf finest sword in kingdom. [Br. Lit.: *Beowulf*]

24. **Vincent de Paul, St.** worked and gave prodigiously of himself to poor. [Christian Hagiog.: Attwater, 337]

25. **widow's mite** poor woman's contribution of all she had. [*N.T.*: *Mark*, 12: 42–44; *Luke* 21:2–4]

268. **GENIUS (See also WISDOM.)**

1. **Aquinas, St. Thomas** (1225–1274) preeminent mind of medieval church. [Eur. Hist.: Bishop, 273–274]

2. **Aristotle** (384–322 B.C.) famous Greek philosopher of *a priori* reasoning. [Gk. Hist.: NCE, 147]

3. **Aronnax, Prof.** scholarly mental giant; Capt. Nemo's captive guest. [Fr. Lit.: *Twenty Thousand Leagues Under the Sea*]

4. **Nemo, Captain** epitome of the genius in science fiction; inventor and creator of fabulous submarine, *Nautilus*. [Fr. Lit.: *Twenty Thousand Leagues Under the Sea*]

269. **GENOCIDE (See also BRUTALITY, MASSACRE.)**

1. **Auschwitz** largest, most efficient Nazi extermination camp. [Ger. Hist.: *Hitler*, 958–959, 970, 1123]

2. **Babi Yar** ravine near Kiev where Nazis slaughtered 10,000 Jews. [Russ. Hist.: Wigoder, 56]

3. **Bergen-Belsen** Nazi slave labor and extermination camp. [Ger. Hist.: *Hitler*, 1187, 1188]

4. **Buchenwald** showcase of Nazi atrocities. [Ger. Hist.: *Hitler*, 1055]

5. **Dachau** primarily work camp, experienced share of Nazi horrors. [Ger. Hist.: *Hitler*, 1055]

6. **Final Solution** Nazi plan decided fate of 6,000,000 Jews. [Ger. Hist.: *Hitler*, 1037–1061]

7. **Holocaust** extermination of European Jewry (1933–1945). [Jew. Hist.: Wigoder, 266–267]

8. **Lublin** Nazi extermination camp. [Ger. Hist.: *Hitler*, 970]

9. **Majdanek** Nazi extermination camp. [Ger. Hist.: Wigoder, 113]

10. **My Lai** American army division annihilates population of entire Vietnamese hamlet (March 16, 1968). [Am. Hist.: Kane, 450]

11. **Ravensbrueck** women's concentration camp in Poland. [Ger. Hist.: Shirer, 1275]

12. **Sachsenhausen** Nazi concentration camp. [Ger. Hist.: Shirer, 375]

13. **Six Million Jews** testimony to efficacy and atrocity of Final Solution. [Eur. Hist.: *Hitler*, 1123]

14. **Treblinka** Nazi extermination camp. [Ger. Hist.: *Hitler*, 970]

15. **Wannsee Conference** "Final Solution" plotted and scheduled. [Ger. Hist.: Wigoder, 619]

16. **Zyklon B** hydrogen cyanide; valued by Nazis for its killing efficiency. [Ger. Hist.: *Hitler*, 970]

270. **GENTLENESS**

1. **Brown, Matilda** meek, mild heroine. [Br. Lit.: *Cranford*]

2. **Casper the Friendly Ghost** meek little ghost who desires only to make friends. [Comics: Horn, 162]

3. **Cordelia** gentle daughter of Lear. [Br. Lit.: *King Lear*]

4. **Eliante** her kind heart contrasted with Celimene's caustic wit. [Fr. Lit.: *Le Misanthrope*]

5. **Gentle Ben** massive but extremely tame bear. [TV: Terrace, I, 302]

6. **mallow** traditional symbol of gentleness or mildness. [Plant Symbolism: *Flora Symbolica*, 175]

7. **March, Beth** the domestic, sensitive, sweater-knitting March daughter. [Am. Lit.: *Little Women*]

8. **Virgilia** meek, gentle wife of Coriolanus. [Br. Lit.: *Coriolanus*]

9. **Wilkes, Melanie** gentle, mild-mannered, dutiful Southern wife. [Am. Lit.: *Gone With the Wind*]

271. **GENUINENESS**

1. **acid test** test of genuineness for gold; not destructive of genuine metal. [Assaying: Brewer *Dictionary*, 7]

2. **Bible** name used by Christians for their Scriptures; "the real source of truth." [Christianity: *NCE*, 291]

3. **Gospel** one of the four biographies of Jesus Christ that begin the New Testament; thus, "the real beginning of Christianity." [Christianity: *NCE*, 1112]

4. **Pure, Simon** young quaker who Colonel Feignwell impersonates to marry Pure's ward. [Am. Lit.: *A Bold Stroke for a Wife*, Brewer *Handbook*, 1008]

5. **the Real McCoy** probably originally McKay, a Scotch whisky; the term now alludes to the "first or best of its kind" or "the actual one." [Pop. Culture: Payton, 409]

6. **To Tell the Truth** question-and-answer probe to determine which of three people is the "the real McCoy." [TV: Terrace, II, 383]

272. **GHOST**

1. **Alonzo the Brave** appears as ghost to lover. [Br. Lit.: "Alonzo the Brave" in Walsh *Modern*, 14]

2. **the Angels of Mons** a spectral army of angels that supposedly came between German and British forces (1914). [Br. and Fr. Hist.: Wallechinsky, 447]

3. **Bhta** haunter of cemeteries; attendant of Shiva. [Hindu Myth.: Parrinder, 45]

4. **Casper** meek little ghost who desires only to make friends. [Am. Comics: "Casper the Friendly Ghost" in Horn, 162]

5. **Drury Lane Theater Ghost** said to bring great acting success to those who see it. [Br. Folklore: Wallechinsky, 446]

6. **Epworth Poltergeist** supposedly invaded the house of Rev. Samuel Wesley. [Am. Folklore: Wallechinsky, 446]

7. **Flying Dutchman** ghost ship purportedly sailed off Cape of Good Hope. [Folklore: Brewer *Note-Book*, 335]

8. **the Ghost of Charles Rosmer** itinerant peddler returns to the property where he was murdered. [Folklore: Wallechinsky, 446]

9. **the Ghost of Christmas Past** Scrooge's first monitor; spirit presenting past. [Br. Lit.: *A Christmas Carol*]

10. **the Ghost of Christmas Present** Scrooge's second monitor; spirit presenting present. [Br. Lit.: *A Christmas Carol*]

11. **the Ghost of Christmas Yet to Come** Scrooge's third monitor; spirit presenting future. [Br. Lit.: *A Christmas Carol*]

12. **the Ghost of Hamlet's Father** appears to the prince, states he was murdered by Claudius and demands revenge. [Br. Lit.: *Hamlet*]

13. **the Ghost's Walk** spirit and step of Lady Morbury Dedlock. [Br. Lit.: *Bleak House*]

14. **Glas, Bodach** ghostly bearer of evil tidings. [Br. Lit.: *Waverley*]

15. **the Headless Horseman** phantom who scares Ichabod Crane out of his wits. [Am. Lit.: *The Legend of Sleepy Hollow and Other Stories*]

16. **Homunculus** formless spirit of learning. [Ger. Lit.: *Faust*]

17. **Kirby, George and Marian** ghosts who occupy Topper's house. [TV: "Topper" in Terrace II, 381]

18. **Marley** the friendly ghost who helps Ebenezer Scrooge become more benevolent. [Br. Lit.: *A Christmas Carol*]

19. **Nighe, Bean** ghost of a woman who died in childbirth. [Scot. Folklore: Briggs, 15–16]

20. **Phantom, The** mysterious, ghostlike foe of injustice in a mythical African-Asian country. [Am. Comics: Horn, 551]

21. **Phantom of the Opera, The** deformed man haunts opera house for vengeance. [Am. Cinema: Halliwell, 562]

22. **Quint, Peter and Miss Jessel** former lovers return to haunt house. [Am. Lit.: *The Turn of the Screw*]

23. **Short Hoggers of Whittinghame** ghost of baby murdered by his mother cannot rest because he is "nameless." [Br. Folklore: Briggs, 363–364]

24. **Vermilion Phantom** ghost rumored to have appeared at various times in French history, such as before deaths of Henry IV and Napoleon. [Fr. History: Wallechinsky, 445]

25. **White House Ghost** several people supposedly saw Abraham Lincoln's ghost there. [Am. Folklore: Wallechinsky, 447]

26. **White Lady** ghost seen in different castles and palaces belonging to Prussia's royal family. [Prussian Folklore: Brewer *Handbook*, 1207]

27. **White Lady of Avenel** "a tutelary spirit." [Br. Lit.: *The Monastery*, Brewer *Handbook*, 1208]

28. **White Lady of Ireland** the domestic spirit of a family; intimates approaching death with shrieks. [Irish Folklore: Brewer *Handbook*, 1208]

29. **Wild Huntsman** spectral hunter with dogs who frequents the Black Forest. [Ger. Folklore: Brewer *Handbook*, 1207]

273. **GIANTISM (See also TALLNESS.)**

1. **Albion** son of Neptune and ancestor of England. [Br. Lit.: *Faerie Queene*]

2. **Alcyoneus** one of the Titans. [Gk. Myth.: Kravitz, 17]

3. **Aloeidae** name given to twins Otus and Ephialtes. [Gk. Myth.: Kravitz, 17]

4. **Anakim** race of tall men routed by Joshua. [*O.T.: Numbers* 13:32–33]

5. **Antaeus** colossal wrestler slain by Hercules. [Gk. Myth.: Brewer *Dictionary*, 38]

6. **Antigonus** giant nicknamed the Hand-Tosser. [Belgian Legend: Walsh *Classical*, 25]

7. **Ascapart** thirty feet tall; defeated by Sir Bevis. [Medieval Romance: Walsh *Classical*, 34]

8. **Atlas** Titan condemned to support world on his shoulders. [Gk. Myth.: Brewer *Handbook,* 13]

9. **Babe, the Blue Ox** Paul Bunyan's gigantic animal-of-all-work. [Am. Folklore: Spiller, 720]

10. **Balan** strong and courageous colossus. [Span. Lit.: *Amadis de Gaul*]

11. **Balor** Formorian giant with evil eye. [Irish Myth.: Benét, 76]

12. **Beaver, Tony** equals mythical exploits of Paul Bunyan. [Am. Lit.: *Up Eel River*]

13. **Bellerus** a Cornish giant. [Br. Lit.: Brewer *Handbook,* 108]

14. **Blunderbore** nursery tale giant killed by Jack. [Br. Lit.: Brewer *Dictionary,* 128]

15. **Brobdingnag** country of people twelve times the size of men. [Br. Lit.: *Gulliver's Travels*]

16. **Bunyan, Paul** legendary lumberjack who accomplished prodigious feats. [Am. Folklore: Brewer *Dictionary,* 163]

17. **Cardiff giant** a gypsum statue passed off as a petrified prehistoric man till revealed as a hoax (1869). [Am. Hist.: *EB* (1963), 9: 533]

18. **Clytius** son of Uranus and Gaea. [Gk. Myth.: Kravitz, 64]

19. **Colossos** a gigantic brazen statue 126 ft. high executed by Charês for the harbor at Rhodes. [Gk. Hist.: Brewer *Handbook,* 226]

20. **Cormoran** nursery tale giant felled by Jack. [Br. Lit.: Brewer *Dictionary,* 262]

21. **Cyclopes** race of one-eyed, gigantic men. [Gk. Lit.: *Odyssey;* Arab. Lit.: *Arabian Nights,* "Sindbad the Sailor," Third Voyage]

22. **Egil** giant who watched over Thor's goats. [Norse Myth.: *LLEI,* I: 327]

23. **Enceladus** powerful giant whose hisses cause volcanic eruptions. [Gk. Myth.: Kravitz, 88]

24. **Ephialtes and Otus** nine fathoms tall; threatened to battle Olympian gods. [Gk. Myth.: Leach, 39; Gk. Lit.: *Iliad*]

25. **Ferragus** the Portuguese giant who took the empress Bellisant under his care. [Br. Lit.: "Valentine and Orson" in Brewer *Handbook,* 364]

26. **Foawr** stone-throwing slaughterer of cattle. [Br. Folklore: Briggs, 178]

27. **Galapos** giant slain by King Arthur. [Br. Lit.: *History of Arthur,* Brewer *Handbook,* 400]

28. **Gargantua** royal giant who required 17,913 cows for personal milk supply. [Fr. Lit.: *Gargantua and Pantagruel*]

29. **Glumdalca, Queen** captive giantess in love with Tom. [Br. Lit.: *Tom Thumb*]

30. **Gog and Magog** two Cornish giants taken captive by Brutus, legendary founder of Britain. [Br. Legend: Brewer *Dictionary*, 471]

31. **Goliath** towering Philistine giant slain by youthful David. [*O.T.: I Samuel* 17:49–51]

32. **Jack-in-Irons** gigantic figure that attacks lonely wayfarers. [Br. Folklore: Briggs, 237]

33. **Jolly Green Giant** trademark comes alive in animated commercials. [Am. Advertising: Misc.]

34. **Jotunn** race of giants frequently in conflict with gods. [Norse Myth.: Leach, 559]

35. **King Kong** giant ape brought to New York as "eighth wonder of world." [Am. Cinema: Payton, 367]

36. **Long Meg of Westminster;** 16th-century giantess. [Br. Hist.: Espy, 337]

37. **Lubbard Fiend** brownie of gigantic size. [Br. Folklore: Briggs, 270–272]

38. **Miller, Maximilian Christopher** the Saxon giant. [Br. Hist.: Brewer *Handbook*, 706]

39. **Mimir** gigantic god of primeval ocean. [Norse Myth.: Leach, 728]

40. **Morgante** ferocious giant converted to Christianity. [Ital. Lit.: *Morgante Maggiore*, Wheeler, 248]

41. **Nephilim** race dwelling in Canaan before Israelites. [*O.T.: Genesis* 6:4]

42. **Og** giant who attacked Israelites. [*O.T.: Deuteronomy* 3:2]

43. **Orgoglio** a hideous giant, as tall as three men; son of Earth and Wind. [Gk. Myth.: Brewer *Handbook*, 780]

44. **Orion** colossus of great beauty and hunting skill. [Gk. and Rom. Myth.: Wheeler, 271]

45. **Pantagruel** gigantic, virtuous king who needed 4,600 cows to nurse him. [Fr. Lit.: *Gargantua and Pantagruel*]

46. **Polyphemus** cruel monster; one of the Cyclopes. [Gk. Lit.: *Odyssey;* Rom. Lit.: *Aeneid*]

47. **Titans** lawless children of Uranus and Gaea. [Gk. Myth.: Brewer *Dictionary*, 1086]

48. **Tityus** son of Zeus; body covered nine acres. [Gk. and Rom. Myth.: Wheeler, 368]

49. **Typhon** fire-breathing colossus. [Gk. and Rom. Myth.: Wheeler, 373]

50. **Utgard** residence of colossi. [Norse Myth.: Brewer *Dictionary*, 1120]

51. **Ymir** father of the giant race. [Norse Myth.: Wheeler, 395]

274. **GLAMOUR (See also ELEGANCE.)**

1. **Cleopatra** name of several queens and princesses of the Ptolemies of Egypt; the name is frequently used to epitomize glamour. [Egypt. Hist. and Pop Culture: Misc.]

275. **GLUTTONY**

1. **Aguecheek, Sir Andrew** gluttonous and lascivious fop. [Br. Lit.: *Twelfth Night*]

2. **belly** prominent indication of overeating. [Folklore: Jobes, 200]

3. **Biggers, Jack** one of the best known "feeders" of eighteenth-century England. [Br. Hist.: Wallechinsky, 377]

4. **crab** loves to devour oysters. [Medieval Animal Symbolism: White, 210–211]

5. **Dagwood** relieves tensions by making and eating gargantuan sandwiches. [Comics: "Blondie" in Horn, 118]

6. **Fat Freddy** character who loves food more than anything else. [Comics: "The Fabulous Furry Freak Brothers" in Horn, 239–240]

7. **Gargantua** enormous eater who ate salad lettuces as big as walnut trees. [Fr. Lit.: Brewer Handbook, 406]

8. **Gastrolaters** people worshiped food in the form of Manduce. [Fr. Lit.: *Pantagruel*]

9. **hedgehog** attribute of gourmandism personified. [Animal Symbolism: Hall, 146]

10. **Jones, Nicely Nicely** Damon Runyon's Broadway glutton. [Am. Lit. and Drama: *Guys and Dolls*]

11. **Jughead** character renowned for his insatiable hankering for hamburgers. [Comics: "Archie" in Horn, 87]

12. **Laphystius** epithet of Zeus, meaning "gluttonous." [Gk. Myth. Zimmerman, 292–293]

13. **Lucullus** Roman epicure chiefly remembered for his enormous consumption of food. [Rom. Hist.: Payton, 406]

14. **lupin** traditional symbol of voracity. [Plant Symbolism: *Flora Symbolica*, 175]

15. **Manduce** idol worshiped by the Gastrolaters. [Fr. Lit.: *Pantagruel*]

16. **Pantagruel** son of Gargantua noted for his continual thirst. [Fr. Lit.: Jobes, II, 1234]

17. **Snorkel, Sergeant** character devoted to God, country, and belly. [Comics: "Beetle Bailey" in Horn, 106]

18. **Stivic, Michael "Meathead"** Archie's son-in-law; has insatiable appetite. [TV: "All in the Family" in Terrace, I, 47]

19. **Willey, Walter** servant who achieved fame through his public gluttony. [Br. Hist.: Wallechinsky, 378]

20. **Wimpy, J. Wellington** Popeye's companion, a corpulent dandy with a tremendous capacity for hamburgers. [Comics: "Thimble Theater" in Horn, 657–658]

21. **Winnie-the-Pooh** lovable, bumbling devourer of honey. [Children's Lit.: *Winnie-the-Pooh*]

22. **Wood, Nicholas** his gastronomic abilities inspired poems and songs; at one historic sitting, he consumed all the edible meat of a sheep. [Br. Hist.: Wallechinsky, 378]

23. **Wood, Willy** "ate up cream cheese, roast beef, piecrust"; incessant eater. [Nurs. Rhyme: Baring-Gould, 158]

24. **Yogi Bear** character with insatiable appetite; always stealing picnic baskets from visitors to Jellystone Park. [Am. Comics: Misc.; TV: Terrace, II, 448–449]

276. GOD

1. **Abba** title of reverence for God the Father. [*N.T.: Mark* 14:36; *Romans* 8:15]

2. **Adonai** spoken in place of the ineffable Yahweh. [Judaism: NCE, 22]

3. **Aesir** the Teutonic pantheon. [Norse Myth.: Leach, 17]

4. **Ahura Mazda (Ormuzd, Ormazd)** the spirit of good and creator of all things. [Zoroastrianism: Payton, 11]

5. **Allah** Arabic name of the Supreme Being. [Islam: Benét, 24]

6. **Amen-Ra** national and chief god of Egyptians. [Egypt. Myth.: Leach, 42]

7. **Ancient of Days** scriptural epithet for God. [*O.T.: Daniel* 7:9]

8. **Assur** principal god. [Assyrian Myth.: Benét, 59]

9. **Brahman** supreme soul of the universe. [Hindu Phil.: Parrinder, 50]

10. **Buddha** "the Enlightened One"; mystical supremacy. [Hinduism: Payton, 108]

11. **the Creator** common sobriquet for God. [Pop. Usage: Misc.]

12. **El** rare Biblical appellation of the Lord. [Judaism: Wigoder, 169]

13. **Elohim** spoken in place of the ineffable Yahweh. [Judaism: *NCE*, 22]

14. **Jehovah** the ancient Hebrew name for God. [Heb. Lang.: *NCE*, 1407]

15. **Ormuzd** supreme deity and embodiment of good. [Persian Myth.: Wheeler, 272]

16. **Osiris** supreme deity and ruler of eternity. [Ancient Egyptian Myth.: Benét, 745]

17. **rays, garland of** emblem of God the Father. [Christian Iconog.: Jobes, 374]

18. **Shekinah** equivalent for Lord in Aramaic interpretation of Old Testament. [Targumic Lit.: Brewer *Dictionary*, 991]

19. **Tetragrammaton** Hebrew word for Lord: YHWH; pronunciation forbidden. [Judaism: Wigoder, 593]

20. **Yahweh** reconstruction of YHWH, ancient Hebrew name for God. [Heb. Lang.: *NCE*, 3019]

277. **GOODNATUREDNESS (See also CHEERFULNESS.)**

1. **Booth, Amelia** good-natured heroine. [Br. Lit.: *Amelia*]

2. **Boythorn, Laurence** amiable, pleasant character. [Br. Lit.: *Bleak House*]

3. **Cadwallader, Rev. Mr.** pleasant and cheery rector. [Br. Lit.: *Middlemarch*]

4. **Cheshire Cat** imperturbable cat with perpetual grin. [Br. Lit.: *Alice's Adventures in Wonderland*]

5. **Coverley, Sir Roger de** soul of amiability. [Br. Lit.: *The Spectator*, Walsh *Modern*, 108]

6. **Good Joe** personification for a good-hearted, obliging person. [Pop. Culture: Payton, 278]

7. **Herf, Jimmy** newspaper reporter as everybody's friend. [Am. Lit.: *The Manhattan Transfer*]

8. **jasmine** traditional representation of a pleasant nature. [Flower Symbolism: *Flora Symbolica*, 175]

9. **white mullein** indicates amiability. [Flower Symbolism: *Flora Symbolica*, 178]

GOODNESS (See KINDNESS.)

278. **GOSSIP (See also SLANDER.)**

1. **assembly of women** symbolizes gossip in dream context. [Dream Lore: Jobes, 143]

2. **Blondie and Tootsie** two characters continually gossiping from morning to night. [Comics: "Blondie" in Horn, 118]

3. **Duchess of Berwick** rumor-jabbering woman upsets Lady Windermere. [Br. Lit.: *Lady Windermere's Fan*, Magill, I, 488–490]

4. **Norris, Mrs.** Fanny's aunt, the universal type of busybody. [Br. Lit.: *Mansfield Park*, Magill, I, 562–564]

5. **Peyton Place** New Hampshire town where everyone knows everyone else's business. [Am. Lit.: *Peyton Place*, Payton, 523]

GOURMANDISM (See EPICUREANISM.)

GRACIOUSNESS (See COURTESY, HOSPITALITY.)

279. GRATITUDE

1. **agrimony** traditional symbol for gratitude. [Flower Symbolism: *Flora Symbolica*, 172]

2. **Canticle of the Sun, The** St. Francis of Assisi's pantheistic hymn of thanks. [Christian Hagiog.: Bishop, 296]

3. **Hannah** jubilantly thankful to God for giving son. [*O.T.: I Samuel* 1:21–28, 2:1–10]

4. **Noah's altar** built to thank God for safe landing. [*O.T.: Genesis* 8:20–21]

5. **Thanksgiving Day** American holiday acknowledging God's favor. [Am. Culture: Brewer *Dictionary*, 1071]

280. GREED (See also STINGINESS.)

1. **Almayer's Folly** lust for gold leads to decline. [Br. Lit.: *Almayer's Folly*]

2. **Alonso** Shakespearean symbol of avarice. [Br. Lit.: *The Tempest*]

3. **Barak's wife** agrees to sell shadow, symbol of her fertility. [Aust. Opera: R. Strauss, *Woman Without a Shadow*, Westerman, 432]

4. **Béline** fans husband's hypochondria to get his money. [Fr. Lit.: *Le Malade Imaginaire*]

5. **Brown, Joe** turns in partner Joe Christmas for reward money. [Am. Lit.: *Light in August*]

6. **Common Lot, The** the get-rich-quick club. [Am. Lit.: *The Common Lot*, Hart, 369]

7. **Crawley, Pitt** inherits, marries, and hoards money. [Br. Lit.: *Vanity Fair*]

8. **Financier, The** riches as raison d'être. [Am. Lit.: *The Financier*, Magill, I, 280–282]

9. **Gehazi** behind master's back, takes money he declined. [*O.T.:* *II Kings* 5:21–22]

10. **Grandet, Eugénie** wealth as raison d'être. [Fr. Lit.: *Eugénie Grandet*, Magill, I, 258–260]

11. **Griffiths, Clyde** insatiable desire for wealth causes his downfall. [Am. Lit.: *An American Tragedy*]

12. **Hoard, Walkadine** hastily marries courtesan posing as wealthy widow. [Br. Lit.: *A Trick to Catch the Old One*]

13. **Kibroth-hattaavah** Hebrew place name: where greedy were buried. [*O.T.: Numbers,* 11:33–35]

14. **Lucre, Pecunious** duped into succoring profligate nephew by lure of a fortune. [Br. Lit.: *A Trick To Catch the Old One*]

15. **Mammon** avaricious fallen angel. [Br. Lit.: *Paradise Lost*]

16. **Mammon, Sir Epicure** avaricious knight; seeks philosopher's stone for Midas touch. [Br. Lit.: *The Alchemist*]

17. **Mansion, The** shows material advantages of respectability winning over kinship. [Am. Lit.: *The Mansion*, Hart, 520]

18. **Midas** greedy king whose touch turned everything to gold. [Classical Myth.: Bulfinch, 42–44]

19. **Naboth's Vineyard** another's possession gotten, by hook or crook. [*O.T.: I Kings,* 21]

20. **New Grub Street** place of ruthless contest among moneymongers. [Br. Lit.: *New Grub Street*, Magill, I, 647–649]

21. **Osmond, Gilbert** marries Isabel Archer for her money. [Am. Lit.: *The Portrait of a Lady*, Magill, I, 766–768]

22. **Overreach, Sir Giles** grasping usurer, unscrupulous and ambitious. [Br. Lit.: *A New Way to Pay Old Debts*, Wheeler, 275]

23. **Pardoner's Tale** three brothers kill each other for treasure. [Br. Lit.: *Canterbury Tales,* "Pardoner's Tale"]

24. **pig** medieval symbol of avarice. [Art: Hall, 247]

25. **Putnam, Abbie** marries old man in anticipation of inheritance. [Am. Lit.: *Desire Under the Elms*]

26. **Scrooge, Ebenezer** byword for greedy miser. [Br. Lit.: *A Christmas Carol*]

27. **Sisyphus** condemned to impossible task for his avarice. [Gk. Myth.: Wheeler, 1011]

281. **GRIEF**

1. **Adonais** Shelley's elegy for John Keats. [Br. Lit.: "Adonais" in Benét, 10]

2. **Aedon** changed to nightingale for murdering son; her song funereal. [Gk. Legend: *NCE*, 24]

3. **Aegiale** (**Aegle**) her tears of grief become amber. [Gk. Myth.: Kravitz, 6]

4. **All Souls' Day** holy day of prayer for repose of departed souls. [Christianity: Brewer *Dictionary*, 1021]

5. **arms reversed** visual symbol of grieving. [Heraldry: Jobes, 128]

6. **Artemisia** (fl. 4th century B.C.) built Mausoleum to commemorate husband. [Gk. Hist.: Walsh *Classical*, 32]

7. **Canens** Janus's daughter; cried herself to death over disappearance of husband, Picus. [Rom. Myth.: Zimmerman, 49]

8. **Clementine** forty-niner's drowned daughter; "lost and gone forever." [Am. Music: Leach, 236]

9. **cypress** symbol of mourning. [Flower Symbolism: Jobes, 402]

10. **dandelion** symbol of grief. [Flower Symbolism: Jobes, 413]

11. **Eos** inconsolably weeps for slain son, Memnon. [Gk. Myth.: Brewer *Dictionary*, 1065]

12. **Hyacinthus** beautiful youth, accidentally killed; from his blood sprang flower marked with letters AI, a lament. [Gk. Myth: Howe, 134]

13. **In Memoriam** Tennyson's tribute to his friend, A. H. Hallam. [Br. Lit.: Harvey, 808]

14. **Kaddish** a prayer said for a close relative. [Judaism: Jobes, II, 901]

15. **Kinah** woeful dirge recited on Tishah b'Av. [Judaism: Wigoder, 342]

16. **Kumalo, Rev. Stephen** Zulu clergyman saddened by fate of fellow blacks. [South African Lit.: *Cry, the Beloved Country*]

17. **Libbeus the Apostle** gentlest apostle, dies from despair at Christ's death. [Ger. Lit.: *The Messiah*]

18. **Lycidas** Milton's elegy for his friend, Edward King (1637). [Br. Lit.: *NCE*, 1781]

19. **marigold** symbol of grief. [Flower Symbolism: *Flora Symbolica*, 175]

20. **Niobe** weeps unceasingly for her murdered children. [Gk. Myth.: Wheeler, 259]

21. **On My First Son** Ben Jonson's short poem mourning the death of his first son. [Br. Lit.: Norton, 243]

22. **Pietà** representation of sorrowing Virgin with dead Christ. [Art: Hall, 246]

23. **poppy** symbol of consolation. [Flower Symbolism: *Flora Symbolica*, 176; Kunz, 329]

24. **Rachel** massacre of innocents fulfills prophecy that she will weep. [*N.T.: Matthew* 2:18; *Jeremiah* 31:15]

25. **red on blue** symbol of death and mourning. [Chinese Art: Jobes, 357]

26. **shivah** seven days of grieving following close relative's burial. [Judaism: Wigoder, 550]

27. **swallow** bird that cried "consolation" at Lord's crucifixion. [Animal Symbolism: Brewer *Dictionary,* 1050]

28. **Tishah be'Av** (9th of Av) Jewish day of lamentation for destruction of Temple. [Judaism: Wigoder, 51]

29. **Wailing Wall** Western wall where Jews lament the destruction of the Second Temple of Jerusalem. [Judaism: *EB,* X: 627]

30. **weeping willow** symbolizes grief at loss. [Flower Symbolism: *Flora Symbolica,* 178]

282. GROWTH

1. **acorn** used to symbolize the beginning of growth. [Pop. Culture: Misc.]

2. **mustard seed** kingdom of Heaven thus likened; for phenomenal development. [*N.T.: Matthew* 13:31–32]

283. GUARDIANSHIP (See also PROTECTIVENESS.)

1. **Argus** hundred-eyed giant guarding Io. [Gk. Myth.: Leach, 72]

2. **Argus Panoptes** all-seeing herdsman with one hundred eyes. [Gk. Myth.: Walsh *Classical,* 29]

3. **battle ax** symbol of wardship. [Western Folklore: Jobes, 163]

4. **beefeater** popular name for a Yeoman of the Guard or Yeoman Warder of the Tower of London. [Br. Hist.: Payton, 88]

5. **Bodhisattva** enlightened one deferring Nirvana to help others. [Buddhism: Parrinder, 48]

6. **brother's keeper, my** Cain denies the responsibility. [*O.T.: Genesis* 4:9]

7. **Cardea** protects children from witches. [Rom. Myth.: Leach, 191]

8. **Cerberus** three-headed dog, guards gate to Hades. [Gk. Myth.: Zimmerman, 55]

9. **cherubim** defended tree of life with flaming swords. [*O.T.: Genesis* 3:24]

10. **cock** watchful church-tower sitter. [Christian Symbolism: Appleton, 21]

11. **Cybele** protector of cities and mother-goddess. [Phrygian Myth.: Avery, 345]

12.   **Delphyne** half-woman, half-beast; guarded Zeus while imprisoned by Typhon. [Gk. Myth.: Howe, 78]

13.   **Egil** giant who watched over Thor's goats. [Norse Myth.: *LLEI*, I: 327]

14.   **Erytheis** stood vigil over golden apples of Hesperides. [Gk. Myth.: *LLEI*, I: 327]

15.   **eunuch** castrated guardian of Eastern harems. [Arab. Culture: Jobes, I, 530–531]

16.   **Fafnir** dragon guarding the Nibelung's gold. [Ger. Opera: Wagner, *Siegfried*, Westerman, 240–241]

17.   **fairy godmother** mythical being who guards children from danger and rewards them for good deeds. [Folklore: Misc.]

18.   **Faithful Eckhardt** old man; warns people of death procession on Maundy Thursday. [Ger. Folklore: *LLEI*, I: 281]

19.   **Ferohers** tutelary angels. [Persian Myth.: *LLEI*, I: 328]

20.   **fiery swords** brandished by cherubim safeguarding tree of life. [*O.T.: Genesis* 3:24]

21.   **Fisher King** guardian of the Grail. [Ger. Legend, *Parzival*; Arthurian Legend: Walsh *Classical*, 227]

22.   **Fylgie** guardian spirit assigned to each human for life. [Norse Myth.: *LLEI*, I: 328]

23.   **Garm** ferocious watchdog at gate of Hell. [Norse Myth.: *LLEI*, I: 328]

24.   **guardian angel** term for Christian namesake who watches over a young child. [Christianity: Misc.]

25.   **Heimdall** guardian of Bifrost; distinguished for acute vision and hearing. [Norse Myth.: Leach, 488]

26.   **Ladon** hundred-headed dragon; guarded apples of the Hesperides. [Rom. Myth.: Zimmerman, 145]

27.   **lion** sleeps with eyes open. [Christian Symbolism: Appleton, 59]

28.   **Mahub Ali** horse-dealer in charge of Kim. [Br. Lit.: *Kim*]

29.   **Nana** gentle old dog; guards the Darling children. [Br. Lit.: *Peter Pan*]

30.   **the Palace Guard** sobriquet for the zealous spokesmen-defenders of the Nixon Administration. [Am. Hist.: *The Palace Guard*]

31.   **palladium** a "safeguard"; Troy believed safe while statue of Pallas Athene remained. [Gk. Lit.: *Iliad*; Espy, 40]

32.   **raven** guardian of the dead. [Christian Folklore: Mercatante, 159]

33.   **Swiss Guards** papal praetorian guard instituted by Julius II. [Ital. Hist.: Plumb, 218, 254]

34. **wyvern** protector of treasure and wealth. [Heraldry: Halberts, 40]

284. **GUIDANCE (See also COUNSEL.)**

1. **Anthony, Mr.** gave guidance to supplicants on radio show. [Am. Radio: "Ask Mr. Anthony" in Buxton, 99]

2. **Baloo** bear who teaches Mowgli jungle law. [Br. Lit.: *The Jungle Books*]

3. **Dear Abby** column of moral or psychological advice; syndicated since 1956. [Pop. Culture: Payton, 185]

4. **Deborah** under her aegis, Barak routed the Canaanites. [*O.T.: Judges* 4:4–10]

5. **Dix, Dorothea** (1870–1951) syndicated columnist who gave advice to the lovelorn. [Am. Pop. Culture: Misc.]

6. **lamp** Word of God showing the way. [Christian Symbolism: *O.T.: Psalms* 119:105]

7. **Landers, Ann** (1918–   ) syndicated columnist who gives advice on personal problems. [Pop. Culture: Misc.]

8. **Mentor** Odysseus's friend and advisor. [Gk. Lit.: *Odyssey*]

9. **Ten Commandments** God's precepts for man's life. [*O.T.: Exodus* 20:3–17; *Deuteronomy* 5:7–21]

285. **GUIDE**

1. **Akela** leader of wolfpack. [Br. Lit.: *The Jungle Books*]

2. **Anubis** "Pathfinder"; conducted dead to judgment before Osiris. [Egyptian Myth.: Jobes, 105]

3. **Baedeker** series of guidebooks for travelers. [Travel: NCE, 207]

4. **Beatrice** Dante's beloved's soul; directs him in Paradise. [Ital. Lit.: *Divine Comedy*, Magill, I, 211–213]

5. **Cicero** Dante's cicerone through the Inferno. [Ital. Lit.: *Divine Comedy*]

6. **Cumaean sibyl** famous prophetess; leads Aeneas through underworld. [Rom. Lit.: *Aeneid*]

7. **dolphin** transported blessed souls to islands of dead. [Gk. and Rom. Myth.: Appleton, 31]

8. **Jack the Porpoise** led ships through treacherous strait off New Zealand. [Br. Hist.: Wallechinsky, 128]

9. **Judas goat** a goat used to lead sheep to slaughter. [Eur. Culture: Misc.]

10. **lighthouse at Pharos** 400 ft. tall; beacon visible 300 miles at sea. [World Hist.: Wallechinsky, 257]

11. **Palinurus** pilot of Aeneas. [Rom. Lit.: *Aeneid*]

12. **pillar of cloud, pillar of fire** Jehovah leads way to promised land. [*O.T.: Exodus* 13:21–22]

13. **star of Bethlehem** guiding light to Jesus for the Magi. [Christian Symbolism: *N.T.: Matthew*, 2:9]

14. **Tiphys** pilot of the Argonauts. [Rom. Myth.: Brewer *Dictionary*, 1085]

286. **GULLIBILITY**

1. **Georgette** Mary Richards' coworker and Ted Baxter's wife; epitomizes gullibility. [TV: "The Mary Tyler Moore Show" in Terrace, II, 70]

2. **Oswald** believes Edmund's false charges against Edgar. [Br. Lit.: *King Lear*]

3. **Othello** "thinks men honest that but seem to be so." [Br. Lit.: *Othello*]

4. **Peachum, Polly** among others, believes she is Macheath's wife. [Br. Opera: *The Beggar's Opera*]

5. **Simple Simon** credulous booby. [Nurs. Rhyme: Opie, 387]

H

287. **HAIR**

1. **Absalom** hair entangled in branches, he was left dangling. [O.T.: II Samuel 18:9]

2. **Aslaug** used hair as cloak to meet king. [Norse Myth.: Walsh Classical, 35]

3. **Beatles** famous English rock group whose initial appeal was derived partly from their moplike haircuts. [Br. Hist.: NCE, 253]

4. **Bes** shaggy-haired, shortlegged god with tail. [Egyptian Myth.: Leach, 138]

5. **Buffalo Bill** (William F. Cody, 1846–1917) American cowboy and showman whose image was fortified by his long blond hair. [Am. Hist.: NCE, 390]

6. **Cousin Itt** Addams's relative; four feet tall and completely covered with blond hair. [TV: "The Addams Family" in Terrace, I, 29]

7. **Custer, General George** (1839–1876) American army officer whose image included long, yellowish hair. [Am. Hist.: NCE, 701]

8. **Enkidu** hirsute companion of Gilgamesh. [Babyl. Myth.: Gilgamesh]

9. **Godiva, Lady** (d. 1057) Leofric's long golden-tressed wife who rode nude through Coventry. [Br. Hist.: Payton, 274]

10. **Gruagach** "the hairy one"; fairy lady. [Scot. Folklore: Briggs, 206–207]

11. **hippies** 1960s "dropouts of American culture" usually identified with very long hair adorned with flowers. [Popular Culture: Misc.]

12. **Mullach, Meg** long-haired and hairy-handed brownie. [Scot. Folklore: Briggs, 284–285]

13. **Rapunzel** her golden tresses provide access to tower loft. [Ger. Fairy Tale: Rapunzel]

14. **Samson** the Hercules of the Israelites; rendered powerless when Delilah cut off his hair. [O.T.: Judges 13–16]

HAPPINESS (See JOY.)

288. **HARMONY**

1. **Concordia** goddess of harmony, peace, and unity. [Rom. Myth.: Kravitz, 65]

2. **Harmony** child of ugly Hephaestus and lovely Aphrodite; union of opposites. [Gk. Myth.: Espy, 25]

3. **Polyhymnia** muse of lyric poetry; presided over singing. [Gk. Myth.: Brewer *Dictionary*, 849]

4. **yin-yang** complementary principles that make up all aspects of life. [Chinese Trad.: *EB*, X: 821]

289. **HATRED**

1. **Ahab, Captain** main character whose monomania is an expression of hatred. [Am. Lit.: *Moby Dick*]

2. **basil flower** flower representing hatred of the other sex. [Flower Symbolism: Jobes, 184]

3. **Bigger Thomas** possesses a pathological hatred of white people. [Am. Lit.: *Native Son*, Magill, I, 643–645]

4. **Esau** despised brother for stealing Isaac's blessing. [*O.T.: Genesis* 27:41–42]

5. **Feverel, Sir Austin** after wife left him, he became a womanhater. [Br. Lit.: *The Ordeal of Richard Feverel* Magill, I, 692–695]

6. **Grimes, Peter** a community hounds a man to his death. [Br. Opera: Britten, *Peter Grimes*, Westerman, 536–539]

7. **Medea** legendary sorceress whose hatred came of jealousy. [Gk. Myth.: Payton, 433]

8. **St. John's wort** indicates animosity. [Flower Symbolism: *Flora Symbolica*, 177]

9. **Styx** river of aversion. [Br. Lit.: *Paradise Lost*]

10. **Tulliver, Mr.** instructs children to despise Mr. Wakem. [Br. Lit.: *The Mill on the Floss*, Magill, I, 593–595]

HAUGHTINESS (See ARROGANCE.)

290. **HEADLESSNESS (See also DECAPITATION.)**

1. **Acephali** fabled Libyan nation of men without heads. [Rom. Hist.: Leach, 6]

2. **Alban, St.** carries his head in his hands. [Christian Hagiog.: Brewer *Dictionary*, 18]

3. **Denis of Paris, St.** French patron; carried severed head to burial. [Christian Hagiog.: Attwater, 104–105]

4. **Headless Horseman** spectral figure haunts Sleepy Hollow. [Am. Lit.: *The Legend of Sleepy Hollow*]

291. HEALING (See also MEDICINE.)

1. **Achilles' spear** had power to heal whatever wound it made. [Gk. Lit.: *Iliad*]

2. **Agamede** Augeas' daughter; noted for skill in using herbs for healing. [Gk. Myth.: Zimmerman, 11]

3. **Ahmed, Prince** possessed apple of Samarkand; cure for all diseases. [Arab. Lit.: *Arabian Nights*]

4. **Amahl** cripple cured by accompanying Magi to the Christ child. [Am. Opera: *Amahl and the Night Visitors*, Benét, 28]

5. **Ananias** Lord's disciple restores Saul's vision. [*N.T.: Acts* 9:17–19]

6. **balm in Gilead** metaphorical cure for sins of the Israelites. [*O.T.: Jeremiah* 8:22]

7. **Bethesda** Jerusalem pool, believed to have curative powers. [*N.T.: John* 5:2–4]

8. **copper** Indian talisman to prevent cholera. [Ind. Myth.: Jobes, 369]

9. **coral** cures madness; stanches blood from wound. [Gem Symbolism: Kunz, 68]

10. **emerald** relieves diseases of the eye. [Gem Symbolism: Kunz, 370]

11. **Jesus's five cures** he makes blind beggars see. [*N.T.: Matthew* 9:27–31, 20:31–34; *Mark* 10:46–52; *Luke* 18:35–43; *John* 9:1–34]

12. **sweet fennel** said to remedy blindness and cataracts. [Herb Symbolism; *Flora Symbolica*, 164]

292. HEALTH

1. **agate** symbolizes health; supposed to relieve snake and scorpion bites. [Class. and Medieval Legend: Leach, 27]

2. **Asclepius' cup** symbolizes well-being. [Gk. Myth.: Jobes, 397]

3. **Carna** goddess of physical fitness. [Rom. Myth.: Leach, 192]

4. **Damia** goddess of health. [Gk. Myth.: Jobes, 409]

5. **Hygeia** goddess of health; daughter and personification of Asclepius. [Gk. Myth.: Kravitz, 123]

6. **Hygeia's cup** symbol of fertility and fitness. [Gk. Myth.: Jobes, 396–397]

293. **HEARTLESSNESS** (See also CRUELTY, RUTHLESSNESS.)

1. **Chester, Sir John** towards son's love affair. [Br. Lit.: *Barnaby Rudge*]

2. **Clare, Angel** cannot forgive Tess's past. [Br. Lit.: *Tess of the D'Urbervilles*]

3. **Estella** trained by Miss Havisham to take advantage of men. [Br. Lit.: *Great Expectations*]

4. **Ettarre** encourages knight's love to gain his tournament prize. [Br. Lit.: *Idylls of the King*, "Pelleas and Ettarre"]

5. **Gerard, Lieutenant Philip** unfeeling in singleminded pursuit of Kimble. [TV: "The Fugitive" in Terrace, I, 290]

6. **Gessler** sentenced Tell to shoot apple off son's head. [Swiss Legend: Brewer *Dictionary*, 1066; Ital. Opera: Rossini, *Wilhelm Tell*]

7. **Hatto** for hardheartedness to poor during famine, eaten by mice. [Ger. Legend: *LLEI*, I: 290]

8. **Javert** coldhearted in his relentless pursuit of Valjean. [Fr. Lit.: *Les Misérables*]

9. **La Belle Dame Sans Merci** cruel and heartless lady. [Br. Lit.: "La Belle Dame Sans Merci" in Walsh *Modern*, 51]

10. **Turandot** in revenge for dishonor to ancestor. [Ital. Opera: Puccini, *Turandot*, Westerman, 368]

294. **HEAVEN** (See also PARADISE.)

1. **Aaru** abode of blessed dead and gods. [Egyptian Myth.: Benét, 1]

2. **Abraham's bosom** reward for the righteous. [*N.T.: Luke* 16:23]

3. **Anu (An)** Babylonian god of heaven. [Babyl. Myth.: Benét, 41]

4. **Asgard** abode of the gods. [Norse Myth.: Walsh *Classical*, 34]

5. **Avalon** the blissful otherworld of the dead. [Celtic Myth.: *NCE*, 194]

6. **Beulah** allegorical name for Israel. [*O.T.: Isaiah* 62:4–5]

7. **Dilmun** dwelling of gods where sun rose. [Sumerian Myth.: Gaster, 24]

8. **Elysian Fields** home of the blessed after death. [Gk. Myth.: Kravitz, 88]

9. **Elysium** abode of the blessed after death. [Gk. Myth.: Zimmerman, 94; Gk. Lit.: *Odyssey*]

10. **Fortunate Isles (Happy Isles)** otherworld for heroes favored by gods. [Gk. Myth.: *NCE*, 861]

11. **garden of the Hesperides** in this garden grew a tree with golden apples. [Gk. Myth.: Zimmerman, 109]

12. **Happy Hunting Ground** translation of Indian name for heaven. [North Am. Indian Myth.: Misc.]

13. **Holy City** poetical name for heaven. [World Rel.: *NCE*, 1213]

14. **Land of the Leal** abode of the blessed dead. [Scot. Myth.: Misc.]

15. **Mount Zion** celestial city. [Br. Lit.: *Pilgrim's Progress*]

16. **New Jerusalem** new paradise; dwelling of God among men. [*N.T.: Revelation* 21:2]

17. **Olympus** abode of the chief gods. [Gk. Myth.: Espy, 22]

18. **Paradise** poetic name for heaven. [World Rel.: *NCE*, 1213]

19. **Valhalla** celestial banquet hall for departed war heroes. [Norse Myth.: Brewer *Dictionary*, 1122]

HEIGHT (See GIANTISM, TALLNESS.)

295. **HELL (See also UNDERWORLD.)**

1. **Abaddon** place of destruction. [*N.T.: Revelation* 9:11; Br. Lit.: *Paradise Lost*]

2. **Gehenna** place of eternal suffering. [*O.T.: II Kings* 23:10]

3. **Hades** the great underworld. [Gk. Myth.: *NCE*, 1219]

4. **Hinnom** valley of ill repute that came to mean hell. [Judaism: *NCE*, 1244]

5. **Naraka** realm of torment for deceased wicked people. [Buddhism, Hindu Myth.: Brewer *Dictionary*, 745]

6. **Pandemonium** chief city of Hell. [Br. Lit.: *Paradise Lost*]

7. **Sheol** (or **Tophet**) gloomy place of departed, unhappy souls. [Judaism: *NCE*, 1219]

296. **HELPFULNESS (See also KINDNESS.)**

1. **Bauchan** hobgoblin often helpful to man. [Scot. Folklore: Briggs, 19]

2. **Bodachan Sabhaill** barn brownie who threshed for old men. [Scot. Folklore: Briggs, 29]

3. **bwbachod** Welsh equivalent of brownies; helpful domestically. [Welsh Folklore: Briggs, 55–56]

4. **Dorcas** made garments for widows. [*N.T.: Acts* 9:39]

5. **Good Samaritan** man who helped half-dead victim of thieves after a priest and a Levite had "passed by." [*N.T.: Luke* 10:33]

6. **Killmoulis** brownie that haunted mill, helping miller. [Br. Folklore: Briggs, 246–247]

7. **Phynnodderee** benevolent Manx brownie of great strength. [Manx Folklore: Brewer *Dictionary*, 830]

8. **Robin Round-cap** domestic spirit who helped with chores. [Br. Folklore: Briggs, 344]

9. **Simon the Cyrenian** made to help bear Christ's cross to Calvary. [*N.T.: Matthew* 27:32; *Luke* 23:26]

297. HENPECKED

1. **Belphegor** fiend turned man; henpecked by wife. [Ital. Lit.: *Belphegor*, Walsh *Classical*, 53]

2. **Dithers, Mr.** Dagwood's irascible boss; fears only his demanding wife. [Comics: "Blondie" in Horn, 118]

3. **Fondlewife** old banker, dotingly submissive to wife. [Br. Lit.: *The Old Bachelor*]

4. **Jiggs** nouveau riche; forever ducking nagging wife Maggie's rolling pin. [Comics: "Bringing Up Father" in Horn, 132]

5. **Mitty, Walter** daydreaming, henpecked husband. [Am. Lit.: "The Secret Life of Walter Mitty" in Cartwell, 606–610]

6. **Syntax, Doctor** harried and hectored clergyman takes off for the good life. [Br. Lit.: *Doctor Syntax*, LLEI, 1: 279]

7. **Tesman, George** Hedda's scholarly husband; jumps at her command. [Nor. Lit.: *Hedda Gabler*]

HERESY (See APOSTASY.)

298. HEROISM (See also BRAVERY.)

1. **Achilles** Greek hero without whom Troy could not have been taken. [Gk. Lit.: *Iliad*]

2. **Aeneas** Trojan hero; legendary founder of Roman race. [Rom. Lit.: *Aeneid*]

3. **Argonauts** those accompanying Jason to fetch Golden Fleece. [Gk. Myth.: Parrinder, 26]

4. **Arthur** king and hero of Scotland, Wales, and England. [Arthurian Legend: Parrinder, 28]

5. **Bellerophon** rider of Pegasus; conquered monsters and Amazons. [Gk. Myth.: Parrinder, 42; Kravitz, 43]

6. **Beowulf** saved Danes from monster Grendel. [Br. Lit.: *Beowulf*]

7. **Cid** Spanish knight renowned for exploits against Moors. [Span. Hist.: *EB*, 4: 615–616]

8. **Cuchulain** "the Achilles of the Gael." [Irish Myth.: Benét, 239–240]

9. **David** boy who slew Goliath. [*O.T.: Samuel:* 18:4–51]

10. **Hector** King Priam's son; dies fighting for Troy. [Gk. Lit.: *Iliad*]

11. **Hereward the Wake** last of the English; dies defending homeland. [Br. Lit.: *Hereward the Wake*, Magill, I, 367–370]

12. **Hornblower, Captain Horatio** victorious captain of HMS *Lydia* and HMS *Sutherland*. [Br. Lit.: *Captain Horatio Hornblower*]

13. **Jason** leader of the Argonauts. [Gk. Myth.: Payton, 347]

14. **Prometheus** stole divine fire for man's sake. [Gk. Myth.: Espy, 33]

15. **Richard the Lion-Hearted** (1157–1199) nicknamed the Black Knight; performer of valorous deeds. [Br. Hist: *EB*, VIII: 566; Br. Lit.: *Ivanhoe*]

16. **Roland** chief paladin of Charlemagne; renowned for his prowess. [Fr. Lit.: *NCE*, 2344]

17. **Samson** hero of Israel. [*O.T.: Judges* 13–16]

299. HIGHSPIRITEDNESS

1. **Gashouse Gang** boisterous Cardinals ballclub of the 1930s. [Am. Sports: Shankle, 167]

2. **the Gay Nineties (Naughty Nineties)** the 1890s; the *fin-de-siècle* epoch when traditional Victorian religiosity was flouted. [Am. and Br. Hist.: Payton, 264]

3. **Hal, Prince** led boisterous life in the company of Falstaff. [Br. Lit.: *I Henry IV*]

4. **Nickleby, Nicholas** adventurous student facing adversities of life. [Br. Lit.: *Nicholas Nickleby*]

5. **Roaring Twenties** decade of exuberance (1920s). [Am. Hist.: Flexner, 309]

300. HIGHWAYMAN (See also OUTLAWRY, THIEVERY.)

1. **Band of Merry Men** Robin Hood's brigands. [Br. Lit.: *Robin Hood*]

2. **Beane, Sawney** English highwayman whose gang slew and ate their victims. [Brit. Folklore: Misc.]

3. **Duval, Claude** 17th-century British highwayman; subject of ballads. [Br. Legend: Harvey, 256]

4. **Faggus, Tom** stole, especially from the Doone clan. [Br. Lit.: *Lorna Doone*, Magill, I, 524–526]

5. **Hood, Robin** outlaw; stole from rich to give to poor. [Br. Lit.: *Robin Hood; Ivanhoe*]

6. **King, Tom** the "Gentleman Highwayman"; associate of Dick Turpin. [Br. Hist.: Brewer *Note-Book*, 363]

7. **Macheath, Captain** highwayman hero of the opera. [Br. Lit.: *Beggar's Opera*]

8. **Moon's men** highwaymen; worked their crimes by night. [Br. Lit.: *I Henry IV*]

9. **Rob Roy** Robin Hood of Scotland. [Br. Lit.: *Rob Roy*]

10. **Twitcher, Jemmy** treacherous and crafty brigand. [Br. Lit.: *Beggar's Opera*]

11. **Turpin, Dick** (1706–1739) enjoyed short and brutal career as horsestealer and highwayman. [Br. Hist.: *NCE*, 2808]

301. HOMECOMING

1. **Odyssey** concerning Odysseus's difficulties in getting home after war. [Gk. Myth.: *Odyssey*]

302. HOMOSEXUALITY

1. **Bilitis** putative singer of Sapphic lyrics. [Fr. Lit.: *Les Chansons de Bilitis, NCE*, 1621]

2. **Christopher Street** magazine for homosexuals. [Am. Pop. Culture: Misc.]

3. **City and the Pillar, The** portraying a young gay separated from "normal" people. [Am. Lit.: *The City and the Pillar*]

4. **Ganymede** beautiful shepherd entrances Jupiter. [Rom. Lit.: *Metamorphoses*]

5. **Gay Liberation** organization that supports equal rights in jobs, housing, etc. for homosexuals. [Am. Pop. Culture: Misc.]

6. **Oglethorpe, John** his sexual preference causes marital problems. [Am. Lit.: *The Manhattan Transfer*]

7. **Sappho** Greek poetess from Lesbos; hence, *lesbian*. [Gk. Hist.: Brewer *Dictionary*, 962]

303. HONESTY (See also RIGHTEOUSNESS, VIRTUOUSNESS.)

1. **Alethia** ancient Greek personification of truth. [Gk. Myth.: Zimmerman, 18]

2. **Better Business Bureau** nationwide system of organizations investigating dishonest business practices. [Am. Commerce: Misc.]

3. **bittersweet** traditional symbol of truth. [Plant Symbolism: *Flora Symbolica*, 172]

4. **Boffin, Nickodemus** despite personal loss, endows patron's son. [Br. Lit.: *Our Mutual Friend*]

5. **Bunker, Edith** her uprightness frequently conflicts with Archie's opportunism. [TV: "All in the Family" in Terrace, I, 47–48]

6. **chrysanthemum** symbol of truth. [Flower Symbolism: *Flora Symbolica*, 173; Kunz, 330]

7. **Cranmer, Thomas** a meek, patient, honest churchman. [Br. Lit.: *Henry VIII*]

8. **Diogenes** (c. 412–323 B.C.) philosopher; fabled lantern-carrying searcher for an honest man. [Gk. Hist.: Hall, 104]

9. **Edgar** truthful, straightforward character; does no evil. [Br. Lit.: *King Lear*]

10. **John of Gaunt** overly blunt uncle of Richard II. [Br. Lit.: *Richard II*]

11. **Lenox, John** his straight-forward dealings win Harum's approval. [Am. Lit.: *David Harum*]

12. **Lincoln, Abraham** (1809–1865) 16th U.S. president; nicknamed "Honest Abe." [Am. Hist.: Kane, 525]

13. **Melantius** honest soldier; trusts everyone until shown otherwise. [Br. Lit.: *The Maid's Tragedy*]

14. **open book** signified spreading of truth by text and doctrine. [Christian Symbolism: Appleton, 13]

15. **Pure, Simon** character in Centlire play (1718). [Br. Lit.: *Bold Stroke for a Wife*]

16. **Trelawney, Squire** sincere, genuine ship-owner; benevolent authority. [Br. Lit.: *Treasure Island*]

17. **Truman, Harry** (1884–1972) 33rd U.S. president who, despite much controversy over his policies, is remembered for impeccable honesty and plain speaking. [Am. Hist.: *NCE*, 2793]

18. **truth serum** drug inducing one to speak uninhibitedly. [Science: Brewer *Dictionary*, 1105]

19. **Una** personification of honesty; leads lamb and rides white ass. [Br. Lit.: *Faerie Queene*]

20. **Washington, George** (1732–1799) first U.S. president; reputed to have said, "Father, I cannot tell a lie." [Am. Hist.: *NCE*, 2933]

21. **white chrysanthemum** traditional symbol of truth. [Flower Symbolism: Jobes, 333]

304. **HOPE** (See also OPTIMISM.)

1. **anchor** emblem of optimism; steadfastly secured the soul in adversity. [*N.T.*: *Hebrews*, 6:18–19]

2. **cinquefoil** traditional representation of hope. [Flower Symbolism and Heraldry: Jobes, 341]

3. **Emigrants, The** shows Norwegians in Dakota wheatlands striving for better life. [Nor. Lit.: *The Emigrants*, Magill, I, 244–246]

4. **flowering almond** symbol of spring; blooms in winter. [Flower Symbolism: Jobes, 71]

5. **hawthorn** symbol of optimism. [Flower Symbolism: *Flora Symbolica*, 174; Kunz, 328]

6. **Iceman Cometh, The** "The lie of the pipe dream is what gives life." [Am. Lit.: *The Iceman Cometh*]

7. **Of Mice and Men** portrays a philosophy that humans are made of hopes and dreams. [Am. Lit.: *Of Mice and Men*]

8. **rainbow** God's assurance He would not send another great flood. [*O.T.*: *Genesis*, 9:12–16]

9. **snowdrop** symbol of optimism. [Flower Symbolism: *Flora Symbolica*, 177; Kunz, 326]

HOPELESSNESS (See DESPAIR.)

305. **HORROR**

1. **Addams, Charles** (1912–   ) famed cartoonist of the macabre. [Am. Comics: *NCE*, 19]

2. **Bhairava** (m), **Bhairav** (f) terrible forms of Shiva and spouse. [Hindu Myth.: Parrinder, 44]

3. **the Black Death** plague whose unprecedented mortality was incomprehensible to medieval mind. [Eur. Hist.: Bishop, 379–382]

4. **Bosch, Hieronymus** (c. 1450–1516) paintings contain grotesque representations of evil and temptation. [Art Hist.: Osborne, 149]

5. **Cabinet of Dr. Caligari, The** thrilling horror story told by a madman. [Ger. Cinema: Halliwell, 119]

6. **Danse Macabre** Saint-Saëns' musical depiction of a dance of the dead. [Music Hist.: Thompson, 1906]

7. **Disasters of War** Goya's violent protest against French occupation of Spain. [Art. Hist.: Osborne, 497]

8. **Dracula, Count** vampire terrifies Transylvanian peasants and London circle. [Br. Lit.: *Dracula*]

9. **dragonwort** traditional representation of horror. [Flower Symbolism: Jobes, 469]

10. **Exorcist, The** supernatural horror story about a girl possessed by the devil (1974). [Am. Cinema: Halliwell, 247]

11. **Jaws** box office sensation about a killer shark (1975). [Am. Cinema: Halliwell, 380]

12. **mandrake** traditional representation of horror. [Plant Symbolism: *Flora Symbolica*, 175]

13. **Phantom of the Opera, The** story of an angry, disfigured composer who haunts the sewers beneath the Paris Opera House. [Am. Cinema: Halliwell, 562]

14. **Pit and the Pendulum, The** study in bone-chilling terror. [Am. Lit.: "The Pit and the Pendulum" in *Portable Poe*, 154–173]

15. **Psycho** Hitchcock's classic horror film. [Am. Cinema: *NCE*, 1249]

16. **snakesfoot** indicates shocking occurrence. [Flower Symbolism: *Flora Symbolica*, 177]

306. HORSE

1. **Al Borak** white horse Muhammad rode to the seven heavens. [Islam: Leach, 172]

2. **Arion** fabulous winged horse; offspring of Demeter and Poseidon. [Gk. Myth.: Zimmerman, 31]

3. **Arundel** Bevis's incomparable steed. [Br. Lit.: *Bevis of Hampton*]

4. **Assault** famous horse in history of thoroughbred racing. [Am. Hist.: *NCE*, 1273]

5. **Balius** immortal steed of Achilles. [Gk. Myth.: Kravitz, 44]

6. **Black Beauty** story of a horse has become a children's classic. [Br. Lit.: *Black Beauty*, Payton, 80]

7. **Bucephalus** wild steed, broken by Alexander to be his mount. [Gk. Hist.: Leach, 167]

8. **centaur** beast that is half-horse, half-man. [Gk. Myth.: Mercatante, 201–202]

9. **Citation** famous horse in history of thoroughbred racing. [Am. Hist.: *NCE*, 1273]

10. **Flicka** a lioness among horses. [TV: "My Friend Flicka" in Terrace, II, 125]

11. **Gallant Fox** famous horse in history of thoroughbred racing. [Am. Hist.: *NCE*, 1273]

12. **Grane** Brünnhilde's war horse, presented to Siegfried. [Ger. Opera: Wagner, *Götterdämmerung*, Westerman, 244]

13. **Gringalet** Gawain's steed. [Br. Lit.: *Sir Gawain and the Green Knight*]

14. **Hambletonian** famous trotting horse after which race for three-year-old trotters is named. [Am. Culture; Mathews, 769]

15. **Hippolytus, St.** patron saint of horses. [Christian Hagiog.: Brewster, 367]

16. **Houyhnhnms** race of horses that represent nobility, virtue, and reason. [Br. Lit.: *Gulliver's Travels*]

17. **Man o' War ("Big Red")** famous racehorse foaled at Belmont Stables. [Am. Hist.: Payton, 421]

18. **Mr. Ed** the talking horse. [TV: Terrace, II, 116–117]

19. **Native Dancer** famous horse in history of thoroughbred racing. [Am. Hist.: *NCE*, 1273]

20. **Pegasus** winged mount of Bellerophon. [Gk. Myth.: Hall, 238]

21. **Rosinante** Don Quixote's mount. [Span. Lit.: *Don Quixote*]

22. **Scout** Tonto's horse. [TV: "The Lone Ranger" in Terrace, II, 34; Radio: "The Lone Ranger" in Buxton, 143]

23. **Seabiscuit** famous horse in history of thoroughbred racing. [Am. Hist.: *NCE*, 1273]

24. **Seattle Slew** famous horse in history of thoroughbred racing. [Am. Hist.: *NCE*, 1273]

25. **Secretariat** famous horse in history of thoroughbred racing. [Am. Hist.: *NCE*, 1273]

26. **Silver** the Lone Ranger's trusty steed. [Radio: "The Lone Ranger" in Buxton, 143–144; TV: Terrace, II, 34–35]

27. **Tony** Tom Mix's "Wonder Horse." [Radio: "Tom Mix" in Buxton, 241–242]

28. **Topper** Hopalong Cassidy's faithful horse. [Cinema and TV: "Hopalong Cassidy" in Terrace, I, 369]

29. **Trigger** Roy Roger's horse. [TV: "The Roy Rogers Show" in Terrace, II, 260]

30. **Whirlaway** famous horse in history of thoroughbred racing. [Am. Hist.: *NCE*, 1273]

307. HOSPITALITY

1. **Abigail** undoes husband's unneighborliness with fare for David's troops. [O.T.: *I Samuel* 25:23–27]

2. **Abraham** graciously receives and treats three wayfarers. [O.T.: *Genesis* 18:1–15]

3. **Acestes** Sicilian king; entertains Aeneas. [Rom. Lit.: *Aeneid*]

4. **Alcandre** Polybus' wife; entertains Helen and Menelaus on their way home from Troy. [Gk. Lit.: *Odyssey*]

5. **Bailley, Harry** "Mr. Congeniality". [Br. Lit.: *Canterbury Tales*]

6. **Boniface** jovial innkeeper; name became generic for restaurateur. [Br. Drama: *The Beaux' Stratagem;* Espy, 129]

7. **the fatted calf** best calf killed for feast to celebrate return of prodigal son. [N.T.: *Luke* 15:13]

8. **Gatsby, Jay** character who serves nothing but the best to his guests. [Am. Lit.: *The Great Gatsby*]

9. **the Glorious Appollers** known for their cordiality and sociability. [Br. Lit.: *Old Curiosity Shop*]

10. **Julian the Hospitalor** set up famed hospice for weary travelers. [Medieval Romance: Hall, 181]

11. **Lot** treated and feted two disguised angels. [O.T.: *Genesis*, 19:1–3]

12. **Lycus** by hospitably entertaining Hercules, earned his gratitude and military assistance. [Gk. Myth.: Zimmerman, 156]

13. **oak** symbol of graciousness. [Flower Symbolism: *Flora Symbolica*, 176]

14. **Philemon and Baucis** poor couple welcomes disguised gods refused by rich households. [Rom. Lit.: *Metamorphoses*]

HUGENESS (See GIANTISM.)

308. **HUMBUGGERY (See also TRICKERY.)**

1. **Barnum, P. T.** (1810–1891) circus owner whose sideshows were sometimes fraudulent; wrote *Humbugs of the World*. [Am. Hist.: *NCE*, 234]

2. **Bilko, Sergeant** bunco artist extraordinaire. [TV: "You'll Never Get Rich" in Terrace II, 452–453]

3. **Face** cunning butler, sets up scam in master's absence. [Br. Lit.: *The Alchemist*]

4. **Mandeville** supposed author of an exaggerated travelogue. [Br. Lit.: *Voyage of Sir John Mandeville*, Harvey, 511]

5. **Subtle** charlatan, posing as alchemist, bilks hapless victims. [Br. Lit.: *The Alchemist*]

6. **Wizard of Oz** false wizard takes up residence in Emerald City. [Am. Lit.: *The Wonderful Wizard of Oz*]

309. **HUMILITY (See also MODESTY.)**

1. **Bernadette Soubirous, St.** humble girl to whom Virgin Mary appeared. [Christian Hagiog.: Attwater, 65–66]

2. **Bonaventura, St.** washes dishes even though a cardinal. [Christian Hagiog.: Hall, 50]

3. **broom** traditional representation of humility. [Plant Symbolism: *Flora Symbolica*, 167]

4. **Bruno, St.** pictured with head bent as sign of humbleness. [Christian Hagiog.: Hall, 53]

5. **cattail** used by da Vinci as symbol of humility. [Plant Symbolism: Embolden, 25]

6. **Elizabeth of Hungary, St.** meek princess renounced world, cared for sick. [Christian Hagiog.: Attwater, 112]

7. **Job** abases self in awe of the Lord. [*O.T.: Job* 40:3–5; 42:1–6]

8. **John the Baptist** feels unworthy before Christ. [*N.T.: Mark* 1:7; *Luke* 3:16]

9. **small bindweed** traditional representation of humility. [Plant Symbolism: *Flora Symbolica* 172]

HUMOROUSNESS (See WITTINESS.)

310. **HUNGER**

1. **Biafra** secessionist state of western Africa in which, during war with Nigeria, more than 1,000,000 people died of starvation (1968). [African Hist.: *NCE*, 290]

2. **Erysichthon** condemned by Demeter to perpetual insatiety. [Gk. Myth.: Kravitz, 93]

3. **Lazarus** the beggar full of sores. [*N.T.: Luke* 16:19–31]

4. **Potato Famine** estimated 200,000 Irish died (1846). [Irish Hist.: Brewer *Note-Book*, 705]

5. **Twist, Oliver** beseechingly asks workhouse-master for more gruel. [Br. Lit.: *Oliver Twist*]

311. **HUNTING**

1. **Agraeus** epithet of Apollo, meaning "hunter." [Gk. Myth.: Zimmerman, 26]

2. **Agrotera** epithet of Artemis, meaning "huntress." [Gk. Myth.: Zimmerman, 32]

3. **Artemis** (Rom. **Diana**) moon goddess; virgin huntress. [Gk. Myth.: Kravitz, 36]

4. **Atalanta** famous huntress; slew the Centaurs. [Gk. Myth.: Leach, 87]

5. **Britomartis** Cretan nymph; goddess of hunters and fishermen. [Gk. Myth.: Zimmerman, 43]

6. **Green Hills of Africa** portrays big game-hunting coupled with literary digressions. [Am. Lit.: *Green Hills of Africa*]

7. **Hubert, St.** patron saint; encountered stag with cross in horns. [Christian Hagiog.: Brewster, 473–474]

8. **Jorrocks** irrepressible pseudo-aristocratic cockney huntsman. [Br. Lit.: *Jorrock's Jaunts and Jollies*]

9. **Nimrod** Biblical hunter of great prowess. [*O.T.: Genesis* 10:9; Br. Lit.: *Paradise Lost*]

10. **NRA** (National Rifle Association of America) organization that encourages sharpshooting and use of firearms for hunting. [Am. Pop. Culture: *NCE*, 1895]

11. **Orion** hunter who pursued the Pleiades. [Classical Myth.: Zimmerman 184–185]

12. **Sagittarius** the Archer of the Zodiac; used occasionally to symbolize hunting. [Astrology: Payton, 594]

13. **Stymphalian birds** venomous Arcadian flock shot by Hercules; sixth Labor. [Gk. and Rom. Myth.: Hall, 149]

312. HYPOCHONDRIA

1. **Argan** character who suffers imaginary ills; determined to be an invalid. [Fr. Lit.: *Le Malade Imaginaire*]

2. **Usher, Roderick** hypochondriac who invites friend to visit and comfort him. [Am. Lit.: "Fall of the House of Usher" in Benét, 338]

313. HYPOCRISY (See also PRETENSION.)

1. **Alceste** judged most social behavior as hypocritical. [Fr. Lit.: *Le Misanthrope*]

2. **Ambrosio** self-righteous abbot of the Capuchins at Madrid. [Br. Lit.: *Ambrosio, or The Monk*]

3. **Angelo** externally austere but inwardly violent. [Br. Lit.: *Measure for Measure*]

4. **Archimago** enchanter, disguised as hermit, wins confidence of Knight. [Br. Lit.: *Faerie Queene*]

5. **Arsinoé** false prude. [Fr. Lit.: *The Misanthrope*]

6. **Atar Gul** trusted domestic; betrays those he serves. [Fr. Lit.: *Atar Gul*, Walsh *Modern*, 32]

7. **Bigotes** 12th-century French order regarded as hypocritical. [Fr. Hist.: Espy, 99]

8. **Blifil** Allworthy's nephew; talebearer and consummate pietist. [Br. Lit.: *Tom Jones*]

9. **Blood, Col. Thomas** (1628–1680) false in honor and religion. [Br. Lit.: *Peveril of the Peak*, Walsh *Modern*, 61]

10. **Boulanger, Ralph** Emma's lover pretends repentance to avoid commitment. [Fr. Lit.: *Madame Bovary*]

11. **Boynton, Egeria** religious charlatan. [Am. Lit.: *Undiscovered Country*]

12. **Buncombe County** insincere speeches made solely to please this constituency by its representative, 1819–1821. [Am. Usage: Misc.]

13. **Cantwell, Dr.** lives luxuriously by religious cant. [Br. Lit.: *The Hypocrite,* Brewer *Handbook,* 175]

14. **Célimène** ridicules people when absent; flatters them when present. [Fr. Lit.: *Le Misanthrope*]

15. **Chadband, Rev.** pharisaic preacher; thinks he's edifying his hearers. [Br. Lit.: *Bleak House*]

16. **Christian, Edward** conspirator; false to everyone. [Br. Lit.: *Peveril of the Peak,* Walsh *Modern,* 96]

17. **crocodile tears** crocodile said to weep after devouring prey. [Western Folklore: Jobes, 383; Mercatante, 9–10]

18. **Dimmesdale, Arthur** acted the humble minister for seven years while former amour suffered. [Am. Lit.: *The Scarlet Letter*]

19. **the Gallanbiles** pretend piety on Sabbath but demand dinner. [Br. Lit.: *Nicholas Nickleby*]

20. **Gashford** humble manner masks sly, shirking character. [Br. Lit.: *Barnaby Rudge*]

21. **Haskell, Eddie** gentleman with adults, troublemaker behind their backs. [TV: "Leave it to Beaver" in Terrace, II, 18–19]

22. **Heep, Uriah** the essence of insincerity. [Br. Lit.: *David Copperfield*]

23. **Honeythunder, Luke** his philanthropy hid animosity. [Br. Lit.: *Edwin Drood*]

24. **Manders** self-righteous pastor agrees to blackmail. [Nor. Lit.: *Ghosts*]

25. **Martext, Sir Oliver** a "most vile" hedge-priest. [Br. Lit.: *As You Like It*]

26. **Mawworm** sanctimonious preacher. [Br. Lit.: *The Hypocrite,* Brewer *Handbook,* 687]

27. **newspeak** official speech of Oceania; language of contradictions. [Br. Lit.: *1984*]

28. **Pecksniff** pretentious, unforgiving architect of double standards. [Br. Lit.: *Martin Chuzzlewit*]

29. **Pharisees** sanctimonious lawgivers do not practise what they preach. [N.T.: *Matthew* 3:7; 23:1–15; *Luke* 18:9–14]

30. **Potemkin village** false fronts constructed to deceive. [Russ. Hist.: Espy, 339]

31. **Sainte Nitouche** sanctimonious and pretentious person (Fr. *n'y touche*). [Fr. Usage: Brewer *Dictionary,* 760]

32. **Snawley** sanctimonious hypocrite; placed stepsons in Dotheboys Hall. [Br. Lit.: *Nicholas Nickleby*]

33. **Square, Mr.** Tom's tutor; spouts hypocritically about the beauty of virtue. [Br. Lit.: *Tom Jones*]

34. **Tartuffe** swindles benefactor by pretending religious piety. [Fr. Lit.: *Tartuffe*]

35. **Vicar of Bray** changes religious affiliation to suit reigning monarch. [Br. Folklore: Walsh *Classical*, 61]

36. **the Whelp** nickname for hypocritical Tom Gradgrind. [Br. Lit.: *Hard Times*]

37. **whited sepulchres** analogy in Jesus's denunciation of Pharisees' sanctimony. [*N.T.: Matthew* 23:27]

I

314. IDENTIFICATION

1. **Emmaus** where two disciples discover identity of Jesus. [*N.T.: Luke* 24:13–35]
2. **Euryclea** Ulysses' nurse; recognized him by scar on thigh. [Gk. Lit.: *Odyssey*]
3. **Longinus** centurion finally sees Christ as son of God. [*N.T.: Matthew* 27:54; *Mark* 15:39; *Luke* 23:47; Christian Legend: Hall, 193]
4. **Orestes** recognized by Iphigenia at the moment of his sacrifice. [Gk. Lit.: *Iphigenia in Tauris*, Kitto, 327–347]
5. **Passover** Jewish festival; blood of sacrificed lambs placed on houses of the Israelites to prevent death of their firstborn. [*O.T.: Exodus* 12:3–13]
6. **Sakuntala** (fl. 40) recognized as queen on return of lost ring. [Sanskrit Lit.: *Abhijnanasakuntala*, Brewer *Dictionary*, 955]
7. **shibboleth** word used by Gileadites to identify Ephraimites who could not pronounce *sh*. [*O.T.: Judges* 12:4–6]
8. **Simeon** recognizes young Jesus as messiah. [*N.T.: Luke* 2:22–34]
9. **Stanley, Henry** (1841–1904) American journalist finds explorer, Dr. Livingstone, in Africa (1871). [Am. Hist.: Van Doren, 263]
10. **Ulysses' bow** Penelope recognizes husband by his ability to bend Ulysses' bow. [Gk. Lit.: *Ulysses*]

315. IDOLATRY

1. **Aaron** responsible for the golden calf. [*O.T.: Exodus* 32]
2. **Ashtaroth** Canaanite deities worshiped profanely by Israelites. [*O.T.: Judges* 2:12]
3. **Baalim** Canaanite deities worshiped profanely by Israelites. [*O.T.: Judges* 2:11]
4. **Baphomet** fabled image; allegedly a Templar fetish. [Medieval Legend: Walsh *Classical*, 46]
5. **David** King of Israel who was held in reverence after he slew Goliath. [*O.T.: Samuel* 17:4–51]
6. **golden calf** idol made by Aaron in Moses's absence. [*O.T.: Exodus* 32:2–4]
7. **Jehu** obliterates the profane worship of Baal. [*O.T.: II Kings* 10:29]

8. **Jeroboam** forsook worship of God; made golden calves. [*O.T.*: *I Kings* 12:28–33]

9. **Moloch** deity to whom parents sacrificed their children. [*O.T.*: *II Kings* 23:10]

10. **Parsis** religious community of India; worship fire along with other aspects of nature. [Hindu. Rel.: *NCE*, 2075]

316. **IGNORANCE** (See also **STUPIDITY.**)

1. **Am ha-Arez** those negligent in or unobservant of Torah study. [Judaism: Wigoder, 26]

2. **avidya** ignorance as cause of suffering through desire. [Hindu Phil.: Parrinder, 36]

3. **Deane, Lucy** unaware of fiancé Stephen's obvious relationship with Maggie. [Br. Lit.: *The Mill on the Floss*]

4. **Dunsmen** opposers of Renaissance learning (14th century); hence, *dunce*. [Br. Hist.: Espy, 116]

5. **Islayev, Arkady** so entrenched in work, oblivious to wife's infidelities. [Russ. Lit.: *A Month in the Country*]

6. **It Pays to Be Ignorant** panelists fail to answer such questions as "Which player on a baseball team wears a catcher's mask?" [Am. Radio: Buxton, 120]

7. **Lennie** big, strong, simple-minded ranch hand. [Am. Lit.: *Of Mice and Men*, Magill, I, 672–674]

8. **Newman, Alfred E.** cartoon character personifying ignorance as bliss: "What, me worry?" [Comics: "Mad" in Horn, 442]

9. **Parable of the Cave** cave dwellers see only the shadows of reality. [Gk. Phil.: *Republic*]

10. **Peppermint Patty** cartoon character habitually stumped by teacher and forever failing exams. [Comics: "Peanuts" in Horn, 543]

11. **Scarecrow** goes to Wizard of Oz to get brains. [Am. Lit.: *The Wonderful Wizard of Oz*]

12. **Schweik** cheerful, feeble-minded character; the antithesis of German militarism. [Czech Lit.: *The Good Soldier Schweik*, Magill, IV, 390–392]

13. **Sweat Hogs** class of incorrigible students majoring in remedial education. [TV: "Welcome Back, Kotter" in Terrace, II, 423]

317. **ILLEGITIMACY**

1. **bend sinister** supposed stigma of illegitimate birth. [Heraldry: Misc.]

2. **Clinker, Humphry** servant of Bramble family turns out to be illegitimate son of Mr. Bramble. [Br. Lit.: *Humphry Clinker*, Payton, 324]

3. **Edmund** illegitimate son of Earl of Gloucester; conspires against father. [Br. Hist.: *King Lear*]

318. **ILLUSION (See also APPEARANCES, DECEIVING.)**

1. **Barmecide feast** imaginary feast served to beggar by prince. [Arab. Lit.: *Arabian Nights*, "The Barmecide's Feast"]

2. **Dubois, Blanche** felt she and Mitch were above others. [Am. Lit.: *A Streetcar Named Desire*]

3. **Emperor's New Clothes** supposedly invisible to unworthy people; in reality, nonexistent. [Dan. Lit.: *Andersen's Fairy Tales*]

4. **Fata Morgana** esp. in the Straits of Messina: named for Morgan le Fay. [Ital. Folklore: Espy, 14]

5. **Glass Menagerie, The** drama of St. Louis family escaping reality through illusion (1945). [Am. Lit.: *The Glass Menagerie*, Magill, III, 418–420]

6. **Herbert, Niel** Mrs. Forrester's affairs destroyed his image of her. [Am. Lit.: *A Lost Lady*]

7. **Hudibras** English Don Quixote; opponent of repressive laws. [Br. Lit.: *Hudibras*, Espy, 204]

8. **Marshland, Jinny** saw philanderer Brad Criley as true lover. [Am. Lit.: *Cass Timberlane*]

9. **mirage** something illusory, such as an imaginary tree and pond in the midst of a desert. [Pop. Usage: Misc.]

10. **Mitty, Walter** imagines self in brilliant and heroic roles. [Am. Lit.: "The Secret Life of Walter Mitty" in Cartwell, 606–610]

11. **Quixote, Don** attacks windmills thinking them giants. [Span. Lit.: *Don Quixote*]

12. **Snoopy** imaginative dog. [Comics: "Peanuts" in Horn, 542–543]

13. **Xanadu** place appearing in Coleridge's dream; where Kubla Khan "did/A stately pleasure-dome decree." [Br. Lit.: "Kubla Khan" in Payton, 744]

319. **IMBALANCE**

1. **Leaning Tower of Pisa** belltower in Pisa, Italy; gradually tilting. [Ital. Architecture: Misc.]

320. **IMMORTALITY** (See also AGELESSNESS.)

1. **Admetus** granted everlasting life when wife Alcestis dies in his place. [Gk. Myth.: *NCE*, 54]

2. **amber axe** symbol of everlasting life. [Western Folklore: Jobes, 82]

3. **amrita** beverage conferring immortality. [Hindu Myth.: Parrinder, 19]

4. **ankh** talisman ensuring everlasting life. [Egyptian Myth.: Jobes, 99]

5. **apples of perpetual youth** admit Norse gods to eternal life. [Norse Myth.: Benét, 43]

6. **cedar** symbol of everlasting life. [Western Folklore: Jobes, 301]

7. **Chiron** immortal centaur. [Gk. Myth.: Kravitz, 58]

8. **cicada** symbol of eternal life. [Chinese Folklore: Jobes, 338]

9. **cypress** symbol of eternal life. [Flower Symbolism: Jobes, 402]

10. **cypress coffin** symbolizes everlasting life; used for burials of heroes. [Gk. and Egyptian Folklore: Leach, 272]

11. **fan palm** emblem of eternal life among early Christians. [Plant Symbolism: Embolden, 25–26]

12. **globe amaranth** flower of immortality. [Flower Symbolism: *Flora Symbolica*, 172]

13. **greybeard-grow-young** magical lake plant; its scent conferred everlasting life. [Babyl. Myth.: *Gilgamesh*]

14. **Luggnagg** imaginary island; inhabitants immortal but lack immortal health. [Br. Lit.: *Gulliver's Travels*]

15. **nectar** drink of gods; bestows eternal life. [Gk. and Rom. Myth.: Brewer *Dictionary*, 75)]

16. **scarab** dung-beetle; said to carry secret of eternal life. [Egyptian Legend: Brewer *Dictionary*, 967]

17. **serpent** sheds skin to renew its life. [Gk. Myth.: Gaster, 37]

18. **Struldbrugs** race "cursed" with gift of deathlessness. [Br. Lit.: *Gulliver's Travels*]

19. **tree of life** eat of its fruit and live forever. [*O.T.: Genesis*, 3:22]

20. **Utnapishtim** blessed by Enlil with everlasting life. [Babyl. Myth.: *Gilgamesh*]

21. **Wandering Jew** doomed to live forever for scorning Jesus. [Fr. Lit.: *The Wandering Jew*]

22. **Xanthus and Balius** Achilles' horses. [Gk. Lit.: *Iliad*]

23. **yew** traditionally planted in churchyards; symbol of deathlessness. [Br. Legend: Brewer *Dictionary*, 1171]

321. **IMPERIALISM**

1. **White Man's Burden** imperialist's duty to educate the uncivilized. [Br. Hist.: Brewer's *Dictionary*, 1152]

322. **IMPERTINENCE**

1. **Bunny, Bugs** cartoon character who is impertinent toward everyone. [Comics: Horn, 140]

2. **McCarthy, Charlie** dummy who is impertinent toward master, Edgar Bergen. [Radio: "The Edgar Bergen and Charlie McCarthy Show" in Buxton, 76–77]

3. **Pierce, Hawkeye** wisecracking medic with an insult for everyone. [TV: "M°A°S°H" in Terrace, II, 71–72]

IMPETUOUSNESS (See RASHNESS.)

323. **IMPOSSIBILITY (See also UNATTAINABILITY.)**

1. **belling the cat** mouse's proposal for warning of cat's approach; application fatal. [Gk. Lit.: *Aesop's Fables*]

2. **east and west** since one direction is relative to the other, "never the twain shall meet." [Pop. Usage: Misc.]

3. **leopard's spots** beast powerless to change them. [*O.T.: Jeremiah* 13:23]

IMPOTENCE (See WEAKNESS.)

324. **IMPRISONMENT**

1. **Alcatraz Island** former federal maximum security penitentiary, near San Francisco; "escapeproof." [Am. Hist.: Flexner, 218]

2. **the Altmark** German prison ship in World War II. [Br. Hist.: Brewer *Dictionary*, 27]

3. **Andersonville** in southwest Georgia; imprisoned Union soldiers died under wretched conditions. [Am. Hist.: *NCE*, 99]

4. **Attica** well-known prison in Attica, New York; remembered for its riot (1971). [Am. Hist.: *NCE*, 182]

5. **ball and chain** originally penological, now generalized symbol. [Western Folklore: Jobes, 176]

6. **Bastille** Paris prison stormed on July 14, 1789. [Fr. Hist.: Worth, 21]

7. **Birdman of Alcatraz** Robert F. Stroud (1890–1963), convicted murderer, became ornithologist in prison. [Am. Culture: Misc.]

8. **Black Hole of Calcutta** Indian dungeon in which overcrowding suffocated prisoners. [Br. Hist.: Harbottle, 45–46]

9. **Cereno, Benito** captain held captive by mutinous slaves. [Am. Lit.: *Benito Cereno*]

10. **Count of Monte Cristo** Edmond Dantès; wrongly imprisoned in the dungeons of Château D'If. [Fr. Lit.: *The Count of Monte Cristo*, Magill, I, 158–160]

11. **Devil's Island** Guiana island penal colony (1852–1938); Alfred Dreyfus among famous prisoners there. [Fr. Hist.: *NCE*, 754]

12. **Droma** chain forged to fetter wolf, Fenris. [Norse Myth.: *LLEI*, I: 326]

13. **Enormous Room, The** portrays three months behind bars in France. [Am. Lit.: *The Enormous Room*]

14. **Fortunato** walled up to die in catacomb niche. [Am. Lit.: "The Cask of Amontillado" in *Portable Poe*, 309–316]

15. **Fotheringay** Mary Stuart's final prison and place of execution (1587). [Br. Hist.: Grun, 260]

16. **Hogan's Heroes** incarcerated in Stalag 13, unlikeliest of POW camps. [TV: Terrace, I, 357–358]

17. **Leavenworth** the oldest military prison (est. 1874); also the name of a state penitentiary. [Am. Hist.: *NCE*, 984]

18. **Manette, Dr.** lost memory during 18-year term in France. [Br. Lit.: *A Tale of Two Cities*]

19. **Man in the Iron Mask** mystery prisoner; legendary contender for Louis XIV's throne. [Fr. Hist.: Brewer *Note-Book*, 460, 555]

20. **Newgate** famed jail of London in centuries past. [Br. Hist.: Brewer *Dictionary*, 754]

21. **Prisoner of Chillon, The** poem by Lord Byron; based on imprisonment of François de Bonnivard. [Br. Lit.: Benét, 817]

22. **San Quentin** famous western California prison (established in 1852); the subject of many songs. [Am. Hist.: *NCE*, 2419]

23. **Sing Sing** notoriously harsh state prison at Ossining, New York. [Am. Hist.: Flexner, 219]

24. **Tower of London** famed as jail. [Br. Hist.: Brewer *Dictionary*, 1094]

25. **Valjean, Jean** spent nineteen years in prison for stealing loaf of bread. [Fr. Lit.: *Les Misérables*]

325. INCEST

1. **Amnon** ravishes his sister, Tamar. [O.T.: *II Samuel* 13:14]

2. **Antiochus** sexually active with daughter. [Br. Lit.: *Pericles*]

3. **Canace** Aeolus's daughter; committed suicide after relations with brother. [Gk. Myth.: Zimmerman, 49]

4. **Clymenus** Arcadian who violated his daughter, Harpalyce. [Gk. Myth.: Zimmerman, 65]

5. **Electra** bore great, passionate love for father, Agamemnon. [Gk. Myth.: Zimmerman, 92; Gk. Lit.: *Electra, Orestes*]

6. **Engstrand, Regina** Oswald's half-sister and chosen lover. [Nor. Lit.: *Ghosts*]

7. **Giovanni and Annabella** brother-sister romance. [Br. Lit.: *'Tis Pity She's a Whore*]

8. **Harpalyce** bears child by father, Clymenus. [Gk. Myth.: Howe, 114]

9. **Jocasta** unknowingly marries her son, Oedipus. [Gk. Lit.: *Oedipus Rex*]

10. **Judah** unknowingly has relations with daughter-in-law. [*O.T.*: *Genesis* 38:15–18]

11. **Lot** impregnates his two daughters. [*O.T.*: *Genesis* 19:36]

12. **Myrrha** mother of Adonis; daughter of Adonis's father. [Gk. Myth.: Brewer *Dictionary*, 741]

13. **Niquee and Anasterax** sister and brother live together in incest. [Span. Lit.: *Amadis de Gaul*]

14. **Oedipus** unknowingly marries mother and fathers four sons. [Gk. Lit.: *Oedipus Rex*]

15. **Tower, Cassandra (Cassie)** had relations with Dr. Tower, her father. [Am. Lit.: *King's Row*, Magill, I, 478–480]

16. **Warren, Nicole** suffers after having had sexual relations with father. [Am. Lit.: *Tender Is the Night*]

INCORRUPTIBILITY (See HONESTY.)

326. **INDECISION**

1. **Cooke, Ebenezer** his irresolution usually leads to catatonia. [Am. Lit.: *The Sot-Weed Factor*]

2. **the Graduate** college man with absolutely no direction. [Am. Lit.: *The Graduate*]

3. **Hamlet** "To be or not to be . . . ." [Br. Lit.: *Hamlet*]

4. **hung jury** cannot decide guilt or innocence. [Am. Hist.: Misc.]

5. **Libra** 7th constellation of the Zodiac; those born under Libra may be indecisive. [Astrology: Payton, 389]

6. **Theramenes** shilly-shallying oligarch; nicknamed Cothurnus, i.e., ambipedal boot. [Gk. Hist.: Brewer *Dictionary*, 960]

7. **Whiffle, Peter** would-be writer, cursed with indecision, accomplishes nothing. [Am. Lit.: *Peter Whiffle*, Magill, I, 739–741]

327. **INDEPENDENCE**

1. **Bastille Day** July 14; French national holiday celebrating the fall of the Bastille prison (1789). [Fr. Hist.: *NCE*, 245]

2. **Declaration of Independence** by delegates of the American Thirteen Colonies announcing U.S. independence from Great Britain (1776). [Am. Hist.: *NCE*, 733]

3. **Huggins, Henry** self-reliant boy; earns money for toys. [Children's Lit.: *Henry Huggins*]

4. **Independence Day** Fourth of July; U.S. patriotic holiday celebrating the Declaration of Independence. [Am. Hist.: *NCE*, 990]

5. **Maine** often thought of as the state of "independent Yankees." [Pop. Culture: Misc.]

6. **Mugwumps** Republican party members who voted independently. [Am. Hist.: Jameson, 337]

7. **Quebec** Canada's French-speaking province has often attempted to attain independence from rest of country. [Canadian Hist.: *NCE*, 2555]

8. **white oak** indicates self-sufficiency. [Flower Symbolism: *Flora Symbolica*, 178]

328. **INDIFFERENCE**

1. **Antoinette, Marie** (1755–1793) queen of France to whom is attributed this statement on the solution to bread famine: "Let them eat cake." [Fr. Hist.: *NCE*, 1696]

2. **Bastienne** unsuccessful ploy to win back Bastien. [Ger. Opera: Mozart, *Bastien and Bastienne*, Westerman, 83]

3. **Defarge, Madame** knitted while executions were taking place. [Br. Lit.: *A Tale of Two Cities*]

4. **Laodicean** inhabitant of ancient Greek city, Laodicea; people noted for indifferent attitude toward religion. [Gk. Hist.: *NCE*, 1529]

5. **Nero** (37–68) Roman Emperor who is reported to have fiddled while Rome burned. [Rom. Hist.: Misc.]

6. **New York City** often thought of as a metropolis of cold, uncaring people. [Pop. Culture: Misc.]

7. **Oblomov** passed life in torpor; symbolically, died sleeping. [Russ. Lit.: *Oblomov*]

8. **senvy** indicates apathy and noncaring. [Flower Symbolism: *Flora Symbolica*, 177]

329. **INDIVIDUALISM** (See also EGOTISM.)

1. **Beaumont, Ned** gambler-detective solves murder case in unorthodox manner. [Am. Lit.: *The Glass Key*, Magill, I, 307–308]

2. **Different Drummer** Thoreau's eloquent prose poem on the inner freedom and individualistic character of man. [Am. Lit.: *NCE*, 2739]

3. **Longstocking, Pippi** eccentric young girl who sets her own standards. [Children's Lit.: *Pippi Longstocking*]

330. **INDUCEMENT**

1. **Electra** incited brother, Orestes, to kill their mother and her lover. [Gk. Myth.: Zimmerman, 92; Gk. Lit.: *Electra, Orestes*]

2. **Hezekiah** exhorts Judah to stand fast against Assyrians. [*O.T.: II Chronicles* 32:6–8]

3. **Lantier, Etienne** exhorts fellow miners to massive strike. [Fr. Lit.: *Germinal*]

4. **Mannon, Lavinia** 20th-century Electra in New England. [Am. Lit.: *Mourning Becomes Electra*]

5. **Salome** beguilingly prompts decapitation of John the Baptist. [*N.T.: Mark* 6:22–28]

6. **Tricoteuses** sobriquet of battle-exhorting women at French Convention. [Fr. Hist.: Brewer *Dictionary*, 1100]

7. **Tyrtaeus** (fl. 7th century B.C.) elegist; roused Spartans to Messenian triumph. [Gk. Hist.: Brewer *Dictionary*, 1111]

331. **INDUSTRIOUSNESS**

1. **ant** works hard to prepare for winter while grasshopper plays. [Gk. Lit.: *Aesop's Fables*, "The Ant and the Grasshopper"]

2. **beaver** perpetually and eagerly active. [Western Folklore: Jobes, 192]

3. **bee** proverbial busyness refers to ceaseless activity of worker bees. [Western Folklore: Jobes, 445]

4. **beehive** heraldic and verbal symbol. [Western Folklore: Jobes, 193]

5. **grindstone** or grind common metaphor for industriousness. [Pop. Culture: Misc.]

6. **red clover** symbolic of diligence. [Flower Symbolism: Jobes, 350]

7. **Saturday's child** works hard for his living. [Nurs. Rhyme: Opie, 309]

8. **Stakhanov, Aleksey** (1905–   ) Russian worker who "overachieved"; increased daily output enormously. [Russ. Hist.: *NCE*, 2606]

9. **third little pig** builds his house of bricks while his two brothers fritter away their time. [Children's Lit.: *The Three Little Pigs*]

332. INEPTITUDE (See also AWKWARDNESS.)

1. **Brown, Charlie** meek hero unable to kick a football, fly a kite, or win a baseball game. [Comics: "Peanuts" in Horn, 543]

2. **Dogberry** officious, inept constable. [Br. Lit.: *Much Ado About Nothing*]

3. **Fife, Barney** deputy who can't be trusted with loaded gun. [TV: "The Andy Griffith Show" in Terrace, I, 55–56]

4. **George of the Jungle** bungling do-gooder. [TV: Terrace, I, 305 –306]

5. **Gilligan** whose every action reeks of incompetence. [TV: "Gilligan's Island" in Terrace, I, 312–313]

6. **Halftrack, General** the ultimate in inept officers. [Comics: "Beetle Bailey" in Horn, 105–106]

7. **Hound, Huckleberry** bungler trying to find niche; always fails. [TV: "The Huckleberry Hound Show" in Terrace, I, 367–377]

8. **Klink, Colonel** naive official in charge of prisoner-of-war camp. [TV: "Hogan's Heroes" in Terrace, I, 357–358]

9. **Orbaneja** obliged to label painted objects for identification. [Span. Lit.: *Don Quixote*]

10. **the Peter Principle** book stating, "in a Hierarchy, every employee tends to rise to the level of his incompetence." [Am. Lit.: *The Peter Principle*, Payton, 522]

11. **Sad Sack** who can't do anything right. [Comics: "The Sad Sack" in Horn, 595–596]

12. **Scarecrow** can't live up to his name. [Am. Lit.: *The Wonderful Wizard of Oz*; Am. Cinema: Halliwell, 780]

13. **Schultz, Sergeant** bumbling assistant to Colonel Klink at Stalag 13. [TV: "Hogan's Heroes" in Terrace, I, 357–358]

14. **Toody and Muldoon** twin antitheses of "New York's Finest." [TV: "Car 54, Where Are You?" in Terrace, I, 138–139]

15. **Tumbleweeds** world's most incompetent sheriff. [Comics: Horn, 673]

333. INEXPENSIVENESS

1. **bargain basement** sale of old stock at highly discounted prices. [Pop. Culture: Misc.]

2. **flea market** yard sale of used items at low prices. [Pop. Culture: Misc.]

3. **Five and Ten** popular sobriquet for various department stores, which at one time sold no item for more than a dime. [Pop. Culture: Misc.]

4. **Louisiana Purchase** about one third the area of the U.S. bought from Napoleon for $15 million (1803). [Am. Hist.: Jameson, 293]

5. **Manhattan** Manhattan Indians sold the island to Dutch West India Company supposedly for about $24 worth of merchandise (1626). [Am. Hist.: Jameson, 305]

6. **Mickey Mouse** squeaky-voiced cartoon hero; the term is often used in alluding to things of minor significance or expense. [Am. Cinema: *EB, VI:* 862; Am. Pop. Culture: Misc.]

7. **Seward's Folly** Alaska, purchased from Russia by Henry Seward for 2 cents an acre (1867). [Am. Hist.: Payton, 610]

8. **tag sale** yard sale of used items, usually at very low prices. [Pop. Culture: Misc.]

9. **Woolworth's** international five-and-dime store. [Am. Commerce: *NCE,* 3004]

334. INEXPERIENCE (See also INNOCENCE, NAIVENESS.)

1. **Bowes, Major Edward** (1874–1946) originator and master of ceremonies of the Amateur Hour on radio. [Am. Radio: Buxton, 149–150]

2. **Gong Show, The** variety show in which beginners try to prove their abilities. [TV: Misc.]

3. **greenhorn** a raw, inexperienced person; especially a new cowboy. [Pop. Culture: Misc.]

4. **Mack, Ted** (1904–1976) host of a television show starring amateurs. [TV: "Ted Mack and the Original Amateur Hour" in Terrace, II, 347]

5. **Newcome, Johnny** any unpracticed youth, especially new military officers. [Br. Folklore: Wheeler, 258]

6. **plebe** (plebeian) first or lowest class, especially at U.S. Military and Naval Academies. [Pop. Culture: Misc.]

7. **rookie** a novice; often an athlete playing his first season as a member of a professional sports team. [Sports: Misc.]

INFERTILITY (See BARRENNESS.)

INFIDELITY (See also ADULTERY, CUCKOLDRY, FAITHLESS-
NESS.)

335. INFORMER

1. **Battus** revealed theft by Mercury; turned to touchstone. [Gk.
   and Rom. Myth.: Walsh *Classical,* 47]

2. **Chambers, Whittaker** (1901–1961) chief witness in perjury trial
   of Alger Hiss (1949). [Am. Hist.: *NCE,* 501]

3. **Dean, John W., III** (1938–   ) chief witness and informer
   against Nixon in the Watergate hearings. [Am. Hist.: *NCE,*
   2939]

4. **Judas Iscariot** led armed band to Gethsemane and showed
   them which one was Jesus. [*N.T.: Matthew* 26:46–50; *Mark*
   14:42–45; *Luke* 22:47–48; *John* 18:1–8]

5. **Morgan le Fay** reveals Lancelot and Guinevere's affair to
   Arthur. [Arthurian Legend: Harvey, 559]

6. **Nolan, Gypo** betrays friend to police for subsistence money.
   [Irish Lit.: *The Informer*]

7. **Peachum, Mr.** informer and fence for stolen goods. [Br. Lit.:
   The Beggar's Opera]

8. **Teresa, Vincent** wrote a book in which he revealed inner
   workings of the Mafia. [Am. Lit.: *My Life in the Mafia.*]

9. **Valachi, Joe** (1903–1971) New York gangster who revealed the
   inner operations of the Mafia. [Am. Hist.: *Facts* (1971), 436]

336. INGRATITUDE

1. **Anastasie and Delphine** ungrateful daughters do not attend
   father's funeral. [Fr. Lit.: *Père Goriot*]

2. **Glencoe, Massacre of** Campbell clan, having accepted hospitality of the MacDonalds for more than a week, attacked their
   hosts, killing 38. [Scot. Hist.: *EB,* IV: 573]

3. **Goneril and Regan** two evil daughters of King Lear; their
   monstrous ingratitude upon receiving his kingdom drives him
   mad. [Br. Lit.: *King Lear*]

4. **Lucius** enjoyed Timon's generosity; refuses him loan when
   poor. [Br. Lit.: *Timon of Athens*]

5. **Lucullus** Timon's false friend; forgets all too easily his generosity. [Br. Lit.: *Timon of Athens*]

6. **Sempronius** shared in Timon's bounty; denies him loan when
   poor. [Br. Lit.: *Timon of Athens*]

7. **ten lepers** of the ten lepers cleansed by Jesus, only one returned to thank him. [*N.T.: Luke* 11–19]

337. INHOSPITALITY

1. **Nabal** rudely refuses David's messengers' request for food. [*O.T.: I Samuel* 25:10–11]

338. INJUSTICE

1. **American concentration camps** 110,000 Japanese-Americans incarcerated during WWII. [Am. Hist.: Van Doren, 487]

2. **Bassianus** murdered after being falsely accused. [Br. Lit.: *Titus Andronicus*]

3. **Bean, Judge Roy** (1825–1904) his brand of justice was the only "law west of the Pecos." [Am. Hist.: *WB*, 2, 137]

4. **Ben Hur** wrongly accused of attempted murder. [Am. Lit.: *Ben Hur*, Hart, 72]

5. **Bligh, William** (1754–1817) naval officer accused of practising unfair and illegal cruelties. [Br. Hist.: *EB*, II: 82; Am. Lit.: *Mutiny on the Bounty*]

6. **Bok, Yakov** Jew falsely accused of ritual murder in Russia. [Am. Lit.: *The Fixer*]

7. **Budd, Billy** courmartialed and unjustly hanged as mutineer and murderer. [Am. Lit.: *Billy Budd*]

8. **Child of the Cord** defendants brought before the *Vehmgerichte*. [Ger. Hist.: Brewer *Note-Book*, 166]

9. **Dred Scott decision** majority ruling by Supreme Court that a slave is property and not a U.S. citizen (1857). [Am. Hist.: Payton, 203]

10. **Dreyfus, Capt. Albert** (1859–1935) imprisoned on Devil's Island on falsified espionage charges. [Fr. Hist.: Wallechinsky, 60]

11. **Eurydice** Orpheus's wife; taken to underworld before her time. [Gk. Myth.: Magill, I, 700–701]

12. **Hippolytus** falsely accused by stepmother of rape after he rejected her advances. [Rom. Lit.: *Aeneid; Metamorphoses*]

13. **hops** symbol of injustice. [Flower Symbolism: *Flora Symbolica*, 174; Kunz, 330]

14. **Jedburgh Justice** Scottish version of lynch law. [Scot. Hist.: Brewer *Note-Book*, 468]

15. **Jim Crow laws** among other rulings, prevented interstate travel by Negroes. [Am. Hist.: Van Doren, 485]

16. **kangaroo court** moblike tribunal, usually disregarding principles of justice. [Pop. Culture: Misc.]

17. **Lydford law** "hang first; try later." [Br. Hist.: Espy, 160]

18. **Lynch, Judge** (1736–1796) personification of mob law, summary execution. [Am. Hist.: Leach, 561]

19. **Martius and Quintus** falsely accused of Bassianus' murder. [Br. Lit.: *Titus Andronicus*]

20. **Mohicans** Indian tribe driven off homeland. [Am. Hist.: Hart, 515]

21. **Ox-Bow Incident** three innocent men lynched for cattle rustling. [Am. Lit.: *The Ox-Bow Incident*]

22. **Queen of Hearts** "first the sentence, and then the evidence!" [Br. Lit.: *Alice's Adventures in Wonderland*]

23. **Rubashov, Nicholas** punished for crimes he never committed. [Br. Lit.: *Darkness at Noon*]

24. **Sacco and Vanzetti** accused and executed for murder (1927); their guilt has been largely disputed. [Am. Hist.: Allen, 59–61]

25. **the Stamp Act** unfair revenue law imposed upon American colonies by Britain (1765). [Am. Hist.: Jameson, 475]

26. **Valjean, Jean** imprisoned nineteen years for stealing loaf of bread. [Fr. Lit.: *Les Misérables*]

27. **Vehmgerichte** medieval Westphalian tribunals; judges abused juridical powers. [Ger. Hist.: Brewer *Dictionary*, 1124]

339. **INNOCENCE (See also INEXPERIENCE, NAIVENESS.)**

1. **Adam and Eve** naked in Eden; knew no shame. [*O.T.: Genesis* 2:25]

2. **Arjuna** Sanskrit name means sinless. [Hindu Myth.: Benét, 50]

3. **Babes in the Wood** innocent children are lost in the wood and die. [Br. Lit.: *Babes in the Wood*, Walsh *Classical*, 42]

4. **basin and ewer** Pilate's guiltlessness signified by washing of hands. [*N.T.: Matthew* 27:24]

5. **Budd, Billy** friendly sailor; held in warm affection by crew. [Am. Lit.: *Billy Budd*]

6. **Christabel** free of evil. [Br. Lit.: "Christabel" in Walsh *Modern*, 95]

7. **Cinderella** with fairy godmother's aid, poor maligned girl wins prince's heart. [Fr. Fairy Tale: *Cinderella*]

8. **Cio-Cio-San** believes marriage to Pinkerton is real. [Ital. Opera: Puccini, *Madama Butterfly*, Westerman, 357]

9. **daisy** symbol of blamelessness. [Flower Symbolism: *Flora Symbolica*, 173; Kunz, 328]

10. **Delano, Amasa** naive, goodhearted captain rescues captive captain from mutineers. [Am. Lit.: *Benito Cereno*]

11. **Desdemona** blamelessness martyred through slander. [Br. Lit.: *Othello*]

12. **Hallyard, St.** Norwegian martyred in defense of guiltless woman. [Christian Hagiog.: Attwater, 165]

13. **Heidi** has instinct for goodness. [Children's Lit.: *Heidi*]

14. **lamb** attribute of young woman; personification of guiltlessness. [Art: Hall, 161]

15. **Minnie** female saloonkeeper in mining town; never been kissed. [Ital. Opera: Puccini, *Girl of the Golden West*, Westerman, 360–361]

16. **Pedro** in marrying former mistress of enemy. [Ger. Opera: d'Albert, *Tiefland*, Westerman, 371–374]

17. **Pinch, Tom** guileless, with unbounded goodness of heart. [Br. Lit.: *Martin Chuzzlewit*]

18. **Susanna** unjustly condemned for adultery; later acquitted. [*Apocrypha: Daniel and Susanna*]

INQUISITIVENESS (See CURIOSITY.)

INSANITY (See MADNESS.)

340. **INSECURITY**

1. **Hamlet** introspective, vacillating Prince of Denmark. [Br. Lit.: *Hamlet*]

2. **Linus** cartoon character who is lost without his security blanket. [Comics: "Peanuts" in Horn, 542–543]

INSEPARABILITY (See FRIENDSHIP.)

INSOLENCE (See ARROGANCE.)

341. **INSPIRATION**

1. **Aganippe** fountain at foot of Mt. Helicon, consecrated to Muses. [Gk. Myth.: *LLEI*, I: 322]

2. **angelica** traditional representation of inspiration. [Herb Symbolism: *Flora Symbolica*, 164]

3. **Calliope** Muse of heroic poetry. [Gk. Myth.: Zimmerman, 47]

4. **Castalia** Parnassian spring; regarded as source of inspiration. [Gk. Myth.: Zimmerman, 52]

5. **Clio** Muse of history. [Gk. Myth.: Zimmerman, 64]

6. **dove** source of afflatus. [Art: Hall, 161]

7. **Dulcinea (del Toboso)** country girl, whom Quixote apotheosizes as guiding light. [Span. Lit.: *Don Quixote*]

8. **Erato** Muse of lyric poetry, love poetry, and marriage songs. [Gk. Myth.: Zimmerman, 97]

9. **Euterpe** Muse of music and lyric poetry. [Gk. Myth.: Zimmerman, 105]

10. **Hippocrene** Mt. Helicon spring regarded as source of poetic inspiration. [Gk. Myth.: *NCE*, 1246]

11. **lactating breast** representation of poetic and musical impulse. [Art: Hall, 161]

12. **Melpomene** Muse of tragedy (tragic dramas). [Gk. Myth.: Zimmerman, 163]

13. **palm, garland of** traditional identification of a Muse. [Gk. Myth.: Jobes, 374]

14. **Pegasus** steed of the Muses; symbolizes poetic inspiration. [Gk. Myth.: Espy, 32]

15. **Polyhymnia** or **Polymania** Muse of sacred song, oratory, lyric, singing, and rhetoric. [Gk. Myth.: Zimmerman, 216]

16. **Stroeve, Blanche** her body inspired Strickland to paint nude portrait. [Br. Lit.: *The Moon and Sixpence*, Magill, I, 621–623]

17. **Terpsichore** Muse of choral song and dancing. [Gk. Myth.: Zimmerman, 260]

18. **Thalia** Muse of comedy. [Gk. Myth.: Zimmerman, 261]

19. **tongues of fire** manifestation of Holy Spirit's descent on Pentecost. [*N.T.: Acts* 2:1–4]

20. **Urania** Muse of astronomy. [Gk. Myth.: Zimmerman, 284]

342. **INTELLIGENCE (See also WISDOM.)**

1. **IQ** (intelligence quotient) controversial measurement of intelligence by formula which compares mental age with chronological age. [Western Education.: *EB*, V: 376]

2. **Mensa International** organization whose members have IQs in the top two percent of the general population. [Am. Pop. Culture: *EB*, VI: 793]

3. **Stanford-Binet Intelligence Scale** test used to measure IQ; designed to be used primarily with children. [Am. Education: *EB*, IX: 521]

INTEMPERANCE (See DRUNKENNESS.)

INTIMIDATION (See BULLYING.)

INTOXICATION (See DRUNKENNESS.)

343. INTRIGUE (See also CONSPIRACY.)

1. **Borgias** 15th-century family who stopped at nothing to gain power. [Ital. Hist.: Plumb, 59]

2. **Ems dispatch** Bismarck's purposely provocative memo on Spanish succession; sparked Franco-Prussian war (1870). [Ger. Hist.: *NCE*, 866]

3. **Machiavelli, Nicolò** (1469–1527) author of book extolling political cunning. [Ital. Hist.: *The Prince*]

4. **Mannon, Lavinia** undoes adulterous mother by brainwashing brother. [Am. Lit.: *Mourning Becomes Electra*]

5. **Mission Impossible** team of investigators with Byzantine *modus operandi*. [TV: "Mission Impossible" in Terrace, II, 100–101]

6. **Paolino** has cohort woo his covertly wed wife. [Ital. Opera: Cimarosa, *The Secret Marriage*, Westerman, 63]

7. **Phormio** slick lawyer finagles on behalf of two men. [Rom. Lit.: *Phormio*]

8. **Ruritania** imaginary pre-WWI kingdom, rife with political machinations. [Br. Lit.: *Prisoner of Zenda*]

9. **X Y Z Affair** thinly disguised extortion aroused anti-French feelings (1797–1798). [Am. Hist.: Jameson, 564]

344. INVENTIVENESS

1. **Archimedes** (287–212 B.C.) invented military engine which saved Syracuse. [Gk. Hist.: Hall, 31]

2. **Bell, Alexander Graham** (1847–1922) inventor of telephone (1876). [Am. Hist.: Jameson, 46]

3. **the Connecticut Yankee** made mechanical devices in the sixth century. [Am. Lit.: *A Connecticut Yankee in King Arthur's Court*]

4. **Dictynna** invented fishermen's nets. [Gk. Myth.: Kravitz, 79]

5. **Edison, Thomas Alva** (1847–1931) inventor of many electrical devices. [Am. Hist.: Jameson, 157]

6. **Erechtheus** inventor of chariots. [Gk. Myth.: Kravitz, 91]

7. **Franklin, Benjamin** (1706–1790) gave us lightning rod, bifocals, stove, etc. [Am. Hist.: Jameson, 836]

8. **Goldberg, Rube** (1883–1970) designed elaborate contraptions to effect simple results. [Am. Hist.: Espy, 111]

9. **Leonardo da Vinci** (1452–1519) created prototypes for parachutes, submarines, tanks, helicopters. [Ital. Hist.: Plum, 185–200]

345. **INVISIBILITY**

1. **Abaris** magic arrow made him invisible. [Gk. Myth.: Benét, 1]
2. **agate** confers this power. [Rom. Folklore: Brewer *Dictionary*, 15]
3. **Cheshire cat** vanishes at will; grin the last feature to go. [Br. Lit.: *Alice's Adventures in Wonderland*]
4. **chrysoprase** put in mouth, renders bearer invisible. [Gem Symbolism: Kunz, 67–68]
5. **fern seed** makes bearer invisible. [Western Folklore: Brewer *Dictionary*, 406]
6. **glory, hand of** severed hand of hanged man renders bearer invisible. [Western Folklore: Leach, 477]
7. **Gyges's ring** confers this power. [Gk. Folklore: Brewer *Dictionary*, 497]
8. **Harvey** six-foot rabbit invisible to everyone but the play's protagonist. [Am. Lit.: Benét, 444]
9. **heliotrope** effective if drunk with proper invocations. [Medieval Folklore: Boland, 43]
10. **Invisible Man** (Griffin) character made invisible by chemicals. [Br. Lit.: *Invisible Man*]
11. **Mambrino's Helmet** golden helmet makes wearer invisible. [Span. Lit.: *Don Quixote*]
12. **Perseus's helmet** made him invisible when he killed Medusa. [Gk. Myth.: *Metamorphoses*]
13. **Reynard the Fox's ring** when ring becomes green, Reynard is invisible. [Medieval Lit.: *Reynard the Fox*]
14. **tarnkappe** cloak taken from the Nibelungs by Siegfried grants the wearer invisibility and strength. [Ger. Lit.: *Nibelungenlied*]

346. **IRASCIBILITY** (See also **ANGER, EXASPERATION, SHREWISHNESS.**)

1. **Caius, Dr.** irritable physician. [Br. Lit.: *Merry Wives of Windsor*]
2. **Donald Duck** cantankerousness itself. [Comics: Horn, 216–217]
3. **Elisha** sics bears on boys for their jibing. [O.T.: *II Kings* 2:23–24]
4. **Findlay, Maude** out-spoken, oft-married, liberated woman. [TV: "Maude" in Terrace, II, 79–80]

5. **Granny** cantankerous matriarch of the Clampett family. [TV: "The Beverly Hillbillies" in Terrace, I, 93–94]

6. **Hotspur** Sir Henry Percy, so named for his fiery character. [Br. Lit.: *I Henry IV*]

7. **Houlihan, Hot Lips** resident termagant of M A S H 4077th. [TV: "M°A°S°H" in Terrace, II, 70–71]

8. **Nipper, Susan** sharp-tongued nurse of Florence Dombey. [Br. Lit.: *Dombey and Son*]

9. **Tybalt** irascible foil to peacemaking Benvolio. [Br. Lit.: *Romeo and Juliet*]

10. **yellow bile** humor effecting temperament of irritability. [Medieval Physiology: Hall, 130]

347. **IRONY** (See also LAST LAUGH.)

1. **Alvaro** attempt to disarm accidentally causes opponent's death. [Ital. Opera: Verdi, *La Forza del Destino*, Westerman, 316]

2. **Arrigo** fight for freedom means opposing new found father. [Ital. Opera: Verdi, *Sicilian Vespers*, Westerman, 308–309]

3. **Artemidorous** presents Caesar with scroll outlining conspiracy; it remains unopened. [Br. Lit.: *Julius Caesar*]

4. **Barabas** perishes in trap he set for Turks. [Br. Lit.: *The Jew of Malta*]

5. **Bazaroff** reformed radical; dies accidentally. [Russ. Lit.: *Fathers and Sons*]

6. **Bel-Ami** subtitled: "The History of a Scoundrel." [Fr. Lit.: *BelAmi*]

7. **Bigger Thomas** finds freedom through killing and life's meaning through death. [Am. Lit.: *Native Son*, Magill, I, 643–645]

8. **Carlos, Don** loves bride he procured for his father. [Ital. Opera: Verdi, *Don Carlos*, Westerman, 319]

9. **Cassandra** true prophet, doomed to go unbelieved. [Gk. Myth.: Espy, 40]

10. **Catch-22** pleading insanity to leave army indicates sanity. [Am. Lit.: *Catch-22*]

11. **Claudius** emperor-scholar in soldier-worshiping nation. [Br. Lit.: *I, Claudius*]

12. **Così fan tutte** illustrates comically some shortcomings of feminine fidelity. [Ger. Opera: Mozart, *Così fan tutte*, Westerman, 97–98]

13. **Creon** victim of his own harsh tyranny. [Gk. Lit.: *Antigone*]

14. **Defender of the Faith** Henry VIII's pre-Reformation title, conferred by Leo X. [Br. Hist.: Benét, 258]

15. **Gaigern, Baron** attempts to rob ballerina; becomes her lover. [Ger. Lit.: *Grand Hotel*]

16. **Harmony Society** embraced communism and celibacy; the latter caused their extinction. [Am. Hist.: Hart, 349]

17. **John of Balue** imprisoned in an iron cage he invented. [Br. Lit.: *Quentin Durward*]

18. **Magic Mountain, The** sanatorium as escape from "insane world." [Ger. Lit.: *The Magic Mountain*, Magill, I, 545–547]

19. **Mayor of Casterbridge, The** Henchard dies in care of man he tyrannized. [Br. Lit.: *The Mayor of Casterbridge*, Magill, I, 571–573]

20. **Otternschlag, Dr.** attempting suicide, discovers will to live. [Ger. Lit.: *Grand Hotel*]

21. **Pagliacco** clown forced to be funny despite breaking heart. [Ital. Opera: Leoncavallo, *Pagliacci*, Espy, 339]

22. **Pattern, Sir Willoughby** egoist's actions lead to self-defeat. [Br. Lit.: *The Egoist*, Magill, I, 241–242]

23. **Popeye** murderer; hanged for murder he did not commit. [Am. Lit.: *Sanctuary*]

24. **Rachel** executed as Jewess; revealed to be Christian clergyman's daughter. [Fr. Opera: Halévy, *The Jewess*, Westerman, 168]

25. **Rigoletto** arranges murder of daughter's seducer; she dies instead. [Ital. Opera: Verdi, *Rigoletto*, Westerman, 299–300]

26. **R.U.R.** robots, manufactured for man's ease, revolt. [Czech. Lit.: *R.U.R.*]

27. **sails** Theseus forgets white sails; his father Aegeus kills himself. [Gr. Myth: *NCE*, 2732]

28. **Sitzkrieg** "phony war"; lull between Polish conquest and invasion of France. [Eur. Hist.: *Hitler*, 815–819]

29. **Tithonus** given eternal life but not eternal youth. [Gk. Myth.: Brewer *Dictionary*, 1087]

30. **War of 1812** Jackson's New Orleans victory occurred after treaty was signed. [Am. Hist.: Hart, 893]

348. IRREPRESSIBILITY

1. **Bell for Adano, A** Joppolo's stress on democracy overcomes superior's arrogance. [Am. Lit.: *A Bell for Adano*]

2. **Grapes of Wrath, The** Ma cries, "We ain' gonna die out." [Am. Lit.: *The Grapes of Wrath*]

3. **Little Orphan Annie** a most irrepressible waif. [Comics: Horn, 459]

4. **March, Augie** man's "refusal to lead a disappointed life." [Am. Lit.: *The Adventures of Augie March*]

IRRESOLUTION (See INDECISION.)

349. **IRRESPONSIBILITY** (See also CARELESSNESS, FORGET-FULNESS.)

1. **Alectryon** changed to cock because he forgot to warn Mars of sun's rising. [Rom. Myth.: *LLEI*, I: 322]

2. **Belch, Sir Toby** Olivia's riotous, reckless uncle. [Br. Lit.: *Twelfth Night*]

3. **Bovary, Emma** irresponsible, careless character; betrays husband. [Fr. Lit.: *Madame Bovary*]

4. **Capp, Andy** negligent of marital obligations. [Comics: Horn, 82–83]

5. **Falstaff, Sir John** misuses "the King's press damnably." [Br. Lit.: *II Henry IV*]

6. **Google, Barney** neglects wife for race horse. [Comics: Horn, 99–100]

7. **Palinurus** sleeping helmsman, falls overboard. [Rom. Lit.: *Aeneid*]

8. **Paragon, Mary Anne** careless servant of David and Dora. [Br. Lit.: *David Copperfield*]

9. **Trulliber, Parson** satire on one who does not do his job. [Br. Hist.: *Joseph Andrews*, Espy, 131]

350. **IRREVERSIBILITY**

1. **crossing the Rubicon** Caesar passes point of no return into Italy. [Rom. Hist.: Brewer *Dictionary*, 941]

2. **Humpty Dumpty** all the King's men failed to reassemble him. [Nurs. Rhyme: *Mother Goose*, 40]

351. **ISOLATION** (See also REMOTENESS.)

1. **Alcatraz Island** "The Rock"; former federal prison in San Francisco Bay. [Am. Hist.: Flexner, 218]

2. **Aschenbach, Gustave von** spiritual and emotional solitude combine in writer's deterioration. [Ger. Lit.: *Death in Venice*]

3. **Count of Monte Cristo** Edmond Dantès imprisoned in the dungeons of Chateau D'If for 14 years. [Fr. Lit.: *The Count of Monte Cristo*, Magill, I, 158–160]

4. **Crusoe, Robinson** man marooned on a desert island for 24 years. [Brit. Lit.: *Robinson Crusoe*, Magill, I, 839–841]

5. **Dickinson, Emily** (1830–1886) secluded within the walls of her father's house. [Am. Lit.: Hart, 224]

6. **Hermit Kingdom** Korea, when it alienated itself from all but China (c. 1637–c. 1876). [Korean Hist.: *NCE*, 1233]

7. **Magic Mountain, The** suspended in time, which exists in flat world below. [Ger. Hist.: *The Magic Mountain*, Magill, I, 545–547]

8. **Man Without a Country, The** story of man exiled from homeland. [Am. Lit.: *The Man Without a Country*, Magill, I, 553–557]

9. **Olivia** "abjured the company and sight of men." [Br. Lit.: *Twelfth Night*]

10. **Selkirk, Alexander** (1676–1721) marooned on Pacific island; thought to be prototype of Robinson Crusoe. [Scot. Hist.: *EB*, IX: 45]

11. **Sleepy Hollow** out-of-the-way, old-world village on Hudson. [Am. Lit.: "Legend of Sleepy Hollow" in Benét, 575]

12. **Stylites** medieval ascetics; resided atop pillars. [Christian Hist.: Brewer *Dictionary*, 1045]

13. **Stylites, St. Simeon** lived 36 years on platform atop pillar. [Christian Hagiog.: Attwater, 309]

J

352. **JEALOUSY** (See also **ENVY**.)

1. **adder's tongue** flower symbolizes jealousy. [Western Folklore: Jobes, 31]

2. **Arnolphe** representative of jealous middle age. [Fr. Lit.: *L'Ecole des Femmes*]

3. **Bartolo, Dr.** jealous and suspicious tutor. [Fr. Lit.: *Barber of Seville*]

4. **Calchas** dies from grief on encountering even wiser soothsayer. [Gk. Myth.: *LLEI*, I: 325]

5. **Callirrhoë** demands of husband former wife's necklace and robe. [Gk. Legend: *NCE*, 55]

6. **Cephalus and Procris** young married couple plagued by jealousy. [Gk. Myth.: Hall, 62]

7. **Deianira** kills husband Hercules for suspected affair with Iole. [Gk. Myth.: Leach, 303]

8. **Dionyza** jealously plots Marina's murder. [Br. Lit.: *Pericles*]

9. **Donald Duck** frustrated character jealous of Mickey Mouse. [Comics: Horn, 216–217]

10. **Ferrando** of Manrico's influence on Leonora. [Ital. Opera: Verdi, *The Troubadour*, Westerman, 302]

11. **Golaud** jealousy leads to the murder of his brother, Pelléas. [Fr. Opera: Debussy, *Pelléas and Mélisande*, Westerman, 196]

12. **green-eyed monster** epithet. [Br. Lit.: *Othello*]

13. **Kitelys** man and wife each laughably suspicious of the other's fidelity. [Br. Lit.: *Every Man in His Humour*]

14. **Leontes** of wife and Polixenes. [Br. Lit.: *The Winter's Tale*]

15. **Medea** sends husband Jason's new bride poisoned cloak. [Gk. Lit.: *Medea*; Fr. Lit.: *Médée*]

16. **Oberon** King of Fairies; jealous of wife's attachments. [Br. Lit.: *A Midsummer Night's Dream*]

17. **Othello** smothers Desdemona out of jealousy. [Br. Lit.: *Othello*]

18. **Polyphemus** crushes lover's lover. [Rom. Lit.: *Metamorphoses*]

19. **Pozdnishef, Vasyla** murders wife in fit of insane resentment. [Russ. Lit.: *The Kreutzer Sonata*, Magill, I, 481–483]

20. **Shabata, Frank** mistrusted everyone who showed kindness to wife, Marie. [Am. Lit.: *O Pioneers!*, Magill, I, 663–665]

21. **wild ass** signifies jealousy. [Animal Symbolism: Jobes, 142]

22. **yellow** color symbolizing jealousy. [Western Folklore: Jobes, 1704]

23. **yellow rose** indicates jealousy. [Flower Symbolism: *Flora Symbolica*, 177]

JESTER (See CLOWN.)

353. **JOKE, PRACTICAL (See also MISCHIEVOUSNESS.)**

1. **April Fool's Day** April 1st; a day for playing practical jokes on the unsuspecting. [Western Folklore: Payton, 34]

2. **Barmecide feast** beggar given empty dishes, imaginary food. [Arab. Lit.: *Arabian Nights*, "The Barmecide's Feast"]

3. **Hop-Frog's king** "had an especial admiration for *breadth* in a jest." [Am. Lit.: "Hop-Frog" in Portable Poe, 317–329]

4. **Merygreeke, Matthew** mischievously puts Ralph up to wooing widow. [Br. Lit.: *Ralph Roister Doister*]

5. **Old Jackanapes** fills Miss Pussy's apple pies with frogs. [Children's Lit.: *The Golden Hen*, Fisher, 232–233]

6. **Panurge** conniving scoundrel whose forte was practical joking. [Fr. Lit.: *Pantagruel*]

7. **Pulver, Ensign** devised mechanisms to needle to skipper. [Am. Lit.: *Mister Roberts*, Magill, I, 605–607]

354. **JOURNEY (See also QUEST, WANDERING.)**

1. **Beagle** name of the ship in which Charles Darwin made his five-year voyage. [Br. Hist.: NCE, 721–722]

2. **Canterbury Tales** pilgrimage from London to Canterbury during which tales are told. [Br. Lit.: *Canterbury Tales*]

3. **Childe Harold** makes pilgrimage throughout Europe for liberty and personal revelation. [Br. Lit.: "Childe Harold's Pilgrimage" in Magill, IV, 127–129]

4. **Christian** travels to Celestial City with cumbrous burden on back. [Br. Lit.: *Pilgrim's Progress*]

5. **Christopher, St.** patron saint; aided wayfarers across river. [Christian Hagiog.: Attwater, 85]

6. **Conestoga wagon** famed covered wagon taking pioneers to West before railroads. [Am. Hist.: NCE, 623]

7. **Dante and Virgil** travel through Hell, Purgatory, Paradise. [Ital. Lit.: *Divine Comedy*, Magill, I, 211–213]

8. **Everyman** makes pilgrimage to God, unaccompanied by erstwhile friends. [Br. Lit.: *Everyman*]

9. **Exodus** departure of Israelites from Egypt under Moses. [O.T.: *Exodus*]

10. **Hakluyt, Richard** (c. 1552–1616) English geographer and publisher of eyewitness accounts of more than 200 voyages of exploration. [Br. Hist.: *EB*, 8: 553–554]

11. **Heart of Darkness** adventure tale of journey into heart of the Belgian Congo. [Br. Lit.: *Heart of Darkness*, Magill, III, 447–449]

12. **Kon-Tiki** primitive raft used by Thor Heyerdahl to cross from Peru to the Tuamotu Islands (1947). [World Hist.: *Kon-Tiki*; NCE, 1238–1239]

13. **Mandeville, Sir John** (fl. 1356) English writer of travelers' voyages around the world. [Br. Hist.: *EB*, VI: 559]

14. **Mayflower** vessel of America's pilgrims (1620). [Am. Hist.: Hart, 530]

15. **Oregon Trail** long ride on horseback from St. Louis to Portland, Oregon. [Am. Hist.: *The Oregon Trail*, Magill, I, 695–698]

16. **petasus** hat; emblem of ancient travelers and hunters. [Gk. Art: Hall, 145]

17. **pilgrimage to Mecca (hajj)** journey every good Muslim tries to make at least once. [Islamic Religion: *WB*, 10: 374–376]

18. **Pilgrim's Progress** Bunyan's allegory of life. [Br. Lit.: Eagle, 458]

19. **Polo, Marco** (1254–1324) Venetian traveler in central Asia and China. [World Hist.: *WB*, 15: 572–573; Ital. Lit.: *Travels of Marco Polo*]

20. **Roughing It** portrays trip from St. Louis across Nevada plains to California. [Am. Lit.: Hart, 729]

21. **Santa Fe trail** caravan route from Missouri to New Mexico. [Am. Hist.: Hart, 743]

22. **Santa Maria, Pinta, and Niña** ships under Columbus in journey to New World. [Span. Hist.: *NCE*, 606]

23. **Syntax, Doctor** leaves home in search of the picturesque. [Br. Lit.: *Doctor Syntax*]

24. **Time Machine, The** adventures of a man who travels through time. [Br. Lit.: Magill, I, 986–988]

25. **Wilderness Road** pioneer route from eastern Virginia to Kentucky. [Am. Hist.: Hart, 924]

355. **JOVIALITY (See also GAIETY.)**

1. **Bob, Captain** Tahitian jailor known for his easy going merriment with prisoners. [Am. Lit.: *Omoo*]

2. **Costigan, Captain J. Chesterfield** jovial, good-humored man. [Br. Lit.: *Pendennis*]

3. **Old King Cole** merry old soul. [Nurs. Rhyme: Opie, 134]

4. **saffron crocus** indicates mirth and laughter. [Flower Symbolism: *Flora Symbolica*, 177]

5. **Tapley, Mark** jolly chief hostler at the Blue Dragon. [Br. Lit.: *Martin Chuzzlewit*]

356. JOY

1. **Auteb** female personification of gladness. [Egypt. Myth.: Jobes, 159]

2. **cinquefoil** indicates gladness. [Flower Symbolism and Heraldry: Jobes, 341]

3. **Euphrosyne** one of Graces; name means 'festivity.' [Gk. Myth.: Kravitz, 96]

4. **gold on red** symbol of felicity and joy. [Chinese Art: Jobes, 357]

5. **Hathor** cow-headed goddess of joy and love. [Egypt. Myth.: Leach, 484]

6. **myrrh** symbol of gladness. [Flower Symbolism: *Flora Symbolica*, 176]

7. **red on green** symbol of felicity and joy. [Chinese Art: Jobes, 357]

8. **wood sorrel** indicates gladness. [Flower Symbolism: *Flora Symbolica*, 177]

357. JUSTICE (See also LAWGIVING.)

1. **Aeacus** a judge of the dead. [Rom. Lit.: *Aeneid*]

2. **Ahasuerus** (519–465 B.C.) Persian king rectifies wrongs done to Jews. [*O.T.: Esther* 8:7–8]

3. **Asha** in moral sphere, presides over righteousness. [Zoroastrianism: Jobes, 138]

4. **blindfold** worn by personification of justice. [Art: Hall, 183]

5. **blue** in American flag, symbolizes justice. [Color Symbolism: Leach, 242; Jobes, 356]

6. **Brown vs. Board of Education** landmark Supreme Court decision barring segregation of schools (1954). [Am. Hist.: Van Doren, 544]

7. **Cambyses, Judgment of** corrupt judge's flayed flesh provides judicial throne. [Gk. Hist.: *Herodotus*]

8. **Carlos, Don** conscience piqued, tries to lift Spanish yoke from Flemish. [Ger. Lit.: *Don Carlos*]

9. **Dike** one of Horae; personification of natural law and justice. [Gk. Myth.: Zimmerman, 85]

10. **Gideon v. Wainwright** established right of all defendants to counsel (1963). [Am. Hist.: Van Doren, 585]

11. **Henry VII** (1457–1509) deliverer of Richard III's just deserts. [Br. Lit.: *Richard III*]

12. **International Court of Justice** main judicial organ of U.N. [World Hist.: *NCE*, 1351]

13. **Libra** sign of the balance, weighing of right and wrong. [Zodiac: Brewer *Dictionary*, 640]

14. **Minos** his justice approved even by the gods; became one of the three judges of the dead. [Gk. Myth.: Zimmerman, 168]

15. **Moran** equitable councillor to King Feredach. [Irish Hist.: Brewer *Dictionary*, 728]

16. **Moran's collar** strangled wearer if he judged unfairly. [Irish Folklore: Brewer *Dictionary*, 728]

17. **Nuremberg Trials** surviving Nazi leaders put on trial (1946). [Eur. Hist.: Van Doren, 512]

18. **Rhadamanthus** made judge in lower world for earthly impartiality. [Gk. Myth.: Brewer *Handbook*, 911]

19. **rudbeckia** indicates fairness. [Flower Symbolism: *Flora Symbolica*, 177]

20. **scales** signify impartiality. [Art: Hall, 183]

21. **scepter** denotes fairness and righteousness. [Heraldry: Halberts, 37]

22. **Solomon** perspicaciously resolves dilemma of baby's ownership. [*O.T.: I Kings* 16–28]

23. **stars, garland of** emblem of equity. [Western Folklore: Jobes, 374]

24. **sword and scales** attributes of St. Michael as devil-fighter and judge. [Christian Symbolism: Appleton, 98]

25. **Valley of Jehoshaphat** where men will be ultimately tried before God. [*O.T.: Joel* 3:2]

26. **World Court** popular name for International Court of Justice which assumed functions of the World Court. [World Hist.: *NCE*, 3006–3007]

27. **Yves, St.** equitable and incorruptible priest-lawyer. [Christian Hagiog.: Attwater, 347]

K

KIDNAPPING (See ABDUCTION.)

KILLING (See MURDER.)

358. KINDNESS (See also GENEROSITY.)

1. **Allworthy, Squire** Tom Jones's goodhearted foster father. [Br. Lit.: *Tom Jones*]

2. **Androcles** relieves lion of thorn in paw and is repaid in arena by lion's failure to attack him. [Rom. Lit.: *Noctes Atticae*, Leach, 55]

3. **the Bachelor** "the universal mediator, comforter, and friend." [Br. Lit.: *Old Curiosity Shop*]

4. **Bishop of Digne** gave starving Valjean food, bed, and comfort. [Fr. Lit.: *Les Misérables*]

5. **Boaz** took benevolent custody of Ruth. [*O.T.: Ruth* 2:8–16]

6. **calycanthus** symbol of compassion. [Plant Symbolism: Jobes, 279]

7. **Carey, Louisa** Philip's loving, sensitive aunt. [Br. Lit.: *Of Human Bondage*, Magill, I, 670–672]

8. **Cuttle, Captain** kindly shelters runaway, Florence Dombey. [Br. Lit.: *Dombey and Son*]

9. **Evilmerodach** Babylonian king; kind to captive king, Jehoiachin. [*O.T.: II Kings* 25:27–29]

10. **Finn, Huckleberry** refuses to turn in Jim, the fugitive slave. [Am. Lit.: *Huckleberry Finn*]

11. **Francis of Assisi, St.** (1182–1226) patron saint and benevolent protector of animals. [Christian Hagiog.: Hall, 132]

12. **Friday's child** loving and giving. [Nurs. Rhyme: Opie, 309]

13. **Glinda** the "Good Witch"; Dorothy's guardian angel. [Am. Lit.: *The Wonderful Wizard of Oz;* Am. Cinema: Halliwell, 780]

14. **Good Samaritan** helps out man victimized by thieves and neglected by other passers-by. [*N.T.: Luke* 10:30–35]

15. **heart** symbol of kindness and benevolence. [Heraldry: Halberts, 30]

16. **Hood, Robin** helps the poor by plundering the rich. [Br. Lit.: *Robin Hood*]

17. **Jesus Christ** kind to the poor, forgiving to the sinful. [*N.T.: Matthew, Mark, Luke, John*]

18. **Joseph of Arimathaea** retrieved Christ's body, enshrouded and buried it. [*N.T.: Matthew* 27:57–61; *John* 19:38–42]

19. **Kuan Yin** goddess of mercy. [Buddhism: Binder, 42]

20. **lemon balm** symbol of compassion. [Herb Symbolism: *Flora Symbolica*, 164]

21. **Merrick, Robert** doing good to others as *raison d'être*. [Am. Lit.: *The Magnificent Obsession*, Magill, I, 547–549]

22. **Nereus** venerable sea god of great kindliness. [Gk. Myth.: *Century Classical*, 744–745]

23. **Old Woman of Leeds** "spent all her time in good deeds." [Nurs. Rhyme: *Mother Goose*, 97]

24. **ox** exhibits fellow-feeling for comrades. [Medieval Animal Symbolism: White, 77–78]

25. **Peggotty, Daniel** kindhearted bachelor who shelters niece and nephew. [Br. Lit.: *David Copperfield*]

26. **Philadelphia** "city of brotherly love." [Am. Hist.: Hart, 651]

27. **Rivers, St. John** takes starving Jane Eyre into his home. [Br. Lit.: *Jane Eyre*]

28. **Strong, Doctor** "the kindest of men." [Br. Lit.: *David Copperfield*]

29. **throatwort** indicates sympathy. [Flower Symbolism: *Flora Symbolica*, 178]

30. **Valjean, Jean** Christlike in his way with man. [Fr. Lit.: *Les Misérables*]

31. **Veronica, St.** from pity, offers Christ cloth to wipe face. [Christian Hagiog.: Attwater, 334]

32. **Vincent de Paul, St.** French priest renowned for his charitable work. [Christian Hagiog.: *NCE*, 2896]

33. **Wenceslas, St.** Bohemian prince noted for piety and generosity. [Eur. Hist.: Brewer *Dictionary*, 1147]

L

359. LABOR

1. **A.F.L.-C.I.O.** (American Federation of Labor–Congress of Industrial Organizations) federation of autonomous labor unions in North America. [Am. Hist.: *NCE*, 84]

2. **Gompers, Samuel** (1850–1924) labor leader; organizer of American Federation of Labor. [Am. Hist.: Jameson, 203]

3. **International Labor Organization (I.L.O.)** agency of the United Nations; aim is to improve labor and living conditions. [World Hist.: *EB*, V: 389–390]

4. **I.W.W.** Industrial Workers of the World [Am. Hist.: Hart, 400]

5. **Marx, Karl** (1818–1883) chief theorist of modern socialism stimulated working class's consciousness. [Ger. Hist.: *NCE*, 1708]

6. **Meany, George** (1894–1980) former president of the A.F.L.-C.I.O. [Am. Hist.: *NCE*, 1733]

7. **National Labor Relations Board** independent agency of U.S. government, supporting labor's right to organize. [Am. Hist.: *NCE*, 1887]

8. **Wobblies** nickname for I.W.W. members. [Am. Hist.: Hart, 400]

360. LAMENESS (See also DEFORMITY.)

1. **Carey, Philip** schoolmates used his clubfoot as object of ridicule. [Br. Lit.: *Of Human Bondage*, Magill, I, 670–672]

2. **Giles, St.** patron of cripples; accidentally hobbled, refused cures. [Christian Hagiog.: Brewster, 392]

3. **Henkies** trows (goblins) who limp when dancing. [Scot. Folklore: Briggs, 219–220]

4. **Hephaestus** blacksmith god; said to have been lamed when ejected from Olympus by Zeus. [Gk. Myth.: Zimmerman, 121]

5. **Mephibosheth** crippled in childhood when nurse dropped him. [*O.T.: II Samuel*, 4:4]

6. **Porgy** crippled Negro beggar of Catfish Row. [Am. Lit.: *Porgy*, Magill, I, 764–766]

7. **Roosevelt, Franklin Delano** (1882–1945) 32nd president of U.S.; stricken with polio and confined to wheelchair. [Am. Hist.: *NCE*, 2355]

8. **Tiny Tim** crippled son of Bob Cratchit. [Br. Lit.: *A Christmas Carol*]

LAMENTATION (See GRIEF.)

361. **LAST LAUGH (See also IRONY.)**

1. **Alcyoneus** giant who threw stone at Hercules; killed when Hercules batted it back. [Gk. Myth.: Zimmerman, 17]

2. **Diomedes** eaten by his own horses, which he had reared on human flesh. [Gk. and Rom. Myth.: Hall, 149]

3. **Fulton's Folly** everybody scoffed at his 1807 steamboat, the "Clermont." [Am. Hist.: Jameson, 190]

4. **Hop-Frog** immolates king and court after repeated insults. [Am. Lit.: "Hop-Frog" in Portable Poe, 317–329]

5. **Magnificent Ambersons, The** Eugene acquires same position George fell from. [Am. Lit.: *The Magnificent Ambersons*]

6. **Mordecai and Haman** latter hanged on gallows he built for former. [*O.T.: Esther* 7:9–10]

7. **Palamon and Arcite** victorious jouster (Arcite) dies in fall; loser wins lady's hand. [Br. Lit.: *Canterbury Tales*, "Palamon and Arcite"]

8. **Pizarro, Don** illegally imprisons Florestan; is later imprisoned himself. [Ger. Opera: Beethoven, *Fidelio*, Westerman, 109–110]

9. **Seward's Folly** ridiculed purchase of Alaska proved wise buy (1867). [Am. Hist.: Van Doren, 254]

10. **Truman, Harry S.** (1884–1972) presidential winner; photographed with Chicago Tribune headline announcing Dewey's victory (1948). [Am. Hist.: *Plain Speaking*, 406]

11. **Tuck, Friar** cajoled to ferry Robin across stream, dumps him returning. [Br. Lit.: *Robin Hood*]

362. **LAUGHTER**

1. **Democritus** (c. 460–c. 370 B.C.) the laughing philosopher. [Gk. Phil.: Jobes, 430]

2. **hyena** rapacious scavenger, known for its maniacal laughter. [Zoology: Misc.]

3. **laughing gas** (nitrous oxide) sweet-smelling, colorless gas; produces feeling of euphoria. [Medicine: Misc.]

4. **Thalia** Muse of comedy [Gk. Myth.: Brewer *Dictionary*, 1071]

363. **LAWGIVING (See also JUSTICE.)**

1. **Draco** (fl. 621 B.C.) codified Athenian law. [Gk. Hist.: Benét, 286]

2. **Hammurabi** Babylonian king (c. 1800 B.C.); established first systematic legal code. [Classical Hist.: *EB*, 8: 598–599]

3. **Justinian** (485–565) ruler of eastern empire; codified Roman law. [Rom. Hist.: *EB*, 10: 362–365]

4. **Minos** scrupulous king and lawgiver of Crete. [Gk. Myth.: Wheeler, 244]

5. **Moses** presents God's ten commandments to Israelites. [*O.T.: Exodus* 20:1–12]

6. **Solon** (c. 639–c. 559 B.C.) Athenian statesman and wise legislator. [Gk. Hist.: Brewer *Dictionary*, 1018]

364. LAZINESS (See also CARELESSNESS.)

1. **Bailey, Beetle** goldbricking army private. [Comics: Horn, 105–106]

2. **Bailey Junior** nonchalant, inefficient boardinghouse page. [Br. Lit.: *Martin Chuzzlewit*]

3. **Belacqua** too slothful in life, he repents after death. [Ital. Lit.: *Divine Comedy*]

4. **Bshyst** demon of sloth. [Zoroastrian Myth.: Leach, 175]

5. **Datchery, Dick** hotel resident with no occupation. [Br. Lit.: *Edwin Drood*]

6. **Jughead** terminally indolent, save when hunger dictates. [Comics: "Archie" in Horn, 87]

7. **Krebs, Maynard G.** for whom "work" is a four-letter word. [TV: "The Many Loves of Dobie Gillis" in Terrace, II, 64–66]

8. **Lake of Idleness** whoever drank thereof, grew immediately "faint and weary." [Br. Lit.: *Faerie Queene*]

9. **Lazybones** popular song by Hoagy Carmichael (1933). [Am. Music: Kinkle, II, 268]

10. **Little Boy Blue** asleep under haystack while livestock roam. [Nurs. Rhyme: *Mother Goose*, 11]

11. **Oblomov** indolent landowner, always in robe and slippers. [Russ. Lit.: *Oblomov*]

12. **phlegm** humor effecting temperament of sluggishness. [Medieval Physiology: Hall, 130]

13. **sloth** arboreal mammal, always associated with sluggishness. [Zoology: Misc.]

14. **Speed** an "illiterate loiterer"; slow-moving servant. [Br. Lit.: *Two Gentlemen of Verona*]

LECHERY (See LUST.)

365. **LEFTHANDEDNESS**

1.   **Ehud** wielded sword sinistrally. [*O.T.: Judges* 3:15, 21]

366. **LEXICOGRAPHY**

1.   **Johnson, Samuel** (1709–1784) literary scholar, creator of first comprehensive lexicographical work of English. [Br. Hist.: *EB,* V: 591]

2.   **Murray, James** (1837–1915) well-known editor of the *Oxford English Dictionary.* [Br. Hist.: *Caught in the Web of Words*]

3.   **Webster, Noah** (1758–1843) philologist and compiler of popular comprehensive American dictionary. [Am. Hist.: Hart, 902]

367. **LIGHT**

1.   **Apollo** god of light. [Gk. Myth.: Espy, 28]

2.   **Asvins** twin gods of light. Hindu Myth.: Benet, 60

3.   **Balder** god of light and peace. Norse Myth.: Leach, 106

4.   **Jesus Christ** "I am the light of the world." N.T.: John 8:12

5.   **Mithras** god of light. [Pers. Myth.: Wheeler, 246]

6.   **patée cross** four spear-headed arms; symbolizes solar light. [Christian Iconog.: Brewer *Dictionary,* 280; Jobes, 386]

368. **LIGHTNING (See also THUNDER.)**

1.   **Agni** god of fire and lightning. [Hindu Myth.: Benét, 15]

2.   **double ax** variation of Jupiter's thunderbolt. [Rom. Myth.: Jobes, 163]

3.   **Elicius** epithet of Jupiter as god of lightning. [Rom. Myth.: Kravitz, 87]

4.   **Franklin, Benjamin** (1706–1790) flew kite in thunderstorm to prove electricity existed in lightning. [Am. Hist.: *NCE,* 1000]

5.   **Jupiter Fulgurator** Jupiter as controller of weather and sender of lightning. [Rom. Myth.: Howe, 147]

6.   **Thor** bravest of gods; protected man from lightning. [Norse Myth.: Brewer *Handbook,* 1099]

LITTLENESS (See DWARFISM, SMALLNESS.)

369. **LONGEVITY (See also ENDURANCE.)**

1.   **Abie's Irish Rose** comedy by Anne Nichols ran for 2327 performances on Broadway. [Am. Lit.: Benét, 3]

2.   **Long Parliament** sat from outbreak of Civil War to Charles II's accession (1640–1660). [Br. Hist.: *EB,* VI: 319–320]

3. **Meet the Press** longest running television program; from 1947 to present. [Am. TV: McWhirter, 234]

4. **Methuselah** son of Enoch; patriarch said to have lived 969 years. [*O.T.: Genesis* 5:21–27]

5. **Mousetrap, The** London play by Agatha Christie, running since 1952. [Br. Lit.: McWhirter, 228]

6. **Roosevelt, Franklin Delano** (1882–1945) 32nd U.S. President; elected to four terms. [Am. Hist.: Hart, 726]

7. **Victoria, Queen** (1819–1901) queen of Great Britain and Ireland (1837–1901). [Br. Hist.: *NCE*, 2886]

370. **LONGSUFFERING (See also PATIENCE.)**

1. **Aspasia** pathetic figure bearing fate with fortitude. [Br. Lit.: *The Maid's Tragedy*]

2. **Burns, Helen** long-suffering victim of school's cruel treatment. [Br. Lit.: *Jane Eyre*]

3. **Canio** must be funny despite rage over wife's unfaithfulness. [Ital. Opera: Leoncavallo, *Pagliacci*, Westerman, 341–342]

4. **Clayhanger, Edwin** makes concessions to wife's greed and irascibility. [Br. Lit.: *The Clayhanger Trilogy*]

5. **Dodsworth, Sam** patiently endures egotism of his childish wife until marriage dissolves. [Am. Lit.: *Dodsworth*]

6. **Griselda** endures husband's cruelty nobly. [Br. Lit.: *Canterbury Tales*, "Clerk's Tale"; Ital. Lit.: *Decameron*, "Dineo's Tale of Griselda"]

7. **oxeye** symbol of long-suffering composure. [Flower Symbolism: *Flora Symbolica*, 176]

8. **Prynne, Hester** stoically endures the ostracism imposed on her for adultery. [Am. Lit.: *The Scarlet Letter*]

9. **Santa Cruz, Jacinta** passively tolerates husband's adultery; rears his bastard. [Span. Lit.: *Fortunata and Jacinta*]

LOQUACITY (See TALKATIVENESS.)

LOSER (See FAILURE.)

371. **LOUDNESS**

1. **boiler factory** proverbial source of noise and confusion. [Am. Culture: Misc.]

2. **breaking of the sound barrier** boom of plane heard exceeding speed of about 750 m.p.h. or Mach 1. [Aviation: Misc.]

3. **Concorde** supersonic jet of British-French design. [Eur. Hist.: *EB*, III: 66]

4. **Joshua** Jericho walls razed by clamorous blasts from his troops' trumpets. [*O.T.: Joshua* 6]

5. **Krakatoa** volcanic explosion on this Indonesian island heard 3000 miles away (1883). [Asian Hist.: *NCE,* 1500]

6. **Stentor** Greek herald with voice of 50 men. [Gk. Myth.: Espy, 39]

372. LOVE

1. **Aengus** one of the Tuatha de Danaan; god of love. [Celtic Myth.: Jobes, 40]

2. **Amor** another name for Cupid. [Rom. Myth.: Kravitz, 19]

3. **Aphrodite** goddess of love and beauty. [Gk. Myth.: Zimmerman, 25–26]

4. **Bast** cat-headed goddess of love and fashion. [Egyptian Myth.: Espy, 20]

5. **Biducht** goddess of love. [Persian Myth.: Jobes, 210]

6. **Cupid (Gk. Eros)** god of love. [Rom. Myth.: Kravitz, 70]

7. **diamond** token of affection, e.g., for engagement. [Gem Symbolism: Jobes, 440–441]

8. **Frigg** Scandinavian goddess of love and fertility. [Norse Myth.: Parrinder, 101]

9. **honeysuckle** symbol of affection. [Flower Symbolism: *Flora Symbolica,* 174; Kunz, 328]

10. **Kama** god of love; Hindu equivalent of Eros. [Hindu Myth.: Brewer *Dictionary,* 661]

11. **Krishna** god who plays flute to enamored milkmaids. [Hindu Myth.: Binder, 23]

12. **myrtle** to Renaissance, its perpetual greenness symbolized everlasting love. [Art: Hall, 219]

13. **pear** symbol of love and tenderness. [Flower Symbolism: *Flora Symbolica,* 176]

14. **red chrysanthemum** symbol of love. [Flower Symbolism: Jobes, 333]

15. **ring** worn on fourth finger, left hand, symbolizes love. [Western Folklore: Brewer *Dictionary,* 919]

16. **rose** traditional symbol of love. [Flower Symbolism: *Flora Symbolica,* 177]

17. **Rules of Courtly Love, The** dos and don'ts manual for medieval lovers. [Eur. Hist.: Bishop, 301]

18. **St. Valentine's Day** (February 14) day of celebration of love. [Western Folklore: Leach, 1153]

19. **Sonnets from the Portuguese** Elizabeth Browning's famous poems celebrating love for her husband (1850). [Br. Lit.: Magill, III, 1007–1009]

20. **sorrel** indicates love and tenderness. [Flower Symbolism: *Flora Symbolica*, 177]

21. **three circles** symbol indicates affection. [Western Folklore: Jobes, 343]

22. **Venus** goddess of love and beauty. [Rom. Myth.: *Aeneid*]

23. **white lilacs** indicates initial feelings of love. [Flower Symbolism: *Flora Symbolica*, 175]

373. LOVE, MATERNAL

1. **asteria** symbol of motherly affection. [Gem. Symbolism: Jobes, 144]

2. **cinquefoil** symbol of motherly love. [Flower Symbolism: Jobes, 341]

3. **Cornelia** indicates that two sons are her jewels. [Rom. Hist.: Hall, 75]

4. **Delphine, Madame** denies motherhood for daughter's marriage. [Am. Lit.: *Madame Delphine*, Hart, 513]

5. **Mary** the Madonna; beatific mother of Christ. [*N.T.: Matthew, Mark, Luke, John;* Christian Iconography: *NCE*, 1709]

6. **red carnation** clove pink, sprung from St. Mary's tears at Calvary. [Christian Legend: Embolden, 23]

7. **Silver Cord, The** Mrs. Phelps's love for sons becomes pathological. [Am. Lit.: Hart, 769]

8. **Venus** provided future protection for Aeneas, her son. [Rom. Myth.: *Aeneid*]

LOVE, PLATONIC (See LOVE, VIRTUOUS.)

374. LOVE, SPURNED

1. **Anaxarete** princess turned to stone for scorning commoner's love. [Gk. Myth.: Zimmerman, 21]

2. **Aoi, Princess** afflicted by husband's amours; declines and dies. [Jap. Lit.: *The Tale of Genji*]

3. **Butterfly, Madame** considered herself Pinkerton's wife; actually his mistress. [Am. Lit.: *Madame Butterfly*, Hart, 513; Ital Opera, *Madama Butterfly*]

4. **Clavdia** thought Hans's proposal foolish and refused him. [Ger. Lit.: *The Magic Mountain*, Magill, I, 545–547]

5. **Cloten** spurned but persistent lover of Imogen. [Br. Lit.: *Cymbeline*]

6. **Conchobar** spurned, the king murders intended's lover and his brothers. [Irish Legend: *LLEI*, I: 326]

7. **Courtly, Sir Hartley** rejected by heiress; she prefers his son. [Br. Lit.: *London Assurance*, Walsh *Modern*, 108]

8. **Dashwood, Elinor** bears rejection with dignity; eventually marries rejecter. [Br. Lit.: *Sense and Sensibility*]

9. **Hermione** rejected by Pyrrhus, who weds Andromache. [Fr. Lit.: *Andromache*]

10. **Hudson, Roderick** sculptor loses Christina Light to rich prince. [Am. Lit.: *Roderick Hudson*]

11. **Hugon, George** rejected by Nana, he stabs himself. [Fr. Lit.: *Nana*, Magill, I, 638–640]

12. **Jason** Medea's lover; leaves her for Glauce. [Gk. Lit.: *Medea*, Magill, I, 573–575]

13. **Maggie** rejected by brother, lover, mother, and neighbors. [Am. Lit.: *Maggie: A Girl of the Streets*, Magill, I, 543–544]

14. **Mellefont** doublecrossed by friend and rejected lover. [Br. Lit.: *The Double-Dealer*]

15. **Newcome, Clive** social conventions forbid him to pursue Ethel. [Br. Lit.: *The Newcomes*, Magill, I, 650–652]

16. **Orestes** spurned suitor of Hermione. [Fr. Lit.: *Andromache*]

17. **Phaedra** feigns rape on being scorned. [Gk. Lit.: *Hippolytus*]

18. **Potiphar's wife** traduces Joseph when seduction of him fails. [*O.T.: Genesis* 39:7–18]

19. **Robin, Fanny** betrayed by Sergeant Troy, her betrothed. [Br. Lit.: *Far From the Madding Crowd*, Magill, I, 266–268]

20. **Touchwood, Lady** dissolute matron rejected by nephew's love. [Br. Lit.: *The Double-Dealer*]

21. **Wiggins, Mahalah** her fiancé changed his mind on their wedding day. [Am. Lit.: *Peter Whiffle*, Magill, I, 739–741]

22. **willow tree** emblem of rejected affection. [Plant Symbolism: "Tit-Willow," *Mikado;* "Willow Song," *Othello*]

23. **Zuleika** traditional name for Potiphar's wife. [Pers. Lit.: Brewer *Dictionary*, 1175]

375. LOVE, TRAGIC (See also DEATH, EARLY.)

1. **Abélard and Héloïse** (Pierre, 1079–1144) (c. 1098–1164) unhappy affair left him castrated, her cloistered. [Eur. Hist.: Bishop, 272]

2. **Annabel Lee** a storm swept her away. [Am. Lit.: "Annabel Lee" in Hart, 35]

3. **Antony and Cleopatra** victims of conflict between political ambition and love. [Br. Lit.: *Antony and Cleopatra*]

4. **Cabot, Eben, and Abbie Putnam** after feuding, recognize love; each imprisoned thereafter. [Am. Lit.: *Desire Under the Elms*]

5. **Clärchen** commits suicide when beloved receives death sentence. [Ger. Lit.: *Egmont*]

6. **Deirdre** when Noisi is betrayed and slain, she kills herself. [Irish Legend: Benét, 259–260]

7. **Dido and Aeneas** with the gods demanding his departure, she commits suicide. [Rom. Lit.: *Aeneid;* Fr. Opera: Berlioz, *The Trojans,* Westerman, 174–176]

8. **Elizabeth** dies when Tannhäuser vows return to Venus. [Ger. Opera: Wagner, *Tannhäuser,* Westerman, 212]

9. **Evangeline and Gabriel** after years of searching, she finds him as he lay dying. [Am. Lit.: "Evangeline" in Hart, 263]

10. **Fields of Mourning** place in underworld where lovers who committed suicide dwell. [Rom. Lit.: *Aeneid*]

11. **Frankie and Johnnie** "sporting woman" shot her man for "doing her wrong." [Pop. Music: Leach, 415]

12. **Galatea and Acis** love shattered by latter's death. [Rom. Lit.: *Metamorphoses*]

13. **Ghismonda and Guiscardo** princess's and commoner's affair fatal upon discovery. [Ital. Lit.: *Decameron*]

14. **Glaucus** loses love, Scylla, when she is made monster. [Rom. Lit.: *Metamorphoses*]

15. **Gráinne** second wife of Fionn, she elopes with Diarmiud; caught by Fionn, Diarmiud is killed. [Irish Legend: *Century Classical,* 509]

16. **Hero and Leander** latter drowns, former kills herself in grief. [Gk. Lit.: *Hero and Leander;* Br. Lit.: *Hero and Leander*]

17. **Hylonome** commits suicide after death of lover, Cyllarus. [Gk. Myth.: Kravitz, 72, 123]

18. **Karenina, Anna** her death destroys Count Vronsky's desire to live. [Russ. Lit.: *Anna Karenina*]

19. **Launcelot, Sir, and Queen Guinevere** exiled by King Arthur, he returns after the King's death to find Guinevere a nun. [Arthurian Legend: *Le Morte d'Arthur*]

20. **Le Sueur, Lucetta** her love for Henchard squelched by his degradation. [Br. Lit.: *The Mayor of Casterbridge,* Magill, I, 571–573]

21. **Mimi** her love for Rodolfo ended by her early death. [Ital. Opera: Puccini, *La Bohème*, Westerman, 348–350]

22. **Norma and Pollio** die together as sacrifices to Druid war god. [Ital. Opera: Bellini, *Norma*, Westerman, 130–131]

23. **Olindo and Sophronia** latter condemned to stake; lover joins her. [Ital. Lit.: *Jerusalem Delivered*]

24. **Onegin, Eugene, and Tatyana** long hopelessly for each other after her marriage to another. [Russ. Lit.: *Eugene Onegin*]

25. **Orpheus and Eurydice** looking back to see if Eurydice was following him to earth, he lost her forever. [Gk. Myth.: Zimmerman, 103]

26. **Paolo and Francesca** slain by his jealous brother, her husband, Giancotto. [Ital. Lit.: *Inferno*]

27. **Pelléas and Mélisande** she married the wrong brother; dies of disappointment. [Fr. Opera: Debussy, *Pelléas and Mélisande*, Westerman, 196]

28. **Pyramus and Thisbe** thinking lover mauled, Pyramus kills himself; upon discovery, Thisbe does likewise. [Rom. Lit.: *Metamorphoses*]

29. **Romeo and Juliet** archetypal star-crossed lovers. [Br. Lit.: *Romeo and Juliet*]

30. **Saint-Preux and Julie d'Etange** passion waxes, but class strictures block marriage. [Fr. Lit.: *The New Helöise*]

31. **Tristan and Iseult** irrevocably enamored; die because of his wife's machinations. [Medieval Legend: *Tristan and Iseult*; Ger. Opera: *Tristan and Iseult*]

32. **Wray, Fay** innocent beauty drives giant gorilla, Kong, to his death. [Am. Cinema: *King Kong*]

376. **LOVE, UNREQUITED**

1. **Bashville** footman; has noble, unrequited affection for heiress. [Br. Lit.: *Cashel Byron's Profession*]

2. **Bede, Adam** thought only of Hetty; she loved another. [Br. Lit.: *Adam Bede*]

3. **Chastelard** died for love of Mary, Queen of Scots. [Br. Lit.: *Chastelard*, Walsh *Modern*, 92]

4. **de Clèves, Princess** secretly loves a man other than her husband. [Fr. Lit.: *La Princesse de Clèves*, Walsh *Modern*, 100]

5. **daffodil** symbol of unrequited love. [Flower Symbolism: Jobes, 405]

6. **Dobson, Zuleika** every Oxford undergraduate falls in love with and despairs over her. [Br. Lit.: *Zuleika Dobson*]

7. **Echo** pined for Narcissus till only voice remained. [Gk. Myth.: Brewer *Dictionary*, 363; Br. Lit.: *Comus*, in Benét, 217]

8. **Krazy Kat** to Ignatz, despite his efforts to dissuade her. [Comics: Horn, 436–437]

9. **Mignon** dies from hopelessness of love for Wilhelm. [Ger. Lit.: *Wilhelm Meister's Apprenticeship*, Walsh *Modern*, 266]

10. **Nureddin** lovesick for Margiana, the Caliph's daughter. [Ger. Opera: Cornelius, *Thief of Baghdad*, Westerman, 256]

11. **Orsino, Count** a priest committed to celibacy; loved by Beatrice. [Br. Lit.: "The Cenci" in Magill, I, 131–133]

12. **Ray, Philip** locks deep within heart his love for Annie. [Br. Lit.: "Enoch Arden" in Magill, I, 249–250]

13. **Sasha** Russian princess hopelessly loved by Orlando. [Br. Lit.: *Orlando*, Magill, I, 698–700]

14. **Standish, Miles** (c. 1584–1656) declared love for Priscilla; received no response. [Am. Lit.: "The Courtship of Miles Standish" in Magill, I, 165–166]

15. **striped carnation** symbol of love's denial. [Flower Symbolism: Jobes, 291]

16. **Treplev, Konstantin** aspiring novelist; hopelessly enamored of actress, commits suicide. [Russ. Lit.: *The Seagull*]

17. **de Vargas, Luis** seminarian falls for father's fiancée. [Span. Lit.: *Pepita Jiménez*]

18. **Zenobia** strong-minded woman; disappointed in love, drowns self. [Am. Lit.: *Blithedale Romance*]

377. LOVE, VICTORIOUS

1. **Ada and Arindal** mortal and fairy permitted to stay together. [Ger. Opera: Wagner, *The Fairies*, Westerman, 202]

2. **Babbie** gypsy wins clergyman despite opposition of town. [Br. Lit.: *The Little Minister*]

3. **Beatrice and Benedick** witty rebels against love; become enamored. [Br. Lit.: *Much Ado About Nothing*]

4. **Bell, Laura** wins Pendennis's love despite his slavish admiration for wealth. [Br. Lit.: *Pendennis*, Magill, I, 726–728]

5. **Bennet, Elizabeth** neither pride nor prejudice can cover up love for Darcy. [Br. Lit.: *Pride and Prejudice*, Magill, I, 180–183]

6. **Cellini and Teresa** their love prevails, despite jealous suitors and duels. [Fr. Opera: Berlioz, *Benvenuto Cellini*, Westerman, 169–170]

7. **Dodsworth, Sam** finally leaves hypocritical wife for true love. [Am. Lit.: *Dodsworth*]

8. **Doone, Lorna** John and Lorna's love wins over many obstacles. [Br. Lit.: *Lorna Doone*, Magill, I, 524–526]

9. **Ernesto and Norina** their schemes permit love to conquer. [Ital. Opera: Donizetti, *Don Pasquale*, Westerman, 123–124]

10. **Ladislaw, Will** finally marries Dorothea, despite her family's protests. [Br. Lit.: *Middlemarch*, Magill, I, 588–591]

11. **Lavinia** after war, affianced to Aeneas. [Rom. Lit.: *Aeneid*]

12. **Nikulaussön, Erlend** despite social convention, he wins Kristin's hand. [Nor. Lit.: *Kristin Lavransdatter*, Magill, I, 483–486]

13. **pierced heart** Renaissance emblem, with motto, "Love conquers all." [Art: Hall, 146]

14. **Pontmercy, Marius** despite grandfather's forbiddance, marries Cosette. [Fr. Lit.: *Les Misérables*]

15. **di Ripafratta, Cavalier** avowed woman-hater falls to innkeeper's feminine charms. [Ital. Lit.: *The Mistress of the Inn*]

16. **Rowena** loved by Ivanhoe, who finally claims her hand. [Br. Lit.: *Ivanhoe*]

17. **Thatcher, Becky** she wins Tom. [Am. Lit.: *Tom Sawyer*]

18. **Western, Jasper** Bumppo relinquishes his claim on Mabel to Jasper, whom Mabel loves. [Am. Lit.: *The Pathfinder*, Magill, I, 715–717]

378. **LOVE, VIRTUOUS**

1. **Aphrodite Urania** patron of ideal, spiritual love. [Gk. Myth.: Espy, 16]

2. **Armande** loves Clitandre platonically; values mind over senses. [Fr. Lit.: *Les Femmes Savantes*]

3. **Athelny, Sally** loves and marries Philip, despite the latter's shortcomings. [Br. Lit.: *Of Human Bondage*, Magill, I, 670–672]

4. **Beatrice** object of Dante's admiration, even after death. [Ital. Lit.: *La Vita Nuova; Divine Comedy*, Walsh *Classical*, 48]

5. **Bergerac, Cyrano de** does not reveal his love for Roxane. [Fr. Lit.: *Cyrano de Bergerac*]

6. **Camille** gives up Armand for his family's sake. [Fr. Lit.: *Camille*]

7. **Cupid's gold arrow** symbolizes noble affection. [Rom. Myth.: Jobes, 397]

8. **Dulcinea** as Quixote's ideal; now, generic for 'sweetheart.' [Span. Lit.: *Don Quixote*, Espy, 128]

9. **Laura** Petrarch's perpetual, unattainable love. [Ital. Lit.: Plumb, 26–32]

10. **Lucretia** model of virtue; raped by son of Tarquin, she kills herself. [Rom. Legend: Daniel, 152]

11. **Murasaki** reared by future husband; causes his reform. [Jap. Lit.: *The Tale of Genji*]

12. **Oriana** faithful and fair beloved for Amadis. [Span. Lit.: *Amadis de Gaul*]

13. **Schouler, Marcus** sets aside love for Trina for McTeague's benefit. [Am. Lit.: *McTeague*, Magill, I, 537–539]

379. LOVERS, FAMOUS

1. **Abélard and Héloïse** (Pierre, 1079–1142) (c. 1098–1164) persecuted 12th-century lovers. [Fr. Hist.: *Century Cyclopedia*, 14]

2. **Atala and Chactas** Indian lovers whose passion goes unconsummated. [Fr. Lit.: *Atala*]

3. **Aucassin and Nicolette** the love story of 12th-century France. [Fr. Lit.: *Aucassin and Nicolette*]

4. **Browning, Robert, and Elizabeth Barrett** (1812–1889) (1806–1861) 19th-century love one of most celebrated of literary romances. [Br. Lit.: Benét, 139]

5. **Celadon and Astree** bywords for lovers in pastoral poetry. [Br. Lit.: *Celadon*, Walsh *Modern*, 91]

6. **Ceyx and Halcyone** to perpetuate love, changed into kingfishers after former's drowning. [Rom. Lit.: *Metamorphoses*]

7. **Daphnis and Chloë** innocent though passionate love of two children. [Gk. Lit.: *Daphnis and Chloë*, Magill, I, 184]

8. **Darby and Joan** inseparable old-fashioned couple. [Br. Lit.: Espy, 335]

9. **Deirdre and Noisi** celebrated lovers of the Ulster Cycle. [Irish Legend: Benét, 259–260]

10. **Della and Jim** each sacrifices greatly for other's Christmas present. [Am. Lit.: "The Gift of the Magi" in Benét, 395]

11. **Edward VIII and Wallis Warfield Simpson** (1894–1972) (1896–   ) British king abdicates throne to marry divorcee (1936). [Br. Hist.: *NCE*, 835]

12. **Helen and Paris** their elopement caused the Trojan war. [Gk. Myth.: *Century Classical*, 525–528, 815–817]

13. **Hero and Leander** love affair on the Hellespont tragically ends with latter's drowning. [Gk. Lit.: *Hero and Leander*; Br. Lit.: *Hero and Leander*]

14. **Jacob and Rachel** he worked fourteen years to win her hand. [O.T.: *Genesis* 29:18]

15. **Lescaut, Manon, and the Chevalier des Grieux** he accompanies Manon to Louisiana when she is exiled for prostitution. [Fr. Lit.: *Manon Lescaut*]

16. **lovebirds** small parrots, traditional symbol of affection. [Am. Culture: Misc.]

17. **Oliver and Jenny** rapturous college relationship leads to blissful marriage. [Am. Lit.: *Love Story*]

18. **Petrarch and Laura** lovers in spirit only. [Ital. Lit.: Plumb, 26–32]

19. **Rinaldo and Armida** virgin witch seeks revenge but falls in love. [Ital. Lit.: *Jerusalem Delivered*]

20. **Romeo and Juliet** young love springs up amidst family feud. [Br. Lit.: *Romeo and Juliet*]

21. **Tristan and Iseult** their pact of undying love has tragic consequences. [Medieval Legend: *Tristan and Iseult*; Ger. Opera: *Tristan and Iseult*]

22. **turtle doves** adoring couple, building their nest. [O.T.: *Song of Songs* 2:12]

23. **Zhivago, Yuri, and Lara** passion stirs between idealistic doctor and nurse during Russian revolution. [Russ. Lit.: *Doctor Zhivago*]

380. **LOYALTY** (See also FRIENDSHIP, PATRIOTISM.)

1. **Achates** companion and faithful friend of Aeneas. [Rom. Lit.: *Aeneid*]

2. **Adam** family retainer; offers Orlando his savings. [Br. Lit.: *As You Like It*]

3. **Aeneas** carried his father Anchises from burning Troy. [Rom. Lit.: *Aeneid*]

4. **alexandrite** type of chrysoberyl typifying undying devotion. [Gem Symbolism: Jobes, 67]

5. **Antony, Mark** Caesar's beloved friend; turns public opinion against Caesar's assassins. [Br. Lit.: *Julius Caesar*]

6. **Argus** Odysseus' dog; overjoyed at Odysseus' return, he dies. [Gk. Lit.: *Odyssey*]

7. **Balderstone, Caleb** servant true to Ravenswoods despite poverty. [Br. Lit.: *The Bride of Lammermoor*]

8. **Bevis** mastiff who "saved his master by his fidelity." [Br. Lit.: *Woodstock*]

9. **Blondel** loyal troubadour to Richard the Lion-hearted; helps him escape. [Br. Lit.: *The Talisman*]

10. **bluebell** symbol of loyalty. [Plant Symbolism: *Flora Symbolica*, 172]

11. **Byam, Roger** remains faithful to Captain Bligh after mutiny. [Am. Lit.: *Mutiny on the Bounty*]

12. **Camillo** as counsellor, exemplifies constancy. [Br. Lit.: *The Winter's Tale*]

13. **Chauvin, Nicolas** (fl. early 19th century) he followed Napoleon through everything. [Fr. Hist.: Wallechinsky, 164]

14. **Chester** Matt Dillon's lame but game sidekick. [TV: "Gunsmoke" in Terrace, I, 331–332]

15. **Chingachgook** ever-devoted to Hawkeye. [Am. Lit.: *The Last of the Mohicans*]

16. **Cordelia** faithful daughter of sea god Llyr [Celtic Myth.: Parrinder, 67]; loyal and loving daughter of King Lear. [Br. Lit.: *King Lear*]

17. **dog** ever pictured at feet of saints; "man's best friend." [Medieval Art: Brewer *Dictionary*, 332; Western Folklore: Misc.]

18. **Dolius** the loyal retainer of Odysseus and Penelope. [Gk. Lit.: *Odyssey*]

19. **Eros** Antony's freed slave; kills himself rather than harm Antony. [Br. Lit.: *Antony and Cleopatra*]

20. **Eumaeus** loyal swineherd of Odysseus. [Gk. Lit.: *Odyssey*]

21. **Faithful Johannes** loyal servant dies for king and is resurrected. [Ger. Fairy Tale: Grimm, 22]

22. **Flavius** loyal and upright steward of Timon. [Br. Lit.: *Timon of Athens*]

23. **Gonzalo** Prospero's "true preserver and a loyal sir." [Br. Lit.: *The Tempest*]

24. **Good-Deeds** only companion who ultimately accompanies Everyman. [Medieval Lit.: *Everyman*]

25. **Horatio** true-blue friend of Hamlet. [Br. Lit.: *Hamlet*]

26. **Horton** "faithful one hundred percent," Horton sits on the Mayzie bird's egg until it is hatched. [Children's Lit.: *Horton Hatches the Egg*]

27. **Iolaus** nephew and trusted companion of Hercules. [Gk. Myth.: Howe, 141]

28. **Jonathan** stalwartly defended David; aided him in escape. [*O.T.: I Samuel* 20:32–34, 42; 23:16]

29. **Kato** loyal servant of the Green Hornet. [Radio: "The Green Hornet" in Buxton, 102–103]

30. **Kent** a "noble and true-hearted" courtier. [Br. Lit.: *King Lear*]

31. **Merrilies, Meg** Henry Bertram's Gypsy-nurse; thoroughly devoted and protective. [Br. Lit.: *Guy Mannering*]

32. **Moniplies, Richard** Nigel's servant; helps him out of imbroglio. [Br. Lit.: *Fortunes of Nigel*]

33. **Panza, Sancho** squire to Don Quixote. [Span. Lit.: *Don Quixote*]

34. **Passepartout** faithful valet of Phileas Fogg. [Fr. Lit.: *Around the World in Eighty Days*]

35. **Podsnap, John** has nationalistic fervor for Britain. [Br. Lit.: *Our Mutual Friend*]

36. **Ruth** devotedly follows mother-in-law to Bethlehem. [*O.T.: Ruth* 1:15–17]

37. **Scipio** Gil Blas' secretary; shares his imprisonment. [Fr. Lit.: *Gil Blas*]

38. **speedwell** indicates female faithfulness. [Flower Symbolism: *Flora Symbolica*, 177]

39. **Suzuki** ever faithful to her mistress, especially in sorrow. [Ital. Opera: Puccini, *Madama Butterfly*, Westerman, 358]

40. **Titinius** Cassius' loyal follower; follows him to death. [Br. Lit.: *Julius Caesar*]

41. **Tom, Uncle** "noble, high-minded, devoutly Christian Negro slave." [Am. Lit.: *Uncle Tom's Cabin*]

42. **Tonto** the Lone Ranger's "Kemo Sabe." [Radio: "The Lone Ranger" in Buxton, 143–144; Comics: Horn, 460; TV: Terrace, II, 34–35]

43. **Wiglaf** stood by Beowulf to fight dragon while others fled. [Br. Lit.: *Beowulf*]

381. LUCK, BAD

1. **albatross** killing it brings bad luck. [Br. Lit.: "Rime of the Ancient Mariner" in Norton, 597–610]

2. **black cat** because of its demonic associations. [Animal Folklore: Jobes, 297]

3. **black ox** sacrificed to Pluto; symbolic of calamity. [Gk. Myth.: Brewer *Dictionary*, 790]

4. **dead man's hand** two aces, two eights; hand Wild Bill Hickok held when murdered. [Am. Slang: Leach, 299]

5. **eclipse** regarded as portent of misfortune. [World Folklore: Leach, 337]

6. **Fawley, Jude** lost everything his heart desired. [Br. Lit.: *Jude the Obscure*]

7. **Flying Dutchman** ominous spectral ship; seen in storms off Cape of Good Hope. [Marine Folklore: *LLEI*, I: 285]

8. **Friday the 13th** regarded as unlucky day. [Western Folklore: Misc.]

9. **Hope diamond** largest blue diamond known; believed to bring bad luck. [Western Culture: *EB*, V: 126]

10. **Jonah** trying to escape God, brought tempest to sea. [*O.T.*: *Jonah* 1:4–12]

11. **ladder** walking under one can bring only misfortune. [Western Folklore: Leach, 598]

12. **mirror** the breaking of one brings seven years of bad luck. [Western Folklore: Cirlot, 211]

13. **opal** unlucky stone; represents the Evil Eye. [Gem Symbolism: Kunz, 148, 320]

14. **Plornish** disaster was his tour de force. [Br. Lit.: *Little Dorrit*]

15. **Seian Horse** ownership fatal. [Rom. Legend: Brewer *Dictionary*, 978]

16. **shirt of Nessus** Centaur's bloodied shirt; given to Heracles as gift by unsuspecting wife, it caused his death. [Gk. Myth.: Benét, 708]

17. **spilt salt** courts evil. [Rom. Myth.: Brewer *Dictionary*, 958; Ital. Art: "Last Supper"]

18. **step on a crack** and break your mother's back; advice to avoid walking on cracks in pavement. [Am. Folklore: Misc.]

19. **thirteen** number attending Last Supper, including Judas; considered unlucky number. [Christian Hist.: Brewer *Dictionary*, 1075; Western Folklore: Misc.]

382. **LUCK, GOOD**

1. **albatross** bird of good luck. [Br. Lit.: "The Rime of the Ancient Mariner" in Norton, 597–610]

2. **bat** symbol of good fortune; bat flesh imparts felicity. [Eastern Folklore: Mercatante, 182]

3. **carnelian** brings luck; drives away evil. [Gem Symbolism: Kunz, 62–63]

4. **crossed fingers** said to bring good luck to a person. [Western Folklore: Misc.]

5. **four-leaf clover** indicates good luck. [Plant Symbolism: Jobes, 350]

6. **gypsum** in egg-shaped form, brings good fortune. [Gem Symbolism: Kunz, 80]

7. **horseshoe** protective talisman placed over doors of churches, stables, etc. [Western Folklore: Leach, 505]

8. **Irish sweepstakes** only lucky people win this famous lottery. [Irish Hist.: *NCE*, 1614]

9. **knock on wood** to bring good luck and ward off bad luck. [Am. Folklore: Misc.]

10. **moonstone** sacred stone; brings good fortune. [Gem Symbolism: Kunz, 97–98]

11. **new penny** placing new penny in gift of purse brings recipient good luck. [Western Folklore: Misc.]

12. **penny** finding one by chance in street brings good luck. [Western Folklore: Misc.]

13. **penny loafer** placing penny in slot at top of shoe brings good fortune. [Am. Folklore: Misc.]

14. **rabbit's foot** proverbial good luck charm. [Western Folklore: Misc.]

15. **red** life-granting color; worn by brides and babies. [Asian Color Symbolism: Binder, 78]

16. **seven** symbolizes good luck in ancient and modern societies. [World Culture: Jobes, 1421–1422]

17. **seventh son** always a lucky or gifted person. [Western Folklore: Leach, 999]

18. **three** symbolizes good luck; most holy of all numbers. [World Culture: Jobes, 1563–1566]

19. **white on red** symbolizes good fortune. [Chinese Art: Jobes, 357]

383. LUST (See also PROFLIGACY, PROMISCUITY.)

1. **Aeshma** fiend of evil passion. [Iranian Myth.: Leach, 17]

2. **Aholah and Aholibah** lusty whores; bedded from Egypt to Babylon. [*O.T.: Ezekiel* 23:1–21]

3. **Alcina** lustful fairy. [Ital. Lit.: *Orlando Furioso*]

4. **Ambrosio, Father** supposedly virtuous monk goatishly ravishes maiden. [Br. Lit.: *The Monk*]

5. **Aphrodite Porne** patron of lust and prostitution. [Gk. Myth.: Espy, 16]

6. **Armida's Garden** symbol of the attractions of the senses. [Ital. Lit.: *Jerusalem Delivered*]

7. **Aselges** personification of lasciviousness. [Br. Lit.: *The Purple Island*, Brewer *Handbook*, 67]

8. **Ashtoreth** goddess of sexual love. [Phoenician Myth.: Zimmerman, 32]

9. **Asmodeus** female spirit of lust. [Jew. Myth.: Jobes, 141]

10. **Balthazar B** shy gentleman afloat on sea of lasciviousness. [Am. Lit.: *The Beastly Beatitudes of Balthazar B*]

11. **Belial** demon of libidinousness and falsehood. [Br. Lit.: *Paradise Lost*]

12. **Bess** Porgy's "temporary" woman; she knew weakness of her will and flesh. [Am. Lit.: *Porgy*, Magill, I, 764–766; Am. Opera: Gershwin, *Porgy and Bess*]

13. **Brothers Karamazov, The** family given to the pleasures of flesh. [Russ. Lit.: *The Brothers Karamazov*]

14. **Caro** loathsome hag; personification of fleshly lust. [Br. Lit.: *The Purple Island*, Brewer *Handbook*, 180]

15. **Casanova** (1725–1798) loving (and likable) libertine. [Ital. Hist.: Espy, 130]

16. **Cleopatra** (69–30 B.C.) Egyptian queen, used sex for power. [Egyptian Hist.: Wallechinsky, 323]

17. **Don Juan** literature's most active seducer: "in Spain, 1003." [Span. Lit.: Benét, 279; Ger. Opera: Mozart, *Don Giovanni*, Espy, 130–131]

18. **dove** attribute of Venus; by extension, carnal passion. [Art: Hall, 109]

19. **elders of Babylon** condemn Susanna when carnal passion goes unrequited. [*Apocrypha: Daniel and Susanna*]

20. **Falstaff, Sir John** fancies himself a lady-killer. [Br. Lit.: *Merry Wives of Windsor*]

21. **Fritz the Cat** a tomcat in every sense. [Comics: Horn, 266–267]

22. **goat** lust incarnate. [Art: Hall, 139]

23. **hare** attribute of sexual desire incarnate. [Art: Hall, 144]

24. **horns** attribute of Pan and the satyr; symbolically, lust. [Rom. Myth.: Zimmerman, 190; Art: Hall, 157]

25. **John of the Funnels, Friar** monk advocating lust. [Fr. Lit.: *Gargantua and Pantagruel*]

26. **Lilith** sensual female; mythical first wife of Adam. [*O.T.: Genesis* 4:16]

27. **long ears** symbol of licentiousness. [Indian Myth.: Leach, 333]

28. **Lothario** heartless libertine and active seducer. [Br. Lit.: *Fair Penitent*, Espy, 129]

29. **Malecasta** personification of wantonness. [Br. Lit.: *Faerie Queene*]

30. **Montez, Lola** (1818–1861) beguiling mistress to the eminent. [Br. Hist.: Wallechinsky, 325]

31. **Obidicut** fiend; provokes men to gratify their lust. [Br. Lit.: *King Lear*]

32. **Pan** man-goat of bawdy and lecherous ways. [Gk. Myth.: Brewer *Dictionary*, 798]

33. **pig** attribute of lust personified. [Art: Hall, 247]

34. **Porneius** personification of fornication. [Br. Lit.: *The Purple Island*, Brewer *Handbook*, 865]

35. **Priapus** monstrous genitals led him on the wayward path. [Rom. Myth.: Hall, 252]

36. **Robinson, Mrs.** middle-aged lady has affair with idealistic young graduate. [Am. Lit.: *The Graduate*; Am. Music: "Mrs. Robinson"]

37. **Salome** in her provocative Dance of the Seven Veils. [Aust. Opera: R. Strauss, *Salome*, Westerman, 417]

38. **Spanish jasmine** flower symbolizing lust. [Flower Symbolism: *Flora Symbolica*, 175]

39. **Villiers, George** first Duke of Buckingham and libidinous dandy. [Br. Lit.: *Waverley*]

40. **Zeus** the many loves of this god has made his name a byword for sexual lust. [Gk. Myth.: Howe, 297–301]

384. **LUXURY (See also WEALTH.)**

1. **angora cat** behavior suggests self-indulgence. [Animal Symbolism: Jobes, 96]

2. **Babylon** ancient city on Euphrates river; famed for its magnificence and culture. [Mid. East. Hist.: *NCE*, 202]

3. **Cadillac** expensive automobile and status symbol. [Trademarks: Crowley *Trade*, 83]

4. **Cartier's** jewelry firm founded by Alfred and Louis Cartier in Paris (1898). [Fr. Hist.: *EB*, 10: 177]

5. **caviar** extremely expensive delicacy of sturgeon's roe; byword for luxurious living. [Western Culture: Misc.]

6. **chinchilla** one of the costliest of furs, made into luxurious coats. [Western Culture: Misc.]

7. **Chivas Regal** expensive Scotch whisky. [Trademarks: Crowley *Trade*, 106]

8. **clover** indicates wealth and ease. [Western Folklore: Jobes, 350]
9. **Cockaigne** fabled land of luxury and idleness. [Medieval Legend: *NCE*, 589]
10. **fat of the land** Pharaoh offers Joseph's family Egypt's plenty. [*O.T.: Genesis* 45:18]
11. **fleshpots of Egypt** where Israelites "did eat bread to the full." [*O.T.: Exodus* 16:3]
12. **grapes** fruit of bacchanalia. [Art: Hall, 142]
13. **green pastures** untroubled life following the Lord. [*O.T.: Psalms* 23:2]
14. **land flowing with milk and honey** promised by God to afflicted Israelites. [*O.T.: Exodus* 3:8; 13:5]
15. **life of Riley** easy and troublefree existence. [Am. Usage: c. 1900 song, "Best of the House is None Too Good for Reilly"; TV: "The Life of Riley" in Terrace, II, 26]
16. **Mercedes Benz** expensive automobile and status symbol. [Trademarks: Crowley *Trade*, 368]
17. **mink coat** highly prized fur apparel; traditionally associated with wealthy ladies. [Western Culture: Misc.]
18. **Pullman car** comfortable, well-appointed railroad sleeping car named for maker. [Am. Hist.: Flexner, 210]
19. **Ritz** elegant and luxurious hotel opened in Paris in 1898 by César Ritz; hence, 'ritzy, putting on the ritz.' [Fr. Hist.: Wentworth, 429]
20. **Rolls Royce** the millionaire's vehicle. [Trademarks: Brewer *Dictionary*, 928]
21. **sable** fur of this mammal produces luxurious, soft fur coats. [Western Culture: Misc.]
22. **Savoy** sumptuous hotel in London; at the time of its opening, it set new standards of luxury. [Br. Hist.: *EB*, 8: 1118]
23. **Tiffany's** jewelry firm founded by Charles Lewis Tiffany; store in New York caters to the wealthy. [Am. Hist.: *EB*, 10: 177]

M

385. MADNESS

1. **Alcithoe** driven mad by Dionysus. [Gk. Myth.: Kravitz, 16]
2. **Alcmeon** driven mad by the Furies. [Gk. Myth.: Kravitz, 16]
3. **Ashton, Lucy** goes mad upon marriage; stabs husband. [Br. Lit.: *Bride of Lammermoor*]
4. **Bedlam** (Hospital of St. Mary of Bethlehem) first asylum for the insane in England; noted for brutal treatment of its patients. [Br. Hist.: *EB*, I: 924]
5. **Belvidera** goes mad when husband dies. [Br. Lit.: *Venice Preserved*, Benét, 1052]
6. **Broteas** angered Artemis; she drove him mad. [Gk. Myth.: Kravitz, 47]
7. **Butes** Dionysus drove him mad. [Gk. Myth.: Kravitz, 48]
8. **Cleese, John** manic comic master with persecution complex. [Br. TV: "Monty Python's Flying Circus" in Terrace, II, 108]
9. **Clementina, Lady** mentally unbalanced; vacillates between love and religion. [Br. Lit.: *Sir Charles Grandison*, Walsh *Modern*, 99]
10. **Dervish (Darwesh)** member of ascetic order; frenzied, whirling dancer. [Muslim Rel.: Parrinder, 75; Jobes, 433]
11. **Dympna, St.** curing of madness attributed to her intercession. [Christian Hagiog.: Attwater, 107]
12. **Elvira** great mad scene caused by betrayal of Arthur. [Ital. Opera: Bellini, *Puritani*, Westerman, 133–135]
13. **Furioso, Bombastes** goes mad upon loss of betrothed. [Br. Opera: Rhodes, *Bombastes Furioso*, Walsh, *Modern*, 64–65]
14. **Gunn, Ben** half-demented castaway. [Br. Lit.: *Treasure Island*]
15. **Leverkühn, Adrian** brilliant musician attains pinnacle; rapidly deteriorates mentally. [Ger. Lit.: *Doctor Faustus*]
16. **Lucia** frustration causes her to murder husband. [Ital. Opera: Donizetti, *Lucia di Lammermoor*, Westerman, 126–127]
17. **Mad Hatter** crazy gentleman who co-hosts mad tea party. [Br. Lit.: *Alice's Adventures in Wonderland*]
18. **March Hare** crazy rabbit who co-hosts mad tea party. [Br. Lit.: *Alice's Adventures in Wonderland*]

19. **McMurphy, Randall Patrick** brash Irishman, lobotomized in asylum after causing numerous scandals. [Am. Lit.: *One Flew Over the Cuckoo's Nest*]

20. **Myshkin, Prince** four years in sanitarium; treated for epilepsy. [Russ. Lit.: *The Idiot*]

21. **O'Bedlam, Bess** female counterpart of Tom O'Bedlam. [Br. Folklore: Walsh *Modern*, 55]

22. **O'Bedlam, Tom** an inmate of London's lunatic asylum. [Br. Folklore: Benét, 3]

23. **Ophelia** goes mad after father's death. [Br. Lit.: *Hamlet*]

24. **Orlando** driven insane by lover's betrayal. [Ital. Lit.: *Orlando Furioso*]

25. **Rochester, Bertha** pyromaniac wife of Edward Rochester. [Br. Lit.: *Jane Eyre*]

26. **Todd, Sweeney** barber returns to England; takes revenge for false conviction by slitting throats of customers. [Br. Folklore: Misc; Br. Lit.: *Sweeney Todd*; Am. Musical Theater: *Sweeney Todd, the Mad Barber of Fleet Street*, in *Facts* (1979), 292.]

27. **Very, Jones** "monomaniac" or "profoundly sane"? [Am. Hist.: Hart, 883]

28. **Wozzeck** thought of blood drives him to murder and suicide. [Aust. Opera: Berg, *Wozzeck*, Westerman, 480–481]

386. **MAGIC (See also ENCHANTMENT.)**

1. **Bleys** magician who taught Merlin arts of sorcery. [Arthurian Legend: Walsh *Classical*, 57]

2. **Houdini, Harry** (1874–1926) famous turn of century American magician and escape artist. [Am. Hist.: *NCE*, 1275]

3. **Merlin** prince of magicians. [Br. Lit.: *Le Morte d'Arthur*]

4. **Prospero** uses magic to achieve ends. [Br. Lit.: *The Tempest*]

MAGNIFICENCE (See SPLENDOR.)

387. **MANNISHNESS (See also BOYISHNESS.)**

1. **Amazon** female warrior. [Gk. Myth.: Parrinder, 18]

2. **Bradamant** female knight-errant. [Ital. Lit.: *Orlando Furioso*]

3. **Brass, Sally** couldn't tell her apart from brother Sampson. [Br. Lit.: *The Old Curiosity Shop*]

4. **Clampett, Elly May** hillbilly amazon. [TV: "The Beverly Hillbillies" in Terrace, I, 93–94]

5. **Omphale** Lydian queen; wore Hercules' lion skin. [Gk. Myth.: Wheeler, 269]

6. **Rosie the Riveter** popular WWII song romanticizing women workers. [Am. Hist.: Flexner, 395]

388. MARKSMANSHIP

1. **Buffalo Bill** (1846–1917) famed sharpshooter in Wild West show. [Am. Hist.: Flexner, 67]
2. **Crotus** son of Pan, companion to Muses; skilled in archery. [Gk. Myth.: Howe, 70]
3. **Deadeye Dick** sobriquet of 1880s cowboy-sharpshooter, Nat Love. [Am. Hist.: Flexner, 41]
4. **Hawkeye** sharpshooting frontier folk hero. [Am. Lit.: *The Last of the Mohicans*]
5. **Hickok, "Wild Bill"** (1837–1876) sharpshooting stage driver and marshal of U.S. West. [Am. Hist.: Flexner, 387]
6. **Hood, Robin** famed throughout land for skill as archer. [Br. Lit.: *Robin Hood*]
7. **Oakley, Annie** (1860–1926) renowned expert gunshooter of Buffalo Bill's Wild West show. [Am. Hist.: Brewer *Dictionary*, 771]
8. **Robin-A-Bobbin** such a bad archer, killed crow while aiming for pigeon. [Nurs. Rhyme: *Mother Goose*, 33]
9. **Tell, William** shot apple off son's head with arrow. [Swiss Legend: Brewer *Dictionary*, 1066; Ital. Opera: Rossini, *William Tell*]

389. MARRIAGE

1. **American linden** symbol of marriage. [Plant Symbolism: *Flora Symbolica*, 182]
2. **Aphrodite Genetrix** patron of marriage and procreation. [Gk. Myth.: Espy, 16]
3. **Benedick** nickname for groom; derived from Shakespeare's Benedick. [Br. Lit.: *Love's Labour's Lost*]
4. **Bridal Chorus** traditional wedding song; from Wagner's *Lohengrin*. [Music: Scholes, 1113]
5. **Cana** wedding feast where Christ made water into wine. [N.T.: John 2:1–11]
6. **epithalamium** poem in honor of bride and groom. [Western Lit.: *LLEI*, 1: 283]
7. **Erato** Muse of bridal songs. [Gk. Myth.: Kravitz, 90]
8. **huppah** bridal canopy in Jewish weddings. [Judaism: Wigoder, 274]

9. **orange blossoms** traditional decoration for brides. [Br. and Fr. Tradition: Brewer *Dictionary*, 784]

10. **quince** in portraits, traditionally held by woman in wedding. [Art: Hall, 257]

11. **rice** newly married couples pelted with rice for connubial good luck. [Western Folklore: Leach, 938]

12. **St. Agnes's Eve** when marriageable girls foresee their future husbands. [Br. Lit.: "The Eve of St. Agnes" in Norton, 686–693]

13. **Wedding March** popular bridal music from Mendelssohn's march in *Midsummer Night's Dream*. [Music: Scholes, 1113]

14. **Wife of Bath** many marriages form theme of her tale. [Br. Lit.: *Canterbury Tales*, "Wife of Bath's Tale]

390. MARTYRDOM (See also SACRIFICE.)

1. **Agatha, St.** tortured for resisting advances of Quintianus. [Christian Hagiog.: Daniel, 21]

2. **Alban, St.** traditionally, first British martyr. [Christian Hagiog: *NCE*, 49]

3. **Andrew, St.** apostle and missionary; condemned to be scourged and crucified. [Christian Hagiog.: Brewster, 4]

4. **arrow and cross** symbol of martyrdom of St. Sebastian. [Christian Iconog.: Attwater, 304]

5. **Brown, John** (1800–1859) abolitionist leader; died for antislavery cause. [Am. Hist.: Hart, 111]

6. **Callista** beautiful Greek convert; executed and later canonized. [Br. Lit.: *Callista*]

7. **carnelian** symbol of St. Sebastian. [Christian Hagiog.: Brewer *Handbook*, I, 411]

8. **Elmo, St.** patron saint of sailors; intestines wound on windlass. [Christian Hagiog.: Attwater, 117]

9. **Golgotha** place of martyrdom or of torment; after site of Christ's crucifixion. [Western Folklore: Espy, 79]

10. **Holy Innocents** male infants slaughtered by Herod. [Christian Hagiog.: Attwater, 179; *N.T.*: *Matthew* 2:16–18]

11. **James Intercisus, St.** cut to pieces for belief in Christianity. [Christian Hagiog.: Brewster, 2]

12. **Jesus Christ** crucified at demand of Jewish authorities. [*N.T.*: *Matthew* 27:24–61; *Mark* 15:15–47; *Luke* 23:13–56; *John* 19:13–42]

13. **Joan of Arc, St.** (1412–1431) burned at stake for witchcraft (1431). [Fr. Hist.: *NCE*, 1417; Br. Lit.: *I Henry VI*]

14. **John the Baptist, St.** Jewish prophet; beheaded at instigation of Salome. [*N.T.: Matthew* 11:1–19; 17:11–13]

15. **More, Sir Thomas** (1478–1535) statesman and humanist; beheaded for opposition to Henry VIII's Act of Supremacy [Br. Hist.: *NCE*, 1830]

16. **Nero's Torches** oil- and tar-smeared Christians implanted and set aflame. [Christian Hist.: Brewer *Note-Book*, 614]

17. **palm** appeared on martyrs' graves. [Christian Symbolism: Appleton, 73]

18. **Perpetua, St., and St. Felicity** gored by wild beasts; slain with swords. [Christian Hagiog.: Attwater, 273]

19. **Peter, St.** apostle crucified upside down in Rome. [Christian Hagiog.: Brewster, 310]

20. **Sacco and Vanzetti** (Nicola, 1891–1927) (Bartolomeo, 1888–1927) perhaps executed more for radicalism than murder (August 22, 1927). [Am. Hist.: Flexner, 311]

21. **Sebastian, St.** Roman soldier; shot with arrows and struck with clubs. [Christian Hagiog.: Brewster, 75]

22. **Stephen, St.** first martyr; stoned as blasphemer. [Christian Hagiog.: Attwater, 313]

23. **sword** instrument of decapitation of early saints. [Christian Symbolism: Appleton, 14]

24. **Thecla, St.** first woman martyr. [Christian Hagiog.: Brewer *Dictionary*, 1072]

25. **Thomas à Becket, St.** (1118–1170) brutally slain in Canterbury cathedral by king's knights. [Br. Hist.: *NCE*, 2735–2736]

391. MASSACRE (See also GENOCIDE.)

1. **Acre** after conquering city, Richard I executed 2700 Muslims (1191). [Eur. Hist.: Bishop, 83–84]

2. **Armenian Massacre** Turks decimated Armenian population, dispersed survivors (1896). [Eur. Hist.: *EB*, I: 525]

3. **Bloody Sunday** seeking audience with Czar, workers receive bullets instead (1905). [Russ. Hist.: *EB*, II: 93]

4. **Boston Massacre** skirmish between British troops and Boston crowd (1770). [Am. Hist.: *EB*, II: 180]

5. **Charge of the Light Brigade** Russians massacre English cavalry at Balaklava (1854). [Eur. Hist.: *NCE*, 212; Br. Lit.: Benét, 186]

6. **Fetterman Massacre** party of 80 frontiersmen ambushed by Indians (1886). [Am. Hist.: *NCE*, 942]

7. **Goliad** 300 slain by Santa Ana in wake of Alamo (1836). [Am. Hist.: Van Doren, 155]

8. **Guernica** bombing of Guernica (1937); memorialized by Picasso's painting. [Span. Hist.: *NCE*, 1158; Art Hist.: Osborne, 867]

9. **Holy Innocents** infant boys massacred in Bethlehem under Herod. [*O.T.: Matthew* 2:16–18]

10. **jawbone of ass** with this, Samson kills 1000 men. [*O.T.: Judges* 15:15]

11. **Katyn Massacre** mass murder of 4250 Polish officers during WWII (c. 1939). [Polish Hist.: *NCE*, 1457]

12. **Lawrence, Kansas** Union stronghold where Quantrill's Confederate band killed more than 150 people (1863). [Am. Hist.: *EB*, VIII: 338]

13. **Massacre of Glencoe** treated hospitably, king's men attempt annihilation of MacDonald clan (1692). [Br. Hist.: Brewer *Note-Book*, 567]

14. **Munich Olympics '72** Arab terrorists brutally killed 11 Israeli athletes. [Jew. Hist.: Wigoder, 462]

15. **My Lai Massacre** murder of 22 Vietnamese villagers by American troops under Lt. William Calley, Jr. (1968). [Am. Hist.: *Facts* (1973) 145]

16. **ox-goad** using this weapon, Shamgar slew 600 Philistines. [*O.T.: Judges* 3:31]

17. **St. Bartholomew's Day Massacre** thousands of French Huguenots murdered for their faith (1572). [Fr. Hist.: *EB*, VII: 775]

18. **St. Valentine's Day Massacre** murder of seven members of a gang of bootleggers in Chicago (1929). [Am. Hist.: *EB*, VII: 797]

19. **Sicilian Vespers** massacre of French (Angevins) by Sicilian nationals (1282). [Ital. Hist.: *NCE*, 2511]

20. **third of May** (1808) Murat's squads executed hundreds of Spanish citizens; memorialized in Goya's painting. [Sp. Hist. and Sp. Art: Daniel, 220]

21. **Whitman Massacre** murder of missionary Marcus Whitman and family by Cayuse Indians (1847). [Am. Hist.: *NCE*, 2972]

22. **Wounded Knee** scene of the slaughter of 200 Sioux Indians (1890). [Am. Hist.: Van Doren, 306]

23. **Wyoming Massacre** colonial militia butchered by Tory-Indian force (1776). [Am. Hist.: Jameson, 564]

MATRICIDE (See MURDER.)

MEDIATION (See PEACEMAKING.)

392. MEDICINE (See also HEALING.)

1. **Acesis** daughter of Asclepius; name means 'healing remedy.' [Gk. Myth.: Kravitz, 37]

2. **Angitia** goddess of healing. [Rom. Myth.: Kravitz, 24]

3. **Antony, St.** invoked against venereal diseases and erysipelas (St. Antony's fire). [Christian Hagiog.: Daniel, 28–29]

4. **Apollo (Phoebus)** patron of medicine. [Gk. Myth.: Kravitz, 28]

5. **Asclepius (Aesculapius)** god of healing. [Gk. Myth.: Kravitz, 37]

6. **caduceus** snake-entwined staff; emblem of medical profession. [Gk. Myth.: Kravitz, 49]

7. **Carmenta** goddess of healing. [Gk. Myth.: Kravitz, 53]

8. **Casey, Ben** one of television's premier doctors. [TV: Terrace, I, 90]

9. **Cosmas, St. and St. Damian** patron saints; brothers, practiced medicine without charge. [Christian Hagiog.: Attwater, 94]

10. **Hippocrates** (c. 460–c. 360 B.C.) Greek physician and "Father of Medicine." [Gk. Hist.: NCE, 1246]

11. **Hippocratic oath** ethical code of medicine. [Western Culture: EB, 11: 827]

12. **Iaso** Asclepius's daughter; personification of his healing power. [Gk. Myth.: Kravitz, 37]

13. **Kildare, Dr.** handsome physician of television melodrama. [Am. TV: Terrace, I, 211]

14. **Mayo Clinic** voluntary association of more than 500 physicians in Rochester, Minnesota. [Am. Hist.: EB, 11: 723]

15. **Paean** physician to the gods. [Gk. Myth.: Espy, 29]

16. **Panacea** daughter of Greek god of healing. [Gk. Myth.: Kravitz, 37]

17. **Roch, St.** (also St. Rock) invoked against infectious diseases; especially in the 15th century, against plague. [Christian Hagiog.: Daniel, 198]

18. **Vitus, St.** invoked against epilepsy and chorea (St. Vitus's dance). [Christian Hagiog.: Attwater, 338]

19. **Welby, Marcus** avuncular doctor of impeccable ethics. [Am. TV: "Marcus Welby, M.D." in Terrace, II, 66]

393. MELANCHOLY (See also GRIEF.)

1. **Acheron** river of woe in the underworld. [Gk. Myth.: Howe, 5]

2. **Anatomy of Melancholy** prose work dealing with various morbid mental states. [Br. Lit.: *Anatomy of Melancholy*]

3. **Barton, Amos** beset by woes. [Br. Lit.: "Sad Fortunes of Amos Barton" in Walsh *Modern*, 45]

4. **black bile** humor effecting temperament of gloominess. [Medieval Physiology: Hall, 130]

5. **blues** melancholy, bittersweet music born among American Negroes. [Am. Music: Scholes, 113]

6. **Cargill, Rev. Josiah** serious, moody, melancholic minister. [Br. Lit.: *St. Ronan's Well*]

7. **Carstone, Richard** driven to gloom by collapse of expectations. [Br. Lit.: *Bleak House*]

8. **cave of Trophonius** oracle so awe-inspiring, consulters never smiled again. [Gk. Myth.: Brewer *Dictionary*, 1103]

9. **Eeyore** alarmingly gloomy, morose donkey. [Children's Lit.: *Winnie-the-Pooh*]

10. **Elegy in a Country Churchyard** meditative poem of a melancholy mood. [Br. Lit.: Harvey, 266]

11. **Ellis Island** immigration center where many families were separated; "isle of tears." [Am. Hist.: Flexner, 193]

12. **Gummidge, Mrs.** "lone lorn creetur" with melancholy disposition. [Br. Lit.: *David Copperfield*]

13. **hare** flesh brings melancholy to those who eat it. [Animal Symbolism: Mercatante, 125]

14. **Jacques** "can suck melancholy out of a song." [Br. Lit.: *As You Like It*]

15. **Mock Turtle** forever weeping and bemoaning his fate. [Br. Lit.: *Alice's Adventures in Wonderland*]

16. **Mudville** no joy here when Casey struck out. [Am. Sports Lit.: "Casey at the Bat" in Turlin, 642]

17. **Orpheus** composed, sang many melancholic songs in memory of deceased Eurydice. [Gk. Myth.: *Orpheus and Eurydice*, Magill, I, 700–701]

18. **Roquentin, Antoine** discomfited by his existence's purposelessness, solitarily despairs. [Fr. Lit.: *Nausea*]

19. **Sad Sack** hapless and helpless soldier; resigned to his fate. [Comics: Horn, 595–596]

20. **Valley of the Shadow of Death** life's gloominess. [*O.T.: Psalms* 23:4]

21. **Wednesday's child** full of woe [Nurs. Rhyme: Opie, 309]

22. **yew tree** symbolizes grief. [Flower Symbolism: *Flora Symbolica*, 178]

394. **MEMORY**

1. **Aethalides** herald of the Argonauts; had perfect memory. [Gk. Myth.: Kravitz, 11]

2. **Balderstone, Thomas** knew all of Shakespeare by heart. [Br. Lit.: *Sketches by Boz*]

3. **Eunoe** river whose water sparks remembrance of kindnesses. [Ital. Lit.: *Purgatory*, 33]

4. **Mneme** Boeotian wellspring which whetted the memory. [Gk. Myth.; Wheeler, 713]

5. **Mnemosyne** goddess of memory; mother of Muses. [Gk. Myth.: Espy, 20]

6. **Munin** one of Odin's ravens; regarded as embodying memory. [Norse Myth.: Leach, 761]

MERCY (See FORGIVENESS.)

395. **MESSENGER**

1. **Aethalides** herald of the Argonauts. [Gk. Myth.: Kravitz, 11]

2. **Alden, John** (1599–1687) speaks to Priscilla Mullins for Miles Standish. [Am. Lit.: "The Courtship of Miles Standish" in Hart, 188–189]

3. **caduceus** Mercury's staff; symbol of messengers. [Rom. Myth.: Jobes, 266–267]

4. **dove** sent by Noah to see if the waters were abated; returns with an olive leaf. [*O.T.: Genesis* 8:8–11]

5. **eagle** symbolic carrier of God's word to all. [Christian Symbolism: Appleton, 35]

6. **Gabriel** announces births of Jesus and John the Baptist. [*N.T.: Luke* 1:19, 26]

7. **Iris** messenger of the gods. [Gk. Myth.: Kravitz, 130; Gk. Lit.: *Iliad*]

8. **Irus** real name was Arnaeus; messenger of Penelope's suitors. [Gk. Lit.: *Odyssey*]

9. **Hermes** (Rom. **Mercury**) messenger of the gods. [Gk. Myth.: Wheeler *Dictionary*, 240]

10. **Munin and Hugin** Odin's two ravens; brought him news from around world. [Norse Myth.: Leach, 761]

11. **Nasby** nickname for U.S. postmasters. [Am. Usage: Brewer *Dictionary*, 745–746]

12. **Pheidippides** ran 26 miles from Marathon to Athens to carry news of Greek defeat of Persians. [Gk. Legend: Zimmerman, 159]

13. **Pony Express** speedy relay mail-carrying system of 1860s. [Am. Hist.: Flexner, 276]

14. **Reuters** news agency; established as telegraphic and pigeon post bureau (1851). [Br. Hist.: Benét, 852]

15. **Revere, Paul** (1735–1818) warned colonials of British advance (1775). [Am. Hist.: 425–426]

16. **staff** symbolic of a courier on a mission. [Christian Symbolism: Appleton, 4]

17. **Stickles, Jeremy** messenger for the king of England (1880s). [Br. Lit.: *Lorna Doone*, Magill, I, 524–526]

18. **Strogoff, Michael** courier of the czar. [Fr. Lit.: *Michael Strogoff*]

19. **thorn** the messenger of Satan. [*N.T.*: *II Corinthians* 12:7]

20. **Western Union** company founded in 1851; provides telegraphic service in U.S. [Am. Hist.: *NCE*, 2958]

396. MIDDLE CLASS (See also PHILISTINISM.)

1. **Babbitt** self-satisfied conformer to middle-class ideas and ideals. [Am. Lit: *Babbitt*]

2. **Forsyte** representative of property-owning class in early 20th century. [Br. Lit.: *The Forsyte Saga*]

397. MILITARISM (See also SOLDIERING.)

1. **Adrastus** leader of the Seven against Thebes. [Gk. Myth.: *Iliad*]

2. **Siegfried** killed many enemies; led many troops to victory. [Ger. Lit. *Nibelungenlied*]

398. MIMICRY

1. **chameleon** lizard able to change the color of its skin to match brown or green surroundings; has come to mean 'inconstant person.' [Western Culture: Misc.]

2. **Costard** apes Elizabethan courtly language. [Br. Lit.: *Love's Labour's Lost*]

3. **Doolittle, Eliza** slum girl taught by professor to imitate upper class. [Br. Lit.: *Pygmalion*]

4. **lyrebird** Australian bird; one of the most famous mimic species. [Ornithology: Sparks, 116]

5. **mockingbird** noted for mimicking songs of other birds; one of the world's most noted singers. [Ornithology: Sparks, 116]

6. **parrot** bird able to mimic human speech; hence, *parrot* 'to repeat or imitate.' [Western Culture: Misc.]

399. MIRACLE

1. **Aaron's rod** flowering rod proved him to be God's choice. [*O.T.: Numbers* 17:8]

2. **Agnes, St.** hair grew to cover nakedness. [Christian Hagiog.: Brewster, 76–77]

3. **Anthony of Padua, St.** believed to have preached effectively to school of fishes. [Christian Legend: Benét, 39]

4. **Cana** at wedding feast, Christ turns water into wine. [*N.T.: John* 2:1–11]

5. **deus ex machina** improbable agent introduced to solve a dilemma. [Western Drama: *LLEI*, I: 279]

6. **Elais** produced olive oil from ground by touch. [Gk. Myth.: Kravitz, 86]

7. **Euphemus** Argonaut; could cross water without getting wet. [Gk. Myth.: Kravitz, 95]

8. **Geppetto** his wish fulfilled when marionette becomes real boy. [Children's Lit.: *Pinocchio;* Am. Cinema: *Pinocchio* in *Disney Films,* 32–37]

9. **Holy Grail** chalice enabled Sir Galahad to heal a cripple. [Br. Lit.: *Le Morte d'Arthur*]

10. **Jesus Christ** as son of God, performed countless miracles. [*N.T.: Matthew, Mark, Luke, John*]

11. **loaves and fishes** Jesus multiplies fare for his following. [*N.T.: Matthew* 14:15–21; *John* 6:5–14]

12. **Lourdes** underground spring revealed to Bernadette Soubirous in visions (1858); major pilgrimage site. [Fr. Hist.: *EB*, VI: 352; Am. Lit.: *Song of Bernadette;* Am. Cinema: "The Song of Bernadette" in Halliwell, 670]

13. **Marah** undrinkably bitter waters, sweetened by Moses. [*O.T.: Exodus* 15:23–25]

14. **Miracle on 34th Street** Santa Claus comes to New York. [Am. Cinema: Halliwell, 493]

15. **parting of the Pamphylean Sea** Alexander's hosts traverse sea in Persian march. [Class. Hist.: Gaster, 238]

16. **parting of the Red Sea** divinely aided, Moses parts the waters for an Israelite escape. [*O.T.: Exodus* 14:15–31]

17. **rod of Moses** transforms into serpent, then back again. [*O.T.: Exodus* 4:24]

400. MIRROR

1. **Alasnam's mirror** indicates to Alasnam a girl's virtue. [Arab. Lit.: *Arabian Nights*, "Prince Zeyn Alasnam"]
2. **Alice's looking-glass** Alice passes through this into dreamland. [Br. Lit.: *Through the Looking-Glass*]
3. **Cambuscan's mirror** warns of impending adversity; indicates another's love. [Br. Lit.: *Canterbury Tales*, "The Squire's Tale"]
4. **Lao's mirror** reflects the looker's mind and thoughts. [Br. Lit.: *Citizen of the World*]
5. **Merlin's magic mirror** allows king to see whatever concerns him. [Br. Lit.: *Faerie Queene*]
6. **Mirror, mirror** magically tells arrogant queen who is the most beautiful of all. [Ger. Fairy Tale: "Snow White" in Grimm, 184]
7. **Perseus's shield** he uses it as a mirror so that he will not have to look directly at Medusa. [Gk. Myth.: Howe, 214]
8. **Prester John's mirror** allows him to see happenings throughout his dominions. [Medieval Legend: Brewer *Handbook*, 710]
9. **Reynard's wonderful mirror** imaginary mirror; reflects doings a mile away. [Medieval Lit.: *Reynard the Fox*]
10. **Vulcan's mirror** showed past, present, and future to viewer. [Br. Lit.: *Orchestra*, Brewer *Handbook*, 710]

401. MISANTHROPY

1. **Ahab, Captain** consumed by hate, pursues whale that ripped off his leg. [Am. Lit.: *Moby Dick*]
2. **Alceste** antisocial hero. [Fr. Lit.: *Le Misanthrope*]
3. **Confidence Man, The** Melville's social satire castigating mankind. [Am. Lit.: *The Confidence Man*, Magill, III, 221–223]
4. **Dryas** hated mankind; avoided public appearances. [Rom. Myth.: Kravitz, 84]
5. **Fuller's thistle** indicates hatred of mankind. [Flower Symbolism: *Flora Symbolica*, 178]
6. **Nemo, Captain** brilliant captain of submarine, "Nautilus"; bitter misanthropy the reason for his undersea seclusion. [Fr. Lit.: *Twenty Thousand Leagues Under the Sea*]
7. **Sub-Mariner** friend of fish, scourge of man. [Comics: Horn, 640]
8. **teasel** indicates hatred of mankind. [Flower Symbolism: *Flora Symbolica*, 178]
9. **Timon** "undone by goodness," turns misanthropic. [Br. Lit.: *Timon of Athens*]

MISBEHAVIOR (See MISCHIEVOUSNESS.)

402. MISCHIEVOUSNESS (See also JOKE, PRACTICAL.)

1. **Ate** goddess of evil and mischief. [Gk. Myth.: Parrinder, 33; Kravitz, 39]

2. **Beaver** mischievous ten-year-old beset by trivial troubles. [TV: "Leave It to Beaver" in Terrace, II, 18–19]

3. **Beg, Little Callum** devilish page. [Br. Lit.: *Waverley*]

4. **Brer Rabbit** clever trickster. [Children's Lit.: *Uncle Remus*]

5. **Brown, Buster** turn-of-the-century *enfant terrible*. [Comics: Horn, 145]

6. **Cercopes** apelike pygmies; tried to steal Hercules' weapons. [Gk. Myth.: Leach, 206]

7. **crocodile** symbolizes naughtiness and chicanery. [Jewish Tradition: Jobes, 382]

8. **Dennis the Menace** latter-day Buster Brown, complete with dog. [Comics: Horn, 201]

9. **Erlking** elf king who works mischief on children. [Ger. Folklore: *LLEI*, I: 283]

10. **Eulenspiegel, Till** legendary peasant known for his pranks. [Ger. Folklore: Benét, 325–326]

11. **Finn, Huckleberry** mischievous, sharp-witted boy has many adventures. [Am. Lit.: *Huckleberry Finn*]

12. **Georgie Porgie** kissed the girls and made them cry. [Nurs. Rhyme: Opie, 185]

13. **Halloween** (Allhallows Eve) youngsters play pranks on the neighbors. [Am. Folklore: Misc.]

14. **Junior (Red Skelton)** "the mean widdle kid." [Radio: "The Red Skelton Show" in Buxton, 197]

15. **Katzenjammer Kids** twin Teutonic terrors. [Comics: "The Captain and the Kids" in Horn, 156–157]

16. **Lampwick** archetypal juvenile delinquent leads Pinocchio astray. [Am. Cinema: *Pinocchio* in *Disney Films*, 32–37]

17. **Little Rascals, The** scamps unite to terrorize adults. [Am. TV: Terrace, II, 31]

18. **Merop's Son** misguided do-gooder. [Gk. and Rom. Myth.: Brewer *Dictionary*, 704]

19. **Moth** "handful of wit"; Armado's "pretty knavish page." [Br. Lit.: *Love's Labour's Lost*]

20. **Nicka-Nan Night** Shrove Tuesday eve when boys play tricks. [Br. Folklore: Brewer *Dictionary*, 756]

21. **Our Gang** group of children in comedy series: always into mischief. [Am. Cinema: Halliwell, 546; Am. TV: "The Little Rascals" in Terrace, II, 31]

22. **Peck's Bad Boy** mischievous boy plays pranks on his father. [Am. Lit.: *Peck's Bad Boy*, Hart, 642]

23. **Peter Rabbit** always ransacking farmer MacGregor's patch. [Children's Lit.: *The Tale of Peter Rabbit*]

24. **pixies** prank-playing fairies; mislead travelers. [Br. Folklore: Briggs, 328–330]

25. **Puck** knavish hobgoblin who plays pranks. [Br. Lit.: *A Midsummer Night's Dream*]

26. **Rooney, Andy** scatterbrained gossoon; makes trouble without trying. [Irish Lit.: *Handy Andy*]

27. **Sawyer, Tom** hookey-playing, imaginative lad of St. Petersburg, Missouri. [Am. Lit.: *Tom Sawyer*]

28. **Wag, Charlie** school-skipping delinquent of penny dreadful. [Br. Lit.: *Charlie Wag, the Boy Burglar*, Opie, 117]

403. MISERLINESS (See also STINGINESS.)

1. **Collyer brothers** (Homer, 1882–1947) (Langely, 1886–1947) wealthy brothers who lived barren and secluded lives in junk-laden Harlem mansion. [Am. Hist.: *Facts* (1947) 116; Am. Lit.: *My Brother's Keeper.*]

2. **Green, Hetty** (1834–1916) "Witch of Wall Street"; financial wizard whose miserliness became legendary. [Am. Hist.: *The Day They Shook the Plum Tree*]

3. **Marner, Silas** cares only to amass gold; robbed of it, he finds new meaning in love for abandoned child. [Br. Lit.: Benét, 930]

4. **Scrooge** "grasping old sinner" who learns that miserliness leads only to loneliness and pain. [Br. Lit.: "A Christmas Carol" in Benét, 196]

404. MISSIONARY

1. **Aubrey, Father** converts savages to Christianity. [Fr. Lit.: *Atala*]

2. **Boniface, St.** missionary to the German infidels in 8th century. [Christian Hagiog.: Brewster, 271]

3. **Davidson, Rev. Alfred** attempts to convert Sadie Thompson to religion but ends up seducing her. [Br. Lit.: "Miss Thompson" in Benét, 675; Am. Cinema: "Rain" in Halliwell, 593]

4. **Livingstone, David** (1813–1873) explorer and missionary in Africa. [Br. Hist.: *NCE*, 1596]

5.   **Patrick, St.** (c. 385–461) early missionary to and patron saint of Ireland. [Christian Hagiog.: Brewster, 138]

6.   **Salvation Army** international religious organization known for its charitable and missionary work. [Christian Rel.: *NCE*, 2408–2409]

7.   **Society of Jesus** Roman Catholic religious order distinguished in foreign missions. [Christian Hist.: *NCE*, 1412]

8.   **Xavier, St. Francis** indefatigable pioneer converter of East Indies. [Christian Hagiog.: Attwater, 141–142]

405.   **MISTRESS (See also COURTESANSHIP, PROSTITUTION.)**

1.   **Abra** favorite concubine of Solomon. [Br. Lit.: *Solomon on the Vanity of the World*, Benét, 3]

2.   **Bains, Lulu** to Elmer Gantry. [Am. Lit.: *Elmer Gantry*]

3.   **Brangwen, Ursula** living with Anton Skrebensky without marriage license causes shock. [Br. Lit.: *The Rainbow*, Magill, I, 800–802]

4.   **Bridehead, Sue** of Jude Fawley; two children by him. [Br. Lit.: *Jude the Obscure*]

5.   **Burden, Joanna** mistress and benefactor to Joe Christmas. [Am. Lit.: *Light in August*]

6.   **Gournay, Mlle. de** Montaigne's "adopted daughter." [Fr. Hist.: Brewer *Handbook*, 633]

7.   **Guinevere, Queen** King Arthur's wife; Sir Launcelot's mistress. [Br. Lit.: *Le Morte d'Arthur*]

8.   **Simonet, Albertine** paramour of narrator. [Fr. Lit.: *Remembrance of Things Past*]

406.   **MOCKERY**

1.   **Abas** changed into lizard for mocking Demeter. [Rom. Myth: *Metamorphoses*, Zimmerman, 1]

2.   **Beckmesser** pompous object of practical jokes. [Ger. Opera: Wagner, *Meistersinger*, Westerman, 226–227]

3.   **crown of thorns** Christ thus ridiculed as king of Jews. [*N.T.*: *Matthew* 27:29; *Mark* 15:17; *John* 19:2–5]

4.   **Ecce Homo** Pilate's presentation of Jesus to Jews. [*N.T.*: *John* 19:4–6]

5.   **I.N.R.I.** ('Isus Nazarnus, Rex Idrum') inscription fastened upon Christ's cross as a mockery. [Christianity: Brewer *Note-Book*, 450]

6.   **Momus** god of blame and ridicule. [Gk. Myth.: Espy, 31]

407. **MODESTY** (See also CHASTITY, HUMILITY.)

1. **Bell, Laura** reserved, demure character. [Br. Lit.: *Pendennis*]
2. **Bianca** gentle, unassuming sister of Kate. [Br. Lit.: *The Taming of the Shrew*]
3. **fig leaves** used to cover Adam and Eve's nakedness. [*O.T.: Genesis* 3:7]
4. **pearl** emblem of discreet shyness. [Gem Symbolism: Kunz, 69]
5. **sweet violet** indicates a modest temperament. [Flower Symbolism: *Flora Symbolica*, 178]

408. **MONEY** (See also FINANCE.)

1. **Brink's** Boston armored car service; robbed of over one million dollars (1950). [Am. Hist.: *Facts* (1950), 24]
2. **Mammon** personification; one cannot serve him and God simultaneously. [*N.T.: Matthew* 6:24: *Luke* 16:9, 11, 13]
3. **Moneta** 'monitress'; epithet of Juno; origin of *mint*. [Rom. Myth.: Espy, 20]
4. **Newland, Abraham** governor of Bank of England; eponymously, banknote. [Br. Hist.: Wheeler, 258]

409. **MONSTER**

1. **Abominable Snowman** enigmatic yeti of the Himalayas. [Tibetan Lore: Wallechinsky, 443]
2. **Aegaeon** gigantic monster with 100 arms, 50 heads. [Gk. and Rom. Myth.: Wheeler, 5]
3. **Argus** hundred-eyed giant who guarded Io. [Gk. Myth. and Rom. Lit.: *Metamorphoses*]
4. **basilisk** lizard supposed to kill with its gaze. [Gk. Myth.: Brewer *Handbook*, 93]
5. **Briareus, Cottus, and Gyges** the three Hecatoncheires (or Centimani), giants each having 50 heads and 100 arms. [Gk. Myth.: Zimmerman, 118]
6. **Brontes** cruel thunder-maker of the three Cyclopes. [Gk. Myth.: Parrinder, 47; Jobes, 251, 400]
7. **Cacus** fire-breathing giant monster. [Rom. Myth.: Kravitz, 49]
8. **Caliban** misshapen "missing link." [Br. Lit.: *The Tempest*]
9. **Cerberus** three-headed watchdog of Hades. [Gk. Myth.: Avery, 270]
10. **Charybdis** Poseidon's daughter; monster of the deep. [Gk. Lit.: *Odyssey*; Rom. Lit.: *Aeneid*]
11. **chimera** mythical creature: goat-lion-dragon; vomited flames. [Classical Myth.: *LLEI*, I: 325]

12. **cockatrice** half-serpent, half-cock; kills with glance. [Heraldry: Brewer *Dictionary*, 243]

13. **Cyclopes** Poseidon's sons, each with one eye in the center of his forehead. [Gk. Lit.: *Odyssey*]

14. **Echidna** half nymph, half snake; never grew old. [Gk. Myth.: Kravitz, 85]

15. **Fenris** frightful wolf, grew sinisterly in size and strength. [Scand. Myth.: *LLEI*, I: 328]

16. **Frankenstein's monster** created from parts of corpses. [Br. Lit.: *Frankenstein*]

17. **Geryon** celebrated monster with three united bodies or three heads. [Rom. Lit.: *Aeneid*]

18. **Gorgons** monsters with serpents for hair and brazen claws. [Gk. Myth.: Zimmerman, 114; Gk. Lit.: *Iliad*]

19. **Grendel** giant in human shape; lives in a murky pond. [Br. Lit.: *Beowulf*]

20. **griffin** fabulous animal, part eagle, part lion. [Gk. Myth. and Art: Hall, 143; Ital. Lit.: *Purgatory*]

21. **harpie** foul-smelling creature; half-vulture, half-woman. [Gk. Myth.: Mercatante, 212–213]

22. **hippocampus** fabulous marine creature; half fish, half horse. [Rom. Myth. and Art: Hall, 154]

23. **hippogriff** offspring of griffin and mare. [Ital. Lit.: *Orlando Furioso*]

24. **Hydra** seven-headed water snake; ravaged Lerna, near Argos. [Gk. and Rom. Myth.: Hall, 149]

25. **Kraken** giant snakelike sea creature. [Dan. Folklore: Mercatante, 194–195]

26. **Ladon** dragon who guarded the Apples of the Hesperides. [Gk. Myth.: Zimmerman, 145]

27. **Lamia** scaly, four-legged, hermaphrodite creature. [Br. Folklore: Briggs, 260–262]

28. **Leviathan** frighteningly powerful sea serpent. [*O.T.: Job* 41; *Psalms* 74:14; 104:26; *Isaiah* 27:1]

29. **Loch Ness monster** "Nessie"; sea serpent said to inhabit Loch Ness. [Scot. Folklore: Wallechinsky, 443]

30. **Medusa** the only mortal Gorgon. [Gk. Myth.: Zimmerman, 161]

31. **Midgard serpent** monstrous serpent that encircles the earth. [Norse Myth.: Leach, 723]

32. **Minotaur** beast with bull's head and man's body. [Gk. Myth.: Brewer *Dictionary*, 714]

33. **Nicor** Scandinavian sea monster; whence, "Old Nick." [Br. Folklore: Espy, 44]

34. **Nidhogg** terrible beast in Nastrond; gnaws ashtree, Yggdrasil. [Norse Myth.: Wheeler, 259]

35. **opinicus** fabulous amalgam of dragon, camel, and lion. [Heraldry: Brewer *Dictionary*, 782]

36. **Orc** monstrous sea creature; devours human beings. [Ital. Lit.: *Orlando Furioso*]

37. **Orthos** two-headed dog; brother of Cerberus. [Gk. Myth.: Zimmerman, 186]

38. **python** huge serpent which sprang from stagnant waters after the Deluge. [Gk. Myth.: Zimmerman, 227]

39. **roc** white bird of enormous size. [Arab. Lit.: *Arabian Nights*, "Second Voyage of Sindbad the Sailor"]

40. **Sagittary** half man, half beast with eyes of fire. [Gk. Myth.: Brewer *Handbook*, 947]

41. **Sasquatch** giant hairy hominid said to lurk about the Pacific Northwest. [Am. Hist.: Payton, 601]

42. **Scylla** half beautiful maiden, half hideous dog. [Gk. Lit.: *Odyssey;* Rom. Lit.: *Metamorphoses*]

43. **666** number of the blasphemous beast with seven heads and ten horns. [*N.T.: Revelation* 13–14]

44. **Sphinx** head and breasts of a woman, body of a dog, and wings of a bird. [Gk. Myth.: Zimmerman, 246; Gk. Lit.: *Oedipus Rex*]

45. **Typhoeus** hundred-headed beast killed by Jovian thunderbolt. [Gk. Myth.: Brewer *Dictionary*, 1111]

46. **werewolf** a man transformed into a wolf. [Eur. Folklore: Benét, 1082]

410. MOON

1. **Artemis** (Rom. **Diana**) goddess of the moon. [Gk. Myth.: Kravitz, 36; Brewer *Dictionary*, 727]

2. **Astarte** (**Ashtoreth**) personification of moon in crescent stage. [Phoenician Myth.: Brewer *Dictionary*, 726–727]

3. **Bast** cat-headed goddess representing sun and moon. [Ancient Egyptian Rel.: Parrinder, 42]

4. **Cynthia** goddess of the moon. [Gk. Myth.: Kravitz, 72]

5. **Endymion** name of man in the moon. [Gk. Myth.: Brewer *Dictionary*, 376–377]

6. **Hecate** personification of the moon before rising and after setting. [Gk. Myth.: Brewer *Dictionary*, 726–727]

7. **Luna** ancient Roman goddess personifying the moon. [Rom. Myth.: Zimmerman, 153]

8. **Petrus** caretaker of Heaven; makes sure moon shines on whole earth. [Ger. Opera: Orff, *The Moon,* Westerman, 115–116]

9. **Phoebe** moon as sister of sun (Phoebus). [Gk. Myth.: Brewer *Dictionary,* 726–727]

10. **Selene** the moon as lover of sleeping shepherd Endymion. [Gk. Myth.: Brewer *Dictionary,* 726–727]

411. MOTHERHOOD

1. **Asherah** mother of the gods; counterpart of Gaea. [Canaanite Myth.: Benét, 57]

2. **Cybele** Great Mother; goddess of nature and reproduction. [Phrygian Myth.: Parrinder, 68; Jobes, 400]

3. **Cynosura** Idaean nymph; nursed the infant Zeus. [Gk. Myth.: Howe, 74]

4. **Danu (Anu)** divine procreator and guardian of gods and mortals. [Celtic Myth.: Parrinder, 72]

5. **Devaki** virgin mother of Krishna. [Hindu Myth.: Parrinder, 76]

6. **Devi** the "great goddess," wife of Shiva; "Mother." [Hindu Myth.: Parrinder, 77]

7. **Gaea** earth and mother goddess. [Gk. Myth.: Zimmerman, 108]

8. **Mary** apotheosized as mother of Christ. [*N.T.: Matthew, Mark, Luke, John*]

9. **Rhea** often titled Great Mother of the Gods. [Gk. Myth.: *NCE,* 1796]

10. **Whistler's mother** popular name for the painter's "Arrangement in Grey and Black, No. 1: The Artist's Mother." [Br. Art: *EB,* 19:814–815]

MOTIVATION (See INDUCEMENT.)

MOURNING (See GRIEF.)

412. MURDER (See also ASSASSINATION, KILLING.)

1. **Abimelech** slew his 70 brothers to become ruler. [*O.T.: Judges* 9:5]

2. **Adrammelech and Sharezer** murder father, Sennacherib, for Assyrian throne. [*O.T.: II Kings* 19:37]

3. **Barnwell, George** noble motives cause him to murder uncle. [Br. Lit.: *Novels by Eminent Hands,* Walsh *Modern,* 44]

4. **Bluebeard** closets away bodies of former wives. [Fr. Fairy Tale: Harvey, 97–98]

5. **Borden, Lizzie** (1860–1927) woman accused of mutilating father and stepmother with ax (1872). [Am. Hist.: Hart, 91]

6. **Boston Strangler** (Albert De Salvo, 1932–   ) strangled thirteen women between 1962 and 1964. [Am. Hist.: Misc.]

7. **Busiris** murders predecessor to gain Egyptian throne. [Gk. Myth: Avery, 231]

8. **Cain** jealous, slays Abel. [O.T.: Genesis 4:8]

9. **Cenci, Beatrice** with brothers, arranges murder of cruel father. [Br. Lit.: The Cenci]

10. **Claudius** murders brother to gain throne. [Br. Lit.: Hamlet]

11. **Danaides** slew husbands on wedding night. [Gk. Myth.: Kravitz, 74]

12. **Donatello** throws Miriam's persecutor over cliff to death. [Am. Lit.: The Marble Faun]

13. **Donegild** killed by Alla for abandoning his wife and son at sea. [Br. Lit.: Canterbury Tales, "Man of Law's Tale"]

14. **Hagen** stabs Siegfried in back; kills Gunther. [Ger. Opera: Wagner, Götterdämmerung, Westerman, 245]

15. **Hines, Doc** kills Joe's father; lets mother die in childbirth. [Am. Lit.: Light in August]

16. **Ibbetson, Peter** a confessed murderer, yet a sensitive, romantic man. [Br. Lit.: Peter Ibbetson, Magill, I, 736–738]

17. **In Cold Blood** nonfiction novel about a brutal, senseless murder in Kansas. [Am. Lit.: In Cold Blood]

18. **Injun Joe** stabs town doctor to death. [Am. Lit.: Tom Sawyer]

19. **Ixion** first murderer of a relative in classical mythology. [Gk. Myth.; Zimmerman, 142; Rom. Lit.: Aeneid]

20. **Jack the Ripper** killed and disemboweled 9 London prostitutes (1888–1889). [Br. Hist.: Brewer Note-Book, 463]

21. **Medea** murdered, among others, her two children. [Gk. Lit.: Century Classical, 684–685]

22. **Michele** murders wife's lover; hides body under cloak. [Ital. Opera: Puccini, The Cloak, Westerman, 362–363]

23. **Modo** fiend presiding over homicide. [Br. Lit.: King Lear]

24. **Mordred, Sir** illegitimate son and treacherous killer of Arthur. [Br. Lit.: Le Morte d'Arthur]

25. **Oedipus** kills father in argument not knowing his identity. [Gk. Lit.: Oedipus Rex]

26. **Orestes** commits matricide to avenge father's honor. [Gk. Lit.: *Electra*]

27. **Porgy** murders Crown, who tried to take Bess. [Am. Opera: Gershwin, *Porgy and Bess*, Westerman, 556]

28. **Raskolnikov** plans and carries out the murder of an old woman pawnbroker. [Russ. Lit.: *Crime and Punishment*]

29. **Rudge** murders master and gardener. [Br. Lit.: *Barnaby Rudge*]

30. **Sikes, Bill** hanged for killing of Nancy. [Br. Lit.: *Oliver Twist*]

31. **Smith, George Joseph** dispatched wives and lovers in bathtubs in 1910s. [Br. Hist.: Wallechinsky, 274]

32. **Sparafucile** his killing of Gilda fulfills curse against Rigoletto. [Ital. Opera: Verdi, *Rigoletto*, Westerman, 300]

33. **Thuggee** religious devotion to Kali involves human strangulation. [Indian Hist.: Brewer *Dictionary*, 1080]

413. **MUSIC**

1. **Apollo** god of music and fine arts. [Gk. Myth.: Zimmerman, 26]

2. **Bragi (Brage)** harpist-god; flowers bloomed, trees budded as he played. [Norse Myth.: Leach, 160]

3. **Cecilia, St.** patron of music and legendary inventor of organ. [Christian Hagiog.: Thompson, 380]

4. **Corybantes** musicians; provided music for goddesses' orgiastic dances. [Gk. Myth.: Kravitz, 67]

5. **Daphnis** shepherd; invented pastoral music to console himself. [Gk. Myth.: Parrinder, 72; Jobes, 414]

6. **Euterpe** Muse of dramatic melody; patroness of flautists. [Gk. Myth.: Brewer *Dictionary*, 385]

7. **Israfel** "none sing so wildly well." [Am. Lit.: "Israfel" in Portable Poe, 606]

8. **Jubal** forebear of all who play harp and pipe. [*O.T.: Genesis* 4:21]

9. **Linus** musician and poet; invented melody and rhythm. [Gk. Myth.: Zimmerman, 152]

10. **Muses** (Rom. **Camanae**) goddesses who presided over the arts. [Gk. Myth.: Howe, 172]

11. **Orpheus** musician, charmed even inanimate things with lyre-playing. [Gk. Myth.: Brewer *Dictionary*, 787]

12. **Polyhymnia** Muse of sacred song. [Gk. Myth.: Howe, 172]

13. **Schroeder** his only wish is to play Beethoven's music on his piano. [Comics: "Peanuts" in Horn, 542–543]

14. **Syrinx** transformed into reeds which pursuing Pan made into pipe. [Gk. Myth.: Hall, 232; Rom. Lit.: *Metamorphoses*]

15. **Tin Pan Alley** *lit.* 1650 Broadway, New York City; *fig.* fount of American popular music. [Am. Music: Thompson, 1105]

414. MUTENESS

1. **Elops** dumb serpent; gives no warning of its approach. [Br. Lit.: *Paradise Lost*]

2. **Henry** bald-headed, pugnosed and silent youngster of comic strip. [Comics: Sheridan, 200]

415. MUTILATION

1. **Absyrtus** hacked to death; body pieces strewn about. [Gk. Myth.: Walsh *Classical*, 3]

2. **Agatha, St.** had breasts cut off. [Christian Hagiog.: Attwater, 34]

3. **Atreus** slew his brother Thyestes's sons and served them to their father at banquet. [Gk. Myth.: Jobes, 153]

4. **Dagon** Philistine idol; falls, losing head and hands. [*O.T.: I Samuel* 5:1–4]

5. **ear and knife** at Christ's betrayal, Peter docked soldier's ear. [Christian Symbolism: *N.T., John* 18:10]

6. **Erasmus, St.** disemboweled, windlass used to wind entrails out of his body. [Art: Daniel, 95]

7. **Jack the Ripper** (late 19th century) dissected his victims. [Br. Hist.: Brewer *Note-Book*, 463]

8. **Monkey's Paw, The** short story in which mangled son is brought back to life *as is* to greedy, foolish old couple with three wishes. [Brit. Lit.: Benét, 511]

9. **Procrustes** made travelers fit bed by stretching or lopping off their legs. [Gk. Myth.: Zimmerman, 221]

10. **Sinis** split victims by fastening them between two bent pines and then letting the pines spring upright. [Gk. Legend: Brewer *Dictionary*, 1005]

MUTINY (See REBELLION.)

416. MYSTERY

1. **abominable snowmen** the yeti of Tibet; believed to exist, yet no sure knowledge concerning them. [Asian Hist.: Wallechinsky, 443–444]

2. **Bermuda Triangle** section of North Atlantic where many planes and ships have mysteriously disappeared. [Am. Hist.: *EB*, I: 1007]

3. **Big Foot (Sasquatch)** man ape similar to the yeti; reputed to have been seen in northwestern U.S. [Am. Hist.: "Yeti" in Wallechinsky, 443–444]

4. **closed book** medieval symbolism for the unknown. [Christian Symbolism: Appleton, 13]

5. **Dark Lady, The** mentioned in Shakespeare's later sonnets; she has never been positively identified. [Br. Lit.: *Century Cyclopedia*, I: 1191]

6. **Easter Island's statues** origin and meaning of more than two hundred statues remain unknown. [World Hist.: Wallechinsky, 443]

7. **E = mc²** physical law of mass and energy; arcanum to layman. [Am. Hist.: Flexner, 298]

8. **Lady or the Tiger, The** Stockton's tale never reveals which fate awaits the youth who dared fall in love with the king's daughter. [Am. Lit.: Benét, 559]

9. **Loch Ness monster** supposed sea serpent dwelling in lake. [Scot. Hist.: Wallechinsky, 443]

10. **Man in the Iron Mask** mysterious prisoner in reign of Louis XIV, condemned to wear black mask at all times. [Fr. Hist.: Brewer *Note-Book*, 460]

11. **Mary Celeste** ship found in mid-Atlantic with sails set, crew missing (1872). [Br. Hist.: Espy, 337]

12. **Mona Lisa** enigmatic smile beguiles and bewilders. [Ital. Art: Wallechinsky, 190]

13. **Roanoke** fate of colony has never been established (1580s). [Am. Hist.: Jameson, 430]

14. **Sphinx** half woman, half lion; poser of almost unanswerable riddle. [Gk. Myth.: Howe, 258; Gk. Lit.: *Oedipus Rex*]

15. **Stonehenge** huge monoliths with lintels in Wiltshire, England, have long confounded modern man as to purpose. [Br. Hist.: Wallechinsky, 442]

16. **U.F.O.** unexplained and unidentified flying object. [Science: Brewer *Dictionary*, 1112]

417. **MYSTICISM**

1. **cabala** Jewish oral traditions, originating with Moses. [Judaism: Benét, 154]

2. **Catherine of Siena, St.** experienced visions from age seven. [Christian Hagiog.: Hall, 59]

3. **Druids** magical priests of Celtic religion; oak cult. [Celtic Rel.: Leach, 325; Jobes, 471]

4. **Hudson, Dr. Wayne** believed power obtained by good deeds and silence. [Am. Lit.: *The Magnificent Obsession*, Magill, I, 547–549]

5. **Ouija** letterboard reveals messages from spirits. [Am. Pop. Culture: Brewer *Dictionary*, 788]

6. **Svengali** Hungarian hypnotist, mesmerizes artist's model who becomes a famous singer under his influence. [Br. Lit.: *Trilby*]

7. **Teresa of Ávila, St.** religious contemplation brought her spiritual ecstasy. [Christian Hagiog.: Attwater, 318]

8. **Zen** Buddhist sect; truth found in contemplation and self-mastery. [Buddhism: Brewer *Dictionary*, 1174]

N

418. **NAIVENESS** (See also **INEXPERIENCE, INNOCENCE.**)

1. **Agnes** young girl, affects to be simple and ingenuous. [Fr. Lit.: *L'Ecole des Femmes*]

2. **babes in the woods** applied to easily deceived or naive persons. [Folklore: Jobes, 169]

3. **beardlessness** traditional representation of innocence and inexperience. [Western Folklore: Jobes, 190]

4. **Carlisle, Lady Mary** couldn't determine true nobility. [Am. Lit.: *Monsieur Beaucaire*, Magill, I, 616–617]

5. **Curlylocks** nursery rhyme heroine exemplifies innocence. [Folklore: Jobes, 398]

6. **Dondi** foster child; confronts world with wide-eyed innocence. [Comics: Horn, 217–218]

7. **Do-Right, Dudley** Canadian mountie do-gooder. [TV: "The Dudley Do-Right Show" in Terrace, I, 229–230]

8. **Errol, Cedric** seven-year-old believes the best of everyone. [Am. Lit.: *Little Lord Fauntleroy*]

9. **Evelina** 17-year-old ingenuously circulates through fashionable London. [Br. Lit.: *Evelina*]

10. **Georgette** Ted Baxter's pretty, ignorant wife. [TV: "The Mary Tyler Moore Show" in Terrace, II, 70–71]

11. **Little Nell** meek little girl reared by grandfather. [Br. Lit.: *The Old Curiosity Shop*]

12. **Miller, Daisy** innocent and ignorant American girl put in compromising European situations. [Am. Lit.: *Daisy Miller*]

13. **Miranda** innocent and noble-minded daughter of Prospero. [Br. Lit.: *The Tempest*]

14. **Schlemihl, Peter** archetypal innocent; sold soul to devil. [Ger. Lit.: *Peter Schlemihl;* Fr. Opera: Westerman, *Tales of Hoffman*, 274–277]

15. **Shosha** narrator's mentally backward and utterly artless wife. [Am. Lit.: *Shosha*]

16. **Topsy** young slave girl; completely naive. [Am. Lit.: *Uncle Tom's Cabin*]

17. **white lilac** flowers indicative of naiveté, callowness. [Flower Symbolism: *Flora Symbolica*, 175]

419. **NATIVITY (See also CHRISTMAS.)**

   1. **Bethlehem** birthplace of Jesus. [*N.T.: Matthew* 2:1]
   2. **Caspar, Melchior, and Balthazar** Magi of the Orient pay homage to infant Jesus. [Christianity: Hall, 6]
   3. **manger** cattle trough which served as crib for Christ. [*N.T.: Luke* 2:7]
   4. **ox and ass** always present in pictures of Christ's birth. [Christian Art: de Bles, 29; *O.T.: Habakkuk* 3:4]
   5. **shepherds** notified by angel of the birth of the Messiah. [*N.T.: Luke* 2:8–17]
   6. **Star of Bethlehem** star in the east which directed the Magi and shepherds to the baby Jesus. [*N.T.: Matthew* 2:9]
   7. **swaddling clothes** in which Mary wraps her new-born infant. [*N.T.: Luke* 2:7]
   8. **three wise men** kings of the Orient, come to worship the baby Jesus. [*N.T.: Matthew* 2:1–2]

NEGLECTFULNESS (See CARELESSNESS.)

NERVOUSNESS (See INSECURITY.)

420. **NIGHT**

   1. **Apepi** leader of demons against sun god; always vanquished by morning. [Egyptian Myth.: Leach, 66]
   2. **Apophis** opponent of sun god Ra. [Egyptian Myth.: Benét, 43]
   3. **Ashtoreth** Moon goddess; Queen of night; equivalent of Greek Astarte. [Phoenician Myth.: Walsh *Classical*, 34–35]
   4. **Cimmerians** half-mythical people dwelling in eternal gloom. [Gk. Lit.: *Odyssey*]
   5. **Erebus** personification and god of darkness. [Gk. Myth.: Brewer *Dictionary*, 381]
   6. **Fafnir** his slaying represents the destruction of night demon. [Norse Myth.: *LLEI*, I: 327]
   7. **Nox** goddess of night. [Rom. Myth.: Wheeler, 261]
   8. **owl** nocturnal bird; Night embodied. [Art: Hall, 231]

421. **NOBLEMINDEDNESS**

   1. **Andrews, Joseph** epitome of the virtuous male. [Br. Lit.: *Joseph Andrews*]
   2. **Banquo** principled and noble compatriot of Macbeth. [Br. Lit.: *Macbeth*]
   3. **Bede, Adam** accepts beloved even after illicit affair. [Br. Lit.: *Adam Bede*]

4. **Camiola** generously pays Bertoldo's ransom. [Br. Lit.: *The Maid of Honor*, Walsh Modern, 84]

5. **Cheeryble Brothers** noble, generous twins. [Br. Lit.: *Nicholas Nickleby*]

6. **Daphnis** afraid of causing pain, does not deflower Chloë. [Ger. Lit.: *Daphnis and Chloë*, Magill, I, 184]

7. **Levin, Konstantine** shows compassion in dealing with peasant laborers. [Russ. Lit.: *Anna Karenina*]

8. **Lohengrin** defeats Telramund in trial by combat; spares him. [Ger. Opera: Wagner, *Lohengrin*, Westerman, 215]

9. **Lord Jim** successful in lifelong efforts to regain honor lost in moment of cowardice. [Br. Lit.: *Lord Jim*]

10. **Newman, Christopher** destroys the evidence that could wreck the man who obstructed his marriage plans. [Am. Lit.: *The American*]

11. **pirates of Penzance** never attacked weaker parties; always freed orphans. [Br. Opera: *The Pirates of Penzance*]

12. **Rienzi** pardons his would-be murderer. [Ger. Opera: Wagner, *Rienzi*, Westerman, 203]

13. **Valjean, Jean** yields to the man who has harassed him unmercifully. [Fr. Lit.: *Les Misérables*]

14. **Wilkes, Ashley** sensitive Southerner who remains true to homeland and wife. [Am. Lit.: *Gone With the Wind*, Magill, III, 424–426.]

422. NOBLE SAVAGE

1. **Chactas** the "noble savage" of the Natchez Indians; beloved of Atala. [Fr. Lit.: *Atala*]

2. **Chingachgook** idealized noble Indian. [Am. Lit.: *The Deerslayer*]

3. **Daggoo** African savage and crew member of the *Pequod*. [Am. Lit.: *Moby Dick*]

4. **noble savage** concept of a simple, pure, and superior man, uncorrupted by civilization. [Western Culture: Benét, 718–719]

5. **Oroonoko** the noble savage enslaved; rebels against captors. [Br. Lit.: *Oroonoko*]

6. **Queequeg** Polynesian prince and Ishmael's comrade aboard whaling vessel, *Pequod*. [Am. Lit.: *Moby Dick*]

NOISE (See LOUDNESS.)

NONCHALANCE (See INDIFFERENCE.)

423. NOSE

1. **Barabas** inventor of infernal machine; possessor of pachydermal snout. [Br. Lit.: *The Jew of Malta*]

2. **Bardolph** for red nose, known as "knight of the burning lamp." [Br. Lit.: *Merry Wives of Windsor*]

3. **Bergerac, Cyrano de** gallant Frenchman; mocked unceasingly for extremely large nose [Fr. Lit.: *Cyrano de Bergerac*]

4. **Durante, Jimmy** ("Schnozzle") (1893–1980) American pianist-comedian with huge nose. [Radio: "The Jimmy Durante Show" in Buxton, 124–125; Am. Cinema: Halliwell, 232]

5. **Kovatzov, Major** loses social eminence when nose self-detaches. [Russ. Lit.: *The Nose*, Kent, 474–497]

6. **Pinocchio** wooden boy's nose grows longer with every lie. [Ital. Lit.: *Pinocchio*; Am. Cinema: *Pinocchio* in *Disney Films*, 32–37]

7. **Rudolph** his red nose lit the way for Santa and his sleigh. [Am. Pop. Music: "Rudolph the Red-Nosed Reindeer"]

NOSINESS (See GOSSIP.)

424. NOSTALGIA

1. **Give My Regards to Broadway** singer sends well-wishes to home town. [Am. Pop. Music: Fordin, 531]

2. **Combray** village of narrator and family. [Fr. Lit.: *Remembrance of Things Past*]

3. **Happy Days** 1950s America viewed through tinted lenses. [TV: Terrace, I, 337–338]

4. **My Ántonia** book in which author recalls her precious childhood years. [Am. Lit.: Magill, I, 630–632]

5. **neiges d'antan** "Where are the snows of yesteryear?" [Fr. Lit.: *Ballade des Dames du temps jadis*, "Villon" in Benét, 1061]

425. NUDITY

1. **Adam and Eve** unashamed in Eden without clothes. [*O.T.*: Genesis 2:25]

2. **Agnes, St.** hair grew to cover her nakedness. [Christian Hagiog.: Daniel, 21]

3. **burlesque show** stage entertainment to which was added striptease dancing. [Am. Hist.: *EB*, II: 383–384]

4. **Digambara** ascetic Jainist sect whose members went naked. [Jainism: *NCE*, 1392]

5. **Godiva Lady** (d. 1057) rode naked through country to secure tax reduction for the people. [Br. Legend: Brewer *Dictionary*, 471]

6. **Gymnosophists** ancient Indian philosophers forsook clothing. [Asian Hist.: Brewer *Note-Book*, 396]

7. **Lee, Gypsy Rose** (1914–1970) American burlesque artiste. [Am. Hist.: Halliwell, 429]

8. **Maja Desnuda** Goya's celebrated picture of woman in the nude. [Span. Art: *Spain*, 246–247]

9. **Playboy centerfold** nubile woman exhibited *au naturel* in centerfold of every issue. [Am. Magazines: *Playboy*]

10. **Venus de Milo** half-naked marble Aphrodite. [Gk. Art: Osborne, 1184]

426. NURSING

1. **Eira** Frigga's attendant; taught science of nursing to women. [Norse Myth.: *LLEI*, I: 327]

2. **Irene** (fl. 3rd century) ministered to St. Sebastian, who was wounded by arrows. [Christian Hagiog.: Hall, 162]

3. **Lellis, St. Camillas de** improved hospitals; patroness of sick and nurses. [Christian Hagiog.: Attwater, 78–79]

4. **Nightingale, Florence** (1820–1910) English nurse; founder of modern nursing. [Br. Hist.: *NCE*, 1943.]

427. NYMPH

1. **Atlantides (Pleiades)** seven daughters of Atlas by Pleione. [Gk. Myth.: Zimmerman, 37]

2. **Camenae** fountain nymphs; identified with Greek Muses. [Rom. Myth.: Zimmerman, 49]

3. **dryads** divine maidens of the woods. [Gk. and Rom. Myth.: Wheeler, 108]

4. **hamadryads** wood nymphs. [Gk. Myth.: Howe, 113]

5. **Hyades** seven daughters of Atlas, entrusted with the care of the infant Dionysus. [Gk. Myth.: Howe, 134]

6. **limoniads** nymphs of meadows and flowers. [Gk. Myth.: Zimmerman, 152]

7. **naiads** divine maidens of lakes, streams, and fountains. [Gk. and Rom. Myth.: Wheeler, 256]

8. **Napaeae** nymphs of woodland glens and vales. [Rom. Myth.: Howe, 174]

9. **Nereids** sea nymphs of the Mediterranean. [Gk. and Rom. Myth.: Wheeler, 257]

10. **Oceanids** sea nymphs of the great oceans. [Gk. and Rom. Myth.: Wheeler, 263]

11. **oreads** divine maidens of the mountains. [Gk. and Rom. Myth.: Wheeler, 270]

O

OBESITY (See FATNESS.)

428. **OBSESSIVENESS**

1. **Ahab** obsessed with whale. [Am. Lit.: *Moby Dick*]
2. **Allmers, Mrs.** obsessed with crippled son. [Nor. Lit.: *Little Eyolf*]
3. **Bounderby, Josiah** single-minded success addict. [Br. Lit.: *Hard Times*]
4. **Cardillac** goldsmith who murders to regain what he created. [Ger. Opera: Hindemith, *Cardillac*, Westerman, 487]
5. **Chillingworth, Roger** "very principle of his life [was] the systematic exercise of revenge." [Am. Lit.: *The Scarlet Letter*]
6. **Defarge, Madame** "everlastingly knitting" before the guillotine as heads fell. [Br. Lit.: *A Tale of Two Cities*]
7. **Gerard, Philip** police lieutenant searches for Kimble without rest. [TV: "The Fugitive" in Terrace, I, 290]
8. **Herman** only goal in life becomes winning at cards. [Russ. Opera: Tchaikovsky, *Queen of Spades*, Westerman, 401]
9. **Javert** personification of law's inexorableness; relentlessly tracks down Valjean. [Fr. Lit.: *Les Misérables*]
10. **Melford, Lydia** could not think of anything but lover Wilson. [Br. Lit.: *Humphry Clinker*, Magill, I, 394–397]
11. **Nemo, Captain** mysterious submarine captain who attempts vengeance against society. [Fr. Lit.: *Twenty Thousand Leagues Under the Sea*]
12. **Tiberius** determined at any cost to become Emperor. [Br. Lit.: *I, Claudius*]

429. **OBSTINACY**

1. **Balmawhapple** bullheaded, blundering Scotch laird. [Br. Lit.: *Waverley*]
2. **Deans, Davie** stern and righteous Presbyterian. [Br. Lit.: *The Heart of Midlothian*]
3. **Gradgrind, Thomas** rigid "man of realities." [Br. Lit.: *Hard Times*]
4. **Grant, Ulysses S.** (1822–1885) 18th U.S. president; nicknamed "Unconditional Surrender." [Am. Hist.: Kane, 523]

5. **Jorkins** intractable, unyielding lawyer. [Br. Lit.: *David Copperfield*]

6. **Mistress Mary** known for being "quite contrary." [Nurs. Rhyme: Baring-Gould, 31]

7. **mule** symbol of obstinacy: "stubborn as a mule." [Folklore: Jobes, 462]

8. **Pharaoh** refuses to heed Moses's mandate from God. [*O.T.: Exodus* 7:13, 22–23, 8:32, 9:7, 12]

OBTUSENESS (See DIMWITTEDNESS.)

ODDNESS (See ECCENTRICITY.)

OLDNESS (See AGE, OLD.)

430. **OMEN (See also PROPHECY.)**

1. **Amasis' ring** discarded ring turns up predicting Polycrates' death. [Gk. Hist.: Benét, 28]

2. **handwriting on the wall** Daniel interprets supernatural sign as Belshazzar's doom. [*O.T.: Daniel* 5:25–28]

3. **Ides of March** 15 March; prophesied as fateful for Caesar. [Br. Lit.: *Julius Caesar*]

4. **merrow** Irish mermaid; her appearance signifies coming storms. [Irish Folklore: Briggs, 290–294]

5. **Mother Carey's chickens** stormy petrels; believed by sailors to be harbingers of storms. [Marine Folklore: Wheeler, 251]

6. **raven** often presages death or catastrophe. [Animal Folklore: Jobes, 213]

7. **waff** wraith whose appearance portends death. [Br. Folklore: Briggs, 425]

8. **white-winged crow** bird of evil omen. [Chinese Folklore: Jobes, 388]

9. **Wotan's ravens** of misfortune, usually fatal. [Ger. Opera: Wagner, *Götterdämmerung*, Westerman, 245]

431. **OMNIPRESENCE (See also UBIQUITY.)**

1. **Allah** supreme being and pervasive spirit of the universe. [Islam: Leach, 36]

2. **Big Brother** all-seeing leader watches every move. [Br. Lit.: *1984*]

3. **eye** God sees all things in all places. [Christian Symbolism: *O.T.: Proverbs* 15:3]

4. **God** transcendant over and immanent in the world. [Christianity and Judaism: *NCE*, 1098–1099]

432. OMNISCIENCE

1. **Ea** shrewd god; knew everything in advance. [Babylonian Myth.: *Gilgamesh*]
2. **God** knows all: past, present, and future. [Christianity and Judaism: *NCE*, 1098–1099]
3. **Santa Claus** he knows who has been bad or good. [Western Folklore: Misc.]
4. **Sphinx** ancient Egyptian symbol of all-knowingness. [Heraldry: Halberts, 38]

433. OPPORTUNISM

1. **Arabella, Lady** squire's wife matchmakes with money in mind. [Br. Lit.: *Doctor Thorne*]
2. **Ashkenazi, Simcha** shrewdly and unscrupulously becomes merchant prince. [Yiddish Lit.: *The Brothers Ashkenazi*]
3. **Butler, Rhett** southerner interested only in personal gain from Civil War. [Am. Lit.: *Gone With the Wind*]
4. **carpetbaggers** northern politicians who settled in the South to control the Negro vote. [Am. Hist.: Jameson, 84]
5. **Cowperwood, Frank A.** capitalist involves politicians in shady dealings. [Am. Lit.: *The Financier*, Magill, I, 280–282]
6. **Peters, Ivy** shyster lawyer capitalizing in New Frontier territory. [Am. Lit.: *A Lost Lady*]
7. **Ravenel, Gontran de** weds peasant's plain daughter to obtain land. [Fr. Lit.: *Mont-Oriol*, Magill, I, 618–620]
8. **Wallingford, "Get-Rich-Quick"** ingenious rascal of high finance; quasi-lawful. [Am. Lit.: *Get-Rich-Quick Wallingford*, Hart, 150]

434. OPTIMISM (See also HOPE.)

1. **Bontemps, Roger** personification of cheery contentment. [Fr. Lit.: "Roger Bontemps" in Walsh *Modern*, 66]
2. **Candide** beset by inconceivable misfortunes, hero indifferently shrugs them off. [Fr. Lit.: *Candide*]
3. **Micawber, Mr.** sanguine gentleman, constantly "waiting for something to turn up." [Br. Lit.: *David Copperfield*]
4. **Pangloss, Dr.** Candide's incurably optimistic tutor. [Fr. Lit.: *Candide*]
5. **Pollyanna** always finds something to be glad about. [Am. Lit.: *Pollyanna;* Am. Cinema: *Pollyanna* in *Disney Films*, 170–172]

435. ORDERLINESS (See also CLEANLINESS.)

1. **Barbara** maid exemplifying personal and domestic neatness. [Br. Lit.: *Old Curiosity Shop*]

2. **Bertram, Sir Thomas** instructor and example of orderliness and moral conduct. [Br. Lit.: *Mansfield Park*, Magill, I, 562–564]

3. **Eunomia** one of Horae; goddess of order and harmony. [Gk. Myth.: Kravitz, 95]

4. **Fogg, Phileas** British gentleman who regimented whole life minutely. [Fr. Lit.: *Around the World in Eighty Days*]

5. **Price, Fanny** appealing heroine keeps unstable house in order. [Br. Lit.: *Mansfield Park*, Magill, I, 562–564]

6. **Robert's Rules of Order** manual of parliamentary procedure by General Robert. [Am. Hist.: Hart, 717]

7. **Unger, Felix** ultra-tidy roommate of the slovenly Oscar. [Am. Drama: *The Odd Couple;* Am. Cinema and TV: "The Odd Couple" in Terrace, II, 160–161]

436. ORPHAN (See also ABANDONMENT.)

1. **Adverse, Anthony** finally, at middle age, discovers origins. [Am. Lit.: *Anthony Adverse*]

2. **Carey, Philip** brought up by stingy uncle and kindly aunt. [Br. Lit.: *Of Human Bondage*, Magill, I, 670–672]

3. **Clickett** the "orfling" from St. Luke's workhouse; Mrs. Micawber's maid-of-all-work. [Br. Lit.: *David Copperfield*]

4. **Cosette** waif indentured to the cruel Thenardiers; saved by the honorable Valjean. [Fr. Lit.: *Les Misérables*]

5. **Dondi** Italian war baby taken in by Americans. [Comics: Horn, 217]

6. **Finn, Huckleberry** his mother dead; his father dies toward end of novel. [Am. Lit.: *Huckleberry Finn*]

7. **Little Orphan Annie** feisty waif succored by paternal Daddy Warbucks. [Comics: Horn, 459]

8. **Twist, Oliver** foundling reared in school of hard knocks. [Br. Lit.: *Oliver Twist*]

9. **Pip** Philip Pirrip, orphaned as an infant. [Br. Lit.: *Great Expectations*]

437. OUTLAWRY (See also HIGHWAYMAN, THIEVERY.)

1. **Bass, Sam** (1851–1878) train robber and all-around desperado. [Am. Hist.: *NCE*, 244]

2. **Billy the Kid** (William H. Bonney, 1859–1881) infamous cold-blooded killer. [Am. Hist.: Flexner, 30]

3. **Bonnie and Clyde** (Bonnie Parker and Clyde Barrow) bank robbers and killers (1930s). [Am. Hist.: Worth, 35]

4. **Cassidy, Butch, and the Sundance Kid** (Henry Brown) (fl. late 19th century) Western outlaws made famous by popular film. [Am. Hist. and Am. Cinema: *Butch Cassidy and the Sundance Kid*, Halliwell, 116]

5. **Dalton gang** bank robbers of late 1800s; killed in shootout (1892). [Am. Hist.: Flexner, 15–16]

6. **Dillinger, John** (1902–1934) murderous gunslinging bank robber of 1930s. [Am. Hist.: Flexner, 290]

7. **Holliday, "Doc"** (fl. late 19th century) outlaw who helped Wyatt Earp fight the Clanton gang (1881). [Am. Hist.: Misc.]

8. **James, Jesse** (1847–1882) romanticized train and bank robber. [Am. Hist.: Flexner, 219]

9. **Ringo, Johnny** (fl. late 19th century) notorious outlaw and gunfighter in the Southwest. [Am. Hist.: Misc.]

10. **Robin Hood** (13th century) legendary outlaw of England who robbed the rich to help the poor. [Br. Hist.: *EB*, VIII: 615–616]

11. **Rob Roy** (Robert MacGregor, 1671–1734) Scottish Highland outlaw remembered in Sir Walter Scott's novel *Rob Roy* (1818). [Scottish Hist.: *EB*, VIII: 619]

12. **Turpin, Dick** (1706–1739) English outlaw who robbed travelers on the road from London to Oxford. [Br. Hist.: *WB*, 19: 425]

13. **Villa, Pancho** (1878–1923) notorious Mexican bandit and revolutionary. [Mex. Hist.: *EB*, X: 435–436]

P

438. **PACIFICATION**

1. **Aegir** sea god, stiller of storms on the ocean. [Norse Myth.: Leach, 16]

2. **Feng** name taken by Odin in capacity of wave-stiller. [Norse Myth.: *LLEI*, I: 328]

3. **Saul and David** David plays his harp to mollify King Saul. [*O.T.: I Samuel* 16:16, 23]

PAIN (See SUFFERING.)

439. **PARADISE (See also HEAVEN, UTOPIA.)**

1. **Bali** Indonesian island; thought of as garden of Eden. [Geography: *NCE*, 215–216]

2. **Brigadoon** magical Scottish village that materializes once every 100 years. [Am. Music: Payton, 100–101]

3. **Canaan** ancient region on Jordan river; promised by God to Abraham. [*O.T.: Genesis* 12:5–10]

4. **Eden** earthly garden of luxury; abode of Adam and Eve. [*O.T.: Genesis* 2:8]

5. **Garden of the Hesperides** quiet garden of the gods where golden apples grew. [Gk. Lit.: *Hippolytus;* Gk. Myth.: Gaster, 25]

6. **Happy Hunting Ground** paradise for American Indians. [Am. Culture: Jobes, 724]

7. **Happy Valley** beautiful spot in Kashmir's Jhelum Valley. [Indian Hist.: Payton, 300]

8. **hissu** where trees bear fruits of lapis lazuli. [Babylonian Lit.: *Gilgamesh*]

9. **Land of the Lotophagi** African land where eating lotos fruit produced amnesia and indolence. [Gk. Lit.: *Odyssey;* Br. Lit.: "The Lotos-Eaters" in Norton, 733–736]

10. **Nirvana** eternal bliss and the end of all earthly suffering. [Indian Religion: Jobes, 1175]

11. **Shangri-la** utopia hidden in the Himalayas. [Br. Lit.: *Lost Horizon*]

12. **Suhkavati** garden of jeweled trees and dulcet-voiced birds. [Buddhist Myth.: Gaster, 24]

13. **Timbuktu** fabled land of wealth and splendor. [Eur. Hist.: Brewer *Dictionary*, 1084]

14. **Tlapallan** land of luxuriance and red sunrise. [Aztec Myth.: Gaster, 25]

440. PASSION OF CHRIST

1. **agony in the garden** Christ confronts His imminent death. [*N.T.: Matthew* 26:36–45; *Mark* 14:32–41]

2. **cock** its crowing reminded Peter of his betrayal. [*N.T.: John* 18:27]

3. **the Cross** upon which Christ was crucified. [*N.T.: Matthew* 27:31–50]

4. **crown of thorns** placed upon Christ's head after scourging. [*N.T.: John* 19:2]

5. **Deposition** Christ is taken from the cross and enshrouded. [*N.T.: Matthew* 27:57–60; Christian Art: Appleton, 55]

6. **dice** cast by Roman guards for Christ's robe. [*N.T.: Matthew* 27:35]

7. **Eloi, Eloi, lama sabachthani?** "My God, my God, why hast thou forsaken me?" Jesus's cry at the ninth hour. [N.T.: *Mark* 15:34]

8. **Entry into Jerusalem** first scene of Passion cycle in painting. [Art: Hall, 114]

9. **Gethsemane** scene of Christ's agony over impending death. [*N.T.: Matthew* 26:36–45; *Mark* 14:32–41]

10. **Golgotha (Calvary)** site of Christ's crucifixion. [*N.T.: Matthew* 27:32]

11. **hammer** Christian symbol for martyrdom, crucifixion. [Christian Symbolism: Jobes, 391, 716]

12. **kiss** means by which Judas identified Jesus. [*N.T.: Matthew* 26:48–50]

13. **ladder** stood upon by Joseph to remove nails holding Christ to the cross. [Christian Symbolism: Appleton, 55]

14. **lantern** held by Judas, leading officers to Christ. [*N.T.: John* 18:3]

15. **Peter's denial** Peter denies Christ three times. [*N.T.: Matthew* 26: 67–75]

16. **pillar and cord** depicted Christ's scourging. [Christian Symbolism: Appleton, 76]

17. **scourges** instruments of Christ's flagellation. [Christian Symbolism: *N.T.: Matthew* 27:26]

18. **seamless robe** Christ's garment, wagered for by Roman soldiers. [N.T.: John 19:23–24]

19. **Simon the Cyrenean** bystander compelled to carry Christ's cross. [N.T.: Matthew 27:32]

20. **spear** weapon plunged into Jesus's side during crucifixion. [N.T.: John 19:34]

21. **sponge** soaked with vinegar and given to thirsting Jesus. [N.T.: John 19:29]

22. **Stations of the Cross** depictions of episodes of Christ's death. [Christianity: Brewer Dictionary, 1035]

23. **stigmata** nail marks of Christ appearing on others. [Christian Hagiog.: Attwater, 136, 146, 211]

24. **30 pieces of silver** price Judas was paid for identifying Christ. [N.T.: Matthew 26:15]

25. **three nails** used to crucify the Lord. [Christian Symbolism: Appleton, 67]

26. **vernicle** Veronica's veil with Jesus's facial image. [Christian Symbolism: Appleton, 107]

27. **Via Dolorosa** road to Calvary. [Christianity: Brewer Dictionary, 112]

28. **vinegar** given to Jesus to drink. [N.T.: Matthew 26:34, 48]

29. **whipping post** scene of Christ's scourging. [N.T.: Matthew 15:15]

441. **PASSION, SENSUAL**

1. **Anteros** Eros's brother; avenger of unrequited love; god of passion. [Gk. Myth.: Zimmerman, 23]

2. **Cleopatra** (69–30 B.C.) alluring and romantic queen of Egypt. [Egypt. Hist.: NCE, 577]

3. **Eros** (Rom. **Cupid**) god of love; whence, word *erotic*. [Gk. Myth.: Zimmerman, 76]

4. **Himeros** god of erotic desire; attendant of Aphrodite. [Gk. Myth.: Howe, 131]

5. **Kama** god of erotic love. [Hindu Myth.: Leach, 569]

6. **The Kiss** sculpture by French sculptor Rodin depicting passionate embrace. [Art: Osborne, 988]

7. **Lolita** twelve-year-old inspires lust in older man. [Am. Lit.: *Lolita*]

8. **ruby** represents intensity of feeling; July birthstone. [Gem Symbolism: Kunz, 28, 319]

442. PASTORALISM

1. **Arcadia** mountainous region of ancient Greece; legendary for pastoral innocence of people. [Gk. Hist.: *NCE*, 136; Rom. Lit.: *Eclogues;* Span. Lit.: *Arcadia*]

2. **Chloë** Arcadian goddess, patronness of new, green crops. [Gk. Myth.: Parrinder, 62]

3. **Daphnis** Sicilian shepherd-flautist; invented bucolic poetry. [Rom. Myth.: *LLEI*, I:326]

4. **Granida and Daifilio** classic idyllic love between princess and shepherd. [Dutch Lit.: *Granida*, Hall, 141]

5. **Pastoral Symphony** Beethoven's Symphony No. 6 in F Major; hymn to nature. [Ger. Music: Thompson, 1634]

6. **Theocritus** poet; rhapsodized over charm of rustic life. [Gk. Lit.: Brewer *Dictionary*, 813]

7. **Walden** Thoreau's classic; advocates a return to nature. [Am. Lit.: Van Doren, 208]

443. PATIENCE (See also LONGSUFFERING.)

1. **Amelia** idealized personification of patience and perseverance. [Br. Lit.: *Amelia*]

2. **dock bloom** symbolizes patience. [Flower Symbolism: Jobes, 454]

3. **Enid** constant and patient wife of Sir Geraint. [Welsh Lit.: *Mabinogion;* Br. Lit.: "Idylls of the King"]

4. **Griselda** lady immortalized for patience and wifely obedience. [Br. Lit.: *Canterbury Tales*, "Clerk of Oxenford's Tale"]

5. **Hermione** bore Leontes' unfounded jealousy, thus gaining his love. [Br. Lit.: *The Winter's Tale*]

6. **Job** underwent trial by God at Satan's suggestion. [*O.T.: Job*]

7. **Penelope** Odysseus' wife; model of feminine virtue, waits twenty years for husband's return. [Gk. Lit.: *Odyssey*]

PATRICIDE (See MURDER.)

444. PATRIOTISM (See also CHAUVINISM, LOYALTY.)

1. **America, Captain** comic-strip character known as the "protector of the American way." [Comics: Horn, 155–156]

2. **American elm** traditional symbol of American patriotism. [Tree Symbolism: *Flora Symbolica*, 182]

3. **Fourth of July** "Independence Day"; day celebrating adoption of the Declaration of Independence. [Am. Hist.: Misc.]

4. **Hale, Nathan** (1755–1776) hero of American revolution; famous for "I regret I have but one life to give for my country." [Am. Hist.: Hart, 341]

5. **Joan of Arc, St.** (1412–1431) heroically followed call to save France. [Christian Hagiog.: Attwater, 187]

6. **nasturtium** symbolizes love of country. [Flower Symbolism: *Flora Symbolica*, 176]

7. **Uncle Sam** personification of U.S. government. [Am. Folklore: Misc.]

445. PATRONAGE (See also PHILANTHROPY.)

1. **Alidoro** fairy godfather to Italian Cinderella. [Ital. Opera: Rossini, *Cinderella*, Westerman, 120–121]

2. **Alphonso, Don** supports Blas in return for political favors. [Fr. Lit.: *Gil Blas*]

3. **Dionysus** inspired men through wine; considered a patron of the arts. [Gk. Myth.: *NCE*, 767]

4. **Fairy Godmother** maternal fairy abets Cinderella in ball preparations. [Fr. Fairy Tale: "Cinderella"]

446. PEACE

1. **Beulah, Land of** resting-place of pilgrims after crossing river of Death. [Br. Lit.: *Pilgrim's Progress*]

2. **Concordia** ancient Roman goddess of peace and domestic harmony. [Rom. Myth.: Zimmerman, 68]

3. **dove** emblem of peace, tenderness, innocence, and gentleness. [Folklore: Brewer *Dictionary*, 340]

4. **Geneva** site of peace conferences (1955, 1960); seat of League of Nations (1920–1946). [Swiss Hist.: *NCE*, 1058]

5. **Goshen, Land of** place of peace and prosperity. [*O.T.: Genesis* 14:10]

6. **Irene** goddess of peace and conciliation. [Gk. Myth.: Espy, 21]

7. **Jesus Christ** prince of peace in Christian beliefs. [*N.T.: Matthew; Mark; Luke; John*]

8. **laurel** traditional emblem of peace. [Plant Symbolism: Jobes, 374]

9. **olive branch** symbol of peace and serenity. [Gk. and Rom. Myth.: Brewer *Handbook*; *O.T.: Genesis*, 8:11]

10. **Pax** goddess of peace. [Rom. Myth.: Zimmerman, 194]

11. **peace pipe** pipe of North American Indians; smoked at conclusion of peace treaties. [Am. Hist.: *NCE*, 427]

12. **Quakers** nonmilitant, gentle, religious sect. [Am. Hist.: Jameson, 189]

447. PEACEMAKING (See also ANTIMILITARISM.)

1. **Agrippa, Menenius** Coriolanus's witty friend; reasons with rioting mob. [Br. Lit.: *Coriolanus*]
2. **Antenor** percipiently urges peace with Greeks. [Gk. Lit.: *Iliad*]
3. **Benvolio** tries to stop Mercutio's fatal clash with Tybalt. [Br. Lit.: *Romeo and Juliet*]
4. **Lysistrata** leads women to use wifely continence to secure peace between countries. [Gk. Lit.: *Lysistrata*]

448. PEDANTRY

1. **Bartleby** copyist in Wall Street office; refuses to do anything but copy documents. [Am. Lit.: "Bartleby the Scrivener"]
2. **Blimber, Cornelia** "dry and sandy with working in the graves of deceased languages." [Br. Lit.: *Dombey and Son*]
3. **Casaubon, Edward** dull pedant; dreary scholar who marries Dorothea. [Br. Lit.: *Middlemarch*]
4. **Caxton, Austin** erudite bookworm. [Br. Lit.: *The Caxtons*]
5. **Choakumchild, Mr.** pedantic master of Gradgrind's school. [Br. Lit.: *Hard Times*]
6. **Conseil** taxonomically talented servant of Prof. Aronnax. [Fr. Lit.: *Twenty Thousand Leagues Under the Sea*]
7. **Dalgetty, Rittmaster Dugald** garrulous pedant. [Br. Lit.: *A Legend of Montrose*]
8. **Fluellen** pedantic Welsh captain and know-it-all. [Br. Lit.: *Henry V*]
9. **Holofernes** shameless pedagogue-schoolmaster. [Br. Lit.: *Love's Labour's Lost*]
10. **Sampson, Dominie** old-fashioned, donnish scholar. [Br. Lit.: *Guy Mannering*]
11. **Scriblerus, Martinus** learned fool. [Br. Lit.: Benét, 909]
12. **Thwackum** selfish and ill-humored clerical pedagogue. [Br. Lit.: *Tom Jones*]

449. PENITENCE

1. **Act of Contrition** prayer of atonement said after making one's confession. [Christianity: Misc.]
2. **Agnes, Sister** former Lady Laurentini; a penitent nun. [Br. Lit.: *The Mysteries of Udolpho*, Freeman, 4]
3. **Canossa** site of Henry IV's submission to Pope Gregory VII (1077). [Eur. Hist.: Grun, 140]

4. **Dimmesdale, Arthur** Puritan minister publicly atones for sin of adultery. [Am. Lit.: *The Scarlet Letter*]

5. **Dismas (Dysmas)** in the Apocryphal gospels, the penitent thief. [Christianity: Benét, 274]

6. **Elul** sixth month of Jewish year; month of repentance. [Judaism: Wigoder, 174]

7. **Flagellants** groups of Christians who practised public flagellation as penance. [Christian Hist.: *NCE*, 959]

8. **Mary Magdalene** abjectly cleans Jesus's feet with tears; dries them with her hair. [*N.T.: Luke* 7:37–50]

9. **Nineveh** townspeople repented for wickedness by fasting and donning sackcloth. [*O.T.: Jonah* 3:5–10]

10. **Pelagius the Repentant, St.** dancing-girl converts to solitary, saintly ways. [Christian Hagiog.: Attwater, 272]

11. **penance** Catholic sacrament, whereby the penitent is absolved of sins by the confessor. [Christianity: *NCE*, 2096]

12. **sable** black fur represents repentance. [Heraldry: Halberts, 37]

13. **sackcloth and ashes** traditional garb of contrition. [*O.T.: Jonah* 3:6; *Esther* 4:1–3; *N.T.: Matthew* 11:21]

14. **scapegoat** sent into wilderness bearing sins of Israelites. [*O.T.: Leviticus* 16:8–22]

15. **Scarlet Sister Mary** seeks divine forgiveness in night of wild prayer. [Am. Lit.: *Scarlet Sister Mary*]

16. **skull** always present in pictures of Mary Magdalene repenting. [Christian Art: de Bles, 29]

17. **Tannhäuser** seeking salvation, takes pilgrimage to Rome. [Ger. Opera: Wagner, *Tannhäuser*, Westerman, 211]

18. **Tenorio, Don Juan** after sinful lifetime, eleventh-hour repentance saves his soul. [Span. Lit.: *Don Juan Tenorio*]

19. **Theodosius** (346–395) Roman Emperor; did public penance before St. Ambrose. [Rom. Hist.: *EB*, 18:272–273]

20. **Twelve Labors of Hercules** undertaken as penance for slaying his children. [Gk. and Rom. Myth.: Hall, 148]

21. **violet** Christian liturgical color; worn during Lent and Advent. [Color Symbolism: Jobes, 357]

22. **Yom Kippur** most sacred Hebrew holy day; the day of atonement. [Judaism: *NCE*, 182]

450. PERFECTION

1. **Giotto's O** perfect circle drawn effortlessly by Giotto. [Ital. Hist.: Brewer *Dictionary*, 463]

2. **golden mean** or section a proportion between the length and width of a rectangle or two portions of a line, said to be ideal. [Fine Arts: Misc.]

3. **hole in one** score of one stroke for a hole in golf. [Sports: *Webster's Sports*, 215]

4. **Jesus Christ** son of God; personification of human flawlessness. [Christian Hist.: *NCE*, 1412]

5. **perfect cadence** where the dominant passes into the harmony of the tonic chord. [Music: Thompson, 333]

6. **perfect contrition** sorrow for sin, coming from a love of God for His own perfections. [Christianity: Misc.]

7. **perfect game** baseball game in which all opposing batters are put out in succession. [Sports: *Webster's Sports*, 311]

8. **perfect number** equal in value to the sum of those natural numbers that are less than the given number but that also divide (with zero remainder) the given number. [Math.: *EB*, VII: 872]

9. **royal flush** best possible hand in poker; one-suited hand from ten to ace. [Cards: Brewer *Dictionary*, 940]

10. **300 game** bowling game of twelve consecutive strikes, scoring maximum 300 points. [Sports: *Webster's Sports*, 311]

451. PERJURY (See also DECEIT.)

1. **Hiss, Alger** (1904–   ) imprisoned for perjury during espionage hearings. [Am. Hist.: *NCE*, 1247]

2. **Oakes** rancher, remembered for his untrustworthy court testimony. [Australian Hist.: Brewer *Dictionary*, 771]

3. **Philip, King** worships "tickling Commodity"; perjures himself. [Br. Lit.: *King John*]

452. PERMANENCE

1. **law of the Medes and Persians** Darius's execution ordinance; an immutable law. [*O.T.: Daniel* 6:8–9]

2. **leopard's spots** there always, as evilness with evil men. [*O.T.: Jeremiah* 13:23; Br. Lit.: *Richard II*]

3. **Nubian's skin** permanently black, as evildoer is permanently evil. [*O.T.: Jeremiah* 13:23]

453. PERSEVERANCE (See also DETERMINATION.)

1. **Ainsworth** redid dictionary manuscript burnt in fire. [Br. Hist.: Brewer *Handbook*, 752]

2. **Call of the Wild, The** dogs trail steadfastly through Alaska's tundra. [Am. Lit.: *The Call of the Wild*]

3. **canary grass** traditional symbol of perseverance. [Plant Symbolism: *Flora Symbolica*, 183]

4. **Goodwood, Caspar** eternal American pursuer of Isabel Archer's hand. [Am. Lit.: *The Portrait of a Lady*, Magill, I, 766–768]

5. **Little Engine That Could** pint-sized locomotive struggles long and hard to surmount hill before succeeding. [Children's Lit.: *Little Engine That Could*]

6. **Moses** Hebrew lawgiver; led his quarrelsome people out of bondage in Egypt. [*O.T.: Exodus; Leviticus*]

7. **Penelope** foils suiters for twenty years while awaiting return of Odysseus. [Gk. Myth.: Kravitz, 182]

8. **Rembrandt to Rembrandt** artist continues to work despite financial failures. [Am. Lit.: "Rembrandt to Rembrandt" in Hart, 703–704]

9. **Santiago** attempts to subdue large fish through harshness of sea and weather. [Am. Lit.: *The Old Man and the Sea*]

10. **snail** symbol of deliberation and steadfastness. [Heraldry: Halberts, 38]

11. **tortoise** perseverance helps him succeed where those inclined to dawdle fail. [Folklore: Jobes, 1590]

12. **Zaretchyn, Nina** sacrifices everything to further career as actress. [Russ. Lit.: *The Seagull*]

454. **PERVERSION (See also BESTIALITY.)**

1. **Humbert, Humbert** middle-aged gentleman crisscrosses America staying in motels with 12-year-old "nymphet." [Am. Lit.: *Lolita*]

2. **Imp of the Perverse** perversity as motive for men's actions. [Am. Lit.: "Imp of the Perverse" in Hart, 402]

3. **Onan** Judah's son; spilled seed upon ground. [*O.T.: Genesis* 38: 9–10]

4. **Sacher-Masoch, Leopold von** (1836–1895) author who derived pleasure from being tortured. [Aust. Hist.: Wallechinsky, 165]

5. **Sade, Marquis de** (1740–1814) jailed for sexual crimes; wrote of sexual cruelty. [Fr. Hist.: Wallechinsky, 165]

455. **PESSIMISM (See also CYNICISM, SKEPTICISM.)**

1. **Calamity Jane** (Martha Jane Canary or Martha Burke, 1852–1903) frontierswoman; mannish prophetess of doom. [Am. Hist.: Flexner, 71]

2. **Cassandra** no credence ever given to her truthful prophecies of doom. [Gk. Myth.: Zimmerman, 51]

3. **Gloomy Gus** one with a pessimistic outlook on the world. [Am. Usage: Misc.]

4. **Heraclitus** (535–475 B.C.) "Weeping Philosopher"; grieved over man's folly. [Gk. Hist.: Brewer *Dictionary*, 1146]

5. **Micaiah** always prophesied misfortune for King Ahab. [*O.T.: I Kings* 22:8]

6. **Murphy's Law** "If anything can go wrong, it will." [Am. Culture: Wallechinsky, 480]

7. **Schopenhauer, Arthur** (1788–1860) German philosopher known for philosophy of pessimism. [Ger. Hist.: *NCE*, 2447]

456. **PHILANTHROPY (See also GENEROSITY, PATRONAGE.)**

1. **Carnegie, Andrew** (1835–1919) steel magnate who believed the rich should administer wealth for public benefit. [Am. Hist.: Jameson, 83]

2. **Guggenheim** 19th- and 20th-century family name of American industrialists and philanthropists. [Am. Hist.: *NCE*, 1159]

3. **Mellon, Andrew** (1855–1937) financier and public official; left large sums for research and art. [Am. Hist.: *NCE*, 1743]

4. **Rhodes, Cecil** (1853–1902) British imperialist; left millions of pounds for public service; notably, the Rhodes scholarships. [Br. Hist.: *NCE*, 2316]

5. **Rockefeller, John D(avison)** (1839–1937) American multimillionaire; endowed many institutions. [Am. Hist.: Jameson, 431]

457. **PHILISTINISM (See also MIDDLE CLASS.)**

1. **Babbitt** anti-intellectual, bourgeois conformist. [Am. Lit.: *Babbitt*]

2. **Grand Hotel** pictures European bourgeoisie in Berlin between wars. [Ger. Lit.: *Grand Hotel*]

3. **Grundy, Mrs.** whose life and doings Dame Ashfield sets store by. [Br. Lit.: *Speed the Plough*]

4. **Philistines** perennial rivals of Israel in Biblical times; looked upon as uncultured by Israelites. [Jewish Hist.: *NCE*, 2132]

458. **PHILOSOPHY**

1. **Aristotle** (384–322 B.C.) eminent Greek philosopher. [Gk. Hist.: *NCE*, 147]

2. **Confucius** (c. 551–479 B.C.) classic Chinese sage. [Chinese Hist.: *NCE*, 625]

3. **Plato** (427–347 B.C.) founder of the Academy; author of *Republic*. [Gk. Hist.: *NCE*, 2165]

4. **Socrates** (469–399 B.C.) Athenian philosopher, propagated dialectic method of approaching knowledge. [Gk. Hist.: *NCE*, 2553]

459. PIANO

1. **Schroeder** compulsively plays the works of Beethoven on his toy piano. [Comics: "Peanuts" in Horn, 543]

PIETY (See RIGHTEOUSNESS.)

460. PIRACY

1. **Barbary Coast** Mediterranean coastline of former Barbary States; former pirate lair. [Afr. Hist.: *NCE*, 229]

2. **Blackbeard** (Edward Teach, d. 1718) colorful, albeit savage, corsair. [Br. Hist.: Jameson, 495]

3. **Conrad, Lord** proud, ascetic but successful buccaneer. [Br. Lit.: *The Corsair*, Walsh *Modern*, 104]

4. **Drake, Sir Francis** (1540–1596) British navigator and admiral; famed for marauding expeditions against Spanish. [Br. Hist.: *NCE*, 793]

5. **Fomorians** mythical, prehistoric, giant pirates who raided and pillaged Irish coast. [Irish Legend: Leach, 409]

6. **Hawkins, Sir John** (1532–1595) British admiral; led lucrative slave-trading expeditions. [Br. Hist.: *NCE*, 1206]

7. **Hook, Captain** treacherous pirate in Never-Never Land. [Br. Lit.: *Peter Pan*]

8. **Jolly Roger** black pirate flag with white skull and crossbones. [World Hist.: Brewer *Dictionary*, 926]

9. **Kidd, Captain William** (1645–1701) British captain; turned pirate over frustrations at maritime trade regulations. [Br. Hist.: *NCE*, 1476]

10. **Lafitte, Jean** (1780–1826) leader of Louisiana band of privateers and smugglers. [Am. Hist.: *NCE*, 1516]

11. **Morgan, Sir Henry** (1635–1688) Welsh buccaneer; took over privateer band after Mansfield's death. [Br. Hist.: *NCE*, 1832]

12. **Silver, Long John** one-legged corsair; leads mutiny on *Hispaniola*. [Br. Lit.: *Treasure Island*]

13. **Singleton, Captain** buccaneer acquires great wealth depredating in West Indies and Indian Ocean. [Br. Lit.: *Captain Singleton*]

PITILESSNESS (See HEARTLESSNESS, RUTHLESSNESS.)

461. POET

 1. **Chaucer, Geoffrey** (c. 1340–1400) author of *The Canterbury Tales, Troilus and Cresida*, etc. [Br. Lit.: Harvey, 161]
 2. **Dante Alighieri** (1265–1321) author of the *Divine Comedy*. [Ital. Lit.: Harvey, 215]
 3. **Sappho** (c. 620–c. 565 B.C.) lyric poet sometimes called the "tenth muse." [Gk. Lit.: Benét, 896–897]
 4. **Shakespeare, William** (1564–1616) English poet. [Br. Lit.: Harvey 745]

462. POETRY

 1. **Bragi** god of verse. [Norse Myth.: Parrinder, 50]
 2. **Calliope** one of the nine Muses. [Gk. Myth.: Jobes, 278; Parrinder, 56]
 3. **Castalia** Parnassian fountain; endowed drinker with poetic creativity. [Gk. Myth.: LLEI, I: 325]
 4. **Daphnis** creator of bucolic poetry. [Gk. Myth.: Kravitz, 75]
 5. **Parnassus** mountains sacred to Muses; hence, abode of poetry. [Gk. Myth.: Hall, 234]

463. POLYGAMY

 1. **Bluebeard** chevalier slays his six wives; seventh evades similar fate. [Fr. Fairy Tale: Harvey, 96–97]
 2. **David** had many wives. [O.T.: I Samuel 25:43–44; II Samuel 3:2–5]
 3. **Lamech** first man to have two wives. [O.T.: Genesis 4:19–20]
 4. **Mongut of Siam, King** 9000 wives and concubines. [Thai. Hist.: Wallechinsky, 279]
 5. **Mormons** religious sect; once advocated plural marriage. [Am. Hist.: NCE, 1833]
 6. **Solomon** 700 wives, princesses, and 300 concubines. [O.T.: I Kings 11:1–8]

464. POSSESSION (See also ENCHANTMENT.)

 1. **Gadarene swine** Jesus sends demons from man to pigs. [N.T.: Matthew 8:28–32; Mark 5:1–13; Luke 8:26–33]
 2. **Legion** man controlled by devils; exorcised by Jesus. [N.T.: Mark 5:9; Luke 8:30]
 3. **Regan** young girl gruesomely infested with the devil. [Am. Lit.: The Exorcist]

465. POVERTY

1. **Aglaus** poorest man in Arcadia, but happier than king. [Gk. Myth.: Kravitz, 13]

2. **Appalachia** West Virginia coal mining region known for its abysmal poverty. [Am. Hist.: NCE, 160]

3. **Apple Annie** apple seller on street corners during Depression. [Am. Hist.: Flexner, 11]

4. **bare feet** symbol of impoverishment. [Folklore: Jobes, 181]

5. **Barnardo Home** one of many homes founded for destitute children. [Br. Hist.: NCE, 233]

6. **Bashmachkin, Akakii Akakiievich** poor clerk saves years for overcoat that is soon stolen. [Russ. Lit.: "The Overcoat" in *The Overcoat and Other Stories*]

7. **Bonhomme, Jacques** nickname for poor French peasants. [Fr. Folklore: Walsh *Classical*, 59]

8. **Booth, Captain** continually in and out of debtor's prison. [Br. Lit.: *Amelia*]

9. **Bung** experiences modified and extreme levels of want. [Br. Lit.: *Sketches by Boz*]

10. **Clare of Assisi, St.** lived entirely on alms; founded "Poor Clares." [Christian Hagiog.: Attwater, 87]

11. **Cratchit, Bob** Scrooge's poorly paid clerk. [Br. Lit.: *A Christmas Carol*]

12. **Crawley, Rev. Josiah** debt-maddened clergyman. [Br. Lit.: *Last Chronicle of Barset*]

13. **Grapes of Wrath, The** about the Joad family; jobless, facing starvation. [Am. Lit.: *The Grapes of Wrath*]

14. **Great Depression** economic crisis of 1929–1933, unprecedented in length and widespread poverty. [Am. Hist.: NCE, 1132]

15. **Grub Street** London street; home of indigent writers. [Br. Hist.: Brewer *Note-Book*, 394]

16. **Hell's Kitchen** section of midtown Manhattan; notorious for slums and high crime rate. [Am. Usage: Misc.]

17. **Hooverville** Depression shantytown arising during Hoover administration. [Amer. Hist.: Flexner, 118]

18. **Hubbard, Old Mother** had not even a bone for her dog. [Nurs. Rhyme: Opie, 317]

19. **Job** lost everything he owned to Satan. [O.T.: Job]

20. **Job's turkey** one-feathered bird even more destitute than its owner. [Can. and Am. Usage: Brewer *Dictionary*, 589]

21. **Lazarus** satisfied with table scraps; dogs licked sores. [N.T.: Luke 16:19–22]

22. **Micawber, Wilkins** optimistic, though chronically penniless and in debt. [Br. Lit.: *David Copperfield*]

23. **Okies** itinerant dust bowl farmers (1930s). [Am. Hist.: Van Doren, 455; Am. Lit.: *The Grapes of Wrath*]

POWER (See AUTHORITY.)

466. **PREDICAMENT**

1. **Dancy, Captain Ronald** must persecute friend to save own skin. [Br. Lit.: *Loyalties*, Magill, I, 533–534]

2. **Gordian knot** inextricable difficulty; Alexander cut the original. [Gk. Hist.: Espy, 49]

3. **Lady or the Tiger, The** hero must choose one of two doors. [Am. Lit.: *The Lady or the Tiger*]

4. **Marta** loves husband; forced into adultery by patron. [Ger. Opera: d'Albert, *Tiefland*, Westerman, 373]

5. **Scylla and Charybdis** two equally dangerous alternatives. [Gk. Lit.: *Odyssey*, Espy, 41]

6. **Symplegades** cliffs at Black Sea entrance; clashed together as ships passed through. [Gk. Myth.: Zimmerman, 251]

467. **PRETENSION (See also HYPOCRISY.)**

1. **Absolon** vain, officious parish clerk. [Br. Lit.: *Canterbury Tales*, "Miller's Tale"]

2. **Armado, Don Adriano de** his language inordinately disproportionate to his thought. [Br. Lit.: *Love's Labour's Lost*]

3. **Chrononhotonthologos** king whose pomposity provoked a fatal brawl with his general. [Br. Lit.: Walsh *Modern*, 96]

4. **Copper, Captain** pretends to great wealth; jewels are counterfeit. [Br. Lit.: *Rule a Wife and Have a Wife*, Walsh *Modern*, 105]

5. **Coriolanus** stiff-necked Roman aristocrat; contemptuous of the common people. [Br. Lit.: *Coriolanus*]

6. **Dodsworth, Fran** shallow industrialist's wife ostentatiously gallivants about Europe. [Am. Lit.: *Dodsworth*]

7. **Dogberry** ostentatiously and fastidiously examines prisoners. [Br. Lit.: *Much Ado About Nothing*]

8. **euphuism** style overly rich with alliteration, figures, and Latinisms. [Br. Lit.: *Euphues*, Espy, 127]

9. **Isle of Lanterns** inhabited by pretenders to knowledge. [Fr. Lit.: *Pantagruel*]

10. **Jourdain, Monsieur** parvenu grandiosely affects gentleman's mien. [Fr. Lit.: *The Bourgeois Gentilhomme*]

11. **Madelon and Cathos** their suitors had to be flamboyant. [Fr. Lit.: *Les Précieuses Ridicules*]

12. **morning glory** symbol of affectation; flower of September. [Flower Symbolism: *Flora Symbolica*, 175; Kunz, 330]

13. **Parolles** boastful villain of affected sentiment and knowledge. [Br. Lit.: *All's Well That Ends Well*]

14. **Pendennis** enters university "posing as moneyed aristocrat." [Br. Lit.: *Pendennis*]

15. **willow herb** indicates affectation. [Flower Symbolism: *Flora Symbolica*, 178]

16. **Yvetot, King of** affects grandeur; kingdom is but a village. [Fr. Legend: Brewer *Dictionary*, 1173]

PRIDE (See BOASTFULNESS, EGOTISM, VANITY.)

468. **PRIZE**

1. **Achsah** Caleb's daughter; promised in marriage to conqueror of Debir. [O.T.: *Joshua* 15:16–19; *Judges* 1:12–15]

2. **blue ribbon** denotes highest honor. [Western Folklore: Brewer *Dictionary*, 127]

3. **Bollingen** annual prize for highest achievement in American poetry. [Am. Lit.: Hart, 88]

4. **Emmy** statuette awarded annually for best achievements in television programing and performance. [TV: Misc.]

5. **Enrico Fermi Award** given for "exceptional and altogether outstanding achievement" in atomic energy. [Am. Hist.: Misc.]

6. **Eva** to marry winner of singing contest. [Ger. Opera: Wagner, *Meistersinger*, Westerman, 225–228]

7. **Goncourt** annual award for best French fiction. [Fr. Lit.: *NCE*, 1106]

8. **Grammy** awarded by the National Academy of Recording Arts and Sciences for the best in the recording field. [Am. Hist.: Misc.]

9. **Guggenheim** annual fellowships for creative work. [Am. Hist.: Hart, 337]

10. **Heisman Trophy** awarded to the outstanding college football player of the year as determined by sportswriters and sportscasters. [Am. Sports: Misc.]

11. **Medal of Freedom** highest award given a U.S. citizen; established 1963. [Am. Hist.: Misc.]

12. **National Book Award** given by the American Academy and Institute of Arts and Letters to outstanding works. [Am. Hist.: Misc.]

13. **Newbery-Caldecott Medal** awarded by the American Library Association for outstanding children's books. [Am. Hist.: Misc.]

14. **Nobel** monetary awards for outstanding contributions benefiting mankind. [World. Hist.: Wheeler, 718]

15. **Oscar** gold statuette awarded to film actors, directors, writers, technicians, etc. [Am. Cinema: Brewer *Dictionary*, 788]

16. **Pulitzer** awards made in letters, music, and journalism. [Am. Hist.: Wheeler, 824]

17. **Silken Threads** the three great prizes of honor in Lilliput. [Br. Lit.: *Gulliver's Travels*]

18. **Tony (Antoinette Perry Award)** presented annually for outstanding work in the theater. [Am. Hist.: Misc.]

PRODIGALITY (See DISSIPATION.)

469. **PROFLIGACY (See also DEBAUCHERY, LUST, PROMISCUITY.)**

1. **Arrowsmith, Martin** simultaneously engaged to Madeline and Leona. [Am. Lit.: *Arrowsmith*]

2. **Bellaston, Lady** wealthy profligate; keeps Tom as gigolo. [Br. Lit.: *Tom Jones*]

3. **Booth, Captain** pleasure-loving prodigal; lacks discipline. [Br. Lit.: *Amelia*]

4. **Casanova, Giovanni Jacopo** (1725–1798) myriad amours made his name synonymous with philanderer. [Ital. Hist.: Benét, 172]

5. **Don Juan** internationally active profligate and seducer. [Ger. Opera: Mozart, *Don Giovanni*, Westerman, 93–95]

6. **Flashman, Harry** British soldier wenches his way around world. [Br. Lit.: *Flashman*]

7. **Genji, Prince** Emperor's dashing and talented bastard woos many. [Jap. Lit.: *The Tale of Genji*]

8. **Iachimo** scorns and craftily tests feminine virtue. [Br. Lit.: *Cymbeline*]

9. **Jones, Tom** manly but all too human young man; has numerous amorous adventures. [Br. Lit.: *Tom Jones*]

10. **Lothario** young rake and seducer. [Br. Lit.: *The Fair Penitent*]

11. **Lyndon, Barry** from bully to dissipative rake and cruel husband. [Br. Lit.: *Barry Lyndon*]

12. **Macheath, Captain** gambler and robber; has scores of illegitimate offspring. [Br. Opera: *The Beggar's Opera*]

13. **Santa Cruz, Juanito** loses his wife, lover, and esteem by philandering. [Span. Lit.: *Fortunata and Jacinta*]

14. **Scales, Gerald** sales representative known for lavish living, gambling, amorality. [Br. Lit.: *The Old Wives' Tale*, Magill, I, 684–686]

15. **Zeus** supreme of Greek gods; extramarital affairs were countless. [Gk. Myth.: Zimmerman, 292]

470. PROLIFICNESS

1. **old woman who lived in a shoe** "had so many children she didn't know what to do." [Nursery Rhyme: Baring-Gould, 85]

2. **rabbit** progenitor of many offspring at short intervals. [Zoology: Misc.]

471. PROMISCUITY (See also PROFLIGACY.)

1. **Aphrodite** promiscuous goddess of sensual love. [Gk. Myth.: Parrinder, 24]

2. **Ashley, Lady Brett** forever falling in love with young men. [Am. Lit.: *The Sun Also Rises*]

3. **Barbarella** scantily dressed, sex-loving, blonde astronaut. [Comics: Horn, 96]

4. **Camille** "a woman of Paris." [Fr. Lit.: *Camille*]

5. **Forrester, Mrs. Marian** traveling husband not enough to fulfill desires. [Am. Lit.: *A Lost Lady*]

6. **Ganconer** fairy who makes love with, then abandons, women. [Br. Folklore: Briggs, 183–184]

7. **Gomer** Hosea's wanton wife. [*O.T.: Hosea* 1:1–3]

8. **Messalina** wife of Emperor Claudius of Rome. [Rom. Hist.: Brewer *Handbook*, 701]

9. **Rogers, Mildred** though a wanton, Philip loved her above all else. [Br. Lit.: *Of Human Bondage*; Magill, I, 670–672]

472. PROPAGANDA

1. **Axis Sally** [Mildred Elizabeth Sisk, (1900–   ) or Rita Louise Zucca, (1912–   )] Nazi broadcaster who urged American withdrawal from WWII. [Am. Hist.: Flexner, 449]

2. **Haw-Haw, Lord** (William Joyce, 1906–1946) British citizen becomes German propagandist in WWII. [Br. Hist.: *NCE*, 1435]

3. **Tokyo Rose** (Iva Ikuko Toguri D'Aquino, 1916–   ) Japanese broadcaster who urged U.S. troops to surrender during WWII. [Am. Hist.: Flexner, 449]

473.   PROPHECY (See also OMEN.)

1.   **augurs** Roman officials who interpreted omens. [Rom. Hist.: Parrinder, 34]

2.   **Balaam** vaticinally speaks with Jehovah's voice. [*O.T.: Numbers* 23:8–10; 24:18–24]

3.   **banshee** Irish spirit who foretells death. [Irish Folklore: Briggs, 14–16]

4.   **Belshazzar's Feast** disembodied hand foretells Belshazzar's death. [*O.T.: Daniel* 5]

5.   **Brave New World** picture of world's condition 600 years from now. [Br. Lit.: *Brave New World*]

6.   **Calamity Jane** (Martha Jane Canary or Martha Burke, 1852–1903) mannish prophetess of doom. [Am. Hist.: Flexner, 71]

7.   **Calpurnia** sees bloody statue of Julius in dream. [Br. Lit.: *Julius Caesar*]

8.   **Carmen** the cards repeatedly spell her death. [Fr. Opera: Bizet, *Carmen*, Westerman, 189–190]

9.   **Cassandra** predicts doom of Troy to brother, Hector. [Br. Lit.: *Troilus and Cressida;* Gk. Myth.: Parrinder, 57]

10.   **Cumaean sibyl** to discover future, leads Aeneas to Hades. [Gk. Lit.: *Aeneid*]

11.   **Delphi** ancient oracular center near Mt. Parnassus. [Gk. Myth.: Parrinder, 74; Jobes, 428]

12.   **Dodona** oldest oracle of Zeus in Greece. [Gk. Myth.: Kravitz, 83]

13.   **Ezekiel** priest and prophet to the Jews during Babylonian captivity. [*O.T.: Ezekiel*]

14.   **Golden Cockerel** its crowing predicts either peace or disaster. [Russ. Opera: Rimsky-Korsakov, *Coq d'Or*, Westerman, 392]

15.   **Guardian Black Dog** sinister omen of death. [Br. Folklore: Briggs, 207–208]

16.   **haruspices** ancient Etruscan seers who divined the future from the entrails of animals. [Rom. Hist.: *EB*, IV: 933]

17.   **Huldah** tells of impending disaster for the idolatrous. [*O.T.: II Kings* 22:14–19]

18.   **I Ching** a book of divination and speculations. [Chinese Lit.: *I Ching*]

19.   **Isaiah** foretells fall of Jerusalem; prophet of doom. [*O.T.: Isaiah*]

20.   **Jeremiah** the Lord's herald. [*O.T.: Jeremiah*]

21. **Joseph** predicted famine from Pharaoh's dreams. [*O.T.: Genesis* 41:25–36]

22. **Muhammad** (570–632) the prophet of Islam. [Islam. Hist.: *NCE*, 1854]

23. **Nostradamus** (1503–1566) startlingly accurate French astrologer and physician. [Fr. Hist.: *NCE*, 1969]

24. **Sibyllae** women endowed with prophetic powers who interceded with gods for men. [Gk. Myth.: Zimmerman, 239]

25. **Smith, Joseph** Mormon prophet; professed visions of new faith. [Am. Hist.: Jameson, 467]

26. **Smith, Valentine Michael** messianic Martian shows earthlings the way. [Am. Lit.: *Stranger in a Strange Land*]

27. **sortes** augury performed by random selection of any book passage. [Br. Hist.: Brewer *Dictionary*, 1020]

28. **Tarot cards** used to tell fortunes. [Magic: Brewer *Dictionary*, 1063]

29. **Tiresias** blind and greatest of all mythological prophets. [Gk. Myth.: Zimmerman, 255; Gk. Lit.: *Antigone; Odyssey; Oedipus Tyrannus*]

30. **Ulrica** foretells Gustavus' murder by his friend Anckarström. [Ital. Opera: Verdi, *Masked Ball*, Westerman, 313–315]

31. **Weird Sisters** three witches who set Macbeth agog with prophecies of kingship. [Br. Lit.: *Macbeth*]

PROSPERITY (See SUCCESS.)

474. **PROSTITUTE (See also COURTESAN, MISTRESS.)**

1. **Adriana** comely girl becomes prostitute to support herself. [Ital. Lit.: *The Woman of Rome*]

2. **Brattle, Carrie** returns home reconciled after life in gutter. [Br. Lit: *The Vicar of Bullhampton*]

3. **Celestina** old, evil procuress hired as go-between. [Span. Lit.: *Celestina*]

4. **La Douce, Irma** leading French prostitute on Pigalle. [Am. Cinema: Halliwell, 460]

5. **Hill, Fanny** frankly erotic heroine of frankly erotic novel. [Br. Lit.: *Memoirs of Fanny Hill.*]

6. **Lulu** keeper of two others on her earnings. [Aust. Opera: Berg, *Lulu*, Westerman, 484]

7. **Maggie** innocent girl, corrupted by slum environment, becomes a prostitute. [Am. Lit.: *Maggie: A Girl of the Streets*, Hart, 514]

8. **Mary Magdalene** repentant prostitute who anointed Jesus's feet. [*N.T.: Luke* 7:36–50]

9. **Nana** beautiful lady who thrived on a troop of men. [Fr. Lit.: *Nana*, Magill, I, 638–640]

10. **Overdone, Mistress** "a bawd of eleven years' continuance." [Br. Lit.: *Measure for Measure*]

11. **Rahab** harlot of Jericho who protected Joshua's two spies. [O.T.: *Joshua* 2]

12. **Thaïs** notorious harlot in Malebolge, Hell's eighth circle. [Ital. Lit.: *Inferno*]

13. **Toast, Joan** a most saintly whore. [Am. Lit.: *The Sot-Weed Factor*]

14. **Warren, Mrs.** raises daughter in comfort and refinement on her bedside earnings. [Br. Lit.: *Mrs. Warren's Profession* in *Plays Unpleasant*]

475. PROTECTION

1. **alum** charm against evil eye. [Egyptian Folklore: Leach, 40]

2. **amethyst** preserved soldiers from harm; gave them victory. [Gem Symbolism: Kunz, 58]

3. **bennet** excludes the devil; used on door frames. [Medieval Folklore: Boland, 56]

4. **blood of the lamb** used to mark houses of the Israelites so they could be passed over. [O.T.: *Exodus* 12:3–13]

5. **chrysoberyl** guards against evil spirits. [Gem Symbolism: Kunz, 65]

6. **cross** used to frighten away devils and protect from evil. [Christian Iconog.: Leach, 265]

7. **daisy** provides protection against fairies. [Flower Symbolism: Briggs, 87]

8. **horseshoe** hung on buildings as defense against fairies. [Br. Folklore: Briggs, 225]

9. **jacinth** guards against plague and wounds. [Gem Symbolism: Kunz, 81]

10. **kolem** rice designs drawn to attract guardianship of gods. [Hinduism: Binder, 61]

11. **magic flute** Tamino's guard against black magic. [Ger. Opera: Mozart, *Magic Flute*, Westerman, 102–104]

12. **malachite** guards wearer from evil spirits, enchantments. [Gem Symbolism: Kunz, 97]

13. **mark of Cain** God's safeguard for Cain from potential slayers. [O.T.: *Genesis* 4:15]

14. **rowan** ash tree which guards against fairies and witches. [Br. Folklore: Briggs, 344]

15. **St. Benedict's cross** charm against disease and danger. [Christian Iconog.: Jobes, 386]

16. **St. Christopher medal** to protect travelers. [Christian Hist.: *NCE*, 552]

17. **St. John's wort** defense against fairies, evil spirits, the Devil. [Br. Folklore: Briggs, 335–336]

18. **sard** guards against incantations and sorcery. [Gem Symbolism: Kunz, 107]

19. **serpentine** guards against bites of venomous creatures. [Gem Symbolism: Kunz, 108]

20. **wood** knocking on it averts dire consequences. [Western Culture: Misc.]

476. **PROTECTIVENESS (See also GUARDIAN.)**

1. **Adams, Parson Abraham** bookish, unworldly protector of the weak and innocent. [Br. Lit.: *Joseph Andrews*]

2. **Darius** (d. 486 B.C.) Persian king; permits and guarantees rebuilding of temple. [*O.T.: Ezra* 6:6–12]

3. **Douglas, the Widow** motherly caretaker of Huck Finn. [Am. Lit.: *Huckleberry Finn*]

4. **Epona (Bubona)** goddess; watched over cattle and horses. [Rom. Myth.: Kravitz, 90]

5. **Evelyn, Aunt** uses influence to keep nephew from war front. [Br. Lit.: *Memoirs of an Infantry Officer*, Magill, I, 579–581]

6. **Genevieve, St.** saved Paris from marauders by intercession. [Christian Hagiog.: Attwater, 147]

7. **Hendon, Miles** disinherited knight takes urchin-prince under wing. [Am. Lit.: *The Prince and the Pauper*]

8. **Ida** nymph who guarded infant Zeus from being eaten by father, Cronus. [Gk. Myth.: Zimmerman, 134]

9. **Jehosheba** secretes future king, Joash, from Athaliah's slaughter. [*O.T.: II Kings* 11:2; *II Chronicles* 22:11]

10. **Knights Templar** society formed to guard pilgrims to Jerusalem. [Medieval Hist.: Brewer *Dictionary*, 1066]

11. **Kuan Yin** protectress of fishermen and housemaids. [Buddhism: Binder, 42]

12. **Magwitch, Abel** saved by Pip; dedicates himself to Pip's future. [Br. Lit.: *Great Expectations*]

13. **Mannering, Guy** paternal helper of friend's daughter and tutor. [Br. Lit.: *Guy Mannering*]

14. **Michael, St.** guardian archangel of the Jews. [*O.T.: Daniel* 10:13, 21; 12:1]

15. **Nicholas, St.** protector of sailors; patron saint of schoolboys. [Christian Hagiog.: Brewster, 12–13]

16. **Old Yeller** friend and watchdog assumes houndly nobility. [Am. Cinema: *Disney Films*, 145–146]

17. **Palladium** colossal statue whose presence insured Troy's safety. [Rom. Legend: Brewer *Dictionary*, 796]

18. **Quasimodo** creature hides Esmeralda in sanctuary to save her. [Fr. Lit.: *The Hunchback of Notre Dame*]

19. **Rahab** conceals two Israelite spies from Jericho authorities. [*O.T.: Joshua* 2:2–6]

20. **ravens** during drought, Elijah fed by black birds. [*O.T.: I Kings* 17:1–6]

21. **Wells Fargo** armored carriers of bullion. [Am. Hist.: Brewer *Dictionary*, 1147]

477. PRUDENCE

1. **five wise virgins** brought lamp oil in case groom arrived late. [*N.T.: Matthew* 25:1–13]

2. **jacinth** endows owner with discretion. [Gem Symbolism: Kunz, 82]

3. **Metis** goddess of caution and discretion. [Rom. Myth.: Wheeler, 242]

4. **mountain ash** symbol of prudence. [Tree Symbolism: *Flora Symbolica*, 176]

478. PRUDERY

1. **Grundy, Mrs.** Ashfields' straitlaced neighbor whose propriety hinders them. [Br. Lit.: *Speed the Plough*]

2. **nice Nelly** excessively modest or prudish woman. [Am. Usage: Misc.]

3. **Quakers** pacifist religious sect, often associated with puritanical behavioral standards. [Am. Hist.: *NCE*, 1017]

4. **Shakers** sect believing in virgin purity. [Christian Hist.: Brewer *Note-book*, 819]

5. **Victorian** one reflecting an unshaken confidence in piety and temperance, as during Queen Victoria's reign. [Am. and Br. Usage: Misc.]

479. PUGILISM

1. **Balboa, Rocky** lower-class Philadelphia boxer wins golden opportunity to fight in prize bout. [Am. Cinema: "Rocky"]

2. **Byron, Cashel** prizefighter; gives up boxing for wealthy lady. [Br. Lit.: *Cashel Byron's Profession*]

3. **Dares** one of Aeneas's companions; noted for his boxing skill. [Rom. Lit.: *Aeneid*]

4. **Entellus** powerful Sicilian boxer; won match for Anchises against Dares. [Rom. Lit.: *Aeneid*]

5. **Eryx** great boxer; killed at own game by challenger, Hercules. [Gk. Myth.: Howe, 97]

6. **Golden Boy** violinist turns boxer for fame, wealth. [Am. Lit.: *Golden Boy*]

7. **Great White Hope** 1910 personification of white peoples' aspirations for a white heavyweight champion. [Am. Hist.: Misc.]

8. **Palooka, Joe** comicdom's great white hope. [Comics: Horn, 343–344]

9. **Queensberry, Marquis of** (Sir John Douglas, 1844–1900) established basic rules of boxing. [Br. Hist.: *NCE*, 2257]

480. PUNCTUALITY

1. **Fogg, Phileas** completes world circuit at exact minute he wagered he would. [Fr. Lit.: *Around the World in Eighty Days*]

2. **Gilbreths** disciplined family brought up to abide by strict, punctual standards. [Am. Lit.: *Cheaper by the Dozen*]

3. **Jones, Casey** legendary railroad engineer; crashes in attempt to arrive in "Frisco" on time. [Am. Folklore: Hart, 431]

4. **Linkinwater, Tim** "punctual as the Counting House Dial." [Br. Lit.: *Nicholas Nickleby*]

5. **Old Faithful** well-known geyser in Yellowstone Park; erupts every 64.5 minutes. [Am. Hist.: *NCE*, 3023]

481. PUNISHMENT

1. **Abijah** Jeroboam's child; taken by God for father's wickedness. [*O.T.: I Kings* 14:12]

2. **Adam** condemned to survive by sweat of brow. [*O.T.: Genesis* 3:19]

3. **Amfortas** sinful life led to perpetual suffering. [Arth. Legend: Walsh *Classical*, 20; Ger. Opera: *Parsifal*]

4. **Ammit** half-hippopotamus, half-lion monster of underworld; ate the sinful. [Egyptian Myth.: Leach, 50]

5. **Ashura** land of punishment for those who die angry. [Jap. Myth.: Jobes, 140]

6. **Atlas** Titan condemned to bear world on shoulders. [Gk. Myth.: Walsh *Classical*, 38]

7. **Born, Bertrand de** Dante has him carry his head as lantern. [Ital. Lit.: *Inferno;* Walsh *Classical,* 55]

8. **Dirae** the Furies; punished crimes and avenged wrongs. [Gk. Myth.: Kravitz, 82, 91–92]

9. **Don Juan** for murder, devoured by fire. [Ger. Opera: Mozart, *Don Giovanni,* Westerman, 95]

10. **Eve** for disobeying God, would suffer in childbirth. [*O.T.: Genesis* 3:16]

11. **flood** for his evilness, man perishes by inundation. [*O.T.: Genesis* 6: 5–8; 7:4]

12. **Herod Agrippa I** was eaten by worms for playing god. [*N.T.: Acts* 12:23]

13. **Ixion** Thessalian king bound to fiery wheel by Zeus. [Gk. and Rom. Myth.: Zimmerman, 142; Rom. Lit.: *Metamorphoses*]

14. **Nadab and Abihu** destroyed by God for offering Him "alien fire." [*O.T.: Leviticus* 10:1–3]

15. **Papageno** for lying, has mouth padlocked. [Ger. Opera: Mozart, *The Magic Flute,* Westerman, 102–104]

16. **plagues on Egypt** God visits Egypt with plagues and epidemics for keeping Israelites in bondage. [*O.T.: Exodus* 8, 12]

17. **Prometheus** for rebelliousness, chained to rock; vulture fed on his liver which grew back daily. [Rom. Myth.: Zimmerman, 221–222]

18. **Prynne, Hester** pilloried and sentenced to wear a scarlet "A" for her sin of adultery. [Am. Lit.: *The Scarlet Letter*]

19. **Sisyphus** condemned in Hades to roll boulder uphill which would immediately roll down again. [Gk. Myth.: Zimmerman, 244; Gk. Lit.: *Odyssey;* Rom. Lit.: *Aeneid*]

20. **Tantalus** for his crimes, sentenced to Hades to be within reach of water he cannot drink. [Gk. Myth.: Zimmerman, 253; Gk. Lit.: *Odyssey*]

21. **Tell, William** ordered to shoot apple placed on son's head for refusing to salute governor's hat. [Ger. Lit.: *William Tell;* Ital. Opera: Rossini, *William Tell;* Westerman, 121–122]

22. **Thyestes** unknowingly eats sons served by vengeful brother. [Rom. Lit.: *Thyestes*]

23. **Tyburn tree** site of the London gibbet. [Br. Hist.: Espy, 169]

24. **Vale of Achor** site of lapidation of Achan, Israelite troublemaker. [*O.T.: Joshua* 7:24–26]

482. **PURITANISM**

1. **Brother Jonathan** 17th-century British nickname for Puritans. [Am. Hist.: Hart, 110]

483. **PURITY (See also MODESTY.)**

1. **almond** symbol of the Virgin Mary's innocence. [*O.T.: Numbers* 17: 1–11; Art: Hall, 14]

2. **crystal** its transparency symbolizes pureness. [Folklore: Jobes, 391]

3. **Galahad, Sir** sole knight who could sit in siege perilous. [Br. Lit.: *Le Morte d'Arthur; Idylls of the King*]

4. **Ivory soap** 99.44% pure. [Trademarks: Crowley *Trade*, 289]

5. **lily** emblematic of the Blessed Virgin Mary. [Christian Symbolism: Appleton, 39]

6. **long unbound hair** custom for unmarried women, virgin saints, brides. [Art: Hall, 144]

7. **sedge** used as symbol of purity in da Vinci paintings. [Plant Symbolism: Embolden, 25]

8. **snow** "pure as the driven snow." [Western Folklore: Misc.]

9. **Star of Bethlehem** indicates pureness. [Flower Symbolism: *Flora Symbolica*, 183]

10. **Virgin Mary** immaculately conceived; mother of Jesus Christ. [*N.T.: Matthew* 1:18–25; 12:46–50; *Luke* 1:26–56; 11:27–28; *John* 2; 19:25–27]

11. **water** archetypal symbol. [Christian Symbolism: Appleton, 109]

12. **water-lily** symbol of innocence of heart; flower of July. [Flower Symbolism: *Flora Symbolica*, 178; Kunz, 329]

13. **white** symbol of virginity; in American flag, purity. [Color Symbolism: Leach, 242]

Q

484. QUACKERY

1. **barber-surgeon** inferior doctor; formerly a barber performing dentistry and surgery. [Medicine: Misc.]

2. **Dulcamara, Dr.** offered bad burgundy as panacea for lovelessness. [Ital. Opera: Donizetti, *Elixir of Love; EB*, 5: 953–954]

3. **Rezio, Dr.** Baratarian court physician; practically starves Sancho Panza in the interest of diet. [Span. Lit.: *Don Quixote*]

4. **Rock, Dr. Richard** fat, 18th-century quack; professed to cure every imaginable disease. [Br. Hist.: Brewer *Handbook*, 888]

5. **Sangrado, Dr.** ignorant physician; believed blood not necessary for life. [Fr. Lit.: *Gil Blas*]

6. **Walker, Dr.** great 18th-century quack, forever advising against disreputable doctors. [Br. Hist.: Brewer *Handbook*, 888]

485. QUARRY

1. **Cerynean stag** captured by Hercules as third Labor. [Gk. and Rom. Myth.: Hall, 149]

2. **Cretan bull** savage bull caught by Hercules as seventh Labor. [Gk. and Rom. Myth.: Hall, 149]

3. **Erymanthian boar** Hercules' fourth Labor: to take this ravaging beast alive. [Gk. and Rom. Myth.: Hall, 149]

4. **fetching Cerberus** Hercules' twelfth Labor: capture the Hadean watchdog. [Gk. and Rom. Myth.: Hall, 150]

5. **Moby Dick** pursued by Ahab and crew of *Pequod*. [Am. Lit.: *Moby Dick*]

6. **Nemean lion** awesome beast strangled by Hercules as first Labor. [Gk. and Rom. Myth.: Hall, 148]

7. **Old Ben** great bear; subject of annual quest by mature men. [Am. Lit.: *The Bear* in *Six Modern Short Novels*]

8. **oxen of Geryon** captured after tremendous obstacles overcome; Hercules' tenth Labor. [Gk. and Rom. Myth.: Hall, 149]

9. **snark** elusive imaginary animal. [Br. Lit.: *The Hunting of the Snark*]

10. **Wolfman** metamorphosed man hunted down by armed men as wild beast. [Am. Lit.: *Wolfman*]

486.   QUEST (See also JOURNEY.)

1. **Dorothy** young girl, lost in dream world, follows the Yellow Brick Road to find the Wizard of Oz. [Am. Lit.: *The Wonderful Wizard of Oz*]

2. **El Dorado** mythical land of gold treasures, object of Spanish expeditions. [Am. Hist.: Jameson, 159]

3. **Golden Fleece** pelt of winged ram sought by Jason and Argonauts. [Rom. Legend: Zimmerman, 113]

4. **grail** its pursuit is central theme of some Arthurian romances. [Br. Lit.: *Le Morte d'Arthur*]

5. **Hippolyta, girdle of** secured after fight with Amazon queen; Hercules' ninth Labor. [Gk. and Rom. Myth.: Hall, 149]

6. **Knights of the Round Table** set out to find the Holy Grail. [Br. Lit.: *Le Morte d'Arthur*]

7. **Ponce de León, Juan** (c. 1460–1521) Spanish explorer; sought the fountain of youth. [Span. Hist.: *NCE*, 2188]

8. **Santiago** old fisherman in search of marlin. [Am. Lit.: *The Old Man and the Sea*]

9. **Telemachus** relentlessly searches for father, Odysseus. [Gk. Lit.: *Odyssey*]

R

487. **RANTING** (See also ANGER, EXASPERATION, IRASCIBILITY.)

1. **Boiler, Boanerges** a zealous, raving preacher. [Br. Lit.: *The Uncommercial Traveller*]

2. **Gantry, Elmer** fire-breathing, hypocritical preacher. [Am. Lit.: *Elmer Gantry*]

3. **Howler, Rev. Melchisedech** ranting loudmouth. [Br. Lit.: *Dombey and Son*]

488. **RAPE**

1. **Amphissa** blinded by father Echetus for having been raped by Aechmodius. [Gk. Myth.: Howe, 23]

2. **Apemosyne** raped by Hermes; killed by brother for immorality. [Gk. Myth.: Zimmerman, 25]

3. **Arne** blinded by stepfather Desmontes after he learned she had been raped and was pregnant. [Gk. Myth.: Howe, 39]

4. **Belinda** violated tonsorially. [Br. Lit.: *The Rape of the Lock*]

5. **Caenis** changed into a man by Poseidon after he raped her. [Gk. Myth.: Zimmerman, 46]

6. **Creusa** raped by Apollo; bore Janus. [Gk. Myth.: Kravitz, 68]

7. **Danaë** Zeus raped her, posing as a golden shower. [Gk. Myth.: Kravitz, 74]

8. **Elvira** peasant girl raped by lusting nobleman. [Span. Lit.: *The King, the Greatest Alcalde*]

9. **Europa** seduced by Jupiter as bull; raped when he changes back. [Rom. Lit.: *Metamorphoses;* Gk. Myth.: Hall, 259]

10. **Lavinia** raped and mutilated by Demetrius and Chiron. [Br. Lit.: *Titus Andronicus*]

11. **Leda** raped by Zeus in form of swan. [Class. Myth.: Zimmerman, 149; Rom. Lit.: *Metamorphoses;* Br. Lit.: *Faerie Queene*]

12. **Lucretia** blackmailed into sex by despicable Sextus; commits suicide afterwards. [Rom. Lit.: *Fasti; Livy;* Br. Lit.: "The Rape of Lucrece"; Art: Hall, 259]

13. **Tamar** raped by her half-brother, Amnon. [*O.T.: II Samuel* 13:11–14]

489. **RASHNESS**

1. **Charge of the Light Brigade** ill-advised British assault at Balaklava, Crimea (1854). [Br. Hist.: Harbottle, 25]

2. **Gilpin, John** rides uncontrollably on fresh steed. [Br. Lit.: *John Gilpin's Ride*]

3. **Icarus** artificial wings destroyed by flying too close to sun. [Gk. Myth.: Kravitz, 126]

4. **Lear** headstrong and "full of changes." [Br. Lit.: *King Lear*]

5. **Uzzah** rashly grabs for Ark of Covenant, a transgression. [*O.T.: II Samuel* 6:6–8]

490. REBELLION

1. **Absalom** conspires to overthrow father, David. [*O.T.: II Samuel* 15:10–18:33]

2. **Bastille Day** celebration of day Paris mob stormed prison; first outbreak of French Revolution (1789). [Fr. Hist.: *EB*, I: 866]

3. **Beer Hall Putsch** early, aborted Nazi coup (1923). [Ger. Hist.: *Hitler*, 198–241]

4. **Boston Tea Party** irate colonists, dressed as Indians, pillage three British ships (1773). [Am. Hist.: Jameson, 58, 495]

5. **Boxer Rebellion** xenophobic Chinese Taoist faction rebelled against foreign intruders (1900). [Chinese Hist.: Parrinder, 50]

6. **Christian, Fletcher** (fl. late 18th century) leader of mutinous sailors against Captain Bligh (1789). [Am. Lit.: *Mutiny on the Bounty*]

7. **Easter Rising** unsuccessful Irish revolt against British (1916). [Irish Hist.: *EB*, III: 760–761]

8. **Gunpowder Plot** aborted plan to blow up British House of Commons (1605). [Br. Hist.: *NCE*, 1165]

9. **Harpers Ferry** scene of Brown's aborted slave uprising. [Am. Hist.: John Jameson, 220]

10. **Hungarian Revolt** iron-curtain country futilely resisted Soviet domination (1956). [Eur. Hist.: Van Doren, 553]

11. **Jacquerie** French peasant revolt, brutally carried out and suppressed (1358). [Fr. Hist.: Bishop, 372–373]

12. **Jeroboam** with God's sanction, establishes hegemony over ten tribes of Israel. [*O.T.: I Kings* 11:31–35]

13. **Korah** rose up against Moses; slain by Jehovah. [*O.T.: Numbers* 16:1–3]

14. **Kralich, Ivan** fugitive from Turkish law; firebrand for Bulgarian independence of Ottoman rule. [Bulgarian Lit.: *Under the Yoke*]

15. **Mutiny on the Bounty** activities of mutineers, Captain Bligh, island wanderings (1789). [Am. Lit.: *Mutiny on the Bounty*]

16. **the Peasants' Revolt** English villeins' attempt to improve their lot (1381). [Br. Hist.: Bishop, 220–221, 373–374]

17. **Sepoy Rebellion** Indian soldiers' uprising against British rule in India (1857–1858). [Br. Hist.: *NCE*, 1328]

18. **Sheba** led an aborted revolt against King David. [*O.T.: II Samuel* 20: 1–2]

491. REBELLIOUSNESS

1. **Caulfield, Holden** schoolboy at odds with a "phoney" society. [Am. Lit.: *The Catcher in the Rye*]

2. **Dedalus, Stephen** "heretical" youth attempts to throw over Irish politics and religion. [Irish Lit.: *Portrait of the Artist as a Young Man*]

3. **Finn, Huckleberry** unconventional and resourceful runaway boy. [Am. Lit.: *Huckleberry Finn*]

4. **Maheu, Vincent** peaceful coalminer forced into striking for justice. [Fr. Lit.: *Germinal*]

5. **Satan (Lucifer)** the Devil; cast from heaven for rebelling against God. [*O.T.: Isaiah* 14:12; *N.T.: Revelation* 12:7–9; Br. Lit.: *Paradise Lost*]

6. **Scales, Sophia Baines** announcing her desire to be a teacher causes shock (1864). [Br. Lit.: *The Old Wives' Tale*, Magill, I, 684–686]

RECOGNITION (See IDENTIFICATION.)

492. REDHEADEDNESS

1. **Cortés, Hernando** (1485–1547) conquistador received by Montezuma as god because of height and red hair. [Mex. Hist.: *NCE*, 662]

2. **Esau** Isaac's son. [*O.T.: Genesis* 25:25]

3. **Judas Iscariot** so depicted in art. [Christian Icon.: Gaster, 165]

4. **Little Orphan Annie** heroine of comic strip. [Comics: Horn, 459]

493. REFORM

1. **Kennicott, Carol** idealist of social reform, especially village improvement. [Am. Lit.: *Main Street*]

2. **Luther, Martin** (1483–1546) German leader of the Protestant Reformation. [Ger. Hist.: *NCE*, 1631]

494. REFORMATION

1. **Hal, Prince** transformation from rakish prince to responsible king. [Br. Lit.: *II Henry IV*]

2. **Knave of Hearts** vowed he'd steal no more tarts. [Nurs. Rhyme: Baring-Gould, 152]

3. **Moses the Black, St.** rascally thief; converted, became ordained priest. [Christian Hagiog.: Attwater, 247–248]

4. **La Sacristaine** repents of sin and rejoins convent. [Medieval Legend: Walsh *Classical*, 48]

5. **Saul** becomes Christian proselytizer after Lord's visitation. [*N.T.: Acts* 9:1–22]

6. **Scrooge, Ebenezer** Christmas becomes a merry affair when he abandons his miserliness. [Br. Lit.: *A Christmas Carol*]

7. **Thaïs** Alexandrian courtesan; converted to Christianity. [Medieval Legend: Walsh *Classical*, 307]

8. **Vinicus** lustful Roman becomes devout Christian. [Polish Lit.: *Quo Vadis*, Magill, I, 797–799]

495. REFUGE (See also CONCEALMENT.)

1. **Adullam** cave where David hid from Saul. [*O.T.: I Samuel* 22:1]

2. **Alsatia (white friars)** London monastery; former refuge for lawless characters. [Br. Hist.: Walsh *Modern*, 15]

3. **Bezer-in-the-wilderness** one of the appointed cities of sanctuary for unintentional murderers. [*O.T.: Joshua* 20:8]

4. **Golan** appointed city of sanctuary for unintentional murderers. [*O.T.: Joshua* 20:8]

5. **Kedesh** city of sanctuary for unintentional murderers. [*O.T.: Joshua* 20:7]

6. **Kiriath-arba** city of sanctuary for unintentional murderers. [*O.T.: Joshua* 20:7]

7. **Noah's Ark** preserves Noah's family and animals from flood. [*O.T.: Genesis* 6:7–9]

8. **Ramoth** city of sanctuary for unintentional murderers. [*O.T.: Joshua* 20:8]

9. **Schechem** city of sanctuary for unintentional murderers. [*O.T.: Joshua* 20:7]

496. REGRET (See also REMORSE.)

1. **Epimetheus** Pandora's husband; afterwards thought better of opening box. [Gk. Myth.: Kravitz, 90]

2. **Hale, Nathan** (1755–1776) American Revolutionary spy, hanged by British; regretted only having one life to give for country. [Am. Hist.: *NCE*, 1176]

3. **Moses** led his people to threshold of promised land but could not enter. [*O.T.: Deuteronomy* 34:1–4]

4. **Nebo, Mt.** from which Moses views promised land he cannot enter. [*O.T.: Deuteronomy* 34:1–4]

5. **raspberry** symbol of regret and grief. [Flower Symbolism: *Flora Symbolica*, 177]

497. REJUVENATION

1. **Aeson** in extreme old age, restored to youth by Medea. [Rom. Myth.: *LLEI*, I: 322]

2. **Dithyrambus** epithet of Dionysus, in allusion to his double birth. [Gk. Myth.: Zimmerman, 88]

3. **Fountain of Youth** fabulous fountain believed to restore youth to the aged. [Western Folklore: Brewer *Handbook*, 389]

4. **sage** a rejuvenator; said to stop gray hair. [Herb Symbolism: *Flora Symbolica*, 165]

498. REMORSE (See also REGRET.)

1. **Deianira** commits suicide out of remorse for unwittingly having killed husband, Hercules. [Gk. Myth.: Benét, 709]

2. **Jocasta** commits suicide when she realizes she has married son, Oedipus. [Gk. Lit.: *Oedipus Rex*]

3. **Mannon, Orin** crazed by guilt for inciting mother's suicide. [Am. Lit.: *Mourning Becomes Electra*]

4. **Oedipus** blinds self upon learning of his crimes. [Gk. Lit.: *Oedipus Rex*]

5. **Othello** commits suicide from guilt for wife's murder. [Br. Lit.: *Othello*]

499. REMOTENESS (See also ISOLATION.)

1. **Antarctica** continent surrounding South Pole. [Geography: *NCE*, 113–115]

2. **Dan to Beersheba** from one outermost extreme to another. [*O.T.: Judges* 20:1]

3. **Darkest Africa** in European and American imaginations, a faraway land of no return. [Western Folklore: Misc.]

4. **end of the rainbow** the unreachable end of the earth. [Western Folklore: Misc.]

5. **Everest, Mt.** Nepalese peak; highest elevation in world (29,028 ft.). [Geography: *NCE*, 907]

6. **Great Divide** great ridge of Rocky Mountains; once thought of as epitome of faraway place. [Am. Folklore: Misc.]

7. **John O'Groat's House** traditionally thought of as the northernmost, remote point of Britain. [Geography: Misc.]

8. **Land's End** the southwestern tip of Britain. [Geography: Misc.]

9. **moon** earth's satellite; unreachable until 1969. [Astronomy: *NCE*, 1824]

10. **North and South Poles** figurative ends of the earth. [Geography: Misc.]

11. **Outer Mongolia** desert wasteland between Russia and China; figuratively and literally remote. [Geography: Misc.]

12. **Pago Pago** capital of American Samoa in South Pacific; thought of as a remote spot. [Geography: Misc.]

13. **Pillars of Hercules** promontories at the sides of Straits of Gibraltar; once the limit of man's travel. [Gk. Myth.: Zimmerman, 110]

14. **Siberia** frozen land in northeastern U.S.S.R.; place of banishment and exile. [Russ. Hist.: *NCE*, 2510]

15. **Tierra del Fuego** archipelago off the extreme southern tip of South America. [Geography: Misc.]

16. **Timbuktu** figuratively, the end of the earth. [Am. Usage: *NCE*, 2749]

17. **Ultima Thule** to Romans, extremity of the world, identified with Iceland. [Rom. Legend: *LLEI*, I: 318]

18. **Yukon** northwestern Canadian territory touching on the Arctic Ocean. [Geography: Misc.]

REPENTANCE (See PENITENCE.)

REPROOF (See CRITICISM.)

500. **RESCUE**

1. **Abishai** saves David from death by Benob. [*O.T.: II Samuel* 21:17]

2. **Andromeda** saved by Perseus from sea monster. [Gk. Myth: Hall, 239; Rom. Lit.: *Metamorphoses*]

3. **Ararat** traditional resting place of Noah's ark after the Flood. [*O.T.: Genesis* 8:4]

4. **Arion** thrown overboard; carried safely to land by dolphins. [Gk. Myth.: *LLEI*, I: 323; Br. Lit.: *Faerie Queene*]

5. **Barry** St. Bernard dog; saved over 40 snowbound people in Alps. [Swiss Hist.: Wallechinsky, 126]

6. **Deucalion** survived Zeus's flood in ark. [Gk. Myth.: Zimmerman, 85]

7. **Diana's statue** saved by Orestes from Scythian thieves. [Gk. Lit.: *Iphigenia in Tauris*]

8. **Dunkirk** combined military-civilian operation rescued 340,000 British troops (1940). [Br. Hist.: Van Doren, 475]

9. **Entebbe** daring Israeli raid freed airline hostages at Ugandan airport (1977). [World Hist.: *Facts* (1977), 487]

10. **Hercules** rescues Alcestis from Hades after her self-sacrifice. [Gk. Lit.: *Alcestis;* Ger. Opera: Gluck, *Alceste,* Westerman, 73–75]

11. **Iphigenia** rescued at the moment of her sacrificial stabbing. [Gk. Myth.: Gayley, 80–81]

12. **Isaac** saved from being sacrificed by angel of the Lord. [*O.T.: Genesis* 22:2–13]

13. **Jonah** saved from drowning in belly of great fish. [*O.T.: Jonah* 1:17]

14. **Macheath** saved from hanging by the king's reprieve. [Ger. Opera: Weill, *Threepenny Opera,* Westerman, 497]

15. **Mignon** rescued by Wilhelm Meister from gypsies. [Fr. Opera: Thomas, *Mignon,* Westerman, 187]

16. **Noah** only man deemed by God worth saving from His destructive flood. [*O.T.: Genesis* 6–10]

17. **oak leaves** used in crown awarded to one who saves a life. [Rom. Tradition: Wheeler, 765]

18. **Peters, Dirk** mutineer; saves Pym and Augustus from starvation. [Am. Lit.: "The Narrative of Arthur Gordon Pym" in Magill, I, 640–643]

19. **Rahab and family** spared from Jericho's destruction for aid rendered to Joshua's army. [*O.T.: Joshua* 6:25]

20. **Sanang** used magic powers to rescue Marco Polo. [Irish Lit.: *Messer Marco Polo,* Magill, I, 584–585]

501. RESOURCEFULNESS

1. **Buck** clever and temerarious dog perseveres in the Klondike. [Am. Lit.: *Call of the Wild*]

2. **Crichton, Admirable** butler proves to be infinite resource for castaway family on island. [Br. Lit.: *The Admirable Crichton*]

3. **Crusoe, Robinson** inventive when shipwrecked on an island. [Br. Lit.: *Robinson Crusoe*]

4. **duck** from ingeniousness of duck in eluding enemies. [Heraldry: Halberts, 26]

5. **Swiss Family Robinson** shipwrecked family carves hospitable life from wilderness. [Children's Lit.: *Swiss Family Robinson*]

6. **Thoreau, Henry David** (1817–1862) example of man's ability to build his own life in the wilderness. [Am. Hist.: *NCE*, 2738]

502. RESURRECTION

1. **Amys and Amyloun** sacrificed children are restored to life. [Medieval Legend: Benét, 31]

2. **Bran** god whose cauldron restored the dead to life. [Welsh Myth.: Jobes, 241]

3. **Dorcas** raised from the dead by St. Peter. [*N.T.: Acts* 9:36–42]

4. **Drusiana** restored to life by John the Evangelist. [Christian Hagiog.: *Golden Legend*]

5. **Dumuzi** god of regeneration and resurrection. [Sumerian Myth.: Jobes, 476]

6. **egg** symbol of Christ's resurrection. [Art: Hall, 110]

7. **Elijah** breathes life back into child. [*O.T.: I Kings* 17:18]

8. **Jairus' daughter** Christ raises her from the dead. [*N.T.: Matthew* 9:18–19; *Mark* 5:21–24; *Luke* 8:40–42]

9. **Jesus Christ** arose from the dead three days after His crucifixion. [*N.T.: Matthew* 28; *Mark* 16; *Luke* 24; *John* 20]

10. **Lazarus** Jesus calls him back to life from the tomb. [*N.T.: John* 11:43–44]

11. **phoenix** fabled bird, rises from its ashes. [Gk. Legend: Brewer *Dictionary*, 829; Christian Symbolism: Appleton, 76]

12. **pomegranate** bursting with seed, it symbolizes open tomb. [Christian Symbolism: Appleton, 77]

13. **scarab** symbol for Ra, sun-god; reborn each day. [Animal Symbolism: Mercatante, 180]

14. **Thammuz** god died annually and rose each spring. [Babyl. Myth.: Brewer *Dictionary*, 1071]

15. **widow's son of Nain** touched by mother's grief, Christ brings him back to life. [*N.T.: Luke* 7:11–17]

503. REUNION

1. **Arafat, Mt.** Adam and Eve met here after 200 years. [Muslim Legend: Benét, 44]

2. **chickweed** flower symbolizing a rejoining. [Flower Symbolism: Jobes, 322]

3. **Esau and Jacob** after many years, they are reconciled. [*O.T.: Genesis* 33:1–4]

4. **Eurydice and Orpheus** reunited despite his backward look. [Ger. Opera: Gluck, *Orpheus and Eurydice*, Westerman, 72]

5. **Joachim and Anna** separated spouses joyfully meet at Jerusalem gate on news of her pregnancy. [Ital. Lit.: *Golden Legend*]

6. **Mary and Elizabeth** the two pregnant women meet after many years and rejoice. [*N.T.: Luke* 1:39–56]

7. **prodigal son and his father** repentant son returns home to a joyous welcome. [*N.T.: Luke* 15:11–32]

504. REVELRY

1. **Bacchanalia** festival in honor of Bacchus, god of wine. [Rom. Religion: *NCE*, 203]

2. **Boar's Head Tavern** scene of Falstaff's carousals. [Br. Lit.: *I Henry IV; II Henry IV*]

3. **Comus** hard-drinking god of festive mirth; whence, *comic*. [Gk. Myth.: Espy, 31]

4. **Dionysia** celebrations honoring the wine god, Dionysus. [Gk. Religion: Avery, 399, 404–408; Parrinder, 80]

5. **Dionysus** (Rom. **Bacchus**) god of wine and revelry. [Gk. Myth.: Parrinder, 39]

6. **Fête Champêtre** erotically tinged painting of picnic scene. [Fr. Art: Daniel, 102]

7. **Goliards** wandering scholar-poets of satirical Latin verse celebrating sensual pleasure. [Medieval Hist.: *NCE*, 1105]

8. **grapes, garland of** traditional headdress of Dionysus (Bacchus). [Gk. and Rom. Myth.: Jobes, 373]

REVENGE (See VENGEANCE.)

REWARD (See PRIZE.)

505. RIBALDRY

1. **Decameron, The** Boccaccio's bawdy panorama of medieval Italian life. [Ital. Lit.: Bishop, 314–315, 380]

2. **Fescennia** Etrurian town noted for jesting and scurrilous verse (Fescennine verse). [Rom. Hist.: *EB*, IV: 112]

3. **Goliards** scholar-poets interested mainly in earthly delights. [Medieval Hist.: Bishop, 292–293]

4. **Iambe** girl who amused Demeter with bawdy stories. [Gk. Myth.: Howe, 136]

RIDICULE (See MOCKERY.)

506. RIGHTEOUSNESS (See also VIRTUOUSNESS.)

1. **Amos** prophet of righteousness. [*O.T.: Amos*]

2. **Astraea** goddess of righteousness. [Gk. Myth.: Walsh *Classical*, 36]

3. **Benedetto, Don** Catholic teacher of moral precepts. [Ital. Lit.: *Bread and Wine*]

4. **Dharma** multi-faceted concept of morality, truth, doctrine. [Hindu Rel.: Parrinder, 77]

5. **Do-Right, Dudley** Canadian mountie who can do no wrong. [TV: "The Dudley Do-Right Show" in Terrace, I, 229–230]

6. **Enoch** traditionally seen as paragon of upright man. [*O.T.: Genesis* 5:21–24]

7. **Everyman** medieval play demonstrating man's salvation dependent on his righteousness. [Br. Lit.: *Everyman*]

8. **Josiah** virtuously reforms Jerusalem's evil ways. [*O.T.: II Kings* 23:1–20]

9. **Noah** only devout man of time; saved from flood. [*O.T.: Genesis* 6: 9–22]

10. **Zosima** elder monk; preaches message of love and forbearance. [Russ. Lit.: *Brothers Karamazov*]

507. RING, MAGIC

1. **Agramant's ring** given to dwarf, Brunello, and stolen. [Ital. Lit.: *Orlando Furioso*]

2. **Andvari's ring** he gave up magic ring to gain liberty. [Norse Myth.: Benét, 35]

3. **Draupnir** Odin's ring; symbol of fertility. [Norse Myth.: *LLEI*, I: 326]

4. **Luned's ring** rendered its wearer invisible. [Welsh Lit.: *Mabinogion*]

5. **Reynard's wonderful ring** tricolored; each color performed different feat. [Medieval Lit.: *Reynard the Fox*]

6. **steel ring** enabled wearer to read the secrets of another's heart. [Br. Lit.: Brewer *Handbook*, 916]

508. RIOT

1. **Attica** city in New York housing state prison; one of the worst prison riots in American history occurred there (1971). [Am. Hist.: *NCE*, 182]

2. **Birmingham riots** melee resulting from civil rights demonstrations (1963). [Am. Hist.: Van Doren, 585–586]

3.   **Boston Massacre** civil uprising fueled revolutionary spirit (1770). [Am. Hist.: Jameson, 57]

4.   **Boston Tea Party** colonists rioted against tea tax (1773). [Am. Hist.: NCE, 341]

5.   **Chicago riots** "police riot" arguably cost Democrats election (1968). [Am. Hist.: Van Doren, 625]

6.   **Donnybrook Fair** former annual Dublin county fair; famous for rioting and dissipation. [Irish Hist.: NCE, 784]

7.   **Germinal** conflict of capital vs. labor: miners strike *en masse*. [Fr. Lit.: *Germinal*]

8.   **Haymarket Riot** Chicago labor dispute erupted into mob scene (1886). [Am. Hist.: Van Doren, 297]

9.   **Kent State** Ohio university where antiwar demonstration led to riot, resulting in deaths of four students (1971). [Am. Hist.: NCE, 1466]

10. **Little Rock** capital of Arkansas; federal troops sent there to enforce ruling against segregation (1957). [Am. Hist.: NCE, 1594]

11. **Luddites** British workers riot to destroy labor-saving machines (1811–1816). [Br. Hist.: NCE, 1626]

12. **Molly Maguires** antilandlord organization; used any means to combat mine owners (1860s, 1870s). [Am. Hist.: Van Doren, 272]

13. **New York Draft Riots** anticonscription feelings resulted in anarchy and bloodshed (1863). [Am. Hist.: Jameson, 429]

14. **Shays' Rebellion** armed insurrection by Massachusetts farmers against the state government (1786). [Am. Hist.: NCE, 2495]

15. **Watts** district in Los Angeles where black Americans rioted over economic deprivation and social injustices (1965). [Am. Hist.: NCE, 1612–1613]

16. **Whiskey Rebellion** uprising in Pennsylvania over high tax on whiskey and scotch products (1794). [Am. Hist.: NCE, 2967]

509.   RIVALRY

1.   **Brom Bones and Ichabod Crane** bully and show-off compete for Katrina's hand. [Am. Lit.: *The Legend of Sleepy Hollow*]

2.   **Capulets and Montagues** bitter feud between these two houses leads to tragedy. [Br. Lit.: *Romeo and Juliet*]

3.   **Diomedes and Troilus** rivals for hand of Cressida. [Br. Lit.: *Troilus and Cressida*]

4.   **Esau and Jacob** struggled even in mother's womb. [O.T.: *Genesis* 25:22]

5. **Eteocles and Polynices** brothers battle for Theban throne. [Gk. Lit.: *Seven Against Thebes*]

6. **Gingham Dog and Calico Cat** stuffed animals eat each other up. [Am. Lit.: "The Duel" in Hollowell]

7. **Guelphs and Ghibellines** perennial medieval Italian feuding political factions. [Ital. Hist.: Plumb, 42–43]

8. **Hatfields and McCoys** 19th-century mountain families carried on endless feud in southern U.S. [Am. Hist.: *NCE*, 942]

9. **Jets and Sharks** teenage gangs fight for supremacy amid the New York tenements. [Am. Lit. and Cinema: *West Side Story*]

10. **Kilkenny cats** contentious felines fight to the death. [Nurs. Rhyme: *Mother Goose*]

11. **Percys and Douglases** the perennial Scottish border feud; recounted in famous ballad "Chevy Chase." [Scot. Hist.: Payton, 141]

12. **Proitus and Acrisius** fought in womb; contended for father's realm. [Gk. Myth.: Gaster, 164]

13. **Richard the Lion-Hearted and Saladin** Christian and Saracen leaders part friends after Crusade. [Br. Lit.: *The Talisman*]

ROBBERY (See THIEVERY.)

RUDENESS (See COARSENESS.)

510. **RUFFIANISM**

1. **droogs** Alex's rough and tough band of hooligans. [Br. Lit.: *A Clockwork Orange*]

2. **Hawkubites** London toughs; terrorized old men, women, and children (1711–1714). [Br. Hist.: Brewer *Note-Book*, 406]

3. **Jackmen** medieval para-military thugs. [Br. Hist.: Brewer *Note-Book*, 463]

4. **Jets and Sharks** hostile street gangs. [Am. Lit. and Cinema: *West Side Story*]

5. **Mohocks** bullies terrorizing London streets in 18th century. [Br. Hist.: Brewer *Dictionary*, 720]

6. **Scowerers** London hooligans, at turn of the 18th century. [Br. Hist.: Brewer *Dictionary*, 972]

7. **Tityre Tus** young bullies in late 17th-century London. [Br. Hist: Brewer *Dictionary*, 1087]

511. **RUSTICITY**

1. **American Gothic** Grant Wood's painting of stern Iowan farming couple. [Am. Art: Osborne, 1215]

2. **Caudill, Boone** epitome of the mountain man. [Am. Lit.: *The Big Sky*]

3. **Currier and Ives** makers of colorful lithographs of scenes of nature and outdoor recreation. [Am. Hist.: *NCE*, 699]

4. **North Woods** forest and lake region; setting for lumberjack legends. [Am. Lit.: Hart, 607]

5. **Petticoat Junction** farce set in rural America. [TV: Terrace, II, 205–206]

6. **shtetl** any small-town Jewish settlement in East Europe. [Jewish Hist.: Wigoder, 552]

512. **RUTHLESSNESS (See also BRUTALITY, CRUELTY, HEART-LESSNESS.)**

1. **Borgia, Cesare** (1476–1507) prototype of Machiavelli's "Prince": intelligent and ruthlessly opportunistic. [Ital. Hist.: Plumb, 59]

2. **Caligula** (12–41) Roman emperor known for terror and cruel autocracy. [Rom. Hist.: *NCE*, 425]

3. **Ivan the Terrible** (1533–1584) his reign was characterized by murder and terror. [Russ. Hist.: *EB*, 9: 1179–1180]

4. **Nero** (37–68) demented Roman emperor; initiated persecutions against the Christians. [Rom. Hist.: *NCE*, 1909]

5. **Robespierre, Maximilien Marie Isidore** (1758–1794) architect of the Reign of Terror (1793–1794). [Fr. Hist.: *EB*, 15: 907–910]

S

513. SACRIFICE (See also MARTYRDOM.)

1. **Adrammelech and Anammelech** Sepharvaite gods to whom children were immolated. [*O.T.: II Kings* 17:31]

2. **Akedah** biblical account of God commanding Abraham's offerings. [Jewish Hist.: Wigoder, 17]

3. **Burghers of Calais** they sacrificed themselves to save city from British siege after Battle of Crécy (1346). [Fr. Hist.: *EB*, II: 447]

4. **Iphigenia** slain to appease Artemis' wrath. [Gk. Myth.: Walsh *Classical*, 156]

5. **Moloch** god to whom idolatrous Israelites immolated children. [*O.T.: II Kings* 23:10; *Jeremiah* 7:31–32, 32:35]

6. **Moriah** site intended for Abraham's offering up of Isaac. [*O.T.: Genesis* 22:2]

7. **suttee** former practice of self-immolation by widow on husband's pyre. [Hinduism: Brewer *Dictionary*, 1049]

8. **Tophet** site of propitiatory immolations to god, Moloch. [*O.T.: II Kings* 23:10; *Jeremiah* 7:31–32]

514. SACRILEGE

1. **abomination of desolation** epithet describing pagan idol in Jerusalem Temple. [*O.T.: Daniel* 9, 11, 12; *N.T.: Mark* 13:14; *Matthew* 24:15]

2. **Aepytus** Arcadian king; entering Poseidon's sanctuary, forbidden to mortals, he is blinded. [Gk. Myth.: Zimmerman, 9]

3. **Beaufort, Cardinal** (1377–1447) haughty churchman; dies execrating God. [Br. Lit.: *II Henry VI*]

4. **cleansing of the temple** sacrilegious money-changers driven out of temple by Christ. [*N.T.: Matthew*, 21:12–13; *Mark*, 11:15–18]

5. **Heliodorus** Syrian official attempted to loot Solomon's temple. [*Apocrypha: II Maccabees* 3]

6. **Hophni and Phinehas** contemptuously abused holiness of sacrifices. [*O.T.: I Samuel* 2:12–17]

7. **Simon Magus** tried to purchase apostolic powers; whence, *simony*. [*N.T.: Acts* 8:18–24]

SADNESS (See MELANCHOLY.)

515. **SALVATION (See also DELIVERANCE.)**

1. **Esther, Queen** intercedes with king for cessation of extermination of Jews. [*O.T.: Esther* 7:8]

2. **Faerie Queene (Gloriana)** gives a champion to people in trouble. [Br. Lit.: *The Faerie Queene*]

3. **Jesus Christ** as savior of souls. [Christian Tradition: Jobes, 330]

4. **Moses** led his people out of bondage. [*O.T.: Exodus*]

SANCTIMONY (See HYPOCRISY.)

SANCTUARY (See REFUGE.)

516. **SAVAGERY**

1. **Apache Indians** once fierce fighting tribe of American West. [Am. Hist.: *NCE*, 123]

2. **bandersnatch** imaginary wild animal of great ferocity. [Br. Lit.: "Jabberwocky" in *Through the Looking-Glass*]

3. **berserkers** ancient Norse warriors; assumed attributes of bears in battle. [Norse Myth.: Leach, 137]

4. **Comanche Indians** warlike tribe of American West. [Am. Hist.: *NCE*, 607]

5. **Crommyonian sow** ravager of the Corinthian countryside. [Gk. Myth.: Benét, 237]

6. **Erymanthian boar** ravaged Arcadian countryside until capture by Hercules. [Gk. Myth.: Jobes, 523]

7. **Huns** Mongolian invaders of western Europe until 453. [Eur. Hist.: Espy, 167]

8. **Magua** a renegade Huron who scalps white men. [Am. Lit.: *The Pathfinder*, Magill, I, 715–717]

9. **mares of Diomedes** lived on human flesh; their capture was Hercules' eighth labor. [Gk. and Rom. Myth.: Hall, 149]

10. **Taras Bulba** savage yet strangely devoted Cossack leader. [Russ. Lit.: *Taras Bulba*, Walsh *Modern*, 77]

11. **Tartars** 13th-century rapacious hordes of Genghis Khan. [Medieval Hist.: Brewer *Dictionary*, 1064]

12. **tiger** aims at annihilating mankind. [Animal Symbolism: Mercatante, 55]

13. **Vandals** 5th-century sackers of Rome and its art. [Ital. Hist.: Espy, 168]

517.   **SCANDAL** (See also **CONTROVERSY**.)

1.   **Abélard, Peter** (1079–c. 1144) French theologian takes Héloïse, abbess, as lover; marries her in secret. [Fr. Hist.: *EB*, I: 18]

2.   **Black Sox Scandal** Chicago White Sox baseball players accused of taking bribes to lose the 1919 World Series. [Sports: *EB*, II: 66]

3.   **Chappaquiddick** car driven by Senator Edward Kennedy plunges off bridge; woman companion dies (1969). [Am. Hist.: *Facts* (1969), 452]

4.   **Edward VIII** (1894–1972) King of Britain whose decision to marry a divorcee forced him to abdicate throne (1936). [Br. Hist.: *NCE*, 835–836]

5.   **$64,000 Question, The** game show discovered to be fixed (1958). [TV: Terrace, II, 295–296]

6.   **South Sea Bubble** fraud is exposed in British South Sea Company (1720). [Br. Hist.: *EB*, IX: 383]

7.   **Teapot Dome** government oil reserves fraudulently leased to private concerns (1922). [Am. Hist.: Flexner, 353]

8.   **Watergate** scandals involving Nixon's administration (1972). [Am. Hist.: Kane, 460–462]

SCAPEGOAT (See **DUPERY**.)

518.   **SCHIZOPHRENIA**

1.   **Haller, Harry** middle-aged man battles two selves. [Ger. Lit.: *Steppenwolf*]

2.   **Jekyll, Dr., and Mr. Hyde** upright physician reduced to animality by potion. [Br. Lit.: *Dr. Jekyll and Mr. Hyde*]

519.   **SEA**

1.   **Aegir** god of the seas. [Norse Myth.: Brewer *Dictionary*, 12]

2.   **Amphitrite** queen of the sea; Poseidon's wife. [Gk. Myth.: *NCE*, 94]

3.   **Bowditch** standard navigational work, *American Practical Navigator;* so called from its compiler, Nathaniel Bowditch. [Am. Hist.: Hart, 97]

4.   **Clement the First, St.** drowned bound to anchor; invoked in marine dedications. [Christian Hagiog.: Attwater, 88]

5.   **Cuchulain** mad with grief, he battles the sea. [Irish Myth.: Benét, 239]

6.   **Dylan** god of waves, which continually mourn him. [Celtic Myth.: Leach, 332; Jobes, 480]

7. **Jones, Davy** personification of the ocean. [Br. and Am. Marine Slang: Leach, 298]

8. **Manannan** Irish god of the sea. [Irish Folklore: Briggs, 280]

9. **mermaid** half-woman, half-fish; seen by sailors. [Western Folklore: Misc.]

10. **Nereids** fifty daughters of Nereus; attendants of Poseidon. [Gk. Myth.: Zimmerman, 174]

11. **Nereus** son of Oceanus; father of the Nereids. [Gk. Myth.: Zimmerman, 174; Gk. Lit.: *Iliad*]

12. **Njorthr** Scandinavian god; protector of sailors and ships. [Norse Myth.: Brewer *Dictionary*, 760]

13. **Oceanids** three thousand daughters of Oceanus and Tethys. [Gk. Myth.: Zimmerman, 178]

14. **Oceanus** Titan and father of the river gods and Oceanids. [Gk. Myth.: Zimmerman, 178]

15. **Poseidon** (Rom. **Neptune**) god of the oceans and all waters. [Gk. Myth.: Wheeler, 257]

16. **Salacia** consort of Neptune and goddess of springs. [Rom. Myth.: Kravitz, 208]

17. **Tethys** goddess-wife of Oceanus. [Gk. Myth.: Brewer *Dictionary*, 1070]

18. **Thetis** sea deity and mother of Achilles. [Gk. Myth.: Zimmerman, 269; Gk. Lit.: *Odyssey*]

19. **trident** three-pronged fork; attribute of Poseidon. [Gk. Myth.: Hall, 309]

20. **Triton** gigantic sea deity; son and messenger of Poseidon. [Gk. Myth.: Zimmerman, 277; Rom. Lit.: *Aeneid*]

21. **Varuna** god over the waters. [Vedic Myth.: Leach, 1155]

SEASON (See AUTUMN, SPRING, SUMMER, WINTER.)

520. **SEDUCTION (See also FLIRTATIOUSNESS.)**

1. **Armida** modern Circe; sorceress who seduces Rinaldo. [Ital. Lit.: *Jerusalem Delivered*]

2. **Aurelius** Dorigen's nobleminded would-be seducer. [Br. Lit.: *Canterbury Tales*, "The Franklin's Tale"]

3. **Circe** enchantress who turned Odysseus's men into swine; byword for irresistibly fascinating woman. [Gk. Lit.: *Odyssey*; Rom. Lit.: *Aeneid*]

4. **Delilah** fascinating and deceitful mistress of Samson. [O.T.: *Judges* 16]

5. **Dragon Lady** beautiful Chinese temptress. [Comics: "Terry and the Pirates" in Horn, 653]

6. **Europa** seduced by Zeus in form of a white bull. [Gk. Myth.: Kravitz, 96]

7. **Hautdesert, Lady de** tries to seduce Gawain to test his faithfulness. [Br. Lit.: *Sir Gawain and the Green Knight*]

8. **Io** seduced by Jupiter in form of a cloud. [Rom. Myth.: *Metamorphoses*]

9. **Leucosia, Ligeia, and Parthenope** sirens; tried to lure Odysseus and his men to destruction. [Gk. Lit.: *Odyssey*]

10. **Lorelei** siren; lured ships to destruction with singing. [Ger. Folklore: Benét, 599]

11. **Mirandolina** innkeeper artfully seduces misogynist for sport. [Ital. Lit.: *The Mistress of the Inn*]

12. **Sorrel, Hetty** seduced by Arthur Donnithorne. [Br. Lit.: *Adam Bebe*]

SELFISHNESS (See CONCEIT, STINGINESS.)

521. **SELF-SACRIFICE (See also SUICIDE.)**

1. **Aïda** dies with her beloved Radames. [Ital. Opera: Verdi, *Aïda*, Westerman, 325]

2. **Alcestis** offered self up to die in the stead of Admetus. [Gk. Myth.: Leach, 11]

3. **Brooke, Dorothea** gives up Casaubon's fortune for Ladislaw's affection. [Br. Lit.: *Middlemarch*, Magill, I, 588–591]

4. **Camille** gives up Armand so as not to endanger his career. [Fr. Lit.: *La Dame aux Camélias*]

5. **Colamartini, Christina** dies in wilderness attempting to help Paolo. [Ital. Lit.: *Bread and Wine*]

6. **Din, Gunga** water-carrier killed as he rescues narrator of story. [Br. Lit.: "Gunga Din" in Benét, 430]

7. **Dounia** intends to marry Svidrigailov to relieve her brother's poverty. [Russ. Lit.: *Crime and Punishment*]

8. **Eponine** during fight, gives his life to save Marius. [Fr. Lit.: *Les Misérables*]

9. **Fantine** woman becomes prostitute to support daughter. [Fr. Lit.: *Les Misérables*]

10. **Gift of the Magi** husband and wife each give up own treasure to buy the other's Christmas present. [Am. Lit.: "The Gift of the Magi" in Benét, 395]

11. **Gilda** sacrifices self to save her beloved Duke's life. [Ital. Opera: Verdi, *Rigoletto*, Westerman, 300]

12. **des Grieux** accompanies banished Manon to exile in Louisiana. [Fr. Lit.: *Manon Lescaut*]

13. **Hansa, Per** dies in storm on errand of mercy. [Nor. Lit.: *Giants in the Earth*, Magill, I, 303–304]

14. **Jephthah's daughter** accepts father's vow to God to die in exchange for his victory. [*O.T.: Judges* 11:30–40]

15. **Jesus Christ** died on cross to save mankind. [*N.T.: Matthew* 27:24–61]

16. **Kamikaze** WWII Japanese suicide pilots; embodiment of "death before dishonor." [Jap. Hist.: Fuller, III, 618–619]

17. **Madeleine** executed with lover Andrea. [Ital. Opera: Giordano, *Andrea Chénier*, Westerman, 370–371]

18. **Oakhurst, John** kills himself so that three other outcasts may survive. [Am. Lit.: *The Outcasts of Poker Flat*]

19. **Ona** becomes a prostitute to support family. [Am. Lit.: *The Jungle*]

20. **pelican** tears open breast to feed young. [Christian Symbolism: de Bles, 29]

21. **de Posa, Marquis** clears prince's name in conspiracy by indicting himself. [Ger. Lit.: *Don Carlos*]

22. **Susanin, Ivan** leads Poles astray to safeguard tsar; executed. [Russ. Opera: Glinka, *A Life for the Tsar*, Westerman, 379]

SENSUALITY (See BEAUTY, SENSUAL.)

522. **SENTIMENTALITY**

1. **Checkers** dog given as gift to Nixon; used in his defense of political contributions during presidential campaign (1952). [Am. Hist.: Wallechinsky, 126]

2. **Dondi** comic strip in which sentimentality is the main motif. [Comics: Horn, 217–218]

3. **Goody Two Shoes** mawkish girl, overpleased to have two shoes, exclaims her fortune to all. [Nurs. Rhyme: "Little Goody Two Shoes" in Barnhart, 502]

4. **Hardy, Andy** protagonist of 1930s series of sentimental "family" movies. [Am. Cinema: Griffith, 300]

5. **Little Nell** death scene of sweet child epitomizes sentimentality. [Br. Lit.: *Old Curiosity Shop*]

6. **Mary Magdalene** portrayed traditionally in art as weeping; whence, *maudlin*. [Art: Misc.]

7. **Orsino** plays role of languishing lover. [Br. Lit.: *Twelfth Night*]

8. **sob sister** journalist who handles advice to lovelorn column. [Am. Journalism: Brewer *Dictionary*, 1016]

9. **Sweet Adeline** tune of a man's former romance, usually sung in barbershop harmony. [Am. Music: Hart, 823]

10. **Waltons, The** television show of depression-era America softened by nostalgia. [TV: Terrace, II, 418–419]

523. **SERVANT (See also BUTLER.)**

1. **Abigail** helpmeet of King David; traditional name for handmaiden. [*O.T.: I Samuel* 25]

2. **Albert** popular servant's name: assistant, manservant, page-boy. [Br. Lit.: *Loving; By The Pricking of My Thumbs; A Damsel in Distress*]

3. **Brighella** prototype of interfering servant; meddles and gossips. [Ital. Drama: Walsh *Classical*, 62]

4. **Despina** her stratagems control and resolve the plot. [Ital. Opera: Mozart, *Così fan tutte*, Scholes, 259]

5. **Figaro** valet who outwits everyone by his cunning. [Fr. Lit.: *Marriage of Figaro*]

6. **Friday** young Indian rescued by Crusoe and kept as servant and companion. [Br. Lit.: *Robinson Crusoe*]

7. **Ganymede** mortal lad, taken by Zeus to be cupbearer to the gods. [Gk. Myth.: Howe, 106]

8. **Hazel** meddling maid in the Baxter house. [TV and Comics: Terrace, I, 343]

9. **Hebe** cupbearer to the gods; succeeded by Ganymede. [Gk. Myth.: Zimmerman, 117]

10. **Ithamore** purchased by Barabas to betray Governor of Malta. [Br. Drama: *The Jew of Malta*]

11. **Lichas** Hercules' attendant; unknowingly delivers poisoned robe to him. [Rom. Lit.: *Metamorphoses*]

12. **Notburga, St.** Bavarian patroness of domestics; beneficent, though poor. [Christian Hagiog.: Attwater, 257]

13. **Passepartout** Phileas Fogg's rash valet. [Fr. Lit.: *Around the World in Eighty Days*]

14. **Thing** Addams family servant; a disembodied right hand. [TV: "The Addams Family" in Terrace, I, 29]

15. **Xanthias** carries Bacchus's heavy bundles. [Gk. Lit.: *The Frogs*]

16. **Zita, St.** devout and generous domestic; patron saint. [Christian Hagiog.: Attwater, 348]

524. **SEWING AND WEAVING**

1. **Arachne** skilled weaver; changed into spider for challenging Athena to weaving contest. [Gk. Myth.: Zimmerman, 27]

2. **Athena** goddess of spinning and weaving. [Gk. Myth.: Howe, 45]

3. **Marner, Silas** hand-loom weaver who comes, friendless, to Raveloe. [Br. Lit.: Benét, 930]

4. **Penelope** weaves shroud for 20 years, unraveling it each night. [Gk. Lit.: *Odyssey*]

5. **Prynne, Hester** ostracized, sewing becomes her daily preoccupation. [Am. Lit.: *The Scarlet Letter*]

6. **Rumpelstiltskin** dwarf who spun gold from straw to help imprisoned girl. [Ger. Fairy Tale: *Rumpelstiltskin*]

7. **Weavers, The** depicts plight of Silesian weavers. [Ger. Lit.: Benét, 1078]

525. SEX SYMBOL (See BEAUTY, SENSUAL; BUXOMNESS.)

1. **Lace, Miss** 1940s armed forces' pin-up girl from comic strip. [Comics: "Male Call" in Horn, 475]

2. **Petty girl** airbrushed beauty, scantily clad in Esquire's pages. [Am. Lit.: Misc.]

3. **Vargas girl** originally appeared in *Esquire*, later in *Playboy;* created by Alberto Vargas. [Am. Art: *Vargas*]

526. SHEPHERD

1. **Corin** the faithful shepherdess; called "the Virgin of the Grove." [Br. Lit.: "The Faithful Shepherdess" in Brewer *Handbook*, 234]

2. **Daphnis** guards sheep; creator of bucolic poetry. [Gk. Myth.: Kravitz, 75]

3. **Jabal** father of herdsmen. [*O.T.: Genesis* 4:20]

4. **Jesus Christ** the Good Shepherd. [*N.T.: John* 10:11–14]

5. **Little Bo-peep** young shepherdess; searches everywhere for lost flock. [Nurs. Rhyme: Opie, 93]

6. **Little Boy Blue** asleep while his sheep are in the field. [Nurs. Rhyme: Baring-Gould, 46]

527. SHREWISHNESS (See also IRASCIBILITY.)

1. **Caudle, Mrs. Margaret** nagging, complaining wife. [Br. Lit.: *The Curtain Lectures*, Walsh *Modern*, 90]

2. **Dollallolla, Queen** even King Arthur feared his uxorial virago. [Br. Lit: *Tom Thumb the Great*]

3. **Frome, Zenobia (Zeena)** Ethan Frome's hypochondriacal, nagging, belittling wife. [Am. Lit.: *Ethan Frome*]

4. **Galatea** 19th-century version: nags Pygmalion. [Aust. Operetta: von Suppé, *Beautiful Galatea*, Westerman, 285]

5. **Gargery, Mrs.** vixenish wife; keeps husband in thrall. [Br. Lit.: *Great Expectations*]

6. **Katherine** "intolerably curst and shrewd and froward." [Br. Lit.: *The Taming of the Shrew*]

7. **MacStinger, Mrs.** widow; miserable to everyone. [Br. Lit.: *Dombey and Son*]

8. **Peninnah** continually harassed co-wife Hannah about her barrenness. [*O.T.: I Samuel* 1:6]

9. **Sofronia** Norina, disguised for mock marriage, pretends to be virago. [Ital. Opera: Donizetti, *Don Pasquale*, Westerman, 123–124]

10. **Tabitha** Mr. Bramble's virago sister; bent on matrimony. [Br. Lit.: *Humphry Clinker*]

11. **Termagant** tumultuous Muslim deity (male); today, a virago. [Medieval Lit.: Espy, 125]

12. **Xanthippe** Socrates' peevish, quarrelsome wife. [Gk. Hist.: Espy, 114]

SHYNESS (See TIMIDITY.)

SIMILARITY (See TWINS.)

SINFULNESS (See WICKEDNESS.)

528. **SINGER, OPERATIC**

1. **Caruso, Enrico** (1873–1921) world's most celebrated tenor. [Opera Hist.: *NCE*, 469]

529. **SKEPTICISM (See also CYNICISM, PESSIMISM.)**

1. **Bothwell, Sergeant** believes in nothing. [Br. Lit.: *Old Mortality*]

2. **Dawes, Jabez** mischievous brat ridicules Santa's existence. [Am. Lit.: "The Boy Who Laughed at Santa Claus" in Rockwell]

3. **mushroom** symbol of suspicion. [Plant Symbolism: *Flower Symbolica*, 310]

4. **Naaman** at first doubts efficacy of leprosy cure. [*O.T.: II Kings* 5:11–14]

5. **Thomas, St.** wouldn't believe Christ's resurrection until he saw Him; hence, *Doubting Thomas*. [*N.T.: John* 20:24–25]

6. **Windermere, Lady** doesn't believe husband's "virtuous" generosity toward Mrs. Erlynne. [Br. Lit.: *Lady Windermere's Fan*, Magill, I, 488–490]

7. **Zacharias** struck dumb for doubting Gabriel's birth annunciation. [*N.T.: Luke* 1:18–20]

SKINNINESS (See THINNESS.)

530. **SLANDER (See also GOSSIP.)**

1. **Basile** calumniating, niggardly bigot. [Fr. Lit.: *Barber of Seville; Marriage of Figaro*]

2. **Blatant Beast** monster with 100 tongues; calumnious voice of world. [Br. Lit.: *Faerie Queene*]

3. **Candour, Mrs.** the most energetic calumniator. [Br. Lit.: *School for Scandal*]

4. **cobaea vine** symbol of slander. [Flower Symbolism: *Flora Symbolica*, 173]

5. **hellebore** symbol of slander. [Flower Symbolism: *Flora Symbolica*, 174]

6. **Iago** malignant Venetian commander; slanders Cassio to Othello. [Br. Lit.: *Othello*]

7. **Kay, Sir** ill-mannered, mean-spirited, but above all, scurrilous. [Br. Lit.: *Le Morte d'Arthur; Idylls of the King*]

8. **Miriam** made leprous for maligning Moses's marriage to Cushite. [*O.T.: Numbers* 12:9–10]

9. **Shimei** vilifies David, implying he stole Saul's throne. [*O.T.: II Samuel* 16:7–8]

10. **Thersites** dedicated to denigrating his betters. [Gk. Lit.: *Iliad;* Br. Lit.: *Troilus and Cressida*]

SLAUGHTER (See MASSACRE.)

531. **SLEEP**

1. **dormouse** snoozes all through the mad tea-party. [Br. Lit.: *Alice's Adventures in Wonderland*]

2. **Endymion** man kept immortally youthful through eternal sleep. [Gk. Myth.: Howe, 91]

3. **Epimenides** philosopher nods off for 57 years in cave. [Gk. Legend: *LLEI*, I: 283]

4. **hypnale** asp which kills by inducing sleep. [Medieval Animal Symbolism: White, 174]

5. **Hypnos** god of slumber. [Gk. Myth.: Hall, 250]

6. **land of Nod** mythical land of sleep; humorous reference to biblical land in *Genesis*. [Am. and Br. Usage; *O.T.: Genesis* 4:16]

7. **Morpheus** Hypno's son and god of dreams. [Gk. Myth.: Howe, 172]

8. **poppy** attribute of Hypnos, Greek god of sleep. [Art: Hall, 250]

9. **Sandman** induces sleep by sprinkling sand in children's eyes. [Folklore: Brewer *Dictionary*, 966]

10. **Seven Sleepers** youths who fled Decian persecution; slept for more than 200 years. [Christian and Muslim Tradition: Benét, 918]

11. **Sleeping Beauty** enchanted heroine awakened from century of slumber by prince's kiss. [Fairy Tale: Brewer *Dictionary*, 1011]

12. **Snow White** poisoned apple induces her sleep; prince awakens her. [Children's Lit.: Bettelheim, 213]

13. **Somnus** god of sleep; son of Nox. [Rom. Myth.: Wheeler, 349]

14. **Van Winkle, Rip** slept for 20 years, thereby missing war. [Am. Lit.: "Rip Van Winkle" in Hart, 714]

15. **Winkie, Wee Willie** made sure all the children were asleep. [Nurs. Rhyme: Opie, 424]

532. SLEUTHING (See also CRIME FIGHTING.)

1. **Alleyn, Inspector** detective in Ngaio Marsh's many mystery stories. [New Zealand Lit.: Harvey, 520]

2. **Archer, Lew** tough solver of brutal crimes. [Am. Lit.: Herman, 94–96]

3. **Brown, Father** Chesterton's cleric and amateur detective. [Br. Lit.: Herman, 20–21]

4. **Drummond, Bulldog** patriotic Englishman, hero of stories by Sapper. [Br. Lit.: Payton, 108]

5. **Campion, Albert** unpretentious cerebral detective. [Br. Lit.: Herman, 31–33]

6. **Carter, Nick** turn-of-the-century flatfoot. [Radio: "Nick Carter, Master Detective" in Buxton, 173–174]

7. **Chan, Charlie** imperturbable Oriental gumshoe. [Am.Lit.: *Herman*, 36–37; Comics: Horn, 165–166]

8. **Charles, Nick** urbane and witty private detective. [Am. Lit.: *The Thin Man*]

9. **Clouseau, Inspector Jacques** bungling French detective; inexplicably and with great asininity gets his man. [Am. Cinema: "The Pink Panther"]

10. **Columbo** untidy, cigar-smoking mastermind. [TV: "NBC Mystery Movie" in Terrace, II, 141]

11. **deerstalker** fore-and-aft cap, associated with Sherlock Holmes. [Br. Lit.: Walsh *Modern*, 196]

12. **Drew, Nancy** teenage girl supersleuth. [Children's Lit.: *The Hidden Staircase*]

13. **Dupin, Auguste** ratiocinative solver of unsolvable crimes. [Am. Lit.: "The Murders in the Rue Morgue"; "The Mystery of Marie Roget"; "The Purloined Letter" in Portable Poe]

14. **Fell, Dr. Gideon** fat, astute detective in John Dickson Carr's mysteries. [Am. Lit.: Benét, 170]

15. **Fosdick, Fearless** square-jawed, low-paid detective of questionable expertise and unquestionable obtuseness. [Comics: "Li'l Abner" in Horn, 450]

16. **Hardy Boys** teenagers solve crimes and mysteries with detective father. [Children's Lit.: *Clue in the Embers; Twisted Claw; Tower Treasure*]

17. **Hawkshaw** implacable detective with photographic memory. [Br. Lit.: *The Ticket-of-Leave Man*, Barnhart, 546]

18. **Holmes, Sherlock** the great detective; famous for deductive reasoning. [Br. Lit.: Payton, 316]

19. **inverness** coat with cape; emblem of Sherlock Holmes. [Br. Costume and Lit.: Espy, 267]

20. **Lane, Drury** Barney Ross's deaf ex-actor and amateur detective. [Am. Lit.: Herman, 105]

21. **Lecoq, Monsieur** meticulous detective; pride of French Sureté. [Fr. Lit.: *Monsieur Lecoq*]

22. **Lestrade** bungling Scotland Yard foil to Sherlock Holmes. [Br. Lit.: Payton, 387]

23. **Lupin, Arsène** murderer turned detective. [Fr. Lit.: Herman, 20]

24. **magnifying glass** traditional detective equipment; from its use by Sherlock Holmes. [Br. Lit.: Payton, 473]

25. **Maigret, Inspector** studiously precise detective; bases his work solidly on police methods. [Fr. Lit.: Herman, 114]

26. **Mannix** private eye with unorthodox style. [TV: Terrace, II, 62]

27. **Marlowe, Philip** hard-boiled but engaging private eye. [Am. Lit.: *The Big Sleep; Farewell, My Lovely; The Long Goodbye*]

28. **Marple, Miss** sweet old lady, tougher than she seems. [Br. Lit.: Herman, 51–55]

29. **Mason, Perry** attorney busier with detection than law. [Am. Lit.: Herman, 71–74]

30. **Mayo, Asey** the "codfish Sherlock." [Am. Lit.: Herman, 122–124]

31. **McGee, Travis** tough private eye and tougher private avenger. [Am. Lit.: Herman, 92–94]

32. **Pinkertons** famous detective agency; founded in 1850. [Am. Hist.: Jameson, 392]

33. **Poirot, Hercule** brainy, dandified genius in Christie mysteries. [Br. Lit.: Herman, 51–55]

34. **Pollifax, Mrs.** redoubtable widow joins the C.I.A. [Am. Lit.: *A Palm for Mrs. Pollifax*]

35. **Queen, Ellery** dilettantish private investigator. [Am. Lit.: Herman, 105]

36. **the Rabbi** Rabbi David Small solves crimes using his Talmudic training. [Am. Lit.: *Friday the Rabbi Slept Late*]

37. **the Saint** dashing diviner of knotty puzzles. [Radio: Buxton, 206; TV: Terrace, II, 264]

38. **Spade, Sam** hard-boiled private eye. [Am. Lit.: Herman, 79–82]

39. **Strangeways, Nigel** urbane solver of intricate crimes. [Br. Lit.: Herman, 37–38]

40. **Thatcher, John Putnam** charming, civilized, urbane detective. [Am. Lit.: Herman, 86–87]

41. **Tibbs, Virgil** California's brilliant, black detective. [Am. Lit.: *In the Heat of the Night*]

42. **Tracy, Dick** square-chinned detective of realistic police strip. [Comics: Horn, 206]

43. **Vance, Philo** impressively learned, polished, and urbane detective. [Am. Lit.: Herman, 22, 126–127]

44. **Wimsey, Lord Peter** Shakespeare-quoting gentleman turned amateur detective. [Br. Lit.: Herman, 113–114]

45. **Wolfe, Nero** corpulent, lazy, but persevering crime-solver. [Am. Lit.: Herman, 119–122]

533. **SMALLNESS (See also DWARFISM.)**

1. **Alice** nibbles a magic mushroom to become a pygmy. [Br. Lit.: *Alice's Adventures in Wonderland*]

2. **Alphonse** petite page to Mr. Wititterly. [Br. Lit.: *Nicholas Nickleby*]

3. **Andorra** small state of 191 square miles, between France and Spain. [Eur. Hist.: *NCE*, 100]

4. **Anon, Mr.** a deformed and hunchbacked midget. [Br. Lit.: *Memoirs of a Midget*, Magill, I, 577–579]

5. **hop-o'-my-thumb** generic term for a midget or dwarf. [Folklore: Brewer *Dictionary*, 544]

6. **Liechtenstein** central European principality, comprising 65 square miles. [Eur. Hist.: *NCE*, 1578]

7. **Lilliputians** race of pygmies living in fictitious kingdom of Lilliput. [Br. Lit.: *Gulliver's Travels*]

8. **Little Tich** midget music-hall comedian of late 1800s. [Br. Hist.: Brewer *Dictionary*, 1082]

9. **Luxembourg** duchy of 999 square miles in Western Europe. [Eur. Hist.: *NCE*, 1632]

10. **M., Miss** a pretty, perfectly formed midget. [Br. Lit.: Magill, I, 577–579]

11. **Mowcher, Miss** kindhearted hairdresser of small stature. [Br. Lit.: *David Copperfield*]

12. **Pepin the Short** first Frankish king; progenitor of Carolingian dynasty. [Eur. Hist.: Bishop, 20, 25]

13. **Quilp, Daniel** small man with giant head and face. [Br. Lit.: *Old Curiosity Shop*]

14. **Rhode Island** smallest of the fifty states; nicknamed "Little Rhodie." [Am. Hist.: *NCE*, 2315]

15. **Stareleigh, Justice** "a most particularly short man." [Br. Lit.: *Pickwick Papers*]

16. **Thumb, Tom** (1838–1883) stage name for the midget Charles Sherwood Stratton. [Am. Hist.: Benét, 1016]

17. **Zacchaeus** little man took to tree to see Christ. [*N.T.: Luke* 19:3–4]

SNOBBERY (See ARROGANCE, PRETENSION.)

534. **SOLDIERING (See also MILITARISM.)**

1. **Atkins, Tommy** nickname for English soldiers. [Br. Folklore: Walsh *Modern*, 33]

2. **Bailey, Beetle** hapless private who resists authority and seeks easy way out. [Comics: Horn, 105–106]

3. **Ellyat, Jack** from Connecticut: Union trooper undergoes many hardships. [Am. Lit.: "John Brown's Body" in Magill, I, 445–448]

4. **G.I. Joe** any American soldier. [Am. Military Slang: Misc.]

5. **Good Soldier Schweik** simple, innocent Czech soldier in the Austrian army during World War I. [Czech Lit.: *The Good Soldier: Schweik*, Magill, IV, 390–392]

6. **Janissaries** elite Turkish infantry. [Turk. Hist.: Fuller, I, 499, 508]

7. **Sad Sack** whose travails reflect those of all soldiers. [Comics: Horn, 595–596]

8. **West Point** home of the United States Military Academy. [Am. Hist.: Hart, 907]

9. **Wingate, Clay** from Georgia: Confederate counterpart of Jack Ellyat. [Am. Lit.: "John Brown's Body" in Magill, I, 445–448]

535. SONG, PATRIOTIC

1. **America** song known to every pupil across the land. [Am. Music: Van Doren, 144]

2. **America the Beautiful** patriotic song by Katherine Bates glorifying national ideals (1893). [Am. Music: Scholes, 30]

3. **Battle Hymn of the Republic** Union's Civil War rallying song. [Am. Music: Van Doren, 228]

4. **Deutschland über Alles** German national anthem. [Ger. Music: Misc.]

5. **God Save the Queen** official national anthem of the British Commonwealth. [Br. Music: Scholes, 408]

6. **John Brown's Body** Union rallying hymn during Civil War. [Am. Music: Jameson, 257]

7. **Maple Leaf Forever!** Canadian national song (1867). [Can. Music: Scholes, 597]

8. **Marseillaise** French national anthem. [Fr. Music: Misc.]

9. **Maryland, My Maryland** song expressing sentiments of Southern cause during Civil War (1861). [Am. Music: Scholes, 602]

10. **O Canada!** national song of Canada, popular among French Canadians. [Can. Music: Scholes, 699]

11. **O Deutschland, Hoch in Ehren!** war song of the Germans in 1914. [Ger. Music: Scholes, 700]

12. **Over There** George M. Cohan's song of American entry into WWI. [Am. Music: Flexner, 417]

13. **Rule, Britannia!** patriotic British song (1740). [Br. Music: Scholes, 897–898]

14. **Star-Spangled Banner, The** national anthem of the United States. [Am. Music: Scholes, 980]

15. **Tipperary** war song popular in British Army in World War I. [Br. Music: Scholes, 1025]

16. **Watch on the Rhine, The** (Die Wacht am Rhein) popular national song of Germany. [Ger. Music: Scholes, 1111]

17. **Wearing of the Green, The** patriotic song of Ireland (1797). [Irish Music: Scholes, 1111]

18. **When Johnny Comes Marching Home** Southern Civil War rallying song. [Am. Music: Van Doren, 228–229]

19. **Yankee Doodle** Revolutionary War paean of American glory. [Nurs. Rhyme: Opie, 439]

SORROW (See GRIEF.)

536. **SOUTH**

1. **Confederacy** government of 11 Southern states that left the Union in 1860. [Am. Hist.: *EB*, III: 73]

2. **Dixie** popular name for Southern states in U.S. and for song. [Am. Hist.: *EB*, III: 587]

3. **Gone With the Wind** archetypal novel about the South. [Am. Lit.: *Gone With the Wind*]

4. **gray** color of the uniform of the Confederate soldier. [Am. Hist.: *NCE*, 566]

5. **grits** coarsely ground hominy served in traditional Southern breakfast. [Am. Culture: Misc.]

6. **Johnny Reb** a Confederate soldier or a resident of the Confederate states. [Am. Usage: Misc.]

7. **Mason-Dixon Line** boundary between Pennsylvania and Maryland that came to divide the slave (southern) states from the free (northern) states. [Am. Hist.: *NCE*, 1714]

8. **Spanish moss** silvery gray plant whose threadlike fronds hang from trees in the South. [Am. Culture: *EB*, IX: 400–401]

9. **Stars and Bars** flag of the Confederate States of the U.S. [Am. Hist.: *EB*, III: 73]

10. **wisteria** woody vine found in Southern gardens. [Am. Culture: *EB*, X: 716]

SPEED (See SWIFTNESS.)

537. **SPINSTERHOOD**

1. **Grundy, Miss** prim and proper schoolteacher, continually vexed by her students' antics. [Comics: "Archie" in Horn, 87]

2. **Havisham, Miss** old spinster; always wore her bridal dress though jilted on wedding day. [Br. Lit.: *Great Expectations*]

3. **Throssel, Miss Phoebe** a spinster with marriage continually on her mind. [Br. Lit.: *Quality Street*, Magill, I, 793–795]

538. **SPLENDOR**

1. **Bucentaur** opulent Venetian ship of state. [Ital. Hist.: Plumb, 257]

2. **Crystal Palace** huge museum and concert hall made of iron and glass at Great Exhibition (1851). [Br. Hist.: *NCE*, 692]

3. **dahlia** symbol of splendor. [Plant Symbolism: *Flora Symbolica,* 168]

4. **Hanging Gardens of Babylon** Nebuchadnezzar's huge terraces, built to placate wife. [World Hist.: Wallechinsky, 255]

5. **Khan, Kubla** (1215–1294) splendors of imperial court dazzled Polo entourage. [Asian Hist.: *EB,* 10: 541–543]

6. **magnolia** symbol of magnificence. [Flower Symbolism: *Flora Symbolica,* 175]

7. **Taj Mahal** fabulous tomb of Shah Jahan's wife. [Indian Hist.: Wallechinsky, 317]

8. **Tutankhamun's tomb** full of treasures of Egyptian pharaoh (c. 1350 B.C.). [Egypt. Hist.: Osborne, 1164]

9. **Versailles** luxurious palace of French kings; outside Paris. [Fr. Hist.: Brewer *Dictionary,* 1127]

539. SPRING

1. **Flora** goddess of this season. [Rom. Myth.: Hall, 130]

2. **flowers** represent this season. [Art: Hall, 129]

3. **garlanded girl** personification of spring. [Art: Hall, 130]

4. **peep frogs** their voices welcome the season. [Am. Culture: Misc.]

5. **Persephone** personification of spring. [Gk. Myth.: Cirlot, 252]

6. **robin** harbinger of spring. [Western Culture: Misc.]

7. **swallow** harbinger of the spring season. [Animal Symbolism: Mercatante, 164]

8. **turtle doves** "voice of the turtle is heard." [*O.T.: Song of Songs* 2:12]

9. **Venus** goddess of this season. [Rom. Myth.: Hall, 130]

10. **Ver** personification; portrayed as infantile and tender. [Rom. Myth.: *LLEI,* I: 322]

540. SPYING

1. **Bond, James** Agent 007: super spy, super hero. [Br. Lit.: Herman, 27]

2. **C.I.A.** (Central Intelligence Agency) U.S. intelligence agency. [Am. Hist.: *NCE,* 492]

3. **Cly, Roger** old servant of Darnay; became a spy. [Br. Lit.: *A Tale of Two Cities*]

4. **Hannay, Richard** opponent of foreign evil. [Br. Lit.: Herman, 38–39]

5. **Hushai the Archite** sent by David to inveigle Absalom's confidence. [*O.T.: II Samuel* 15:34]

6. **KGB** the Committee of State Security, USSR agency (begun 1954) with responsibility for espionage and counter–espionage. [*EB*, V; 780]

7. **Kuryakin, Illya** taciturn, blond partner of Solo from U.N.C.L.E. [TV: "The Man from U.N.C.L.E." in Terrace, II, 60]

8. **Mata Hari** (1876–1917) courtesan executed by French for German espionage (1917). [Ger. Hist.: *EB*, VI: 683]

9. **Muir, Lieutenant Davy** garrison quartermaster discovered to be French spy. [Am. Lit.: Magill, I, 715–717]

10. **NKVD** People's Commisariat of Internal Affairs, USSR police agency (1934–1943) that carried out purges of the 1930s. [*EB*, VII: 366]

11. **Palmer, Harry** anti-hero of *The Ipcress File*. [Am. Cinema: Herman, 28–29]

12. **Secret Agent, The** Conrad's novel of the intrigues of a foreign secret agent (1907). [Br. Lit.: Magill, III, 949–951]

13. **Smersh** acronym for Smert Shpionam (Death to Spies), a section of the KGB. [*EB*, IX: 283]

14. **Solo, Napoleon** suave and debonair agent for U.N.C.L.E. [TV: "The Man from U.N.C.L.E." in Terrace, II, 60]

541. STINGINESS (See also GREED, MISERLINESS.)

1. **Benny, Jack** (1894–1974) the king of penny pinchers. [Radio: "The Jack Benny Program" in Buxton, 122–123; TV: Terrace, 402]

2. **Carey, William** Philip's penny-pinching, smugly religious uncle. [Br. Lit.: Magill, I, 670–672]

3. **Euclio** parsimonious and distrustful man hoards gold treasure. [Rom. Lit.: *The Pot of Gold*]

4. **Pitt, Crawley** inherits, marries, and hoards money. [Br. Lit.: *Vanity Fair*]

5. **Sieppe, Trina** begrudged every penny she spent. [Am. Lit.: *McTeague*]

STOICISM (See LONGSUFFERING.)

542. STORYTELLING

1. **Aesop** semi-legendary fabulist of ancient Greece. [Gk. Lit.: Harvey, 10]

2. **Mother Goose** originally a fictitious nursery rhyme spinner from Perrault, later a Bostonian authoress. [Fr. Lit.: Brewer *Handbook*, 732]

3. **Münchäusen, Baron** traveler grossly embellishes his experiences. [Ger. Lit.: Harvey, 565]

4. **Ovid** (Publius Ovidius Naso, 43 B.C.–A.D. 17) great storyteller of classical mythology. [Rom. Lit.: Zimmerman, 187]

5. **Remus, Uncle** narrator of animal tales in Old South. [Am. Lit.: *Nights with Uncle Remus*]

6. **Sandy** told endless tales as she and Boss traveled. [Am. Lit.: *A Connecticut Yankee in King Arthur's Court*]

7. **Scheherazade** forestalls her execution with 1,001 tales. [Arab. Lit.: *Arabian Nights*]

543. **STRENGTH (See also BRAWNINESS.)**

1. **acorn** heraldic symbol of strength. [Heraldry: Jobes, 27]

2. **Atlas** Titan condemned to bear heavens on shoulders. [Gk. Myth.: Walsh *Classical*, 38]

3. **Atlas, Charles** (1892–1972) 20th-century strongman; went from "98-pound weakling" to "world's strongest man." [Am. Sports: Amory, 38–39]

4. **Babe** Paul Bunyan's blue ox; straightens roads by pulling them. [Am. Lit.: Fisher, 270]

5. **Bionic Man** superman of the technological age. [TV: "The Six Million Dollar Man" in Terrace, II: 294–295]

6. **buffalo** heraldic symbol of power. [Heraldry: Halberts, 21]

7. **Bunyan, Paul** legendary woodsman of prodigious strength. [Am. Folklore: *Paul Bunyan*]

8. **Cratos** name literally means power. [Gk. Myth.: Jobes, 378]

9. **Cyclopes** one-eyed giants; builders of fortifications. [Gk. Myth.: Avery, 346]

10. **Hercules** his twelve labors revealed his godlike powers. [Rom. Myth.: Howe, 122]

11. **Katinka, the Powerful** a female Man Mountain Dean. [Am. Comics: "Toonerville Folks" in Horn, 668]

12. **Little John** oak of a man in Robin Hood's band. [Br. Lit.: *Robin Hood*]

13. **meginjardir** Thor's belt; doubled his power. [Norse Myth.: Brewer *Dictionary*, 1076]

14. **Milo of Croton** renowned athlete. [Gk. Myth.: Hall, 209]

15. **Samson** possessed extraordinary might which derived from hair. [*O.T.: Judges* 16:17]

16. **Superman** caped superhero and modern-day Hercules. [Comics: Horn, 642–643]

STRIFE (See **DISCORD.**)

STUBBORNNESS (See **OBSTINACY.**)

544. **STUPIDITY** (See also **DIMWITTEDNESS, IGNORANCE.**)

1. **Abdera** maritime city whose inhabitants were known proverbially for their stupidity. [Gk. Folklore: Benét, 2]
2. **donkey** chooses cuckoo's singing over nightingale's. [Ger. Folklore and Poetry: Brentano and Arnim, *Des Knaben Wunderhorn; NCE*, 363]
3. **Dull, Anthony** archexample of stupidity. [Br. Lit.: *Love's Labour's Lost*]
4. **Elbow** ignorant, blundering constable. [Br. Lit.: *Measure for Measure*]
5. **pomegranate** symbol of foolishness. [Flower Symbolism: *Flora Symbolica*, 176]
6. **Simple Simon** simpleton of bumptious ways. [Nurs. Rhyme: Opie, 385]
7. **Slender** "though well-landed, an idiot." [Br. Lit.: *Merry Wives of Windsor*]
8. **Smith, Knucklehead** dummy with self-referring name. [TV: "Winchell and Mahoney" in Terrace, II, 190–192]
9. **Snerd, Mortimer** a real dummy. [Radio: "The Edgar Bergen and Charlie McCarthy Show" in Buxton, 76–77]
10. **Stephen** simpleton; made gapingstock by all. [Br. Lit.: *Every Man in His Humour*]
11. **three wise men of Gotham** fools momentarily afloat in a light bowl. [Nurs. Rhyme: Opie, 193]

545. **SUBJUGATION**

1. **Cushan-rishathaim** Aram king to whom God sold Israelites. [*O.T.: Judges* 3:8]
2. **Gibeonites** consigned to servitude in retribution for trickery. [*O.T.: Joshua* 9:22–27]
3. **Ham** Noah curses him and progeny to servitude. [*O.T.: Genesis* 9:22–27]
4. **Jabin** Canaanite king to whom God sold Israelites. [*O.T.: Judges* 4:1]
5. **Nebuchadnezzar** Babylonian king, plunders Jerusalem; carries people into exile. [*O.T.: II Kings* 24:10–16]

546. SUBSTITUTION

1. **Arsinoë** put her own son in place of Orestes; her son was killed and Orestes was saved. [Gk. Myth.: Zimmerman, 32]

2. **Barabbas** robber freed in Christ's stead. [*N.T.: Matthew* 27:15–18; Swed. Lit.: *Barabbas*]

3. **Canty, Tom** young beggar takes to throne in prince's stead. [Am. Lit.: *The Prince and the Pauper*]

4. **Edward, Prince of Wales** kingling becomes urchin in clothing exchange. [Am. Lit.: *The Prince and the Pauper*]

5. **George, Tobey** after Marcus's death, replaces him as Katie's "son." [Am. Lit.: *The Human Comedy*]

6. **Hagar** thinking herself barren, Sarah offers slave to Abraham. [*O.T.: Genesis* 16:1–4]

7. **Leah** deceptively given to Jacob, instead of Rachel. [*O.T.: Genesis* 29:22–25]

8. **whipping boy** surrogate sufferer for delinquent prince. [Eur. Hist.: Brewer *Note-Book*, 942]

547. SUCCESS

1. **Alger, Horatio** (1834–1899) writer of boys' stories where heroes win fame and fortune. [Am. Hist.: Hart, 19]

2. **Browndock, Miss** "made her fortune in no time at all." [Br. Lit.: *Nicholas Nickleby*]

3. **McVey, Hugh** from poor white to leading manufacturer. [Am. Lit.: *Poor White*, Magill, I, 762–764]

4. **O Pioneers!** realistic success story of those who fathered nation. [Am. Lit.: *O Pioneers!*, Magill, I, 663–665]

5. **Ragged Dick** hero of Alger's rags-to-riches epic. [Am. Lit.: Van Doren, 807]

6. **white cloud** indicates high achievement. [Western Folklore: Jobes, 350]

7. **wolf** symbol of success on coats of arms. [Heraldry: Halberts, 16]

548. SUFFERING

1. **aloe** symbol of suffering. [Flower Symbolism: Jobes, 71]

2. **Andersonville** horrible Civil War prison and final resting place of 12,926 Union soldiers. [Am. Hist.: Jameson, 18]

3. **Bataan** site of U.S.-Filipino army "death march" (1943). [Am. Hist.: *EB*, I: 867–868]

4. **Black hole of Calcutta** 146 Britishers imprisoned in small, stifling room (1756). [Br. Hist.: Harbottle, 45–46]

5. **Concentration Camps** where millions of Jews were starved, experimented on, and exterminated by Nazis (1939–1945). [Eur.Hist.: Misc.]

6. **Gethsemane** garden east of Jerusalem where Jesus suffered in anguished fatigue. [*N.T.: Matthew* 26:36; *Mark* 14:32]

7. **Hiroshima** where the atomic bomb was dropped (August 6, 1945). [Am. Hist.: Fuller, III, 626]

8. **Io** having been changed into a heifer by Zeus, pestered by gadfly sent by Hera. [Gk. Myth.: Espy, 292]

9. **J.B.** Job's trials in modern setting and idiom. [Am. Lit.: *J.B.*]

10. **Job** beset with calamities. [*O.T.: Job* 1:13–22; 2:6–10]

11. **Mauperin, Renée** undergoes lingering and anguished death from guilt. [Fr. Lit.: *Renée Mauperin*]

12. **Orestes** persecuted and tormented by Furies. [Gk. Myth.: Wheeler, 271; Gk. Lit.: *The Eumenides*]

13. **Prometheus** chained to rock while vulture fed on his liver. [Gk. Myth.: Zimmerman, 221]

14. **Raft of the Medusa, The** realistically portrays anguished ship's crew. [Fr. Art: Daniel, 166]

15. **Tantalus** condemned to Tartarus with food and water always just out of reach; hence, *tantalize*. [Gk. Myth.: Zimmerman, 253]

16. **Valley Forge** winter quarters of Washington's underfed, underclothed Continental army (1778). [Am. Hist.: Jameson, 519]

549. SUICIDE (See also SELF-SACRIFICE.)

1. **Ajax (the greater)** kills himself in rage over loss of Achilles' armor. [Rom. Lit.: *Aeneid*]

2. **Antigone** imprisoned, kills herself in despair. [Gk. Lit.: *Antigone*]

3. **Calista** stabs herself on disclosure of adultery. [Br. Lit.: *The Fair Penitent*]

4. **Cassandra** commits suicide to escape the Athenians. [Fr. Opera: Berlioz, *The Trojans*, Westerman, 174]

5. **Charmian** kills herself after mistress Cleopatra's death. [Br. Lit.: *Antony and Cleopatra*]

6. **Deianira** accidentally kills husband, Hercules; kills herself out of guilt. [Gk. Myth.: Kravitz, 76]

7. **Dido** kills herself when Aeneas abandons her. [Rom. Myth.: Avery, 392–393; Rom. Lit.: *Aeneid*]

8. **Enobarbus** kills himself for deserting Antony. [Br. Lit.: *Antony and Cleopatra*]

9. **Erigone** hangs himself in grief over father's murder. [Gk. Myth.: Kravitz, 91]

10. **Evadne** immolates herself on husband's funeral pyre. [Gk. Myth.: Kravitz, 100]

11. **Javert** French inspector drowns himself to escape self-perpetuating torment. [Fr. Lit.: *Les Misérables*]

12. **Jonestown** in Guyana; scene of mass-murder and suicides. [Am. Hist.: *Facts* (1978), 889–892]

13. **Kamikaze** WWII Japanese pilot corps plunge own planes into enemy ships in banzai attacks. [Jap. Hist.: Fuller, III, 618–619]

14. **Karenina, Anna** throws herself in front of approaching train. [Russ. Lit.: *Anna Karenina*]

15. **Panthea** kills herself upon death of lover, Abradates. [Gk. Lit.: Walsh *Classical*, 3]

16. **Phaedra** Athenian queen drinks poison after confessing guilt. [Fr. Lit.: *Phaedra*,Magill, I, 741–742]

17. **Saul** falls on sword to avoid humiliation of capture. [*O.T.*: *I Samuel* 31:4–6]

18. **Vane, Sibyl** young actress kills herself after Dorian's betrayal. [Irish Lit.: *The Picture of Dorian Gray*, Magill, I, 746–748]

550. SUMMER

1. **Aestas** personification of summer; portrayed as youthful and sprightly. [Rom. Myth.: *LLEI*, I: 322]

2. **Ceres** goddess of the season. [Rom. Myth.: Hall, 130]

3. **cricket** symbol of summer; weather prognosticator. [Insect Symbolism: Jobes, 382]

4. **naked girl with fruit** personification of summer. [Art: Hall, 130]

5. **sickle and sheaf of corn** representational of the season. [Art: Hall, 129]

551. SUN (See also LIGHT.)

1. **Apollo** sun god; his chariot ride spanned morning to night. [Gk. Myth.: Benét, 42]

2. **Aton (Aten)** solar deity worshiped as the one god by Amenophis IV. [Egypt. Myth.: Parrinder, 33]

3. **Bast** cat-headed goddess representing sun and moon. [Egypt. Myth.: Parrinder, 41]

4. **Belenus** sun god. [Celtic Myth.: Parrinder, 42]

5. **Buto** goddess and mother of the sun and moon. [Egypt. Myth. Kravitz, 48]

6. **cock** Helios's sacred bird; sacrificed to the sun in Mexico. [Rom. and Mex. Myth.: Leach, 239]

7. **Cuchulain** sun-figure and powerful fighter. [Irish Myth.: Parrinder, 68]

8. **double ax** symbol of the sun. [Hindu and Western Folklore: Cirlot, 22]

9. **eagle** symbol represents the sun. [Gk. Myth.: Brewer *Dictionary*, 358]

10. **fire** representation of the sun. [Western Symbolism: Cirlot, 105–106]

11. **gold** color of the sun's rays. [Color Symbolism: Jobes, 357]

12. **Helios** sun in its astronomic aspects; aspect of Apollo. [Gk. Myth: Espy, 28]

13. **Hyperion** Titan and father of the sun. [Gk. Myth.: Zimmerman, 132]

14. **lion** symbol of the sun gods; corresponds to the sun. [Western Symbolism: Cirlot, 189–190]

15. **Mithra (Mithras)** god of sunlight. [Persian Myth.: *EB*, VI: 944–945]

16. **Phaëthon** Apollo's son; foolishly attempted to drive sun chariot. [Gk. Myth.: Zimmerman, 202]

17. **Phoebus** epithet of Apollo as the sun god. [Gk. Myth.: Benét, 42]

18. **Ra** personification of the sun. [Egypt. Myth.: Parrinder, 235]

19. **Sol** the sun god. [Rom. Myth.: Zimmerman, 245]

552. SURPRISE

1. **Operation Z** Japanese plan for Pearl Harbor attack. [Jap. Hist.: Toland, 177–178, 183–187]

2. **Pearl Harbor** site of surprise attack on American fleet by the Japanese (December 7, 1941). [Am. Hist.: Fuller, III, 455–456]

3. **thief in the night** analogy to the Lord's unexpected coming. [*N.T.: I Thessalonians* 5:2]

4. **truffle** indicates the unexpected. [Flower Symbolism: *Flora Symbolica*, 178]

553. SURVIVAL (See also ENDURANCE.)

1. **Alive** story of the survivors of plane crash in the Andes. [Am. Lit.: *Alive*]

2. **Comanche** horse; sole survivor of Little Big Horn massacre (1876). [Am. Hist.: Wallechinsky, 126]

3. **Crusoe, Robinson** only survivor of shipwreck. [Br. Lit.: *Robinson Crusoe*]

4. **Deucalion** survives flood that destroys human race. [Gk. Myth.: Howe, 80]

5. **Donner Party** survivors of group of emigrants to California (1846–1847). [Am. Hist.: *NCE*, 783–784]

6. **Lot** allowed by God to escape the conflagration of Sodom and Gomorrah. [*O.T.: Genesis* 13:1–12]

7. **Mellitias, St.** of "Forty Martyrs," the only one to survive icy ordeal. [Christian Hagiog.: Attwater, 133–134]

8. **Noah** chosen by God to escape the deluge. [*O.T.: Genesis* 5–9]

554. SUSTENANCE

1. **Amalthaea** goat who provided milk for baby Zeus. [Gk. Myth.: Leach, 41]

2. **ambrosia** food of the gods; bestowed immortal youthfulness. [Gk. Myth.: Kravitz, 19]

3. **locusts and wild honey** John the Baptist's meager fare in wilderness. [*N.T.: Matthew* 3:4; *Mark* 1:6]

4. **manna** given by the Lord to the Israelites. [*O.T.: Exodus* 16: 14–15]

555. SWIFTNESS

1. **Al Borak** horse who carried Muhammad from Mecca to Jerusalem overnight. [Muslim Tradition: Walsh *Classical*, 13–14]

2. **Argo** swift, magic ship of the Argonauts. [Gk. Myth.: Avery, 145]

3. **Atalanta** heroine; fleet of foot; defeated by trickery. [Gk. Myth.: Walsh *Classical*, 36–37; Br. Lit.: *Atalanta*]

4. **Bayard** swiftest horse in the world. [Medieval and Renaissance Legend: Brewer *Dictionary*, 86]

5. **Camilla** Volscian queen; could run over cornfield without bending blades. [Rom. Lit.: *Aeneid*]

6. **cheetah** fastest four-footed animal alive; can reach 60 mph. [Zoology: Misc.]

7. **Hermes** (Rom. **Mercury**) messenger god; ran on the wings of the wind. [Gk. Myth.: Zimmerman, 124]

8. **Jehu** Israelite king noted for his rapid chariot driving. [*O.T.: II Kings* 9]

9. **Laelaps** hound so swift, it always overtook its quarry. [Gk. Myth.: Howe, 149]

10. **Pacolet's horse** enchanted steed of unparalleled quickness. [Fr. Lit.: *Valentine and Orson; LLEI*, 1: 304]

11. **Pheidippides** (fl. 490 B.C.) ran 26 miles to Athens to announce Greek victory over Persians. [Gk. Legend: Zimmerman, 159]

12. **Road Runner** foxy bird who continually zooms out of the coyote's reach. [TV: "The Road Runner Show" in Terrace, 247]

13. **Superman** superhero; faster than a speeding bullet. [Comics: Horn, 642; TV: "Adventures of Superman" in Terrace, I, 37–38]

14. **winged petasus** Mercury's cap; symbolic of speed. [Gk. and Rom. Myth.: 145]

556. SWORD

1. **Almace** sabre of Turpin. [Fr. Lit.: *The Song of Roland*]

2. **Angurvadel** of Frithjof; blazed in war, gleamed dimly in peace. [Norse Myth.: *LLEI*, I: 323]

3. **Balisarda** made by sorceress for killing Orlando. [Ital. Lit.: *Orlando Furioso*, Benét, 75]

4. **Balmung** mighty sword belonging to Siegfried. [Ger. Lit.: *Nibelungenlied*]

5. **Barbamouche** Climborin's sabre. [Fr. Lit.: *The Song of Roland*]

6. **Colada** El Cid's two-hilted, solid gold sword. [Span. Lit.: *Song of the Cid*]

7. **Damocles, sword of** sword hung by a single hair over his head. [Rom. Lit.: Brewer *Handbook*, 257]

8. **Durindana (Durendal)** Orlando's unbreakable sword. [Ital. Lit.: *Morgante Maggiore*, Brewer *Handbook*, 309]

9. **Excalibur** Arthur's enchanted sword; extracting it from stone won him crown. [Br. Lit.: *Le Morte d'Arthur*]

10. **Fragarach** the "Answerer"; Lug's mighty blade could pierce any armor. [Irish Myth.: Leach, 415]

11. **Gram** belonged to Sigmund; broken by Odin. [Norse Lit.: *Volsung Saga*]

12. **Gramimond** Valdabrun's sabre. [Fr. Lit.: *The Song of Roland*]

13. **Hauteclaire** Oliver's trusty sabre. [Fr. Lit.: *The Song of Roland*]

14. **Joyeuse** Charlemagne's sword; buried with him. [Fr. Lit.: Brewer *Dictionary*, 594]

15. **Marmorie** Grandoyne's sabre. [Fr. Lit.: *The Song of Roland*]

16. **Merveilleuse** Doolin of Mayence's remarkably sharp sword. [Fr. Lit.: Wheeler, 241]

17. **Mimung** magic sword lent by Wittich to Siegfried. [Norse Myth.: Wheeler, 244]

18. **Mordure** Arthur's all-powerful sword, made by Merlin. [Br. Lit.: *Faerie Queene*]

19. **Morglay** Bevis's sword. [Br. Lit.: *Bevis of Hampton*]

20. **Murgleys** Ganelon's sabre. [Fr. Lit.: *The Song of Roland*]

21. **Notung** Sigmund's promised sword, found in ash tree; later, Siegfried's. [Ger. Opera: Wagner, *Valkyrie*, Westerman, 236]

22. **Precieuse** sabre of the pagan, Baligant. [Fr. Lit.: *The Song of Roland*]

23. **Rosse** Alberich's gift to Otwit; frighteningly fine-edged. [Norse Myth.: Brewer *Dictionary*, 936]

24. **Sanglamore** Braggadocio's big, bloody glaive. [Br. Lit.: *Faerie Queene*]

25. **Sautuerdu** Malquiant's sabre. [Fr. Lit.: *The Song of Roland*]

26. **Tizona** dazzling, golden-hilted sword of the Cid. [Span. Lit.: *Song of the Cid*]

27. **Zulfagar** sword of Ali, Muhammad's son. [Islamic Legend: Brewer *Handbook*, 1066]

SYCOPHANCY (See FLATTERY.)

T

557. **TACITURNITY**

1. **Barkis** warmhearted but taciturn husband of Peggoty. [Br. Lit: *David Copperfield*]

2. **Bartleby the Scrivener** "I prefer not to" was his constant refrain and all he ever said. [Am. Lit.: "Bartleby the Scrivener"]

3. **Bert and I** taciturn "down-Easterners." [Am. Culture: Misc.]

4. **Coolidge, Calvin** (1872–1933) 30th U.S. president; nicknamed "Silent Cal." [Am. Hist.: Frank, 99]

5. **Laconian** inhabitant of ancient country of Laconia; people noted for pauciloquy. [Gr. Hist.: *NCE*, 1514]

558. **TALKATIVENESS**

1. **Balwhidder** kind but loquacious Presbyterian clergyman. [Br. Lit.: *Annals of the Parish*]

2. **Bates, Miss** goodhearted purveyor of trivia and harmless gossip. [Br. Lit.: *Emma*]

3. **Bernstein, Baroness** (Beatrix Esmond) loquaciously amusing, venomous, or coarse character. [Br. Lit.: *The Virginians*]

4. **blarney stone** whoever kisses the stone "will never want for words." [Irish Folklore: Leach, 147]

5. **cicada** symbol of talkativeness because of its constant, strident noise. [Folklore: Jobes, 338]

6. **daisies** the flowers chatter incessantly at Alice. [Children's Lit.: *Through the Looking-Glass*]

7. **Echo** beautiful nymph who, by her constant talk, kept Hera away from Zeus. [Gk. Myth.: Howe, 89]

8. **Kenge, Mr.** garrulous soldier; nicknamed "conversation Kenge." [Br. Lit.: *Bleak House*]

9. **Old Woman of Gloucester** talkative woman displeased with her more talkative parrot. [Nurs. Rhyme: *Mother Goose*, 112]

10. **parrot** chattering bird; mimics human speech. [Animal Symbolism: Mercatante, 157]

11. **Polonius** wordy, "wretched, rash, intruding fool." [Br. Lit.: *Hamlet*]

12. **Trim, Corporal** dutiful attendant of Uncle Toby; distinguished for volubility. [Br. Lit.: *Tristram Shandy*]

559.   TALLNESS (See also GIANTISM.)

1.   **Chrysler Building** in New York City; one of the tallest buildings in the world. [Architecture: Misc.]

2.   **Colossus of Rhodes** statue of Apollo; wonder of ancient world. [Gk. Hist.: Osborne, 256]

3.   **Eiffel Tower** built in 1889 in Paris. [Architecture: *NCE*, 843]

4.   **elevator shoe** shoe with insole designed to increase wearer's height. [Am. Pop. Culture: Misc.]

5.   **Empire State Building** New York's famous skyscraper. [Architecture: *NCE*, 865]

6.   **giraffe** tallest of animals. [Zoology: *NCE*, 1088]

7.   **redwoods** giant trees (sequoias) of Pacific Coast. [Botany: *NCE*, 2477]

8.   **Sears Tower** in Chicago; one of America's tallest buildings. [Architecture: Misc.]

9.   **Woolworth Building** in New York City; erected by Frank Woolworth in 1913; tallest building until Empire State Building (1930–1931). [Architecture: *NCE*, 3004]

10.   **World Trade Center** New York's giant twin edifices. [Architecture: Payton, 742]

560.   TARDINESS

1.   **Dagwood** comic strip character; chronically late at the office. [Comics: "Blondie" in Horn, 118]

2.   **ten o'clock scholar** schoolboy who habitually arrives late. [Nurs. Rhyme: Opie, 378]

3.   **White Rabbit** pocket watch-carrying rabbit chattering, "I'm late, I'm late, for a very important date." [Br. Lit.: *Alice's Adventures in Wonderland*]

561.   TEACHING (See also EDUCATION.)

1.   **Aristotle** (384–322 B.C.) Greek philosopher who tutored Alexander the Great. [Gk. Hist.: *NCE*, 147]

2.   **Bhaer, Professor** teaches writing to Jo; eventually marries her. [Am. Lit.: *Little Women*]

3.   **Brooks, Miss** (Connie) popular TV show features a harried Miss Brooks as high school teacher. [TV: "Our Miss Brooks" in Terrace, II, 174]

4.   **Chips, Mr.** lovable and didactic schoolteacher. [Br. Lit.: *Goodbye, Mr. Chips*]

5.   **Chiron** knowledgeable Centaur; instructed Achilles, Jason, and Asclepuis. [Gk. Myth.: Parrinder, 62]

6. **Grundy, Miss** Archie's grumpy high school teacher. [Am. Comics: "Archie" in Horn, 87]

7. **Kotter, Gabe** teacher of Special Guidance Remedial Academics. [TV: "Welcome Back, Kotter" in Terrace, II, 423]

8. **Moffat, Miss** teacher in Welsh mining town. [Br. Lit.: *The Corn Is Green; NCE*, 2982]

9. **Pangloss** character who taught Candide "metaphysico-theologo-cosmolonigology." [Fr. Lit.: *Candide*]

10. **Peach, Miss** whimsical schoolmarm copes with grammar-school students. [Comics: Horn, 495–496]

11. **Porpora** famous music master of Consuelo and Haydn. [Fr. Lit.: *Consuelo*, Magill, I, 156–158]

12. **Silenus** knowledgeable tutor of Bacchus. [Rom. Myth.: Daniel, 213]

13. **Socrates** (469–399 B.C.) Greek philosopher; tutor of many, such as Aristotle and Plato. [Gk. Hist.: *NCE*, 2553]

562. TEENAGER

1. **Aldrich, Henry** teenaged film character of the 1940s. [Am. Cinema: Halliwell, 337]

2. **American Bandstand** durable and popular TV show; teenagers are featured performers. [TV: Terrace, I, 52]

3. **Archie** the eternal comic-book teenager. [Comics: Horn, 87]

4. **Caulfield, Holden** sensitive, troubled teenager has nervous breakdown. [Am. Lit.: *Catcher in the Rye*]

5. **Gidget** archetypal teenage girl. [TV: Terrace, I, 311–312]

6. **Gillis, Dobie** 1950s and 1960s teenager struggling to postpone adulthood. [TV: "The Many Loves of Dobie Gillis" in Terrace, II, 64–66]

7. **Hardy, Andy** teenaged son of a "typical family" in a small midwestern town. [Am. Cinema: Halliwell, 323]

563. TEMPERANCE

1. **Alcoholics Anonymous (AA)** organization founded to help alcoholics (1934). [Am. Culture: *EB*, I: 448)

2. **amethyst** provides protection against drunkenness; February birthstone. [Gem Symbolism: Kunz, 58–59]

3. **Anti-Saloon League** successfully led drive for Prohibition (1910s). [Am. Hist.: Flexner, 357]

4. **Jonadab** enjoined his people to abstinence. [*O.T.: Jeremiah* 35: 5–11]

5. **Nation, Carry** (Amelia Moore) (1846–1911) hatchet-wielding saloon wrecker. [Am. Hist.: Flexner, 253]

6. **Prohibition** (1919–1933) period when selling and consuming liquor was against the law. [Am. Hist.: *NCE*, 2710]

7. **Rechabites** pastoral people who abstained from all wines. [*O.T.: Jeremiah* 35:5–19]

8. **Samson** consecrated to God in abstinence. [*O.T.: Judges* 13:4–5]

9. **Volstead Act** 18th Amendment, passed by Congress to enforce Prohibition (1919). [Am. Hist.: Flexner, 286]

10. **Woman's Christian Temperance Union** society of militant housewives against drinking (20th century). [Am. Hist.: Flexner, 357]

564. TEMPTATION

1. **apple** as fruit of the tree of knowledge in Eden, has come to epitomize temptation. [*O.T.: Genesis* 3:1–7; Br. Lit.: *Paradise Lost*]

2. **forbidden fruit** God prohibits eating from Tree of Knowledge. [*O.T.: Genesis* 2:16–17]

3. **quince** symbol of temptation [Flower Symbolism: *Flora Symbolica*, 176]

4. **Satan** offers world to Jesus in exchange for His obeisance. [*N.T.: Matthew* 4:8–11]

5. **serpent** coaxes Eve to eat forbidden fruit. [*O.T.: Genesis* 3:1–5]

TERROR (See HORROR.)

565. TERRORISM

1. **Al Fata** Palestine Liberation movement's terrorist organization. [Arab. Hist.: Wigoder, 186]

2. **Baader-Meinhof gang** German terrorists. [Ger. Hist.: *Facts* (1978), 114–115]

3. **Black Panthers** militant black revolutionists and civil-rightists. [Am. Hist.: Flexner, 46]

4. **Gestapo** Nazi secret police; executors of "Final Solution." [Ger. Hist.: Wigoder, 211]

5. **IRA** the Irish Republican Army; long history of terror and violence. [Irish Hist.: *NCE*, 1365–1366]

6. **Ku Klux Klan** post-Civil War white supremecist organization used terrorist tactics against blacks. [Am. Hist.: *NCE*, 1505]

7. **Nazis** (National Socialism) spread fear and terror throughout Hitler's Germany. [Ger. Hist.: *NCE*, 1894]

8. **Red Brigade** Italian terrorist group; assassinated Aldo Moro (1978). [Ital. Hist.: *Facts* (1978), 133]

9. **Reign of Terror** (1793–1794) revolutionary government made terror its means of suppression, by edict (September 5, 1793). [Fr. Hist.: *EB*, IX: 904]

10. **Symbionese Liberation Army** small terrorist group that kidnapped Patty Hearst (1974–1975). [Am. Hist.: *Facts* (1974), 105]

11. **Weathermen** American terrorist group against the "Establishment." [Am. Hist.: *Facts* (1972), 384]

566. TEST

1. **Arthur, King** (c. 950–1000) becomes King of England by pulling sword from stone. [Arth. Legend: *NCE*, 159]

2. **Carmel, Mt.** site of contest between Elijah and Baal priests. [*O.T.: I Kings* 18:19–40]

3. **Cuban missile crisis** President Kennedy called Krushchev's bluff, forcing dismantling of missile sites (1962). [Am. Hist.: Van Doren, 581–582]

4. **J.B.** testing of contemporary Job. [Am. Lit.: *J.B.*]

5. **Job** tormented to test devoutness. [*O.T.: Job* 1, 2]

6. **Judgment of God** medieval trial by combat or ordeal. [Eur. Hist.: Leach, 561]

7. **K'ung Fu** Confucian-based sect demands rigid tests for membership. [TV: Terrace, I, 448]

8. **ordeal by fire** noble accused of crime holds red-hot iron or walks blindfolded and barefoot over red-hot plowshares to prove his innocence. [Br. Hist.: Brewer *Handbook*, 779]

9. **Turandot** solver of riddles wins Turandot; failure brings death. [Ital. Opera: Puccini, *Turandot*, Westerman, 367–368]

567. THEATER

1. **Abbey Theatre** home of famed Irish theatrical company. [Irish Hist.: *NCE*, 3]

2. **Bolshoi** Moscow's premier ballet company. [Russ. Hist.: *NCE*, 327]

3. **Broadway** famous theatrical district at New York's Times Square. [Am. Hist.: Hart, 107]

4. **Carnegie Hall** New York's venerable theater for concert-goers. [Am. Hist.: *NCE*, 460]

5. **Comédie-Française** (Théâtre-Français) world's oldest established national theater. [Fr. Hist.: *EB*, III: 33]

6. **Drury Lane** London street famed for theaters; the theatrical district. [Br. Hist.: Herbert, 1321]

7. **Federal Theater** provided employment for actors, directors, writers, and scene designers (1935–1939). [Am. Hist.: *NCE*, 932]

8. **Garrick Theatre** famous London playhouse; named for David Garrick. [Br. Lit.: *NCE*, 1048]

9. **Globe Theatre** playhouse where Shakespeare's plays were performed. [Br. Lit.: *NCE*, 1094]

10. **Habima Theater** national theater of Israel; its troupe is famous for passionate acting style. [Israeli Hist.: *NCE*, 1170]

11. **Lincoln Center** New York's modern theater complex. [Am. Hist.: *NCE*, 1586]

12. **Metropolitan Opera House** famous theater in New York City; opened in 1883. [Am. Hist.: *NCE*, 1761]

13. **Old Vic** London Shakespeare theater (1914–1963). [Br. Hist.: *NCE*, 1999]

14. **Radio City Music Hall** New York City's famous cinema; home of the Rockettes. [Am. Hist.: *NCE*, 2338]

15. **La Scala (Teatro alla Scala)** "Theater at the Stairway"; Milan opera house; built 1776. [Ital. Hist.: *EB*, VI: 57]

16. **Shubert Alley** heart of Broadway; named after the three Shubert brothers. [Am. Hist.: Herbert, 1322]

17. **Winter Garden** a famous old theater in New York City. [Am. Hist.: Payton, 738]

568. **THIEVERY (See also GANGSTERISM, HIGHWAYMAN, OUT-LAWRY.)**

1. **Alfarache, Guzmán de** picaresque, peripatetic thief; lived by unscrupulous wits. [Span. Lit.: *The Life of Guzmán de Alfarache*]

2. **Armstrong, Johnnie** Scottish Robin Hood; robbed only the English. [Br. Hist.: Walsh *Classical*, 31–32]

3. **Autolycus** master robber. [Gk. Myth.: Leach, 96]

4. **Barabbas** thief released instead of Jesus to appease crowd. [*N.T.: Matthew* 27:16–26; *Mark* 15:7–15; *John* 18:40]

5. **Cacus** Vulcan's three-headed, thieving son. [Rom. Myth.: Benét, 154]

6. **Compeyson** accomplished criminal; swindles, forges, and steals. [Br. Lit.: *Great Expectations*]

7. **Crackit, Toby** a housebreaker; burglarizes Chertsey. [Br. Lit.: *Oliver Twist*]

8. **Dawkins, John** London pickpocket and thief. [Br. Lit.: *Oliver Twist*]

9. **Fagin** he trained young boys to become thieves. [Br. Lit.: *Oliver Twist*]

10. **Gradgrind, Tom** thief; robbed Bounderby's Bank. [Br. Lit.: *Hard Times*]

11. **Hood, Robin** took from the rich and gave to the poor. [Br. Lit.: *Robin Hood*]

12. **Knave of Hearts** "stole the tarts" made by Queen of Hearts. [Nurs. Rhyme: Baring-Gould, 152]

13. **Mercury** god of thieves. [Gk. Myth.: Wheeler, 240]

14. **Nicholas's Clerks** slang for thieves. [Br. Usage: Brewer *Handbook*, 754; Br. Lit.: *I Henry IV; II Henry IV*]

15. **Nym** humorous thief and rogue. [Br. Lit.: *Merry Wives of Windsor; Henry V*]

16. **Raffles** leading Victorian criminal-hero. [Br. Lit.: Herman, 19–20]

17. **Sikes, Bill** Fagin's thieving associate. [Br. Lit.: *Oliver Twist*]

18. **Taffy** Welshman who "stole a piece of beef." [Nurs. Rhyme: Baring-Gould, 72–73]

19. **Turpin, Dick** (1706–1739) English housebreaker and highwayman. [Br. Hist.: Brewer *Dictionary*, 1108]

20. **Valentine, Jimmy** a romanticized burglar. [Am. Lit: *Alias Jimmy Valentine*, Espy, 337]

21. **Valjean, Jean** stole a loaf of bread; sentenced to 19 years in jail. [Fr. Lit.: *Les Misérables*]

569. THINNESS

1. **Crane, Ichabod** Sleepy Hollow's gaunt schoolmaster. [Am. Lit.: *Legend of Sleepy Hollow*]

2. **Dartle, Rosa** Mrs. Steerforth's gaunt companion. [Br. Lit.: *David Copperfield*]

3. **Oyl, Olive** Popeye's skinny girlfriend. [Comics: "Thimble Theater" in Horn, 657–658]

4. **Sprat, Jack** "He could eat no fat." [Nurs. Rhyme: Opie, 238]

570. THUNDER (See also LIGHTNING.)

1. **Bromius** epithet of Dionysus, meaning 'thunder.' [Gk. Myth.: Zimmerman, 43]

2. **Brontes** cruel Cyclops who controls the weather; able to cause great thunder. [Gk. Myth.: Parrinder, 47; Jobes, 241, 400]

3. **Donar** god of thunder; corresponds to Thor. [Ger. Myth.: Leach, 321]

4. **Indra** thunder god and controller of weather. [Vedic Myth.: Leach, 521]

5. **Mjolnir** Thor's hammer. [Norse Myth.: Brewer *Dictionary*, 1076]

6. **Thor** god of thunder. [Norse Myth.: Leach, 1109]

571. TIME

1. **Antevorta** goddess of the future. [Rom. Myth.: Kravitz, 24]

2. **Cronos** (Rom. **Saturn**) Titan; god of the world and time. [Gk. and Rom. Myth.: Kravitz, 69]

3. **dance of Shiva** symbolizes the passage of time. [Hindu Tradition: Cirlot, 76]

4. **Father Time** classic personification of time with scythe and hourglass. [Art: Hall, 119]

5. **ring** represents the cyclical nature of time. [Pop. Culture: Cirlot, 273–274]

6. **river** represents the irreversible passage of time. [Pop. Culture: Cirlot, 274]

7. **Skulda** Norn of future time. [Norse Myth.: Wheeler, 260]

8. **Urda** Norn of time past. [Norse Myth.: Wheeler, 260]

9. **Verdandi** Norn of time present. [Norse Myth.: Wheeler, 260]

10. **white poplar** traditional symbol of time. [Flower Symbolism: *Flora Symbolica*, 178]

TIMELESSNESS (See AGELESSNESS, IMMORTALITY.)

572. TIMIDITY (See also COWARDICE.)

1. **Alden, John** (c. 1599–1687) too timid to ask for Priscilla's hand in marriage. [Am. Lit.: "The Courtship of Miles Standish" in Benét, 230]

2. **Bergson, Emil** could only express love for Marie in secret thoughts. [Am. Lit.: *O Pioneers!*, Magill, I, 663–665]

3. **Blushington, Edward** upon taking marriage vows, he needs wine to say "I do." [Br. Lit.: *The Bashful Man*, Walsh *Modern*, 62–63]

4. **Cowardly Lion** biggest "pussycat" in the forest. [Am. Lit.: *The Wonderful Wizard of Oz*]

5. **Crane, Ichabod** timorous schoolteacher. [Am. Lit.: *The Legend of Sleepy Hollow*]

6. **Cyclamen** traditional symbol of timidity. [Flower Symbolism: Jobes, 400]

7. **Florimel** feared "the smallest monstrous mouse that creeps on floor." [Br. Lit.: *Faerie Queene*]

8. **Little Dorrit** withdrawn, self-effacing seamstress. [Br. Lit.: *Little Dorrit*]

9. **Little Miss Muffet** frightened away by a spider. [Nurs. Rhyme: Opie, 323]

10. **Milquetoast, Casper** the timid soul; easily controlled by others. [Comics: *The Timid Soul*, Espy, 141]

11. **Mitty, Walter** timid, henpecked husband. [Am. Lit.: Payton, 448]

12. **Peepers, Mr.** shy character in TV series. [TV: Terrace, II, 118–119]

13. **peony** symbol of shyness and timidity. [Flower Symbolism: *Flora Symbolica*, 176]

14. **Piglet** diffident little pig; tremulously courageous. [Children's Lit.: *Winnie-the-Pooh*]

15. **rush** indicates docility and diffidence. [Flower Symbolism: *Flora Symbolica*, 177]

573. TOUGHNESS

1. **Kojak** tough, New York City plainclothes detective. [TV: Terrace, 445]

2. **Nolan, Jim** hard-bitten, he rouses fellow migrant workers to strike. [Am. Lit.: *In Dubious Battle*]

574. TRANSFORMATION

1. **Actaeon** surprised Artemis bathing and was changed by her into a stag. [Gk. Myth.: Jobes, 28]

2. **Adonis** killed by a boar, he was changed into an anemone by Venus. [Gk. Lit.: *Metamorphoses*]

3. **Alectryon** changed into rooster by angry Ares; required, thereby, to announce forever the coming of the sun. [Gk. Myth.: Zimmerman, 17]

4. **Arachne** won weaving contest against Athena, who then changed her into a spider. [Gk. Myth.: Jobes, 116]

5. **Arethusa** changed into stream by Artemis to save her from river god, Alpheus. [Gk. Myth.: Zimmerman, 29]

6. **Ascalaphus** turned into an owl by Demeter. [Gk. Myth.: Kravitz, 37]

7. **Callisto** nymph that Zeus transformed into a bear. [Gk. Myth.: Walsh *Classical*, 28]

8. **Chelone** changed into tortoise for refusing to attend wedding of Zeus and Hera. [Gk. Myth.: Zimmerman, 59]

9. **Crocus** distressed by unrequited love, changed by Hermes into a saffron plant. [Gk. Myth.: Avery, 338]

10. **Daphne** turned into laurel tree to escape Apollo. [Gk. Myth.: Kravitz, 75]

11. **Derceto** nature deity; became mermaid when Mopsus pursued her. [Philistine Myth.: Jobes, 433; Avery, 389]

12. **Dirce** changed by gods into a fountain. [Gk. Myth.: Zimmerman, 88]

13. **Eurydice** transformed into a bacchante to suit enamored Zeus. [Fr. Operetta: Offenbach, *Orpheus in Hades*, Westerman, 271–272]

14. **Galatea** statue of woman fashioned by Pygmalion and brought to life by Aphrodite. [Gk. Myth.: Jobes, 623]

15. **Hulk, the** the monster that David Banner becomes when angered. [Comics and TV: Horn, 324]

16. **Io** changed into heifer by Zeus because of Hera's jealousy. [Gk. Myth.: Zimmerman, 137]

17. **Lot's wife** disobeyed God's order not to look back; she became a pillar of salt. [*O.T.: Genesis* 19:26]

18. **Midas** everything he touched turned to gold. [Gk. Myth.: Zimmerman, 167]

19. **Orlando** born a man in 1588, dies a woman in 1928. [Br. Lit. *Orlando*, Magill, I, 698–700]

20. **Periclymenus** had the power to assume any form. [Gk. Myth.: Zimmerman, 199]

21. **Philomela (Philomena)** changed by gods into nightingale. [Gk. Myth.: Zimmerman, 205–206]

22. **Phoulca** bogey-beast taking many forms; e.g., horse, bat, eagle. [Irish Folklore: Briggs, 326–327]

23. **Pinocchio** changed from mischievous puppet to loving boy. [Ital. Lit.: *The Adventures of Pinocchio*]

24. **Proteus** has ability to change shape. [Gk. Myth.: Kravitz, 201]

25. **pumpkin** turned into coach by Cinderella's fairy godmother. [Fr. Fairy Tale: *Cinderella*]

26. **Tebrick, Silvia Fox** changed from dignified woman into wild fox. [Am. Lit.: *Lady into Fox*, Magill, I, 486]

27. **Tippetarius** boy changed into Ozma, Queen of Oz. [Children's Lit.: *The Land of Oz*]

28. **Tiresias** saw two snakes copulating and was changed into a woman. [Gk. Myth.: Jobes, 1576]

29. **transubstantiation** changing of bread to body of Christ. [Christian Theol.: Brewer *Dictionary*, 1097]

30. **Veretius** Welsh king changed into wolf by St. Patrick. [Br. Legend: Brewer *Dictionary*, 1148]

31. **Zeus** assumed many forms to indulge his passions. [Zimmerman, 292–293]

575. **TREACHERY (See also TREASON.)**

1. **Aaron** plots downfall of Titus. [Br. Lit.: *Titus Andronicus*]

2. **Achitophel** traitorous Earl of Shaftesbury. [Br. Lit.: *Absalom and Achitophel*]

3. **Agravain, Sir** traitorous with Modred against Arthur. [Br. Lit.: *Le Morte d'Arthur*]

4. **Antenor** assigned to hell for actions defeating Troy. [Gk. Myth.: Avery, 106; Ital. Lit.: Dante, *Inferno*, Walsh *Classical*, 24]

5. **Antonio** schemes against his brother Prospero. [Br. Lit.: *The Tempest*]

6. **Ascalaphus** Hadean gardener; informs on Persephone, learning of her potential departure. [Gk. Myth.: Zimmerman, 33]

7. **Baanah and Rechab** Ishbosheth's captains decapitate him in bed. [*O.T.: II Samuel* 4:5–7]

8. **Bellerophon letter** letter, given in pretended friendship, denounces bearer. [Folklore: Walsh *Classical*, 52]

9. **Brutus, Decius** committed treachery against friend Caesar. [Br. Lit.: *Julius Caesar*]

10. **Cantwell, Dr.** treacherous towards Lady Lambert; arrested as swindler. [Br. Lit.: *The Hypocrite*, Walsh *Modern*, 85–86]

11. **Charrington, Mr.** antique-store keeper sets up lovers for captors. [Br. Lit.: *1984*]

12. **Chuzzlewit, Jonas** tries to poison father. [Br. Lit.: *Martin Chuzzlewit*]

13. **Claudius** conspired to kill Hamlet's father and marry his mother. [Br. Lit.: *Hamlet*]

14. **cock crow** before third crowing, Peter thrice denies Christ. [*N.T.: Matthew* 26:34, 74–75]

15. **Cortés, Hernando** (1485–1547) repaid Montezuma's courtesy by murdering him. [Span. Hist.: *EB*, 5: 194–196]

16. **Delilah** divulged secret of Samson's strength to Philistines. [*O.T.: Judges* 16:19–20]

17. **Ephialtes** Greek betrayer of Spartans at Thermopylae. [Gk. Hist.: Kravitz, 89]

18. **Ganelon** the Judas among Charlemagne's paladins. [Fr. Lit.: *Song of Roland; LLEI*, I: 286; Ital. Lit.: *Inferno*; Br. Lit.: *Canterbury Tales*, "Nun's Priest's Tale"]

19. **Iago** soldier discredits Desdemona's fidelity. [Br. Lit.: *Othello*]

20. **Joab** murders two fellow commanders; sides with usurper, Adonijah. [*O.T.: I Kings* 2:32]

21. **Judas Iscariot** betrayer of Jesus. [*N.T.: Matthew* 26:14–16, 20–25, 47–56; 27:3–10]

22. **Maskwell** cunning doublecrosser; betrays friend and lover. [Br. Lit.: *The Double-Dealer*]

23. **Modred** revolted against King Arthur. [Arth. Legend: Brewer *Handbook*, 714–715; Br. Lit.: *Idylls of the King*]

24. **Morgan le Fay** tricks Accolon into stealing Excalibur. [Arth. Legend: *Le Morte d'Arthur,* Walsh *Classical,* 3]

25. **Pearl Harbor** Japan, while negotiating in Washington, bombs Hawaii (December 7, 1941). [Am. Hist.: Fuller, III, 455–456]

26. **perfidious Albion** Napoleon's epithet for England, "perfide Albion." [Fr. Hist.: Misc.]

27. **redheadedness** from Judas Iscariot; so depicted in art. [Christian Iconog.: Gaster, 165]

28. **Rosencrantz and Guildenstern** Hamlet's traitorous friends; "adders fang'd." [Br. Lit.: *Hamlet*]

29. **Saturninus** connives and plots politically; kills Titus. [Br. Lit.: *Titus Andronicus*]

30. **Schoolmaster of Falerii** Etruscan teacher, after delivering children to Romans, is rebuffed. [Rom. Hist.: Hall, 119]

31. **Sebastian** plots to murder Alonso and Gonzalo. [Br. Lit.: *The Tempest*]

32. **Thermopylae** shown the back door, Persians destroyed Spartans (480 B.C.). [Gk. Hist.: Harbottle, 248]

33. **30 pieces of silver** price paid Judas to deliver Jesus. [Christian Symbolism: *N.T.: Matthew* 26:15]

34. **Uriah letter** Uriah carries David's letter ordering his own death. [*O.T.: II Samuel* 11:15]

35. **whale** lures fish to mouth with sweet breath. [Animal Symbolism: Mercatante, 27]

36. **woman in red** Dillinger's mysterious girl friend; alerted FBI to his whereabouts. [Am. Hist.: Flexner, 291]

37. **yellow** color marking doors of convicted traitors. [Fr. Legend: Brewer *Dictionary*, 1171]

576. TREASON (See also TREACHERY.)

1. **Arnold, Benedict** (1741–1801) American Revolutionary general who plotted surrender of West Point to British. [Am. Hist.: Benét, 52]

2. **Burgundy, Duke of** fights for English, then joins French. [Br. Lit.: *I Henry VI*]

3. **Carne, Caryl** traitor to country. [Br. Lit.: *Springhaven*]

4. **Christian, Colonel William** executed for treason. [Br. Lit.: *Peveril of the Peak,* Walsh *Modern,* 96]

5. **Edmund** "a most toad-spotted traitor." [Br. Lit.: *King Lear*]

6. **Quisling, Vidkun** (1887–1945) Norwegian fascist leader; persuaded Hitler to attack Norway. [Nor. Hist.: Flexner, 444]

7. **Vichy** seat of collaborationist government after German occupation (1941). [Fr. Hist.: Brewer *Dictionary,* 1128]

577. **TREASURE**

1. **Ali Baba** uses magic to find thieves' storehouse of booty. [Arab. Lit.: *Arabian Nights,* "Ali Baba and the Forty Thieves"]

2. **Comstock Lode** richest silver vein in world. [Amer. Hist.: Flexner, 177]

3. **El Dorado** legendary land of gold in South America. [Span. Myth.: *NCE,* 846]

4. **Fort Knox** U.S. depository of gold bullion. [Am. Hist.: *NCE,* 984]

5. **forty-niners** participants in California gold rush of 1849. [Am. Hist.: *LLEI,* I: 270]

6. **Golconda** fabled Indian city, meaning "source of great wealth." [Indian Hist.: *NCE,* 1101]

7. **Kidd, Captain** (c. 1645–1701) pirate captures prizes and buries treasure. [Am. Lit.: Hart, 444]

8. **King Solomon's mines** in Africa; search for legendary lost treasure of King Solomon. [Br. Lit.: *King Solomon's Mines*]

9. **Legrand, William** uncovers chest of gold by deciphering parchment. [Am. Lit.: "The Gold Bug" in *Tales of Terror and Fantasy*]

10. **Mother Lode** name applied to gold-mining region of California. [Am. Hist.: Hart, 569]

11. **the Nibelung** more gold and jewels than wagons could carry. [Ger. Lit.: *Nibelungenlied*]

12. **Nostromo** inadvertently gains hoard of silver ingots. [Br. Lit.: *Nostromo*]

13. **Ophir** Red Sea area noted for gold. [*O.T.: I Kings* 9:28; 10:11; 22:48]

14. **Sutter's Mill** site of first strike precipitating Gold Rush. [Am. Hist. Flexner, 175]

15. **Treasure Island** search for buried treasure ignited by discovery of ancient map. [Br. Lit.: *Treasure Island*]

16. **Treasure of the Sierra Madre** in Mexico, written by the reclusive, pseudonymous B. Traven. [Am. and Mex. Lit.: *The Treasure of the Sierra Madre*]

17. **U.S. Mint** repository of U.S. gold reserve. [Am. Hist.: *NCE*, 1787]

578. TRICKERY (See also CUNNING, DECEIT, HUMBUGGERY.)

1. **Bunsby, Captain Jack** trapped into marriage by landlady. [Br. Lit.: *Dombey and Son*]

2. **Delilah** tricks Samson into revealing secret of his strength. [*O.T.: Judges* 16:6–21]

3. **gerrymander** political chicanery aimed at acquiring votes. [Am. Hist.: Jameson, 199]

4. **Gibeonites** obtained treaty with Joshua under false pretenses. [*O.T.: Joshua* 9:3–15]

5. **Jacob** through guile, obtained blessing intended for Esau. [*O.T.: Genesis* 27:18–29]

6. **Loge (Loki)** enables Wotan to overpower Alberich, gain Rhine-gold. [Ger. Opera: Wagner, *Das Rheingold*, Westerman, 232]

7. **Malatesta** schemes outwit miser; enable young lovers to wed. [Ital. Opera: Donizetti, *Don Pasquale*, Westerman, 123–124]

8. **Rebekah** encouraged son Jacob to deceive father for blessing. [*O.T.: Genesis* 27:5–17]

9. **Serpina** dupes bachelor employer into marrying her. [Ital. Opera: Pergolesi, *La Serva Padrona*, Westerman, 61]

579. TRINITY

1. **botonné cross** symbolizes Father, Son, and Holy Ghost. [Christian Iconog.: Jobes, 386]

2. **equilateral triangle** perfect geometrical representation of triune God. [Christian Symbolism: Appleton, 102]

3. **iris** emblem of the trinity in da Vinci's "Madonna of the Rocks." [Plant Symbolism: Embolden, 26]

4. **fleur-de-lis** symbol of the trinity; resembles lily. [Christian Symbolism: *EB*, IV: 182]

5. **shamrock** St. Patrick's legendary symbol of triune God. [Christian Symbolism: Appleton, 87]

6. **Sign of the Cross** signifying Father, Son, and Holy Ghost. [Christianity: *NCE*, 2786]

7. **trefoil (clover)** emblem of the Trinity. [Christian Symbolism: Cirlot, 50–51]

8. **Trimurti** Hindu triad of Brahma, Vishnu, and Siva. [Hinduism: Brewer *Dictionary*, 1101]

580. TRUMPET

1. **Gabriel** angel who will blow the trumpet to announce the coming of Judgment Day. [Christian Trad.: *Century Cyclopedia*, 1667]

TRUTH (See HONESTY.)

581. TURNING POINT

1. **Alamogordo** site of first A-bomb explosion; heralded atomic age (1945). [Am. Hist.: Flexner, 11]
2. **Barbarossa** disastrous invasion of Russia; sealed Nazi fate (1941–1943). [Eur. Hist.: *Hitler*, 888–921, 922–955]
3. **Caesar crosses Rubicon** defying Roman law, Caesar moves to consolidate power (49 B.C.). [Rom. Hist.: *EB*, 3: 575–580]
4. **Cannonade of Valmy** dawn of modern warfare (1792). [Eur. Hist.: Fuller, II, 346–369]
5. **Crécy** first European use of gunpowder (by British) in battle (1346). [Eur. Hist.: Bishop, 382–385]
6. **D-Day** Allied invasion of France during WWII (June 6, 1944). [Eur. Hist.: Fuller, III, 562–567]
7. **El Alamein** "Desert Fox" outfoxed; Allies gained upper hand (1943). [Eur. Hist.: Fuller, III, 494–502]
8. **Fall of Constantinople** associated with end of Middle Ages (1453). [Eur. Hist.: Bishop, 398]
9. **Gettysburg, Battle of** the deathblow of the Confederacy (1863). [Am. Hist.: Jameson, 199]
10. **Golden Spurs, Battle of** early victory of infantry over mounted knights (1302). [Eur. Hist.: *EB*, IV: 608]
11. **Hastings, Battle of** Norman conquest; last successful invasion of Britain (1066). [Br. Hist.: Harbottle, 107]
12. **Khe Sanh** savage siege marks turning point in Vietnam (1968). [Am. Hist.: Van Doren, 620]
13. **Magna Charta** beginning of British democratic system (1215). [Br. Hist.: Bishop, 49–52, 213]
14. **Moon Landing** astronauts Armstrong and Aldrin make history (1969). [Am. Hist.: *NCE*, 2579–2581]
15. **Marston Moor** deciding battle of British Civil War (1644). [Br. Hist.: Harbottle, 154]
16. **Midway** decisive American victory over Japanese in WWII (1942). [Am. Hist.: Fuller, III, 470–477]

17. **95 Theses** Martin Luther presented his theses at Wittenberg (1517). [Eur. Hist.: *EB*, 11: 188–196]

18. **Origin of the Species** Darwin's revolutionary theory of human evolution (1859). [Science: *NCE*, 721–722]

19. **Spanish Armada** Britain supplanted Spain as master of the sea. [Br. Hist.: Harbottle, 19]

20. **theory of relativity** Einstein's contribution to the space-time relationship. [Science: *NCE*, 843–844]

21. **Tours** Arab onslaught halted by Franks under Charles Martel (732). [Eur. Hist.: Bishop, 19]

582. **TWINS (See also DOUBLE.)**

1. **Alcmena's sons** born in single delivery but conceived by two men. [Rom. Lit.: *Amphitryon*]

2. **Antipholus** identically named sons of Aegeon and Emilia. [Br. Lit.: *Comedy of Errors*]

3. **Apollo and Artemis** twin brother and sister; children of Leta and Zeus. [Gk. Myth.: *NCE*, 125–126]

4. **Bobbsey Twins** two sets of twins share adventures. [Children's Lit.: *Bobbsey Twins' Mystery at Meadowbrook*]

5. **Castor and Pollux** sons of Leda and Zeus, placed in heaven as constellation Gemini. [Gk. Myth.: Zimmerman, 52]

6. **Comedy of Errors** based on Plautus, with two sets of twins. [Br. Lit.: *Comedy of Errors*]

7. **Dioscuri (Castor and Pollux)** Spartan brothers. [Gk. Myth.: Avery, 408; Leach, 314]

8. **Donny, the Misses** twin principals of Greenleaf boarding school. [Br. Lit.: *Bleak House*]

9. **Dromio** Dromio of Ephesus; Dromio of Syracuse. [Br. Lit.: *Comedy of Errors*]

10. **Esau and Jacob** Rebekah's quarrelsome infants. [*O.T.: Genesis* 25:22–26]

11. **de Franchi, Lucien and Louis** one twin innately feels what happens to other. [Fr. Lit.: *The Corsican Brothers*]

12. **Gemini (Castor and Pollux)** zodiacal twins; [Gk. Myth.: *NCE*, 1056]

13. **Katzenjammer Kids** early comic strip featured incorrigible twins. [Comics: "The Captain and the Kids" in Horn, 421]

14. **Menaechmi, The** comedy, by Plautus, about mistakes involving identical twins. [Rom. Lit.: *The Menaechmi*]

15. **Perez and Zerah** born to Tamar; conceived by father-in-law, Judah. [*O.T.: Genesis* 38:29–30]

16. **Romulus and Remus** suckled by she-wolf; founded Rome. [Rom. Myth.: Wheeler, 320]

17. **Tweedledum and Tweedledee** identical characters in children's fantasy. [Br. Lit.: *Through the Looking-Glass*]

18. **two circles** symbol of twins; in particular, Castor and Pollux [Gk. Myth.: Jobes, 343]

583. TYRANNY

1. **Big Brother** omnipresent leader of a totalitarian nightmare world. [Br. Lit.: *1984*]

2. **Creon** rules Thebes with cruel decrees. [Gk. Lit.: *Antigone*]

3. **Gessler** Austrian governor treats Swiss despotically; shot by Tell. [Ital. Opera: Rossini, *William Tell*, Westerman, 121–122]

4. **Necho, Pharaoh** oppresses Jerusalem by exaction of harsh taxes. [*O.T.: II Kings* 23: 33–35]

5. **pig** mean, sadistic tyrant; epitome of human horridness. [Br. Lit.: *Animal Farm*]

6. **Queen of Hearts** dictatorial ruler who chops off subjects' heads. [Br. Lit.: *Alice's Adventures in Wonderland*]

7. **Rehoboam** bitterly repressed his people. [*O.T.: I Kings* 12:12–16]

8. **salamander** Francis I's symbol of absolute dictatorial power. [Animal Symbolism: Mercatante, 19]

U

584. **UBIQUITY** (See also **OMNIPRESENCE.**)

1. **Burma-Shave** their signs seen as "verses of the wayside throughout America." [Am. Commerce and Folklore: Misc.]
2. **Coca-Cola** soft drink found throughout the world. [Trademarks: Crowley *Trade*, 115]
3. **Gideon Bible** bible placed in hotel rooms and other establishments throughout the world. [Am. Hist.: *NCE*, 291]
4. **Howard Johnson's** restaurant-motel chain throughout America; buildings recognized by their bright orange roofs. [Trademarks: Crowley *Trade*, 274]
5. **Kilroy** fictitious American soldier; left inscription, "Kilroy was here," everywhere America fought. [Am. Mil. Folklore: Misc.]
6. **McDonald's** fast-food restaurant chain throughout the world; recognized by golden arches. [Am. Culture: Misc.]

585. **UGLINESS**

1. **Avagddu** ugly child of Tegid Voel and Cerridwen. [Celtic Folklore: Parrinder, 35]
2. **Balkis** hairy-legged type of Queen of Sheba. [Talmudic Legend: Walsh *Classical*, 45]
3. **Bendith Y Mamau** stunted, ugly fairies; kidnapped children. [Celtic Folklore: Briggs, 21]
4. **Berchta** beady-eyed, hook-nosed crone with clubfoot and stringy hair. [Ger. Folklore: Leach, 137]
5. **Black Annis** cannibalistic hag with blue face and iron claws. [Br. Folklore: Briggs, 24]
6. **Duessa** witch, stripped of lavish disguise, found to be hideous hag. [Br. Lit.: *Faerie Queene*]
7. **Ethel** buck-toothed, gangly teenager in love with idler, Jughead. [Comics: "Archie" in Horn, 37]
8. **Euryale and Stheno** the immortal Gorgons; had serpents for hair and brazen claws. [Gk. Myth.: Zimmerman, 114]
9. **Frankenstein's monster** ugly monster. [Br. Lit.: *Frankenstein*, Payton, 254]
10. **gargoyles** medieval European church waterspouts; made in form of grotesque creatures. [Architecture: *NCE*, 1046]
11. **Gorgons** snake-haired, winged creatures of frightful appearance. [Gk. Myth.: Howe, 108]

12. **Gross, Allison** repulsive witch "in the north country." [Scot. Ballad: *Childe Ballads*]

13. **Medusa** creature with fangs, snake-hair, and protruding tongue. [Gk. Myth.: Hall, 206]

14. **Quasimodo** "Nowhere on earth a more grotesque creature." [Fr. Lit.: *The Hunchback of Notre Dame*]

15. **Spriggans** grotesque fairies; "dourest and most ugly set of sprights." [Br. Folklore: Briggs, 380–381]

16. **Ugly Duchess** repulsive woman with pocket-shaped mouth. [Br. Lit.: *Alice's Adventures in Wonderland*]

17. **Ugly Duckling** ugly outcast until fully grown. [Fairy Tale: Misc.]

18. **Witch of Wookey** repulsive hag curses boys and girls. [Br. Legend: Brewer *Dictionary*, 1164]

586. **UNATTAINABILITY (See also IMPOSSIBILITY.)**

1. **Elixir of Life** fabulous potion conferring immortality. [Medieval Legend: Brewer *Dictionary*, 371]

2. **Fountain of Youth** legendary fountain of eternal youth. [World Legend: Brewer *Dictionary*, 432]

3. **perpetual motion machine** machine operating of itself forever. [World Legend: Brewer *Dictionary*, 823]

4. **Philosopher's Stone** substance supposed to convert base metal to gold. [Medieval Legend: Brewer *Dictionary*, 829]

587. **UNDERWORLD (See also HELL.)**

1. **Aidoneus** epithet of Hades. [Gk. Myth.: Zimmerman, 14]

2. **Amenti** hidden world where the sun sets. [Egypt. Myth.: Leach, 42]

3. **Anunnaki** lesser Sumerian underworld deities. [Sumerian Myth.: Benét, 41]

4. **Aornum** entrance through which Orpheus descended to Hades. [Gk. Myth.: Zimmerman, 25]

5. **Aralu** desolate land of no return. [Babyl. Myth.: Leach, 69]

6. **Avernus, Lake** entrance to the maw. [Rom. Lit.: *Aeneid;* Art: Hall, 147]

7. **Dis** god of nether world; identified with Pluto. [Rom. Myth.: Leach, 315]

8. **Duat** one of the Egyptian abodes of the dead. [Egypt. Myth.: Benét, 290]

9. **Ereshkigal** queen of underworld; Persephone equivalent. [Sumerian Myth.: Benét, 319–320]

10. **Hades** realm of departed spirits. [Gk. Myth.: Brewer *Dictionary*, 499]

11. **Hel** ruled over world of the dead. [Norse Myth.: Leach, 488]

12. **Nergal** god ruling the world of dead. [Sumerian and Akkadian Myth.: Parrinder, 203]

13. **Niflheim** region of perpetual cold and darkness; afterworld. [Norse Myth.: Wheeler, 259]

14. **oak leaves, garland of** emblem of Hecate, goddess of the underworld. [Gk. Myth.: Jobes, 374]

15. **Orcus** nether world of the dead. [Rom. Myth.: Wheeler, 270]

16. **Pluto** god of underworld. [Gk. Myth.: Howe, 224]

17. **Sheol** abode of the dead. [Hebrew Theology: Brewer *Dictionary*, 499]

18. **Styx** river of Hades across which souls of dead must travel. [Gk. Myth.: Howe, 259]

19. **Tartarus** infernal regions. [Gk. Myth.: Hall, 147]

UNFAITHFULNESS (See FAITHLESSNESS.)

UNGRATEFULNESS (See INGRATITUDE.)

UNKINDNESS (See CRUELTY, INHOSPITALITY.)

588. **UNSCRUPULOUSNESS (See also TRICKERY.)**

1. **Blas, Gil** educated rogue on warpath for self-gain. [Fr. Lit.: *Gil Blas*]

2. **Brass, Sampson** unprincipled attorney. [Br. Lit.: *Old Curiosity Shop*]

3. **Bray, Walter** to clear his debts to old Gride, arranges to have Gride marry his daughter. [Br. Lit.: *Nicholas Nickleby*]

4. **Butler, Rhett** war profiteer; morality not a concern. [Am. Lit.: *Gone With the Wind*]

5. **Claudio** asks sister to sacrifice her virtue to save his life. [Br. Lit.: *Measure for Measure*]

6. **Duroy, George** climbs to wealth by exploiting wife's disgrace. [Fr. Lit.: *Bel-Ami*]

7. **Henchard, Michael** offers wife and child for sale. [Br. Lit.: *The Mayor of Casterbridge*]

8. **Livia** she poisoned whoever interfered with her plans. [Br. Lit.: *I, Claudius*]

9. **Prince, The** practicality in power; end justifies means. [Ital. Lit.: *The Prince*]

10. **Tweed, William Marcy "Boss"** (1823–1878) corrupt politico; controlled New York City government (1863–1871). [Am. Hist.: Jameson, 511]

11. **Winterset, Duke de** commonly described as "an English scoundrel." [Am. Lit.: *Monsieur Beaucaire*, Magill, I, 616–617]

589. UNSELFISHNESS

1. **Arden, Enoch** returned castaway; keeps identity secret from wife to preserve her "new life" happiness. [Br. Lit.: *Enoch Arden*]

2. **Bartholomea Capitanio and Vincentia Gerosa, Sts.** founded order to nurse sick, teach young. [Christian Hagiog.: Attwater, 58]

3. **Bergerac, Cyrano de** composed eloquent love letters for another. [Fr. Lit.: *Cyrano de Bergerac*]

4. **Cratchit, Bob** ill-paid clerk; uncomplainingly supports large family. [Br. Lit.: *A Christmas Carol*]

5. **Goriot, Père** generosity to daughters caused his own poverty. [Fr. Lit.: *Père Goriot*]

590. UNSOPHISTICATION (See also NAIVENESS.)

1. **Adams, Parson** industrious curate; good-naturedly unsophisticated. [Br. Lit.: *Joseph Andrews*]

2. **Agnès** ignorant girl; unaware of world's and guardian's wiles. [Fr. Lit.: *L'Ecole des Femmes*]

3. **Barefoot Boy** adventures of rural boyhood. [Am. Lit.: Hart, 57]

4. **Beverly Hillbillies** the rustication of California's wealthy Beverly Hills. [TV: Terrace, I, 93–94]

5. **brown ass** traditional symbol signifying lack of culture. [Animal Symbolism: Jobes, 142]

6. **Dogpatch** town of illiterate country folk. [Comics: "Li'l Abner" in Horn, 450]

7. **Donn, Arabella** Jude's wife; a vulgar country girl. [Br. Lit.: *Jude the Obscure*]

8. **Geese of Brother Philip** sheltered lad believes father's explanation of girls. [Ital. Lit.: *Decameron*, Hall, 135]

9. **Grand Fenwick, Duchy of** minuscule backward European kingdom that "bites the world's tail." [Am. Lit.: *The Mouse That Roared*]

10. **Grand Ole Opry** country-western music performance hall and radio show; "back-country" motif. [Radio: Buxton, 100–101]

11. **Green, Verdant** callow Oxford freshman; victim of practical jokes. [Br. Lit.: *The Adventures of Mr. Verdant Green*, Brewer *Dictionary*, 1126]

12. **Kadiddlehopper, Clem** character who epitomizes naiveness. [Radio: "The Red Skelton Show" in Buxton, 197]

13. **Li'l Abner** naive comic strip character. [Comics: Horn, 450–451]

14. **Miller, Daisy** her American ways caused scandal in Rome. [Am. Lit.: *Daisy Miller*]

15. **Okies** Californians' derogatory name for Oklahoma immigrants; meaning "ignorant tramps." [Am. Lit.: *The Grapes of Wrath*]

16. **Pyle, Gomer** innocent character in Marine Corps situation comedy. [TV: "Gomer Pyle, U.S.M.C." in Terrace, I, 319]

17. **Snerd, Mortimer** ventriloquist's dummy personifies unsophistication. [Radio: "The Edgar Bergen and Charlie McCarthy Show" in Buxton, 7–77]

UNWORLDLINESS (See ASCETICISM.)

USELESSNESS (See FUTILITY.)

591. **USURPATION**

1. **Adonijah** presumptuously assumed David's throne before Solomon's investiture. [O.T.: *I Kings* 1:5–10]

2. **Anschluss** Nazi takeover of Austria (1938). [Eur. Hist.: *Hitler*, 590–627]

3. **Athaliah** steals throne by killing all royal line. [O.T.: *II Kings* 11:1]

4. **Frederick** arrogated dominions of his brother. [Br. Lit.: *As You Like It*]

5. **Glorious Revolution** James II deposed; William and Mary enthroned (1688). [Br. Hist.: *EB*, 3: 248]

6. **Godunov, Boris** (c. 1551–1605) cunningly has tsarevich murdered; gallantly accepts throne. [Russ. Lit.: *Boris Godunov*; Russ. Opera: Moussorgsky, *Boris Godunov*]

7. **Menahem** murders Shallum and enthrones himself. [O.T.: *II Kings* 15:14]

8. **Otrepyev, Grigory** baseborn monk assumes dead tsarevich's identity and throne. [Russ. Lit.: *Boris Gudonov*; Russ. Opera: Moussorgsky, *Boris Godunov*]

592. **USURY**

1. **Fledgeby** cowardly and deceitful moneylender. [Br. Lit.: *Our Mutual Friend*]

2. **Gride, Arthur** extorting moneylender. [Br. Lit.: *Nicholas Nickleby*]

3. **Milo** loaned gold for huge interest rates and sexual favors. [Gk. Lit.: *The Golden Ass*]

4. **Nickleby, Ralph** avaricious and ungentlemanly moneylender. [Br. Lit.: *Nicholas Nickleby*]

5. **Shylock** shrewd, avaricious moneylender. [Br. Lit.: *Merchant of Venice*]

593. **UTOPIA (See also HEAVEN, PARADISE, WONDERLAND.)**

1. **Abbey of Thelema** Rabelais' vision of the ideal society. [Fr. Lit.: *Gargantua*, Plumb, 394]

2. **Altneuland** future Jewish state; "if willed, no fairytale." [Hung. Lit.: *Altneuland*, Wigoder, 21]

3. **Amaurote** chief city in Utopia. [Br. Lit.: *Utopia*]

4. **Annfwn** land of perpetual beauty and happiness where death is unknown. [Welsh Myth.: Leach, 91]

5. **Atlantis** legendary island; inspired many Utopian myths. [Western Folklore: Misc.]

6. **Brook Farm** literary, socialist commune intended to be small utopia (1841–1846). [Am. Hist.: Jameson, 63]

7. **El Dorado** legendary place of fabulous wealth. [Am. Hist.: Espy, 335]

8. **Helicon Home Colony** socialist community founded by Upton Sinclair. [Am. Hist.: *NCE*, 2524]

9. **Looking Backward, 2000–1887** utopian novel (1888). [Am. Lit.: Benét, 598]

10. **Nephelococcygia** ethereal wonderland of castles; secure from gods. [Gk. Lit.: *The Birds*]

11. **Never Never Land** fictional home. [Br. Lit.: *Peter Pan*, Espy, 339]

12. **New Harmony** cooperative colony founded by Robert Owen in Indiana (1825). [Am. Hist.: *EB*, X: 315]

13. **Oneida** founded by John Humphrey Noyes in New York; based on extended family system. [Am. Hist.: *EB*, X: 315]

14. **Republic, The** Plato's dialogue describes the ideal state. [Gk. Lit.: Benét, 850]

15. **Saint-Simonism** sociopolitical theories advocating industrial socialism. [Fr. Hist.: Brewer *Dictionary*, 955]

16. **Seven Cities of Cibola** the land of the Zuñis (New Mexico); great wealth sought by Coronado. [Mex. Myth.: Payton, 614]

17. **Shangri-la** earthly paradise in the Himalayas. [Br. Lit.: *Lost Horizon*]

18. **Utopia** More's humanistic treatise on the ideal state (1516). [Br. Lit.: *Utopia*]

V

VALOR (See BRAVERY.)

594. VANITY (See also CONCEIT, EGOTISM.)

1. **Barnabas, Parson** conceited and weak clergyman. [Br. Lit.: *Joseph Andrews*]

2. **Bottom, Nick** self-important weaver. [Br. Lit.: *A Midsummer Night's Dream*]

3. **Cassiopeia** claimed her beauty was greater than that of the Nereids. [Gk. Myth.: Leach, 196]

4. **Eglantine, Madame** distinguished by her feminine delicacy and seeming worldliness. [Br. Lit.: *Canterbury Tales*, "The Prioress's Tale"]

5. **March, Amy** beautiful, vain, spoiled girl. [Am. Lit.: *Little Women*]

6. **mirror** attribute of vainglory. [Art: Hall, 211]

7. **Narcissus** fell in love with own image. [Gk. Myth.: Howe, 174]

8. **peacock** conceit personified. [Animal Symbolism: Hall, 239]

9. **Turveydrop, Mr.** conceited father of Prince. [Br. Lit.: *Bleak House*]

10. **Zion, Daughters of** Lord reacts harshly to their wanton finery. [*O.T.: Isaiah* 3:16–26]

595. VENGEANCE

1. **Absalom** kills half-brother, Amnon, for raping sister, Tamar. [*O.T.: II Samuel* 13:28–29]

2. **Acamas** Aeneas's companion; kills Promachus to avenge brother's murder. [Gk. Lit.: *Iliad*]

3. **Acarnan and Amphoterus** enabled by Zeus to grow to manhood in single day to avenge father's murder. [Gk. Myth.: Zimmerman, 2]

4. **Achilles** avenges Patroclus's death by brutally killing Hector. [Gk. Lit.: *Iliad*]

5. **Agag** mutilated by Samuel to requite Israelite slaughter. [*O.T.: I Samuel* 15:33]

6. **Ahab** mad captain seeks revenge on whale. [Am. Lit.: *Moby Dick*]

7. **Alastor** epithet applied to Zeus and others as avenger. [Gk. Myth.: *NCE*, 49]

8. **Alfio** takes vengeance on Turiddu for adultery with his wife. [Ital. Opera: Mascagni, *Cavalleria Rusticana*, Westerman, 338–339]

9. **Atreus** cuckolded by brother, serves him his sons for dinner. [Rom. Lit.: *Thyestes*, Brewer *Dictionary*, 1081]

10. **Balfour, Ebenezer** takes vengeance on David, whose father stole Ebenezer's woman. [Brit. Lit.: *Kidnapped*]

11. **Chillingworth, Roger** tortures Dimmesdale for adultery. [Am. Lit.: *The Scarlet Letter*]

12. **Colomba** will not rest until father's murder is avenged. [Fr. Lit.: *Colomba*]

13. **Coppelius** destroys Olympia because of bad check. [Fr. Opera: Offenbach, *Tales of Hoffmann*, Westerman, 275]

14. **cry of blood** innocent victim's blood calls for justice. [*O.T.*: *Genesis* 4:10; Br. Lit.: *Richard II*]

15. **Dantes, Edmond** waits 14 years to get even with rivals. [Fr. Lit.: *The Count of Monte-Cristo*]

16. **Dirae** avenging goddesses or Furies. [Rom. Myth.: *LLEI*, I: 326]

17. **Don Carlos** takes vengeance upon Alvaro, alleged murderer of his father. [Ital. Opera: Verdi, *La Forza del Destino*, Westerman, 316–317]

18. **Electra** gets even with her father's murderers. [Gk. Lit.: *Electra*]

19. **eye for an eye** Moses's *lex talionis*. [*O.T.*: *Exodus* 21:23–25; *Leviticus* 24:20; *Deuteronomy* 19:21]

20. **Falke, Dr.** avenges his public humiliation by Eisenstein. [Aust. Operetta: J. Strauss, *Die Fledermaus*, Westerman, 278]

21. **Hamlet** must avenge murder of his father. [Br. Lit.: *Hamlet*]

22. **Herodias** spitefully effects decapitation of John the Baptist. [*N.T.*: *Mark* 6:19–26]

23. **Joab** kills Abner, murderer of his brother. [*O.T.*: *II Samuel* 3:27]

24. **Lisbeth (Cousin Bette)** swears to get back at the Hulots. [Fr. Lit.: *Cousin Bette*, Magill, I, 166–168]

25. **Malta, The Jew of** Christian-hating merchant's betrayal of Malta. [Br. Lit.: *The Jew of Malta*]

26. **Medea** uses poisoned nightgown to kill Jason's new wife. [Fr. Opera: Cherubini, *Medea*, Westerman, 81]

27. **Montresor** redresses insult by entombing insulter in catacomb niche. [Am. Lit.: "The Cask of Amontillado" in *Portable Poe*, 309–316]

28. **Nemesis** daughter of Night, brought retribution upon haughty. [Gk. Myth.: Hall, 221]

29. **Rigoletto** wreaks vengeance on daughter-seducing Duke of Mantua. [Ital. Opera: Verdi, *Rigoletto*, Westerman, 300]

30. **Sextus** kills Ptolemy for the murder of Pompey. [Br. Opera: *Julius Caesar in Egypt*, Westerman, 52–53]

31. **Shere Khan** tiger forever trying to pursue, kill Mowgli. [Br. Lit.: *The Jungle Books*]

32. **Tamora** plots to avenge son by murdering the Andronicus family. [Br. Lit.: *Titus Andronicus*]

33. **Titus Andronicus** seeks revenge against Saturninus, Chiron, and Demetrius. [Br. Lit.: *Titus Andronicus*]

34. **trefoil** traditional symbol of vengeance. [Flower Symbolism: *Flora Symbolica*, 178]

596. VERSATILITY

1. **Franklin, Benjamin** (1706–1790) American statesman, inventor, printer, author, scientist. [Am. Hist.: Benét, 366]

2. **jack-of-all-trades** epitome of the versatile worker of trades. [Pop. Culture: Misc.]

3. **Jefferson, Thomas** (1743–1826) writer of Declaration of Independence; inventor, scholar, president. [Am. Hist.: Jameson, 256–257]

4. **Leonardo da Vinci** (1452–1519) painter, sculptor, architect, musician, scientist, engineer. [Ital. Hist.: *NCE*, 1561–1562]

597. VICTORY

1. **Arc de Triomphe** arch built in Paris by Napoleon to celebrate his conquests (1806–1836). [Fr. Hist.: Misc.]

2. **Arch of Trajan** triumphal monument by emperor (c. 100). [Rom. Hist.: Misc.]

3. **bay leaves** wreath used as victor's crown. [Heraldry: Halberts, 20]

4. **Beethoven's 5th** symphony with theme, which is Morse code for V, symbolizing victory. [Western Culture: Misc.]

5. **elephant** pack animal for Romans during successful Punic wars. [Animal Symbolism: Hall, 111]

6. **Greek cross** symbol of Christ's triumph over death. [Christian Iconog.: Jobes, 386]

7. **laurel wreath** traditional symbol of victory, recognition, and reward. [Gk. and Rom. Hist.: Jobes, 374]

8. **Nike (Victoria)** winged goddess of triumph. [Gk. Myth.: Brewer *Dictionary*, 757]

9. **palm** sign of triumph. [*N.T.: Revelation* 7:9]

10. **V-E Day** Allies accept Germany's surrender in WWII (May 8, 1945). [World Hist.: Van Doren, 506]

11. **V-J Day** Allies accept Japan's surrender in WWII (August 15, 1945). [World Hist.: Van Doren, 507]

598. VILLAINY (See also EVIL, WICKEDNESS.)

1. **d'Acunha, Teresa** portrait of devilish Spanish servant and kidnapper. [Br. Lit.: *The Antiquary*]

2. **Bligh, Captain** (1754–1817) sadistic, heavy-handed captain of the *Bounty* [Am. Lit.: *Mutiny on the Bounty*]

3. **Bluto (Brutus)** Popeye's archenemy. [Comics: "Thimble Theater" in Horn, 657–658]

4. **Boris and Natasha** duo of dirty dealers. [TV: "Rocky and His Friends" in Terrace, II, 252–253]

5. **Dalgarno, Lord** young profligate nobleman; betrays Lady Hermione, slanders Nigel. [Br. Lit.: *Fortunes of Nigel*]

6. **Dastardly, Dick** popular personification of a villain. [Comics: "Dastardly and Motley" in Terrace, I, 185]

7. **Fagin** iniquitous old man; employs youngsters as thieves. [Br. Lit.: *Oliver Twist*]

8. **Foulfellow, J. Worthington** sly fox cajoles Pinocchio onto stage. [Am. Cinema: *Pinocchio* in *Disney Films*, 32–37]

9. **Iago** slanders Desdemona; precipitates tragedy. [Br. Lit.: *Othello*]

10. **Legree, Simon** cruel slavemaster of Uncle Tom. [Am. Lit.: *Uncle Tom's Cabin*]

11. **Mime** tries to poison Siegfried and get Nibelung treasure. [Ger. Opera: Wagner, *Siegfried*, Westerman, 241]

12. **Montserrat, Conrade de** attempts to assassinate king; detected by Kenneth's hound. [Br. Lit.: *The Talisman*]

13. **Mother St. Agatha** prioress abets lustful monk's plot to punish runaway. [Br. Lit.: *The Monk*]

14. **Murdour** reprehensible scoundrel; cuckolds and kills Bevis's father. [Br. Lit.: *Bevis of Hampton*]

15. **Oil Can Harry** a study in dastardliness. [Comics: "Mighty Mouse" in Horn, 492; TV: "The Mighty Mouse Playhouse" in Terrace, II, 96]

16. **Pizarro, Don** illegally imprisons and starves Florestan; plans murder. [Ger. Opera: Beethoven, *Fidelio,* Westerman, 109–110]

17. **Plantagenet, Richard** murders Somerset. [Br. Lit.: *II Henry VI*]

18. **the Queen** "a crafty devil"; "hourly coining plots." [Br. Lit.: *Cymbeline*]

19. **Scarpia** offers mock execution for Tosca's affections. [Ital. Opera: Puccini, *Tosca,* Westerman, 352–354]

20. **Sheriff of Nottingham** traditional badman; thwarted in attempts to capture Robin Hood. [Br. Lit.: *Robin Hood*]

21. **Tello, Don** lustful nobleman; sates his passion on Elvira. [Span. Lit.: *The King, the Greatest Alcalde*]

22. **deVille, Cruella** witchlike rich lady dognaps 99 dalmatians for coat-making. [Am. Cinema: *101 Dalmatians* in *Disney Films,* 181–184]

VINDICTIVENESS (See VENGEANCE.)

VIOLENCE (See BRUTALITY, CRUELTY.)

599. **VIOLIN**

1. **Nero** (37–68) emperor said to have fiddled while Rome burned (64). [Rom. Hist.: Misc.]

600. **VIRGINITY (See also CHASTITY, PURITY.)**

1. **Agnes, St.** patron saint of virgins. [Christian Hagiog.: Brewer *Dictionary,* 16]

2. **Cecilia, St.** consecrated self to God, bridegroom followed suit. [Christian Hagiog.: Attwater, 81–82]

3. **Chrysanthus and Daria, Sts.** sexless marriage for glory of God. [Christian Hagiog.: Attwater, 86]

4. **Drake, Temple** chastity makes her the object of attacks. [Am. Lit.: *Sanctuary*]

5. **garden, enclosed** wherein grow the red roses of chastity. [Christian Symbolism: *De Virginibus,* Appleton, 41]

6. **Josyan** steadfastly retains virginity for future husband. [Br. Lit.: *Bevis of Hampton*]

7. **lily** symbol of Blessed Virgin; by extension, chastity. [Christian Symbolism: Appleton, 57–58]

8. **Lygia** foreign princess remains chaste despite Roman orgies. [Polish Lit.: *Quo Vadis,* Magill, I, 797–799]

9. **red and white roses, garland of** emblem of virginity, esp. of the Virgin Mary. [Christian Iconog.: Jobes, 374]

10. **ostrich egg** symbolic of virgin birth. [Art: Hall, 110]

11. **Vestals** six pure girls; tended sacred fire to Vesta. [Rom. Hist.: Brewer *Dictionary,* 1127]

12. **Virgin Mary, Blessed** mother of Jesus. [Christianity: *NCE,* 1709]

601. VIRILITY (See also BEAUTY, MASCULINE, BRAWNINESS)

1. **Fury, Sergeant** archetypal he-man. [Comics: "Sergeant Fury and His Howling Commandos" in Horn, 607–608]

2. **Henry, John** a "natchal man" from Black River country. [Am. Lit.: Hart, 428]

3. **Macomber, Francis** Hemingway's hero assumes manhood by assertive act. [Am. Lit.: *The Short Happy Life of Francis Macomber,* Magill, IV, 1130–1133]

4. **Marlboro Man** cigarette advertising campaign established new symbol of virility. [Am. Pop. Culture: Misc.]

5. **Priapus** male generative power personified. [Gk. Myth.: Espy, 27, 224]

6. **rooster** symbol of maleness. [Folklore: Binder, 85]

7. **stag** symbol of maleness. [Animal Symbolism: Mercatante, 59–60]

602. VIRTUOUSNESS (See also HONESTY, RIGHTEOUSNESS.)

1. **Andrews, Pamela** epitome of the virtuous female rewarded. [Br. Lit.: *Pamela*]

2. **Andromache** thinks only of family; rejects king's advances. [Fr. Lit.: *Andromache*]

3. **Apostrophia** epithet of Aphrodite, meaning "rejecter of sinful passion." [Gk. Myth.: Misc.]

4. **Christian** John Bunyan's virtuous, well-traveled hero. [Br. Lit.: *Pilgrim's Progress*]

5. **Erlynne, Mrs.** gains socially admirable title of "good woman." [Br. Lit.: *Lady Windermere's Fan,* Magill, I, 488–490]

6. **Galahad, Sir** noblest and purest knight of the Round Table. [Br. Lit.: *Le Morte d'Arthur*]

7. **Guyon, Sir** embodiment of virtuous self-control. [Br. Lit.: *Faerie Queene*]

8. **Marina** "a piece of virtue." [Br. Lit.: *Pericles*]

9. **Nickleby, Kate** pure-minded sister of Nicholas; repulses all advances. [Br. Lit.: *Nicholas Nickleby*]

10. **Susanna** rejects advances of elderly men. [*Apocrypha: Susanna*]

11. **Tuesday's child** full of grace. [Nurs. Rhyme: Opie, 309]

12. **Wilkes, Melanie** virtuous, long-suffering wife of Ashley. [Am. Lit.: *Gone With the Wind*]

VOLUPTUOUSNESS (See BUXOMNESS.)

VORACITY (See GLUTTONY.)

603. **VOYEURISM** (See also EAVESDROPPING.)
1. **Actaeon** turned into stag for watching Artemis bathe. [Gk. Myth.: Leach, 8]
2. **elders of Babylon** watch Susanna bathe. [*Apocrypha: Susanna;* Art: Daniel, 217]
3. **Gyges** king's bodyguard requested secretly to view queen undressing. [Gk. Lit.: Avery, 507–508]
4. **Peeping Tom** illicitly glanced at the naked Godiva. [Br. Legend: Brewer *Dictionary*, 815]

604. **VULNERABILITY**
1. **Achilles** warrior vulnerable only in his heel. [Gk. Myth.: Zimmerman, 4]
2. **Antaeus** only vulnerable if not touching ground. [Gk. and Rom. Myth.: Hall, 151]
3. **Balder** conquerable only with mistletoe. [Norse Myth.: Walsh *Classical*, 43]
4. **Diarmuid** Irish Achilles, killed through cunning Fionn's deceit. [Irish Myth.: Jobes, 443; Parrinder, 79]
5. **Maginot Line** French fortification zone along German border; thought impregnable before WWII. [Fr. Hist.: *NCE*, 1658]
6. **Samson** strength derived from his hair; betrayed by Delilah. [*O.T.: Judges* 16]
7. **Siegfried** vulnerable in only one spot on his back. [Ger. Opera: Wagner, *Götterdämmerung,* Westerman, 245]
8. **Siegfried Line** German fortification zone opposite the Maginot Line between Germany and France. [Ger. Hist.: *WB*, 17: 370]
9. **Superman** invulnerable except for Kryptonite. [TV: "The Adventures of Superman" in Terrace, I, 38; Comics: Horn, 642]

W

605. WANDERING (See also BOHEMIANISM, JOURNEY.)

1. **Ahasueras** German name for the Wandering Jew. [Ger. Lit.: Benét, 1071]

2. **Ancient Mariner** Coleridge's wandering sailor. [Br. Lit.: "The Rime of the Ancient Mariner" in Norton, 597–610]

3. **Aniara** spaceship condemned to perpetual earth orbit. [Swed. Opera: Blomdahl, *Aniara*, Westerman, 562]

4. **Argonauts** sailed with Jason in search of Golden Fleece. [Gk. Myth.: Howe, 36]

5. **Bedouin** a nomadic desert Arab. [Br. Folklore: Espy, 98]

6. **Cain** punished by God to life of vagrancy. [*O.T.: Genesis* 4:12]

7. **Candide** a wanderer in search of best of all possible worlds. [Fr. Lit.: *Candide*]

8. **Cocytus** Hadean river where unburied were doomed to roam for 100 years. [Gk. Myth.: Benét, 210]

9. **Eulenspiegel, Till** roams Low Countries as soldier and deliverer. [Ger. Folklore: Benét, 325–326]

10. **Goedzak, Lamme** accompanies Eulenspiegel on his circumambulations. [Ger. Folklore: Benét, 325–326]

11. **Goliards** wandering scholar-poets of 12th-century Europe. [Medieval Hist.: *NCE*, 1105]

12. **Gulliver, Lemuel** visits fabulous lands. [Br. Lit.: *Gulliver's Travels*]

13. **Gynt, Peer** Norwegian farmer drifts around without purpose. [Nor. Lit.: *Peer Gynt*, Magill, I, 722–724]

14. **Gypsy** member of nomadic people who usually travel in small caravans. [Eur. Hist.: *NCE*, 1168]

15. **Ishmael** "the wanderer" aboard Ahab's ship. [Am. Lit.: *Moby Dick*]

16. **Kwai Chang Caine** Shaolin priest wanders throughout America. [TV: "Kung Fu" in Terrace I, 449]

17. **Labre, St. Benedict** itinerant holy beggar. [Christian Hagiog.: Attwater, 64]

18. **land of Nod** condemned to vagabondage, Cain settles here. [*O.T.: Genesis* 4:16]

19. **Lord Jim** a marked man's wanderings to regain his honor. [Am. Lit.: *Lord Jim*]

20. **Melmoth the Wanderer** to win souls, he is cursed to roam earth after death. [Br. Lit.: *Melmoth the Wanderer*]

21. **Nolan, Philip** transferred from ship to ship; never lands. [Am. Lit.: "The Man Without a Country" in Benét, 632]

22. **Odysseus (Ulysses)** the wandering hero of the Trojan War. [Gk. Lit.: *Odyssey*]

23. **Omoo** Polynesian word for an island rover. [Am. Lit.: *Omoo*]

24. **Ossian** a legendary, wandering Irish bard. [Irish Lit.: Harvey, 603]

25. **Route 66** adventure series of two young men wandering along highway Route 66. [TV: Terrace, II, 259]

26. **Siddharta** character who wanders in search of "inner truth." [Ger. Lit.: *Siddharta*]

27. **Wandering Jew** condemned to eternal wandering for mocking Christ. [Christian Legend: *NCE*, 2926; Fr. Lit.: *Wandering Jew*]

606. **WAR** (See also BATTLE.)

1. **Amazons** race of female warriors. [Gk. Myth.: Zimmerman, 19]

2. **Ares (Mars)** god of war. [Gk. Myth.: Kravitz, 31]

3. **Athena (Rom. Minerva)** goddess of war. [Gk. Myth.: Howe, 44]

4. **battle ax** symbol of military conflict. [Western Folklore: Jobes, 163]

5. **Bellona** Mars's charioteer and sister. [Rom. Myth.: Leach, 135]

6. **Durga** malignant goddess of war. [Hinduism: Leach, 330]

7. **Enyo** goddess of battle and attendant of Ares. [Gk. Myth.: Howe, 91]

8. **Guernica** painting by Picasso depicting horror of war. [Art: Osborne, 866–867]

9. **Huitzilopochtli** war god of ancient Mexicans. [Mex. Myth.: Harvey, 403]

10. **Myrmidon** one of the fierce Thessalonians who fought in the Trojan War under their king, Achilles. [Gk. Myth.: *Iliad*]

11. **Neman** form of Irish war goddess, Badb (also Morrigan or Macha). [Irish Folklore: Briggs, 308]

12. **Odin** god who presided over feasts of slain warriors. [Norse Myth.: Brewer *Dictionary*, 774]

13. **red cloud** indicates military conflict. [Eastern Folklore: Jobes, 350]

14. **Tyr** god of victory in war. [Norse Myth.: Leach, 1147]

15. **Valkyries** Odin's warrior maidens. [Norse Myth.: Leach, 1154]

607. **WARNING**

1. **Canterbury bells** fairies' church bells; relied on for vigilance. [Flower Symbolism: *Flora Symbolica*, 167]

2. **Capitoline geese** squawked obstreperously at sight of invader mounting rampart. [Rom. Hist.: Benét, 166]

3. **cock** crows at trespassers; morning call routs evil spirits. [Folklore: White, 150; Mercatante, 173–175]

4. **crow's cry** warning of death or illness. [Western Folklore: Jobes, 388]

5. **fiery cross** traditional Highlands call to arms. [Scot. Hist.: Brewer *Note-Book*, 324–325]

6. **Laocoön** Trojan priest warns citizens not to accept wooden horse. [Rom. Lit.: *Aeneid*]

7. **Olivant** Roland's ivory horn; sounded to summon Charlemagne. [Fr. Lit.: *The Song of Roland*]

8. **Revere, Paul** (1735–1818) famous American patriot who warned, "The British are coming" (1775). [Am. Hist.: Jameson, 425–426]

608. **WATER**

1. **Adad** storm god; helped cause the Flood. [Babyl. Myth.: Benét, 7]

2. **Adam's ale** water; only drink in Paradise. [Folklore: Brewer *Dictionary*, 9]

3. **Alpheus** river god. [Gk. Myth.: Zimmerman, 18]

4. **Apsu** personification of fresh water. [Babyl. Myth.: Benét, 4]

5. **Arethusa** changed into stream by Artemis to save her from Alpheus. [Gk. Myth.: Zimmerman, 29]

6. **Cyane** turned into a fountain by Hades. [Gk. Myth.: Kravitz, 70]

7. **Dirce** turned into a fountain at death. [Gk. Myth.: Kravitz, 82–83]

8. **Galatea** grieving, turned into a fountain. [Gk. Myth.: *Metamorphoses*]

9. **Jupiter Pluvius** dispenser of rain. [Rom. Myth.: Espy, 22]

10. **Neptune** in allegories of the elements, personification of water. [Art: Hall, 128]

11. **undine** female water spirit. [Medieval Hist.: Brewer *Dictionary*, 1115]

609. **WEAKNESS (See also TIMIDITY, VULNERABILITY.)**

1. **Gertrude** "Frailty, thy name is woman!" [Br. Lit.: *Hamlet*]

2. **Henry VI** dominated by queen and vassal; shirks responsibilities. [Br. Lit.: *Henry VI*]

3. **John, King** without grandeur, strength, or any regal quality. [Br. Lit.: *King John*]

4. **Milquetoast, Casper** the original "Timid Soul"; afraid of calling soul his own. [Comics: Horn, 663]

5. **Mitty, Walter** epitome of weak-spirited man. [Am. Lit.: "The Secret Life of Walter Mitty" in Payton, 448]

6. **musk** traditional symbol of weakness. [Plant Symbolism: *Flora Symbolica*, 176]

7. **Pilate, Pontius** yields to clamoring of Jews, hands Jesus over. [*N.T.: Matthew* 27:24–26; *Luke* 23:16–25; *John* 19:1–16]

8. **Warren, Nicole** relies on Dick for stability and identity. [Am. Lit.: *Tender Is the Night*]

610. **WEALTH (See also LUXURY.)**

1. **Abu Dhabi** Persian Gulf sheikdom overflowing with petrodollars. [Mid-East Hist.: *NCE*, 9]

2. **Big Daddy** wealthy Mississippi landowner of humble origins. [Am. Lit.: *Cat on a Hot Tin Roof*]

3. **black and gold** symbol of financial prosperity. [Heraldry: Jobes, 222]

4. **buttercup** traditional symbol of wealth. [Plant Symbolism: *Flora Symbolica*, 167]

5. **Cave of Mammon** abode of god of riches. [Br. Lit.: *Faerie Queene*]

6. **Corinth** ancient Greek city; one of wealthiest and most powerful. [Gk. Hist. and Myth.: Zimmerman, 69]

7. **Croesus** Lydian king; name became synonymous with riches. [Gk. Myth.: Kravitz, 69]

8. **Dives** rich man who ignored poor man's plight; sent to Hell. [*N.T.: Luke* 16:19–31]

9. **Erichthonius** world's richest man in classical times. [Gk. Myth.: Kravitz, 91]

10. **Fortunatus' purse** luckless man receives gift of inexhaustible purse. [Ital. Fairy Tale: *LLEI*, I: 286]

11. **Fuggers** 16th-century German financiers. [Ger. Hist.: *NCE*, 1023–1024]

12. **Hughes, Howard** (1905–1976) eccentric millionaire; lived as recluse. [Am. Hist.: *NCE*, 1284]

13. **Midas** Phrygian king; whatever he touched became gold. [Gk. and Rom. Myth.: Wheeler, 24]

14. **Plutus** cured god dispenses fortunes equally to all men. [Gk. Lit.: *Plutus*]

15. **Rockefeller, John D(avison)** (1839–1937) oil magnate; name has become synonymous with "rich." [Am. Hist.: Jameson, 431]

16. **Solomon** fabulous riches garnered from gifts and tolls. [*O.T.: I Kings* 10:14–25]

17. **Timon** rich Athenian; ruined by his prodigal generosity to friends. [Br. Lit.: *Timon of Athens*]

18. **turquoise** seeing turquoise after a new moon brings wealth. [Gem Symbolism: Kunz, 345]

19. **Warbucks, Daddy** adventurous soldier of fortune and richest man in world. [Comics: "Little Orphan Annie" in Horn, 459]

20. **wheat stalk** traditional symbol of wealth. [Flower Symbolism: *Flora Symbolica*, 178]

611. WHITENESS

1. **ermine** winter stoat; said to die if whiteness is soiled. [Art: Hall, 115]

2. **Moby Dick** white whale pursued relentlessly by Captain Ahab; "It was the whiteness of the whale that above all things appalled me." [Am. Lit.: *Moby Dick*]

3. **pale horse** ridden by Death. [*N.T.: Revelation* 6:8]

4. **white belt of wampum** giving one was giving the deepest pledge of honor. [Am. Indian Trad.: Misc.]

5. **white forked flame** holiest flame on the altar. [Persian Folklore: Misc.]

6. **White Steed of the Prairies** charger who led the wild horses before the West was tamed. [Am. Indian Legend: Misc.]

7. **white stone** marked a joyful day. [Rom. Trad.: Misc.]

612. WHOLESOMENESS

1. **Armstrong, Jack** "the all-American boy." [Radio: Buxton, 121–122]

2. **Brady Bunch, The** widower and widow marry, producing an instant, wholesome family of eight. [TV: Terrace, I, 115]

3. **Miss America** annual beauty contest features wholesome contestants. [Am. Hist.: Allen, 56–57]

4. **Ozzie and Harriet** series portraying the wholesome, American family. [TV: "The Adventures of Ozzie and Harriet" in Terrace, I, 34]

5. **Waltons, The** poor, rural family in the 1930s; they extol chastity, honesty, family unity, and love. [TV: Terrace, II, 418]

613. **WICKEDNESS** (See also EVIL, VILLAINY.)

1. **Admah and Zeboyim** cities destroyed by God for citizens' sinfulness. [*O.T.: Deuteronomy* 19:23]

2. **Ahab** honored false gods, usurped others' land; byword for baseness. [*O.T.: I Kings* 17:29–34; 21:25]

3. **Bluebeard** murders six wives; a personification of wickedness. [Fr. Lit.: Walsh *Classical,* 58]

4. **Jezebel** urged husband, Ahab, to evildoing. [*O.T.: I Kings* 21:25]

5. **Manasseh** idolatrously and murderously leads Jerusalem astray. [*O.T.: II Kings* 21:2–4, 9]

6. **Sodom and Gomorrah** cities of iniquity destroyed by God's wrath. [*O.T.: Genesis* 19:24]

614. **WIFELINESS** (See also DOMESTICITY.)

1. **Amoret** Sir Scudamore's wife; loving and ever-devoted. [Br. Lit.: *Faerie Queene*]

2. **Arundhati** example of the ideal Hindu wife. [Hindu Legend: Benét, 56]

3. **Billy Boy** question-and-answer ballad pointing up merits of possible bride. [Br. and Am. Folklore: Leach, 139]

4. **Martha** personification of the busy housekeeper. [*N.T.: Luke* 10:39]

5. **Penelope** a model of wifely virtue. [Gk. Lit.: *Odyssey*]

615. **WILD WEST**

1. **Apache** North American Indians of Southwest who fought against frontiersmen. [Am. Hist.: *NCE,* 123]

2. **Arapaho** North American Plains Indians living along the Platte and Arkansas rivers. [Am. Hist.: *EB,* I: 477–478]

3. **Bass, Sam** (1851–1878) desperado whose career inspired ballads. [Am. Hist.: *NCE,* 244]

4. **Bean, Judge Roy** (c. 1825–1903) legendary frontier judge who ruled by one law book and a six-shooter. [Am. Hist.: *NCE,* 252]

5. **Big Valley, The** portraying cattle-owning aristocrats of the Wild West. [TV: Terrace, I, 99–100]

6. **Billy the Kid** (William H. Bonney, 1859–1881) Brooklyn-born gunman of the Wild West. [Am. Hist.: Worth, 27]

7. **Bonanza** saga of the Cartwright family. [TV: Terrace, I, 111–112]

8. **Boom Town** originally, a western town that prospered suddenly, usually because of gold mines nearby. [Am. Hist.: Misc.]

9. **boot hill** typical graveyard of gunfighters and their victims. [Am. Folklore: Misc.]

10. **Bowie knife** throwing weapon invented by James or Rezin Bowie, frontiersmen in Texas. [Am. Folklore: *EB*, II: 207]

11. **Broken Arrow** a series depicting Indian–white man exploits. [TV: Terrace, I, 122]

12. **Bury Me Not on the Lone Prairie** popular song about life in the West. [Am. Culture: Misc.]

13. **Calamity Jane** (Martha Jane Canary Burke, c. 1852–1903) extraordinary markswoman and pony express rider. [Am. Hist.: *NCE*, 418]

14. **California Trail** route used by pioneers, extending from Wyoming to Sacramento. [Am. Hist.: *WB*, 21: 440f]

15. **Carson, Kit (Christopher)** (1809–1868) frontiersman, guide, and Indian fighter in the West and Southwest. [Am. Hist.: *NCE*, 466]

16. **Cheyenne** North American Indians who made up part of the Wild West scene. [Am. Hist.: *NCE*, 562]

17. **Cheyenne** cowboy of the strong, silent type. [TV: Terrace, I, 153–154]

18. **Chisholm Trail** route used by traders and drovers bringing cattle from Texas to Kansas. [Am. Hist.: *NCE*, 543]

19. **circuit rider** frontier Methodist preacher who served "appointments" (services) in cabins, schoolhouses, and even taverns. [Am. Hist.: *NCE*, 561]

20. **Cochise** (c. 1815–1874) Apache Indian chief who led the fight against white men in the Southwest. [Am. Hist: *NCE*, 589]

21. **Cody, "Buffalo Bill"** (1846–1917) ex-Army scout who joined and led a famous Wild West show. [Am. Hist.: *NCE*, 390]

22. **Colt .45** six-shot revolver invented by Samuel Colt and used throughout the West. [Am. Hist.: *WB*, 4: 684–685]

23. **Comanche** North American Indian tribe; often figured in Wild West stories. [Am. Hist.: *NCE*, 607]

24. **Comstock Lode** richest silver deposit in U.S.; famous during frontier days. [Am. Hist.: *NCE*, 418]

25. **Conestoga wagon** horse-drawn freight wagon; originated in the Conestoga Creek region in Pennsylvania. [Am. Hist.: *EB*, III: 72]

26. **Crazy Horse** (1842–1877) Indian chief who led Sioux against the white man in the northern plains. [Am. Hist.: *EB*, III: 225–226]

27. **Custer's Last Stand** U.S. troops led by Col. Custer are massacred by the Indians at Little Big Horn, Montana (1877). [Am. Hist.: *NCE*, 701]

28. **Deadwood Gulch** Wild West city in South Dakota where graves of Hickok and Annie Oakley are located. [Am. Hist.: *NCE*, 729]

29. **Death Valley Days** vignettes depicting frontier life. [TV: Terrace, I, 195]

30. **Dillon, Matt** frontier marshal of Dodge City. [TV: "Gunsmoke" in Terrace, I, 331]

31. **Dodge City** onetime rowdy cowboy town under supervision of Bat Masterson and Wyatt Earp. [Am. Hist.: *NCE*, 776]

32. **Earp, Wyatt** (1848–1929) U.S. cowboy, lawman, and gunfighter. [Am. Hist.: *NCE*, 819]

33. **Geronimo** (1829–1909) renegade Indian of the Wild West. [Am. Hist.: *NCE*, 1076]

34. **ghost town** town left vacant after gold strike; common during frontier days. [Am. Hist.: *NCE*, 1080]

35. **Gunsmoke** Wild West television epic with Dodge City setting. [TV: Terrace, I, 331–332]

36. **Hickok, "Wild Bill"** (1837–1876) famous marshal of the West. [Am. Hist.: Hart, 371]

37. **High Noon** western film in which time is of the essence. [Am. Cinema: Griffith, 396–397]

38. **Holliday, "Doc"** (fl. late 19th century) outlaw who helped Wyatt Earp fight the Clanton gang at O.K. Corral. [Am. Hist.: Misc.]

39. **Home on the Range** popular song about the West "where the buffalo roam" and "the deer and the antelope play." [Am. Culture: Misc.]

40. **Indian Territory** area set aside for the Indians by the U.S. government. [Am. Hist.: *NCE*, 1331]

41. **James, Jesse** (1847–1882) American outlaw of the Wild West. [Am. Hist.: *NCE*, 1395]

42. **the Lone Ranger** masked hero of the Wild West. [TV: Terrace, II, 34–35; Radio: Buxton, 143–144]

43. **Oakley, Annie** (1860–1926) sharpshooter; major attraction of Buffalo Bill's show. [Am. Hist.: *NCE*, 1982]

44. **O.K. Corral** scene of famous gunfight between Wyatt Earp and the Clanton gang (1881). [Am. Hist.: *WB*, 6: 9]

45. **Oregon Trail** wagon-train route used by pioneers, extending from Missouri to the Oregon Territory. [Am. Hist.: *NCE*, 2016]

46. **Paladin** archetypal gunman who leaves a calling card. [TV: "Have Gun, Will Travel" in Terrace, I, 341]

47. **Pecos Bill** giant folk hero famed for cowboy exploits. [Am. Lit.: Hart, 643]

48. **Pony Express** relay mail service during frontier days. [Am. Hist.: *NCE*, 2190]

49. **prairie schooner** horse-drawn wagon used by pioneers; its white canvas top resembled a schooner sailing on the prairie. [Am. Hist.: *NCE*, 2209]

50. **Rawhide** series depicting cowboys as cattle-punchers along the Santa Fe trail. [TV: Terrace, II, 235]

51. **Ringo, Johnny** (fl. late 19th century) notorious outlaw who fought many gun battles in the Southwest. [Am. Hist.: Misc.]

52. **Santa Fe Trail** wagon-train route extending from Independence, Missouri to Santa Fe, New Mexico. [Am. Hist.: *NCE*, 2421]

53. **Shane** a classic, serious western film about a pioneer family protected by a mysterious stranger. [Am. Cinema: Halliwell, 651]

54. **Sioux** confederation of North American Indian tribes; last battle fought at Wounded Knee. [Am. Hist.: *NCE*, 2527]

55. **Sitting Bull** (1831–1890) Indian chief who united the Sioux tribes against the white men. [Am. Hist.: *EB*, IX: 243–244]

56. **Texas Rangers** established in 1835, a mounted fighting force to maintain law and order in the West. [Am. Hist.: *NCE*, 2723]

57. **Tombstone** Arizona town known for its outlaws, prospectors, and gun battles (1800s). [Am. Hist.: *EB*, X: 36]

58. **Wells Fargo** company that handled express service to western states; often robbed by outlaws. [Am. Hist.: *NCE*, 2953]

59. **Winchester 73** repeating rifle manufactured by Oliver Winchester and widely used by the settlers of the West. [Am. Hist.: *EB*, X: 699]

616. WIND

1. **Aeolian harp** musical instrument activated by winds. [Gk. Myth.: Jobes, 40]

2. **Aeolus** steward of winds; gives bag of winds to Odysseus. [Gk. Myth: Kravitz, 10; Gk. Lit.: *Odyssey*]

3. **Afer (Africus)** southwest wind. [Gk. Myth.: Kravitz, 11]

4. **Apeliotes (Lips)** east or southeast wind. [Gk. Myth.: Kravitz, 27]

5. **Aquilo** equivalent of Boreas, the Greek north wind. [Rom. Myth.: Kravitz, 30]

6. **Argestes** name of the east wind. [Gk. Myth.: Kravitz, 32]

7. **Aura** goddess of breezes. [Gk. Myth.: Kravitz, 42]

8. **Auster** the southwest wind. [Rom. Myth.: Kravitz, 42]

9. **Boreas** god of the north wind. [Gk. Myth.: Parrinder, 49]

10. **Caicas** the northeast wind. [Gk. Myth.: Kravitz, 50]

11. **chinook** warm winter wind which descends the leeward side of the Rockies; known to cause intense, quick rise in temperature. [Meteorology: *EB*, II: 862]

12. **cordonazo:** hurricane-force wind of Central America; name derives from shortening of Spanish phrase meaning "lash of St. Francis." [Meteorology: *EB*, III: 147]

13. **Corus** god of the north or northwest wind. [Rom. Myth.: Jobes, 374]

14. **Eurus (Volturnus)** the southeast wind. [Gk. Myth.: Kravitz, 97, 238]

15. **Favonius** ancient Roman personification of west wind. [Rom. Myth.: Howe, 103]

16. **Gentle Annis** weather spirit; controls gales on Firth of Cromarty. [Scot. Folklore: Briggs, 185]

17. **gregale (Euroclydon)** cold, northeast wind over the central Mediterranean. [Meteorology: *EB*, IV: 724; *N.T.: Acts* 27:14]

18. **haboob** hot, moist wind of Saharan summers; known to create extremely high walls of sand. [Meteorology: *EB*, IV: 825]

19. **levanter** pronounced westerly wind over the Strait of Gibraltar; known to bring eastbound planes to a halt. [Meteorology: *EB*, VI: 175]

20. **Mudjekeewis** Indian chief; held dominion over all winds. [Am. Lit.: "Hiawatha" in Benét, 466]

21. **Njord** god of the north wind. [Norse Myth.: Wheeler, 260]

22. **northeaster (nor'easter)** strong northeast wind associated with coastal storms of New England and the Canadian Maritimes; often causes much damage. [Meteorology: *EB*, VII: 401]

23. **norther** strong, cold wind which causes the temperature to plummet as far south as Central America. [Meteorology: *EB*, VII: 402]

24. **Ruach** isle of winds. [Fr. Lit.: *Pantagruel*]

25. **samn** scorching Arabian whirlwind; name derives from Arabic word for "poison wind." [Meteorology: *EB*, VIII: 838]

26. **sirocco** warm, moisture-laden wind that blows from the Sahara over southern Europe; once associated with abnormal behavior. [Meteorology: *EB*, IX: 238]

27. **southerly buster** Australian local wind known to cause precipitous drops in temperature. [Meteorology: *EB*, IX: 238]

28. **williwaw** violent local wind that afflicts the Strait of Magellan each winter. [Meteorology: *EB*, X: 690]

29. **Zephyrus** the west wind. [Gk. Myth.: Kravitz, 38, 242]

617. **WINE**

1. **Andros** center for worship of Bacchus, wine god. [Rom. Myth.: Hall, 16]

2. **Bacchus** oenological god. [Rom. Myth.: Hall, 37, 142]

3. **Beaujolais** a wine-growing region in France; often a medium-dry, fruity burgundy. [Fr. Hist.: *NCE*, 2990]

4. **Bordeaux** French city whose wines (especially Médoc, Graves, Sauternes, Saint Émilion) are world-known. [Fr. Hist.: *EB*, II: 162]

5. **Burgundy** region of France that produces fine, natural wines. [Fr. Hist.: *NCE*, 2989]

6. **Catawba** grape grown in the eastern U.S., producing a medium-dry white wine. [Am. Hist.: Misc.]

7. **Chablis** village in central France known for the white wine which bears its name. [Fr. Hist.: *NCE*, 497]

8. **chalice** cup holding wine at Eucharist. [Christian Tradition: *Mark* 14:23]

9. **Champagne** province in northeastern France renowned for its sparkling wine. [Fr. Hist.: *EB*, II: 724]

10. **Chianti** the best-known Italian wine. [Ital. Hist.: *NCE*, 2990]

11. **Dionysus** god of the vine and its enlightening powers. [Gk. Myth.: Avery, 404–408; Parrinder, 80]

12. **Finger Lakes** the region in New York state where many eastern wines are made. [Am. Hist.: *NCE*, 2990]

13. **Liber and Libera** ancient Italian god and goddess of wine and vine cultivation. [Rom. Myth.: Howe, 154]

14. **Liebfraumilch** the best-known Rhine wine. [Ger. Hist.: *NCE*, 2990]

15. **Marsala** a sweet, amber wine made in Sicily. [Ital. Hist.: *NCE*, 2990]

16. **Médoc** a red Bordeaux wine. [Fr. Hist.: *NCE*, 2990]

17. **Napa Valley** greatest wine-producing region of the United States. [Am. Hist.: *NCE*, 2990]

18. **Naxian Groves** vineyards celebrated for fine vintages. [Gk. Hist.: Brewer *Handbook*, 747]

19. **Oeneus** Calydonian king; first to cultivate grapes. [Rom. Myth.: Hall, 142]

20. **port** fortified sweet wine made from grapes grown in the Douro valley in Portugal. [Port. Hist.: *NCE*, 2194]

21. **Rhine valley** region of Germany that produces fine, natural wines. [Ger. Hist.: *NCE*, 2990]

22. **Riesling** grape grown in Germany and California, producing a dry or sweet white wine. [Ger. Hist.: Misc.]

23. **Rioja** Spain's most widely exported wine. [Span. Hist.: *NCE*, 2990]

24. **sherry** dry fortified wine, originally made from grapes grown in Andalusia, Spain. [Span. Hist.: *NCE*, 2501]

25. **Tokay** region of Hungary that produces natural wines. [Hung. Hist.: *NCE*, 2889]

26. **Valpolicella** a dark, rich red wine from Veneto. [Ital. Hist.: *NCE*, 2990]

27. **Vouvray** village in central France known for its medium-dry white wine. [Fr. Hist.: Misc.]

618. WINTER

1. **Boreas** the north wind; associated with winter. [Rom. Myth.: Hall, 130]

2. **crane** pictorial emblem in Buddhist tradition. [Animal Symbolism: Jobes, 378]

3. **Ded Moroz** personification of winter; "Grandfather Frost." [Russ. Folklore: Misc.]

4. **goat** zodiacally belongs to December; hence, winter. [Astrology: Hall, 139]

5. **Hiems** personification; portrayed as old and decrepit. [Rom. Myth.: *LLEI*, I: 322]

6. **Jack Frost** personification of winter. [Pop. Culture: Misc.]

7. **Old Man Winter** personification of winter. [Pop. Culture: Misc.]

8. **old man wrapped in cloak** personification of winter. [Art: Hall, 130]

9. **Persephone** the period of her stay (winter) with Hades. [Gk. Myth.: Espy, 28]

619. WISDOM (See also GENIUS.)

1. **Amenhotep** (fl. 14th century B.C.) pictured as bearded man holding papyrus roll. [Ancient Egypt. Art: Parrinder, 18]

2. **Athena** (Rom. **Minerva**) goddess of wisdom. [Gk. and Rom. Myth.: Brewer *Dictionary*, 713]

3. **Augustine, St.** (354–430) patron saint of scholars; voluminous theological author. [Christian Hagiog.: Brewster, 384–385]

4. **Balder** most beautiful, luminescent, and wise god. [Norse Myth.: Parrinder, 40]

5. **blue salvia** traditional symbol of wisdom; indicates mature judgment. [Flower Symbolism: *Flora Symbolica*, 177]

6. **Bodhi** knowledge by which one attains Nirvana. [Buddhism: Parrinder, 48]

7. **Bragi** god of wisdom, poetry, and eloquence. [Norse Myth: Parrinder, 50]

8. **Chiron** knowledgeable Centaur; instructed Achilles, Jason, and Asclepius. [Gk. Myth.: Parrinder, 62]

9. **Confucius** (551–479 B.C.) Chinese philosopher and writer. [Chinese Hist.: Parrinder, 65]

10. **Enki** god of wisdom; counterpart of Akkadian Ea. [Sumerian Myth.: Parrinder, 90]

11. **Fudo** Japanese god of wisdom. [Jap. Myth.: Leach, 427]

12. **Ganesha** god of wisdom. [Hindu Myth.: Leach, 440]

13. **gold** symbol of sagacity. [Color Symbolism: Jobes, 356]

14. **Hiawatha** "wise man"; legendary founder of Iroquois Confederacy. [Am. Hist.: Jameson, 229; Am. Lit.: "Hiawatha" in Benét, 466]

15. **Jerome, St.** Latin doctor of Church; preeminent biblical scholar. [Christian Hagiog.: Attwater, 185]

16. **Mimir** guardian of well of wit and wisdom. [Norse Myth.: Wheeler, 244]

17. **Odin** god; drank from fountain, became all-knowing. [Norse Myth.: Brewer *Dictionary*, 774]

18. **owl** associated with Athena, goddess of wisdom. [Gk. Myth.: Hall, 231]

19. **Nebo** god of sagacity; inventor of writing. [Babyl. Myth.: Brewer *Dictionary*, 749]

20. **Nestor** sage counselor and just king of Pylos. [Gk. Hist.: Wheeler, 257; Gk. Lit.: *Iliad*]

21. **Plato** (427–347 B.C.) Greek philosopher revered for wisdom. [Gk. Hist.: *NCE*, 2165]

22. **scroll** early form of manuscript; symbolic of learning. [Christian Symbolism: Appleton, 85]

23. **Socrates** (469–399 B.C.) wise and respected teacher adept at developing latent ideas. [Gk. Hist.: *EB*, 16: 1001–1005]

24. **Solomon** invested by God with unprecedented sagacity. [*O.T.:* *I Kings* 3:7–13; 4:29–34]

25. **tree of the knowledge of good and evil** eat of its fruit and know all. [*O.T.: Genesis* 2:9; 3:6]

26. **white mulberry** traditional symbol of wisdom. [Tree Symbolism: *Flora Symbolica*, 176]

620. WITCHCRAFT (See also ENCHANTMENT.)

1. **Alcina** Circelike spellmaker; defeated by good magic. [Br. Opera: Handel, *Alcina*, Westerman, 54–55]

2. **Baba Yaga** cannibalistic crone; stone-breasted companion of devil. [Russ. Folklore: Leach, 100]

3. **Brocken** Harz peak; rendezvous for the Sabbat on Walpurgis Night. [Ger. Folklore: Leach, 165]

4. **Broom Hilda** witch as cigar-smoking, love-starved crone. [Comics: Horn, 134]

5. **Circe** turns Odysseus's men into animals. [Gk. Myth.: *Odyssey*]

6. **Hecate** mysterious goddess of Hades; associated with sorcery. [Gk. Myth.: Howe, 115]

7. **Kundry** sorceress; ugly messenger of the Grail castle. [Ger. Legend: *Parzival;* Ger. Opera: *Parsifal*]

8. **Pamphile** applies ointment to change into eagle. [Rom. Lit.: *The Golden Ass*]

9. **Rosemary's baby** through witchcraft, child born with horns and tail. [Am. Lit.: *Rosemary's Baby*]

10. **Salem, Massachusetts** locale of frenzied assault on supposed witches (1692). [Am. Hist.: Jameson, 442; Am. Lit.: *The Crucible*]

11. **Samantha** good witch married to a mortal. [TV: "Bewitched" in Terrace, I, 94–95]

12. **Walpurgis Night** traditional German witches' sabbath. [Ger. Folklore: *NCE*, 2918]

13. **Weird Sisters** demon-women; predict Macbeth's fate. [Br. Lit.: *Macbeth*]

14. **Witch of Endor** conjures up Samuel for distressed Saul. [*O.T.: I Samuel* 28:3–25]

15. **Witches' Hammer** manual for recognizing telltale marks of witches (15th century). [Eur. Hist.: Brewer *Note-Book*, 952]

621. WITTINESS

1. **Bennet, Elizabeth** lively and clever character. [Br. Lit.: *Pride and Prejudice*]

2. **Boyet** "wit's pedler" and "an ape of form." [Br. Lit.: *Love's Labour's Lost*]

3. **Mercutio** clever, comic foil to Romeo. [Br. Lit.: *Romeo and Juliet*]

622. WONDERLAND (See also HEAVEN, PARADISE, UTOPIA.)

1. **Annwn** land of joy and beauty without disease or death. [Welsh Lit.: *Mabinogion*]

2. **Atlantis** fabulous and prosperous island; legendarily in Atlantic Ocean. [Gk. Myth.: Leach, 89]

3. **Avalon** island where dead King Arthur was carried. [Arth. Legend and Br. Lit.: *Le Morte d'Arthur; Idylls of the King; The Once and Future King*]

4. **Istakhar, mountains of** lair of Eblis; beautiful treasure land. [Br. Lit.: *Vathek*]

5. **Middle-earth** an old-fashioned name for "world": scene of J. R. R. Tolkien's fantasies. [Br. Lit.: *The Hobbit; The Lord of the Rings*]

6. **Munchkinland** domain of little people in Oz. [Am. Lit.: *The Wonderful Wizard of Oz*]

7. **Narnia** scene of fantasies by C. S. Lewis. [Br. Lit.: *Prince Caspian*]

8. **Never Never Land** magic land of lost boys and Indians. [Br. Lit.: *Peter Pan*]

9. **Oz** fabulous kingdom over the rainbow. [Am. Lit.: *The Wonderful Wizard of Oz*]

10. **Xanadu** site of Kubla Khan's "pleasure dome." [Br. Lit.: "Kubla Khan" in Benét, 555]

623. WRITINGS, SACRED

1. **Avesta** book of teachings of Zoroaster. [Zoroastrianism: Leach, 97]

2. **Bhagavad-Gita** part of *Mahabharata:* most important Hindu scripture. [Hindu Rel.: Parrinder, 43]

3. **Book of Mormon** supplementary bible of the Latter-Day Saints. [Am. Hist.: Payton, 455]

4. **Book of the Dead** instructions for the Art of Dying. [Ancient Egypt. Rel.: Parrinder, 49]

5. **Dead Sea Scrolls** papyrus scrolls containing texts of Old Testament, found in 1947. [Mid-East Hist.: *NCE*, 729]

6. **Eddas** bible of ancient Scandinavian religion; two separate collections. [Norse Lit.: Jobes, 490; Parrinder, 87]

7. **the Holy Bible** name used by Christians for their scriptures. [Christianity: *NCE*, 291]

8. **Koran (Quran)** the sacred book of Islam. [Islam: *NCE*, 1496]

9. **Mahabharata** long Sanskrit epic poem on theology and morals. [Indian Lit.: *Mahabharata*]

10. **Talmud** Jewish civil and religious law, including the Mishna. [Judaism: Payton, 661]

11. **the Vedas** oldest scriptures of Hinduism. [Hinduism: *NCE*, 2870]

X

624. **XENOPHOBIA**

1. **Boxer Rebellion** Chinese rising aimed at ousting foreign interlopers (1900). [Chinese Hist.: Van Doren, 334–335]

2. **the Hermit Kingdom** Korea; so called for 300-year closed-door policy. [Am. Hist.: Van Doren, 286]

3. **House Un-American Activities Committee** conducted witch hunts to purge government of unwanted aliens. [Am. Hist.: *NCE*, 1641]

4. **Know-Nothing Party** aimed at WASP control of government by depriving naturalized Americans and Roman Catholics of political rights. [Am. Hist.: Payton, 371]

5. **McCarthyism** from U.S. Senator McCarthy who acted out morbid fear of aliens, especially Communists. [Am. Hist.: Payton, 409]

6. **New Orleans riots** anti-Italian mobs lynched 11 immigrants after Sicilian murder trial (1891). [Am. Hist.: Van Doren, 309]

7. **Sacco and Vanzetti** (Nicola, 1891–1927) (Bartolomeo, 1888–1927) Italian anarchists convicted in controversial murder trial (1921). [Am. Hist.: Van Doren, 411]

Y

625.   **YOUTH** (See also **CHILDREN.**)

1.   **Agni** Vedic light god; embodies eternal youth. [Vedic Myth.: *LLEI*, I: 322]

2.   **Freya** goddess of eternal youth. [Ger. Myth. and Opera: Wagner, *Rheingold*, Westerman, 232]

3.   **Hebe (Juventas)** goddess of the young. [Gk. and Rom. Myth.: Hall, 146]

4.   **primrose** symbol of early youth. [Flower Symbolism: *Flora Symbolica*, 176; Kunz, 327]

Z

626. ZANINESS

1. **Allen, Gracie** (1902–1964) actress who played scatterbrained wife of George Burns. [TV: "The George Burns and Gracie Allen Show" in Terrace, I, 303–304]

2. **Ball, Lucille** (1910–   ) American comedienne; "unchallenged queen of scatterbrains." [TV: "I Love Lucy" in Terrace, I, 383]

3. **Caesar, Sid** (1922–   ) pillar of zany fifties xomedy. [TV: "Your Show of Shows" in Terrace, II, 290–291]

4. **Harvard Lampoon** mocking, satirical periodical. [Am. Pop. Culture: Misc.]

5. **Hellzapoppin** Olsen and Johnson's "screamlined revue" described by one drama critic as a "demented vaudeville brawl." [Am.Theater: Misc.]

6. **the Keystone Kops** slapstick film comedians specializing in wild chases (1912–1920). [Am. Cinema: Halliwell, 399]

7. **Krazy Kat** tremendously zany, popular comic character that delighted Jazz Age intellectuals. [Comics: Payton, 372; "Krazy Kat" in Horn, 436]

8. **Mad Magazine** popular publication featuring zany approach to life. [Am. Pop. Culture: Misc.]

9. **Monty Python's Flying Circus** ingenious, satiric show that uses both live action and animation. [Br. and Am. TV: Terrace, II, 108]

10. **Sales, Soupy** (1926–   ) American entertainer; children's "funny man." [TV: "The Soupy Sales Show" in Terrace, II, 305]

11. **Skelton, Red** (1910–   ) comedian with zaniness personified in characters such as Freddie the Freeloader and Clem Kaddiddlehopper. [TV: "The Red Skelton Show" in Terrace, II, 238]

12. **the Three Stooges** (Moe Howard, 1897–1975) (Shemp Howard, 1895–1955) (Larry Fine, 1902–1975) masters of slapstick in the extreme. [TV: Terrace, II, 366]

627. ZEAL

1. **Bows, Mr.** crippled fiddler with intense feelings. [Br. Lit.: *Pendennis*]

2. **Cedric of Rotherwood** zealous about restoring Saxon independence. [Br. Lit.: *Ivanhoe*]

3. **Faustus, Doctor** zealous for universal knowledge; sells soul to Lucifer. [Medieval Legend and Ger. Lit.: *Faust;* Br. Lit.: *Doctor Faustus*]

4. **flaming heart** attribute of St. Augustine; symbol of religious fervor. [Art: Hall, 123]

5. **Merridew, Jack** boy with lust for authority and killing. [Brit. Lit.: *Lord of the Flies*]

6. **Olsen, Jimmy** eager-beaver cub reporter and Superman's friend. [Comics: "Superman" in Horn, 341]

7. **Palace Guard** term used in alluding to Richard Nixon's zealous, ardent staff, with reference to Watergate and cover-up. [Am. Pop. Culture: Misc.]

8. **white dittany** traditional symbol of zeal. [Flower Symbolism: *Flora Symbolica,* 173]

628. ZODIAC

1. **Aquarius** water-bearer (Jan. 20–Feb. 18). [Astrology: Hall, 314]

2. **Aries** ram (Mar. 21–Apr. 19). [Astrology: Hall, 314]

3. **Cancer** crab (June 21–July 22). [Astrology: Hall, 314]

4. **Capricorn** goat (Dec. 22–Jan. 19). [Astrology: Hall, 315]

5. **Gemini** twins (May 21–June 20). [Astrology: Hall, 314]

6. **Leo** lion (July 23–Aug. 22). [Astrology: Hall, 315]

7. **Libra** balance (Sept. 23–Oct. 22). [Astrology: Hall, 315]

8. **Pisces** fishes (Feb. 19–Mar. 20). [Astrology: Hall, 314]

9. **Sagittarius** archer (Nov. 22–Dec. 21). [Astrology: Hall, 315]

10. **Scorpio** scorpion (Oct. 23–Nov. 21). [Astrology: Hall, 315]

11. **Taurus** bull (Apr. 20–May 20). [Astrology: Hall, 314]

12. **Virgo** virgin (Aug. 23–Sept. 22). [Astrology: Hall, 315]

397

Bibliography

The Abbot
Scott, Sir Walter. *The Abbot*. Dutton, 1969.

Absalom and Achitophel
Dryden, John. *Absalom and Achitophel,* ed. James and Helen Kinsley. Oxford U.P., 1961.

The Absentee
Edgeworth, Maria. *The Absentee* in *Castle Rackrent*. Dutton, 1960.

Ackerman
Ackerman, A.S.E. *Popular Fallacies*. Gale, 1970.

Adam Bede
Eliot, George. *Adam Bede*. Washington Square Press, 1971.

The Admirable Crichton
Barrie, James M. *The Admirable Crichton* in *English Drama in Transition, 1880–1920,* ed. Henry F. Salerno. Pegasus, 1968.

Adonais
Shelley, Percy B. *Adonais, an Elegy on the Death of John Keats,* ed. Thomas J. Wise. AMS Press, 1886.

The Adventures of Augie March
Bellow, Saul. *The Adventures of Augie March*. Fawcett World, 1973.

The Adventures of Pinocchio
Collodi, Carlo. *The Adventures of Pinocchio*. Macmillan, 1972.

The Adventures of the Little Wooden Horse
Williams, Ursala. *The Adventures of the Little Wooden Horse*. Penguin, 1975.

Aeneid
Vergil. *Aeneid,* 2nd edition, tr. and ed. Frank Copley. Bobbs-Merrill, 1975.

Aesop's Fables
Aesop. *Aesop's Fables,* tr. Samuel Croxall and Roger L'Estrange. Brownlow, 1969.

Against The Grain
Huysmans, Joris Karl. *Against the Grain*. Dover, 1969.

The Age of Innocence
Wharton, Edith. *The Age of Innocence*. Scribner, 1968.

Ah Sin
Harte, Bret, and Mark Twain. *Ah Sin* in *The Complete Works of Bret Harte*. Chatto and Windus, 1880–1912.

Alastor
Shelley, Percy B. *Alastor: Or the Spirit of Solitude, and Other Poems.* ed. Bertram Dobell. AMS Press, n.d.

Alcestis
Euripides. *Alcestis,* tr. William Arrowsmith. Oxford U.P., 1915.

The Alchemist
Jonson, Ben. *The Alchemist*. Hill and Wang, 1966.

Alice's Adventures in Wonderland
Carroll, Lewis. *Alice's Adventures in Wonderland*. Viking Press, 1975.

Alive
Read, Piers P. *Alive*. Avon, 1975.

L'Allegro
Milton, John. "L'Allegro" in *L'Allegro and Il Penseroso*. Southwest Book Services, 1976.

Allen
Allen, Frederick Lewis. *Only Yesterday*. Bantam, 1959.

All for Love
Dryden, John. *All for Love,* ed. John J. Enck. Crofts, 1966.

All Quiet on the Western Front
Remarque, Erich Maria. *All Quiet on the Western Front*. Fawcett World, 1969.

All the King's Men
Warren, Robert Penn. *All the King's Men*. Random House, 1960.

All's Well That Ends Well
Shakespeare, William. *All's Well that Ends Well,* ed. G. K. Hunter. Barnes & Noble, 1966.

Almayer's Folly
Conrad, Joseph. *Almayer's Folly*. Bentley, 1971.

Amadis de Gaul
Amadis de Gaul, tr. Edwin Place and Herbert Behm. Univ. Press of Kentucky, 1974.

Ambrosio
Lewis, Matthew G. *Ambrosio, or The Monk*. Avon, 1975.

Amelia
Fielding, Henry. *Amelia*. Dutton, 1978.

The American
James, Henry. *The American*, ed. Joseph Beach and Quentin Anderson. Holt, Rinehart, and Winston, 1949.

The American Dream
Albee, Edward. *The American Dream*. Coward, 1961.

The American Scene
James, Henry. *The American Scene*. Indiana U.P., 1968.

Amory
Amory, Cleveland, ed. *International Celebrity Register*. Celebrity Register Ltd., 1959.

Amphitryon
Dryden, John. *Amphitryon* in *The Dramatic Works*, ed. M. Summers. 6 vols. Gordian, 1968.

Amphitryon
Molière, Jean B. *Amphitryon*, tr. Oscar Mandel. Spectrum, 1977.

Amphitryon
Plautus. *Amphitryon: Three Plays in New Verse Translation*. Univ. of North Carolina Press, 1974.

Amphitryon 38
Giraudoux, Jean. *Amphitryon 38* in *Giraudoux: Three Plays*, tr. La Farge and Judd. Hill and Wang, 1964.

Anatole
Titus, Eve. *Anatole*. McGraw-Hill, 1956.

Anatomy of Melancholy
Burton, Robert. *Anatomy of Melancholy*. R. West, 1923.

Andersen's Fairy Tales
Andersen, Hans Christian. *Andersen's Fairy Tales*. Macmillan, 1963.

Androcles and the Lion
Shaw, George Bernard. *Androcles and the Lion*. Penguin, 1951.

Andromache
Euripides. *Andromache*, ed. P.T. Stevens. Oxford U.P., 1971.

Andromaque
Racine, Jean B. *Andromaque*, ed. Philip Koch. Prentice-Hall, 1969.

Animal Farm
Orwell, George. *Animal Farm*. Harcourt, 1954.

Anna Karenina
Tolstoy, Leo. *Anna Karenina*. Bantam, 1977.

Annals
Tacitus. *Annals*, ed. F.R. Goodyear. Cambridge U.P., 1972.

Annals of the Parish
Galt, John. *Annals of the Parish: Or the Chronicles of Dalmailing During the Ministry of Reverend Micah Balwhidder Written by Himself*, ed. James Kinsley. Oxford U.P., 1967.

Anne Frank
Frank, Anne. *Anne Frank: Diary of a Young Girl*. Doubleday, 1967.

Anne of Green Gables
Montgomery, L.M. *Anne of Green Gables*. Bantam, 1976.

Ant and Bee
Banner, Angela. *Ant and Bee*. Franklin Watts, 1958.

Anthony Adverse
Allen, Hervey. *Anthony Adverse*. Holt, 1958.

Antigone
Anouilh, Jean. *Antigone*. Larousse, 1966.

Antigone
Sophocles. *Antigone*, tr. Richard Braun. Oxford U.P., 1973.

The Antiquary
Scott, Sir Walter. *The Antiquary*. Dutton, 1955.

Antony and Cleopatra
Shakespeare, William. *Antony and Cleopatra*, ed. C.J. Gianakaris. William C. Brown, 1969.

Apocrypha
Apocrypha. *New English Bible*. Oxford U.P., 1970.

Appleton
Appleton, Leroy, and Stephen Bridges. *Symbolism in Liturgical Art.* Scribner, 1959.

Appointment in Samarra
O'Hara, John. *Appointment in Samarra.* Popular Library, 1976.

Arabel's Raven
Aiken, Joan. *Arabel's Raven.* Dell, 1975.

Arabian Nights
Book of a Thousand Nights and One Night, tr. Powys Mathers. St. Martin's Press, 1972.

La Arcadia
de Vega, Lope. *La Arcadia,* ed. E.S. Morby. Castalia, c. 1975.

Arcadia
Greene, Robert. *Arcadia* in *The Life and Complete Works in Prose and Verse of Robert Greene.* Printed for private circulation, 1881–86.

Arcadia
Sannazaro, Jacopo. *Arcadia and Piscatorial Eclogues,* tr. Ralph Nash. Wayne State U.P., 1966.

Arcadia
Sidney, Philip. *Arcadia.* Penguin, 1977.

archy and mehitabel
Marquis, Don. *archy and mehitabel.* Doubleday, 1970.

The Ark
Benary-Isbert, Margot. *The Ark.* Harcourt, 1953.

Arms and the Man
Shaw, George Bernard. *Arms and the Man.* Bantam, 1968.

Around the World in Eighty Days
Verne, Jules. *Around the World in Eighty Days.* Oxford U.P., 1959.

Arrowsmith
Lewis, Sinclair. *Arrowsmith.* Harcourt, 1949.

Ars Poetica
Horace. *Ars Poetica* in *Collected Works of Horace,* tr. Dunsany and Oakley. Dutton, 1961.

Arthur Mervyn
Brown, Charles Brockton. *Arthur Mervyn,* ed. W. Bertho ff. Holt, 1966.

Ash Wednesday
Eliot, T.S. *Ash Wednesday* in *The Complete Poetry and Plays, 1909–1950.* Harcourt, 1952.

As I Lay Dying
Faulkner, William. *As I Lay Dying.* Random House, 1964.

L'Assommoir
Zola, Emile. *L'Assommoir.* Penguin, 1970.

As You Like It
Shakespeare, William. *As You Like It,* ed. Agnes Latham. Barnes & Noble, 1975.

Atala
de Chateaubriand, René. *Atala.* Prentice-Hall, 1965.

Atalanta
Swinburne, A.C. *Atalanta in Calydon.* Scholarly Press, reprint of 1923 ed.

The Atheist's Tragedy
Tourneur, Cyril. *The Atheist's Tragedy,* ed. Brian Morris and Roma Gill. Norton, 1976.

Atlas Shrugged
Rand, Ayn. *Atlas Shrugged.* New American Library, 1970.

Attwater
Attwater, Donald. *Penguin Dictionary of Saints.* Penguin, 1965.

Aucassin and Nicolette
Aucassin and Nicolette & Other Medieval Romances & Legends, ed. Eugene Mason. Dutton, 1958.

Auden
Replogle, Justin. *Auden's Poetry.* Univ. of Washington Press, 1971.

Avery
Avery, Catherine B. *The New Century Handbook of Greek Mythology and Legend.* Appleton-Century-Crofts, 1972.

The Awkward Age
James, Henry. *The Awkward Age.* Penguin, 1974.

Babbitt
Lewis, Sinclair. *Babbitt.* Harcourt, 1949.

Bailey

Bailey, Nathaniel. *Universal Etymological English Dictionary.* Alfred Adler Institute, 1969.

Balchin

Balchin, Nigel. "Guy Fawkes" in *British History Illustrated*, October 1975, pp. 2–13.

Ballet Shoes

Streatfeild, Noel. *Ballet Shoes.* Random House, 1950.

Balthazar B

Donleavy, J.P. *The Beastly Beatitudes of Balthazar B.* Dell, 1968.

Bambi

Salten, Felix. *Bambi.* Grosset and Dunlap, 1969.

Barabbas

Lagerkvist, Pär. *Barabbas.* Bantam, 1968.

The Barber of Seville

Beaumarchais, Pierre A. *The Barber of Seville*, tr. B.P. Ellis. AHM, 1966.

Baring-Gould

Baring-Gould, William S., and Ceil Baring-Gould. *The Annotated Mother Goose.* Bramhall House, 1962.

Barnaby Rudge

Dickens, Charles. *Barnaby Rudge.* Dutton, 1972.

Barnhart

New Century Handbook of English Literature, ed. Clarence Barnhart. Appleton-Century-Crofts, 1967.

Baron Münchhausen

Baron Münchhausen: Fifteen Truly Tall Tales. Retold by Doris Orgel. Addison Wesley, 1971.

Baron Münchhausen's Narrative

Raspe, Rudolph Erich. *Baron Münchhausen's Narrative.* Brentano's, 1907.

Barren Ground

Glasgow, Ellen. *Barren Ground.* Hill and Wang, 1957.

Barry Lyndon

Thackeray, William Makepeace. *Memoirs of Barry Lyndon, Esq.* Univ. of Nebraska Press, 1962.

Bartleby

Melville, Herman. "Bartleby the Scrivener" in *Complete Works*, ed. Howard Vincent. Hendricks House, 1947.

Bartlett

Bartlett's Familiar Quotations, 14th ed., revised E.M. Beck. Little, Brown, 1968.

Baxter

Baxter, John. *Sixty Years of Hollywood.* A.S. Barnes, 1973.

Baydo

Baydo, A. *Topical History of the United States.* Prentice-Hall, 1974.

A Bear Called Paddington

Bond, Michael. *A Bear Called Paddington.* Dell, 1968.

Beau James

Fowler, Gene. *Beau James.* Viking Press, 1949.

The Beauties of English Poesy

Goldsmith, Oliver. *The Beauties of English Poesy.* W. Griffin, 1767.

The Beaux' Stratagem

Farquhar, George. *The Beaux' Stratagem.* British Book Centre, 1975.

Beggar on Horseback

Kaufmann, George, and Marc Connelly. *Beggar on Horseback.* Scholarly Press, 1925.

Beggar's Opera

Gay, John. *The Beggar's Opera*, ed. Peter Lewis. Barnes & Noble, 1973.

Bel Ami

de Maupassant, Guy. *Bel Ami*, tr. Douglas Parmee. Penguin, 1975.

A Bell for Adano

Hersey, John. *A Bell for Adano.* Bantam, 1970.

Benét

The Reader's Encyclopedia, 2nd edition. William Rose Benét. Thomas Y. Crowell, 1965.

Benito Cereno

Melville, Herman. *Benito Cereno* in *Eight Short Novels*, ed. Dean Flower. Fawcett World, 1970.

Benvenuto Cellini

Cellini, Benvenuto. *The Autobiography of Benvenuto Cellini*, tr. John Symonds. Doubleday, 1960.

Benya Krik, the Gangster
Babel, Isaac. *Benya Krik, the Gangster and Other Stories,* ed. Avrahm Yarmolinsky. Schocken Books, 1969.

Beowulf
Beowulf, tr. Burton Raffel. New American Library, 1963.

The Bermuda Triangle
Berlitz, Charles. *The Bermuda Triangle.* Avon, 1977.

Bettelheim
Bettelheim, Bruno. *The Uses of Enchantment.* Vintage Books, 1977.

Bevis of Hampton
Unknown. *Bevis of Hampton.* Penguin, 1974.

The Big Sky
Guthrie, A.B., Jr. *The Big Sky.* Bantam, 1972.

The Big Sleep
Chandler, Raymond. *The Big Sleep.* Random House, 1976.

Billy Budd
Melville, Herman. *Billy Budd.* Doubleday, 1970.

Binder
Binder, Pearl. *Magic Symbols of the World.* Hamlyn, 1972.

Birds
Aristophanes. *Birds.* Chandler, 1968.

Birth of Tragedy
Nietzsche, Friedrich. *The Birth of Tragedy,* tr. Francis Golffing. Doubleday, 1956.

Bishop
Bishop, Morris. *The Horizon Book of the Middle Ages,* ed. Norman Kotker, et al. American Heritage, 1968.

Black Beauty
Sewell, Anna. *Black Beauty.* Macmillan, 1962.

The Black Cauldron
Alexander, Lloyd. *The Black Cauldron.* Dell, 1969.

Black Oxen
Atherton, Gertrude. *Black Oxen.* Folcroft Library, 1923.

Blanchard
Blanchard, R. H. *Handbook of Egyptian Gods and Mummy Amulets.* Attic Books, 1974.

Bleak House
Dickens, Charles. *Bleak House.* Holt, 1970.

Blue Willow
Gates, Doris. *Blue Willow.* Viking Press, 1969.

Blunt
Blunt, Rev. John Henry. *Dictionary of Sects, Heresies, Ecclesiastical Parties, and Schools of Religious Thought.* Gale, 1974.

The Blythedale Romance
Hawthorne, Nathaniel. *The Blythedale Romance* in *Works,* vol. 5. Houghton Mifflin, 1882–91.

Bobbsey Twins
Hope, Laura Lee. *Bobbsey Twins' Mystery at Meadowbrook.* Grosset and Dunlap, 1963.

Boland
Boland, Bridget. *Gardener's Magic and Other Old Wives' Lore.* Farrar, 1977.

Bold Stroke for a Wife
Centlivre, Susannah. *Bold Stroke for a Wife,* ed. Thalia Stathas. Univ. of Nebraska Press, 1968.

Bombaugh
Bombaugh, Charles C. *Gleanings for the Curious from the Harvest Fields of Literature.* Gale, 1970.

Bombaugh *Facts*
Bombaugh, Charles C. *Facts and Fancies for the Curious.* Gale, 1968.

The Book of Three
Alexander, Lloyd. *The Book of Three.* Holt, 1964.

Boris Godunov
Pushkin, Alexandre. *Boris Godunov,* tr. Philip Barbour. Greenwood Press, 1976.

The Borrowers
Norton, Mary. *The Borrowers.* Harcourt, 1965.

The Bostonians
James, Henry. *The Bostonians.* Penguin, 1974.

Le Bourgeois Gentilhomme
Molière, Jean P. *Le Bourgeois Gentilhomme* in *Oeuvres Complètes.* Gallimard, 1971.

Brand
Ibsen, Henrik. *Brand*. Dutton, 1959.

Brave New World
Huxley, Aldous. *Brave New World*. Harper & Row, 1969.

Bray
Bray, Frank Chapin. *Bray's University Dictionary of Mythology*. Apollo Editions, 1964.

Bread and Wine
Silone, Ignazio. *Bread and Wine*. Harper, 1937.

Breakfast of Champions
Vonnegut, Kurt. *Breakfast of Champions*. Dell, 1974.

Brewer Dictionary
Brewer, E. Cobham. *Brewer's Dictionary of Phrase and Fable*, ed. Ivor H. Evans. Harper, 1971.

Brewer Handbook
Brewer, E. Cobham. *The Reader's Handbook*. Gale, 1966.

Brewer Miracles
Brewer, E. Cobham. *A Dictionary of Miracles*. Gale, 1966.

Brewer Note-Book
Brewer, E. Cobham. *The Historic Note-Book*. Gale, 1966.

Brewton
Brewton, John E. and Sara W. *Index to Children's Poetry*. H.W. Wilson, 1965.

Brewster
Brewster, H. Pomeroy. *Saints and Festivals of the Christian Church*. Gale, 1974.

The Bride of Lammermoor
Scott, Sir Walter. *The Bride of Lammermoor*. Dutton, 1972.

The Bridge of San Luis Rey
Wilder, Thornton. *The Bridge of San Luis Rey*. Harper, 1967.

The Bridge Over the River Kwai
Boulle, Pierre. *The Bridge Over the River Kwai*. Bantam, 1970.

Brief Lives
Aubrey, John. *Brief Lives or Minutes of Lives*, ed. Edward G. McGehee. Oxford U.P., 1972.

Briggs
Briggs, Katherine. *An Encyclopedia of Fairies: Hobgoblins, Brownies, Bogies and Other Supernatural Creatures*. Pantheon, 1977.

The Broken Heart
Ford, John. *The Broken Heart*, ed. Brian Morris. Hill and Wang, 1966.

The Bronze Bow
Speare, Elizabeth. *The Bronze Bow*. Houghton Mifflin, 1972.

Brothers Ashkenazi
Singer, Israel Joshua. *The Brothers Ashkenazi*. Knopf, 1936.

The Brothers Karamazov
Dostoevski, Fyodor. *The Brothers Karamazov*. Bantam, 1971.

Browne
Browne, Ray B., and Marshall Fishwick, eds. *Icons of America*. Popular Press, 1978.

Bulfinch
Bulfinch, Thomas. *Age of Fable*. Dutton, 1969.

Bungalow Mystery
Keene, Carolyn. *The Bungalow Mystery*. Grosset and Dunlap, 1930.

Bussy D'Ambois
Chapman, George. *Bussy D'Ambois*, ed. Maurice Evans. Hill and Wang, 1966.

Buxton
Buxton, Frank, and Bill Owen. *The Big Broadcast: 1920–1950*. Avon, 1973.

By Love Possessed
Cozzens, James Gould. *By Love Possessed*. Fawcett World, 1973.

By the Pricking of My Thumbs
Christie, Agatha. *By the Pricking of My Thumbs*. Pocket Books, 1975.

The Cabala
Wilder, Thornton. *The Cabala*. Avon, 1975.

Cain
Byron, George. *Cain in Byron: Poetical Works*, ed. Frederick Page and John Jump. Oxford U.P., 1970.

Callista
Newman, John H. *Loss and Gain: The Story of a Convert, 1848,* ed. Robert L. Wolff. Garland, 1975.

Call of the Wild
London, Jack. *The Call of the Wild.* AMSCO School Publications, 1969.

Camille
Dumas, Alexandre, fils. *Camille,* tr. Matilde Heron. Books for Libraries, 1976.

Campbell *Creative*
Campbell, Joseph. *The Masks of God: Creative Mythology.* Viking Press, 1968.

Campbell *Encyclopedia*
Campbell, Oscar J. *A Shakespeare Encyclopedia.* Methuen, 1966.

Campbell *Hero*
Campbell, Joseph. *Hero With a Thousand Faces.* Princeton U.P., 1968.

Campbell *Occidental*
Campbell, Joseph. *The Masks of God: Occidental Mythology.* Viking Press, 1964.

Campbell *Oriental*
Campbell, Joseph. *The Masks of God: Oriental Mythology.* Viking Press, 1962.

Campbell *Primitive*
Campbell, Joseph. *The Masks of God: Primitive Mythology.* Viking Press, 1959.

Candida
Shaw, George Bernard. *Candida.* Penguin, 1974.

Candide
Voltaire. *Candide,* ed. G.R. Havens. Holt, 1969.

Cannery Row
Steinbeck, John. *Cannery Row.* Viking Press, 1945.

Canterbury Tales
Chaucer, Geoffrey. *The Canterbury Tales,* tr. David Wright. Random House, 1965.

Captain Brassbound's Conversion
Shaw, George Bernard. *Captain Brassbound's Conversion* in *Four Plays by Shaw.* Dell, 1957.

Captain Hatteras
Verne, Jules. *At the North Pole: The Adventures of Captain Hatteras.* Aeonian Press, 1976.

Captain Horatio Hornblower
Forester, C.S. *Captain Horatio Hornblower.* Little, Brown, 1939.

Captain Singleton
Defoe, Daniel. *Captain Singleton: The Life, Adventures & Pyracies of the Famous Captain Singleton.* Oxford U.P., 1973.

Carmen
Mérimée, Prosper. *Carmen,* ed. Pierre de Beaumont. Odyssey, 1969.

Cartwell
Cartwell, Van H., and Charles Grayson. *The Golden Argosy.* Dial, 1955.

Carved Lions
Molesworth, Mary. *The Carved Lions.* Dutton, 1964.

Case
Case, Brian, and Stan Britt. *The Illustrated Encyclopedia of Jazz.* Harmony, 1978.

Cashel Byron's Profession
Shaw, George Bernard. *Cashel Byron's Profession,* ed. Stanley Weintraub. Southern Illinois U.P., 1968.

Cass Timberlane
Lewis, Sinclair. *Cass Timberlane.* Random House, 1945.

The Castle
Kafka, Franz. *The Castle.* Random House, 1974.

Castle of Llyr
Alexander, Lloyd. *Castle of Llyr.* Holt, 1966.

The Catcher in the Rye
Salinger, J.D. *The Catcher in the Rye.* Bantam, 1970.

Catch-22
Heller, Joseph. *Catch-22.* Simon and Schuster, 1961.

Cat on a Hot Tin Roof
Williams, Tennessee. *Cat on a Hot Tin Roof.* New Directions, 1975.

Caught in the Web of Words
Murray, K.M. *Caught in the Web of Words.* Yale U.P., 1977.

The Caxtons
Bulwer-Lytton, Edward. *The Caxtons: A Family Picture.* Scholarly Press, 1971.

The Celebrated Jumping Frog of Calaveras County
Twain, Mark. *The Celebrated Jumping Frog of Calaveras County.* Gregg, 1969.

Celestina
De Rojas, Fernando. *Celestina.* Dutton, 1959.

The Cenci
Shelley, Percy B. *The Cenci,* ed. Roland A. Duerksen. Bobbs-Merrill, 1970.

Century Classical
New Century Classical Handbook, ed. C.B. Avery and J. Johnson. Appleton-Century-Crofts, 1962.

Century Cyclopedia
New Century Cyclopedia of Names, ed. Clarence L. Barnhart and William D. Halsey. Appleton-Century-Crofts, 1954.

Century English
Barnhart, Clarence L. *New Century Handbook of English Literature,* rev. ed. Appleton-Century-Crofts, 1967.

Chambers
Chambers, Robert. *The Book of Days.* Gale, 1967.

Charlotte's Web
White, E.B. *Charlotte's Web.* Harper, 1952.

Cheaper By the Dozen
Gilbreth, Frank, and Ernestine Carey. *Cheaper By the Dozen.* Crowell, 1963.

Child
Child, Heather, and Dorothy Colles. *Christian Symbols: Ancient and Modern.* Scribner, 1971.

Childe Ballads
Traditional Tunes of the Childe Ballads, ed. Bertrand H. Bronson. 4 vols. Princeton U.P., 1959 (Vol. 1), 1962 (Vol. 2), 1966 (Vol. 3), 1972 (Vol. 4).

Children of Green Knowe
Boston, Lucy M. *The Children of Green Knowe.* Harcourt, 1967.

A Child's Christmas in Wales
Thomas, Dylan. *A Child's Christmas in Wales.* New Directions, 1959.

Chitty-Chitty-Bang-Bang
Fleming, Ian. *Chitty-Chitty-Bang-Bang.* Random House, 1964.

A Christmas Carol
Dickens, Charles. *A Christmas Carol.* Dutton, 1972.

Christmas Stories
Dickens, Charles. *Christmas Stories* in *New Oxford Illustrated Dickens.* Oxford U.P., 1956.

Cinderella
Perrault, Charles. *Cinderella.* Henry Walck, 1971.

Cinq-Mars
de Vigny, Alfred. *Cinq-Mars; or, a Conspiracy under Louis XIII.* Howard Fertig, 1978.

Cirlot
Cirlot, J.E. *Dictionary of Symbols,* 2nd ed. Philosophical Library, 1972.

Citizen of the World
Goldsmith, Oliver. *Citizen of the World.* Dutton, Everyman, n.d.

The City and the Pillar
Vidal, Gore. *The City and the Pillar.* Dutton, 1965.

Clockwork Orange
Burgess, Anthony. *A Clockwork Orange.* Ballantine, 1976.

The Clouds
Aristophanes. *The Clouds,* ed. William Arrowsmith. New American Library, 1970.

Clue in the Embers
Dixon, Franklin W. *The Clue in the Embers.* Grosset and Dunlap, 1956.

A Cold Wind Blowing
Willard, Barbara. *A Cold Wind Blowing.* Dutton, 1973.

Colomba
Mérimée, Prosper. *Colomba.* French and European Pubn., 1963.

Colonel Sheperton's Clock
Turner, Philip. *Colonel Sheperton's Clock.* Collins, 1966.

Comedy of Errors
Shakespeare, William. *The Comedy of Errors*, ed. R.A. Foakes. Barnes & Noble, 1968.

Common Sense
Paine, Thomas. *Common Sense*. Penguin, 1976.

Communist Manifesto
Marx, Karl, and Friedrich Engels. *The Communist Manifesto*. Penguin, 1968.

The Compleat Angler
Walton, Izaak. *The Compleat Angler*. Dutton, Everyman, n.d.

Confessions
De Quincey, Thomas. *Confessions of an English Opium Eater*. New American Library, 1966.

Coningsby
Disraeli, Benjamin. *Coningsby: or The New Generation*. Scholarly Press, 1976.

A Connecticut Yankee in King Arthur's Court
Twain, Mark. *A Connecticut Yankee in King Arthur's Court*. Harper & Row, n.d.

The Conquest of Granada
Dryden, John. *The Conquest of Granada, or Almanzor and Almahide* in *Dryden: Three Plays*, ed. George Saintsbury. Hill and Wang, 1957.

Coriolanus
Shakespeare, William. *Coriolanus*, ed. B.H. Kemball-Cook. Oxford U.P., 1954.

Corpus Delicti
Herman, Linda, and Beth Stiel. *Corpus Delicti of Mystery Fiction*. Scarecrow Press, 1974.

Corsican Brothers
Dumas, Alexandre, père. *The Corsican Brothers*. Methuen, 1904.

Corson
Corson, Hiram. *Index of Proper Names and Subjects to Chaucer's Canterbury Tales*. Folcroft Library Editions, 1973.

Cott
Cott, Ted. *Victor Book of Musical Fun*. Simon and Schuster, 1945.

The Count of Monte-Cristo
Dumas, Alexandre, père. *The Count of Monte-Cristo*. Hart, 1975.

Cousin Pons
Balzac, Honoré de. *Cousin Pons*. French and European Pubn., 1962.

Cranford
Gaskell, Elizabeth. *Cranford*, ed. Elizabeth P. Watson. Oxford U.P., 1972.

Cricket on the Hearth
Dickens, Charles. *Cricket on the Hearth*. Frederick Warne, 1956.

Crime and Punishment
Dostoyevsky, Fyodor. *Crime and Punishment*. tr. Constance Garnett. Random House, Vintage, 1955.

Critique of Hegel's "Philosophy of Right"
Marx, Karl. *Critique of Hegel's "Philosophy of Right,"* ed. J. O'Malley. Cambridge U.P., 1970.

Crowley
Crowley, Ellen T. *Acronyms, Initialisms, and Abbreviations Dictionary*, 5th ed. Gale, 1976; annual supplements.

Crowley Trade
Crowley, Ellen. *Trade Names Dictionary*. Gale, 1974.

The Crucible
Miller, Arthur. *The Crucible: Text & Criticism*, ed. Gerald Weales. Viking Press, 1971.

Cry, The Beloved Country
Paton, Alan. *Cry, The Beloved Country*. Scribner, 1948.

Curious George
Rey, Hans A. *Curious George*. Houghton Mifflin, 1951.

Cyclops
Cyclops in *Euripides; The Complete Greek Tragedies*, ed. D. Grene and R. Lattimore, vol. 3. Univ. of Chicago Press, 1955 ND59.

Cymbeline
Shakespeare, William. *Cymbeline*. Oxford U.P., 1972.

Cyrano
Rostand, Edmond. *Cyrano de Bergerac*, tr. Anthony Burgess. Knopf, 1971.

Daisy Miller
James, Henry. *Daisy Miller and Other Stories*. Airmont, 1968.

La Dame aux Camélias
Dumas, Alexandre, fils. *La Dame aux Camélias*. French and European Pubn., 1955.

A Damsel in Distress.
Wodehouse, P.G. *A Damsel in Distress*. British Book Centre, 1956.

Daniel
Daniel, Howard. *Encyclopaedia of Themes and Subjects in Painting*. Thames and Hudson, 1971.

Darrel of the Blessed Isles
Bacheller, Irving A. *Darrel of the Blessed Isles*. Grosset, 1903.

Davenport
Davenport, Adams W. *Dictionary of English Literature*. Gale, 1966.

David Copperfield
Dickens, Charles. *David Copperfield*. Dutton, 1953.

Davidson
Davidson, H.R. Ellis. *Gods and Myths of Northern Europe*. Penguin, 1964.

Dawson
Dawson, Lawrence H. *Nicknames and Pseudonyms*. Gale, 1974.

The Day They Shook the Plum Tree
Lewis, Arthur H. *The Day They Shook the Plum Tree*. Pocket Books, 1975.

Dead Souls
Gogol, Nikolai. *Dead Souls*. tr. Andrew MacAndrew. New American Library, Signet, 1961.

Death in the Afternoon
Hemingway, Ernest. *Death in the Afternoon*. Scribner, 1932.

Death in Venice
Mann, Thomas. *Death in Venice*. Knopf, 1965.

Death of a Salesman
Miller, Arthur. *Death of a Salesman*. Viking Press, 1967.

de Bles
de Bles, Arthur. *How to Distinguish the Saints in Art*. Art Culture Pubn., 1925.

Decameron
Boccaccio, Giovanni. *The Decameron*, tr. G.H. McWilliam. Penguin, 1972.

The Deerslayer
Cooper, James Fenimore. *The Deerslayer*. Macmillan, 1962.

de Mille
de Mille, Agnes. *The Book of the Dance*. Golden Press, 1963.

de Purucker
de Purucker, G. *Occult Glossary*. Theosophical U.P., 1956.

Desire Under the Elms
O'Neill, Eugene. *Desire Under the Elms* in *Three Plays*. Random House, 1959.

Dictionary of Facts
The Standard Dictionary of Facts. Frontier Press, 1924.

Disney Films
Maltin, Leonard. *The Disney Films*. Bonanza Books, 1973.

Divine Comedy
Dante Alighieri. *The Divine Comedy*. Random House, 1955.

Dr. Breen's Practice
Howells, William D. *Doctor Breen's Practice*. Scholarly Press, 1970.

Doctor Faustus
Mann, Thomas. *Doctor Faustus*. Knopf, 1948.

Doctor Faustus
Marlowe, Christopher. *Doctor Faustus*. New American Library, 1969.

Doctor Syntax
Hamilton, Harlan W. *Dr. Syntax*. Kent State U.P., 1969.

Doctor Thorne
Trollope, Anthony. *Doctor Thorne*. Harcourt, 1962.

Dodsworth
Lewis, Sinclair. *Dodsworth*. New American Library, 1971.

A Doll's House
Ibsen, Henrik. *A Doll's House*. Dutton, 1954.

Dombey and Son
Dickens, Charles. *Dombey and Son*. Penguin, 1975.

Dominic
Steig, William. *Dominic*. Farrar, 1972.

Don Carlos
Schiller, Friedrich. *Don Carlos,* tr. Charles E. Passage. Ungar, 1959.

Don Juan Tenorio
Zorilla y Moral, José. *Don Juan Tenorio,* ed. Nicholson B. Adams. Prentice-Hall, 1971.

Don Quixote
Cervantes, Miguel de. *Don Quixote.* Airmont, 1967.

Don Segundo Sombra
Guiraldes, Ricardo. *Don Segundo Sombra,* tr. Angela B. Dellepiane. Prentice-Hall, 1971.

The Double-Dealer
Congreve, William. *The Double-Dealer.* British Book Centre, 1974.

Down to Earth
Wrightson, Patricia. *Down to Earth.* Harcourt, 1965.

Dr. Doolittle
Lofting, Hugh. *The Story of Dr. Doolittle.* Lippincott, 1920.

Dracula
Stoker, Bram. *Dracula.* Doubleday, 1959.

Dry Guillotine
Belbenoit, René. *Dry Guillotine.* Dutton, 1938.

Dunkling
Dunkling, Leslie. *The Guinness Book of Names.* Guinness Superlatives, 1974.

Eagle
Eagle, Dorothy, ed. *The Concise Oxford Dictionary of English Literature,* 2nd ed. Oxford U.P., 1970.

Eastman
Eastman, Mary H. *Index to Fairy Tales, Myths, and Legends.* F.W. Faxon, 1926.

EB

Encyclopaedia Britannica. Encyclopaedia Britannica, 1977. [Roman numerals refer to Micropaedia; Arabic numerals refer to Macropaedia.]

EB (1963)

Encyclopaedia Britannica. Encyclopaedia Britannica, 1963.

EB (1978)
1978 Book of the Year: Events of 1977. Encyclopaedia Britannica, 1978.

Eclogues
Virgil. *Eclogues,* ed. H.E. Gould. St. Martin's Press, 1967.

L'Ecole des Femmes
Molière, Jean P. *L'Ecole des Femmes.* French and European Pubn., 1964.

Edgar
Edgar, M.G., ed. *Treasury of Verse for Little Children.* Crowell, 1946.

Edwin Drood
Dickens, Charles. *Edwin Drood and Master Humphrey's Clock.* Dutton, 1970.

Eggenberger
Eggenberger, David. *A Dictionary of Battles From 1479 b.c. to the Present.* Thomas Y. Crowell, 1967.

Egmont
Goethe, Johann W. Von. *Egmont,* tr. Willard Trask. Barron's, 1960.

The Egoist
Meredith, George. *The Egoist.* Penguin, 1979.

Electra
Euripides. *Electra,* tr. Gilbert Murray. Oxford U.P., 1905.

Eliot
Eliot, T.S., ed. *A Choice of Kipling's Verse.* Faber and Faber, 1963.

Elmer Gantry
Lewis, Sinclair. *Elmer Gantry.* New American Library, Signet, 1971.

Emboden
Emboden, W.A. *A Renaissance Botanist: Leonardo da Vinci. Hortulus Aliquando,* Winter 1975–76, pp. 13–30.

Emma
Austen, Jane. *Emma.* New American Library, 1964.

Emperor Jones
O'Neill, Eugene. *Emperor Jones.* Prentice-Hall, 1960.

Enoch Arden
"Enoch Arden" in *Tennyson,* ed. Kingsley Amis. Penguin, 1973.

The Epicurean
Moore, Thomas. *The Epicurean.* Miller, 1875.

Espy
Espy, Willard R. *O Thou Improper, Thou Uncommon Noun.* Clarkson N. Potter, 1978.

Eugene Aram
Bulwer-Lytton, Edward. *Eugene Aram* in *Works*. Wanamaker, n.d.

Eugene Onegin
Pushkin, Alexander. *Eugene Onegin,* ed. Avrahm Yarmolinsky, tr. Babette Deutsch. Penguin, 1975.

The Eunuch
Terence. *The Eunuch,* tr. Frank O. Copley. Bobbs-Merrill, 1965.

Evans
Evans, Bergen. *Dictionary of Mythology, Mainly Classical.* Centennial Press, 1970.

Evelina
Burney, Fanny. *Evelina.* W.W. Norton, 1965.

Everyman
Everyman, ed. A.C. Cawley. Barnes & Noble, 1970.

Every Man in His Humour
Jonson, Ben. *Every Man in His Humour.* British Book Centre, 1974.

The Exorcist
Blatty, William P. *The Exorcist.* Harper & Row, 1971.

Faber
Faber Book of English Verse, ed. John Hayward. Faber and Faber, 1958.

Fables
Fontaine, Jean de la. *Fables,* tr. Edward Marsh. Dutton, 1966.

Facts
Facts on File. Facts on File, various years.

Faerie Queene
Spenser, Edmund. *Faerie Queene,* ed. P.C. Bayley. Oxford U.P., 1965–66.

Fair Maid of Perth
Scott, Sir Walter. *The Fair Maid of Perth* in *Complete Works.* Houghton, 1923.

The Fair Penitent
Rowe, Nicholas. *The Fair Penitent,* ed. Malcolm Goldstein. Univ. of Nebraska Press, 1969.

The Fall
Camus, Albert. *The Fall.* Knopf, 1957.

Farewell, My Lovely
Chandler, Raymond. *Farewell, My Lovely.* Random House, 1976.

Family from One End Street
Garnett, Eve. *Family from One End Street.* Vanguard, 1960.

A Farewell to Arms
Hemingway, Ernest. *A Farewell to Arms.* Scribner, 1967.

Far Out the Long Canal
De Jong, Meindert. *Far Out the Long Canal.* Harper, 1964.

Fasti
Ovid. *Fasti,* ed. Cyril Bailey. Oxford U.P., 1921.

Fatal Curiosity
Lillo, George. *Fatal Curiosity,* ed. William H. McBurney. Univ. of Nebraska Press, 1967.

Father Christmas
Briggs, Raymond. *Father Christmas.* Coward, 1973.

Fathers and Sons
Turgenev, Ivan. *Fathers and Sons,* tr. R. Edmonds. Penguin, 1975.

Faust
Goethe, Johann W. von. *Faust,* tr. Walter Kaufmann. Doubleday, 1961.

Feminine Mystique
Friedan, Betty. *The Feminine Mystique.* Norton, 1974

Les Femmes Savantes
Molière, Jean B. *Les Femmes Savantes,* ed. H. Gaston Hall. Oxford U.P., 1974.

Fentress
Fentress, Calvin. "Ram Dass, Nobody Special" in *New Times,* September 4, 1978, pp. 37–47.

Ferguson
Ferguson, George. *Signs and Symbols in Christian Art.* Oxford U.P., 1954.

Fifteen
Cleary, Beverly. *Fifteen.* William Morrow, 1956.

Finn Family Moomintroll
Jansson, Tove. *Finn Family Moomintroll.* Henry Walck, 1965.

Finnegans Wake
Joyce, James. *Finnegans Wake*. Viking Press, 1959.

Fisher
Fisher, Margery. *Who's Who in Children's Books*. Holt, 1975.

The Five Hundred Hats of Bartholomew Cubbins
Seuss, Dr. *The Five Hundred Hats of Bartholomew Cubbins*. E.M. Hale, 1938.

Five on a Treasure Island
Blyton, Enid. *Five on a Treasure Island*. Atheneum, 1972.

Five Weeks in a Balloon
Verne, Jules. *Five Weeks in a Balloon*. Aeonian Press, reprint of 1869 ed.

The Fixer
Malamud, Bernard. *The Fixer*. Dell, 1966.

Flashman
Fraser, George Macdonald. *Flashman*. New American Library, 1969.

Flexner
Flexner, Stuart Berg. *I Hear America Talking*. Van Nostrand, 1976.

Flight of the Doves
Macken, Walter. *The Flight of the Doves*. Macmillan, 1970.

Flora Symbolica
Flora Symbolica, reprinted in *Sex in the Garden*, ed. Tom Riker. Morrow, 1976.

Foerster
Foerster, Norman, ed. *American Poetry and Prose*. Houghton Mifflin, 1970.

Follow My Black Plume
Trease, Geoffrey. *Follow My Black Plume*. Vanguard Press, 1963.

Fordin
Fordin, Hugh. *The World of Entertainment! Hollywood's Greatest Musicals*. Doubleday, 1975.

The Forsyte Saga
Galsworthy, John. *The Forsyte Saga*. Scribner, 1933.

Fortunata and Jacinta
Galdos, Benito Perez. *Fortunata and Jacinta*, tr. Lester Clark. Penguin, 1975.

Fortunes of Nigel
Scott, Sir Walter. *The Fortunes of Nigel*. Dutton, 1965.

For Whom the Bell Tolls
Hemingway, Ernest. *For Whom the Bell Tolls*. Scribner, 1940.

Four Major Plays
Ibsen, Henrik. *Four Major Plays*, vol. 2, tr. Rolf Fjelde. New American Library, 1970.

Frank
Frank, Sid. *The Presidents: Tidbits & Trivia*. Hammond, 1975.

Frankenstein
Shelley, Mary W. *Frankenstein: Or, the Modern Prometheus*, ed. James H. Rieger. Bobbs-Merrill, 1974.

Franny and Zooey
Salinger, J.D. *Franny and Zooey*. Bantam, 1969.

Freeman
Freeman, William. *Dictionary of Fictional Characters*, rev. Fred Urquhart. The Writer, 1974.

Friar Bacon
Greene, Robert. *Friar Bacon and Friar Bungay*. British Book Centre, 1975.

Friday the Rabbi Slept Late
Kemelman, Harry. *Friday the Rabbi Slept Late*. Crown, 1964.

The Frogs
Aristophanes. *The Frogs and Other Plays*, tr. David Barrett. Penguin, 1964.

Fuller
Fuller, J.F.C. *A Military History of the Western World*, 3 vols. Funk & Wagnalls, 1956.

Fyfe
Fyfe, Thomas Alexander. *Who's Who in Dickens*. Gryphon Books, 1971.

The Gambler
Dostoevsky, Feodor. *The Gambler*, ed. Edward Wasiolek, tr. Victor Terras. Univ. of Chicago Press, 1972.

A Game of Dark
Mayne, William. *A Game of Dark*. Dutton, 1971.

Gardener's Dog
de Vega, Lope. *The Gardener's Dog* in *Four Plays of Lope de Vega*. Hyperion Press, 1978.

Gargantua and Pantagruel
Rabelais, Fran c,ois. *Gargantua and Pantagruel*, tr. John M. Cohen. Penguin, 1955.

Gaster
Gaster, Theodore, ed. *Myth, Legend, and Custom in the Old Testament*. Harper, 1969.

Gayley
Gayley, Charles Mills. *The Classic Myths in English Literature and Art*. Milford House, 1974.

Gemini
Kipling, Rudyard. *Gemini* in *Soldiers Three*. Doubleday, 1909.

Gentleman's Agreement
Hobson, Laura Z. *Gentleman's Agreement*. Simon and Schuster, 1947.

Gentlemen Prefer Blondes
Loos, Anita. *Gentlemen Prefer Blondes*. Boni and Liveright, 1925.

George
Turnbull, Agnes. *George*. E.M. Hale, 1965.

Germinal
Zola, Emile. *Germinal*. New American Library, 1970.

Ghost of Thomas Kempe
Lively, Penelope. *The Ghost of Thomas Kempe*. Dutton, 1973.

Ghosts
Ibsen, Henrik. *Ghosts*. Avon, 1965.

Gil Blas
Le Sage, Alain René. *The Adventures of Gil Blas of Santillane*. Hyperion, 1977.

Giles Goat-Boy
Barth, John. *Giles Goat-Boy*. Fawcett Crest, 1966.

Gilgamesh
Gilgamesh: A Verse Narrative, ed. Herbert Mason. New American Library, 1972.

Ginger Pye
Estes, Eleanor. *Ginger Pye*. Harcourt, 1972.

Go Down, Moses
Faulkner, William. *Go Down, Moses*. Random House, 1973.

God Bless You, Mr. Rosewater
Vonnegut, Kurt. *God Bless You, Mr. Rosewater*. Dell, 1974.

God's Little Acre
Caldwell, Erskine. *God's Little Acre*. Viking Press, 1933.

The Golden Ass
Apuleius, Lucius. *The Golden Ass*, tr. Jack Lindsay. Indiana U.P., 1962.

Golden Boy
Odets, Clifford, and William Gibson. *Golden Boy*. Atheneum, 1965.

Golden Legend
De Voragine, Jacobus. *Golden Legend*. Arno Press, 1941.

Golden Mary
Dickens, Charles. "The Wreck of the 'Golden Mary' TH" in *Christmas Stories* in *New Oxford Illustrated Dickens*. Oxford U.P., 1956.

Golden Treasury
Untermeyer, Louis, ed. *Golden Treasury of Poetry*. Golden Press, 1959.

Goldfinger
Fleming, Ian. *Goldfinger*. Macmillan, 1966.

Golenpaul
Golenpaul, Ann. *Information Please Almanac: Atlas and Yearbook, 1975*. Information Please Almanac, 1975.

Gone With the Wind
Mitchell, Margaret. *Gone With the Wind*. Avon, 1974.

The Good Earth
Buck, Pearl. *The Good Earth*. Pocket Books, 1975.

The Graduate
Webb, Charles. *The Graduate*. New American Library, 1971.

Granger
Granger, Edith. *Granger's Index to Poetry and Recitation*. Books for Libraries, 1974.

Grapes of Wrath
Steinbeck, John. *Grapes of Wrath*. Bantam Books, 1970.

Great Expectations
Dickens, Charles. *Great Expectations,* ed. Angus Calder. Penguin, 1965.

The Great Gatsby
Fitzgerald, F. Scott. *The Great Gatsby.* Scribner, 1920.

The Green Carnation
Hichens, Robert. *The Green Carnation,* ed. Stanley Weintraub. Univ. of Nebraska Press, 1970.

The Green Hills of Africa
Hemingway, Ernest. *The Green Hills of Africa.* Scribner, 1935.

Grendel
Gardner, John. *Grendel.* G.K. Hall, 1972.

Griffith
Griffith, Richard, and Arthur Mayer. *The Movies.* Simon and Schuster, 1957.

Grimm
Grimms' Tales for Young and Old, tr. Ralph Manheim. Doubleday, 1977.

Grinding It Out
Kroc, Ray, and Robert Anderson. *Grinding It Out: The Making of McDonald's.* Contemporary Publishing, 1977.

Grove
Grove's Dictionary of Music and Musicians, 5th ed. St. Martin's Press, 1954.

Grun
Grun, Bernard. *The Timetables of History.* Simon and Schuster, 1975.

Guirand
Guirand, Felix. *New Larousse Encyclopedia of Mythology.* Putnam, 1973.

Gulliver's Travels
Swift, Jonathan. *Gulliver's Travels,* ed. L.A. Landa. Houghton Mifflin, 1960.

The Guns of August
Tuchman, Barbara W. *The Guns of August.* Bantam, 1976.

Guy Mannering
Scott, Sir Walter. *Guy Mannering.* Dutton, 1954.

Guzmán de Alfarache
Aleman, Mateo. *The Life of Guzmán de Alfarache.* Knopf, 1924.

Hall
Hall, James. *Dictionary of Subjects and Symbols in Art.* Harper, 1974.

Halliwell
Halliwell, Leslie. *The Filmgoer's Companion.* Hill and Wang, 1977.

Hamlet
Shakespeare, William. *Hamlet,* ed. George Rylands. Oxford U.P., 1947.

The Happy Lion
Duvoisin, Roger. *The Happy Lion.* McGraw-Hill, 1954.

Harbottle *Battles*
Harbottle, Thomas Benfield. *Dictionary of Battles.* Gale, 1966.

Hard Times
Dickens, Charles. *Hard Times,* ed. David Craig. Penguin, 1969.

Handy Andy
Lover, Samuel. *Handy Andy; A Tale of Irish Life.* Appleton, 1904.

Hans Breitmann's Ballads
Leland, Charles G. *Hans Breitmann's Ballads.* Dover, 1914.

The Happy Hooker
Hollander, Xaviera. *The Happy Hooker.* Dell, 1972.

Harding's Luck
Nesbit, Edith. *Harding's Luck.* British Book Centre, 1974.

Hardwick
Hardwick, Michael. *A Literary Atlas and Gazetteer of the British Isles.* Gale, 1973.

Harris
Harris, Brice, ed. *Restoration Plays.* Modern Library, 1966.

Hart
Hart, James D., ed. *The Oxford Companion to American Literature,* 4th ed. Oxford U.P., 1965.

Harvey
Harvey, Sir Paul, ed. *The Oxford Companion to English Literature,* 4th edition. rev. Dorothy Eagle. Oxford U.P., 1967.

The Haunted House
Dickens, Charles. *The Haunted House* in *Christmas Stories from Household Words and All the Year Round.* n.d.

Havelok the Dane
Havelok the Dane, ed. Ian Serraillier. Walck, 1967.

The Heart Is a Lonely Hunter
McCullers, Carson. *The Heart Is a Lonely Hunter.* Bantam, 1970.

The Heart of Midlothian
Scott, Sir Walter. *The Heart of Midlothian.* Dutton, 1956.

The Heathen Chinee
Harte, Bret. "The Heathen Chinee," usually known as "Plain Language from Truthful James" in *The Complete Works of Bret Harte.* Chatto and Windus, 1880–1912.

Hedda Gabler
Ibsen, Henrik. *Hedda Gabler and Other Plays,* tr. Eva LeGallienne and Norman Ginsbury. Dutton, Everyman, 1976.

Heidi
Spyri, Johanna. *Heidi.* Penguin, 1971.

Helene
Euripides. *Helene,* ed. A.M. Dale. Oxford U.P., 1967.

Heloïse and Abelard
Moore, George. *Heloïse and Abelard.* Liveright, 1945.

Hemingway
Hemingway, Ernest. *Short Stories of Ernest Hemingway.* Scribner, 1938.

Henderson the Rain King
Bellow, Saul. *Henderson the Rain King.* Fawcett World, 1974.

Henry and Beezus
Cleary, Beverly. *Henry and Beezus.* William Morrow, 1952.

I Henry IV
Shakespeare, William. *I Henry IV,* ed. George L. Kittredge and Irving Ribner. John Wiley, 1966.

II Henry IV
Shakespeare, William. *II Henry IV.* Oxford U.P., 1970.

Henry V
Shakespeare, William. *Henry V.* Oxford U.P., 1971.

I Henry VI
Shakespeare, William. *I Henry VI.* Oxford U.P., 1970.

II Henry VI
Shakespeare, William. *II Henry VI.* Oxford U.P., 1970.

III Henry VI
Shakespeare, William. *III Henry VI,* ed. George L. Kittredge and Irving Ribner. John Wiley, 1969.

Henry VIII
Shakespeare, William. *Henry VIII.* Oxford U.P., 1971.

Henry Esmond
Thackeray, William M. *Henry Esmond.* Dutton, 1972.

Henry Huggins
Cleary, Beverley. *Henry Huggins.* William Morrow, 1950.

Herbert
Herbert, Ian. *Who's Who in the Theatre.* Gale, 1977.

A Herd of Deer
Dillon, Eilis. *A Herd of Deer.* Funk & Wagnalls, 1970.

Herman
Herman, Linda, and Beth Stiel. *Corpus Delicti of Mystery Fiction.* Scarecrow Press, 1974.

Hero and Leander
Marlowe, Christopher. *Hero and Leander.* Johnson Reprint, 1972.

Hero and Leander
Musaeus. *Hero and Leander,* tr. F.L. Lucas. Golden Cockerel Press, 1977.

Herzog
Bellow, Saul. *Herzog.* Fawcett World, 1974.

Hiawatha
Longfellow, Henry Wadsworth. *The Song of Hiawatha.* Tuttle, 1975.

The Hidden Staircase
Keene, Carolyn. *The Hidden Staircase.* Grosset and Dunlap, 1930.

Hippolytus
Euripides. *Hippolytus,* tr. Robert Bagg. Oxford U.P., 1973.

History of John Bull
Arbuthnot, John. *History of John Bull.* Oxford U.P., 1976.

Hitler
Toland, John. *Adolf Hitler.* Ballantine Books, 1976.

H.M.S. Pinafore
Gilbert, W. S. "H.M.S. Pinafore" in *The Complete Works of Gilbert and Sullivan*. Norton, 1976.

The Hobbit
Tolkien, J.R.R. *The Hobbit*. Houghton Mifflin, 1973.

Hollowell
Hollowell, Lillian. *A Book of Children's Literature*. Rinehart, 1950.

Hone
Hone, William. *The Table Book*. Gale, 1966.

Hone Everyday
Hone, William. *The Everyday Book*. Gordon, 1967.

The Hope of the Katzekopfs
Paget, Frances E., and William Churne. *The Hope of the Katzekopfs: A Fairy Tale*. Johnson Reprints, 1968.

Horn
Horn, Maurice. *The World Encyclopedia of Comics*. Chelsea House, 1976.

Horton Hatches the Egg
Seuss, Dr. *Horton Hatches the Egg*. Random House, 1940.

The Hound of the Baskervilles
Doyle, A. Conan. *The Hound of the Baskervilles*. Dell, 1959.

House of Arden
Nesbit, Edith. *House of Arden*. Dutton, 1968.

The House of Sixty Fathers
de Jong, Meindert. *The House of Sixty Fathers*. Harper, 1956.

The House of the Seven Gables
Hawthorne, Nathaniel. *The House of the Seven Gables*. Harcourt, 1970.

Howe
Howe, George, and Harrer, G. A. *A Handbook of Classical Mythology*. Gale, 1970.

How the People Sang the Mountains Up
Leach, Maria. *How the People Sang the Mountains Up*. Viking Press, 1967.

Huckleberry Finn
Twain, Mark. *The Adventures of Huckleberry Finn*. Holt, 1948.

Hugo and Josephine
Gripe, Maria. *Hugo and Josephine*. Dell, 1971.

Humphry Clinker
Smollett, Tobias. *The Expedition of Humphry Clinker*, ed. Lewis M. Knapp. Oxford U.P., 1966.

The Hunchback of Notre Dame
Hugo, Victor. *The Hunchback of Notre Dame*. Dutton, 1953.

The Hunting of the Snark
Carroll, Lewis. *The Hunting of the Snark*. Clarkson N. Potter, 1975.

The Iceman Cometh
O'Neill, Eugene. *The Iceman Cometh*. Random House, 1957.

I Ching
I Ching or the Book of Changes, tr. Peter Legge. Citadel Press, 1971.

I, Claudius
Graves, Robert. *I, Claudius*. Random House, Vintage, 1961.

The Idiot
Dostoyevsky, Fyodor. *The Idiot*. New American Library, Signet, 1969.

Idylls
Theocritus. *Idylls of Theocritus*. Purdue Univ. Studies, 1963.

Idylls of the King
Tennyson, Alfred, Lord. *Idylls of the King*. St. Martin's Press, 1930.

Iliad
Homer. *Iliad*, tr. Robert Fitzgerald. Doubleday, 1975.

Imagines
Philostratrus. *Imagines*. Harvard U.P., 1972.

The Importance of Being Earnest
Wilde, Oscar. *The Importance of Being Earnest*. New York Public Library, 1968.

In Cold Blood
Capote, Truman. *In Cold Blood*. New American Library, 1971.

In Dubious Battle.
Steinbeck, John. *In Dubious Battle*. Bantam, 1970.

Indian Summer
Howells, William Dean *Indian Summer*. Indiana U.P., 1972.

Inferno
Dante Alighieri. *Inferno*. Dutton, 1965.

The Informer
O'Flaherty, Liam. *The Informer*. Triangle Books, 1943.

Ingleby
Ingleby, C.M., et al. *Shakspere AllusionBook: A Collection of Allusions to Shakspere from 1591 to 1700*. Books For Libraries, 1970.

The Injustice Collectors
Auchincloss, Louis. *The Injustice Collectors*. Avon, 1974.

The Inspector General
Gogol, Nikolai. *The Inspector General*. Avon, 1976.

In the Heat of the Night
Ball, John. *In the Heat of the Night*. Harper & Row, 1965.

The Invisible Man
Wells, H.G. *The Invisible Man*. Popular Library, 1972.

Iphigenia in Tauris
Euripides. *Iphigenia in Tauris*, tr. Gilbert Murray. Oxford U.P., 1910.

Iron Giant
Hughes, Ted. *Iron Giant: A Story in Five Nights*. Harper, 1968.

The Iron Lily
Willard, Barbara. *The Iron Lily*. Dutton, 1974.

Ivanhoe
Scott, Sir Walter. *Ivanhoe*. Macmillan, 1962.

Jack
Jack, Alex. *The New Age Dictionary*. Kanthaka Press, 1976.

Jack Sheppard
Ainsworth, William. *Jack Sheppard*. Century, 1909.

Jacobowsky & Der Oberst
Werfel, Franz. *Jacobowsky & Der Oberst*. Irvington, 1961.

Jameson
Jameson, J. Franklin. *Dictionary of United States History*. Gale, 1971.

Jane Eyre
Bronte, Charlotte. *Jane Eyre*. Dutton, 1963.

J.B.
MacLeish, Archibald. *J.B.* Houghton Mifflin, 1958.

Dr. Jekyll and Mr. Hyde
Stevenson, Robert L. *Dr. Jekyll and Mr. Hyde*. Dutton, Everyman, 1962.

Jerusalem Delivered
Tasso, Torquato. *Jerusalem Delivered*. Putnam, 1963.

Jew of Malta
Marlowe, Christopher. *The Jew of Malta* in *Marlowe: Five Plays*, ed. Havelock Ellis. Hill and Wang, 1956.

Jobes
Jobes, Gertrude. *Dictionary of Mythology, Folklore, and Symbols*— Parts 1 & 2. Scarecrow Press, 1962.

John Brent
Winthrop, Theodore. *John Brent*, ed. H. Dean Propst. College and Univ. Press, 1970.

John Gabriel Borkman
Ibsen, Henrik. *John Gabriel Borkman* in *Four Major Plays*, tr. Rolf Fjelde, vol. 2. New American Library, 1970.

John Gilpin's Ride
Cowper, William. *John Gilpin's Ride*. Watts, 1967.

Johnny Tremain
Forbes, Esther. *Johnny Tremain*. Dell, 1969.

Johnson
Johnson, Rossiter. *Dictionary of Famous Names in Fiction, Drama, Poetry, History and Art*. Gale, 1974.

Jonathan Livingston Seagull
Bach, Richard. *Jonathan Livingston Seagull*. Macmillan, 1970.

Jorrock's Jaunts & Jollities
Surtees, Robert S. *Jorrock's Jaunts and Jollities*, ed. Herbert Van Thal. Dufour, 1969.

Joseph Andrews
Fielding, Henry. *Joseph Andrews*. Norton, 1958.

Josh
Southall, Ivan. *Josh*. Macmillan, 1972.

Joy
Joy, Charles Rhind. *Harper's Topical Concordance*, rev. ed. Harper, 1962.

Jude the Obscure
Hardy, Thomas. *Jude the Obscure*. St. Martin's Press, 1977.

Judgment Day
Farrell, James T. *Judgment Day*. Avon, 1973.

Julius Caesar
Shakespeare, William. *Julius Caesar*, ed. T.S. Dorsch. Barnes & Noble, 1964.

The Jungle
Sinclair, Upton. *The Jungle*. New American Library, 1973.

The Jungle Books
Kipling, Rudyard. *The Jungle Books*. Grosset and Dunlap, 1950.

Jurgi
Jurgi, E.J. *Great Religions of the Modern World*. Princeton U.P., 1946.

Kaganoff
Kaganoff, Benzion C. *A Dictionary of Jewish Names and Their History*. Schocken Books, 1977.

Kalevala
Loenrot, Elias. *Kalevala*, tr. Francis P. Magoun. Harvard U.P., 1963.

Kane
Kane, Joseph Nathan. *Facts About the Presidents*. Ace Books, 1976.

Karst
Karst, Gene, and Martin J. Jones, Jr. *Who's Who in Professional Baseball*. Arlington House, 1973.

Keddie
Keddie, William. *Cyclopaedia of Literary and Scientific Anecdote*. Gryphon, 1971.

Kent
Kent, Leonard J. *The Collected Tales and Plays of Nikolai Gogol*. Pantheon, 1964.

Kidnapped
Stevenson, Robert L. *Kidnapped*. New American Library, 1959.

Killikelly
Killikelly, Sarah H. *Curious Questions*. Gale, 1968.

King John
Shakespeare, William. *King John*, ed. E.A. Honingmann. Barnes & Noble, 1965.

King Lear
Shakespeare, William. *King Lear*, in *William Shakespeare: The Complete Works*, ed. Peter Alexander. Collins, 1951.

King of the Golden River
Ruskin, John. *King of the Golden River*. Dover, 1974.

King Quotations
King, William F. *Classical and Foreign Quotations*. Gale, 1968.

The King, the Greatest Alcalde
de Vega, Lope. *The King, the Greatest Alcalde*. in *Poet Lore* 29 (1918): 379–446.

King Things
King, Edmund F. *Ten Thousand Wonderful Things*. Gale, 1970.

Kinkle
Kinkle, Roger D. *The Complete Encyclopedia of Popular Music and Jazz, 1900–1950*. 4 vols. Arlington House, 1974.

Kipps
Wells, H.G. *Kipps*. Dell, 1968.

Kitto
Kitto, H.D.F., *Greek Tragedy: A Literary Study*. Doubleday, 1954.

Kon-Tiki
Heyerdahl, Thor. *Kon-Tiki*. Washington Square Press, 1973.

Koran
Koran, tr. N.J. Dawood. Penguin, 1964.

Kravitz
Kravitz, David. *Who's Who in Greek and Roman Mythology*. Clarkson N. Potter, 1975.

Kubla Khan
Coleridge, Samuel Taylor. "Kubla Khan, A Vision in a Dream" in *Collected Works of Samuel T. Coleridge*. Princeton U.P., 1972.

Kunz
Kunz, George Frederick. *The Curious Lore of Precious Stones*. Dover, 1971.

Kwong
Kwong, Ki Chaou. *Dictionary of English Phrases*. Gale, 1971.

The Lady or the Tiger
Stockton, Frank. *The Lady or the Tiger and Other Stories*. Mss Information Co., 1972

Lahue
Lahue, Kalton C. *World of Laughter: The Motion Picture Comedy Short, 1910–1930*. Univ. of Oklahoma Press, 1972.

The Land of Oz
Baum, L. Frank. *The Land of Oz*. Airmont, 1968.

The Lark and the Laurel
Willard, Barbara. *The Lark and the Laurel*. Harcourt, Bruce, Jovanovich, 1970.

The Last Chronicle of Barset
Trollope, Anthony. *The Last Chronicle of Barset*, ed. Arthur Mizener. Houghton Mifflin, 1964.

The Last Days of Pompeii
Bulwer-Lytton, Edward. *The Last Days of Pompeii* in *Works*. Wanamaker, n.d.

Latham
Latham, Edward. *Dictionary of Names, Nicknames, and Surnames*. Gale, 1966.

Laughlin
Laughlin, William H. *Laughlin's Fact Finder—People, Places, Things, Events*. Parker, 1969.

Leach
Leach, Maria, ed. *Funk & Wagnalls Standard Dictionary of Folklore, Mythology, and Legend*. Funk & Wagnalls, 1972.

Leaves of Grass
Whitman, Walt. *Leaves of Grass*. Norton, 1968.

The Legend of Sleepy Hollow
Irving, Washington. *The Legend of Sleepy Hollow and Other Stories*. Airmont, 1964.

A Legend of Montrose
Scott, Walter. *A Legend of Montrose* in *Complete Works*. Houghton, 1923.

Leonard
Leonard, Thomas M. *Day by Day: the Forties*. Facts on File, 1977.

Lie Down In Darkness
Styron, William. *Lie Down In Darkness*. Viking Press, 1957.

The Life of John Buncle
Amory, Thomas. *The Life of John Buncle, Esq., 1756–1766*, ed. Michael F. Shugrue. Garland, 1974.

Light in August
Faulkner, William. *Light in August*. Random House, 1967.

The Lion, the Witch, and the Wardrobe
Lewis, C.S. *The Lion, The Witch, and The Wardrobe*. Macmillan, 1970.

Little
Little, Charles. *Historical Lights: 6000 Quotations*. Gale, 1968.

Little Blue and Little Yellow
Lionni, Leo. *Little Blue and Little Yellow*. Astor-Honor, 1959.

Little Dorrit
Dickens, Charles. *Little Dorrit*, ed. John Holloway. Penguin, 1967.

The Little Engine That Could
Piper, Watty. *The Little Engine That Could*. Platt, 1976.

Little Eyolf
Ibsen, Henrik. *Little Eyolf* in *Ibsen: The Complete Major Prose Plays*. Farrar, Straus, and Giroux, 1978.

The Little House
Burton, Virginia. *The Little House*. Houghton Mifflin, 1943.

Little House in The Big Woods
Wilder, Laura Ingalls. *Little House in The Big Woods*. Harper & Row, 1953.

The Little Lame Prince
Mulock, Dinah. *The Little Lame Prince and his Travelling Cloak*. Hale, 1909.

Little Lord Fauntleroy
Burnett, Frances H. *Little Lord Fauntleroy*. Biblio Distribution Centre, 1975.

The Little Minister
Barrie, J.M. *The Little Minister*. Airmont, 1968.

Little Old Mrs. Pepperpot ·
Proysen, Alf. *Little Old Mrs. Pepperpot*. Astor-Honor, 1960.

Little Red Fox
Uttley, Allison. *Little Red Fox and the Wicked Uncle*. Bobbs-Merrill, 1963.

The Little Steam Roller
Greene, Grahame. *The Little Steam Roller*. Doubleday, 1975.

Little Tim
Ardizzone, Edward. *Little Tim and the Brave Sea Captain*. Henry Walck, 1955.

Little Women
Alcott, Louisa May. *Little Women*. Grosset and Dunlap, 1947.

Livy
Livy. *Livy*, ed. T.A. Dorey. Univ. of Toronto Press, 1971.

LLEI
The Lincoln Library of Essential Information. 2 vols. The Frontier Co., 1972.

Lolita
Nabokov, Vladimir. *Lolita*. Berkeley Pub. Co., 1975.

The Long Goodbye
Chandler, Raymond. *The Long Goodbye*. Ballantine, 1977.

The Long Voyage
Dickens, Charles. "The Long Voyage" in *Reprinted Pieces*. Dutton, 1970.

Look Homeward, Angel
Wolfe, Thomas. *Look Homeward, Angel*. Scribner, 1929.

Lord Jim
Conrad, Joseph. *Lord Jim*. Doubleday, 1927.

Lord of Burleigh
Tennyson, Alfred, Lord. "Lord of Burleigh" in *Poems of Tennyson*, ed. Christopher Ricks. Norton, 1972.

Lord of the Flies
Golding, William. *Lord of the Flies*. Putnam, 1959.

Lord of the Rings
Tolkien, J.R.R. *Lord of the Rings*. Houghton Mifflin, 1974.

Lost Horizon
Hilton, James. *Lost Horizon*. Washington Square Press, 1972.

A Lost Lady
Cather, Willa. *A Lost Lady*. Random House, Vintage, 1972.

The Lost World
Doyle, Arthur Conan. *The Lost World*. Random House, 1959.

Lothair
Disraeli, Benjamin. *Lothair*, ed. Vernon Bogdanor. Oxford U.P., 1975.

Louie's Lot
Hildrick, E.W. *Louie's Lot*. D. White, 1968.

Love's Labour's Lost
Shakespeare, William. *Love's Labour's Lost*, ed. Richard W. David. Barnes & Noble, 1966.

Love Story
Segal, Erich. *Love Story*. Harper & Row, 1970.

Loving
Green, Henry. *Loving*. Dufour, 1949.

Lucy Brown and Mr. Grimes
Ardizzone, Edward. *Lucy Brown and Mr. Grimes*. Henry Walck, 1971.

Lurie
Lurie, Charles N. *Everyday Sayings*. Gale, 1968.

Lusiads
Camoes, Luis de. *Lusiads*. Southern Illinois U.P., 1963.

Lysistrata
Aristophanes. *Lysistrata*, tr. Douglass Parker. New American Library, 1970.

Macbeth
Shakespeare, William. *Macbeth*, ed. R.W. Dent. William C. Brown, 1969.

Mabinogion
The Mabinogion, tr. Jeffrey Gantz. Penguin, 1976.

Macleod
Macleod, Ann, adapt. *English Fairy Tales*. Paul Hamlyn, 1965.

Madame Bovary
Flaubert, Gustave. *Madame Bovary*, ed. Charles I. Weir. Holt, 1948.

Maggie: A Girl of the Streets
Crane, Stephen. *Maggie: A Girl of the Streets*. Fawcett World, 1978.

The Magician's Nephew
Lewis, C.S. *The Magician's Nephew*. Macmillan, 1970.

Magill
Magill, Frank. *Masterpieces of World Literature in Digest Form.* 4 vols. Harper & Row, 1960.

The Magnificent Ambersons
Tarkington, Booth. *The Magnificent Ambersons.* Avon, 1973.

Mahābhārata
Mahābhārata, tr. Chakravarthi V. Narasimhan. Columbia U.P., 1973.

The Maid's Tragedy
Beaumont, Francis, and John Fletcher. *The Maid's Tragedy,* ed. Andrew J. Gurr. Univ. of California Press, 1969.

Main Street
Lewis, Sinclair. *Main Street.* Signet Classics, 1971.

Major Bradford's Town
Melville, Doris Johnson. *Major Bradford's Town: A History of Kingston.* Town of Kingston, Mass., 1976.

Le Malade Imaginaire
Molière, Jean B. *Le Malade Imaginaire.* French and European Pubn., 1964.

The Maldonado Miracle
Taylor, Theodore. *The Maldonado Miracle.* Doubleday, 1973.

The Maltese Falcon
Hammett, Dashiell. *The Maltese Falcon.* Random House, 1972.

Manhattan Transfer
Dos Passos, John. *Manhattan Transfer.* Houghton Mifflin, 1963.

Manon Lescaut
Prevost, Antoine. *Manon Lescaut,* tr. Helen Waddell. Hyperion, 1977.

Manxmouse
Gallico, Paul. *Manxmouse.* Coward, McCann and Geoghegan, 1968.

The Marble Faun
Hawthorne, Nathaniel. *The Marble Faun.* Ohio State U.P., 1968.

Marianne Dreams
Storr, Catherine. *Marianne Dreams.* Penguin, 1975.

The Marriage of Figaro
Beaumarchais, P.A. *The Marriage of Figaro,* tr. B.P. Ellis. AHM Publishing, 1966.

Martin Chuzzlewit
Dickens, Charles. *Martin Chuzzlewit,* ed. P.N. Furbank. Penguin, 1975.

Martin Eden
London, Jack. *Martin Eden.* Macmillan, 1957.

Martin Pippin
Farjeon, Eleanor. *Martin Pippin in the Apple Orchard.* Lippincott, 1961.

Martinus Scriblerus
Pope, Alexander, et al. *Memoirs of Martinus Scriblerus* in *The Works of Alexander Pope,* ed. J.W. Croker, Vol. 10. Gordian Press, 1967.

Marvin
Marvin, Frederic Rowland. *The Last Words of Distinguished Men and Women.* Gale, 1970.

Mary Poppins
Travers, Pamela L. *Mary Poppins.* Harcourt Brace Jovanovich, 1972.

Master of Ballantrae
Stevenson, Robert L. *Master of Ballantrae.* Dutton, 1972.

Mathews
Mathews, Mitford, ed. *Dictionary of Americanisms on Historical Principles.* Univ. of Chicago Press, 1951.

Mayers
Mayers, William F. *Chinese Reader's Manual.* Gale, 1968.

The Mayor of Casterbridge
Hardy, Thomas. *The Mayor of Casterbridge.* Norton, 1977.

McWhirter
McWhirter, Norris, and Ross McWhirter. *Guinness Book of World Records.* Bantam, 1975.

Measure for Measure
Shakespeare, William. *Measure for Measure,* ed. R.E. Houghton. Oxford U.P., 1970.

Medea
Euripides. *Medea,* ed. Alan Elliott. Oxford U.P., 1969.

Médée
Anouilh, Jean. *Médée.* French and European Pubn., 1953.

Meg and Mog
Nicoll, Helen. *Meg and Mog.* Atheneum, 1973.

Mein Kampf
Hitler, Adolf. *Mein Kampf,* tr. Ralph Manheim. Houghton Mifflin, 1962.

Melmoth the Wanderer
Maturin, Charles R. *Melmoth the Wanderer.* Univ. of Nebraska Press, 1961.

Memoirs of Fanny Hill
Cleland, John. *Memoirs of Fanny Hill.* New American Library, Signet, n.d.

Menaechmi
Plautus. *Menaechmi,* tr. Frank O. Copley. Bobbs-Merrill, 1956.

Mencken
Mencken, H.L. *The American Language,* abridged R.I. McDavid. Knopf, 1963.

Mercatante
Mercatante, Anthony S. *The Zoo of the Gods: Animals in Myth, Legend, and Fable.* Harper & Row, 1974.

The Merchant of Venice
Shakespeare, William. *The Merchant of Venice,* ed. John R. Brown. Barnes & Noble, 1964.

The Merry Wives of Windsor
Shakespeare, William. *The Merry Wives of Windsor,* ed. H.J. Oliver. Barnes & Noble, 1971.

Messiah
Klopstock, F.G. *Messiah.* Collyer, 1769–71.

Metamorphoses
Ovid. *Metamorphoses,* tr. Rolfe Humphries. Indiana U.P., 1955.

Michael Strogoff
Verne, Jules. *Michael Strogoff.* Airmont, 1964.

Middlemarch
Eliot, George. *Middlemarch.* Macmillan, 1966.

Midshipman Quinn
Styles, Showell. *Midshipman Quinn.* Vanguard, 1958.

A Midsummer Night's Dream
Shakespeare, William. *A Midsummer Night's Dream,* ed. Sally Freeman. Gordon and Breach, 1975.

Mike Mulligan
Burton, Virginia Lee. *Mike Mulligan and His Steam Shovel.* Houghton Mifflin, 1977.

Miller
Miller, Sim, ed. *The Rolling Stone Illustrated History of Rock & Roll.* Random House, 1976.

The Misanthrope
Molière, Jean B. *The Misanthrope,* tr. Bernard D. Grebanier. Barron's, 1959.

Misc.
Includes items of a proverbial nature and/or of common knowledge.

The Miser
Molière Jean B. *The Miser,* tr. Wallace Fowlie. Barron's, 1965.

Les Misérables
Hugo, Victor. *Les Misérables.* French and European Pubn., 1951.

Mistress Masham's Repose
White, Terence H. *Mistress Masham's Repose.* Putnam, 1960.

The Mistress of the Inn
Goldoni, Carlo. *The Mistress of the Inn.* Moscow Art Theater series of Russian plays, 1923.

Moby Dick
Melville, Herman. *Moby Dick,* ed. Harold Beaver. Penguin, 1975.

A Modern Midas
Jōkai, Mor. *A Modern Midas.* J.W. Lovell, 1886.

The Moffats
Estes, Eleanor. *The Moffats.* Harcourt Brace Jovanovich, 1968.

The Monastery
Scott, Sir Walter. *The Monastery.* Dutton, 1969.

The Monk
Lewis, Matthew. *The Monk.* Avon, 1975.

Monmouth
Geoffrey of Monmouth. *History of the Kings of Britain,* ed. Charles Dunn. Dutton, 1958.

Monsieur Beaucaire
Tarkington, Booth. *Monsieur Beaucaire.* McClure, Phillips, 1900.

Monsieur Lecoq
Gaboriau, Emile. *Monsieur Lecoq,* ed.
E.F. Bleuler. Dover, 1975.

A Month in the Country
Turgenev, Ivan. *A Month in the Country.* French, 1957.

Moody
Moody, Sophy. *What Is Your Name*
Gale, 1976.

Mopsa, The Fairy
Ingelow, Jean. *Mopsa, The Fairy.* Dutton, 1964.

Le Morte d'Arthur
Malory, Thomas. *Le Morte d'Arthur,*
ed. Janet Cowen. Penguin, 1975.

Mostly Mary
Rae, Gwynneth. *Mostly Mary.* Avon,
1972.

Mother Goose
The Real Mother Goose. Rand McNally, 1955.

Mourning Becomes Electra
O'Neill, Eugene. *Mourning Becomes
Electra.* Random House, 1931.

The Mourning Bride
Congreve, William. *The Mourning
Bride, Poems, and Miscellanies.* Somerset Pubn., n.d.

The Mouse That Roared
Wibberley, Leonard. *The Mouse That
Roared.* Little, Brown, 1955.

Mr. Polly
Wells, H.G. *The History of Mr. Polly,*
ed. Gordon Ray. Houghton Mifflin,
1961.

Mrs. Easter's Parasol
Drummond, V.H. *Mrs. Easter's Parasol.* Faber and Faber, 1944.

Mrs. Frisby
O'Brien, Robert C. *Mrs. Frisby and
the Rats of NIMH.* Atheneum, 1975.

Much Ado About Nothing
Shakespeare, William. *Much Ado
About Nothing,* ed. Charlton Hinman.
Oxford U.P., 1972.

Mulberry Street
Seuss, Dr. *And to Think That I Saw It
on Mulberry Street.* E.M. Hale, 1937.

Murder in the Cathedral
Eliot, T.S. *Murder in the Cathedral.*
Harcourt Brace Jovanovich, 1964.

Mutiny on the Bounty
Nordhoff, Charles B., and James N.
Hall. *Mutiny on the Bounty.* Washington Square Press, 1975.

My Brother's Keeper
Davenport, Marcia. *My Brother's
Keeper.* Scribner, 1954.

My Father's Dragon
Gannett, Ruth. *My Father's Dragon.*
Random House, 1948.

My Friend Flicka
O'Hara, Mary. *My Friend Flicka.* Lippincott, 1973.

My Life in the Mafia
Teresa, Vincent C., with Thomas C.
Renner. *My Life in the Mafia.* Doubleday, 1973.

My Side of the Mountain
George, Jean. *My Side of the Mountain.* Dutton, 1967.

Mysterious Island
Verne, Jules. *Mysterious Island.* Pendulum Press, 1974.

The Namesake
Hodges, C. Walter. *The Namesake: A
Story of King Alfred.* Coward, McCann and Geoghegan, 1964.

Nares
Nares, Robert. *Glossary of Words,
Phrases, Names, and Allusions in the
Works of English Authors.* Gale, 1966.

Native Son
Wright, Richard. *Native Son.* Harper
& Row, 1940.

Nausea
Sartre, Jean-Paul. *Nausea,* tr. Lloyd
Alexander. New Directions, 1959.

NCE
The New Columbia Encyclopedia, ed.
William H. Harris and Judith S. Levey. Columbia U.P., 1975.

A Nest of Simple Folk
O'Faolain, Sean. *A Nest of Simple
Folk.* Viking Press, 1934.

The Newcomes
Thackeray, William Makepeace. *The
Newcomes.* Bradbury and Evans, 1854
ND55.

New Héloise
Rousseau, Jean-Jacques. *La Nouvelle
Héloise.* Penn. State U.P., 1968.

Nibelungenlied
Nibelungenlied, tr. Frank G. Ryder. Wayne State U. P., 1962.

Nicholas Nickleby
Dickens, Charles. Nicholas Nickleby. Dutton, 1957.

Nigger of the Narcissus
Conrad, Joseph. The Nigger of the Narcissus. Macmillan, 1962.

The Night Before Christmas
Moore, Clement. The Night Before Christmas. Grosset and Dunlap, 1970.

Nine Tailors
Sayers, Dorothy. Nine Tailors. Harcourt Brace Jovanovich, 1966.

1984
Orwell, George. 1984. New American Library, 1971.

Noctes Atticae
Gellius. Noctes Atticae, ed. P. K. Marshall. Oxford U.P., 1968.

Noddy and His Car
Blyton, Enid. Noddy and His Car. British Book Centre, 1974.

Norton
Eastman, et al. The Norton Anthology of Poetry. Norton, 1970.

Norton Literature
Norton Anthology of English Literature, 3rd edition. 2 vols. Norton, 1974.

Norton Modern
Norton Anthology of Modern Poetry, ed. Richard Ellmann and Robert O'Clair. Norton, 1973.

Nostromo
Conrad, Joseph. Nostromo. Modern Library, 1951.

N.T.
New Testament. New English Bible. Oxford U.P., 1970.

Number One
Dos Passos, John. Number One. Queens House, 1977.

Oblomov
Goncharov, Ivan. Oblomov, tr. Natalie Duddington. Dutton, 1972.

The Odd Couple
Simon, Neil. The Odd Couple. Random House, 1966.

Odyssey
Homer. Odyssey, tr. Robert Fitzgerald. Doubleday, 1974.

Oedipus Rex
Sophocles. Oedipus Rex, tr. Gilbert Murray. Oxford U.P., 1948.

Oedipus Tyrannus
Sophocles. Oedipus Tyrannus. Norton, 1970.

Of Mice and Men
Steinbeck, John. Of Mice and Men. Bantam, 1970.

The Old Batchelour
Congreve, William. The Old Batchelour. British Book Centre, 1974.

The Old Curiosity Shop
Dickens, Charles. The Old Curiosity Shop, ed. A. Easson. Penguin, 1972.

The Old Man and the Sea
Hemingway, Ernest. The Old Man and the Sea. Scribner, 1961.

Old Mortality
Scott, Sir Walter. Old Mortality, ed. Angus Calder. Penguin, 1975.

Oliver Twist
Dickens, Charles. Oliver Twist, ed. Kathleen Tillotson. Oxford U.P., 1966.

Omoo
Melville, Herman. Omoo. Northwestern U.P., 1968.

On the Road
Kerouac, Jack. On the Road. Viking Press, 1978.

The Once and Future King
White, T.H. The Once and Future King. Putnam, 1958.

One Day in the Life of Ivan Denisovich
Solzhenitzyn, Alexandr. One Day in the Life of Ivan Denisovich, tr. Aitken Gillon. Farrar, 1971.

One Flew Over the Cuckoo's Nest
Kesey, Ken. One Flew Over the Cuckoo's Nest. New American Library, 1975.

Opie
Opie, Iona and Peter. Oxford Dictionary of Nursery Rhymes. Oxford U.P., 1951.

Orestes
Aeschylus. *Oresteia,* tr. Robert Fagles. Bantam, 1977.

Origin of the Species
Darwin, Charles. *Origin of the Species.* Macmillan, 1962.

Orlando Furioso
Ariosto, Ludovico. *Orlando Furioso,* tr. John Harrington. Oxford U.P., 1972.

Orlando Innamorato
Bojardo, Matteo Maria. *Orlando Innamorato.* Sansoni, 1892.

Oroonoko
Behn, Aphra. *Oroonoko; Or, The Royal Slave.* Norton, 1973.

Osborne
Osborne, Harold, ed. *The Oxford Companion to Art.* Oxford U.P., 1970.

O.T.
Old Testament. *New English Bible.* Oxford U.P., 1970.

Othello
Shakespeare, William. *Othello,* ed. J. Leeds Barroll. William C. Brown, 1971.

Our Mutual Friend
Dickens, Charles. *Our Mutual Friend,* ed. Stephen Gill. Penguin, 1971.

The Outcasts of Poker Flat
Harte, Bret. *The Outcasts of Poker Flat and Other Tales.* New American Library, Signet, 1961.

The Overcoat
Gogol, Nikolai. *The Overcoat and Other Stories.* Knopf, 1950.

Overland Launch
Hodges, C. Walter. *The Overland Launch.* Coward, McCann and Geoghegan, 1969.

The Owl Service
Garner, Alan. *The Owl Service.* Henry Walck, 1968.

The Ox-Bow Incident
Clark, Walter van Tilberg. *The Ox-Bow Incident.* New American Library, 1943.

Oxford English Dictionary
The Oxford English Dictionary, ed. J.A. Murray, et al. Oxford U.P., 1970.

Paddle-to-the-Sea
Holling, Holling C. *Paddle-to-the-Sea.* Houghton Mifflin, 1941.

The Palace Guard
Rather, Dan, and Gary P. Gates. *The Palace Guard.* Harper & Row, 1975.

A Palm for Mrs. Pollifax
Gilman, Dorothy. *A Palm for Mrs. Pollifax.* Doubleday, 1973.

Pamela
Richardson, Samuel. *Pamela.* Norton, 1958.

Pansies
Lawrence, D.H. *Pansies.* P.R. Stephensen, 1929.

Pantagruel
Rabelais, François. *Pantagruel.* French and European Pubn., 1964.

Papillon
Charrière, Henri. *Papillon.* Pocket Books, 1973.

Paradise Lost
Milton, John. *Paradise Lost,* ed. Scott Elledge. Norton, 1975.

Parish
Parish, James Robert. *Actors' Television Credits, 1950–1972.* Scarecrow Press, 1973.

Parrinder
Parrinder, Geoffrey. *Dictionary of Non-Christian Religions.* Westminster Press, 1971.

Parzival
Von Eschenbach, Wolfram. *Parzival.* Random House, 1961.

Patience
Gilbert, W.S. "Patience" in *The Complete Works of Gilbert and Sullivan.* Norton, 1976.

A Pattern of Roses
Peyton, K.M. *A Pattern of Roses.* Thomas Y. Crowell, 1973.

Payton
Payton, Geoffrey. *Webster's Dictionary of Proper Names.* G. & C. Merriam, 1970.

Pendennis
Thackeray, William M. *The History of Pendennis.* Harper, 1864.

Pensées
Pascal, Blaise. *Pensées*, tr. A.J. Krailsheimer. Penguin, 1966.

Pepita Jimenez
Valera, Juan. *Pepita Jimenez*, tr. Harriet De Onis. Barron's, 1965.

Perceval
de Troyes, Chrétien. *Le Roman de Perceval*. Droz, 1959.

Père Goriot
Balzac, Honoré de. *Père Goriot*. Modern Library, 1950.

Pericles
Shakespeare, William. *Pericles*, ed. F.D. Hoeniger. Barnes & Noble, 1963.

Peter Churchmouse
Austin, Margot. *Peter Churchmouse*. Dutton, 1941.

The Peterkin Papers
Hale, Lucretia. *The Peterkin Papers*. Dover, 1960.

Peter Pan
Barrie, James M. *Peter Pan*. Grosset and Dunlap, 1970.

Peter Schlemihl
Chamisso, Adelbert von. *Peter Schlemihl's Remarkable Story*, ed. Fred Honig. Arc Books, 1964.

Phormio
Terence. *Phormio*, tr. Frank O. Copley. Bobbs-Merrill, 1958.

Phyfe
Phyfe, William Henry P. *5000 Facts and Fancies*. Gale, 1966.

Pickwick Papers
Dickens, Charles. *Pickwick Papers*, ed. Robert L. Patten. Penguin, 1975.

The Picture of Dorian Gray
Wilde, Oscar. *The Picture of Dorian Gray*. Dell, 1956.

Pierce
Pierce, Gilbert Ashville. *The Dickens Dictionary*. Haskell House, reprint of 1878 ed.

Pilgrim's Progress
Bunyan, John. *Pilgrim's Progress*. Holt, 1949.

The Pilot
Cooper, James Fenimore. *The Pilot*. Townsend, 1859.

Pinky Pye
Estes, Eleanor. *Pinky Pye*. Harcourt, 1958.

Pinocchio
Collodi, Carlo. *Pinocchio*, tr. E. Harden. Penguin, Puffin, 1972.

Pippi Longstocking
Lindgren, Astrid. *Pippi Longstocking*. Viking Press, 1950.

The Pirates of Penzance
Gilbert, W.S. and Arthur Sullivan. "The Pirates of Penzance" in *The Complete Plays of Gilbert and Sullivan*. Norton, 1976.

The Pit
Norris, Frank. *The Pit: A Story of Chicago*. Bentley, 1971.

The Plague
Camus, Albert. *The Plague*. Random House, 1972.

Plain Speaking
Miller, Merle. *Plain Speaking*. Berkley, 1974.

Plays of Strindberg
Strindberg, August. *Plays of Strindberg*, tr. Michael Meyer, 2 vols. Random House, 1976.

Plays Unpleasant
Shaw, George Bernard. *Plays Unpleasant*. Penguin, 1950.

Pliny
Pliny. *Natural History*, 11 vols. Harvard U.P., 1962.

Plumb
Plumb, J.H. *The Horizon Book of the Renaissance*, ed. Richard Ketchum, et al. American Heritage, 1961.

Plutarch's Lives
Plutarch. *Plutarch's Lives*, ed. Edmund Fuller. Dell, 1968.

Plutus
Aristophanes. *Plutus*. W.B. Clive, 1889.

Poe
Poe, Edgar A. *Collected Works of Edgar Allan Poe, vol. 1: Poems*, ed. Thomas O. Mabbott. Harvard U.P., 1969.

Pollyanna
Porter, Eleanor. *Pollyanna*. A.L. Burt, 1913.

Pope
Pope, Alexander. *Poems of Alexander Pope,* ed. John Butt. Yale U.P., 1963.

Portable Poe
Poe, Edgar Allan. *The Portable Edgar Allan Poe,* ed. Philip Van Doren Stern. Viking Press, 1972.

Portrait of the Artist as a Young Man
Joyce, James. *A Portrait of the Artist as a Young Man.* Penguin, 1977.

Potiphar Papers
Curtis, George W. *The Potiphar Papers.* AMS Press, 1970.

Pot of Gold
Plautus. *The Pot of Gold and Other Plays,* tr. E.F. Watling. Penguin, 1965.

Les Précieuses Ridicules
Molière, Jean P. *Les Précieuses Ridicules.* French and European Pubn., 1965.

Pride and Prejudice
Austen, Jane. *Pride and Prejudice.* Oxford U.P., 1975.

The Prince
Machiavelli, Niccolo. *The Prince.* St. Martin's Press, 1964.

The Prince and the Pauper
Twain, Mark. *The Prince and the Pauper.* Macmillan, 1962.

Prince Caspian
Lewis, C.S. *Prince Caspian.* Macmillan, 1951.

Prince Prigio
Lang, Andrew. *Prince Prigio and Prince Ricardo.* Dutton, 1961.

The Prisoner of Zenda
Hope, Anthony. *The Prisoner of Zenda.* New American Library, 1974.

Private Lives
Coward, Noel. *Private Lives.* Doubleday, 1930.

Profiles in Courage
Kennedy, John F. *Profiles in Courage.* Harper & Row, 1964.

Psychomachia
Prudentius. "Psychomachia" in *Works.* Harvard U.P., 1942.

Puck of Pook's Hill
Kipling, Rudyard. *Puck of Pook's Hill.* Dover, 1968.

Pumping Iron
Gaines, Charles, and George Butler. *Pumping Iron.* Simon and Schuster, 1974.

Pygmalion
Shaw, George Bernard. *Pygmalion.* New American Library, 1975.

Queenie Peavy
Burch, Robert. *Queenie Peavy.* Viking Press, 1966.

Quennell
Quennell, Peter, and Hamish Johnson. *Who's Who in Shakespeare.* Weidenfeld and Nicholson, 1973.

Quentin Durward
Scott, Sir Walter. *Quentin Durward.* Dutton, 1965.

Rabbit Hill
Lawson, Robert. *Rabbit Hill.* Dell, 1968.

Racketty Packetty House
Burnett, Frances Hodgson. *Racketty Packetty House.* Lippincott, 1975.

Radford
Radford, Edwin. *Unusual Words and How They Came About.* Philosophical Library, 1946.

Ragan
Ragan, David. *Who's Who in Hollywood.* Arlington House, 1976.

Ragged Dick
Alger, Horatio. *Ragged Dick and Mark the Match Boy.* Macmillan, 1962.

Raggedy Ann Stories
Gruelle, John B. *Raggedy Ann Stories.* Volland, 1918.

The Railway Children
Nesbit, Edith. *The Railway Children.* British Book Centre, 1974.

Ralph Roister Doister
Udall, Nicholas. *Ralph Roister Doister.* J.M. Dent, 1901.

Ramage French
Ramage, Crauford Tait. *Familiar Quotations from French and Italian Authors.* Gale, 1968.

Ramage German
Ramage, Crauford Tait. *Familiar Quotations from German and Spanish Authors.* Gale, 1968.

Ramage *Greek*
Ramage, Crauford Tait. *Familiar Quotations from Greek Authors.* Gale, 1968.

Ramayana
Valmiki. *Ramayana,* tr. Chakravarti Rajagopalachari. InterCulture, 1974.

The Rape of Lucrece
Shakespeare, William. *The Rape of Lucrece.* British Book Centre, 1974.

Rape of the Lock
Pope, Alexander. *The Rape of the Lock,* ed. J.S. Cunningham. Oxford U.P., 1966.

Rapunzel
Grimm Brothers. *Rapunzel.* Crowell, 1975.

Rebecca of Sunnybrook Farm
Wiggin, Kate Douglas. *Rebecca of Sunnybrook Farm.* Macmillan, 1962.

The Red Badge of Courage
Crane, Stephen. *The Red Badge of Courage.* Macmillan, 1966.

Redburn
Melville, Herman. *Redburn.* Northwestern U.P., 1969.

The Red Pony.
Steinbeck, John. *The Red Pony.* Viking Press, 1959.

The Rehearsal
Villiers, George. *The Rehearsal.* Folcroft, 1976.

The Relapse
Vanbrugh, John. *The Relapse,* ed. Curt Zimansky. Univ. of Nebraska Press, 1970.

Reliques
Percy, Thomas. *Reliques of Ancient English Poesy,* ed. Henry B. Wheatley. Dover, 1966.

Remembrance of Things Past
Proust, Marcel. *Remembrance of Things Past.* Random House, 1934.

Renée Mauperin
de Goncourt, Edmond and Jules. *Renée Mauperin.* Fasquelle, 1920.

The Republic
Plato. *The Republic,* ed. Allan Bloom. Basic Books, 1968.

The Rescuers
Sharp, Margery. *The Rescuers.* Dell, 1974.

The Return of the Native
Hardy, Thomas. *The Return of the Native.* New American Library, Signet, 1973.

Reynard the Fox
Reynard the Fox, ed. Roy Brown. Abelard-Schuman, 1969.

RHD
The Random House Dictionary of the English Language, ed. Jess Stein, et al. Random House, 1973.

Richard II
Shakespeare, William. *Richard II.* Oxford U.P., 1966.

Richard III
Shakespeare, William. *Richard III,* ed. R.E. Houghton. Oxford U.P., 1965.

Riders to the Sea
Synge, John Millington. *Riders to the Sea.* Irish Academic Press, 1972

The Rime of the Ancient Mariner
Coleridge, Samuel Taylor. "The Rime of the Ancient Mariner" in *the Oxford Book of English Verse,* ed. A. Quiller-Couch. Oxford U.P., 1939.

The Ring and the Book
Browning, Robert. *The Ring and the Book.* Dutton, 1962.

The Ring of the Nibelung
Wagner, Richard. *The Ring of the Nibelung.* Scribner, 1975.

The Rise of Silas Lapham
Howells, William Dean. *The Rise of Silas Lapham.* Indiana U.P., 1971.

The Rivals
Sheridan, Richard B. *The Rivals.* Oxford U.P., 1968.

Rob Roy
Scott, Sir Walter. *Rob Roy.* Dutton, 1973.

Robin Hood
Robin Hood, ed. J. Ritson. Rowman, 1972.

Robinson Crusoe
Defoe, Daniel. *Robinson Crusoe,* ed. J. Donald Crowley. Oxford U.P., 1972.

Rockwell
Norman Rockwell's Christmas Book, ed. Lena Tabori Fried and Ruth Eisenstein. Abrams, 1977.

Roderick Hudson
James, Henry. *Roderick Hudson.* Houghton Mifflin, 1977.

Roderick Random
Smollett, Tobias. *Roderick Random.* New American Library, 1964.

Rogers
Rogers, May. *The Waverly Dictionary.* Gale, 1967.

Roller Skates
Sawyer, Ruth. *Roller Skates.* Dell, 1969.

Romeo and Juliet
Shakespeare, William. *Romeo and Juliet,* ed. Maynard Mack and Robert Boynton. Hayden, 1975.

Romola
Eliot, George. *Romola* in *The Complete Works of George Eliot.* Harper, n.d.

The Rose and the Ring
Thackeray, William Makepeace. *The Rose and the Ring.* Pierpont Morgan Library, 1947.

Rosie's Walk
Hutchins, Pat. *Rosie's Walk.* Macmillan, 1968.

Rosemary's Baby
Levin, Ira. *Rosemary's Baby.* Random House, 1967.

Rovin
Rovin, Jeff. *The Great Television Series.* A.S. Barnes, 1977.

Roxana, the Fortunate Mistress
Defoe, Daniel. *Roxana, the Fortunate Mistress.* Oxford U.P., 1964.

Roxy
Eggleston, Edward. *Roxy.* Gregg Press, 1968.

The Royal Family
Kaufmann, George S., and Edna Ferber. *The Royal Family.* French, 1929.

Rumpelstiltskin
Grimm Brothers. *Rumpelstiltskin.* Scholastic Book Service, 1974.

R.U.R.
ˇCapek, Karel. *R.U.R.* Oxford U.P., 1961.

Ship of Fools
Porter, Katherine Anne. *Ship of Fools.* Norton, 1972.

Ryland
Ryland, Frederick. *Chronological Outlines of English Literature.* Gale, 1968.

Sacco-Vanzetti Case: A Transcript
Sacco-Vanzetti Case: A Transcript of the Trial of Nicola Sacco and Bartolomeo Vanzetti in the Courts of Massachusetts and Subsequent Proceedings, 1920–27. 2nd edition. ed. Paul P. Appel. Appel, 1969.

St. Ronan's Well
Scott, Sir Walter. *St. Ronan's Well* in *Complete Works.* Houghton, 1923.

Saints and Festivals
Brewster, H. Pomeroy. *Saints and Festivals of the Christian Church.* Gale, 1974.

Samson Agonistes
Milton, John. "Samson Agonistes" in *Compact Milton,* ed. H.S. Taylor. Barron's, 1967.

Sanctuary
Faulkner, William. *Sanctuary.* New American Library, 1968.

Sann
Sann, Paul. *Fads, Follies and Delusions of the American People.* Crown Publishers, 1967.

Sartoris
Faulkner, William. *Sartoris.* Random House, 1966.

Sartor Resartus
Carlyle, Thomas. *Sartor Resartus.* Scholarly Press, 1977.

The Saturdays
Enright, Elizabeth. *The Saturdays.* Dell, 1966.

Satyricon
Petronius. *Satyricon.* New American Library, 1960.

The Scarlet Letter
Hawthorne, Nathaniel. *The Scarlet Letter: A Romance.* Oxford U.P., 1965.

The Scarlet Pimpernel
Orczy, Emmuska. *The Scarlet Pimpernel*. New American Library, 1974.

Scarlet Sister Mary
Peterkin, Julie. *Scarlet Sister Mary*. Berg, 1929.

Scholes
Scholes, Percy A., ed. *The Oxford Companion to Music*, 10th edition. rev. John Owen Ward. Oxford U.P., 1972.

The School for Scandal
Sheridan, Richard B. *The School for Scandal*, ed. C.J. Price. Oxford U.P., 1971.

The School for Wives
Molière, Jean P. *The School for Wives*, tr. Richard Wilbur. Harcourt, Brace Jovanovich, 1972.

The Seagull
Chekhov, Anton. *The Seagull*, tr. Jean-Claude Van Itallie. Harper & Row, 1977.

Second Shepherds' Play
Second Shepherds' Play in *Specimens of Pre-Shaksperian Drama*, ed. J.M. Manly, vol. 1. Dover, 1967.

The Secret Garden
Burnett, Frances H. *The Secret Garden*. Lippincott, 1962.

The Secret Language
Nordstrom, Ursula. *The Secret Language*. Harper, 1960.

Sense and Sensibility
Austen, Jane. *Sense and Sensibility*. Oxford U.P., 1975.

Septimus and the Danedyke Mystery
Chance, Stephen. *Septimus and the Danedyke Mystery*. Nelson, 1973.

Seraphina
Harris, Mary K. *Seraphina*. Faber, 1960.

Seven Against Thebes
Aeschylus. *Seven Against Thebes*, ed. Christopher Dawson. Prentice-Hall, 1970.

Sexual Politics
Millett, Kate. *Sexual Politics*. Avon, 1973.

Shamela Andrews
Baker, Sheridan. *Shamela and Joseph Andrews*. Thomas Y. Crowell, 1972.

Sharp
Sharp, Harold and Marjorie Z. *Index to Characters in the Performing Arts*. 4 vols.: Part 1—Non-Musical Plays, 1966; Part 2—Opera & Musical Productions, 1969; Part 3—Ballets A to Z and Symbols, 1972; Part 4—Radio and Television, 1973. Scarecrow Press.

Shepard
Shepard, Leslie. *History of Street Literature*. Gale, 1973.

Sheridan
Sheridan, Martin. *Comics and Their Creators*. Hyperion Press, 1971.

Sherlock Holmes
Baring-Gould, William S. *The Annotated Sherlock Holmes*. Clarkson N. Potter, 1967.

Shirer
Shirer, William L. *The Rise and Fall of the Third Reich*. Fawcett World, 1972.

Short Friday
Singer, Isaac Bashevis. *Short Friday*. Fawcett Crest, 1964.

Shosha
Singer, Isaac Bashevis. *Shosha*. Farrar, Straus & Giroux, 1978.

Siddhartha
Hesse, Hermann. *Siddhartha*. tr. Hilda Rosner. New Directions, 1951.

The Silver Chair
Lewis, C.S. *The Silver Chair*. Macmillan, 1970.

Simon
Simon, George T. *Simon Says: The Sights and Sounds of the Swing Era 1935–1955*. Galahad Books, 1971.

Simplicissimus
von Grimmelshausen, H.J.C. *Simplicissimus the Vagabond*, tr. A.T. Goodrich. Folcroft, 1978.

Sir Gawain and the Green Knight
Sir Gawain and the Green Knight in *The Age of Chaucer* [Vol. I, *Penguin Guide to English Literature*]. Penguin, 1954.

Sir Launcelot Greaves
Smollett, Tobias. *Sir Launcelot Greaves,* ed. David Evans. Oxford U.P., 1973.

Sirga
Guillot, Rene. *Sirga.* S.G. Phillips, 1959.

Six Modern Short Novels
Six Great Modern Short Novels. Dell, 1964.

The Sketch Book of Geoffrey Crayon, Gentleman
Irving, Washington. *The Sketch Book of Geoffrey Crayon, Gentleman.* Twayne, 1978.

Sketches by Boz
Dickens, Charles. *Sketches by Boz.* Dutton, 1968.

Slaughterhouse-Five
Vonnegut, Kurt. *Slaughterhouse-Five.* Dell, 1971.

The Small House at Allington
Trollope, Anthony. *The Small House at Allington.* Dutton, 1972.

Smith
Garfield, Leon. *Smith.* Pantheon, 1967.

Smithsonian
Smithsonian, November 1977.

Snark
Carroll, Lewis. *The Hunting of the Snark.* Clarkson N. Potter, 1975.

The Snowy Day
Keats, Ezra Jack. *The Snowy Day.* Viking Press, 1962.

Sobel
Sobel, Bernard. *The New Theatre Handbook and Digest of Plays.* Crown, 1959.

Soldiers of Fortune
Davis, Richard Harding. *Soldiers of Fortune.* Scholarly Press, 1971.

Song of Igor's Campaign
Song of Igor's Campaign, tr. Vladimir Nabokov. McGraw-Hill, 1975.

Song of Roland
The Song of Roland, tr. Dorothy Sayers. Penguin, 1957.

Song of the Cid
Song of the Cid, tr. J.G. Markley. Bobbs-Merrill, 1961.

Sophocles Two
Sophocles Two, ed. David Grene and Richard Lattimore. Univ. of Chicago Press, 1957.

Sordello
Browning, Robert. "Sordello" in *Poems of Robert Browning,* ed. Donald Smalley. Houghton Mifflin, 1956.

The Sot-Weed Factor
Barth, John. *The Sot-Weed Factor.* Bantam, 1969.

Southwick Quizzism
Southwick, Albert P. *Quizzism and Its Key.* Gale, 1970.

Spain
Spain: A History in Art, ed. Bradley Smith. Doubleday, 1971.

Sparks
Sparks, John. *Bird Behavior.* Bantam, 1971.

Spevack
Spevack, Marvin. ed. *Harvard Concordance to Shakespeare.* Belknap, 1974.

Spiller
Spiller, Robert, et al. *Literary History of the United States,* 3rd ed. Macmillan, 1963.

Spoon River Anthology
Masters, Edgar Lee. *Spoon River Anthology.* Macmillan, 1968.

Sports Illustrated
"Inside the Eagle's Nest" in *Sports Illustrated,* February 15, 1979, pp. 142–143.

Springhaven
Blackmore, Richard. *Springhaven.* Harper., 1887.

The Spy
Cooper, James Fenimore. *The Spy.* Popular Library, 1971.

Stalky and Company
Kipling, Rudyard. *Stalky and Company.* Dell, 1968.

Stauffer
Stauffer, Francis H. *The Queer, the Quaint, and the Quizzical.* Gale, 1968.

Stefansson
Stefansson, Vilhjalmur. *Adventures in Error.* Gale, 1970.

Steppenwolf
Hesse, Hermann. *Steppenwolf.* Holt, Rinehart, Winston, 1970.

Stimpson
Stimpson, George W. *Nuggets of Knowledge.* Gale, 1970.

Stimpson *Questions*
Stimpson, George W. *Popular Questions Answered.* Gale, 1970.

The Stone-Faced Boy
Fox, Paula. *The Stone-Faced Boy.* Scholastic Book Service, 1972.

Stories
Cheever, John. *The Stories of John Cheever.* Knopf, 1978.

The Story About Ping
Flack, Marjorie. *The Story About Ping.* Viking, 1970.

The Story of Ferdinand
Leaf, Munro. *The Story of Ferdinand.* Viking Press, 1969.

Stranger in a Strange Land
Heinlein, Robert. *Stranger in a Strange Land.* Putnam, 1972.

Strawberry Girl
Lenski, Lois. *Strawberry Girl.* Lippincott, 1945.

A Streetcar Named Desire.
Williams, Tennessee. *A Streetcar Named Desire.* New Directions, 1947.

The Sun Also Rises
Hemingway, Ernest. *The Sun Also Rises.* Scribner, 1926.

Swiss Family Robinson
Wyss, Johann. *Swiss Family Robinson.* Grosset and Dunlap, 1970.

Sylvester and the Magic Pebble
Steig, William. *Sylvester and the Magic Pebble.* Dutton, 1973.

Sylvestre Bonnard
France, Anatole. *The Crime of Sylvestre Bonnard.* Dodd Mead, 1924.

The Tale of Benjamin Bunny
Potter, Beatrix. *The Tale of Benjamin Bunny.* Dover, 1974.

The Tale of Genji
Murasaki, Lady Shikibu. *The Tale of Genji.* Modern Library, 1960.

The Tale of Peter Rabbit
Potter, Beatrix. *The Tale of Peter Rabbit.* Dover, 1972.

A Tale of Two Cities
Dickens, Charles. *A Tale of Two Cities,* ed. George Woodcock. Penguin, 1970.

Tales of Hoffmann
Hoffmann, E.T.A. *Tales of Hoffmann,* tr. Michael Bullock. Frederick Ungar, 1963.

Tales of Terror
Poe, Edgar Allan. *Tales of Terror and Fantasy.* Dutton, 1972.

Tales of the Genii
Tales of the Genii, tr. James Ridley. Harrap, 1919.

The Talisman
Scott, Sir Walter. *The Talisman.* Dutton, 1972.

The Taming of the Shrew
Shakespeare, William. *The Taming of the Shrew,* ed. George L. Kittredge and Irving Ribner. John Wiley, 1966.

Tartarin de Tarascon
Daudet, Alphonse. *Tartarin de Tarascon.* French and European Pubn., 1965.

Tartuffe
Molière, Jean. *Tartuffe,* ed. Hallam Walker. Prentice-Hall, 1969.

Tarzan of the Apes
Burroughs, Edgar Rice. *Tarzan of the Apes.* Grosset and Dunlap, 1973.

Taylor
Taylor, Margaret Fisk. *A Time to Dance.* United Church Press, 1967.

The Tempest
Shakespeare, William. *The Tempest,* ed. Leonard Nathanson. William C. Brown, 1969.

Tender Is the Night
Fitzgerald, F. Scott. *Tender Is the Night.* Scribner, 1960.

Terrace
Terrace, Vincent. *The Complete Encyclopedia of Television Programs, 1947–1976.* 2 vols. A.S. Barnes, 1976.

Tess of the D'Urbervilles
Hardy, Thomas. *Tess of the D'Urbervilles,* ed. Scott Elledge. Norton, 1966.

Thebaid
Statius. *The Thebaid*. Adolt M. Hakkert, 1968.

The Thin Man
Hammett, Dashiell. *The Thin Man*. Random House, 1972.

This Side of Paradise
Fitzgerald, F. Scott. *This Side of Paradise*. Scribner, 1920.

Thompson
Thompson, Oscar. *International Cyclopedia of Music and Musicians*, 10th rev. ed. Dodd, 1975.

Thorne *Facts*
Thorne, Robert. *Fugitive Facts*. Gale, 1969.

The Three Musketeers
Dumas, Alexandre, père. *The Three Musketeers*. Hart, 1975.

Three Princes of Serendip
Hodges, Elizabeth J. *Three Princes of Serendip*. Atheneum, 1964.

The Three Royal Monkeys
de la Mare, Walter. *The Three Royal Monkeys*. Knopf, 1948.

The Three Toymakers
Williams, Ursula Moray. *The Three Toymakers*. Hamish Hamilton, 1945.

Through the Looking-glass
Carroll, Lewis. *Through the Looking-glass*. Random House, 1946.

Thyestes
Seneca. *Thyestes*, tr. Moses Hadas. Bobbs-Merrill, 1957.

Tiger at the Gates
Giraudoux, Jean. *Tiger at the Gates*. Oxford U.P., 1955.

Till Ulenspiegel
DeCoster, Charles T. *The Legend of the Glorious Adventures of Tyl Ulenspiegel in the Land of Flanders and Elsewhere.*Hyperion Press, 1978.

Timbs
Timbs, John. *Historic Ninepins*. Gale, 1969.

Timbs *Things*
Timbs, John. *Things Not Generally Known*. Gale, 1968.

Time of Trial
Burton, Hester. *Time of Trial*. Dell, 1970.

The Time Machine
Wells, H.G. *The Time Machine*. Bantam, 1968.

Timon of Athens
Shakespeare, William. *Timon of Athens*, ed. H.J. Oliver. Barnes & Noble, 1958.

'Tis Pity She's A Whore
Ford, John. *'Tis Pity She's A Whore*. Hill and Wang, 1969.

Titus Andronicus
Shakespeare, William. *Titus Andronicus*, ed. J.C. Maxwell. Barnes & Noble, 1968.

Tobacco Road
Caldwell, Erskine. *Tobacco Road*. New American Library, Signet, 1970.

Toby Tyler
Otis, James. *Toby Tyler*. Scholastic Book Service, 1972.

To Have and Have Not
Hemingway, Ernest. *To Have and Have Not*. Scribner, 1937.

Toland
Toland, John. *The Rising Sun*. Bantam Books, 1971.

Tom Brown's School Days
Hughes, Thomas. *Tom Brown's School Days*. Airmont, 1968.

Tom Jones
Fielding, Henry. *Tom Jones*, ed. W. Somerset Maugham. Fawcett World, 1969.

Tom Sawyer
Twain, Mark. *Tom Sawyer*. Washington Square Press, 1972.

Tom Thumb the Great
Fielding, Henry. *Tom Thumb and the Tragedy of Tragedies*. Univ. of California Press, 1970.

Tom's Midnight Garden
Pearce, Philippa. *Tom's Midnight Garden*. Lippincott, 1959.

Torrie
Johnson, Annabel and Edgar. *Torrie*. Harper & Row, 1960.

Tortilla Flat
Steinbeck, John. *Tortilla Flat*. Viking Press, 1935.

The Tower Treasure
Dixon, Franklin W. *The Tower Treasure*. Grosset and Dunlap, 1927.

Traveller
Goldsmith, Oliver. *Traveller, Or, a Prospect of Society*. British Book Centre, 1975.

Travels of Marco Polo
Polo, Marco. *Travels of Marco Polo*. Dutton, Everyman, 1954.

Treasure Island
Stevenson, Robert Louis. *Treasure Island*. Macmillan, 1962.

Treat
Treat, Roger. *The Encyclopedia of Football*. A.S. Barnes, 1977.

The Trial
Kafka, Franz. *The Trial*. Random House, 1969.

A Trick to Catch the Old One
Middleton, Thomas. *A Trick to Catch the Old One*. Univ. of California Press, 1968.

Trilby
DuMaurier, George. *Trilby*. Dutton, 1953.

Tristan
Von Strassburg, Gottfried. *Tristan*, tr. Arthur T. Hatto. Penguin, 1960.

Tristan and Isolde
Wagner, Richard. *Tristan and Isolde: Complete Orchestral Score*. Dover, 1973.

Troilus and Cressida
Shakespeare, William. *Troilus and Cressida*, ed. Arthur Quiller-Couch, et al. Cambridge U.P., 1969.

The Trojan Women
Euripides. *The Trojan Women*, tr. Gilbert Murray. Oxford U.P., 1915.

Tropic of Cancer
Miller, Henry. *Tropic of Cancer*. Ballantine, 1975.

Turkin
Turkin, Hy, and S.C. Thompson. *The Official Encyclopedia of Baseball*, 9th ed. A.S. Barnes, 1977.

Turner
Turner, Michael R., and Anthony Miall, eds. *The Parlour Song Book*. Viking Press, 1972.

The Turn of the Screw
James, Henry. *The Turn of the Screw*. Dell, 1956.

Twelfth Night
Shakespeare, William. *Twelfth Night*, ed. T.H. Howard-Hill. William C. Brown, 1969.

Twelve Famous Plays
Twelve Famous Plays of the Restoration and Eighteenth Century. Modern Library, 1933.

The Twenty-One Balloons
DuBois, William Pène. *The Twenty-One Balloons*. Dell, 1969.

Twenty Thousand Leagues Under the Sea
Verne, Jules. *Twenty Thousand Leagues Under the Sea*, tr. Mendor Brunetti. New American Library, Signet, 1969.

The Twisted Claw
Dixon, Franklin D. *The Twisted Claw*. Grosset and Dunlap, 1939.

Two Gentlemen of Verona
Shakespeare, William. *Two Gentlemen of Verona*, ed. George L. Kittredge and Irving Ribner. John Wiley, 1969.

Tyler, Wilkin, and Skee
Burch, Robert. *Tyler, Wilkin, and Skee*. Dell, 1971.

Uncle Remus
Harris, Joel C. *Uncle Remus: His Songs and Sayings*. Grosset and Dunlap, 1974.

Uncle Tom's Cabin.
Stowe, Harriet Beecher. *Uncle Tom's Cabin*. Dutton, 1961.

Uncle Vanya
Chekhov, Anton. *Uncle Vanya*. Avon, 1974.

The Uncommercial Traveller
Dickens, Charles. *The Uncommercial Traveller*. Dutton, 1970.

Understood Betsy
Fisher, Dorothy. *Understood Betsy*. Grosset and Dunlap, 1970.

Under the Yoke
Vazov, Ivan. *Under the Yoke*. Heinemann, 1912.

The Undiscovered Country
Howells, William D. *The Undiscovered Country.* Scholarly Press, 1971.

Universal Dictionary
Bailey, Nathan. *Universal Etymological English Dictionary.* Adler's Foreign Books, 1969.

Up Eel River
Montague, Margaret P. *Up Eel River.* Arno, facsimile of 1928 ed.

Upstairs, Downstairs
Hawkesworth, John. *Upstairs, Downstairs.* Ulverscroft, 1976.

Utopia
More, St. Thomas. *Utopia,* ed. Edward Surtz. Yale U.P., 1964.

V.
Pynchon, Thomas. *V.* Lippincott, 1961.

Van Doren
Van Doren, Charles, et al., eds. *Webster's Guide to American History.* G. & C. Merriam, 1971.

Vanity Fair
Thackeray, William M. *Vanity Fair.* Dutton, 1972.

Vargas
Austin, Reid, and Alberto Vargas. *Vargas.* Crown, 1980.

Vathek
Beckford, William. *Vathek.* Oxford U.P., 1970.

The Velveteen Rabbit
Williams, Margery. *The Velveteen Rabbit.* Doubleday, 1958.

The Vicar of Bullhampton
Trollope, Anthony. *The Vicar of Bullhampton.* Oxford U.P., 1975.

The Vicar of Wakefield
Goldsmith, Oliver. *The Vicar of Wakefield.* Dutton, 1956.

The Village
Bunin, Ivan. *The Village,* tr. I. Hapgood. Fertig, 1975.

Villon
Villon. *Poems,* tr. Peter Dale. St. Martin's Press, 1973.

The Virginians
Thackeray, William M. *The Virginians.* Smith, Elder, 1886.

La Vita Nuova
Dante's Vita Nuova, tr. Mark Musa. Indiana U.P., 1973.

Vizetelly
Vizetelly, Frank H., and Leander J. DeBekker. *Desk-Book of Idioms and Idiomatic Phrases in English Speech and Literature.* Gale, 1970.

Volsung Saga
Volsung Saga, tr. William Morris. Macmillan, 1962.

Voyage of the 'Dawn Treader'
Lewis, C.S. *The Voyage of the 'Dawn Treader.'* Macmillan, 1970.

Voyage to the Moon
Verne, Jules. *Voyage to the Moon.* Harmony Books, 1977.

Walden
Thoreau, Henry David. *Walden.* Macmillan, 1966.

Wallechinsky
Wallechinsky, David, et al. *The Book of Lists.* William Morrow, 1977.

Walsh Information
Walsh, William S. *A Handy Book of Curious Information.* Gale, 1970.

Walsh Classical
Walsh, William S. *Heroes and Heroines of Fiction: Classical, Medieval, Legendary.* Gale, 1966.

Walsh Curiosities
Walsh, William S. *A Handy Book of Literary Curiosities.* Gale, 1966.

Walsh Modern
Walsh, William S. *Heroes and Heroines of Fiction: Modern Prose and Poetry.* Gale, 1966.

The Wandering Jew
Sue, Eugène. *The Wandering Jew.* Modern Library, n.d.

The Water Babies
Kingsley, Charles. *The Water Babies.* Hart, 1977.

Watership Down
Adams, Richard. *Watership Down.* Macmillan, 1974.

Waverley
Scott, Sir Walter. *Waverley.* Dutton, 1969.

Webster's Sports
Webster's Sports Dictionary. G. & C. Merriam, 1976.

Wells
Wells, Carolyn. A Whimsey Anthology. Gale, 1976.

Wentworth
Wentworth, Harold, and S.B. Flexner. Dictionary of American Slang, 2nd supplemented ed. Thomas Y. Crowell, 1975.

Werner Bischof
Capa, Cornell. Werner Bischof. Grossman, 1974.

Westerman
Westerman, Gerhart von. Opera Guide. Dutton, 1968.

West Side Story
Bernstein, Leonard, et al. West Side Story. Random House, 1958.

What Makes Sammy Run
Schulberg, Budd. What Makes Sammy Run Random House, 1941.

Wheeler
Wheeler, William A. Dictionary of the Noted Names of Fiction. Gale, 1966.

Wheeler Allusions
Wheeler, William A. Familiar Allusions. Gale, 1966.

Where the Wild Things Are
Sendak, Maurice. Where the Wild Things Are. Harper & Row, 1963.

White
White, T.H. The Book of Beasts. Jonathan Cape, 1954.

The White Archer
Houston, James. The White Archer: An Eskimo Legend. Harcourt Brace Jovanovich, 1967.

The White Devil
Webster, John. The White Devil. Chandler, 1961.

White Fang
London, Jack. White Fang. Macmillan, 1935.

White Jacket
Melville, Herman. White Jacket. Holt, 1967.

Wieland
Brown, Charles Brockden. Wieland. Harcourt Brace Jovanovich, 1969.

Wigoder
Wigoder, Geoffrey, ed. Encyclopedic Dictionary of Judaica. Leon Amiel, 1974.

Wild Jack
Christopher, John. Wild Jack. Macmillan, 1974.

William Tell
Schiller, Friedrich Von. William Tell, tr. Sidney E. Kaplan. Barron's, 1954.

William the Dragon
Donnison, Polly. William the Dragon. Coward, McCann and Geoghegan, 1973.

The Wind in the Willows
Grahame, Kenneth. The Wind in the Willows. Dell, 1969.

Wind, Sand and Stars
De Saint-Exupéry, Antoine. Wind, Sand and Stars. Harcourt Brace Jovanovich, 1967.

Winesburg, Ohio
Anderson, Sherwood. Winesburg, Ohio. Viking Press, 1960.

Winnie-the-Pooh
Milne, A.A. Winnie-the-Pooh, Dell, 1974.

The Winter's Tale
Shakespeare, William. The Winter's Tale, in William Shakespeare: The Complete Works, ed. Peter Alexander. Collins, 1951.

The Witch's Daughter
Bawden, Nina. The Witch's Daughter. Lippincott, 1966.

A Wizard of Earthsea
LeGuin, Ursula. A Wizard of Earthsea. Bantam, 1975.

The Wolfman
Dreadstone, Carl. The Wolfman. Berkley, 1977.

The Woman of Rome
Moravia, Alberto. The Woman of Rome, tr. Lydia Holland. Manor Books, 1948.

The Wonderful Adventures of Nils
Lagerlof, Selma. The Wonderful Adventures of Nils. Pantheon, 1947.

The Wonderful Adventures of Paul Bunyon
The Wonderful Adventures of Paul Bunyon, retold by Louis Untermeyer. Heritage, c. 1945.

The Wonderful Wizard of Oz
Baum, L. Frank. *The Wonderful Wizard of Oz*. Random House, 1972.

The Wondrous Tale of Alroy
Disraeli, Benjamin. *The Wondrous Tale of Alroy*. Carey, Lea, and Blanchard, 1833.

Woods
Woods, George Benjamin, and Jerome Buckley, eds. *Poetry of the Victorian Period*. Scott Foresman, 1955.

Woodstock
Scott, Sir Walter. *Woodstock*. Dutton, 1969.

WB
World Book Encyclopedia. World Book-Childcraft International, 1979.

Yankee Thunder
Shapiro, Irwin. *Yankee Thunder: The Legendary Life of Davy Crockett*. Julian Messner, 1944.

The Yearling
Rawlings, Marjorie K. *The Yearling*. Scribner, 1962.

You Can't Go Home Again
Wolfe, Thomas. *You Can't Go Home Again*. Harper, 1940.

The Young Manhood of Studs Lonigan
Farrell, James T. *The Young Manhood of Studs Lonigan* in *Studs Lonigan: A Trilogy*. Vanguard, c. 1932–35.

Zeely
Hamilton, Virginia. *Zeely*. Macmillan, 1971.

Zimmerman
Zimmerman, J.E. *Dictionary of Classical Mythology*. Harper & Row, 1964.

Index

Aeneid, 201.1
Aengus, 372.1
Aenon, 54.1
Aeolian harp, 616.1
Aeolus, 11.1, 616.2
Aepytus, 514.2
Aeshma, 383.1
Aesir, 276.3
Aeson, 497.1
Aesop, 542.1
Aestas, 550.1
Aethalides, 394.1, 395.1
Aether, 11.2
Afer (Africus), 616.3
A.F.L.-C.I.O., 359.1
Africa, Darkest, 499.3
After Six, Inc., 191.1
Agag, 595.5
Agamede, 291.2
Aganippe, 341.1
agate, 292.1, 345.2
agate, black, 75.7
Agatha, St., 390.1, 415.2
Agathocles, 160.1
Aged P., 144.1
Agenor, 75.3
Agib, 69.1
Agincourt, 56.2
Aglaia, 57.1
Aglaonice, 70.1
Aglaus, 465.1
Agnes, 418.1, 590.2
Agnes, Sister, 449.2
Agnes, St., 95.1, 399.2, 425.2, 600.1
Agni, 242.1, 368.1, 625.1
Agnus Dei, 101.1
Agobard, 24.1
agony in the garden, 440.1
Agraeus, 311.1
Agramant's ring, 507.1
Agravain, Sir, 575.3
Agricola, 115.1
agrimony, 279.1
Agrippa, Menenius, 447.1
Agrotera, 311.2
Aguecheek, Sir Andrew, 251.2, 275.1
Ahab, 428.1, 595.6, 613.2
Ahab, Captain, 289.1, 401.1
Ahasueras, 605.1

Ahasuerus, 357.2
Ahmed, Prince, 291.3
Aholah and Aholibah, 28.1, 383.2
Ah Puch, 145.1
Ahriman, 208.1
Ahura Mazda (Ormuzd, Ormazd), 276.4
Aïda, 521.1
Aidoneus, 587.1
Aidos, 116.1
Aimwell, 150.1
Ainsworth, 453.1
Ajax (the greater), 70.2, 549.1
Ajax (the lesser), 112.1
Akawi-ko, 220.2
Akedah, 513.2
Akela, 285.1
Aladdin's lamp, 224.1
Alalcomeneus, 243.2
Alamo, 56.3
Alamogordo, 581.1
Alaric, 115.2
Alasnam's mirror, 95.8, 400.1
Alastor, 595.7
Alban, St., 290.2, 390.2
albatross, 381.1, 382.1
Alberich, 7.1, 183.1
Alberich's curse, 208.2
Albert, 523.2
Albigenses, 28.2, 37.1
Albion, 81.1, 273.1
Al Borak, 306.1, 555.1
Alcandre, 307.4
Alcatraz Island, 324.1, 351.1
Alceste, 313.1, 401.2
Alcestis, 521.2
Alcimedon, 127.1
Alcina, 383.3, 620.1
Alcithoe, 385.1
Alcmena, 5.1
Alcmena's sons, 582.1
Alcmeon, 385.2
Alcoholics Anonymous (AA), 12.1, 563.1
Alcyoneus, 273.2, 361.1
Aldegonde, Lord St., 72.1
Alden, John, 395.2, 572.1

Alden, John, and Miles Standish, 259.24
Aldine Classics, 243.3
Aldrich, Henry, 562.1
ale, Adam's, 608.2
Alecto, 19.1
Alectryon, 349.1, 574.3
Alethia, 303.1
Alexander the Great, 115.3
Alexander VI, 147.1
alexandrite, 380.4
Alexis, St., 37.2
Alfarache, Guzmán de, 568.1
Al Fata, 565.1
Alfio, 595.8
Alger, Horatio, 15.1, 547.1
Algernon, Moncrieff, and Jack Worthing, 150.23
Ali Baba, 111.1, 577.1
Alice, 224.2, 533.1
Alice's looking-glass, 400.2
Alidoro, 194.1, 445.1
Alison, 5.2
Alive, 89.1, 553.1
Allah, 128.2, 276.5, 431.1
Allen, Gracie, 164.1, 626.1
Alleyn, Inspector, 532.1
Allmers, Mrs., 428.2
All Quiet on the Western Front, 22.1
All Souls' Day, 281.4
Allworthy, Squire, 358.1
Almace, 556.1
Almanach de Gotha, 33.1
Almayer's Folly, 280.1
Almeira, 19.2
almond, 483.1
almond blossom, 246.1
almond, flowering, 304.4
Alnaschar's daydream, 250.2
aloe, 548.1
Aloeidae, 273.3
Alonso, 280.2
Alonzo the Brave, 272.1
Alpha Centauri, 80.1
Alpheus, 608.3
Alphonse, 533.2

Alphonseand Gaston, 125.1
Alphonso, Don, 445.2
Alsatia (white friars), 495.2
Al Sirat, 79.1
Altamont, Col. Jack, 252.2
altar, Noah's, 279.4
Altmark, the, 324.2
Altneuland, 593.2
alum, 475.1
Alvaro, 347.1
Alving, Mrs., 235.1
Amadis of Gaul, 100.1
Amahl, 291.4
Amahl and the Night Visitors, 102.1
Amaimon, 161.3
Amalekites, 197.1
Amalthaea, 554.1
Amalthea's horn, 3.1
amaranth, globe, 320.12
Amaryllis, 61.1
Amasis' ring, 430.1
Amaurote, 79.2, 593.3
Amaziah, 244.2
Amazon, 387.1
Amazons, 606.1
amber, 35.1
amber axe, 320.2
Ambrose, St., 193.1
ambrosia, 554.2
Ambrosio, 313.2
Ambrosio, Father, 383.4
Amelia, 220.3, 267.2, 443.1
Amenhotep, 619.1
Amen-Ra, 276.6
Amenti, 587.2
America, 535.1
America, Captain, 444.1
American Bandstand, 562.2
American concentration camps, 338.1
American elm, 444.2
American Gothic, 511.1
American linden, 389.1
American pasque flower, 248.1
American Scene, The, 263.1

America the Beautiful, 535.2
amethyst, 67.1, 475.2, 563.2
Amfortas, 481.3
Am ha-Arez, 316.1
Amish, 44.1
Ammit, 481.4
Amneris, 200.1
Amnon, 325.1
Amoco Cadiz, 167.1
Amor, 372.2
Amoret, 614.1
Amoret (Amoretta), 57.2
Amos, 506.1
Amos and Andy, 162.2, 259.3
Amphissa, 488.1
Amphitrite, 519.2
Amphitryon and Jupiter, 179.1
Amphoterus, Acarnan and, 595.3
amrita, 320.3
Amylion, Amys and, 259.4, 502.1
Amys and Amylion, 259.4, 502.1
anaconda, 143.1
Anakim, 273.4
Anammelech, Adrammelech and, 513.1
Ananias, 150.2, 291.5
Ananias Club, 150.3
Anastasia and Orizella, 200.2
Anastasie and Delphine, 336.1
Anasterax, Niquee and, 325.13
Anatomy of Melancholy, 393.2
Anaxarete, 374.1
Anchises, 69.2, 70.3
anchor, 304.1
Ancient Mariner, 605.2
Ancient of Days, 276.7
Andermatt, Christiane, 5.3, 55.1
Andersonville, 324.3, 548.2
Andorra, 533.3

Andras, 170.1
Andret, 186.1
Andrews, Joseph, 60.3, 421.1
Andrews, Pamela, 602.1
Andrew, St., 390.3
Androcles, 358.2
Andromache, 220.4, 602.2
Andromeda, 500.2
Andros, 617.1
Andvari, 183.2
Andvari's ring, 507.2
Andy, Amos and, 162.2, 259.3
anemone, 52.3
anemone, blue, 246.2
angel, guardian, 18.4, 283.24
Angelica, 62.1, 221.1, 341.2
Angelica, Suor, 254.1
Angelo, 313.3
angel of light, 150.4
Angels of Mons, the, 272.2
Angitia, 392.2
angora cat, 384.1
Angry Young Men, 174.2
Angstrom, Harry "Rabbit," 262.1
Angur-boda, 167.2
Angurvadel, 556.2
Aniara, 605.3
ankh, 320.4
Ankou, 145.2
Anna, Joachim and, 503.5
Annabella, Giovanni and, 325.7
Annabel Lee, 58.1, 375.2
Annfwn, 593.4
Annwn, 622.1
Anon, Mr., 533.4
A. N. Other, 207.1
Anschluss, 591.2
Anselmo, 136.1
ant, 331.1
Antaeus, 273.5, 604.2
Antarctica, 499.1
Antenor, 122.2, 447.2, 575.4
Anteros, 441.1

Antevorta,571.1
Anthea, 247.1
Anthesteria, 247.2
Anthony, Mr., 284.1
Anthony of Padua, St., 399.3
Anthony, St., 37.3
Antichrist, 197.2
Anti-Defamation League, 24.2
Antietam, 56.4
Antigone, 175.3, 549.2
Antigonus, 273.6
Antiochus, 325.2
Antiphates, 89.2
Antipholus, 582.2
Anti-Saloon League, 563.3
Antisthenes, 139.1
antler dance, 237.1
antlers, 134.2
Antoinette, Marie, 148.1, 328.1
Antonio, 267.3, 575.5
Antony and Cleopatra, 375.3
Antony, Mark, 193.2, 380.5
Antony, St., 392.3
Anu, 237.2
Anu (An), 294.3
Anubis, 145.3, 285.2
Anunnaki, 587.3
Aoi, Princess, 374.2
Aornum, 587.4
Apache, 615.1
Apache Indians, 516.1
Apaches, 208.3
Apaturia, 150.5
Apeliotes (Lips), 616.4
Apemantus, 139.2
Apemosyne, 488.2
Apepi, 420.1
Aphesius, 154.1
Aphrodite, 58.2, 237.3, 372.3, 471.1
Aphrodite Genetrix, 389.2
Aphrodite Porne, 383.5
Aphrodite Urania, 378.1
Apis, 83.1
Apollo, 60.4, 367.1, 413.1, 551.1

Apolloand Artemis, 582.3
Apollo (Phoebus), 392.4
Apollyon, 161.4, 208.4
Apophis, 157.2, 420.2
Apostrophia, 602.3
Appalachia, 465.2
apple, 564.1
Apple Annie, 30.2, 465.3
apple blossom, 248.2
apple of discord, 170.2
apple pie, 16.1
Appleseed, Johnny, 30.3, 267.4
apples of perpetual youth, 320.5
apples of Sodom, 150.6
Appomattox Courthouse, 151.1
April Fool's Day, 353.1
Apsu, 128.3, 608.4
aquamarine, 67.2
Aquarius, 628.1
Aquilo, 616.5
Aquinas, St. Thomas, 268.1
Arabella, Lady, 433.1
Arabian Nights, 224.3
Arachne, 35.2, 524.1, 574.4
Arafat, Mt., 503.1
Aralu, 587.5
Aramati, 220.5
Aram, Eugene, 158.2
Arapaho, 615.2
Ararat, 500.3
Arbaces, 150.7
Arbela, 56.5
Arcadia, 442.1
Arc de Triomphe, 597.1
Archer, Isabel, 191.2
Archer, Lew, 532.2
Archie, 562.3
Archimago, 150.8, 208.5, 313.4
Archimedes, 171.1, 344.1
Arch of Trajan, 597.2
Arcite, Palamon and, 361.7
Arden, Enoch, 91.1, 589.1
Areopagitica, 257.1
Areopagus, 122.3

Ares, 606.2
Arethusa, 574.5, 608.5
Argan, 312.1
Argestes, 616.6
Argo, 555.2
Argonauts, 298.3, 605.4
Argus, 127.2, 283.1, 380.6, 409.3
Argus Panoptes, 283.2
Ariadne, 205.2
Arians, 28.3
Aries, 628.2
Arindal, Ada and, 377.1
Arion, 306.2, 500.4
Aristaeus, 226.1
Aristarchus of Samos, 43.1
Aristotle, 268.2, 458.1, 561.1
Arjuna, 339.2
Ark, Noah's, 495.7
ark of bulrushes, 111.2
Arlington National Cemetery, 86.2
Armada, Spanish, 151.2
Armado, 70.4
Armado, Don Adriano de, 467.2
Armageddon, 56.6, 159.3, 195.1
Armande, 378.2
Armenian Massacre, 391.2
Armida, 520.1
Armida, Rinaldo and, 379.19
Armida's Garden, 383.6
Armilus, 197.3
Armleder, 24.3
Arms and the Man, 22.2
arms reversed, 281.5
Armstrong, Jack, 612.1
Armstrong, Johnnie, 568.2
Armstrong, Neil, 243.4
Army Bomb Plot, 219.1
Arne, 488.3
Arnold, Benedict, 576.1
Arnolphe, 150.9, 352.2
Aronnax, Prof., 268.3
Arrigo, 347.2
arrow and cross, 390.4

arrow, Cupid's gold, 378.7
Arrow of Azrael, 145.4
Arrowsmith, Martin, 469.1
Arsinoë, 220.6, 313.5, 546.1
Artemidorous, 347.3
Artemis (, 95.2, 98.1, 311.3, 410.1
Artemis, Apollo and, 582.3
Artemisia, 281.6
Artful Dodger, 135.1
Arthur, 298.4
Arthur, King, 100.2, 566.1
Arundel, 306.3
Arundhati, 614.2
Aruru, 128.4
Arveragus, 134.3
Ascalaphus, 574.6, 575.6
Ascapart, 273.7
Aschenbach, Gustave von, 351.2
Asclepius (Aesculapius), 392.5
Asclepius' cup, 292.2
Aselges, 383.7
Asgard, 294.4
ash, mountain, 477.4
Asha, 357.3
Asherah, 411.1
ashes, dust and, 145.18
ashes, sackcloth and, 449.13
Ashkenazi, Simcha, 433.2
Ashley, Lady Brett, 191.3, 471.2
Ashman, 226.2
Ashmedai, 157.3
Ashtaroth, 315.2
Ashton, Lucy, 385.3
Ashtoreth, 383.8, 420.3
Ashura, 481.5
Asia, 255.1
Askr, 128.5
Aslaug, 287.2
Asmodeus, 135.2, 157.4, 383.9
Aspasia, 123.1, 370.1
asphodel flower, 145.5
assassins, 39.1, 223.2

Assault, 306.4
ass, Balaam's, 38.1
ass, brown, 590.5
ass, jawbone of, 391.10
ass, ox and, 419.4
ass, wild, 352.21
assembly of women, 278.1
Assumption of Virgin Mary, 36.1
Assur, 276.8
Astarte, 58.3, 237.4, 410.2
Astarte's dove, 237.5
aster, China, 220.12
asteria, 373.1
Asterius, 63.1
Astraea, 506.2
Astree, Celadon and, 379.5
Asvins, 367.2
Atala and Chactas, 379.2
Atalanta, 196.1, 311.4, 555.3
Atargatis' dove, 237.6
Atar Gul, 313.6
Ate, 208.6, 402.1
Athaliah, 591.3
Athelny, Sally, 378.3
Athena, 127.3, 237.7, 524.2, 606.3, 619.2
Atkins, Tommy, 534.1
Atlantic City, 265.1
Atlantides (Pleiades), 427.1
Atlantis, 166.1, 593.5, 622.2
Atlas, 273.8, 481.6, 543.2
Atlas, Charles, 76.1, 543.3
atomic bomb (A-bomb), 159.4
Aton (Aten), 551.2
Atreus, 415.3, 595.9
Atropos, 145.6
Atropos, Clotho, and Lachesis, 229.2
Attica, 324.4, 508.1
Attila, 115.4
Aubrey, Father, 404.1
Auburn, 1.1
Aucassin and Nicolette, 379.3

Auge, 98.2
Augean stables, 240.1
Augsburg, Peace of, 204.1
augurs, 473.1
Augustine, St., 619.3
auk, great, 215.4
Auld Ane, 161.5
Auld Hornie, 161.6
Auld Lang Syne, 225.1
Aura, 616.7
Aurae, 11.3
Aurelius, 520.2
Aurora, 142.2
Auschwitz, 269.1
Auster, 616.8
Austerlitz, 56.7, 151.3
Auteb, 356.1
Autolycus, 135.3, 568.3
Autumnus, 46.1
Avagddu, 585.1
Avalon, 294.5, 622.3
Avernus, Lake, 587.6
Avesta, 623.1
Avidyā, 208.7, 316.2
Avignon, 120.1
ax, battle, 283.3, 606.4
ax, double, 237.23, 368.2, 551.8
axe, amber, 320.2
Axis Sally, 472.1
Azazel, 161.7
Azrael, 145.7
Azrael, Arrow of, 145.4

B

Baader-Meinhof gang, 565.2
Baal, 237.8
Baalim, 315.3
Baanah and Rechab, 575.7
Baba Yaga, 620.2
Babbie, 377.2
Babbitt, 396.1, 457.1
Babe, 543.4
Babel, 114.1
Babes in the Wood, 339.3
babes in the woods, 418.2
Babe, the Blue Ox, 273.9

Big Bull Market, 258.2
Big Daddy, 610.2
Big-endians, 28.4
Big Foot (Sasquatch), 416.3
Biggers, Jack, 275.3
Bigger Thomas, 289.3, 347.7
Big John, 76.2
Bigotes, 313.7
Big Valley, The, 615.5
Bikini and Eniwetok, 159.5
bilberry, 150.10
Bildad, Eliphaz, and Zophar, 130.4
bile, black, 393.4
bile, yellow, 346.10
Bilitis, 302.1
Bilko, Sergeant, 308.2
Bill of Rights, 257.3
Billy Boy, 614.3
Billy the Kid, 437.2, 615.6
bindweed, small, 309.9
Bionic Man, 543.5
Birch, Harvey, 75.6
Birdman of Alcatraz, 66.1, 324.7
birds, Stymphalian, 311.13
Birmingham riots, 508.2
Biron, 173.4
Birotteau, César, 53.1
Birth of a Nation, The, 120.2
Bishop of Digne, 254.2, 358.4
bitterroot, 248.3
bittersweet, 303.3
black, 145.10, 208.8
black agate, 75.7
black and gold, 610.3
Black Annis, 585.5
Blackbeard, 132.2, 460.2
Black Beauty, 306.6
black bile, 393.4
black cat, 381.2
Black Death, 172.1, 305.2
Black Death pogroms, 24.6
black dog, 208.9

black-eyed susan, 248.4
Black Friday, 53.2, 118.2
Black Hand, the, 266.1
black heart, 208.10
Black Hole of Calcutta, 324.8, 548.4
Black Hundreds, 24.7
black ox, 381.3
Black Panthers, 565.3
black poodle, 208.11
black poplar, 75.8
Black Prince, 82.1
Black Sox, 78.1
Black Sox Scandal, 517.2
Black Tuesday, 53.3
black widow spider, 143.3
Blakeney, Percy, 173.5, 251.3
blarney stone, 558.4
Blas, Gil, 588.1
Blatant Beast, 530.2
Bleys, 386.1
Blifil, 313.8
Bligh, Captain, 91.2, 132.3, 598.2
Bligh, William, 338.5
Blimber, Cornelia, 448.2
blindfold, 357.4
Blind Pew, 69.3
Blodenwedd, 57.5
Blondel, 380.9
Blondie, 260.1
Blondie and Tootsie, 278.2
blood, 97.2
Blood, Col. Thomas, 313.9
blood, cry of, 595.14
blood libel, 24.8
blood of the lamb, 475.4
bloodstone, 67.3
Bloody Sunday, 391.3
bloom, dock, 443.2
Bloomer, Amelia, 235.3
blossom, almond, 246.1
blossom, apple, 248.2
blossom, crabapple, 58.5
blossom, orange, 248.22
blossom, peach, 248.24
blossoms, orange, 95.9, 237.37, 389.9
Bludyer, Mr., 130.1

blue, 357.5
blue, red on, 281.25
blue anemone, 246.2
Bluebeard, 412.4, 463.1, 613.3
bluebell, 380.10
bluebonnet, 248.5
Blue Boy, 189.1
blue cornflower, 246.3
blue laws, 93.1
blue ribbon, 468.2
blues, 393.5
blue salvia, 619.5
blue-stocking, 235.4
Bluffe, Captain, 70.7
Blunderbore, 273.14
Blushington, Edward, 572.3
Bluto (Brutus), 598.3
boa constrictor, 143.4
Boadicea (Boudicca), 75.9
boar, Erymanthian, 485.3, 516.6
Boar's Head Tavern, 504.2
Boatswain, 177.1
Boaz, 358.5
Bobadill, Captain, 70.8, 126.2
bobbed hair, 218.4
Bobbin, Robbin and, 231.13
Bobbsey Twins, 582.4
Bob, Captain, 355.1
Bobchinsky and Dobchinsky, 182.1
Bodachan Sabhaill, 296.2
Bodach Glas, 145.11
Bodhi, 619.6
Bodhisattva, 198.2, 283.5
Bodine, Jethro, 164.2
Boffin, Nickodemus, 303.4
Boiler, Boanerges, 487.1
boiler factory, 371.1
Bokim, 133.1
Bok, Yakov, 24.9, 338.6
Bold Beauchamp, 75.10
Boleyn, Anne, 148.3
Bolingbroke, Henry, 135.5
Bolívar, Simón, 154.2

Bollingen, 468.3
Bolo, Miss, 130.2
Bolshoi, 567.2
bolton, 244.3
bomb, atomic, 159.4
bomb, hydrogen, 159.14
bomb, neutron, 159.20
Bona Dea, 95.3, 184.1,
  237.10
Bona Mater, 184.2
Bonanza, 615.7
Bonaventura, St., 309.2
Bond, James, 540.1
Bones, Brom, 173.6
bones, devil's, 265.10
Bonhomme, Jacques,
  465.7
Boniface, 307.6
Boniface, St., 404.2
bonnet, 185.2
Bonnie and Clyde, 437.3
Bontemps, Roger, 434.1
book, closed, 416.4
book, open, 303.14
book, sealed, 111.5
Book of Mormon, 252.3,
  623.3
Book of the Courtier,
  100.4
Book of the Dead, 623.4
Boom Town, 615.8
Boone, Daniel, 261.1
Boop, Betty, 245.1
Booth, Amelia, 277.1
Booth, Captain, 465.8,
  469.3
Boot Hill, 86.3, 615.9
Booze, 181.5
Bordeaux, 617.4
Borden, Lizzie, 412.5
Boreas, 616.9, 618.1
Borgia, Cesare, 135.6,
  512.1
Borgia, Lucrezia, 62.2
Borgias, 343.1
Boris and Natasha, 598.4
Borkman, John Gabriel,
  155.1
Born, Bertrand de, 481.7
Borromeo, Charles, 44.2
Boru, Brian, 154.3
Bosch, Hieronymus,
  305.4

Boston, 93.2
Bostonians, The, 235.5
Boston marathon, 196.2
Boston Massacre, 391.4,
  508.3
Boston Strangler, 412.6
Boston Tea Party, 490.4,
  508.4
Boswell, James, 65.1
Bothwell, Sergeant, 529.1
botonné cross, 579.1
Bottom, 194.2
Bottom, Nick, 38.2,
  594.2
Boulanger, Ralph, 313.10
Bounderby, Josiah, 428.3
Bountiful, Lady, 267.7
Bourse, 241.1
Bovary, Charles, 73.2
Bovary, Emma, 5.5, 72.3,
  216.1, 349.3
Bow Bells, 108.1
Bowditch, 519.3
Bowdler, Thomas, 93.3
Bowery, the, 12.3, 147.4,
  158.3
Bowes, Major Edward,
  334.1
Bowie, Jim, 261.2
Bowie knife, 615.10
Bows, Mr., 627.1
bow, Ulysses', 314.10
Boxer Rebellion, 490.5,
  624.1
Boyet, 621.2
Boyne, Battle of the,
  151.5
Boynton, Egeria, 313.11
Boynton, Nanny, 187.2
Boy Scouts, 10.1, 124.1
Boythorn, Laurence,
  277.2
Bradamant, 387.2
Brady Bunch, The, 612.2
Brady, "Diamond Jim,"
  265.5
Braggadocchio, 70.9
Bragi, 193.4, 462.1, 619.7
Bragi (Brage), 413.2
Brahman, 276.9
Brahmin, 33.3
Braille, Louis, 69.4
Brainworm, 173.7

Bran, 145.12, 502.2
branch, olive, 446.9
Brandimante, 220.7
Branghtons, the, 107.1
Brangwen, Ursula, 405.3
Brant, Capt. Adam, 5.6
Brass, Sally, 387.3
Brass, Sampson, 588.2
Brattle, Carrie, 474.2
Brave New World, 473.5
Bray, Walter, 588.3
bread, 101.2
bread basket, 226.5
breaking of the sound
  barrier, 371.2
breast, 237.11
breast, lactating, 341.11
Breck, Alan, 75.11
Breitmann, Hans, 176.1
Brer Fox, 135.7
Brer Rabbit, 402.4
Briareus, Cottus, and
  Gyges, 409.5
Brick, 12.4
Bridal Chorus, 389.4
Bridehead, Sue, 405.4
Bridge, Brooklyn, 79.5
Bridge, Golden Gate,
  79.6
Bridge, London, 79.7
Bridge, River Kwai, 79.8
Bridge of San Luis Rey,
  The, 79.4, 229.3
Bridge of Sighs, 113.2
Brid'oison, Judge, 85.1
Bridoison, Taiel de, 94.1
Brigadoon, 439.2
Brighella, 523.3
Brink's, 408.1
Briseis, 220.8
Britomart, 95.4, 220.9
Britomartis, 311.5
Broadway, 567.3
Brobdingnag, 273.15
Brocken, 620.3
Broken Arrow, 615.11
Brom Bones and
  Ichabod Crane, 509.1
Bromius, 570.1
Brontes, 409.6, 570.2
Brooke, Dorothea, 521.3
Brook Farm, 593.6
Brooklyn Bridge, 79.5

Brooks, Miss, 561.3
broom, 309.3
Broom Hilda, 620.4
Broteas, 385.6
Brother Jonathan, 16.4,
    207.2, 482.1
brothers, Collyer, 403.1
brothers, Joseph's,
    118.10, 200.6
Brothers Karamazov,
    The, 383.13
brother's keeper, my,
    283.6
brothers, Montgolfier,
    243.23
brothers, Sullivan, 158.9
Browdie, John, 76.3
brown, 55.3
brown ass, 590.5
Brown, Buster, 402.5
Brown, Charlie, 21.1,
    219.2, 332.1
Browndock, Miss, 547.2
Brown, Father, 532.3
Browning, Robert, and
    Elizabeth Barrett, 379.4
Brown, Joe, 280.5
Brown, John, 154.4,
    390.5
Brown, Matilda, 270.1
Brown vs. Board of
    Education, 357.6
Brummel, Beau, 251.4
Brummel, George B.
    (Beau Brummel), 227.1
Brunhild, 19.4, 150.11,
    175.4
Bruno, St., 309.4
Brutus, 39.2, 118.3
Brutus, Decius, 575.9
Bryan, William Jennings,
    152.1
Bshyst, 364.4
bubbles, 77.2
Bucentaur, 538.1
Bucephalus, 306.7
Buchanan, Daisy, 62.3
Buchanan, Tom, 5.7
Buchenwald, 269.4
Buchis, 83.2
Buck, 177.2, 501.1
Budd, Billy, 338.7, 339.5
Buddenbrooks, 149.1

Buddha, 198.3, 276.10
buffalo, 267.8, 543.6
Buffalo Bill, 287.5, 388.1
Bulge, Battle of the,
    56.9, 151.6
bull, 75.12, 132.4, 267.9
bull, Cretan, 83.3, 485.2
bulldog, 160.3
Bullet, 177.3
Bull, John, 81.3
Bull Run, 56.11
Bull's-eye, 177.4
Bullwinkle, 164.3
bulrushes, ark of, 111.2
Bumble, Mr., 132.5
Bumppo, Natty, 261.3
Buncombe County,
    313.12
Bundren, Addie, 262.3
Bung, 465.9
Bunion Derby, 219.3
Bunker, Archie, 64.2
Bunker, Edith, 164.4,
    303.5
Bunker Hill, 56.12
Bunny, Benjamin, 6.2
Bunny, Bugs, 135.8,
    322.1
Bunsby, Captain Jack,
    578.1
Bunter, 87.2
Bunthorne, Reginald,
    112.2
Bunyan, Paul, 76.4,
    273.16, 543.7
Buonafede, 182.2
Burchell, Mr., 173.8,
    267.10
Burden, Joanna, 405.5
Burghers of Calais, 513.3
Burgundy, 617.5
Burgundy, Duke of,
    576.2
burlesque show, 425.3
Burley, John, 176.2
Burlingame, Henry,
    173.9
Burma-Shave, 584.1
Burns, Helen, 370.2
Bury Me Not on the
    Lone Prairie, 615.12
Busiris, 412.7
Butes, 385.7

Butler, Rhett, 433.3,
    588.4
Butler, Theodosius, 112.3
Buto, 551.5
buttercup, 610.4
Butterfly, Madame, 374.3
butterfly orchis, 264.1
Buttermilk, Little
    Johnny, 150.12
bwbachod, 296.3
Byam, Roger, 91.3,
    380.11
Byron, Cashel, 479.2
Byron, Lord, 146.1

C

cabala, 417.1
Cabala, The, 33.4
Cabinet of Dr. Caligari,
    The, 305.5
Cabot, Eben, and Abbie
    Putnam, 375.4
Cabrini, St. Frances,
    243.7
Caca, 242.2
Cacus, 409.7, 568.5
cadence, perfect, 450.5
Cadillac, 384.3
caduceus, 392.6, 395.3
Cadwallader, Rev. Mr.,
    277.3
Caedmon, 243.8
Caenis, 488.5
Caesar crosses Rubicon,
    581.3
Caesar, Julius, 40.1,
    115.6
Caesar, Sid, 626.3
Cagliostro, 256.1
Caicas, 616.10
Cain, 52.4, 412.8, 605.6
Cain, mark of, 475.13
Caius, Dr., 346.1
Calamity Jane, 455.1,
    473.6, 615.13
Calandrino, 182.3
Calantha, 255.2
Calchas, 352.4
Caleb, 220.42
calf, golden, 208.17,
    315.6
Caliban, 89.4, 409.8

Calidore, Sir, 100.5
California Joe, 261.4
California Trail, 615.14
Caligula, 512.2
Calista, 549.3
Calliope, 193.5, 341.3, 462.2
Callirrhoë, 352.5
Callista, 390.6
Callisto, 574.7
Call of the Wild, The, 453.2
Calmady, Sir Richard, 153.1
Calpurnia, 473.7
Calvary (Golgotha), 145.13
calycanthus, 358.6
Camacho, 134.4
Cambridge, 188.2
Cambuscan's mirror, 400.3
Cambyses, Judgment of, 357.7
camellia, 248.6
camellia, white, 57.19
Camenae, 427.2
Camilla, 221.2, 555.5
Camilla, Mrs., 150.13
Camille, 378.6, 471.4, 521.4
Camillo, 380.12
Camiola, 421.4
Camors, 176.3
Campion, Albert, 532.5
Camptown Races, 265.6
Cana, 389.5, 399.4
Canaan, 439.3
Canace, 325.3
Canadian Mounties, 129.1
canary grass, 453.3
can-can, 245.2
Cancer, 628.3
Candida, 220.10
Candide, 434.2, 605.7
Candour, Mrs., 530.3
Canens, 281.7
Canio, 370.3
Canisius, St. Peter, 152.2
Cannae, 56.13
Cannes, 238.1

Cannonade of Valmy, 581.4
Canossa, 449.3
Canterbury bell, 220.43, 607.1
Canterbury Tales, 354.2
Canticle of the Sun, The, 279.2
cantua, 246.4
Cantwell, Dr., 313.13, 575.10
Canty, Tom, 546.3
Canute, 115.7
cap, green, 53.4
Capitoline geese, 607.2
Capone, Al "Scarface," 266.2
Capp, Andy, 108.2, 181.6, 349.4
cap, Phrygian, 257.17
Capricorn, 628.4
caps, coonskin, 218.7
Capulets and Montagues, 509.2
Capys, 168.1
Cardea, 283.7
Cardiff giant, 273.17
Cardillac, 428.4
cardinal flower, 222.1
cards, Tarot, 473.28
CARE, 9.2
Carey, Louisa, 358.7
Carey, Philip, 153.2, 360.1, 436.2
Carey, William, 541.2
Cargill, Rev. Josiah, 393.6
Carker, James, 192.1
Carker, John, 219.4
Carlisle, Lady Mary, 418.4
Carlos, Don, 347.8, 357.8
Carmel, Mt., 566.2
Carmen, 221.3, 473.8
Carmenta, 98.3, 392.7
Carna, 292.3
carnation, 246.5
carnation, red, 373.6
carnation, scarlet, 248.32
carnation, striped, 376.15
carnation, yellow, 35.16
Carne, Caryl, 576.3
Carnegie, Andrew, 456.1

Carnegie Hall, 567.4
carnelian, 382.3, 390.7
Caro, 383.14
Carolina yellow jessamine, 248.7
carols, 102.3
carp, 75.13
Carpetbaggers, 213.2, 433.4
Carpo, 46.3
Carson, Kit, 615.15
Carstone, Richard, 393.7
car-stuffing, 218.5
Carter, Nick, 532.6
Carter, Sergeant, 210.1
Cartier's, 384.4
Carton, Sidney, 176.4
Caruso, Enrico, 528.1
Casanova, 383.15
Casanova, Giovanni Jacopo, 469.4
Casaubon, Edward, 448.3
Casby, Christopher, 213.3
Casey, Ben, 392.8
Caspar, Melchior, and Balthazar, 419.2
Casper, 272.4
Casper the Friendly Ghost, 270.2
Cassandra, 168.2, 347.9, 455.2, 473.9, 549.4
Cassidy, Butch, and the Sundance Kid, 437.4
Cassio, 182.4
Cassiopeia, 594.3
Cassius, 118.4
Castalia, 341.4, 462.3
Castiglione, Baldassare, 124.2
Castlewood, Francis Esmond, 176.5
Castor and Pollux, 259.6, 582.5
cat, 104.2, 157.6, 190.2
cat, angora, 384.1
cat, belling the, 323.1
cat, black, 381.2
Cat, Cheshire, 277.4, 345.3
cat, Morris the, 228.3
Catawba, 617.6

Cody, "Buffalo Bill," 615.21
coffin, cypress, 320.10
Colada, 556.6
Colamartini, Christina, 521.5
collar, Moran's, 357.16
college, cow, 226.8
Collins, Mr., 244.7
Collyer brothers, 403.1
Colomba, 595.12
Colossos, 273.19
Colossus of Rhodes, 559.2
Colt .45, 615.22
Columbine, 245.4, 250.5
columbine, Rocky Mountain, 248.29
Columbo, 532.10
Columbus, Christopher, 214.1
Comanche, 553.2, 615.23
Comanche Indians, 516.4
Combray, 424.2
Comédie-Française, 567.5
Comedy of Errors, 582.6
Common Lot, The, 280.6
Common Market, 121.1
common thistle, 44.5
Compeyson, 568.6
Compleat Angler, The, 119.1
Comstock, Anthony, 93.4
Comstock Lode, 577.2, 615.24
Comus, 504.3
Conachar, 126.4
Concentration Camps, 548.5
concentration camps, American, 338.1
Conchobar, 374.6
Concorde, 371.3
Concordia, 288.1, 446.2
Conestoga wagon, 354.6, 615.25
Confederacy, 536.1
Confidence Man, The, 401.3
Confucius, 458.2, 619.9
Connecticut Yankee, the, 344.3
Conqueror Worm, 145.16

Conrad, Lord, 460.3
Conseil, 448.6
Conservative party, 117.1
Constance, 15.3
Constantinople, Fall of, 581.8
Constitutum Constantini, 252.5
Consus, 122.4, 265.9
contrition, perfect, 450.6
Conway, Hugh, 2.4
Cooke, Ebenezer, 21.2, 326.1
Coolidge, Calvin, 557.4
coonskin caps, 218.7
Copernicus, Nicholas, 43.2
Copia, 3.2
Coppelius, 595.13
copper, 291.8
Copper, Captain, 467.4
Copperfield, David, Peggotty, and Clara, 259.19
copperhead, 143.6
coral, 291.9
Coral Sea, 56.14
coral snake, 143.7
cord, pillar and, 440.16
Cordelia, 270.3, 380.16
cordonazo:, 616.12
coreopsis, 97.3
Corey, Giles, 255.3
Corin, 526.1
Corinth, 610.6
Coriolanus, 35.4, 467.5
Cormoran, 273.20
Cornelia, 373.3
Cornelius, 54.2
Cornelius, Valdes and, 116.3
cornflower, blue, 246.3
corn, sheaf of, and sickle, 550.5
cornucopia, 3.3, 46.4
Coronis, 221.4
Cortés, Hernando, 115.10, 492.1, 575.15
Corus, 616.13
Corybantes, 114.3, 413.4
Cory, Richard, 29.3
Cosa Nostra, 266.3
Cosette, 436.4

Così fan tutte, 347.12
Cosmas, St. and St. Damian, 392.9
Costard, 398.2
Costello, Lou, 164.5
Costigan, Captain J. Chesterfield, 355.2
Cottus, Briareus, and Gyges, 409.5
Count of Monte Cristo, 324.10, 351.3
Coup de Jarnac, 126.5
Courtenay, Miles, 100.7
court, kangaroo, 338.16
Courtly Love, The Rules of, 372.17
Courtly, Sir Hartley, 374.7
Court of St. James's, 81.4
Cousin Itt, 287.6
Coverley, Sir Roger de, 100.8, 277.5
Cowardly Lion, 126.6, 572.4
cow college, 226.8
Cowperwood, Frank A., 433.5
cowslip, 57.6
coyote, 262.4
crab, 275.4
crabapple blossom, 58.5
Crackit, Toby, 568.7
crack, step on a, 381.18
crane, 618.2
Crane, Ichabod, 48.2, 569.1, 572.5
Crane, Ichabod, and Brom Bones, 509.1
Cranmer, Thomas, 303.7
Cratchit, Bob, 465.11, 589.4
Crater, Judge, 166.4
Cratos, 543.8
Cratus, 69.5
Crawley, Pitt, 280.7
Crawley, Rev. Josiah, 465.12
Crawley, Sir Pitt, 107.3
Crazy Horse, 615.26
Crazy Ivar, 37.9
Creakle, Mr., 132.6
Creator, the, 276.11

deus ex machina, 399.5
Deutschland über Alles, 535.4
Devaki, 411.5
de Vargas, Luis, 376.17
Devi, 411.6
deVille, Cruella, 598.22
devil's bones, 265.10
Devil's Island, 52.5, 324.11
Devils, Prince of the, 161.13
Dharma, 506.4
Dhisana, 3.7
diamond, 67.4, 80.2, 372.7
diamond, Hope, 381.9
Diana's statue, 500.7
Diarmuid, 604.4
dice, 440.6
Dickinson, Emily, 351.5
Dick, Mr., 187.3
Dickon, 124.3
Dick Van Dyke Show, The, 178.2
Dictynna, 344.4
Dido, 135.12, 549.7
Dido and Aeneas, 375.7
Dien Bien Phu, 151.8
Different Drummer, 329.2
Digambara, 425.4
Dike, 357.9
Dillinger, John, 437.6
Dillon, Matt, 49.2, 615.30
Dilmun, 294.7
Dimmesdale, Arthur, 313.18, 449.4
Din, Gunga, 521.6
dinosaur, 215.2
Diocletian, 132.8
Diogenes, 37.10, 139.5, 177.7, 303.8
Diomedes, 361.2
Diomedes and Sthenelus, 259.9
Diomedes and Troilus, 509.3
Diomedes, mares of, 516.9
Dionysia, 504.4

Dionysus, 226.11, 445.3, 504.5, 617.11
Dionyza, 352.8
Dioscuri (Castor and Pollux), 582.7
Dirae, 481.8, 595.16
Dirce, 574.12, 608.7
di Ripafratta, Cavalier, 377.15
Dis, 587.7
Disasters of War, 305.7
discord, apple of, 170.2
Discordia, 170.3
disease, Legionnaires', 172.6
Dismas (Dysmas), 449.5
Dithers, Mr., 210.3, 297.2
Dithyrambus, 497.2
dittany, 98.4
dittany, white, 627.8
Diver, Dick, 149.2
Dives, 157.9, 610.8
Divine Comedy, 201.3
Dix, Dorothea, 284.5
Dixie, 536.2
Dobbin, Captain William, 48.3
Dobchinsky, Bobchinsky and, 182.1
Dobson, Zuleika, 376.6
dock bloom, 443.2
Doctors' Plot, 118.6
Dodge City, 615.31
dodo, 215.3
Dodona, 473.12
Dodsworth, Fran, 467.6
Dodsworth, Sam, 174.4, 370.5, 377.7
Doeg the Edomite, 211.2
dog, 380.17
dogbane, 150.15
dog, black, 208.9
Dog, Guardian Black, 473.15
Dogberry, 332.2, 467.7
Dogberry and Verges, 112.6
Dogpatch, 590.6
dog returning to his vomit, 250.6
dogwood, 248.9
Dolius, 135.13, 380.18

Dollallolla, Queen, 527.2
doll, Kewpie, 218.13
Doll's House, A, 235.6
Dolor, 249.2
dolphin, 285.7
Dominic, 177.8
Domino, Antoine "Fats," 231.3
Dôn, 237.22
Donald Duck, 346.2, 352.9
Donar, 570.3
Donatello, 152.7, 412.12
Donatists, 28.6
Don Carlos, 595.17
Dondi, 418.6, 436.5, 522.2
Donegild, 412.13
Don Juan, 383.17, 469.5, 481.9
donkey, 544.2
Donn, Arabella, 590.7
Donna Reed Show, The, 178.3
Donner Party, 89.6, 553.5
Donnybrook Fair, 508.6
Donny, the Misses, 582.8
Doolittle, Doctor, 187.4
Doolittle, Eliza, 108.3, 162.7, 398.3
Doone, Lorna, 58.6, 377.8
Dorcas, 296.4, 502.3
Do-Right, Dudley, 418.7, 506.5
Doritis, 3.8
dormouse, 531.1
Dorothy, 224.6, 486.1
Dotheboys Hall, 44.6
double ax, 237.23, 368.2, 551.8
double bar cross, 45.6
Double, Edmund, 231.4
Douglas, the Widow, 476.3
Dounia, 521.7
dove, 220.15, 341.6, 383.18, 395.4, 446.3
dove and lily, 20.1
dove, Astarte's, 237.5
dove, Atargatis', 237.6

Evangeline, 167.6, 220.18
Evangeline and Gabriel, 375.9
Eve, 243.13, 481.10
Eve, Adam and, 30.1, 52.2, 128.1, 175.2, 339.1, 425.1
Evelina, 418.9
Evelyn, Aunt, 476.5
Everest, Mt., 499.5
Everyman, 354.8, 506.7
Evilmerodach, 358.9
ewer, basin and, 339.4
Excalibur, 556.9
Exodus, 354.9
Exorcist, The, 305.10
extreme unction (last rites), 145.20, 225.2
eye, 431.3
eye for an eye, 595.19
eyes, scales falling from, 198.8
Ezekiel, 7.4, 473.13

F

Fabio, 6.4
Fabius, 135.14
Face, 87.5, 308.3
factory, boiler, 371.1
Faerie Queene (Gloriana), 201.4, 515.2
Fafnir, 283.16, 420.6
Faggus, Tom, 300.4
Fagin, 568.9, 598.7
fair, cherry, 77.3
fairy godmother, 283.17, 445.4
Faithful Eckhardt, 283.18
Faithful Johannes, 380.21
Fakirs, 37.11, 223.3
Fala, 177.9
Falke, Dr., 595.20
Fall of Constantinople, 581.8
Fall, The, 263.5
Falstaff, Sir John, 70.11, 126.7, 349.5, 383.20
Famine, Potato, 310.4
fan, 245.7

Fannie and Edmund Bertram, 259.10
fan palm, 320.11
Fantasia, 224.7
Fantine, 521.9
Farewell to Arms, A, 22.3
fasces, 45.8
fatal raven, 195.3
Fatal Vespers, 167.7
Fata Morgana, 94.2, 318.4
Fat Freddy, 275.6
Father Time, 7.5, 571.4
Fatima, 136.4
fat of the land, 384.10
fatted calf, the, 254.4, 307.7
Fauntleroy, Little Lord, 189.2
Faustus, Doctor, 15.4, 136.5, 627.3
Favonius, 616.15
Fawkes, Guy, 118.8
Fawley, Jude, 381.6
Fear of Flying, 199.1
feast, Barmecide, 233.1, 318.1, 353.2
Feast, Belshazzar's, 233.2, 473.4
feast, Lucullan, 233.4
Feast, Trimalchio's, 233.7
Federal Theater, 567.7
feet, bare, 465.4
Fell, Dr., 35.8
Fell, Dr. Gideon, 532.14
Fenella, 182.7
Feng, 438.2
fennel, sweet, 291.12
Fenris, 409.15
Ferdinand, 83.4
Ferguson, Samuel, 51.1
fern, 246.12
fern seed, 345.5
Ferohers, 283.19
Ferragus, 273.25
Ferrando, 352.10
Fescennia, 505.2
Feste, 106.3
fetch, 179.3
fetching Cerberus, 485.4
Fête Champêtre, 504.6

Fetterman Massacre, 391.6
Feverel, Sir Austin, 289.5
Fiacre, St., 172.2, 226.12
Fideal, 157.10
Fields of Mourning, 375.10
Fiend, Lubbard, 273.37
fiery cross, 64.3, 607.5
fiery swords, 283.20
Fife, Barney, 332.3
54-40 or Fight!, 170.5
Figaro, 135.15, 523.5
fig leaves, 407.3
figs, garland of, 237.24
Final Solution, 24.10, 269.6
Financier, The, 280.8
Finches of the Grove, 202.2
Findlay, Maude, 235.8, 346.4
Finger Lakes, 617.12
fingers, crossed, 382.4
Finn, Huckleberry, 6.5, 358.10, 402.11, 436.6, 491.3
fire, 551.10
Fire, Great Chicago, 167.3, 242.6
fire, ordeal by, 566.8
Fire, St. Anthony's, 172.10
fire, St. Elmo's, 80.4
fire and water, 52.7
firebranded foxes, 159.8
Fires of Smithfield, 28.9
First Families of Virginia, 33.5
First Noel, The, 102.9
fish, 101.5, 237.25
Fisher King, 283.21
fishes, loaves and, 399.11
Fitzgerald, F. Scott, 176.10
Five and Ten, 333.3
Five by Five, Mr., 231.6
five wise virgins, 477.1
flagellants, 223.4, 449.7
flagpole sitting, 218.8
flag, red, 141.5
flag, white, 151.17

flame lily, 246.13
flame, white forked,
    611.5
flaming heart, 627.4
Flanders Field, 86.5
Flashman, Harry, 84.4,
    469.6
Flavius, 380.22
flea market, 333.2
Fledgeby, 592.1
fleshpots of Egypt,
    384.11
fleur-de-lis, 246.14, 579.4
Flicka, 306.10
Flintstones, The, 178.4
Flite, Miss, 187.5
flood, 481.11
Flood, Deucalion's, 167.5
Flood, Johnstown, 167.10
Flora, 539.1
Flora, Miles and, 208.23
Flora, Zephyr and, 247.4
Florian, 242.5
Florimel, 572.7
flower, asphodel, 145.5
flower, basil, 289.2
flower, cardinal, 222.1
flowering almond, 304.4
flower of saguaro cactus,
    248.10
flowers, 539.2
flowers and fruit,
    garland of, 237.26
flowers, garland of,
    237.27
flowers, spring, 185.9
Fluellen, 448.8
flute, magic, 475.11
Flutter, Sir Fopling,
    251.5
Flying Dutchman, 272.7,
    381.7
flytrap, white, 150.32
Foawr, 273.26
Fogg, Phileas, 6.6, 228.1,
    435.4, 480.1
Fomorians, 460.5
Fondlewife, 297.3
foot, rabbit's, 382.14
Foppington, Lord, 251.6
forbidden fruit, 30.5,
    564.2
Ford, 173.15

foreskins, 100 Philistine,
    212.2
forget-me-not, 248.11
Forrester, Mrs. Marian,
    471.5
Forsyte, 396.2
Fort Knox, 577.4
Fort Sumter, 56.16
Fortuna, 94.3
Fortunate Isles (Happy
    Isles), 294.10
Fortunato, 324.14
Fortunatus' purse, 610.10
forty-niners, 577.5
Fosdick, Fearless, 532.15
Fotheringay, 324.15
Fotis, 88.2
Foulfellow, J. Worthing-
    ton, 598.8
Fountain of Youth,
    497.3, 586.2
Four Horsemen of the
    Apocalypse, 27.2, 159.9
Four Hundred, the, 33.6
four-leaf clover, 382.5
Fourth of July, 16.7,
    257.10, 444.3
fox, 135.16
foxes, firebranded, 159.8
Fragarach, 556.10
Francesca, Paolo and,
    375.26
Franciscans, 37.12
Francis de Sales and
    Jane Frances de
    Chantal, Sts., 259.14
Francis of Assisi, St.,
    358.11
frangipani, 246.15
Frank, Anne, 24.11,
    146.3
Frankenstein's monster,
    409.16, 585.9
Frankie and Johnnie,
    221.7, 375.11
frankincense, gold, and
    myrrh, 102.11
Franklin, Benjamin, 65.3,
    171.4, 344.7, 368.4,
    596.1
Frasquita, 245.8
Freaks, 153.4
Fred and Ethel, 259.11

Frederick, 591.4
Free Soil Party, 25.3
French, Mr., 87.6
French willow, 75.16
Freya, 58.9, 226.13,
    237.28, 625.2
Friday, 523.6
Friday and Robinson
    Crusoe, 259.12
Friday's child, 358.12
Friday the 13th, 381.8
Frigg, 372.8
Frigga, 184.5
frisbees, 218.9
Fritchie, Barbara, 75.17
Fritz the Cat, 383.21
frogs, peep, 539.4
Frollo, Claude, 78.2
Frome, Ethan, 199.2,
    226.14
Frome, Zenobia (Zeena),
    527.3
Frost, Jack, 109.2
fruit, forbidden, 30.5,
    564.2
fruit, naked girl with,
    550.4
fruit and flowers,
    garland of, 237.26
Fudd, Elmer, 19.6, 162.9
Fudo, 619.11
Fuggers, 610.11
Fugitive, The, 205.7
Fuller's thistle, 401.5
Fulton's Folly, 250.7,
    361.3
funeral, Valentino's,
    258.6
Furioso, Bombastes,
    385.13
Fury, Sergeant, 601.1
Fylgie, 283.22

G

Gabriel, 18.3, 20.3,
    395.6, 580.1
Gabriel, Evangeline and,
    375.9
Gadarene swine, 464.1
Gaea, 184.6, 226.15,
    411.7
Gagarin, Yury, 243.14

Gaigern, Baron, 347.15
Galahad, Sir, 483.3, 602.6
Galapos, 273.27
Galatea, 58.10, 527.4, 574.14, 608.8
Galatea and Acis, 375.12
Galilee, 101.6
Galileo, 43.3
Gallanbiles, the, 313.19
Gallant Fox, 306.11
Gallipoli, 151.9
Gambrinus, 181.7
game, perfect, 450.7
Ganconer, 471.6
Gandhi, Mohandas K., 37.13
Ganelon, 575.18
Ganesha, 619.12
gang, Baader-Meinhof, 565.2
gang, Dalton, 437.5
Gang, Detroit Purple, 266.4
Gang, Gashouse, 299.1
Gantry, Elmer, 206.1, 256.2, 487.2
Ganymede, 302.4, 523.7
garden, Adonis', 77.1
Garden, Armida's, 383.6
garden, enclosed, 600.5
garden of the Hesperides, 294.11, 439.5
Gargantua, 273.28, 275.7
Gargery, Mrs., 527.5
gargoyles, 585.10
garlanded girl, 539.3
garland of figs, 237.24
garland of flowers, 237.27
garland of flowers and fruit, 237.26
garland of grape leaves, 237.29
garland of grapes, 504.8
garland of oak leaves, 587.14
garland of palm, 341.13
garland of rays, 142.8, 276.17
garland of red and white roses, 600.9

garland of stars, 36.7, 357.23
garland of wheat ears, 3.12, 226.26
garland of wool and narcissi, 229.14
Garm, 283.23
garnet, 67.6
Garrick Theatre, 567.8
Gascon, 70.12
Gashford, 313.20
Gashouse Gang, 299.1
gas, laughing, 362.3
Gaston, Alphonse and, 125.1
Gastrolaters, 275.8
Gatsby, Jay, 13.2, 34.2, 202.3, 307.8
Gautama, 198.5
gavel, 45.9
Gawain, 75.18
Gawain, Sir, 100.12
Gay Liberation, 302.5
Gay Nineties (Naughty Nineties), the, 299.2
Gay 90s, 264.2
Gaza Strip, 170.6
Geddes, 106.4
geese, Capitoline, 607.2
Geese of Brother Philip, 590.8
Gehazi, 280.9
Gehenna, 295.2
Geiger counter, 141.1
Gemini, 582.12, 628.5
Genesis, 128.8, 243.15
Geneva, 446.4
Genevieve, St., 476.6
Genghis Khan, 115.12
Genji, Prince, 469.7
Genseric, 115.13
Gentle Annis, 616.16
Gentle Ben, 270.5
Gentleman's Agreement, 24.12
George of the Jungle, 332.4
George, St., 81.5
George, Tobey, 546.5
Georgette, 286.1, 418.10
Georgie Porgie, 402.12
Geppetto, 399.8

Gerard, Lieutenant Philip, 293.5
Gerard, Philip, 428.7
Geritol, 7.6
Germinal, 508.7
Geronimo, 615.33
gerrymander, 578.3
Gerstein, Kurt, 168.3
Gertie the Dinosaur, 243.16
Gertrude, 609.1
Geryon, 409.17
Geryon, oxen of, 485.8
Gessler, 293.6, 583.3
Gestapo, 82.7, 208.16, 565.4
Gethsemane, 440.9, 548.6
Gettysburg, 56.17, 86.6
Gettysburg Address, 77.4, 193.9
Gettysburg, Battle of, 581.9
Ghibellines, Guelphs and, 509.7
Ghismonda and Guiscardo, 375.13
Ghost, Drury Lane Theater, 272.5
Ghost of Charles Rosmer, the, 272.8
Ghost of Christmas Past, the, 272.9
Ghost of Christmas Present, the, 272.10
Ghost of Christmas Yet to Come, the, 272.11
Ghost of Hamlet's Father, the, 272.12
Ghost's Walk, the, 272.13
ghost town, 615.34
giant, Cardiff, 273.17
Giants in the Earth, 226.16
Gibeath-haaraloth, 103.4
Gibeonites, 545.2, 578.4
G.I. Bill, 9.3
Gibson girl, 58.11
Gideon, 154.7
Gideon Bible, 584.3
Gideon v. Wainwright, 357.10
Gidget, 562.5
Gift of the Magi, 521.10

Gift of the Magi, The, 102.10

G.I. Joe, 534.4

Gila monster, 143.8, 143.8

Gilbreths, 480.2

Gilda, 2.5, 521.11

Gildersleeve, Throckmorton P., 210.4

Giles, St., 360.2

Gilgamesh, 167.8, 201.5

Gilligan, 332.5

Gilligan's Island, 91.6

Gillis, Dobie, 562.6

Gilpin, John, 489.2

Gingham Dog and Calico Cat, 509.6

ginseng, 26.2

Giotto's O, 450.1

Giovanni and Annabella, 325.7

giraffe, 559.6

girl, garlanded, 539.3

girl, Gibson, 58.11

girl, naked, with fruit, 550.4

girl, Petty, 525.2

Girl Scouts, 10.2

girl, Vargas, 525.3

Give My Regards to Broadway, 424.1

Glas, Bodach, 272.14

Glass Menagerie, The, 318.5

Glaucus, 60.8, 375.14

Gleason, Jackie, 231.7

Glencoe, Massacre of, 336.2, 391.13

Glendower, Owen, 70.13

Glinda, 358.13

globe, 45.10

globe amaranth, 320.12

Globe Theatre, 567.9

Gloomy Gus, 455.3

Glorious Appollers, the, 307.9

Glorious Revolution, 591.5

glory, hand of, 345.6

Gloucester, 69.7

Glumdalca, Queen, 273.29

gnome, 184.7

Gnosticism, 28.10

goat, 383.22, 618.4

goat, Judas, 150.18, 285.9

Gobbo, Launcelot, 106.5

God, 128.9, 431.4, 432.2

Godfather, 266.6

Godiva, Lady, 287.9, 425.5

Godmother, Fairy, 283.17, 445.4

God Save the Queen, 81.6, 535.5

Godunov, Boris, 591.6

Goedzak, Lamme, 605.10

Gog and Magog, 27.3, 273.30

Golan, 495.4

Golaud, 352.11

Golconda, 577.6

gold, 551.11, 619.13

Goldberg, Rube, 344.8

gold, black and, 610.3

Golden Ass, The, 38.5

Golden Bells, 58.12

Golden Boy, 479.6

Golden Calf, 208.17, 315.6

Golden Cockerel, 473.14

Golden Fleece, 486.3

Golden Gate Bridge, 79.6

golden handshake, 225.3

Golden Horde, 115.14

golden mean, 450.2

golden poppy, 248.12

goldenrod, 248.13

Golden Spurs, Battle of, 581.10

golden wattle, 246.16, 246.16

gold fish-swallowing, 218.10

gold, frankincense, and myrrh, 102.11

gold on red, 356.4

gold on white, 33.7

Gold Rush, 258.3

gold watch, 225.4

Golgotha (Calvary), 390.9, 440.10

Goliad, 391.7

Goliards, 504.7, 505.3, 605.11

Goliath, 76.5, 273.31

Gomer, 471.7

Gomorrah, Sodom and, 147.13, 159.24, 613.6

Gompers, Samuel, 359.2

Goncourt, 468.7

Goneril and Regan, 221.8, 336.3

Gone With the Wind, 536.3

Gong Show, The, 334.2

Gonsalve, Inigo and, 111.3

Gonzalo, 380.23

Good-Deeds, 380.24

Good Earth, The, 226.17

Good Joe, 277.6

Good Samaritan, 296.5, 358.14

Good Shepherd, 101.7

Good Soldier Schweik, 534.5

Goodwood, Caspar, 453.4

Goody Two Shoes, 522.3

Goofy, 48.4

Google, Barney, 265.11, 349.6

Goops, 107.4

Gordian knot, 466.2

Gorgons, 409.18, 585.11

Goriot, Père, 589.5

Goshen, 3.9

Goshen, Land of, 446.5

Gospel, 271.3

Go Tell It On The Mountain, 257.11

Gotham, three wise men of, 544.11

Götterdämmerung, 27.4, 159.10

Gournay, Mlle. de, 405.6

Graces, 57.9

Gradgrind, Thomas, 429.3

Gradgrind, Tom, 568.10

Graduate, the, 326.2

Graeae, the, 69.8

grail, 486.4

Gráinne, 375.15

Gram, 556.11

Gramimond, 556.12

Grammy, 468.8
Grandet, Eugénie, 263.6, 280.10
Grand Fenwick, Duchy of, 590.9
Grand Hotel, 457.2
Grand, Joseph, 250.8
Grand Ole Opry, 590.10
Grand Tour, the, 188.5
Crane, 306.12
Granida and Daifilio, 442.4
Granny, 346.5
Grant's Tomb, 86.7
Grant, Ulysses S., 429.4
grape leaves, garland of, 237.29
grape, Oregon, 248.23
grapes, 384.12
grapes and vine leaves, 46.5
grapes, garland of, 504.8
Grapes of Wrath, The, 348.2, 465.13
grass, canary, 453.3
Grasshopper, 90.1, 260.2
Grauman's Chinese Theater, 222.3
gray, 536.4
Gray, Dorian, 8.2, 29.5
great auk, 215.4
Great-Aunt Dymphna, 187.6
Great Chicago Fire, 242.6
Great Depression, 465.14
Great Divide, 499.6
Great Emancipator, The, 257.12
Great Exhibition, the, 243.17
Great Gatsby, The, 149.3
Great Giant of Henllys, 157.11
Great Pyramid of Cheops, 86.8
Great Schism, the, 170.7
Great Train Robbery, The, 243.18
Great White Hope, 479.7
Greek cross, 597.6
green, 200.4, 237.30
Green, Hetty, 403.2

green, red and, 102.23
green, red on, 356.7
Green, Verdant, 590.11
green, white and, 185.10
green cap, 53.4
green-eyed monster, 352.12
Green Giant, Jolly, 273.33
Green Hills of Africa, 311.6
greenhorn, 334.3
green pastures, 384.13
Greenwich Village, 71.1
gregale (Euroclydon), 616.17
Grendel, 409.19
Gretel, Hansel and, 89.7, 205.8
greybeard-grow-young, 320.13
Grey, Lady Jane, 77.5, 146.4, 148.4
Gride, Arthur, 592.2
griffin, 409.20
Griffiths, Clyde, 280.11
Grimes, Peter, 289.6
Grim Reaper, 145.21
grindstone, 331.5
Gringalet, 306.13
Gringoire, 48.5
Griselda, 370.6, 443.4
grits, 536.5
Gross, Allison, 585.12
Grosvenor, Archibald, 112.7
Gruagach, 287.10
Grub Street, 465.15
Grundy, Miss, 537.1, 561.6
Grundy, Mrs., 64.4, 457.3, 478.1
Guadalcanal, 56.18
guardian angel, 18.4, 283.24
Guardian Black Dog, 473.15
Guelphs and Ghibellines, 509.7
Guernica, 391.8, 606.8
Guggenheim, 456.2, 468.9

Guilbert, Brian de Bois, 132.9
Guillotin, Joseph, 148.5
Guinevere and Sir Launcelot, 375.19
Guinevere, Queen, 5.11, 405.7
Guiscardo, Ghismonda and, 375.13
Gulliver, Lemuel, 6.7, 605.12
Gummidge, Mrs., 393.12
Gunn, Ben, 91.7, 385.14
Gunpowder Plot, 118.9, 219.7, 490.8
Gunsmoke, 615.35
Gutenberg, Johannes, 243.19
Guyon, Sir, 602.7
Gyges, 603.3
Gyges, Briareus, and Cottus, 409.5
Gyges's ring, 345.7
Gymnosophists, 425.6
Gynt, Peer, 605.13
gypsum, 382.6
Gypsy, 605.14

H

Habanera, 245.9
Habima Theater, 567.10
haboob, 616.18
Hades, 295.3, 587.10
Hagar, 546.6
Hagar and Ishmael, 52.8
Hagen, 412.14
Hague, Frank, 156.1
Haight-Ashbury, 71.2
Hail, Mary, 20.4
hair, bobbed, 218.4
hair, long unbound, 483.6
Hakluyt, Richard, 354.10
Halcyone, Ceyx and, 379.6
Hale, Nathan, 75.19, 444.4, 496.2
Halftrack, General, 332.6
Halitherses, 66.2
Haller, Harry, 518.1
Halley, Edmond, 43.4
Halloween, 402.13

Judgment of God, 566.6
Juggernaut, 159.16
Jughead, 275.11, 364.6
jujube, 253.3
Julia, 173.20
Julia, Donna, 5.13
Julian the Hospitalor, 236.3, 307.10
Julie, Miss, 245.11
Juliet, Romeo and, 146.7, 375.29, 379.20
Jungle, The, 240.2
Junior (Red Skelton), 402.14
Junkers, 33.8
Juno, 11.4
Jupe, 106.10
Jupiter, Amphitryon and, 179.1
Jupiter Fulgurator, 368.5
Jupiter Pluvius, 608.9
jury, hung, 326.4
Justinian, 363.3
Jutland, 56.21

K

K., 262.6
Kaddish, 281.14
Kadiddlehopper, Clem, 590.12
Kaldi, 171.5
Kalevala, 201.8
Kali, 145.24
Kama, 372.10, 441.5
Kamikaze, 521.16, 549.13
kangaroo court, 338.16
Karenina, Anna, 5.14, 375.18, 549.14
karma, 229.7
Katherine, 527.6
Katinka, the Powerful, 543.11
Kato, 380.29
Katyn Massacre, 391.11
Katzenjammer Kids, 402.15, 582.13
Kay, Sir, 70.14, 530.7
Keats, John, 146.5
Kedesh, 495.5
Keep the Home Fires Burning, 178.7

Keller, Helen, 69.10, 144.3, 160.7
Kelly, Emmett, 106.11
Kenge, Mr., 558.8
Kenneth, Sir, 173.21
Kennicott, Carol, 493.1
Kent, 380.30
Kent State, 508.9
Kewpie doll, 218.13
key, 220.22
keys, 45.11
Keystone Kops, the, 626.6
KGB, 540.6
Khan, Kubla, 538.5
Khe Sanh, 581.12
Khnum, 128.11
Kibroth-hattaavah, 280.13
Kidd, Captain William, 460.9, 577.7
Kildare, Dr., 392.13
Kilkenny cats, 509.10
Killmoulis, 296.6
Kilroy, 584.5
Kim, 6.9
Kinah, 281.15
king and his ministers, 231.10
King Cotton, 226.18
King Kong, 273.35
King, Martin Luther, Jr., 193.10
King of Kings, 101.8
King Solomon's mines, 577.8
King, Tom, 300.6
Kirby, George and Marian, 272.17
Kiriath-arba, 495.6
Kishinev, 24.17
kismet, 229.8
kiss, 440.12
kiss, Mafia's, 225.8
Kiss, The, 441.6
Kitelys, 352.13
Kitty Hawk, 47.1
Klingsor, 208.20
Klink, Colonel, 332.8
Klondike, the, 258.4
Knave of Hearts, 494.2, 568.12
knife, Bowie, 615.10
knife, ear and, 415.5

Knights of the Round Table, 100.14, 486.6
Knights Templar, 476.10
knock on wood, 382.9
knot, Gordian, 466.2
Know-Nothing Party, 624.4
Koch, Ilse, 82.12
Kojak, 129.4, 573.1
Ko-Ko, 211.3, 232.6
kolem, 475.10
Kon-Tiki, 6.10, 354.12
Kookie, 251.7
Köpenick, 173.22
Korah, 490.13
Koran (Quran), 623.8
Kore, 226.19
Kotter, Gabe, 561.7
Kovatzov, Major, 423.5
Kowalski, Stanley, 84.6, 210.5
Krakatoa, 371.5
Kraken, 409.25
Kralich, Ivan, 490.14
Kramden, Ralph, 210.6
Kramer, Josef, 82.13
Krasov, Kuzma Ilich, 174.6
Krazy Kat, 376.8, 626.7
Krebs, Maynard G., 364.7
Kriemhild, 58.15
Krik, Benya, 266.5
Kringle, Kris, 102.16
Krishna, 372.11
Kristallnacht, 24.18, 159.17
Kuan Yin, 358.19, 476.11
Ku Klux Klan (KKK), 64.8, 217.4, 565.6
Kumalo, Rev. Stephen, 281.16
Kundry, 620.7
K'ung Fu, 566.7
Kuryakin, Illya, 540.7
Kwai Chang Caine, 605.16

L

La Belle Dame Sans Merci, 293.9

Lescaut, 139.6

Lescaut, Manon, 123.3, 260.3

Lescaut, Manon, and the Chevalier des Grieux, 379.15, 379.15

Lessways, Hilda, 32.3

Lestrade, 532.22

Le Sueur, Lucetta, 375.20

Lethe, 253.4

letters, chain, 218.6

letter, Uriah, 575.34

Leucippus, 173.24

Leucosia, Ligeia, and Parthenope, 520.9, 520.9

levanter, 616.19

Leverkühn, Adrian, 385.15

leviathan, 27.5, 409.28

Levin, Konstantine, 421.7

Lewis, 112.10

Lexington, 56.22

Libbeus the Apostle, 281.17

Liber and Libera, 617.13

Liberator, 25.6

Liberty Bell, 16.8

Libra, 326.5, 357.13, 628.7

Lichas, 523.11

Lidice, 159.18

Liebfraumilch, 617.14

Liechtenstein, 533.6

life of Riley, 384.15

Ligeia, Leucosia, and Parthenope, 520.9

light, angel of, 150.4

Lightfoot, Martin and Hereward, 259.16

lighthouse at Pharos, 285.10

Light in August, 64.10

Li'l Abner, 48.6, 590.13

lilac, purple, 248.26

lilac, white, 372.23, 418.17

lilies of the field, 57.13

Lilith, 98.8, 383.26

Lilliputians, 533.7

lily, 246.20, 483.5, 600.7

lily, dove and, 20.1

lily, flame, 246.13

lily, sego, 248.33

lily, white, 185.11

lily of the valley, 246.21

limbo, 253.5

Limkins, Mr., 231.11

limoniads, 427.6

Lincoln, Abraham, 25.7, 154.9, 303.12

Lincoln Center, 567.11

Lindbergh, Charles, 243.21

linden, 246.22

linden, American, 389.1

Lindisfarne, 56.23

Linkinwater, Tim, 228.2, 480.4

Linus, 340.2, 413.9

lion, 101.10, 255.5, 283.27, 551.14

lion, Nemean, 485.6

lions' mouths, 113.4

lips, bee-stung, 218.3

Lisa, 200.8

Lisbeth (Cousin Bette), 595.24

Lismahago, Lieutenant Obadiah, 6.11

Little Annie Fanny, 88.3

Little Bighorn, 151.10

Little Bo-peep, 90.2, 526.5

Little Boy Blue, 90.3, 364.10, 526.6

Little Buttercup, 29.6

Little Caesar, 266.7

Little Dorrit, 572.8

Little Emily, 192.3

Little Engine That Could, 160.8, 453.5

Little John, 543.12

Little Miss Muffet, 572.9

Little Nell, 418.11, 522.5

Little Orphan Annie, 8.3, 137.1, 348.3, 436.7, 492.4

Little Prince, The, 224.10

Little Rascals, The, 402.17

Little Rock, Arkansas, 64.11, 508.10

Little Tich, 533.8

Little Tramp, 219.8

Livia, 588.8

Livingstone, David, 404.4

loaves and fishes, 399.11

lobelia, 208.21

Loch Ness monster, 409.29, 416.9

Locket, Lucy, 90.4

Lockit, Lucy, 155.4

locust, 191.6

locusts and wild honey, 554.3

Lodge, Mr., 210.7

Loge (Loki), 578.6

Lohengrin, 421.8

Lolita, 62.7, 441.7

Lollards, 28.13

Loman, Willy, 174.7, 199.3, 219.9

Lombard Street, 241.3

London Bridge, 79.7

Lone Ranger, the, 129.5, 173.25, 615.42

long ears, 383.27

Long, Huey P., 156.2

Longinus, 314.3

Long Meg of Westminster;, 273.36

Long Parliament, 369.2

Longstocking, Pippi, 187.8, 329.3

long unbound hair, 483.6

Lonigan, Studs, 149.5

Looking Backward, 2000–1887, 593.9

looking-glass, Alice's, 400.2

Lord Jim, 421.9, 605.19

Lord Jim, Marlow and, 259.17

Lord of Misrule, 102.17

Lord of the Dance, 101.11

Lord of the Flies, 145.26

Lord of the Manor of Tyburn, 211.4

Lord of the Rings, The, 224.11

Lorelei, 194.6, 520.10

Lost in Space, 91.8

Lost Weekend, The, 12.7

Mannon, Lavinia, 330.4, 343.4

Mannon, Orin, 498.3

Man of Sorrows, 101.12

Manon, 221.9

Man o' War ("Big Red"), 306.17

Mansion, The, 280.17

Man Without a Country, The, 351.8

Maon, wilderness of, 111.6

maple leaf, 246.24

Maple Leaf Forever!, 535.7

Marah, 399.13

Marathon, 56.25

marathon, Boston, 196.2

marathon dancing, 196.6, 218.14

marathon eating, 218.15

Marcella, 58.16

March, Amy, 594.5

March, Augie, 174.8, 348.4

March, Beth, 146.6, 270.7

March Hare, 385.18

March, Meg, 178.9

"March to the Sea," Sherman's, 159.23

Mardi Gras, 264.3

mares of Diomedes, 516.9

Margaret of Anjou, 132.12

Marguerite, 36.5

Marie Antoinette, 58.17

marigold, 281.19

Marina, 602.8

Marion, Francis, 135.21

marjoram, 26.5

Mark, 206.4

market, flea, 333.2

Mark, King, 134.9

mark of Cain, 475.13

Marlboro Man, 601.4

Marley, 272.18

Marlow and Lord Jim, 259.17

Marlowe, Philip, 532.27

Marmorie, 556.15

Marneffe, Madame, 123.4

Marner, Silas, 403.3, 524.3

Marple, Miss, 532.28

Marsala, 617.15

Marseillaise, 535.8

Marshall Plan, 9.5

Marshland, Jinny, 318.8

Marston Moor, 581.15

Marta, 466.4

Martano, 126.9

Martext, Sir Oliver, 313.25

Martha, 614.4

Martha, St., 178.10

Martius and Quintus, 338.19

Marx, Karl, 359.5

Mary, 373.5, 411.8

Mary and Elizabeth, 503.6

Mary Celeste, 1.5, 416.11

Maryland, My Maryland, 535.9

Mary Magdalene, 133.3, 449.8, 474.8, 522.6

Mary Mouse, 104.5

M*A*S*H, 85.5

mask, 150.22

Maskwell, 575.22

Mason-Dixon Line, 536.7

Mason, Perry, 49.4, 152.8, 532.29

Massacre, Armenian, 391.2

Massacre, Boston, 391.4, 508.3

Massacre, Fetterman, 391.6

Massacre, Katyn, 391.11

Massacre, My Lai, 269.10, 391.15

Massacre of Glencoe, 391.13

Massacre, St. Bartholomew's Day, 391.17

Massacre, St. Valentine's Day, 391.18

Massacre, Whitman, 391.21

Massacre, Wyoming, 391.23

Master Leonard, 161.16

mastodon, 215.8

Mata Hari, 540.8

Mater Matuta, 98.10

Matthew, 206.5

Matthew, Master, 182.8

Matthias, 254.5

Maugis, 194.7

Mauperin, Renée, 548.11

Maurya, 158.5

Maverick, 265.15

Mawworm, 313.26

May, third of, 391.20

Mayday, 141.2

Mayeux, 153.5

Mayflower, 16.9, 110.3, 248.19, 354.14

Mayo, Asey, 532.30

Mayo Clinic, 392.14

Mayor of Casterbridge, The, 347.19

McCarthy, Charlie, 322.2

McCarthyism, 624.5

McCarthy, Senator Joseph, 217.5

McCoys, Hatfields and, 509.8

McDonald, Ronald, 106.12

McDonald's, 584.6

McGarrett, Steve, 129.6

McGee, Travis, 532.31

McMurphy, Randall Patrick, 385.19

McTeague, 76.7, 84.7

McVey, Hugh, 547.3

Meany, George, 359.6

Mecca, pilgrimage to, 354.17

Medal of Freedom, 468.11

Medal of Honor, 75.26

medal, St. Christopher, 475.16

Medea, 289.7, 352.15, 412.21, 595.26

Medes and Persians, law of the, 452.1

Medicare, 9.6

Médoc, 617.16

Medusa, 148.8, 409.30, 585.13

Meet the Press, 369.3

Megaera, 19.10

meginjardir, 543.13
Mein Kampf, 24.19
Melantius, 303.13
Melchior, Caspar, and Balthazar, 419.2
Meleager, 229.10
Melford, Lydia, 428.10
Melibee, 254.6
Mélisande, Pelléas and, 375.27
Mellefont, 374.14
Mellitias, St., 553.7
Mellon, Andrew, 456.3
Melmoth the Wanderer, 605.20
Melpomene, 341.12
melting pot, 16.10
Melusina, 158.6
Menaechmi, The, 582.14
Menahem, 78.6, 591.7
Menelaus, 134.10
Mengele, Dr. Joseph, 82.14
Mensa International, 342.2
Mentor, 122.7, 284.8
Mephibosheth, 360.5
Mephistopheles, 161.17, 208.22
Mercedes Benz, 384.16
Mercury, 568.13
Mercury, Sosia and, 179.6
Mercutio, 621.3
Merlin, 386.3
Merlin's magic mirror, 400.5
mermaid, 519.9
Merop's Son, 402.18
Merrick, Robert, 358.21
Merridew, Jack, 627.5
Merrilies, Meg, 380.31
merrow, 430.4
Merry-Andrew, 106.13
Merry Mount, 260.4
Merveilleuse, 556.16
Merygreeke, Matthew, 353.4
Messalina, 471.8
mess of pottage, 78.7
Methuselah, 7.7, 369.4
Metis, 477.3

Metropolitan Opera House, 567.12
Mezentius, 132.13
Micaiah, 455.5
Micawber, Mr., 434.3
Micawber, Mrs. Emma, 220.25
Micawber, Wilkins, 465.22
mice, three blind, 69.21
Michael, 18.5
Michaelmas daisy, 225.9
Michael, St., 476.14
Michal, 130.6
Michele, 412.22
Mickey Mouse, 333.6
Midas, 38.6, 280.18, 574.18, 610.13
Middle-earth, 622.5
Midgard, 184.9
Midgard serpent, 409.31
Midway, 56.26, 581.16
Mighty Casey, 219.10
Mignon, 376.9, 500.15
mignonette, 246.25
Mikado of Japan, the, 217.6
Miles and Flora, 208.23
Miles Gloriosus, 70.16
milk and honey, land of, 3.10, 384.14
Miller, Daisy, 418.12, 590.14
Miller, Maximilian Christopher, 273.38
Millionaire, The, 224.12
Milo, 592.3
Milo of Croton, 543.14
Milquetoast, Casper, 572.10, 609.4
Milvain, Jasper, 190.3
Mime, 598.11
Mimi, 375.21
Mimir, 273.39, 619.16
Mimung, 556.17
min, 28.14
miniskirt, 218.16
mink coat, 384.17
Minnesota Fats, 231.12
Minnie, 265.16, 339.15
Minos, 357.14, 363.4
Minotaur, 83.5, 409.32
Miracle, Dr., 194.8

Miracle on 34th Street, 102.18, 399.14
mirage, 318.9
mi'raj, 36.6
Miranda, 418.13
Mirandolina, 520.11
Miriam, 13.5, 530.8
mirror, 381.12, 594.6
mirror, Alasnam's, 95.8, 400.1
mirror, Cambuscan's, 400.3
mirror, Merlin's magic, 400.5
Mirror, mirror, 400.6
mirror, Prester John's, 400.8
mirror, Reynard's wonderful, 400.9
mirror, Vulcan's, 400.10
Misanthrope, 260.5
Miss America, 58.18, 234.3, 612.3
missile crisis, Cuban, 566.3
Mission Impossible, 343.5
Mississippi Bubble, the, 256.3
Mister Keen, 166.9
mistletoe, 102.19, 248.20
Mistress Mary, 429.6
Mite, Sir Matthew, 176.12
Mithra (Mithras), 551.15
Mithras, 367.5
Mitty, Walter, 224.13, 297.5, 318.10, 572.11, 609.5
Mjolnir, 570.5
M., Miss, 533.10
Mneme, 394.4
Mnemosyne, 394.5
moa, 215.9
Moby Dick, 485.5, 611.2
mockingbird, 398.5
Mock Turtle, 393.15
Modest Proposal, A, 89.11
Modo, 412.23
Modred, 575.23
Moe, 210.8
Moechus, 5.16
Moffat, Miss, 561.8

95 Theses, 581.17
Niobe, 35.10, 133.4, 281.20
Nipper, Susan, 346.8
Niquee and Anasterax, 325.13
Nirvana, 439.10
Nisus and Euryalus, 259.18
Nixon, Richard, 150.27
Njord, 616.21
Njorthr, 519.12
NKVD, 540.10
Noah, 181.9, 205.13, 500.16, 506.9, 553.8
Noah's altar, 279.4
Noah's Ark, 495.7
Nobel, 468.14
noble savage, 422.4
Noisi, Deirdre and, 379.9
Nolan, Gypo, 335.6
Nolan, Jim, 573.2
Nolan, Philip, 52.11, 605.21
Nora, 235.11
Norina, Ernesto and, 377.9
Norma and Pollio, 375.22
Normandy Invasion, 56.29
Norns, 229.13
Norris, Mrs., 278.4
North and South Poles, 499.10
northeaster (nor'easter), 616.22
norther, 616.23
North Star, 25.8, 80.3
North Woods, 511.4
Nostradamus, 41.4, 473.23
Nostromo, 577.12
Nosy Parker, 136.8
Notburga, St., 523.12
Notung, 556.21
Nox, 420.7
NRA, 311.10
Nubian's skin, 452.3
Number One, 190.6
number, perfect, 450.8
Nureddin, 376.10

Nuremberg Egg, 105.2
Nuremberg Laws, 24.20
Nuremberg Trials, 357.17
nutmeg, wooden, 256.6
Nydia, 69.13
Nym, 568.15

O

oak, 307.13
oak, white, 327.8
Oakes, 451.2
Oakhurst, John, 521.18
oak leaves, 500.17
oak leaves, garland of, 587.14
Oakley, Annie, 74.3, 388.7, 615.43
Oakmen, 183.7
O'Bedlam, Bess, 385.21
O'Bedlam, Tom, 385.22
Oberlin College, 243.25
Oberon, 194.9, 352.16
Obidicut, 383.31
Oblomov, 328.7, 364.11
Oblomov, Ilya, 72.6
O Canada!, 535.10
Oceanids, 427.10, 519.13
Oceanus, 519.14
Ochs, Baron, 107.6
Ocnus, the rope of, 263.8
O Come, All Ye Faithful, 102.21
Octa, 142.7
Odd Couple, The, 49.6
O Deutschland, Hoch in Ehren!, 535.11
Odilia, St., 69.14
Odin, 226.20, 606.12, 619.17
Odysseus (Ulysses), 135.23, 605.22
Odyssey, 201.12, 301.1
Oedipus, 52.12, 69.15, 325.14, 412.25, 498.4
Oeneus, 617.19
Of Mice and Men, 263.9, 304.7
Og, 273.42
O'Gill, Darby, 224.15
Oglethorpe, John, 302.6

O'Hanlon, Virginia, 174.9
O'Hara, Scarlett, 58.19, 245.13
Oholiab, Bezalel and, 127.4
Oil Can Harry, 598.15
O.K. Corral, 615.44
Okies, 465.23, 590.15
Okinawa, 56.30
Old Ben, 485.7
Old Bogy, 157.14
Oldbuck, Jonathan, 23.2
Old Faithful, 480.5
Old Jackanapes, 353.5
Old King Cole, 355.3
Old Lady of Threadneedle Street, 241.4
Old Man Winter, 618.7
old man wrapped in cloak, 618.8
Old Mother Hubbard, 262.7
Old Nick, 161.19
Old Scratch, 161.20
Old Vic, 567.13
Old Woman of Gloucester, 558.9
Old Woman of Leeds, 358.23
Old Woman of Surrey, 258.5
old woman who lived in a shoe, 237.35, 470.1
Old Yeller, 476.16
Olenska, Countess Ellen, 71.4
Olindo and Sophronia, 375.23
O Little Town of Bethlehem, 102.22
Olivant, 607.7
olive branch, 446.9
olive branches, 99.1
Oliver and Jenny, 379.17
Olivia, 351.9
Olsen, Jimmy, 627.6
Olympus, 294.17
Omoo, 605.23
Omphale, 387.5
Ona, 521.19

Posthumus, 52.14
Potato Famine, 310.4
Potemkin village, 313.30
Potiphar's wife, 374.18
Potsdam Conference, 121.9
pottage, mess of, 78.7
potter's field, 86.10
Povey, Constance Baines, 72.7
Powler, Peg, 208.27
Pozdnishef, Madame, 5.17
Pozdnishef, Vasyla, 352.19
prairie schooner, 615.49
prajna, 198.6
Praxidice, 241.5
Precieuse, 556.22
Prester John's mirror, 400.8
Priapus, 153.6, 383.35, 601.5
Price, Fanny, 435.5
Pride's Purge, 52.15
Prigio, Prince, 112.16
primrose, 625.4
Prince of Wales, 179.4
Prince, The, 588.9
Priscillianism, 37.17
Prism, Miss, 90.6
Prisoner of Chillon, The, 324.21
Prisoner of Zenda, The, 2.7
Procris, Cephalus and, 352.6
Procrustes, 82.17, 415.9
prodigal son, 176.14, 254.8
prodigal son and his father, 503.7
Profiles in Courage, 75.29
Prohibition, 12.8, 563.6
Proitus and Acrisius, 509.12
Prometheus, 113.6, 128.12, 196.7, 242.10, 298.14, 481.17, 548.13
Proserpina, 2.8
Prospero, 386.4
protea, 246.28

Proteus, 574.24
Protocols of the Elders of Zion, 24.21
Prufrock, J. Alfred, 7.10, 199.4
Prynne, Hester, 5.18, 370.8, 481.18, 524.5
Pry, Paul, 136.10, 186.4
Psyche, Cupid and, 136.2
Psycho, 305.15
Ptolemy, 43.6
Puck, 402.25
Pulitzer, 468.16
Pullman car, 384.18
Pulver, Ensign, 353.7
Pumblechook, 49.7
pumpkin, 574.25
pumpkin pie, 16.13
Pure, Simon, 271.4, 303.15
Purim, 154.14
Puritanism, 44.7
Puritans, 169.3
purple, 45.15
purple and yellow, 185.7
Purple Heart, 75.30
purple lilac, 248.26
purse, Fortunatus', 610.10
Purvis, Melvin, 129.9
Putnam, Abbie, 280.25
Putnam, Abbie, and Eben Cabot, 375.4
Pygmalion, 127.12
Pylades and Orestes, 259.22
Pyle, Gomer, 590.16
Pym, Arthur Gordon, 6.14
Pyramus and Thisbe, 375.28
Pyrrhic victory, 151.15
Pythias, Damon and, 259.8
python, 143.12, 409.38

Q

Quakers, 22.4, 446.12, 478.3
quarterback, Monday morning, 130.7

Quasimodo, 153.7, 476.18, 585.14
Quebec, 327.7
Queen, Ellery, 532.35
Queen of Hearts, 338.22, 583.6
Queen of Sheba, 62.12
Queen of Spades, The, 265.20
Queensberry, Marquis of, 479.9
Queen, the, 598.18
Queequeg, 422.6
Queer Street, 53.10
Quilp, Daniel, 533.13
quince, 389.10, 564.3
Quint, Peter, 208.28
Quint, Peter and Miss Jessel, 272.22
Quintus, Martius and, 338.19
Quisling, Vidkun, 576.6
Quixote, Don, 100.18, 318.11

R

Ra, 551.18
rabbit, 185.8, 237.40, 470.2
Rabbi, the, 532.36
rabbit's foot, 382.14
raccoon coats, 218.19
Rachel, 281.24, 347.24
Rachel, Jacob and, 379.14
Rachel weeping for her children, 133.5
Radio City Music Hall, 567.14
Raffles, 568.16
Raft of the Medusa, The, 548.14
Ragged Dick, 15.10, 547.5
Raggedy Ann, 97.6
Ragmaid, 61.5
Ragnarok, 159.21
Rahab, 474.11, 476.19
Rahab and family, 500.19
Raid of Ruthven, 2.9
raids, panty, 218.18

Salome, 62.13, 140.4, 330.5, 383.37
Salt River, 151.12
salt, spilt, 381.17
Salus, St. Simeon, 187.13
Salvation Army, 10.4, 267.18, 404.6
salvia, blue, 619.5
Sam and Eric, 179.5
Samantha, 620.11
Samarkand, 56.36
samn, 616.25
sampaguita, 246.32
Sampson, Dominie, 448.10
Samson, 69.19, 75.34, 287.14, 298.17, 543.15, 563.8, 604.6
Sanang, 500.20
Sanātana Dharma, 198.7
Sanballat and Tobiah, 130.8
Sandman, 531.9
Sandy, 177.15, 542.6
San Francisco earthquake, 167.13
Sanglamore, 556.24
Sangrado, Dr., 484.5
San Quentin, 324.22
Santa Claus, 102.25, 267.19, 432.3
Santa Cruz, Jacinta, 370.9
Santa Cruz, Juanito, 469.13
Santa Fe trail, 354.21, 615.52
Santa Maria, Pinta, and Niña, 354.22
Santiago, 160.10, 453.9, 486.8
Santuzza, 1.6
sapphire, 67.12, 95.11
Sappho, 302.7, 461.3
Sarah, 55.9
Saratoga (Stillwater), 56.37
sard, 475.18
sardonyx, 67.13
Sarn, Prudence, 153.8
Sasha, 376.13
Sasquatch, 409.41

Satan (Lucifer), 161.22, 197.4, 208.30, 491.5, 564.4
Saturday's child, 331.7
Saturnalia, 147.10
Saturninus, 575.29
Satyricon, 147.11
Saul, 175.5, 494.5, 549.17
Saul and David, 438.3
Sautuerdu, 556.25
savage, noble, 422.4
SAVAK, 82.19
Savonarola, 156.4
Savoy, 384.22
Sawyer, Tom, 6.15, 29.8, 135.27, 402.27
scales, 357.20
scales falling from eyes, 198.8
Scales, Gerald, 469.14
Scales, Sophia Baines, 491.6
scales, sword and, 357.24
scallop shell, 54.4
scapegoat, 449.14
scarab, 320.16, 502.13
Scaramouche, 70.22, 126.12
Scarecrow, 316.11, 332.12
scarlet carnation, 248.32
scarlet letter, 5.19
Scarlet Sister Mary, 449.15
Scarpia, 598.19
scepter, 45.17, 357.21
Schechem, 495.9
Scheherazade, 135.28, 194.13, 542.7
Schlemihl, Peter, 418.14
Schoolmaster of Falerii, 575.30
Schopenhauer, Arthur, 455.7
Schouler, Marcus, 378.13
Schroeder, 413.13, 459.1
Schubert, Franz, 146.8
Schultz, Sergeant, 332.13
Schwanda, 194.14
Schweik, 316.12
Scipio, 380.37
Scopes trial, 120.9
Scorpio, 628.10

Scotland Yard, 129.10
Scottsboro Case, 120.10
scourges, 440.17
Scout, 306.22
Scowerers, 510.6 ·
scrap of paper, 120.11
Scriblerus, Martinus, 448.11
scroll, 619.22
Scrooge, Ebenezer, 102.26, 280.26, 403.4, 494.6
Scylla, 409.42
Scylla and Charybdis, 141.8, 466.5
scythe, 145.33
Seabiscuit, 306.23
sealed book, 111.5
seamless robe, 440.18
Sears Tower, 559.8
SEATO, 121.10
Seattle Slew, 306.24
Sebastian, 575.31
Sebastian, St., 390.21
Secret Agent, The, 540.12
Secretariat, 306.25
Secretary, the, 85.7
Sedan, 56.38, 151.13
sedge, 483.7
seed, fern, 345.5
seed, mustard, 282.2
seeds, willow, 26.9
sego lily, 248.33
Seian Horse, 381.15
Selene, 410.10
Selkirk, Alexander, 91.9, 351.10
Sempronius, 336.6
senvy, 328.8
Sepoy Rebellion, 490.17
sepulchres, whited, 313.37
Serannes, Theodore de, 173.32
Serbonian Bog, 114.8
Sergius III, 147.12
serpent, 135.29, 320.17, 564.5
serpentine, 475.19
Serpina, 578.9
seven, 382.16

Seven Cities of Cibola, 593.16
Seven Dwarfs, 183.9
Seven Sisters, 188.12
Seven Sleepers, 531.10
seventh son, 382.17
Seward's Folly, 250.12, 333.7, 361.9
Sextus, 68.5, 595.30
Shabata, Frank, 352.20
Shakers, 44.8, 223.6, 478.4
Shakespeare, William, 461.4
Shallum, 118.12
shamrock, 246.33, 264.5, 579.5
Shane, 615.53
Shangri-la, 439.11, 593.17
Sharezer, Adrammelech and, 412.2
shark, 143.14
Sharks, Jets and, 509.9, 510.4
Sharpless, 262.9
Shawn, Ted, and Ruth St. Denis, 140.3
Shays' Rebellion, 508.14
sheaf of corn, sickle and, 550.5
Sheba, 490.18
Shekinah, 276.18
Shelby, George, 25.9
Shelley, Percy Bysshe, 146.9
shell, scallop, 54.4
Shemaiah, 78.8
Shem and Japheth, 124.5
Sheol, 295.7, 587.17
shepherds, 419.5
Shere Khan, 232.9, 595.31
Sheriff of Nottingham, 598.20
Sherman's "March to the Sea," 159.23
sherry, 617.24
shibboleth, 314.7
shield, Perseus's, 400.7
Shimei, 530.9
Shimerda, Antonia, 226.22
shirt of Nessus, 381.16

Shiva, 128.13
Shiva, dance of, 571.3
shivah, 281.26
shoe, elevator, 559.4
shoes, saddle, 218.21
Short Hoggers of Whittinghame, 272.23
Shosha, 418.15
showy lady slipper, 248.34
shtetl, 511.6
Shubert Alley, 567.16
Shylock, 592.5
Siberia, 52.18, 499.14
sibyl, Cumaean, 285.6, 473.10
Sibyllae, 473.24
Sicilian Vespers, 391.19
sickle and sheaf of corn, 550.5
Siddharta, 236.5, 605.26
Sidonians, 127.13
Siegfried, 173.33, 397.2, 604.7
Siegfried Line, 604.8
Sieppe, Trina, 541.5
Sign of the Cross, 579.6
Sikes, Bill, 412.30, 568.17
Silent Majority, 16.14
Silent Night, 102.27
Silenus, 181.10, 561.12
Silken Threads, 468.17
silky, 178.14
Silly Putty, 218.22
Silvanus, 226.23
Silver, 306.26
Silver Cord, The, 373.7
Silver, Long John, 460.12
Silver, Mattie, 97.8
silver, 30 pieces of, 440.24, 575.33
Simeon, 314.8
Simonet, Albertine, 405.8
Simonetta, 58.20
Simon Magus, 514.7
Simon the Cyrenean, 440.19
Simon the Cyrenian, 296.9
Simple Simon, 286.5, 544.6

Simplicissimus, 6.16
Simpson, Wallis Warfield, and Edward VIII, 379.11
Singin' in the Rain, 97.9
Singleton, Captain, 460.13
Sing Sing, 324.23
Sinis, 415.10
Sinon, 135.30, 150.30
Sioux, 615.54
Sirens, 194.15
Sirius, 80.5
sirocco, 616.26
Sisyphus, 262.10, 280.27, 481.19
Sitting Bull, 615.55
Sitzkrieg, 347.28
Six-Day War, 77.7
Six Million Jews, 269.13
$64,000 question, the, 517.5
skateboards, 218.23
skeleton, 145.34
Skelton, Red, 626.11
skid row, 12.9, 219.12
Skimpole, Horace, 190.7
skin, Nubian's, 452.3
Skulda, 571.7
skull, 145.35, 449.16
skull and crossbones, 141.9, 145.36
Skvoznik-Dmukhanovsky, Anton Antonovich, 182.11
Sleeping Beauty, 194.16, 531.11
Sleepy Hollow, 351.11
Slender, 544.7
sloth, 364.13
Slough of Despond, 158.8
Slout, Mr., 132.15
Slurk, Mr., 112.17
Sly, Christopher, 181.11
small bindweed, 309.9
Small, Lennie, 48.7
Smersh, 540.13
Smike, 1.7
Smiley, Jim, 265.21
Smilin' Jack, 47.4
Smith, Cyrus, 91.10
Smithfield, Fires of, 28.9

10 Downing Street, 81.9
ten lepers, 336.7
ten o'clock scholar, 560.2
Tenorio, Don Juan, 449.18
Teresa, Cellini and, 377.6
Teresa of Ávila, St., 417.7
Teresa, Vincent, 335.8
Tereus, 89.14
Termagant, 527.11
Terpsichore, 140.5, 341.17
Tesman, George, 297.7
Tess of the D'Urbervilles, 61.6
test-tube baby, 98.12
Tethys, 519.17
Tetragrammaton, 276.19
Teufelsdroeckh, Herr, 23.3
Texan, 70.23
Texas Rangers, 129.13, 615.56
Thaïs, 123.7, 474.12, 494.7
Thalia, 57.17, 341.18, 362.4
Thalia, 341
thalidomide, 153.9
Thammuz, 502.14
Thanatos (Mors), 145.38
Thanksgiving, 16.17, 233.5
Thanksgiving Day, 3.11, 279.5
Thatcher, Becky, 377.17
Thatcher, John Putnam, 532.40
Theater, Federal, 567.7
Theater, Habima, 567.10
Theatre, Abbey, 567.1
Theatre, Garrick, 567.8
Theatre, Globe, 567.9
Thecla, St., 390.24
Themis, 98.13
Theocritus, 442.6
Theodosius, 449.19
Theon, 130.9
theory of relativity, 581.20
Theramenes, 326.6

Thermopylae, 56.40, 575.32
Thersites, 530.10
Theseus, 75.35, 205.17
Theseus and Pirithoüs, 259.25
Thespis, 4.1
Thestylis, 61.7
Thetis, 519.18
thief in the night, 552.3
Thing, 523.14
thin ice, 141.14
Thinker, The, 119.2
third little pig, 135.32, 331.9
third of May, 391.20
thirteen, 381.19
30 pieces of silver, 440.24, 575.33
Thirty Years War, 159.25
Thisbe, Pyramus and, 375.28
thistle, 246.34
thistle, common, 44.5
thistle, Fuller's, 401.5
Thomas à Becket, St., 390.25
Thomas, St., 31.3, 529.5
Thor, 368.6, 570.6
Thoreau, Henry David, 501.6
thorn, 395.19
thorns, crown of, 406.3, 440.4
Thoth, 145.39
Thousandfurs, 173.35
Thraso, 70.24
three, 382.18
three blind mice, 69.21
three circles, 372.21
300 game, 450.10
Three Musketeers, The, 259.26
three nails, 440.25
Three Princes of Serendip, 94.7
Three Stooges, the, 626.12
three wise men, 419.8
three wise men of Gotham, 544.11
throatwort, 358.29

Throgmorton Street, 241.7
throne, 45.19
Throssel, Miss Phoebe, 537.3
Thuggee, 412.33
Thumb, Tom, 533.16
Thummin, Urim and, 94.8
Thumper, 138.3
Thursday, Margaret, 1.9
Thwackum, 448.12
Thyestean banquet, 89.15, 233.6
Thyestes, 481.22
Tibbs, Virgil, 532.41
Tiberge and the Chevalier, 259.27
Tiberius, 428.12
Tierra del Fuego, 499.15
Tiffany's, 384.23
tiger, 516.12
tiger, saber-toothed, 215.11
Timberlane, Cass, 254.9
Timbuktu, 439.13, 499.16
Time Machine, The, 6.19, 354.24
Timon, 401.9, 610.17
Timon of Athens, 37.20
Tinker to Evers to Chance, 121.11
Tin Pan Alley, 413.15
Tiny Tim, 360.8
Tiphys, 285.14
Tipperary, 535.15
Tippetarius, 574.27
Tiresias, 17.3, 69.22, 473.29, 574.28
Tishah be'Av, 281.28
Tisiphone, 19.15
Titania, 194.17
Titanic, 167.14
Titans, 273.47
Tithonus, 347.29
Titinius, 380.40
Titus, 254.10
Titus Andronicus, 595.33
Tityre Tus, 510.7
Tityus, 273.48
Tizona, 556.26
Tlapallan, 439.14